LANGUAGE ARTS
Content and Teaching Strategies

LANGUAGE ARTS

Content and Teaching Strategies

GAIL E. TOMPKINS
California State University, Fresno

KENNETH HOSKISSON
Virginia Polytechnic Institute and State University

Merrill, an imprint of
Macmillan Publishing Company
New York

Collier Macmillan Canada, Inc.
Toronto

Maxwell Macmillan International Publishing Group
New York ◆ *Oxford* ◆ *Singapore* ◆ *Sydney*

Cover art: Leslie Beaber
Editor: Jeff Johnston
Developmental Editor: Linda James Scharp
Production Editor: Ben Ko
Art Coordinator: Vincent A. Smith
Cover Designer: Russ Maselli
Production Buyer: Pamela D. Bennett

This book was set in Bookman.

Photo credits: All photos were taken by author, except the following: Timothy J. Bernard, pages 12, 78, 128, 192, 212, 278, 309, 370, 402, 495, 535; Gail Meese, page 324; and David Strickler, 482.

Macmillan Publishing Company
866 Third Avenue, New York, NY 10022

Collier Macmillan Canada, Inc.

Library of Congress Catalog Card Number: 90-53482
International Standard Book Number: 0-675-22296-6

Printing: 2 3 4 5 6 7 8 9
Year: 1 2 3 4

Credits

Chapter 1. p. 7. "Gismo," Shawn Easton, grade 1, Western Hills Elementary School, Lawton, OK.

Chapter 2. p. 36. "Edith, No!," John McCracken's class, grade 3, Nevin Coppock School, Tipp City, OH. p. 54. From "Selecting software for your LD students" by P. L. Smith and G. E. Tompkins, 1984, *Academic Therapy, 20,* 221–224. Copyright 1984 by Academic Therapy. Adapted by permission.

Chapter 3. p. 89. "Hare-Hair," Jaclyn Cooley, grade 2, Hubbard Elementary School, Noble, OK; p. 90. Down Words, Tissie McClure's class, grade 6, Nicoma Park Intermediate School, Nicoma Park, OK; p. 91. Idiom Poster, Josh Jewell, grade 4, Pioneer Intermediate School, Noble, OK; p. 92. From *Answering Students' Questions about Words,* G. E. Tompkins and D. B. Yaden, 1986, ERIC Clearinghouse on Reading and Communication Skills and the National Council of Teachers of English, Urbana, IL. p. 94. "Tapee," Ben Atwater, grade 5, Whittier Elementary School, Lawton, OK; p. 97. From *Teaching vocabulary to improve reading comprehension* by William F. Nagy, 1988, Urbana, IL: ERIC Clearinghouse on Reading and Communication Skills and the National Council of Teachers of English and the International Reading Association. Copyright 1988 by National Council of Teachers of English. Reprinted by permission.

Chapter 4. pp. 112–118. From "Strategies for more effective listening" by G. E. Tompkins, M. Friend, and P. L. Smith, 1987. In C. R. Personke and D. D. Johnson (Eds.), *Language arts and the beginning teacher,* (chapter 3). Englewood Cliffs, NJ: Prentice Hall. Adapted with permission. p. 117. "Drugs," anonymous, grade 5, Bethel School, Shawnee, OK; p. 123. From "Some examples of doublespeak" by W. D. Lutz, n.d., unpublished ms. distributed by National Council of Teachers of English. From *Listening skills schoolwide: Activities and programs* by T. G. Devine, 1982. Urbana, IL: ERIC Clearinghouse on Reading and Communication Skills and the National Council of Teachers of English. Reprinted by permission. p. 126. "Dream Date," Vera Willey and Linda White's class, grade 5, Lincoln Elementary School, Norman, OK.

Chapter 5. p. 153. From "Storytelling: A bridge from the university to the elementary school to the home" by B. W. Kingore, 1982. *Language Arts, 59,* 28–32. Reprinted with permission. p. 163. "Mr. Kirtley," Tomora Trett, grade 1, Sulphur Elementary School, Sulphur, OK; p. 173. "Dear Diary," Stephanie Camp, grade 4, Ranchwood Elementary School, Yukon, OK; pp. 178–179. "The Lonely Troll," Raymond Butts, Lisa Largent, Jeff Parsons, Kathy Polanewcki, and Larry Rippey, Noble Junior High School, Noble, OK; p. 180. Storyboard, John McCracken's class, grade 3, Nevin Coppock School, Tipp City, OH.

Chapter 6. p. 187. "Friendship," Misty Gregory, grade 4, Monroe Elementary School, Norman, OK; p. 191. Personal Journal, Michael Holzer, grade 3, Jefferson Elementary School, Norman, OK; p. 193. Possible Writing Topics, Chris Edge-Christensen's class, grade 4–5, Whittier Elementary School, Lawton, OK; p. 195. Dialogue Journal, Alisa Richmond, grade 2, Winding Creek Elementary School, Moore, OK; p. 198. Reading Log, Don, grade 2, Monroe Elementary School, Norman, OK; p. 199. Caterpillars Log, Angela Knapple, grade 2, Hubbard Elementary School, Noble, OK; p. 200. "Lab Report," Aaron Ochs, grade 4, Pioneer Intermediate School, Noble, OK; p. 201. Betsy Ross' Diary, Lisa Nye, grade 5, Pioneer Intermediate School, Noble, OK; p. 202. Kindergarten Journals, Brandon Barrett, Becky Lee, Jessica Mendoza, and Marc Trammell, kindergarten, Eisenhower Elementary School, Norman, OK; p. 209. Florence Nightingale cluster, Christina Vinson, grade 5, Horace Mann Elementary School, Duncan, OK. From "RX for writer's block," G. E. Tompkins & D. E. Camp, 1988. *Childhood Education, 64,* 209–214. Reprinted with permission.

Chapter 7. p. 238, 241. From "After your students write, what's next?" by G. E. Tompkins & M. Friend, 1988. *Teaching Exceptional Children, 20,* 4–9. p. 249. "All About the Author," Brian, grade 4, Purcell Elementary School, Purcell, OK.

Chapter 8. p. 268. From *Reading process and practice: From socio-psycholinguists to whole language* by Weaver, 1988. Portsmouth, NH: Heinemann. p. 271. From *Towards a reading-writing classroom* by A. Butler & J. Turbill, 1984. Portsmouth, NH: Heinemann. p. 271. From "A teaching model that develops active reading of expository text" by D. M. Ogle, 1986. *The Reading Teacher.* p. 290. "What can this little bat do?," Shawn Easton, grade 1, Western Hills Elementary School, Lawton, OK; p. 292. "I am the frog," Whitney Mohaffay, grade 1, Norman Christian Academy, Norman, OK.

Chapter 9. p. 341. "The Peacock and the Mouse," Felton Frueh, grade 6, Irving Middle School, Norman,

OK; pp. 342–343. "Suntaria and Lunaria: Rulers of the Earth," Sandra Harris' class, grade 7, Anadarko Middle School, Anadarko, OK.

Chapter 10. p. 352. "Snowy Thoughts," John-David Walles, grade 2, Western Hills Elementary School, Lawton, OK; p. 357. Dinosaur Report, Dustin Smith, grade 4, Western Hills Elementary School, Lawton, OK; p. 358. "G is for Godzilla," Mark Voss, grade 4, Pioneer Intermediate School, Noble, OK; pp. 366–367. "The Goggles Gazette," Janet Kretschmer's class, grade 3, 4, and 5, McGuffey Laboratory School, Oxford, OH; pp. 368–369. "Revolutionary Times," Polly Dwyer and Charlotte Fleetham's class, grade 5, Pioneer Intermediate School, Noble, OK; pp. 374–375. Pen Pal Letter, Allison Dawson, grade 3, Jefferson Elementary School, Norman, OK; p. 376. "Dear Dr. Seuss," Sara Boeheme, grade 1, Lincoln Elementary School, Norman, OK; pp. 378. "Dear William," Adam, grade 3, Jefferson Elementary School, Norman, OK; pp. 382–383. Autobiography, Eddie Heck, grade 2, Hubbard Elementary School, Noble, OK; p. 384. "Daniel Boone," Charles Perez, grade 3, Western Hills Elementary School, Lawton, OK; pp. 384–385. "All about me," Kasey Tompkins, grade 1, Whittier Elementary School, Lawton, OK.

Chapter 11. p. 401. From "Young children's preferences in poetry: A national survey of first, second, and third graders" by C. J. Fisher and M. A. Natarella, 1982. In *Reading in the Teaching of English, 16.* p. 401. From *Children's poetry preferences: A national survey of upper elementary grades* by A. Terry, 1974. Urbana, IL: National Council of Teachers of English. p. 401. From "A survey of the poetry preference of seventh, eighth, and ninth graders" by K. Kutiper, 1985. Unpublished doctoral dissertation, University of Houston. p. 410. "Ghost," Marshall Owen and "What Do You Call an Astronaut?," Tara Dillman, grade 6, Watonga Middle School, Watonga, OK; p. 412. "I Wish," Brandi, grade 2, Washington Irving School, Durant, OK; p. 412. "Yellow is Shiny Galoshes," Sandrea Harris' class, grade 7, Anadarko Middle School, Anadarko, OK; p. 413. "Black," Nancy Reynor, grade 7, Anadarko Middle School, Anadarko, OK; p. 413. "Being heartbroken," Kim Thomas, grade 6, Watonga Middle School, Watonga, OK; p. 414. "If I Were a Tyrannosaurus Rex," Robbie Neal, grade 1, McGuffey Laboratory School, Oxford, OH; p. 414. "I Used to Be a Kernal," Tony Brown and Christina Foster, grade 3, John Adams Elementary School, Lawton, OK; p. 414. "On the American Revolution," Glenda LoBaugh's class, grade 5, Yukon, OK; p. 415. "Thunder Is . . . ," Annette Jacks' class, grade 2, Hubbard Elementary School, Noble, OK; p. 416. "Superman," Mike, grade 7, Anadarko Middle School, Anadarko, OK; p. 416. "Loneliness," Bobby Hoffpauir, grade 8, Watonga Middle School, Watonga, OK; p. 417. "Fast Moving," Eric Embrey, grade 7, Choctaw Junior High School, Choctaw, OK; p. 418. "The Summer Dancers," Amy

Bowen, grade 8, Watonga Middle School, Watonga OK; p. 420. "Baby," Nancy Hutter's class, grade 3, Tioga Elementary School, Bensenville IL; p. 421. "There once Was a For Named Pete," Angela, grade 8, Watonga Middle School, Watonga, OK; p. 422. "The Truck," Jeff, grade 7, Anadarko Middle School, Anadarko, OK; p. 422. "open Up," Angela Eaton, grade 7, Choctaw Junior High School, Choctaw, OK; p. 422. "The Golden Shore," Nikki Newell, grade 7, Anadarko Middle School, Anadarko, OK; p. 423. "Dear Lord," Davis, grade 2, Grand Avenue Elementary School, Chickasha, OK; p. 423. "If I Were in Charge of the World," Brenda Wilkins' class, grade 4, Horace Mann Elementary School, Duncan, OK; p. 425. "Rules about Writing Poetry," Sandra Harris' class, grade 7, Anadarko Middle School, Anadarko, OK; p. 430. "People," Amanda, grade 6, Watonga Middle School, Watonga, OK; p. 431. "The Z was Zipped," Teri Gray and Pam Cottom's classes, grade 4, James Griffith Intermediate School, Choctaw, OK; p. 431. "Elephant Noses," Christopher, kindergarten, McGuffey Laboratory School, Oxford, OH; p. 432. "A Man," Bonnie Kretschmer, grade 4, and "Thoughts after a 40-mile Bike Ride," Roy Wesson, grade 5, McGuffey Laboratory School, Oxford, OH.

Chapter 12. pp. 439–440. From *Spelling: An application of research findings* by R. A. Alfred, 1977. Washington, DC: National Educational Association. Reprinted with permission. From p. 441. From "Reading, writing, and phonology" by C. Chomsky, 1970. *Harvard Educational Review, 40,* pp. 287–309. Copyright 1970 by *Harvard Educational Review.* Adapted with permission. p. 446. From "Developmental spelling: Assessment" by J. R. Gentry (1982). *Diagnostique.* p. 45X. From "Elementary students' invented spellings at the correct stage of spelling development" by M. E. Hitchcock, 1989. Unpublished doctoral dissertation, Norman, OK: University of Oklahoma. Reprinted with permission. From pp. 460–461. Spelling for word mastery by G. E. Cook, M. Esposito, T. Gabrielson, & G. Turner, 1984. Columbus, OH: Merrill. p. 462. From *A writing vocabulary for elementary children* by R. L. Hilleruich, 1978. Springfield, IL: Thomas.

Chapter 13. p. 488. Handwriting Samples, Jennifer Lee, grade 1, Sulphur Elementary School, Sulphur, OK, and Aaron Ochs, grade 4, Pioneer Intermediate School, Noble, OK. p. 474. From *Zaner-Bloser creative growth in handwriting (Grades K–8)* by W. B. Barbe, V. H. Lucas, T. M. Wasylyk, T. M. Hackney, & L. A. Braun, 1984. Columbus: OH. Zaner-Bloser. pp. 476–477. From D'Nealian handwriting (Grades K–8) by D. N. Thurber, 1981. Glenview, IL: Scott, Foresman. Copyright 1981 by Scott, Foresman. Reprinted by permission.

Chapter 14. p. 498. "An Animal and Adjective Alpha–bet Book," Pat Blackburn's class, and "C" page, Trina Hand, grade 2, Western Hills Elementary School, Lawton, OK; From *Understanding language: A primer for the language arts teacher* by J. Malmstrom, 1977. New York: St. Martin's Press.

Chapter 15. pp. 528–529. "My Experiment on Plants," Aaron Ochs, grade 4, Pioneer Intermediate School, Noble, OK; Biography of Ben Franklin, Matthew King, grade 5, Pioneer Intermediate School, Noble, OK; p. 532. Letter to Chris Van Allsburg, Annie Picek, grade 4, Pioneer Intermediate School, Noble, OK; p. 533. "Return to Jumanji," Lori Weaver, grade 4, Pioneer Intermediate School, Noble OK; p. 534. Math Story problem, Suzy Stubblefield, grade 6, Longfellow Middle School, Norman, OK.

Chapter 16. p. 563. Cluster and Autobiography, Ryan Gorman, grade 3, Southgate Elementary School, Moore, OK; p. 566. From "Survival words for disabled readers" by E. A. Polloway & C. H. Polloway, 1981, *Academic Therapy, 16,* (pp. 443–448). Copyright 1981 by PRO-Ed, Inc. Reprinted by permission. p. 578. Idiom, Robert Ochs, grade 3, Hubbard Elementary School, Noble, OK; p. 561. From "Learning disabilities: A puzzlement" by M. Summers, 1977. *Today's Education.* p. 573. From "Doing what comes naturally: Recent research in second language acquisition" by C. Utrzua, 1980. In G. S. Pinnell (Ed) *Discovering language with children,* (pp. 33–38). Urbana, IL: National Council of Teachers of English. Reprinted with permission. p. 574. From "Beginning English reader" by P. C. Gonzales, 1981, *The Reading Teacher, 35,* 154–162. pp. 582–583. From "Launching nonstandard speakers into standard English" by G. E. Tompkins & L. M. McGee, 1983. Language Arts. p. 585. From "spelling and grammar logs" by R. Van de Weghe, 1982. In C. Carter (Ed.), *Non-native and nonstandard dialect students: Classroom practices in teaching English,* 1982–1983. Urbana, IL: National Council of Teachers of English. p. 585. From "Giftedness" by L. Silverman, 1982. In E. L. Meyen (Ed.), *Exceptional children: An alternative resource book,* Denver: Love. Reprinted by permission. p. 591. Activities, Brian Johnson and Brady Toothaker, grade 8, Irving Middle School, Norman, OK.

Appendix E. From "Let's go on a bear hunt! A fresh approach to penmanship drill" by G. E. Tompkins, 1980. *Language Arts, 57,* 782–786. Copyright by National Council of Teachers of English. Reprinted by permission.

To Linnea and Todd with pride and love.
                                    —G.E.T.

To my wife Virginia, and my children,
Heather, Mark, and Tamora.
                                    —K.H.

PREFACE

Language Arts: Content and Teaching Strategies is a language arts methods text designed for preservice and inservice teachers who work (or will work) with students in kindergarten through eighth grade. An integrated or "whole language" approach is taken in the book, based on cognitive, psycholinguistic, and sociolinguistic theories about how children learn, and how they learn language, in particular. An instructional strategy based on these theories is developed in the first chapter and then applied for each language mode: listening, talking, reading, and writing.

Our goal is to present the content of the language arts curriculum and strategies for teaching this content in order for teachers to help students develop communicative competence, the complementary abilities to transmit meaning through talking and writing, and the ability to comprehend meaning through listening and reading. We will discuss language processes, as well as present genuine communication activities to help students develop communicative competence. These activities include conducting oral interviews of community residents; participating in debates on relevant topics; writing stories and sharing these stories with classmates and other genuine audiences; keeping learning logs in science classes; and writing simulated newspapers in conjunction with social studies units. We believe that students must actively engage in whatever it is they are to learn.

This text takes a structured approach because we believe students should *learn* how to use language rather than simply *practice* using language. In the past, teachers have admonished students to listen critically and then assigned them oral reports to give and stories to write. Often the results were disastrous, not because students did not apply themselves, but because they did not know how to comprehend and evaluate the message they listened to, how to prepare and present oral reports, or how to write well-organized and interesting stories.

In the second edition, we have made revisions to reflect the changes that are occurring in how language arts is being taught in elementary schools. The most notable change is the addition of three new chapters. Chapter 3, Words: The Building Blocks of Language, focuses on vocabulary and on how to help students learn and use words effectively. It provides background on the history of the English language, how people learn words and their meanings, and how to teach students about words. In Chapter 8, Reading and Writing Connections, we explore the connections between reading and writing and suggest ways to integrate reading and writing in elementary classrooms. Strategies for making the connection with young children, with authors, with stories, and with informational books are presented. Chapter 15, Extending Language Arts Across the Curriculum, is the third new chapter. Here we discuss how to integrate language arts with literature, social studies, science, and other content areas. We also show how to develop a thematic unit and sample units for primary, middle, and upper grades.

In order to demonstrate how real classroom teachers actually teach language arts, we present a "pro" file in each chapter to spotlight an exemplary teacher who is applying one of the teaching strategies presented in that chapter. Each "pro" file is displayed in a file-folder design and set off from regular text. This feature provides us with the opportunity to recognize 16 of the outstanding teachers across the United States with whom we have had the privilege to work.

A stronger emphasis has been placed on assessment in this edition. The discussion on ways to assess students' learning and how to develop an assessment portfolio has been expanded in the second chapter, and assessment is considered with each listening, talking, reading, and writing teaching strategy presented in the text.

The text has been updated and revised in other ways as well. The book lists have been updated and new titles have been added throughout. One or more figures in each chapter have been designated as "teachers' notebook pages." These figures include practical information about teaching language arts and are presented as pages in a spiral notebook. Also, Chapter 14, Writers' Tools: Grammar, has been rewritten to provide more useful information about how to tie grammar instruction to reading and writing.

This text has been prepared with preservice and inservice teachers in mind, and special features have been included to increase the book's readability. Each chapter begins with a chapter outline, a preview, and points to ponder. To focus readers' attention on key terms, newly introduced terms are italicized and defined in text. Lists of characteristics, trade books, and steps in teaching strategies are presented in figures to spotlight them for readers. A review at the end of each chapter summarizes the main concepts presented in that chapter.

Extension activities are included after the review at the end of each chapter. Readers may apply the information that was presented in the chapter and stretch their knowledge through these activities. Many of the extensions invite readers to observe and interact with students in elementary classrooms while others ask them to prepare instructional materials, to consult outside readings, or to examine how they use language themselves.

Helping students learn to communicate effectively using the language arts is a great challenge facing elementary teachers today, and we hope that the second edition of *Language Arts: Content and Teaching Strategies* will prove to be a useful resource to teachers in meeting this challenge.

Acknowledgements

Many people helped us and encouraged us during the development of this text and during this revision. We offer our heartfelt thanks to each of them. First, we want to thank our graduate and undergraduate students at California State University, Fresno, the University of Oklahoma, and Virginia Tech, who taught us as we taught them. Their insightful questions challenged and broadened our thinking, and their willingness to experiment with the teaching strategies that we were developing furthered our own learning. We owe a special debt of gratitude to Dr. Mary E. Hitchcock of Southeastern Oklahoma State University who spent many hours researching topics, tracking down books and journal articles, and laboriously verifying references for this revision.

We want to express our appreciation to the teachers who invited us into their classrooms and shared their expertise with us. In particular, we want to thank the teachers we have profiled in each chapter: Chapter 1—Betty Jordan, Western Hills Elementary School; Chapter 2—Sally Tsuchiguchi, Viking Elementary School; Chapter 3—Pioneer Intermediate School; Chapter 4—Marie Whiteside, Norseman Elementary School; Chapter 5—Pat Daniel, South Rock Creek School; Chapter 6—Glenna Jarvis, Western Hills Elementary School; Chapter 7—Judy Reeves, Western Hills Elementary School; Chapter 8—Pat Bishop, Heaton Elementary School; Chapter 9—Kathy Brown, Jackson Elementary School; Chapter 10—Mary Ann Commeau, Western Hills Elementary School; Chapter 11—Sandy Harris, Anadarko Middle School; Chapter 12—Judy Kenney, Jackson Elementary School; Chapter 13—Gordon Martindale, Columbia Elementary School; Chapter 14—Kaye Hicks, Western Hills Elementary School; Chapter 15—Brian Bennett, Heaton Elementary School; and Chapter 16—Sue Wuestner, Western Hills Elementary School.

Thanks, too, to the children whose writing samples and photographs appear in the book and to the teachers and administrators who welcomed us into their schools to take photographs and collect writing samples: Max Ballard, Nicoma Park Intermediate School, Nicoma Park, OK; Anita Beard, Norman, OK; Marc Bell, Monroe Elementary School, Norman, OK; Kathy Bending, Highland Elementary School, Downers Grove, IL; Linda Bessett, Sulphur Elementary School, Sulphur, OK; Gracie Branch, Eisenhower Elementary School, Norman, OK; Juli Carson, Jefferson Elementary School, Norman, OK; Shirley Carson, Wayne Elementary School, Wayne, OK; Chris Edge-Christensen, Whittier Elementary School, Lawton, OK, Patty Cejda, Hubbard Elementary School, Noble, OK; Pam Cottom, James Griffith Intermediate School, Choctaw, OK; Jean Davis, James Griffith Intermediate School, Choctaw, OK; Deanie Dillen, Putnam City Schools, Oklahoma City, OK; Polly Dwyer, University of Oklahoma, Norman, OK; Susan Fields, Noble Junior High School, Noble, OK; Charlotte Fleetham, Pioneer Intermediate School, Noble, OK; Parthy Ford, Whittier Elementary School, Lawton, OK; Debbie Frankenberg, Purcell Elementary School, Purcell, OK; Chuckie Garner, Kennedy Elementary School, Norman, OK; Peggy Givens, Watonga Middle School, Watonga, OK; Teri Gray, James Griffith Intermediate School, Choctaw, OK; Garett Griebel, Chickasha, OK; Debbie Hamilton, Irving Middle School, Norman, OK; Lori Hardy, James Griffith Intermediate School, Choctaw, OK; Sandra Harris, Anadarko Middle School, Anadarko, OK; Paula Harrington, Southgate Elementary School, Moore, OK; Ernestine Hightower, Whittier Elementary School, Lawton, OK; Beth Hogh, Pioneer Intermediate School, Noble, OK; Linda Hopper, Wilson Elementary School, Norman, OK; Nancy Hutter, Tioga Elementary School, Bensenville, IL; Annette Jacks, Blanchard Elementary School, Blanchard, OK; Suzie Jennings, Lindsay, OK; Janet Kretschmer, McGuffey Foundation School, Oxford, OH; Helen Lawson,

Deer Creek School, Oklahoma City, OK; Glenda LoBaugh, Ranchwood Elementary School, Yukon, OK; Mark Mattingly, Central Junior High School, Lawton, OK; Carolyn Mays, Garfield Elementary School, Lawton; Pam McCarthy, Hubbard Elementary School, Noble, OK; Tissie McClure, Nicoma Park Intermediate School, Nicoma Park, OK; John McCracken, Nevin Coppock School, Tipp City, OH; Gina McCook, Whittier Middle School, Norman, OK; Mary Oldham, University of Oklahoma, Norman, OK; Teresa Ossenkop, Eisenhower Elementary School, Norman, OK; Sandra Pabst, Monroe Elementary School, Norman, OK; Cindy Perez, John Adams Elementary School, Lawton, OK; JoAnne Pierce, Horace Mann Elementary School, Duncan, OK; Alice Rakitan, Highland Elementary School, Downers Grove, IL; Jelta Reneau and M'Lynn Emanuel, Lincoln Elementary School, Norman, OK; Jenny Reno, Kay Preston, Eunice Edison, Pat Blackburn, Linda Riley, Marilyn Williams, Pat Pittman, Western Hills Elementary School, Lawton, OK; Kim Schmidt, La Petite Academy, Oklahoma City, OK; Becky Selle, Bethel School, Shawnee, OK; Jo Ann Steffen, Nicoma Park Junior High School, Nicoma Park, OK; Gail Warmath, Longfellow Middle School, Norman, OK; Letty Watt, Jefferson Elementary School, Norman, OK; Jeanne Webb, Norman Christian Academy, Norman, OK; MaryBeth Webeler, Highland Elementary School, Downers Grove, IL; Linda White, University of Oklahoma, Norman, OK; Brenda Wilkins, Horace Mann Elementary School, Duncan, OK; Vera Willey, Lincoln Elementary School, Norman, OK; Jean Winters and Diane Lewis, Irving Middle School, Norman, OK; Susie Wood, Marlow, OK. And, thanks, too, to the parents who welcomed us into their homes to take photographs of their children and shared their children's writing with us: Regina Blair, Sherry Bynum, Carole and Bill Hamilton, Martha and Rob Lamm, John and Lois McCracken, Kendra Magness, and Susan Steele.

We also appreciate the support our colleagues and administrators have given us as we have worked on this book. We especially want to thank our colleagues who have encouraged, listened, and shared their ideas with us. For this colleagial support, we are especially grateful. We also want to thank our colleagues who served as reviewers, carefully reading and reacting to the several drafts of this edition: Marilou Sorenson, University of Utah; Joan Glazer, University of Rhode Island; Victoria Chou-Hare, University of Illinois at Chicago; Carol R. Personke, University of Wisconsin; Marilyn T. Gaddis, Southwest Texas State University, San Marcos; LaVerne Warner, Sam Houston State University, Huntsville, Texas; Grant Cioffi, University of New Hampshire; and Lea McGee, Boston University.

Finally, we want to express sincere appreciation to our editors at Macmillan Publishing Company. We want to thank our administrative editor Jeff Johnston for his steadfast support and encouragement and Linda Scharp, our developmental editor, for her wealth of creative ideas, cheer when it was needed most, and, friendship. We also want to thank Ben Ko, our production editor, who moved the book so expertly through the maze of production details, and Molly Kyle, our copyeditor, who wielded her red pen so effectively to fine-tune the manuscript.

CONTENTS

8 ◆ READING AND WRITING CONNECTIONS   265

13 ◆ WRITERS' TOOLS: HANDWRITING   471

14 ◆ WRITERS' TOOLS: GRAMMAR   495

15 ◆ EXTENDING LANGUAGE ARTS ACROSS THE CURRICULUM   519

1 LEARNING AND THE LANGUAGE ARTS

HOW CHILDREN LEARN
    The Cognitive Structure
    Learning
    Implications for Learning Language Arts

HOW CHILDREN LEARN LANGUAGE
    Stages of Language Development
    Development in the Elementary Grades
    Implications for Learning Language Arts

HOW CHILDREN BECOME LITERATE
    Emergent Literacy
    Implications for Learning Language Arts

HOW CHILDREN LEARN LANGUAGE ARTS
    Communicative Competence
    The Four Language Modes
    An Instructional Model

◆ CHAPTER 1 PRESENTS AN OVERVIEW OF THE COGNITIVE,
psycholinguistic, and sociolinguistic learning theories that provide the foundation
for the language arts curriculum presented in this textbook.

◆ AS YOU ARE READING, THINK ABOUT THESE QUESTIONS:

How does knowledge about how children learn affect teaching language arts?

Does knowledge about how children learn to talk relate to the teaching strategies used in elementary classrooms?

How does knowledge about how children become literate compare with how they are taught to read and write?

Based on how children learn language arts, how should language arts programs be developed for elementary students?

Understanding how children learn and particularly how they learn language influences how we teach language arts. The instructional program should never be construed as a smorgasbord of materials and activities; instead, teachers design instruction based on what they know about how children learn. The teacher's role in the elementary classroom is changing. Teachers are now viewed as decision makers, empowered with both the obligation and the responsibility to make curricular decisions. In the language arts program, these curricular decisions have an impact on the content (information being taught) and the teaching strategies (techniques for teaching content). Our approach in this textbook incorporates cognitive, psycholinguistic, and sociolinguistic theories of learning. This approach couples the *constructivist,* or cognitive, theories of learning proposed by Jean Piaget and Jerome Bruner with the psycholinguistic theories developed by Frank Smith, and the sociolinguistic theories of Lev Vygotsky. *Psycholinguistics* is a discipline that combines cognitive psychology with linguistics (the study of language) to focus on the cognitive or mental aspects of language learning. *Sociolinguistics* is a similar combination of disciplines—sociology and linguistics—to emphasize the social and cultural implications of language learning.

❖ HOW CHILDREN LEARN

Jean Piaget (1886–1980) was a Swiss psychologist who developed a new theory of learning, or cognitive development, that radically changed our conceptions of child development and learning. Piaget's theoretical framework (1969) differs substantially from behavioral theories that had influenced education for decades. Piaget describes learning as the modification of students' cognitive structures as they interact with and adapt to their environment. This definition of learning requires a reexamination of the teacher's role. Instead of dispensing knowledge, teachers engage students with experiences and environments that require them to modify their cognitive structures and construct their own knowledge.

Psycholinguists view language as an example of children's cognitive development, of their ability to learn. Young children learn to talk by being immersed in a language-rich environment and without formal instruction. In a period of only three or four years, children acquire a sizable vocabulary and internalize the grammar of language. Preschoolers' oral language development provides a model of language learning that can be used in discussing how children learn to read and write.

Sociolinguists view language learning as social and as a reflection of the culture and community in which students live (Heath, 1983; Vygotsky, 1978, 1986). According to Vygotsky, language helps to organize thought, and children use language to learn as well as to communicate and share experiences with others. Understanding that children use language for social purposes allows teachers to plan instructional activities that incorporate a social component, such as having students share their writing with classmates. And, because children's language and concepts of literacy reflect their cultures and home communities, teachers must respect students' language and appreciate cultural differences in their attitudes toward learning and learning language arts in particular.

The Cognitive Structure

The *cognitive structure* is the organization of knowledge in the brain, and knowledge is organized into category systems called *schemata*. (A single category is called a *schema*.) Within the schemata are three components: categories of knowledge, the features or rules for determining what constitutes a category and what will be included in each category, and a network of interrelationships among the categories (Smith, 1975). These schemata may be compared to a conceptual filing system in which children and adults organize and store the information derived from their past experiences. Taking this analogy further, information is filed in the brain in "file folders." As children learn, they add file folders to their filing system and as they study a topic, that file folder becomes thicker.

As children learn, they invent new categories, and while each person has many similar categories, schemata are personalized according to individual experiences and interests. Some people, for example, may have only one general category, bugs, into which they lump their knowledge of ants, butterflies, spiders, and bees, while other people distinguish between insects and spiders and develop a category for each. Those who distinguish between insects and spiders also develop a set of rules based on the distinctive characteristics of these animals for classifying them into one category or the other. In addition to bug or spider categories, a network of interrelationships connect these categories to other categories. Networks, too, are individualized, depending on each person's unique knowledge and experiences. The category "spiders" might be networked as a subcategory of arachnids, and the class relationship between scorpions and spiders might be made. Other networks, such as a connection to a "poisonous animals" category or a "webs and nests" category could have been made. The networks that link categories, characteristics, and examples with other categories, characteristics, and examples are extremely complex.

As children adapt to their environment, they add new information about their experiences that requires them to enlarge existing categories or to construct new ones. According to Piaget (1969), two processes make this change possible. *Assimilation* is the cognitive process by which information from the environment is integrated into existing schemata. In contrast, *accommodation* is the cognitive process by which existing schemata are modified or new schemata are restructured to adapt to the environment. Through assimilation, children add new information to their picture of the world; through accommodation, they change their picture of the world on the basis of new information.

Learning

The mechanism for cognitive growth or learning is the process of *equilibration* (Piaget, 1975). Encountering something a child does not understand or cannot assimilate causes *disequilibrium,* or cognitive conflict. Disequilibrium typically produces confusion and agitation, feelings that impel children to seek *equilibrium,* or a comfortable balance with the environment. In other words, when confronted with new or discrepant information, children (as well as adults) are intrinsically motivated to try to make sense of it. If the child's schemata can accommodate the new information, then the disequilib-

When students work in cooperative groups, they use language to facilitate their learning.

rium caused by the new experience will motivate the child to learn. Equilibrium is thus regained at a higher developmental level. These are the steps of this process:

1. Equilibrium is disrupted by the introduction of new or discrepant information.
2. Disequilibrium occurs, and the dual processes of assimilation and accommodation function.
3. Equilibrium is attained at a higher developmental level.

If the new information is too difficult, however, and children cannot relate it to what they already know, they will not learn. The important implication for teachers is that new information must be puzzling, challenging, or, to use Piaget's words, "moderately novel." Information that is too easy is quickly assimilated, and information that is too difficult cannot be accommodated and will not be learned. Bybee and Sund (1982) suggest that teachers strive for an optimal mismatch between what children already know and what new information to present.

Prediction occurs as children put their schemata to use in interpreting their environment. They anticipate what will happen if they act in certain ways and predict the results of their actions. When children enter any situation, they organize their behavior according to what they can anticipate, using those schemata that would be appropriate to assimilate whatever in the environment interests them. If their schemata can assimilate all the stimuli in the situation, they relax, because they are in a comfortable state of equilibrium. If there are stimuli in the environment for which they cannot predict the results, however, they will proceed more cautiously, trying to discover the meanings of the stimuli they cannot anticipate. Children seek equilibrium, but they are always undergoing disequilibrium because they cannot assimilate discrepant stimuli without some accommodation.

More recent theories of learning emphasize social interaction. Vygotsky (1978) asserted that children learn by internalizing social relationships, and language is an

❖ "PRO" FILE

MANAGING GROUPS

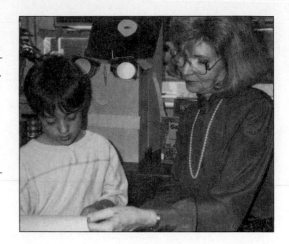

> *"Of course it's not easy to meet the needs of every student, but I try. I want to build on each student's interests while providing opportunities for him or her to listen, talk, read, and write."*
>
> Betty Jordan, First Grade Teacher
> Western Hills Elementary School

PROCEDURE

Shawn is a first grader in my class who is reading and writing well. He's interested in robots, and together we developed a unit on robots especially for Shawn. He is working on these activities:

• Reading three books to learn more about robots
  Debugging Rover (Matthews, 1985)
  Robots A₂Z (Metos, 1980)
  Get Ready for Robots! (Lauber, 1987)

• Making a model of a robot using cardboard boxes
• Writing a story about robots
• Sharing what he has learned with the class

This is a two-week unit for Shawn. He works on these activities while his classmates work individually or in small groups on other language arts activities. He has a file folder in which he keeps his books and papers. Shawn has just finished drafting his story about robots, which he will share with his classmates. He adds his name to the list of students on the chalkboard who have

important part in the learning process. Children's experiences are organized and shaped by society, but rather than merely absorbing these experiences, children negotiate and transform them as a dynamic part of the social context. They learn to talk through interactions with other people and to read and write through interactions with literate children and adults.

Implications for Learning Language Arts

Students interact with their environment and actively construct knowledge using the processes of assimilation and accommodation. Learning takes place when existing

something to share during sharing time this afternoon.

This is Shawn's story about a police officer robot named Gismo, showing his original spellings and lacking a few capital letters and punctuation marks (standard spellings for three words have been added in parentheses):

Gismo

Oces (Once) opon a time there wus a robot how (who) was a police he had saved many lives. He cot lots of creecs (criminals). He was the greatest man ever. One time he went in to a bank and cot a robers and he true (threw) them to neptune he was awared by a gold metel. He wus a HERO.

His classmates are looking forward to listening to the story, and they will clap for him and offer compliments about it. One or two children may even offer a suggestion about how he might improve the story. After today's sharing, Shawn will revise and edit his story before typing the final copy at the computer and binding it to make a book.

ASSESSMENT

When students are working on a variety of activities in the classroom, I am always worried that I won't be able to keep track of everyone's progress. I've devised several strategies that make it a little easier to keep track. First, I talk briefly with each child each morning so I know what each one is doing. I take the first five to ten minutes of our language arts block to make this check. Second, like every other child in the classroom, Shawn keeps a list of the activities he is working on in his unit folder. He checks off each activity as he completes it and has a conference with me to discuss his work. We talk about what he learned and what he will do next. I keep notes about the conferences, lists of the books he has read, and a checklist with the strategies and skills I notice him using in his work and those I need to teach. These two techniques help me to personalize learning for Shawn and my other students.

REFLECTIONS

It would be much easier for me to keep every student on the same page of the same book, but I know they won't learn as much. Shawn needs one type of activity, whereas Kari, Timothy, and the other children need some very different experiences. Right now, I have six groups functioning in the classroom: one group of ten children that I work closely with; Shawn and another student are working independently; and there are three other groups of six, four, and three children.

schemata must be enlarged because of assimilated information and when the schemata must be restructured to account for new experiences being acted on and accommodated.

As students engage in learning activities, they are faced with learning and discovering some new element in an otherwise known or familiar system of information. Students recognize or seek out the information embedded in a situation that makes sense and is moderately novel. By being forced to contend with the novel part of the information, students' schemata are disrupted, or put in a state of disequilibrium. Accommodation of the novel information causes a reorganization of the schemata, resulting in students having more complex schemata and being able to operate on more complex information than was previously possible.

Students learn by relating the known to the unknown as they try to make sense of what they encounter in their environment. Teachers need to tailor instruction to help students relate what they know to what they do not know. The amount of new information in a lesson should be within students' capacity to assimilate and accommodate without experiencing long periods of disequilibrium.

Vygotsky (1978) used the concept of "zone of proximal development" to explain how children learn through social interactions with adults. Adults help children in moving from their actual stage of development toward their potential, and children use language as well as experiences to learn.

In the lessons they prepare for their students, teachers can create optimal conditions for learning. When students do not have the schemata for predicting and interpreting the new information, teachers must help students relate what they know to what they do not know. Therefore, the new information must appear in a situation that makes sense and must be moderately novel; it must not be too difficult for students to accommodate to it.

Students process information or learn using one of three modes: experience, observation, and language (Smith, 1975). Imagine, for example, that a boy has just received a new two-wheel bicycle for his fifth birthday. How will he learn to ride it? Will his parents read him a book about bicycles? Will his father demonstrate how to ride the new bicycle while the boy observes? Will the boy get on his new bicycle and learn to ride it by trial and error? Of course, he will get on the new bicycle and learn to ride it by riding—through direct experience. Later, the father might demonstrate a tricky maneuver his son is having trouble mastering, or the boy may become so interested in bicycling that he will be motivated to read a book to learn more about it. Yet the learning process begins with experience for both in-school and out-of-school learning.

Experience is the most basic, concrete way of learning. According to Piaget (1969), elementary students are concrete thinkers and learn best through active involvement. The second and third learning modes, observation and language, are progressively more abstract and further removed from experience. Activities involving observation and language can be made more meaningful when used in conjunction with direct experience and real-life materials. A list of school experiences using each mode is presented in Figure 1−1.

❖ HOW CHILDREN LEARN LANGUAGE

Language enables children to learn about their world, to understand it, and to control it. As they learn to talk, youngsters implicitly develop knowledge about four language systems: the phonological, syntactic, semantic, and pragmatic systems. Children develop the *phonological,* or sound, system as they learn to pronounce each of the approximately 40 English speech sounds. These individual sounds, called *phonemes,* are represented in print with diagonal lines to differentiate them from *graphemes* (letter or letter combinations). Thus, the first letter in *mother* is written *m,* while the phoneme is written /m/, and the phoneme in *soap* represented by the grapheme *oa* is written /o/.

The second language system is the *syntactic,* or grammar, system. The word *grammar* here means the rules governing how words are combined in sentences as opposed to the grammar of English textbooks or the correct etiquette of language.

Experience	Observation	Language
interviewing	creating filmstrips	brainstorming
manipulating objects	drawing and painting	choral speaking/reading
participating in dramatic	pictures	debating
play	making diagrams,	dictating stories
participating in field	clusters, and story	discussing
trips	maps	listening to audiotapes
participating in role-play	"reading" wordless	listening to stories read
activities	picture books	aloud
using puppets	viewing films, filmstrips,	participating in
using the five senses	and videotapes	conversations
word play activities	viewing charts, maps,	participating in readers'
writing simulated	and models	theater
journals and	viewing plays and	reading
newspapers	puppet shows	taking notes
	viewing and writing	talking
	concrete poetry	writing
	watching	
	demonstrations	
	writing class	
	collaboration stories	

FIGURE 1–1

Activities Using the Three Learning Modes

Children use the syntactic system as they combine words to form sentences and learn to comprehend and produce statements, questions, and other types of sentences during the preschool years.

Another aspect of syntax is *morphology,* the study of word forms. Children quickly learn to combine words and word parts, such as adding -*s* to *dog* to create a plural and -*ed* to *play* to indicate past tense. These words and word parts are *morphemes,* the smallest units of meaning in language. *Dog* and *play* are *free morphemes* because they convey meaning while standing alone. The endings -*s* and -*ed* are *bound morphemes* because they must be attached to free morphemes to convey meaning. Prefixes and suffixes are also bound morphemes. The prefix *un-* in *unhappy* is a bound morpheme, whereas *happy* is a free morpheme because it can stand alone as a word. In addition to combining bound morphemes with free morphemes, two or more free morphemes can be combined to form compound words. *Birthday* is an example of a compound word created by combining two free morphemes.

The third language system is the *semantic,* or meaning, system. Vocabulary and the arrangement of words in sentences are the key components of this system. As children learn to talk, they acquire a vocabulary that is continually increasing through the preschool years. It is estimated that children have a vocabulary of 5000 words by the time they enter school, and they continue to acquire 3000 words each year during the elementary grades. As children acquire vocabulary, they also learn how to string the words together to form English sentences; for instance, children say "The dog has a bone," never "A has dog bone the." In English, word order and the relationships among words are crucial for comprehending the message.

The fourth language system is *pragmatics,* which deals with the social and cultural aspects of language use. People use language for many different *functions,* and how they talk or write varies according to purpose and audience. Language use also varies among social classes, cultural and ethnic groups, and geographic regions. These varieties are known as *dialects.* School is one cultural community, and the language of school is *standard English.* This register is formal, the one used in grammar books, in newspapers and magazines, and by television newscasters. Other forms, including those spoken in urban ghettos, in Appalachia, and by Mexican-Americans in the Southwest, are generally classified as *nonstandard English.* These nonstandard forms of English are alternatives, in which the phonology, syntax, and semantics differ from standard English—they are neither inferior nor substandard. These forms reflect the communities of the speakers, and the speakers communicate as effectively as others who use standard English in their communities. (For more information about standard and nonstandard English, see Chapter 16, "Teaching Students with Special Needs.")

As children learn to talk, read, and write, they learn to control the phonological, syntactic, semantic, and pragmatic language systems. Throughout this book, we will refer to these systems using the terminology introduced in this section. Because the terminology can be confusing, the words and their definitions are reviewed in Figure 1–2.

Stages of Language Development

Young children acquire oral language in a fairly regular and systematic way (Morrow, 1989). All children pass through the same stages, but, because of developmental differences as well as differences in social and cultural backgrounds, they do so at widely different ages (Jaggar, 1985). The ages we mention in this section are estimates, for reference only.

Birth to Age One.   The first real evidence that children are developing language occurs when they speak their first words. Before that time, they experiment with sounds. Typically, during the first year of life, babies vocalize a wide variety of speech-like sounds. The sounds they produce are repeated strings of consonant plus vowel syllables. Amazingly, babies' vocalizations include English sounds as well as sounds heard in German, Russian, Japanese, and other languages. The sounds not common to English gradually drop out, probably as a result of both listening to sounds in the environment and parents' reinforcement of familiar sounds, such as the eagerly awaited *ma-ma* and *da-da.* By nine months, children use a few familiar words such as *milk, doggie,* and *Mommy* to express whole ideas. These first words are most often nouns and invented words, and it is difficult to understand meaning without observing children's accompanying actions or gestures. For example, *ball* may mean "Look, I see a ball," "I want that ball," or "Oops, I dropped my ball, and I can't reach it."

One to Two Years of Age.   Children's vocabularies expand rapidly in this stage, and children begin putting two words together. For example, they may say *bye-bye car* and *allgone cookie.* This language is also known as telegraphic speech,

1. **Phonological System**

phonology	The study of the sounds in a language.
phoneme	The smallest unit of sound.
grapheme	The written representation of a sound using one or more letters.

2. **Syntactic System**

syntax or grammar	The rules governing how words are combined to form sentences.
morphology	The study of morphemes or word forms.
morpheme	The smallest unit of meaning in a language.
free morpheme	A morpheme that can stand alone as a word.
bound morpheme	A morpheme that cannot stand alone as a word and must be attached to a free morpheme.

3. **Semantic System**

semantics	The study of the meaning of a language.

4. **Pragmatic System**

pragmatics	The study of the social and cultural aspects of language.
function	The purpose for which a person uses language.
dialect	Variations in syntax and word choice due to social class, ethnic or cultural group or geographic region.
standard English	The form of English used in textbooks and by television newscasters.
nonstandard English	Other forms of English.

FIGURE 1–2

Terminology of the Four Language Systems

because nonessential words are omitted as they are in telegrams. Children use nouns, verbs, and adjectives—all high information words; they usually omit low information words—prepositions, articles, and conjunctions. Children's speech in this stage is rule-governed, but it is very different from adult speech, thus offering evidence for the psycholinguists' belief that children create their own ways to represent meaning rather than simply imitate adult language.

Two to Three Years of Age. Telegraphic speech begins to evolve into longer utterances and to sound more like adult forms of talk. Word order, the basis of syntax in English, becomes important when children begin to use utterances of three and four words. At this point, grammatical relations such as subject, verb, and object begin to appear in overt syntactic structures. The phonological, syntactic, and semantic systems are constructed as development continues to come closer and closer to the adult form of the language used in their speech communities. Children's vocabularies reach about 1000 words by the end of their third year.

Language is both a means of classifying experiences into categories and communicating experiences to other people.

Three to Four Years of Age. Children now use more complex sentences that include pronouns, adjectives, adverbs, possessives, and plurals. They generalize knowledge about language and then learn about exceptions, such as irregular past-tense markers. At first children use the unmarked form of irregular verbs such as *ate,* as in "I ate my cereal," that they hear in the speech of those around them. Then they perceive that past tense is marked with the *-ed* morpheme and begin to use it with practically all past tense verbs, so that they now say "I eated my cereal." Finally children realize that some verbs are regular, with the past tense marked by *-ed* (as in *talk–talked*), whereas other verbs have different past-tense forms. Then they again say "I ate my cereal." This tendency to overgeneralize the *-ed* past-tense marker of regular verbs continues in some children's speech until age five. Children's vocabularies reach about 1500 words by the end of this year.

Four to Five Years of Age. Children's vocabularies grow to 3000 words, and they have acquired most of the elements of adult language. Sentences are grammatical by adult standards, and children use language for more functions. Their sentences grow in length and complexity; they develop the auxiliary systems and transformations; they develop the ability to change the word order of their sentences to express desired meanings. The initial physical and emotional context of speech with objects, people, events, and locations continues to play an important role in language development.

Five to Six Years of Age.   By age five, children's language is similar to adult language. Most grammatical rules have been mastered, and language patterns are complex. Children use language for a variety of purposes, including to entertain. They can also use language in humorous ways, and their interest in jokes and riddles usually begins at this age.

During the preschool years, parents make an important contribution to language development by expanding and extending children's talk. To the child's utterance, "Dog bark," for example, a parent might respond, "Yes, the dog is barking at the kitty," and provide information about why the dog is barking (Cazden, 1972). This interaction helps the child interpret what is happening in the environment and adds grammatical information. It is a model to learn from, not a sample to copy (Cazden, 1983). Bruner (1978) used the term *scaffold* as a metaphor to explain the value of parents' expansions and extensions of their children's language. Scaffolds are temporary launching platforms that support and encourage children's language development to more complex levels. In addition, Bruner noted that parents use these interactions to keep their children from sliding back once they have moved on to higher platforms and more complex language constructions. Teachers provide a similar type of assistance as they support students in learning language arts (Applebee & Langer, 1983).

Development in the Elementary Grades

Although the most important period in oral language acquisition is the preschool years, children's phonological, syntactic, semantic, and pragmatic development continues in the elementary grades and beyond. They continue to acquire additional sentence patterns; their vocabularies expand tremendously; and they master the remaining sounds of English.

Phonological Development.   Children have mastered a large part of the phonological system by the time they come to school. A few sounds, especially in medial and final positions, however, are not acquired until after age five or six. These sounds include /v/, /th/, /ch/, /sh/, and /zh/. Even at age seven or eight, students still make some sound substitutions, especially in consonant clusters. They may, for example, substitute /w/ for /r/ or /l/, as in *cwack* for *crack* (DeStefano, 1978). When students are learning to read and write, they read words aloud the same way they say them and spell words phonetically, the same way they say them.

Syntactic Development.   Students acquire a variety of sentence patterns during the elementary grades. They begin to construct complex sentences and use embedding techniques to combine ideas. Whereas primary-grade students use the connector *and* to string together a series of ideas, middle- and upper-grade students learn to use dependent clauses and other connectors. A young child might say, "I have a hamster *and* he is brown *and* his name is Pumpkin *and* he likes to run on his wheel," but an older student can embed these ideas: "My brown hamster named Pumpkin likes to run on his wheel." Older students learn to use connectors such as *because, if, unless, meanwhile, in spite of,* and *nevertheless* (Loban, 1976). The constructions students learn to use in their talk also appear in their writing. Ingram (1975) found that fifth- and seventh-grade students used more complex, embedded structures in writing than in talking. This finding makes sense because when students write, they must organize their thoughts and, for efficiency, embed as much information as possible.

Students also learn more about word order in English sentences. Consider these two sentences:

Ann told Tom to leave.
Ann promised Tom to leave.

Who is going to leave? According to the Minimal Distance Principle (MDP), the noun closest to the complement verb (i.e., *to leave*) is the subject of that verb. In the first sentence, *Tom* is the person who will leave. Substitute these other verbs for *told: asked, wanted, tried, urged, commanded, implored.* In each case *Tom* is the person to leave. *Promise* is an exception to the MDP, however, so in the second sentence, it is *Ann* who will leave, not *Tom.* Chomsky (1969) found that primary-grade students overgeneralize the MDP principle and equate *promise* sentences with *tell* sentences. During the middle grades, however, students learn to distinguish the exceptions to the rule.

As students learn to read, they are introduced to the more complex syntactic forms and other conventions found in written language. One form unique to writing is the passive voice. The active voice is almost always used in talk (e.g., "Bobby broke the vase"), rather than the passive voice (e.g., "The vase was broken by Bobby").

Semantic Development. Of the language systems, Lindfors (1980) says that semantic growth is the most vigorous in the elementary grades. Children's vocabulary increases rapidly, perhaps as much as 3000 words per year. At the same time that children are learning new words, they are also learning that many words have more than one meaning. Meaning is usually based on context, or the surrounding words. The common word *run,* for instance, has more than 30 meanings listed in *The Random House Dictionary of the English Language* (Flexner, 1987), and the meaning is tied to the context in which it is used:

Will the mayor *run* for reelection?
The bus *runs* between Dallas and Houston.
The advertisement will *run* for three days.
The plane made a bombing *run.*
Will you *run* to the store and get a loaf of bread for me?
The dogs are out in the *run.*
Oh, no! I got a *run* in my new pair of pantyhose!

Primary-grade students do not have the full, adult meaning of many words; rather, they learn meanings through a process of refinement (Clark, 1971). They add "features" or layers of meaning. In the elementary grades, students use this refinement process to distinguish between pairs of words such as *ask* and *tell* to expand their range of meanings for many common words.

Pragmatic Development.   When children come to school they speak the language of their family and community, and at school they are introduced to standard English, which may be quite similar to or different from their own language dialect. They learn about appropriateness and to vary the language they speak or write according to form, purpose, and audience. M. A. K. Halliday (1973, 1975) has identified seven categories of language function that apply to oral and written language and even to the nonlanguage forms of communication such as gestures and pantomime. These are Halliday's seven categories:

1.   Instrumental language—language to satisfy needs
2.   Regulatory language—language to control the behavior of others
3.   Interactional language—language to establish and maintain social relationships
4.   Personal language—language to express personal opinions
5.   Imaginative language—language to express imagination and creativity
6.   Heuristic language—language to seek information and to find out about things
7.   Informative language—language to convey information

During the elementary grades, students learn to use oral language for a wider range of functions, and they learn written language alternatives for the oral language functions. Figure 1–3 lists some oral and written language alternatives for the seven language functions. Frank Smith (1977) has made a number of observations about how these language functions are learned and applied in school settings:

- Language is learned in genuine communication experiences, rather than through practice activities that lack functional purposes.
- Skill in one language function does not generalize to skill in other functions.
- Language is rarely used for just one function at a time; typically, two or more language functions are involved in talking or writing.
- These language functions involve an audience—listeners for talking and readers for writing.
- Language is one communication alternative; other alternatives include gestures, drawings, pantomime, and rituals.

When children are using language functionally, they are using it for genuine communication and are interacting with others (Pinnell, 1975). These two characteristics of functional language are apparent in both oral and written language.

Function	Oral Language Activity	Written Language Activity
1. Instrumental Language	conversations commercials	notes business letters letters-to-the-editor advertisements
2. Regulatory Language	directions gestures dramatic play	directions classroom rules
3. Interactional Language	conversations sharing discussions	friendly letters pen pal letters courtesy letters dialogue journals
4. Personal Language	discussions debates show and tell sharing commercials	personal journals dialogue journals response to literature activities advertisements
5. Imaginative Language	storytelling readers theater dramatic play role-playing	reading and writing stories and poems writing scripts simulated journals simulated newspapers
6. Heuristic Language	interviews role-playing discussions	learning logs clustering cubing researching and report writing

7. Informative Language	oral reports
	discussions,
		researching and
		  report writing
		reading and writing
		  newspapers
		reading and writing
		  timelines, charts,
		  and maps

FIGURE 1–3

Teacher's Notebook Page: Language Activities Illustrating the Seven Functions of Language

The teacher's role is twofold: to foster a wide range of language use in the classroom, and to find ways to extend children's language in real-life situations. Because children's ability to use one language function does not generalize to ability in other functions, it is essential that students have opportunities to use each of the seven language functions. In her study of the functions of talk in a primary-grade classroom, Pinnell (1975) found that first graders most commonly used interactional language (for social purposes) and rarely used heuristic language (to seek information) when they talked and worked in small groups. Camp (1987) studied seventh graders' language functions during science class and found that students used the same language functions—interactional and heuristic—most commonly and least commonly. These two researchers concluded that students need to experiment with all seven language functions to learn what they can accomplish with language. Some of the language functions may not occur spontaneously in students' talk and writing, and teachers need to plan genuine communication experiences that incorporate all the language functions.

The concept of language functions is relatively new, and research is currently under way that will undoubtedly affect how language arts is taught in the future. For instance, Gere and Abbott (1985) categorized students' talk in writing conferences, and Florio and Clark (1982) examined the language functions in elementary students' compositions. One drawback of much of this research is that several different frameworks are being used to categorize children's language samples, so it is difficult to compare the findings.

Implications for Learning Language Arts

How children learn to talk has important implications for how children learn language arts in school and how teachers teach language arts. These characteristics delineate the sociopsycholinguistic orientation presented in this chapter:

- Children learn to talk by being immersed in the language of their community, not by being taught talking skills in a prescribed sequential order.
- Children construct their own knowledge as they make and test hypotheses, leading to progressive refinements of their talk.
- Children learn and use language for meaningful, functional, and genuine communication purposes.
- Adults provide models and scaffolds to support children's learning.
- Parents and other caregivers expect that children will be successful in learning to talk.

Imagine how different life would be in homes with young children if adults tried to teach children to talk as they have been traditionally taught to read and write. Parents would bring workbooks and charts listing talk skills home from the hospital with the baby. Children would be kept in a quiet room, and parents would first speak to the babies only in single, one-syllable words, then in two-syllable words, and finally in short sentences. Parents would introduce consonant sounds in a particular order, and at some point they would try to use all short vowel words in silly nonsense sentences. Ridiculous, right?

If children learn to talk so well in the short period of three or four years using a natural, immersion approach, why should teachers use an entirely different method to help children learn to read and write only a year or two later? Educators are now recognizing that the strategies parents use to help children learn to talk can be adapted for teaching language arts in the elementary school.

❖ HOW CHILDREN BECOME LITERATE

Literacy used to mean knowing how to read, but the term has been broadened to encompass both reading and writing, so that *literacy* now means the competence "to carry out complex tasks using reading and writing related to the world of work and to life outside the school" (*Cases in Literacy*, 1989, p. 36). Educators are also identifying other literacies that they believe will be needed in the 21st century. Our reliance on radio and television for conveying ideas has awakened us to the importance of "oracy" (the ability to express oneself in and understand spoken language), and visual literacy is receiving a great deal of attention.

The term *literacy* is being used in different ways as well. Teachers are introducing elementary students to computers and developing a "computer literacy." Similarly, math and science educators speak of mathematical and scientific literacies. Hirsch (1987) has called for another type of literacy, "cultural literacy," as a way to introduce children "to the major ideas and ideals from past cultures that have defined and shaped today's society." Rather than a prescription of books to read or concepts to define, however, literacy is a tool, a way to come to learn about the world and a means to participate more fully in society.

Emergent Literacy

Literacy is a process that begins well before the elementary grades and continues into adulthood, if not throughout life. It used to be that five-year-old children came to kindergarten to be "readied" for reading and writing instruction, which would formally begin in first grade. The implication was that there was a point in children's development when it was time to begin teaching them to read. For those not ready, a variety of "readiness" activities would prepare them for reading. Since the 1970s this view has been discredited by teachers' and researchers' observations (Clay, 1989). The children themselves demonstrated that they could retell stories, scribble letters, invent printlike writing, and listen to stories read aloud to them. Some children even taught themselves to read.

This new perspective on how children become literate—that is, how they learn to read and write—is known as *emergent literacy*. Studies from 1966 on have shaped the current outlook (Clay, 1967; Durkin, 1966; Holdaway, 1979; Taylor, 1983; Teale, 1982; Teale & Sulzby, 1989; McGee & Richgels, 1989; Morrow, 1989). Now, researchers are looking at literacy learning from the child's point of view. The age range has been extended to include children as young as twelve or fourteen months of age who

Preschool children gain valuable knowledge about reading and writing when their parents read to them.

listen to stories being read aloud, notice labels and signs in their environment, and experiment with pencils. The concept of literacy has been broadened to include the cultural and social aspects of language learning, and children's experiences with and understandings about written language—both reading and writing—are included as part of emergent literacy.

Teale and Sulzby (1989) paint a portrait of young children as literacy learners with these characteristics:

Children begin to learn to read and write very early in life.

Young children learn the functions of literacy through observing and participating in real-life settings in which reading and writing are used.

Young children's reading and writing abilities develop concurrently and interrelatedly through experiences in reading and writing.

Young children learn through active involvement with literacy materials, by constructing their understanding of reading and writing.

Teale and Sulzby describe young children as active learners who construct their own knowledge about reading and writing with the assistance of parents and other literate persons. These caregivers help by demonstrating literacy as they read and write, by supplying materials, and by structuring opportunities for children to be involved in reading and writing. The environment is positive, with children experiencing reading and writing in many facets of their everyday lives and observing others who are engaged in literacy activities.

Implications for Learning Language Arts

The way children learn about written language is remarkably similar to how they learn to talk. Children are immersed in written language as they are first in oral language. They have many opportunities to see reading and writing taking place for real purposes and to experiment with written language. Through these experiences, children actively construct their knowledge about literacy. As parents and other adults model the processes of reading and writing, they provide a scaffold for children's learning. The "Joint Statement on Literacy Development and Pre-first Grade" presented in Appendix A reinforces these conclusions.

❖ HOW CHILDREN LEARN LANGUAGE ARTS

> It seems to me that the most important general goal for education in the language arts is to enable each child to communicate, as effectively as he or she can, what he or she intends and to understand, as well as he or she can, what others have communicated, intentionally or not. (Brown, 1979, p. 483)

Roger Brown's statement succinctly states the goal for language arts instruction at all grade levels. The teacher's goal, then, is to help students learn to communicate effectively with others through oral and written language.

Communicative Competence

The ability to communicate effectively is known as *communicative competence* (Hymes, 1974), and it involves two components. The first component is the ability to transmit meaning through talking and writing, and the second is the ability to comprehend meaning through listening and reading. Communicative competence also involves pragmatics—students' fluency in the different registers of language as well as knowing when it is socially appropriate to use language in each register. For example, we use informal language with family members and close friends and more formal language with people we know less well or when giving a speech. Similarly, in writing we use different *registers,* or levels of formality. We write letters to close friends in a less formal register than we would use in writing a letter to the editor of the local newspaper.

The content and teaching strategies discussed in this book capitalize on students' cognitive and language abilities to help students develop communicative competence. We emphasize that teachers should provide opportunities for students to use language in situations that are meaningful, functional, and genuine. These three characteristics are important determinants in learning. Walter Loban (1979) echoes our beliefs: "The path to power over language is to use it in genuinely meaningful situations, whether we are reading, listening, writing, or speaking" (p. 485). Vygotsky (1978) concurs: "Reading and writing must be something the child needs" (p. 117); they should be "relevant to life" (p. 118).

We will discuss a variety of language activities for helping students develop communicative competence, such as:

Conducting oral interviews of community residents with special knowledge, interests, or talents

Writing a simulated journal assuming the role of a character while reading a story, autobiography, or informational book

Writing stories using the writing process and then sharing the stories with classmates and other genuine audiences

Analyzing word choice or other aspects of language in the poems they read and write

Compiling class newspapers or simulated newspapers set in the historical period being studied

These activities exhibit the three characteristics of all worthwhile experiences with language. They use language in meaningful rather than contrived situations. They are functional, or real-life, activities. They are genuine rather than artificial activities, such as those typical of workbooks and ditto sheets, because they communicate.

The Four Language Modes

Traditionally, language arts educators have defined *language arts* as the study of the four modes of language: listening, talking, reading, and writing. Thinking is sometimes referred to as the fifth language mode, but, more accurately, it permeates all the language modes.

Beginning at birth, listening is children's first contact with language. Listening instruction is often neglected in elementary classrooms because teachers feel that students have already learned to listen and that instructional time should be devoted to reading and writing. We present an alternative view of listening and listening instruction in Chapter 4, focusing on the following key concepts:

- Listening is a process of which hearing is only one part.
- Students listen for many purposes.
- Students listen differently according to their purpose.
- Students need to learn strategies for the different listening purposes.

As with listening, teachers often neglect instruction in talk during the elementary grades because they feel students already know how to talk. Students need to refine their oral language skills, however, and learn to use talk for more formal purposes. In Chapter 5 we will discuss these key concepts about talk:

- Talk is an essential part of the language arts curriculum.
- Talk is necessary for success in all academic areas.
- Talk ranges from informal conversations and discussions to more formal presentations, including oral reports and debates.
- Drama, including storytelling and role-playing, provides a valuable method of learning and powerful way of communicating.

Until recently, teachers have focused instructional time almost exclusively on reading, but now they are learning to integrate reading with writing and the other language arts. We present the integrated approach throughout this book and focus on reading-writing connections in Chapter 8. Key concepts about reading that will surface in Chapter 8 and throughout this book include the following:

- Reading and writing are interrelated strategic processes.
- Reading allows children to experience and appreciate literature.
- Reading involves both reading aloud to students and students reading independently.
- Informational books are resources for content-area–related language activities (e.g., oral and written research reports).
- Proofreading is a unique type of reading that writers use when they edit their compositions.

The new emphasis on writing focuses on the writing process, and elementary students use this process approach to draft, revise, and share their writing. Chapters 6 through 11 focus on writing, with special emphasis on the writing process. Spelling and handwriting (Chapters 12 and 13) are tools that writers need to communicate effectively with their readers. We will present the following key concepts about writing:

- Informal writing is used as a way to learn and as prewriting.
- Writing is a process in which students cycle recursively through prewriting, drafting, revising, editing, and sharing stages.
- Elementary students experiment with many different written language forms.
- Students learn to write stories, poems, and other forms using literature as a model.
- Spelling and handwriting are tools for writers.

The four language modes can be compared and contrasted in a variety of ways. First, oral versus written: listening and talking are oral, while reading and writing are written. Second, primary versus secondary: the oral language modes are learned in-

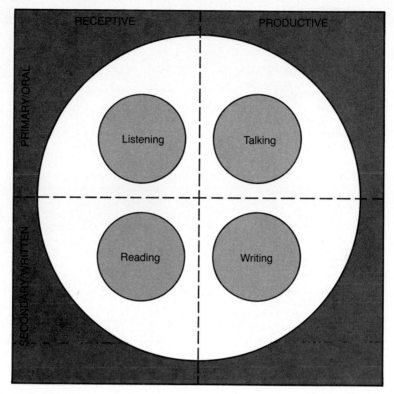

FIGURE 1–4

Relationships Among the Four Language Modes

formally at home before children come to school, whereas the written language modes are typically considered the school's responsibility and are taught more formally. Listening and talking are called primary language modes; reading and writing are called secondary language modes. The third way to compare the modes is receptive versus productive: two language modes, listening and reading, are receptive; talking and writing are productive. In the receptive language modes, students receive or comprehend a message orally through listening or in writing as they read. In the productive language modes, students produce a message, orally or in writing. These three sets of relationships are shown graphically in Figure 1–4.

Even though we will devote chapters to specific language modes, the grouping of the four language modes is both arbitrary and artificial. This arrangement wrongly suggests that there are separate stages of development for each language mode and that children use different mental processes for listening, talking, reading, and writing (Smith, 1979). It has generally been assumed that the four language modes develop in sequence from listening to talking to reading to writing. Although listening is the first form of language to develop, with talking beginning soon after, parents and preschool teachers have recently documented children's early interest in both reading and writing (Baghban, 1984; Bissex, 1980). Also, Carol Chomsky (1971) and other researchers

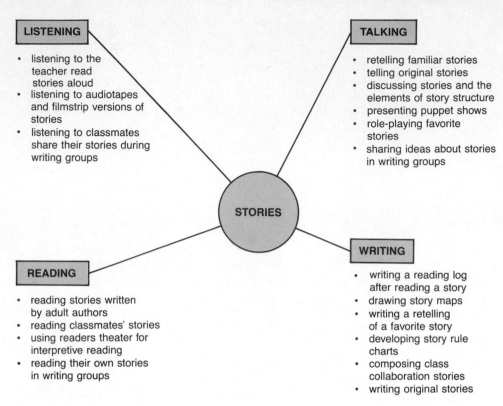

FIGURE 1–5

How the Language Modes Are Used in Learning about Stories

have observed young children experimenting with writing earlier than with reading. On the basis of reports from parents, teachers, and researchers, we can no longer assume that there is a definite sequence in learning and using the four language modes.

This grouping also suggests a division among the language modes, as though they could be used separately. In reality, they are used simultaneously and reciprocally. Almost any language arts activity involves more than one language mode. For instance, in learning about stories, students use all four language modes. They begin by listening when parents and teachers read aloud to them and later by reading stories themselves. Next, they retell familiar as well as original stories. They make puppets to dramatize and role-play favorite stories. From telling stories, they move to writing stories and sharing them with classmates or other genuine audiences. The cluster in Figure 1–5 lists these and other activities for learning about stories that involve all four language modes.

Over a 13-year period, researcher Walter Loban (1976) documented the language growth and development of a group of 338 students from kindergarten through 12th grade (ages 5–18). Two purposes of his longitudinal study were to examine differences between students who used language effectively and those who did not and to identify predictable stages of language development. Three of Loban's conclusions are especially noteworthy to our discussion of the relationship among the language modes. First, Loban reported positive correlations among the four language modes. Second, he found that students with less effective oral language (listening and talking) abilities tended to have less effective written language (reading and writing) abilities. And, third, he found a strong relationship between students' oral language ability and their overall academic ability. Loban's seminal study demonstrates clear relationships among the language modes and emphasizes the need to teach oral language in the elementary school language arts curriculum.

An Instructional Model

Theories of learning and evidence about how children learn language and become literate are useful in developing a model of instruction that can be adapted to various teaching strategies in a language arts program. This model establishes a sequence of instruction for the interaction of students, teacher, and materials in an environment that promotes the assimilation and accommodation of information. Language plays a crucial role in developing concepts as information is presented and discussed. Teachers serve both as a model and a scaffold to support and extend students' learning. The six steps in the sequence of instruction follow.

1. *Initiating.* Teachers introduce the information they want students to use in learning a concept or in understanding some type of information. The initiating step includes the teacher's initial questions, statements, and activities for stimulating interest in the lesson materials and engaging the students' participation. The process of assimilation begins when students are stimulated to participate in the lesson, and it will continue until cognitive conflict occurs.

2. *Structuring.* In this step, teachers structure the information so that students can begin to overcome the cognitive conflict they experience in the initiating step. To overcome cognitive conflict, students begin to enlarge or restructure an existing schema to fit the information, or they begin to develop new schema to organize the information. The information must be moderately novel and must relate in some way to what students already know. Relating new information to what students already know gives teachers greater assurance that students will be able to assimilate and accommodate it. Teachers must explore with students what information they already have in their schemata, because they can only infer students' existing schemata from what they say and do.

3. *Conceptualizing.* Teachers focus students' attention on the relationships among the pieces of information they present. In the structuring step, teachers have located and established the information; in the conceptualizing step, they try to organize and make explicit the relationships among the facts and to further the process of accommodation begun during structuring. When the accommodation process is completed, the existing schemata have been enlarged or a new schema has been developed that fits the new information. In either case, the cognitive conflict that arose in the initiating step has been eliminated.

4. *Summarizing.* Teachers review the major points of the lesson in this step. The material used in the structuring step and the relationships established during the conceptualizing step are organized and summarized for reviewing the concept. This step allows students to make any necessary adjustments in the concept or information and in the new interrelationships established within their cognitive structures. For students who did not complete the accommodation process in the conceptualizing step, summarizing presents another opportunity to accommodate the information.

5. *Generalizing.* Here teachers present information similar to that introduced in the initiating step. The same concept or information is contained in this new material. This step is a check on students' understanding of the concept presented in the lesson. Students demonstrate their understanding by generalizing from the first material to this new material.

6. *Applying.* In this step, students incorporate the concept or information in an activity that allows them to demonstrate their knowledge by using the concept in a novel or unique way.

Using the Instructional Model.   Students do not, of course, learn in such neat little steps. Rather, learning is a process of ebb and flow in which the assimilating and accommodating processes move back and forth as the student grasps pieces of information. Students may grasp a new concept in any of the steps of the instructional model; some students may not learn it at all. Teachers will need to plan additional lessons for the students who do not learn. Whether or not they learn depends on the closeness of the fit between their schemata and the information being presented. Information that does not in some way relate to an existing schema is almost impossible to learn. Information must be just moderately novel to fit students' existing cognitive structures. Some lessons may not lend themselves readily to this six-step sequence of instruction; for certain concepts, one or more of the steps may not be appropriate, and some adjustments may be necessary.

Two applications will illustrate how the teaching strategy can be used with almost any language arts concept: the first is a lesson on fables and the second is on quotation marks.

Fables are brief stories that teach a lesson. Our best-known fables were compiled by Aesop, a Greek slave who lived in the sixth century B.C., but many other civilizations have contributed fables as well. A number of fables have been retold for children, and, recently, children's authors such as Arnold Lobel (1980) have written their own books of fables. The goal of this lesson is for students to read fables, examine how authors construct the stories, and then tell and write their own fables. The lesson is organized around the six steps of the teaching strategy we have discussed. Other activities that would be part of this two-week unit for a fourth-grade class are not included in this plan for the sake of clarity.

1. *Initiating.* The teacher reads several fables such as "The Hare and the Tortoise" and "The Lion and the Mouse" from Hague's *Aesop's Fables* (1985) and explains that these short stories that teach a moral are called fables.

2. *Structuring.* Students and teacher develop a chart listing the characteristics of fables. The list may include these characteristics:

Fables are short.

The characters are usually animals.

The setting is usually rural and not important to the story.

Fables involve only one event.

The moral is usually stated at the end of the story.

The teacher then reads one or two other fables, and the students check that their list of the characteristics of fables is complete.

3. *Conceptualizing.* Students read other fables, and then relate a favorite fable by telling it aloud, by drawing a series of pictures, or in writing.

4. *Summarizing.* The teacher and students review the fables they have read and the list of characteristics they have developed. Then the teacher asks students to write a paragraph explaining what a fable is. Students share their explanations and compare them to the list of characteristics.

5. *Generalizing.* Students read other fables, such as Lobel's *Fables* (1980) or Lionni's *Frederick's Fables* (1985). It is important to include some fables that state the moral implicitly rather than explicitly. Students explain why these stories are or are not fables. The teacher also points out that, although these fables are based on many of the same morals that Aesop used, they were created—not retold—by Arnold Lobel and Leo Lionni.

6. *Applying.* Students write their own fables based on a moral that may be explicitly stated at the end of the story or implied in the story. Students use the writing process to draft, revise, edit, and publish their work. Later they share their fables with classmates or with students in another class who are also reading and writing fables.

The second application focuses on quotation marks. The goal of this lesson is for students to understand what quotation marks mean when they are reading and to be able to use them in their writing. This plan is also organized around the six steps of the teaching strategy. Other activities that would be part of this one-week unit for a second-grade class are omitted to show more clearly the sequence of activities.

1. *Initiating.* The teacher presents a chart with sentences containing direct quotes from *Mice Twice* (Low, 1980), a book the students particularly enjoyed reading (and rereading several times) the previous week. Students and teacher discuss the quotes, and the teacher asks what all the sentences have in common. Students notice that all the sentences include someone talking and are marked with quotation marks.

2. *Structuring.* The teacher presents information about quotation marks, explaining when to use them and that they were invented thousands of years ago to represent two talking lips. The teacher presents a second chart with sentences she

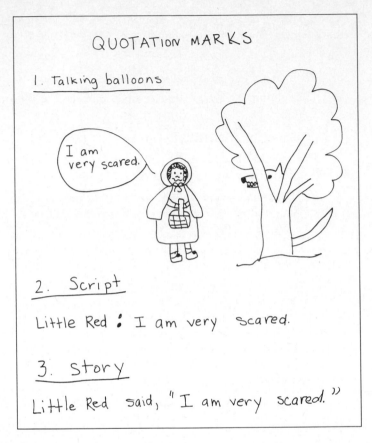

FIGURE 1−6

A Second Grader's Chart on Quotation Marks

has overheard students say during the day. The students work together to add quotation marks.

3.   *Conceptualizing.* Students read *Pinkerton, Behave* by Steven Kellogg (1979), and each student chooses a page in the story to rewrite using quotation marks; for example: The little girl cried, "Pinkerton! Fetch!" Then students add illustrations and share their pages. After the pages have been edited to be sure that quotation marks were used correctly, the pages are collated to make a class collaboration version of the story.

4.   *Summarizing.* Students and teacher review the rules for using quotation marks. To demonstrate their understanding, students pick a favorite story and use a page from the story to develop a chart, as shown in Figure 1−6. First, they draw a picture and use talking balloons to present the dialogue. Next, they rewrite the talk in script form. Finally, they use the narrative (or story) form.

5.   *Generalizing.* Students reread their journals and find four examples of dialogue. They copy the examples and use quotation marks correctly.

Step	Fables Lesson	Quotation Marks Lesson
Initiating	Read several fables and explain that fables are brief stories that teach a lesson.	Share a series of direct quotes from a book students have read recently. Discuss the use of quotation marks.
Structuring	Develop a chart listing the characteristics of fables. Read one or two others and check that the chart includes all characteristics.	Present information about quotation marks and additional quotes without marks for students to add.
Conceptualizing	Have students read other fables, then choose a favorite one to retell orally, with drawings, or in writing.	Find examples of quotations in a story students are reading. Have students each retell a page of the story to make a class collaboration book.
Summarizing	Review the fables already read and the list of characteristics. Ask students to write a paragraph explaining fables.	Review the rules about quotation marks and have students make a chart showing how dialogue written in talking balloons can be rewritten in script and story forms.
Generalizing	Read other stories including some with implicitly stated morals. Have students explain why these stories are or are not fables.	Students find examples of quotations in their journals and recopy them correctly. They check their work with a classmate.
Applying	Students write fables using the writing process and share their fables with other students.	Students compile a book of quotations with examples from literature, students' talk in the classroom, or talk at home.

FIGURE 1–7

Teacher's Notebook Page: Using the Teaching Strategy

6.. *Applying.* Students make a book of quotations from stories they have read or from remarks of classmates or family members. For each quotation, students use quotation marks and other punctuation marks correctly; for example, from *Where the Wild Things Are* (Sendak, 1963), one quotation might be: "I am a wild thing," said Max. These two applications of the teaching strategy are summarized in Figure 1–7.

❖ REVIEW

Language arts instruction should be based on theories and research about how children learn and how they learn language in particular. This chapter presents cognitive, psycholinguistic, and sociolinguistic theories of learning and related research to develop a paradigm for learning and teaching language arts in the elementary grades. The paradigm includes these components:

- Children learn through immersion in their environment.
- Children actively construct their knowledge through interaction with the environment.
- Adults facilitate children's learning through modeling and providing scaffolds.
- Adults expect children to be successful in learning.

The purpose of language arts instruction in the elementary grades is to develop children's communicative competence in the four language modes: listening, talking, reading, and writing. Based on the paradigm, language arts activities should be meaningful, functional, and genuine. Lessons may be based on a six-step teaching model.

❖ EXTENSIONS

1. Observe a language arts lesson being taught in an elementary classroom. Try to determine if the components of the language learning paradigm presented in this chapter are operationalized in the classroom. What conclusions can you draw about students' learning?

2. Observe and tape-record several students' talk. Analyze the development of their phonological, syntactic, semantic, and pragmatic language systems. If possible, compare primary-grade students' language with middle- and upper-grade students' language.

3. Observe in an elementary classroom and listen to students' oral language. Try to identify students' use of each of the seven language functions discussed in this chapter. Also, examine the writing in their writing folders to determine which of the language functions they have used.

4. Interview an elementary teacher and ask how this teacher teaches the four language arts—listening, talking, reading, and writing. Compare the teacher's comments with the information in this chapter.

5. Develop a lesson plan using the teaching strategy presented in this chapter.

❖ REFERENCES

Applebee, A. N., & Langer, J. A. (1983). Instructional scaffolding: Reading and writing and natural language activities. *Language Arts, 60,* 168–175.

Baghban, M. (1984). *Our daughter learns to read and write: A case study from birth to three.* Newark, DE: International Reading Association.

Bissex, G. L. (1980). *Gnys at wrk: A child learns to write and read.* Cambridge, MA: Harvard University Press.

Brown, R. (1979). Some priorities in language arts education. *Language Arts, 56,* 483–484.

Bruner, J. S. (1978). The role of dialogue in language acquisition. In A. Sinclair, R. J. Jarvella, & W. M. Levelt (Eds.), *The child's conception of language,* pp. 241–256. New York: Springer-Verlag.

Bybee, R. W., & Sund, R. B. (1982). *Piaget for educators* (2nd ed.). Columbus, OH: Merrill.

Camp, D. J. (1987). Language functions used by four middle grade students. Unpublished doctoral dissertation. Norman: University of Oklahoma.

Cases in literacy: An agenda for discussion. (1989). Newark, DE: International Reading Association and Urbana, IL: National Council of Teachers of English.

Cazden, C. B. (1972). *Child language and education.* New York: Holt, Rinehart and Winston.

Cazden, C. B. (1983). Adult assistance to language development: Scaffolds, models, and direct instruction. In R. P. Parker & F. A. Davis (Eds.), *Developing literacy: Young children's use of language,* pp. 3–18. Newark, DE: International Reading Association.

Chomsky, C. (1969). *The acquisition of syntax in children from 5 to 10.* Cambridge, MA: MIT Press.

Chomsky, C. (1971). Write now, read later. *Childhood Education, 47,* 296–299.

Clark, E. V. (1971). On the acquisition of the meaning of *before* and *after. Journal of Verbal Learning and Verbal Behavior, 10,* 266–275.

Clay, M. (1967). The reading behavior of five-year-old children: A research report. *New Zealand Journal of Education Studies,* 11–31.

Clay, M. (1989). Forward. In D. S. Strickland & L. M. Morrow (Eds.), *Emerging literacy: Young children learn to read and write.* Newark, DE: International Reading Association.

DeStefano, J. S. (1978). *Language, the learner and the school.* New York: Wiley.

Durkin, D. (1966). *Children who read early.* New York: Teachers College Press.

Flexner, S. B. (1987). *The Random House dictionary of the English language* (2nd ed.). New York: Random House.

Florio, S., & Clark, C. M. (1982). The functions of writing in an elementary classroom. *Research in the Teaching of English, 19,* 115–130.

Gere, A. R., & Abbott, R. D. (1985). Talking about writing: The language of writing groups. *Research in the Teaching of English, 19,* 362–381.

Hague, M. (1985). *Aesop's fables.* New York: Holt, Rinehart and Winston.

Halliday, M. A. K. (1973). *Explorations in the functions of language.* London: Edward Arnold.

Halliday, M. A. K. (1975). *Learning how to mean: Explorations in the development of language.* London: Edward Arnold.

Heath, S. B. (1983). *Ways with words: Language, life, and work in communities and classrooms.* Cambridge: Cambridge University Press.

Hirsch, E. D., Jr. (1987). *Cultural literacy: What every American needs to know.* Boston: Houghton Mifflin.

Holdaway, D. (1979). *The foundations of literacy.* New York: Scholastic.

Hymes, D. (1974). *Foundations in sociolinguistics: An ethnographic approach.* Philadelphia: University of Pennsylvania Press.

Ingram, D. (1975). If and when transformations are acquired by children. In D. P. Dato (Ed.), *Developmental psycholinguistics: Theory and applications,* pp. 99–127. Washington, DC: Georgetown University Press.

Jaggar, A. (1985). Allowing for language differences. In G. S. Pinnell (Ed.), *Discovering language with children,* pp. 25–28. Urbana, IL: National Council of Teachers of English.

Kellogg, S. (1979). *Pinkerton, behave!* New York: Dial.

Lauber, P. (1987). *Get ready for robots!* New York: Crowell.

Lindfors, J. W. (1980). *Children's language and learning.* Englewood Cliffs, NJ: Prentice-Hall.

Lionni, L. (1985). *Frederick's fables*. New York: Pantheon.

Loban, W. (1976). *Language development: Kindergarten through grade twelve* (Research Report No. 18). Urbana, IL: National Council of Teachers of English.

Loban, W. (1979). Relationships between language and literacy. *Language Arts, 56,* 485–486.

Lobel, A. (1980). *Fables*. New York: Harper and Row.

Low, J. (1980). *Mice twice*. New York: Atheneum.

Matthews, E. (1985). *Debugging Rover*. New York: Dodd.

McGee, L. M., & Richgels, D. J. (1989). *Literacy's beginnings: Supporting young readers and writers*. Boston: Allyn and Bacon.

Metos, T. H. (1980). *Robots A_2Z*. New York: Messner.

Morrow, L. M. (1989). *Literacy development in the early years: Helping children read and write*. Englewood Cliffs, NJ: Prentice-Hall.

Piaget, J. (1969). *The psychology of intelligence*. Paterson, NJ: Littlefield, Adams.

Piaget, J. (1975). *The development of thought: Equilibration of cognitive structures*. New York: Viking Press.

Pinnell, G. S. (1975). Language in primary classrooms. *Theory into Practice, 14,* 318–327.

Sendak, M. (1963). *Where the wild things are*. New York: Harper and Row.

Smith, F. (1975). *Comprehension and learning*. New York: Holt, Rinehart and Winston.

Smith, F. (1977). The uses of language. *Language Arts, 54,* 638–644.

Smith, F. (1979). The language arts and the learner's mind. *Language Arts, 56,* 118–125.

Taylor, D. (1983). *Family literacy: Young children learning to read and write*. Exeter, NH: Heinemann.

Teale, W. H. (1982). Toward a theory of how children learn to read and write. *Language Arts, 59,* 555–570.

Teale, W. H., & Sulzby, E. (1989). Emerging literacy: New perspectives. In D. S. Strickland & L. M. Morrow (Eds.), *Emerging literacy: Young children learn to read and write,* pp. 1–15. Newark, DE: International Reading Association.

Vygotsky, L. S. (1978). *Mind in society*. Cambridge, MA: Harvard University Press.

Vygotsky, L. S. (1986). *Thought and language*. Cambridge, MA: MIT Press.

2 TEACHING LANGUAGE ARTS

THE LANGUAGE-RICH CLASSROOM
  The Physical Arrangement
  Textbooks
  Trade Books
  Computers

THE TEACHER'S ROLE
  Planning for Instruction
  Facilitating Student Learning
  Resources for Teachers

ASSESSING STUDENTS' PROGRESS
  Classroom Observations
  Anecdotal Records
  Conferences
  Checklists
  Interviews
  Language Samples
  Across-the-Curriculum Applications

◆ OUR FOCUS NOW SHIFTS FROM HOW CHILDREN LEARN TO HOW teachers support students while they learn. We will describe a language-rich classroom, discuss the teacher's role, and explain how to plan instruction and assess children's learning.

◆ AS YOU ARE READING, THINK ABOUT THESE QUESTIONS:

How should the classroom be arranged to facilitate students' learning?

What materials are needed?

What is the teacher's role?

How do you plan units of instruction?

How should students' learning be assessed?

Language arts instruction should be based on how children learn, how they learn language, and how they become literate. More than 20 years ago, Carl Lefevre (1970) advised that language learning in school should "parallel [children's] early childhood method of learning to speak [their] native tongue—playfully, through delighted experiences of discovery—through repeated exposure to language forms and patterns, by creating imitation and manipulation, and by personal trial and error, with kindly (and not too much) correction from adults" (p. 75). Lefevre's vision is finally becoming a reality as teachers are basing instruction on cognitive, psycholinguistic, and sociolinguistic theories of learning.

A unit on mystery stories, for example, provides the type of language learning experiences that Lefevre suggests. Students begin by reading mystery stories or listening to them read aloud. Many mystery stories have been written for elementary students, who especially enjoy these suspense stories. The *Nate the Great* series by Marjorie Weinman Sharmat (e.g., *Nate the Great Goes Undercover*, 1974) is popular with beginning readers, and middle-grade students enjoy the *Encyclopedia Brown* series by Donald J. Sobol (e.g., *Encyclopedia Brown, Boy Detective*, 1963). Mystery stories have unique characteristics that students can learn to identify after reading and discussing several mysteries. A class of third graders developed the following list of the characteristics of mystery stories:

Mysteries have crimes or problems to solve. Some types of crimes and problems are something lost or stolen, someone killed, or someone kidnapped.

Mysteries have clues. Some examples include torn papers, footprints, fingerprints, dead bodies, and tire tracks.

Mysteries have detectives to solve the crimes or problems. (They *always* solve the crime, too!)

Detectives have unusual names, such as Encyclopedia Brown.

Detectives have something special about them, such as having a dog for an assistant or loving to eat pancakes.

Detectives have special equipment, including magnifying glasses, secret codes, knives and guns, costumes, and masks.

With this information, students are prepared to create their own stories. They write and refine their stories and then publish them as hardcover books. After reading their stories to classmates, students add their stories to the classroom library. Figure 2–1 presents the mystery story this class of third graders composed. The teacher and students working together composed a class story, called a *class collaboration*, which is an effective way to begin writing. After the group writing experience, students write individual stories.

A unit on mysteries provides many opportunities for students to imitate and manipulate language in a situation that is meaningful, functional, and genuine. Moreover, both the mystery stories students read and those they write can later be used for studying specific language skills. Students can, for example, examine how authors use

"Edith, No!"

The mud oozed around Ed Trail's boots as he beached his canoe. It was 10:00 Saturday evening as Ed made his way home through the woods from his fishing trip. He only walked a few steps when . . . SNAP . . . an old trap caught his foot and pulled him down.

As he turned over to free himself, the last thing he saw was a rock.

From the other side of the woods, Sam Baker, well-known detective, was searching for Ed at the request of his worried wife, Sally. He found the place where Ed docked his boat and followed the path from there.

A short distance up the path led Sam to where Ed Trail lay dead with a rock crushing his head.

While Sam was running to tell what had happened, he discovered a torn scarf stuck on a bush. As he observed the scarf, he discovered the initials E. T.

Sam stuck the scarf in his pocket because he knew it was a clue and went to tell Sally Trail what had happened.

Out of breath, Sam arrived at the Trails' and told Sally the horrible details. When Sam showed her the scarf, Sally got a far away look in her eyes and went upstairs. Finding this strange, Sam Baker waited outside the Trail home to see what he might find.

Meanwhile, Sally went upstairs to the room of Aunt Belle who lived with the Trails. Aunt Belle had taken care of Sally as a little girl and knew everything about Sally. Now she was crippled and in a wheel-chair.

"Well, hello dear," said Aunt Belle. "What are you doing here?" "Where are you taking me?" said Aunt Belle worriedly as Sally wheeled her to the stairs. As Sally gave the final shove Aunt Belle screamed . . . .

"EDITH, NO!"

At that moment Sam Baker knew that the initials stood for Sally Edith Trail. The S had been ripped off in her rush to leave the place of the crime.

Sam rushed in just in time to catch Aunt Belle before Sally Edith Trail sent another victim to her death.

Quickly Sam grabbed Sally and took her to the police station.

At the station house the chief found out that Sally killed her husband to keep him from giving all his money to Aunt Belle to take care of her. Sally tried to kill Aunt Belle because she was the only one who could connect Sally with the initials E. T.

Another case wrapped up by Sam Baker.

FIGURE 2–1

A Third-grade Class Collaboration Mystery Story

alliteration, sentence structure, or punctuation, and they can also examine their own stories for similar conventions. Within the context of stories children read and others they write, they can examine how language is used to communicate effectively.

❖ THE LANGUAGE-RICH CLASSROOM

Elementary classrooms should be authentic language environments that encourage students to listen, talk, read, and write; that is, they should be language-rich (Lindfors, 1989). The physical arrangement and materials provided in the classroom play an important role in setting the stage for learning language. In the past, textbooks were the primary instructional material and students sat in desks arranged in rows facing the teacher. Now a wide variety of instructional materials are available in addition to textbooks, including trade books and newspapers. Students' desks are more often arranged in small groups, and classrooms are visually stimulating with signs, posters, charts and other displays related to the units under study. These are components of a language-rich classroom:

- Desks arranged in groups to facilitate cooperative learning
- Classroom libraries stocked with many different kinds of reading materials
- Posted messages about the current day
- Displays of student work and projects
- A chair designated as the author's chair
- Displayed signs, labels for items, and quotations
- Posted directions for activities or use of equipment
- Materials for recording language, including pencils, pens, paper, journals, books, typewriters, computers
- Special places for reading and writing activities
- Reference materials related to literature, social studies, and science units
- A listening center and other audiovisual materials
- A puppet stage or area for presenting plays and storytelling
- Charts on which students record information (e.g., attendance or writing group charts)
- World-related print (e.g., newspapers, maps, calendars)
- Reading and writing materials in primary students' play centers (adapted from Hall, 1987)

These components of a language-rich classroom are elaborated on in Figure 2–2.

The Physical Arrangement

No one physical arrangement best represents a language-rich classroom, but the configuration of any classroom can be modified to include many of the desirable characteristics. First, student desks or tables should be grouped to encourage students to talk, share, and work cooperatively. Separate areas are needed for reading and writing, a classroom library, a listening center, centers for materials related to content area units, and an area for dramatic activities. Kindergarten classrooms also need play centers. At the instructional levels, kindergarten through eighth grade, some variations must occur. Young children have play centers and more work stations, while older students need

---

1. **Arrangement of desks**

   _____ Are desks arranged in groups?
   _____ Does the arrangement facilitate group interaction?

2. **Classroom library**

   _____ Are there four times as many books as there are students in the classroom?
   _____ Are picture books, informational books, poetry, and other types of trade books included?
   _____ Are magazines and newspapers included?
   _____ Were some of the books written by students?

3. **Message center**

   _____ Are schedules and announcements about the current day posted?
   _____ Are some of the messages student-initiated?

4. **Display of student work**

   _____ Do all students have work displayed?
   _____ How much of the student work is less than two weeks old?
   _____ Is there an area where students can display their own work themselves?

5. **Author's chair**

   _____ Is one chair designated as the author's chair for students to use when sharing their writing?
   _____ Is the chair labeled?

6. **Signs, labels and quotations**

   _____ Are equipment and other classroom items labeled?
   _____ Are words, phrases, and sentences posted in the classroom?
   _____ Were some of the signs, labels, and quotes written by students?

7. **Directions**

   _____ Are directions provided so that students can work independently?
   _____ Were some of the directions written by students?

FIGURE 2–2

Characteristics of a Language-rich Classroom

8. Materials for recording language

_____ Are pencils, pens, paper, journals, books, typewriters, computers, and other materials available for recording language?
_____ Do students have to ask permission to use them?

9. Places for reading and writing

_____ Are there special places for reading and writing activities?
_____ Are they quiet and separated from other areas?

10. Reference materials

_____ Are lists, clusters, pictures, charts, books, and other reference materials available for content area study?
_____ Do students use these materials as they work on projects related to the units?

11. Audiovisual materials

_____ Is a listening center available for students to use?
_____ Are other audiovisual materials such as filmstrips, videotapes, and films, and the equipment necessary to use the materials available in the classroom?

12. Dramatic center

_____ Is a puppet stage available in the classroom?
_____ Are art materials for making puppets available?
_____ Is an area available for presenting plays and telling stories?
_____ Are props available?

13. Record collection

_____ Are charts or sheets that call for students to record information used in the classroom?
_____ Do students record the information themselves?

14. World-related print

_____ Do students read and write newspapers, magazines, lists, maps, graphs, calendars, and other forms of world-related print?
_____ Do students collect some of these materials?

15. Display of student projects

_____ Are students' projects with accompanying written explanations and other student-made displays exhibited in the classroom?

16. Play centers

_____ Do play centers in primary-grade classrooms include reading and writing materials?

FIGURE 2–2 (continued)

reference centers with materials related to the units they are studying. The three diagrams in Figure 2–3 suggest ways to make the classroom design language-rich.

Textbooks

Textbooks are one tool for teaching language skills. They are the most accessible resource that teachers have, and they have some benefits:

KINDERGARTEN CLASSROOM

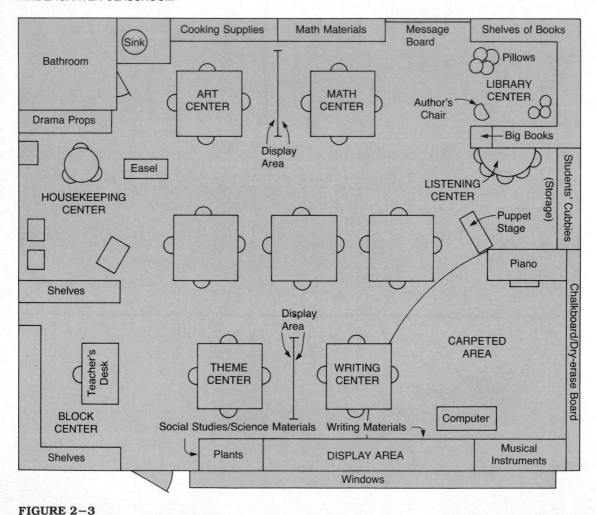

FIGURE 2–3

Diagrams of Classrooms

- Information about language skills
- A sequence of skills for each grade level
- Models and examples
- Practice activities
- Security for beginning teachers

There are also drawbacks, however. The textbook's format is probably its greatest drawback because it is inappropriate for many language activities. Listening, talking,

THIRD GRADE CLASSROOM

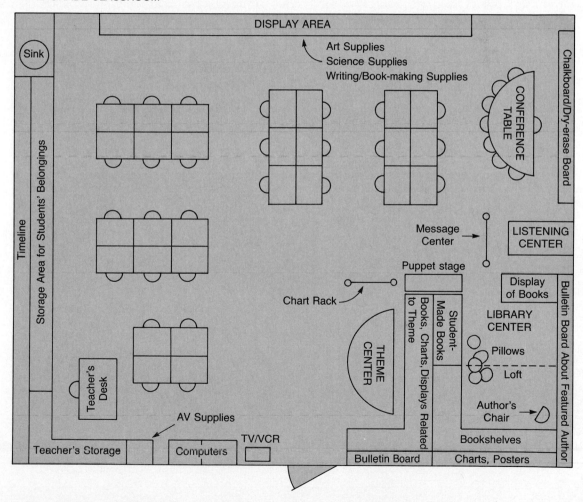

FIGURE 2–3 (*continued*)

reading, and writing activities involve much more than can be contained in a single textbook. Other likely weaknesses are as follows:

- Little attention to listening and talking
- Excessive emphasis on grammar and usage skills
- Emphasis on rote memorization of skills rather than on effective communication
- Focus on correctness rather than on experimentation with language
- Few opportunities to individualize instruction
- Difficulty in connecting textbook activities to across-the-curriculum units

SIXTH GRADE CLASSROOM

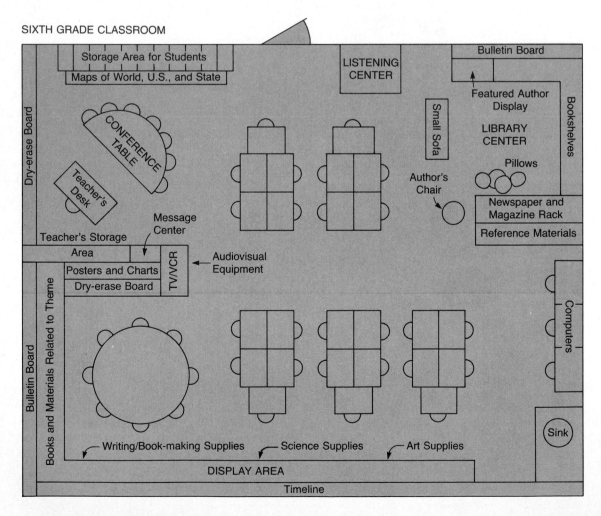

FIGURE 2–3 *(continued)*

Graves (1977) admonished us that textbooks cannot be the only instructional material for teaching language arts. Collections of trade books, tape recordings, puppets, concrete materials, notebooks, paper, and pencils are other necessary materials.

Teachers cannot assume that textbooks are equivalent to the total language arts program. To start on the first page of the language arts textbook on the first day of school and to continue page by page through the textbook fails to consider the students' language needs. Instead, we recommend that textbooks serve as only one resource for the language arts program; for example, textbooks are one resource in teaching about punctuation marks, as illustrated in Figure 2–4, which also suggests many other types of activities that involve more meaningful, functional, and genuine experiences with language.

Several elements must be carefully considered in evaluating language arts textbooks or choosing a textbook series for a school or school district. The conceptual framework of the textbook and the instructional philosophy of its authors are of primary importance. Is the textbook content-centered or child-centered? Textbooks should be consistent with teachers' views of language arts education and how they organize and conduct their classrooms. It is also important to consider whether a textbook incorporates the latest research on how children learn language.

The theoretical orientation is reflected in the content of the textbook, and the content is the second critical consideration. Textbooks that are based on the segmented, content-centered model typically emphasize language skills more than do textbooks based on the child-centered or whole language model. The types of listening, talking, reading, and writing activities that are included are also important. Consider, too, what other types of activities, such as grammar activities, are included and compute the percentage of space devoted to each language mode. Other considerations are whether the textbook invites students to use language in genuine ways or whether the majority of activities involve copying sentences from the textbook or filling in blanks with single letters and words. Teachers must also consider the textbook's physical features, its organization, its adaptability for special students, and its style. Figure 2–5 lists these guidelines. Some of the questions can be answered simply "yes" or "no," whereas others require a more careful and in-depth review.

Trade Books

Trade books are children's books other than textbooks, and thousands of excellent trade books are currently available for elementary students. Types of trade books include picture books, wordless picture books, concept books, chapter books, poetry, biography and autobiography, and informational books.

Picture Books.   *Picture books* are short stories (usually about 32 pages) in which text and illustrations combine to tell the story more effectively than either could alone. The text is minimal, and the illustrations are striking. Many picture books, such as Maurice Sendak's *Where the Wild Things Are* (1963) are appropriate for young children, but some picture books such as Thomas Locker's *The Boy Who Held Back the Sea* (1987) were written with middle-grade students in mind. Fairy tales, myths, and legends have also been retold beautifully as picture books. One example is Trina Schart

Editing

Students work in pairs to edit their own compositions, paying special attention to using punctuation marks correctly. The teacher copies onto a transparency a paragraph from a student's composition or from a tradebook, omitting all punctuation marks. As a class, students read the paragraph and add the necessary punctuation.

Letter Writing

Students write letters to pen pals, paying special attention to using correct punctuation in the letter and on the envelope.

Talk and Punctuation Marks

To help students understand that punctuation marks are used in writing to replace the pauses and voice changes used in speech, have students compose a sentence that could be read equally well as a statement, question, or exclamation. Students read their sentences aloud and classmates identify the implied punctuation marks.

Quotation Marks

Students copy dialogue from cartoons or from tradebooks written with "talking balloons" (e.g., Leo Lionni's *A Flea Story* 1977), writing it first as dialogue and then in narrative form with quotation marks.

Textbooks, Computer Programs, and Learning Games

Students practice using punctuation marks correctly in these drill-and-practice type activities.

Rule Charts

Students work in small groups to develop a chart with rules and examples for each punctuation mark. After the charts are completed, they are hung in the classroom and used for reference.

Journal Writing

Students write the date using correct punctuation before writing each journal entry.

History of the Punctuation Marks

Students investigate the invention of punctuation marks by the ancient Greeks and the meaning behind each mark.

Punctuation Hunt

Students list examples of each use of the punctuation marks in books they are reading or in their own writing. They copy the sentences onto transparencies and share with their classmates using an overhead projector.

Reference Books

Have students read *How to Stop a Sentence and Other Methods of Managing Words* by Nora Gallagher (1982) for information about the uses of punctuation marks. Students compose a class book about punctuation marks, including their history and rules for their use. Examples of correct usage can be taken from tradebooks or created by students. Bind the book and add it to the reference section of the school library.

PUNCTUATION MARKS

FIGURE 2–4

Ways to Teach Students About Punctuation Marks

Physical Features

_____ Is the textbook attractive, durable, and interesting to students?
_____ Do the size, use of margins, print style, and graphics increase the usability of the textbook?
_____ Do the illustrations enhance interest in the textbook?
_____ What supplemental materials (e.g., teacher's editions, resource books, skill handbooks, computer programs, posters, tests) are included with the textbook?

Conceptual Framework

_____ What is the theoretical orientation of the textbook?
_____ Does the textbook reflect the latest research in how language is learned?
_____ Are the instructional goals of the textbook presented clearly?
_____ How well do these goals mesh with your own views of language arts education?

Content

_____ What types of listening, talking, reading, and writing activities are included in the textbook?
_____ How much emphasis is placed on each of the four language models?
_____ How much emphasis is placed on grammar?
_____ Is quality children's literature included in the textbook?
_____ Are the language and language skill activities appropriate for the grade level at which they are presented?
_____ Are activities provided that require students to use language in genuine ways or do most activities require students to only copy sentences from the textbook or fill in the blanks with letters and words?
_____ Are across-the-curriculum activities suggested?
_____ Does the textbook invite student involvement?
_____ Does the textbook encourage students to think critically and creatively?

Organization

_____ How is the textbook organized?
_____ Must each lesson or unit be taught in sequence?
_____ Does the scope and sequence chart provide a reasonable organization of language skills?

Adaptability

_____ Is information provided on how to adapt the textbook to meet students' individual needs?
_____ Can the textbook be adapted for gifted students?
_____ Can the textbook be adapted for learning disabled students?
_____ Can the textbook be adapted for bilingual students or students who speak nonstandard English?

Style

_____ Will students like the writing style of the textbook?
_____ Does the textbook avoid stereotypes and stereotypical language?

FIGURE 2–5

Guidelines for Assessing Language Arts Textbooks

Hyman's *The Sleeping Beauty* (1977). The coveted Caldecott Medal, given annually for the best illustrations in a children's book published during the preceding year, has honored many picture books. A list of books that have won this prestigious award is included in Appendix B.

Wordless Picture Books.   Wordless picture books are similar to picture books but contain no text. The story is told entirely through the pictures, which makes them particularly useful for talk and writing activities. Books such as the hilarious *Frog Goes to Dinner* (Mayer, 1974) and Goodall's wordless retelling of *Little Red Riding Hood* (1988) are popular with primary and middle-grade students. Other books, such as *Anno's U.S.A.* (Anno, 1983) and *The Story of a Castle* (Goodall, 1986), appeal to middle- and upper-grade students because they can be connected to social studies or other content area units.

Concept Books.   *Concept* books are informational books for young children written in the same format as picture books. A phrase or sentence of text is presented on each page with a large photograph or illustration. Gibbons's *The Post Office Book: Mail and How It Moves* (1982) is an informative description of what happens to a letter after it is mailed, and cartoonlike drawings supplement the sparse text. *My Puppy Is Born* (Cole, 1973) uses black-and-white photographs to illustrate a puppy's birth and first eight weeks of life. A very different type of concept book is Burningham's *Opposites* (1985), which presents pairs of opposites (e.g., *hard* and *soft*) illustrated on each two-page spread. ABC books might also be classified as concept books. Although many ABC books are designed for very young children, others are appropriate for elementary students, such as *The National Air and Space Museum ABC* (Mayers, 1986). Crews's concept books are among the most beautiful; in *Carousel* (1982), for example, Crews combines paintings and photographs to create the sounds and sights of a carousel ride.

Informational Books.   *Informational books* provide information on social studies, science, math, art, music, and other topics, and many of these books are available for elementary students. Some are written in a story format, such as *Octopus* (Carrick, 1978), *Castle* (Macaulay, 1977), and *Sugaring Time* (Lasky, 1983) while others are written in a more traditional informational style, with a table of contents, index, and glossary. Examples of traditional informational books are *Money* (Elkin, 1983) and *The Human Body* (Caselli, 1987).

Chapter Books.   *Chapter books* are longer, fictional books written for elementary students in chapter format. Most are written for middle- and upper-grade students, but Arnold Lobel (1970, 1972, 1976, 1979) has written a series of Frog and Toad stories for primary-grade students. Chapter books for middle-grade students include Cleary's Ramona series, for example, *Ramona Quimby, Age 8* (1981), and *Bunnicula* (Howe & Howe, 1979). Upper-grade students enjoy fantasy stories, and Lewis's *The Lion, the Witch and the Wardrobe* (1950) and the other books in the Chronicles of Narnia are favorites. A number of chapter books, such as *Sarah, Plain and Tall* (MacLachlan, 1985) and *The Whipping Boy* (Fleischman, 1986), have received the Newbery Medal for distinguished children's literature. In contrast to the Caldecott Medal, for outstanding illustrations, the Newbery is given for distinguished prose. Appendix B also lists the books that have received this award.

Poetry.   Many delightful books of poetry for children are available today. Some are collections of poems on a single topic written by one poet, such as *Tyrannosaurus Was a Beast* (Prelutsky, 1988) about dinosaurs, and Fleischman's *Joyful Noise: Poems for Two Voices* (1988) about insects. Other collections of poetry on a single topic selected by an author or poet are Hopkins's *Good Morning to You, Valentine* (1976) and Carle's *Animals, Animals* (1989). Two excellent anthologies (collections of poems written by different poets on a variety of topics) are *The Random House Book of Poetry for Children* (Prelutsky, 1983) for younger children and *Knock at a Star: A Child's Introduction to Poetry* (Kennedy & Kennedy, 1982) for older children. Another format for poems is as a picture book with a line or stanza of the poem presented and illustrated on each page. This format is especially good for songs, such as Spier's *The Star-Spangled Banner* (1973), and for poems that were originally written for adults but can be made appropriate for children. Two examples are Longfellow's *Paul Revere's Ride* (Parker, 1985) and *Lewis Carroll's Jabberwocky* (Zalben, 1977).

Biographies and Autobiographies.   Most life-story books are chapter books, such as Hamilton's *Paul Robeson: The Life and Times of a Free Black Man* (1974), but several authors have written shorter biographies that resemble picture books. Perhaps the best-known biographer for younger children is Jean Fritz, who has written biographies of Revolutionary War figures such as *Will You Sign Here, John Hancock?* (1976). A few autobiographies have also been written for children, and one that is popular with upper-grade students is Roald Dahl's *Boy* (1984).

These books can be used in conjunction with or instead of textbooks to teach language arts or any other content area. As an illustration, Figure 2–6 presents a cluster for a unit on the American Revolution, and trade books are an important part of the unit. Students will read biographies and autobiographies, poems, chapter books, and informational books to learn much more about the Revolutionary War and life in

A well-stocked library center is a necessary part of a language-rich classroom.

Biography and Autobiography
Students investigate the role of historical figures in the War by reading a biography or autobiography. Books include D'Aulaires' *Benjamin Franklin* (Doubleday, 1950) and *George Washington* (Doubleday, 1936); Harold Felton's *Deborah Sampson: Soldier of the Revolution* (Dodd, 1976); Jean Fritz's *George Washington's Breakfast* (Coward, 1969), *Traitor, The Case of Benedict Arnold* (Putnam, 1981), *Where Was Patrick Henry on the 29th of May?* (Coward, 1975), *Why Don't You Get a Horse, Sam Adams?* (Coward, 1974), and *Will You Sign Here, John Hancock?* (Coward, 1976); and Joseph Plumb Martin's *Yankee Doodle Boy* (Scott, 1964).

Handwriting
Students copy quotes from the period, such as "Don't fire unless fired upon" (Col. John Parker); "I only regret that I have but one life to lose for my country" (Nathan Hale); and "The British are coming!" (Paul Revere).

Timelines
Students construct a timeline showing the major events leading up to the War and major battles in the War.

Poetry
Students read Henry Wadsworth Longfellow's *Paul Revere's Ride* (Greenwillow, 1985). Compare to Jean Fritz's *And Then What Happened, Paul Revere?* (Coward, 1973). Also, compare Revere's ride in 1775 to Jack Jouett's ride in 1781. Read *Jack Jouett's Ride* by Gail Haley (Viking, 1973).

Simulated Journals
Students keep a simulated journal as an historical figure or a common person who lived during the Revolutionary War era.

Debates
Students stage a debate between "rebels" and "royalists."

Writing
Students write a simulated newspaper that might have been published during the Revolutionary War period.

Spelling
Students examine spellings of the period (e.g., *ye, musick*) that have changed because of the nationalistic spirit of the period and Noah Webster's influence.

REVOLUTIONARY WAR

Chapter Books
Students read stories set in the Revolutionary War era, such as James and Christopher Collier's *My Brother Sam Is Dead* (Four Winds, 1974) and Esther Forbes' *Johnny Tremain* (Houghton Mifflin, 1970). These books can also be read aloud.

Research Reports
Students read informational books about the period to use in preparing oral or written reports. Books include Jean Poindexter Colby's *Lexington and Concord, 1775: What Really Happened* (Hasting House, 1975); Robert Leckie's *The World Turned Upside Down: The Story of the American Revolution* (Putnam, 1973); and Bart McDowell's *The Revolutionary War: America's Fight for Freedom* (National Geographic Society, 1967).

Listening
Students listen to songs of the period including "Yankee Doodle."

Drama
Students role-play key events in the period: Paul Revere's ride, signing the Declaration of Independence, the surrender at Yorktown. Students create a puppet of an historical figure and use the puppet to give a report about the person or to stage a play.

Art
Students view paintings depicting Revolutionary War scenes, such as Grant Wood's "The Midnight Ride of Paul Revere" and Emanuel Gottlieb Leutze's "Washington Crossing the Delaware."

FIGURE 2–6

Cluster for a Unit on the American Revolution

those times than could ever be presented in a social studies textbook. The main draw-back to using trade books is that they are not sequenced and prepackaged as textbooks are. Instead, teachers must make choices and design activities to accompany the books. Similar units incorporating trade books can be developed for almost any content area.

Every elementary classroom should be stocked with trade books that are attractively stored in the library center. These books might be from the teacher's own collection or borrowed from the school or public library. Many of the books should relate to units of study, and these should be changed periodically. Other books for students to read independently are also included in the library center. After studying library centers in classrooms, Leslie Morrow (1989) makes the following ten recommendations:

The library center should be inviting and afford privacy.

The library center should have a physical definition with shelves, carpets, benches, sofas, or other partitions.

Five or six students should fit comfortably in the center at one time.

Two kinds of bookshelves are needed. Most of the collection should be shelved with the spines facing outward, but some books should be set so that the front covers are displayed.

Books should be shelved by category and color-coded by type.

Books written by one author or related to a theme being studied should be displayed prominently, and the displays should be changed regularly.

The floor should be covered with a rug and the area furnished with pillows, beanbag chairs, or comfortable furniture.

The center should be stocked with at least four times as many books as students in the classroom.

A variety of types of reading materials, including books, newspapers, magazines, posters, and charts, should be included in the center.

Attractive posters that encourage reading, especially if they relate to books in the library center, should be added.

These recommendations were based on research in primary-grade classrooms, but would be equally appropriate for middle- and upper-grade students.

Computers

Computers are becoming more and more a part of elementary classrooms. At first, they were used primarily in mathematics, but they have great potential for all areas of the curriculum, including language arts. Several different instructional uses are possible with computers. Robert Taylor (1980) suggests that computers have three educational applications: they can serve as tool, tutor, and tutee.

Perhaps the most valuable application of the computer in the language arts classroom is as a tool. Students can use microcomputers with word-processing programs to write stories, poems, and other writing forms (Dickinson, 1986; Genishi, 1988; De-Groff, 1990). The computer simplifies revising and editing and eliminates the tedium of recopying compositions. Several word-processing programs, such as *The Bank Street Writer* (1982), *The Writing Workshop* (1986), and *QUILL* (1983), have been developed especially for elementary students and are easy to learn to use.

Computers with word-processing programs can be used effectively to record young children's language experience stories (Barber, 1982; Smith, 1985). Teachers take children's dictation as they do in traditional language experience activities, but use a computer rather than paper and pencil. After entering the child's dictation, the child and the teacher read the text and make revisions. Next the text is printed out, and the child can add a drawing. If the child has already drawn a picture, the printout can be cut and taped onto the drawing. The computer simplifies the process of taking children's dictation because teachers can record dictation more quickly than they can write, the dictation can be revised easily, and a clean copy of the revised text can be printed out.

Whereas teachers can use computers to record language experience stories for children, first and second grade students can write their own compositions on the word processor. For an interesting report of first graders writing on a computer, check Phenix and Hannan's article, "Word Processing in the Grade One Classroom" (1984). Their first graders wrote and revised a variety of compositions on computers and "learned that writing does not have to come out right the first time, that it can be manipulated by the author, that a writer has to take risks, that revising is a normal way writing is done" (p. 812).

Students can also use the word processor to write notes and letters to classmates and pen pals. They write these letters on the computer, revise and edit them, and then transmit them using a modem hooked up to the computer. The *QUILL* (1983) word-processing program, for instance, includes a Mailbag for exchanging messages.

A second application is as tutor—a use known as *computer assisted instruction* (CAI). Instructional software programs are available for drill and practice, educational games, simulations, and tutorials. Programmed instruction in language skills such as letter sounds, parts of speech, and affixes is becoming increasingly available. Many of the programs resemble language arts textbook exercises except that they are presented on a monitor screen rather than in a book. Remember, though, that while students enjoy using computers, some activities are little more than electronic workbooks and are subject to the same criticisms as language arts textbooks. High quality software programs can be useful, however, in providing individualized practice on a particular skill.

The number of software programs has grown tremendously in the past few years; some are effective, whereas others are inferior. Chomsky (1984) says the primary criterion in identifying high quality software programs is whether they stimulate students to think about language in new and creative ways. Because of both quality and cost considerations, it is important to preview software carefully before purchasing it. Figure 2–7 offers guidelines for selecting and evaluating language arts software. Students should also help preview software programs and offer opinions and recommendations.

A third computer application is as tutee. Students can learn computer languages, such as *LOGO*, and how to program computers. We will see in Chapter 16 that gifted students particularly benefit from learning computer languages as a way of extending their repertoire of communication modes.

Computer Compatibility

Is the software program compatible with the computer students will be using?
Does the computer have sufficient memory to run the software program?
Which peripherals are needed (e.g., color monitor, printer, voice synthesizer)?

Theoretical Rationale

Is the software consistent with the philosophy of your language arts program?
Can it be integrated into your program to instruct rather than merely to entertain?

Computer Capabilities

Does the software program take advantage of the unique capabilities of the computer?
Does it provide for extensive student interaction?
Does it provide for immediate feedback?
Does it provide for dynamic text display, in which text can be built paragraph by paragraph,
    sentences and words can be highlighted, and text can be moved about?

Frame Display

Is the text in the software program presented in both upper- and lowercase letters?
Is between-line spacing adequate for easy reading?
Do letters resemble regular type rather than stylized lettering?
Are highlighting and other attention-getting devices overused?

Rate of Presentation

Does the student rather than the program control the rate at which text is advanced?

Readability

Is the text (especially the directions) written at students' reading level?

Graphics

Do the illustrations and animation support the instruction or serve only to gain the students' attention?

Game Format

Does the software program require students to learn or practice a skill to play the game successfully
    or can students simply make random choices?
Does it allow students to play against themselves and compete against their previous performances
    rather than against another student?

Instructions to Students

Does the program provide information on each frame of text telling students how to quit the
    program, get help, and see the menu?

Documentation

Does the documentation (or printed materials) accompanying the program contain information on
    objectives, description of the program, the target population, prerequisite language and
    computing skills, suggested introductory and follow-up activities, and the results of field testing
    and validation studies?

FIGURE 2–7

Guidelines for Selecting Language Arts Computer Software
Adapted from Smith & Tompkins, 1984.

Students are eager to use microcomputers with word-processing programs to write stories, poems, and other compositions.

In summarizing the promises and pitfalls of microcomputers in the language arts classroom, Zaharias (1983) concludes that there are two factors restricting the usefulness of this technology. The quantity of available high quality instructional software is still limited, and few computers are available in most elementary schools. Because so few computers are available, students are rarely able to use them regularly. In the next few years, however, educators predict that the availability of high quality software will improve and computers will be added to most elementary classrooms.

THE TEACHER'S ROLE

According to Lindfors (1989), the two fundamental responsibilities of an elementary teacher are to provide a language-rich learning environment in the classroom and to support students in their use of it. It is the teacher's role to make things happen by creating a language arts program that involves students in meaningful, functional, and genuine language activities. One of the best ways to create a language arts program is through thematic units (Goodman, 1986). Units may focus on literature, social studies, science, or another content area.

Planning for Instruction

Good teaching does not simply happen; it requires careful planning and a variety of activities. Activities should simulate the natural type of language learning that students experienced when they were learning to talk. When teachers plan for instruction, they go through several specific steps.

The first step is to identify units of instruction and goals and objectives. Teachers begin by identifying units in literature, social studies, science, and the other content areas they will teach. Sometimes the units are listed in state or district curriculum guides; sometimes they are provided in textbooks; and at other times, teachers choose units they believe are appropriate for their students. Examples of literature units are those that focus on *one author,* such as Tomie de Paola or Beverly Cleary; focus on *one book,* such as *Bridge to Terabithia* (Paterson, 1977); focus on a *genre,* such as mystery stories or biographies; or focus on a *theme,* such as families. Examples of social studies units are Thanksgiving, the American Revolution, and Africa. Weather, plants, and the solar system are examples of science units. Units can also be planned for math, art, and other content areas.

After deciding on the unit, teachers identify the major goal or goals of the unit and the specific objectives. These can be found in curriculum guides and textbooks or can be developed by the teacher. For example, one science unit that is often taught in the elementary grades focuses on weather. The goals and objectives vary according to grade level. The goal for a second grade unit might be for the student to gain an understanding of various types of weather and their effects on people. Objectives for second grade students might include these:

The student will observe daily weather conditions and record information on a weather chart.

The student will explain the uses of weather measurement tools.

The student will describe the effects of different types of weather on people.

The student will explain precautions to take in case of severe weather conditions.

The second step in instruction is to collect materials to use in teaching the unit. After identifying the topic for the unit and the goals and objectives, teachers collect materials, including

- Trade books
- Magazine and newspaper articles
- Textbooks
- Maps, charts, tables
- Films, filmstrips, videotapes
- Community resource persons
- Community resources
- Models, displays, equipment

For the second grade weather unit, teachers might collect a variety of informational books, concept books, picture books, books of poetry; the science textbook; daily newspapers with weather information and maps; charts and posters about weather; filmstrips, films, and videotapes about the weather and of children's stories set in different types of weather; and information from the National Weather Service and local television meteorologists.

Step three is to create a cluster of possibilities. As teachers collect materials related to the unit, ideas for possible activities come to mind, and they begin to list these possibilities. We recommend using a cluster format, as shown in Figure 2–8. Teachers list the activity possibilities according to the categories listed in the figure. For example, for a second grade weather unit, teachers would consider science activities such as

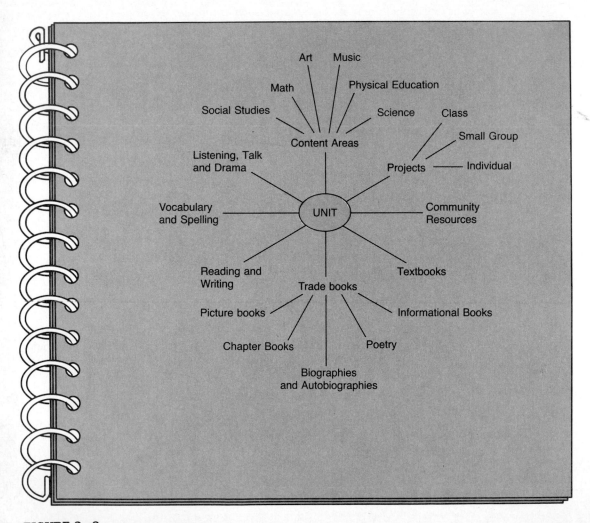

FIGURE 2–8

Teacher's Notebook Page: A Unit Cluster

recording daily temperatures, experiments related to temperature and wind, examining weather instruments, and making wind socks and weather vanes. Possible art activities include making snowflakes or a fog collage (by gluing tissue paper over a scene the students had painted). Words such as *thunderstorms, clouds, evaporation, thermometer, tornado,* and *hurricane* that are related to the unit would be added in the section on Vocabulary and Spelling. As individual projects, students might keep track of the weather for a week or two, make a poster about different kinds of weather, write a book about one kind of weather, read a weather poem to the class, or research a topic related to weather. As a class project, students might write an ABC book about weather. Possible field trips to the National Weather Service or community resource persons such as a television meteorologist might be listed as community resources. Teachers would also list the trade books they had collected related to weather and relevant sections in the science textbook. The completed cluster contains more possibilities than teachers could ever use in one unit, but because of the variety, teachers can select activities for the lesson plan that best meet the needs of this particular class and the amount of time available for the unit. An example of a completed unit cluster on weather is shown in Figure 2–9.

The fourth step is to develop the lesson plan. From the cluster of possibilities, teachers choose which lessons and activities they will use within the time available for the unit, and then they write the lesson plans. Of special importance is planning an initiating activity for the first day and a culminating activity to end the unit. For the second grade weather unit, teachers might show a film about weather to catch the students' interest. A field trip to the National Weather Service or an interview with a TV weather forecaster would be good culminating activities.

Lesson plans are usually written in time blocks. Activities for a unit may be confined to the one time block for the particular subject each day, or they can extend across areas of the curriculum. In the weather unit, for example, reading and writing activities related to the unit can be done as Language Arts, art activities as Art, and science activities as Science. Figure 2–10 presents a week-long excerpt from the lesson plan for the weather unit (and includes only those activities related to the weather unit). Notice that activities may occupy several time blocks each day. You will note that instead of labeling the time blocks as *Language Arts* or *Science,* in the lesson plan, they are labeled Blocks A, B, and C.

Step five is to make plans for assessing learning. The time to decide how to assess students' learning in the unit is during the planning stage, not after the unit has been completed. One way to plan for assessment and grading is to develop a unit checklist identifying the assignments students will complete in class during the unit and how they will be graded. Students receive a copy of the checklist at the beginning of the unit and keep it in their unit folder. Then, as they complete the assignments, they can check them off, and it is easy for the teacher to make periodic checks. At the end of the unit, the teacher collects the unit folders and grades the work. A "Weather Unit Checklist" appropriate for second graders is presented in Figure 2–11. Nine assignments are included on the checklist; students put a check in the left-hand column when they complete each assignment, and the teacher adds the grade in the right-hand column. The assignments take the place of traditional worksheets and will be completed in class—they are not homework assignments. Some assignments will be graded as "done" or "not done," and others will be graded for quality.

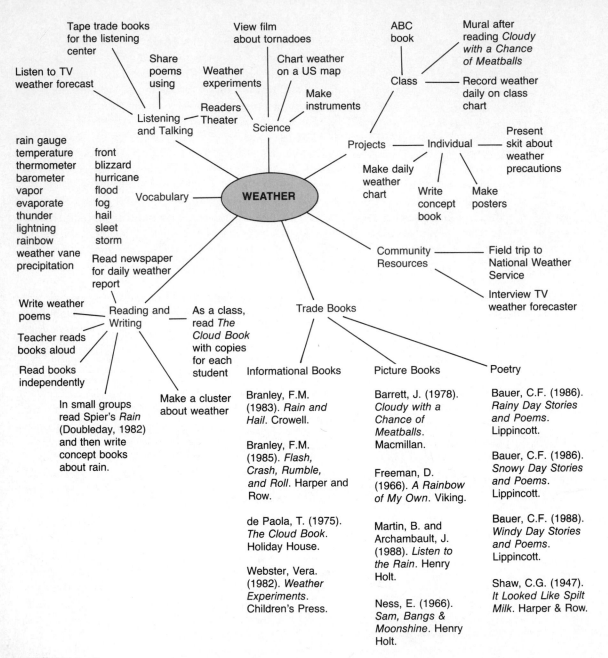

FIGURE 2–9

A Cluster for a Second Grade Weather Unit

	Monday	Tuesday	Wednesday	Thursday	Friday
8:45 - 9:00 Opening	Students read daily weather forecast in newspaper. Mark weather on class calendar and individual calendars. Also, add type of weather to graph.				
Block A 9:00 - 10:30	Finish sharing weather safety posters made last week. Choral reading: "Who Has Seen the Wind?" "I Am Flying". Make cluster on clouds	As a class, read The Cloud Book. (copies for each child.) Write in weather Log. Read aloud: It looked like Spilt Milk	Reread The Cloud Book. Add to the cluster on clouds. Share more information on clouds. Share their information to answer their questions. Read aloud Cloudy with a chance of Meatballs.	Review clouds cluster. Make class book on clouds. Each student makes a page. Paint Mural. Read aloud Cloudy with a chance of Meatballs.	Share draft pages in writing group. Make revisions.
10:30 - 10:45 Break		Go outside to look at clouds - if it is a cloudy day.			
10:45 - 11:30 Math			Talk about thermometers, how to read them, and how to record temperatures		
11:30 - 12:15 Lunch					
12:15 - 12:30 Independent Reading	Students read books chosen from the class collection of weather-related book at the listening center.				
12:30 - 1:00 Fine Arts					
Block B 1:00 - 2:00	Show collection of weather instruments. Discuss uses. Add words to word wall. Which can they make?	Centers 1. Examine instruments. 2. Make weather vane. 3. Make rain gauge. 4. Make wind sock.			View film on "Tools We Use to Measure Weather." Make chart with notes from film.
2:00 - 2:15 Break					
Block C 2:15 - 3:00	View film on "Forecasting the weather." Brainstorm ideas from film. Write in weather log. Talk about interviewing TV weather forecaster.	Write class invitation (review letter format). Discuss interview. Begin list of topics for interview questions.	Develop list of questions students each choose a question to ask. Write questions on cards.	Rehearse interview. Read aloud: I Forecast the weather.	The Interview
3:00 - 3:15 clean up					

FIGURE 2–10

Excerpt from a Lesson Plan

	Weather Unit	
Name_____	Beginning Date_____ Ending Date_____	
	Student's Check	Teacher's Check
1. Keep a daily weather calendar	☐	☐
2. Make a weather instrument and write about it in your Weather Log.	☐	☐
3. Do a weather experiment and write about it in your Weather Log.	☐	☐
4. Read *The Cloud Book* and write in your Weather Log.	☐	☐
5. Write a page for our book about clouds.	☐	☐
6. Make a weather safety poster and share it.	☐	☐
7. Read 2 weather books and write about them in your Weather Log.	☐	☐
8. Read *Rain* and write a poem about rain.	☐	☐
9. Do a weather project. Tell about it.	☐	☐

FIGURE 2–11

An Assessment Checklist for a Second Grade Unit on Weather

Facilitating Student Learning

Teachers play many roles while they facilitate students' learning in the elementary classroom. They instruct, guide, model, assess, support, encourage, respond, insist upon, and explain, to name only a few of the roles. Cazden (1983) categorizes these roles as *scaffolds, models,* and *instruction.*

Just as parents provide support for their children as they learn to talk, teachers also provide temporary supports as students are listening, talking, reading, and writing. For example, teachers serve as guides or coaches as they encourage students who are preparing a puppet show or writing reports. They respond to and reflect on students' writing as any interested audience would. Through these roles, teachers provide a "scaffold" or framework to support students when they tackle complex learning tasks (Applebee & Langer, 1983; Bruner, 1978; Cazden, 1980). As students learn, the need for this scaffolding diminishes, but when they tackle a new concept, the need for support returns. Teachers must continue to be responsive to students' growing competencies to provide this assistance. It is important, too, that teachers appreciate the power of their interactions with students and how they can support students' learning.

In everything they do, teachers are models for students. If you watch children play school at home, you will appreciate just how well children internalize what the teacher models. Teachers model language learning and ways to use language; for instance, they model ways of talking, and how children respond to and interact with classmates often reflects what the teacher has modeled in his or her talk. Teachers model literacy when they read and write along with their classes. When they check a dictionary for the spelling or meaning of a word they are unsure of, they model its use more powerfully than any assignment could.

Teachers also model language learning in more direct ways. When teachers first introduce a new concept, they should model it for students. When teachers introduce the diamante or haiku poetic form, for example, the teacher explains the form and shares several sample poems. Then students compose a poem as a class with the teacher before writing their own poems, and writing the poem as a class is modeling. It is important to point out that the model the teacher supplies is one example to learn from, not a sample to copy (Cazden, 1983). Similarly, teachers first model a writing group conference with a small group of students before students break into groups to share their writing. Modeling is as important in school learning as it was in young children's learning to talk. Students are learning how to "do school" and how to use language in new ways.

Almost everything a teacher does might be called "teaching," and certainly teachers are teaching as they informally support and nurture students' learning and as they model. Another type of teaching is direct teaching, when teachers plan and teach a formal lesson. The instructional model in Chapter 1 is designed for this type of direct teaching, when teachers are helping students learn a new concept or review one that was previously introduced. This instructional model can be used to teach the whole class or small groups of students, and it can be adapted to teach concepts, strategies, and skills related to the four language arts.

Another important component of the teacher's role is to assess student progress, either informally or formally. Teachers assess informally to guide students, to clarify misunderstandings, to monitor progress, and to know when to tear down the scaffold. They also assess students more formally to judge whether they have learned a particular concept and to assign grades. To keep track of 22, 26, or 30 students in a classroom, teachers need a variety of record-keeping techniques.

Resources for Teachers

Teachers are always interested in learning more about how to teach. As you begin teaching, you will want to learn as much as possible about how to teach language arts. Most schools provide inservice or staff development programs, some of which will be devoted to language arts instruction. Two organizations dedicated to improving the quality of instruction in reading and the other language arts are the National Council of Teachers of English (NCTE) and the International Reading Association (IRA). As an undergraduate student majoring in elementary education or as an elementary language arts teacher, you will find that these organizations can help you keep in touch with new ideas in the field. Both organizations publish journals of interest to preservice and classroom teachers with articles suggesting innovative teaching practices, reports of significant research studies, reviews of recently published books of children's literature, techniques for using computers in the classroom, and reviews of professional books and classroom materials. Journals for elementary teachers are *Language Arts,* published by NCTE, and *The Reading Teacher,* published by IRA. The two organizations also publish other journals for high school language arts and reading teachers, college faculty, and researchers. Figure 2–12 lists these and other periodicals of interest to language arts teachers. Most of these journals and magazines invite readers to share their classroom-tested ideas by submitting manuscripts; information for authors appears in each publication that invites unsolicited manuscripts.

NCTE and IRA also organize yearly national conferences, which are held in major cities around the U.S. on a rotating basis. At these conferences, teachers can listen to presentations by well-known authorities in language arts and by children's authors and illustrators, as well as by other classroom teachers who have developed innovative programs in their classrooms. Teachers can also meet in special interest groups to share ideas and concerns. Commercial publishers also display textbooks and other instructional materials at the conferences. In addition, these two organizations have state and local affiliate groups that teachers can join. The affiliates also publish journals and organize conferences. The local groups enable teachers to meet other teachers with similar interests and concerns.

Elementary teachers can also learn more about teaching writing by participation in workshops sponsored by affiliate groups of the National Writing Project (NWP). The NWP began as the Bay Area Writing Project at the University of California at Berkeley in 1974. It was conceived by James Gray and a group of English teachers who wanted to improve the quality of writing instruction in elementary and secondary schools. The NWP has spread to more than 150 affiliate groups located in almost every state and in Canada, Europe, and Asia; for example, the Gateway Writing Project serves the St. Louis area, the Capital Writing Project serves the Washington, D.C., area, and the Oklahoma Writing Project serves the state of Oklahoma. Inservice workshops are scheduled in school districts near each affiliate group. One principle on which the NWP is based is that the best teacher of other teachers is a teacher, and teachers who have been trained by the affiliate groups give presentations at the inservice workshops.

Each NWP affiliate group recruits experienced elementary teachers who have a special interest and/or expertise in teaching writing to participate in special summer training institutes. These teachers then serve as teacher/consultants and make presentations at the inservice workshops. Many NWP affiliate groups also sponsor other workshops and study tours, young author conferences and workshops for student writers, and teacher-as-researcher projects that have direct classroom applications. For additional information about the National Writing Project or for the location of the NWP affiliate group nearest you, contact the National Writing Project, School of Education, University of California, Berkeley, CA 94720.

CBC Features
Children's Book Council, Inc.
67 Irving Place
New York, NY 10003

Childhood Education
Association for Childhood
Education International
11141 Georgia Avenue, Suite 200
Wheaton, MD 20902

The Elementary School Journal
University of Chicago Press
P.O. Box 37005
Chicago, IL 60637

The Good Apple Newspaper
P.O. Box 299
Carthage, IL 62321

The Horn Book
Park Square Building
31 Saint James Avenue
Boston, MA 02116

Language Arts
National Council of Teachers of English
1111 Kenyon Road
Urbana, IL 61801

Learning
530 University Avenue
Palo Alto, CA 94301

The Middle School Journal
National Middle School Association
P.O. Box 14882
Columbus, OH 43214

The New Advocate
480 Washington Street
Norwood, MA 02062

The Reading Teacher
International Reading Association
800 Barksdale Road
P.O. Box 8139
Newark, DE 19711

Teaching K–8
P.O. Box 912
Farmingdale, NY 11737

The WEB: Wonderfully Exciting Books
The Ohio State University
200 Ramseyer Hall
Columbus, OH 43210

Writing Teacher
P.O. Box 791437
San Antonio, TX 78279

FIGURE 2–12

Teacher's Notebook Page: Journals and Magazines for Language Arts Teachers

THEMATIC UNITS

"I believe in integration. I connect stories, informational books, and poems with the units I am teaching. And, I always teach skills within context of the unit. When I separate learning into little compartments, my students don't learn as well. This way works better for me."

Sally Tsuchiguchi, Kindergarten Teacher
Viking Elementary School

PROCEDURE

We're spending about six weeks on an animal unit. Because Easter is coming, I chose *Seven Eggs* by Meredith Hooper (1985) to read today. In this book, seven eggs hatch. A baby penguin cracks out of the first egg; other eggs contain a crocodile, ostrich, lizard, turtle, owl, and the last egg is an Easter egg. I like to share this book with students because they can predict what is going to hatch from the eggs based on what they have learned about animals. Then I read the book a second time, and, as I read, I ask students to select plastic eggs from my Easter basket and open them. Inside the eggs are crocheted finger puppets of each egg-hatching animal. And, the last egg contains little chocolate Easter eggs for the

children to eat. My kindergartners love to open the eggs and find the finger puppets. Because they are so excited about what we're doing, I take the opportunity to ask students to identify the beginning sound of each word, for example, *turtle* begins with *t*. After students identify the beginning sounds, they read the words as I write them on the chalkboard, and, later, they may want to write them in their journals. I ask students to write the name of one animal that was hatched and to draw a picture of the animal in their journal notebooks. Students can copy the animal's name from the chalkboard or write it using invented spelling (original spellings based on children's developing knowledge of sound-symbol relationships). Seanna's journal entry is shown. When she shared her

❖ ASSESSING STUDENTS' PROGRESS

Assessing students' progress in the language arts is a difficult task. Although it may seem fairly easy to develop a criterion-referenced test, administer it, and grade it, tests often measure language *skills* rather than language *use*. It is extremely difficult to measure students' communicative competence with a test. Tests do not measure listen-

P n g n

E g g

work with the other students in the small group, she expanded her writing this way: "A penguin was in the egg."

ASSESSMENT

I observe my kindergartners as they participate in a small group. I check that they are involved in our activity and that they participate willingly. I also note their drawings and writings in their journals as well as their willingness to share what they have written. Sometimes I make notes about these observations in the folders I keep about each child; other times, I make a mental note.

REFLECTIONS

I like to integrate my units across the curriculum. Today's language arts lesson is connected with our animals unit and this week's focus on animals that lay eggs. There are chicken eggs in our incubator, and students observe the eggs each day and turn them. Tomorrow morning I will share information about turtles, penguins, owls, and other animals that lay eggs. After this study, the kindergartners will break into small interest groups, and each group will dictate a page for our book about animals that lay eggs.

ing and talking very well, and a test on punctuation marks, for example, does not indicate students' ability to use punctuation marks correctly in their own writing. Instead, tests typically evaluate students' ability to add punctuation marks to a set of sentences created by someone else, or to proofread and spot punctuation errors in someone else's writing. An alternative and far better approach is to examine how students use punctuation marks in their own writing.

Assessment must be viewed as an integral part of the language arts curriculum. (Goodman, et al., 1989). We suggest seven alternative approaches to documenting children's language development and assessing students' progress. They are classroom observations, anecdotal records, conferences, checklists, interviews, language samples, and across-the-curriculum applications (Baskwill & Whitman, 1988). Information from these approaches together provides a more complete and more personal assessment picture or "portfolio" (Flood & Lapp, 1989). These approaches help teachers get to know students better and to better interpret student learning.

Classroom Observations

Instead of relying on tests, we suggest that teachers become *kid watchers,* a term that Goodman (1978) coined and defined as "direct and informal observation of students." To be an effective kid watcher, teachers must understand how children develop language and understand the role of errors in language learning. In Chapter 1 we described language development as a natural, hypothesis-testing process. Children often make miscues or "errors" as they learn to talk (Goodman & Burke, 1972). They may, for instance, say "keeped" or "goodest" when they are learning rules for forming past tense or superlatives. Instead of errors, however, these words are clues to language development. Children's sentence structure, spelling, and other "errors" provide equally valuable clues to their written language development. Teachers use kid watching spontaneously when they interact with children and are attentive to their behavior and comments. Other observation times should be planned, however, during which the teacher focuses on particular children and makes anecdotal notes about a child's use of language. Students' behavior during testing situations often does not reflect their actual ability to communicate using the language modes.

Anecdotal Records

While teachers kid-watch, they make anecdotal records noting students' performance in listening, talking, reading, and writing activities, as well as questions students ask and concepts and skills they indicate confusion about. These records document students' growth and pinpoint problem areas that need direct instruction from the teacher. A year-long collection of records provides a comprehensive picture of a student's language development. Instead of recording random samples, teachers should choose events that are characteristic of each student. An excerpt from a fifth grade teacher's anecdotal records about one student's progress during a unit on the American Revolution appears in Figure 2–13.

Several organizational schemes are possible, and teachers should use the format that is most comfortable for them. Some teachers make a card file with dividers for each child and write anecdotes on notecards. They feel comfortable jotting notes on these small cards or even carrying around a set of cards in their pockets. Other teachers divide a spiral-bound notebook into sections for each child and write anecdotes in the notebook, which they keep on their desks. A third technique is to write anecdotes on small sheets of paper and clip the sheets into the student's assessment folder.

AMERICAN REVOLUTION UNIT—SIMULATED JOURNALS AND BIOGRAPHIES

March 5	Matthew selected Ben Franklin as historical figure for American Revolution projects.
March 11	Matthew fascinated with information he has found about B. F. Brought several sources from home. Is completing B. F.'s lifeline with many details.
March 18	Simulated journal. Four entries in four days! Interesting how he picked up language style of the period in his journal. Volunteers to share daily. I think he enjoys the oral sharing more than the writing.
March 25	Nine simulated journal entries, all illustrated. High level of enthusiasm.
March 29	Conferenced about cluster for B. F. biography. Well developed with five rays, many details. Matthew will work on "contributions" ray. He recognized it as the least-developed one.
April 2	Three chapters of biography drafted. Talked about "working titles" for chapters and choosing more interesting titles after writing that reflect the content of the chapters.
April 7	Drafting conference. Matthew has completed all five chapters. He and Dustin are competitive, both writing on B. F. They are reading each other's chapters and checking the accuracy of information.
April 12	Writing group. Matthew confused Declaration of Independence with the Constitution. Chapters longer and more complete since drafting conference. Compared with autobiography project, writing is more sophisticated. Longer, too. Reading is influencing writing style—e.g., "Luckily for Ben." He is still somewhat defensive about accepting suggestions except from me. He will make 3 revisions—agreed in writing group.
April 15	Revisions: (1) eliminated "he" (substitute), (2) re-sequenced Chapter 3 (move), and (3) added sentences in Chapter 5 (add).
April 19	Proofread with Dustin. Working hard.
April 23	Editing conference—no major problems. Discussed use of commas within sentences, capitalizing proper nouns. Matthew and Dustin more task-oriented on this project; I see more motivation and commitment.
April 29	Final copy of biography completed and shared with class.

FIGURE 2—13

Excerpt from an Anecdotal Record

Conferences

Teachers often hold short, informal conferences to talk with students about their work or to help them solve a problem related to what they are studying. Most often these conferences concern students' reading or writing activities, but they could be held with the actors in a play or the students working in a small group to create an advertisement or commercial. Conferences can be held at students' desks while the teacher moves around the classroom, at the teacher's desk, or at a special conference table. These are some occasions for and types of conferences:

On-the-spot conferences. Teachers visit briefly with students at their desks to monitor some aspect of the student's work or to check on progress. These conferences are brief; the teacher may spend less than a minute at the student's desk before moving away.

Prereading or prewriting conferences. The teacher and student make plans for reading or writing at the conference. At a prereading conference, they may talk about information related to the book, difficult concepts or vocabulary words related to the reading, or the reading log the student will keep. At a prewriting conference, they may discuss possible writing topics, how to narrow a broad topic, or how to gather and organize information before writing.

Revising conferences. A small group of students and the teacher meet together to get specific suggestions about revising their compositions. These conferences offer student writers an audience to provide feedback on how well they have communicated.

Book discussion conferences. A student (or small group of students) and the teacher meet to discuss the book they have read. They may share entries from their reading logs, discuss the author's use of plot or characters, compare the story to others they have read, or make plans to extend their reading by doing a project.

Editing conferences. In these individual or small-group conferences, the teacher reviews students' proofread compositions and helps them correct spelling, punctuation, capitalization, and other mechanical errors.

Teachers assess students' writing progress during conferences.

Instructional "minilesson" conferences. In these conferences, teachers meet
with individual students to provide special instruction on one or two skills (e.g.,
capitalizing proper nouns, using commas in a series) that are particularly troublesome for certain students.

Assessment conferences. In assessment conferences, the teacher meets with
students after they complete an assignment or project to talk about their
growth as readers or writers and their plans for the next assignment. Teachers
ask students to reflect on their competencies and to set goals.

The teacher's role at conferences is to be listener and guide. Teachers can learn a great
deal about students and their learning if they listen as students talk about their reading,
writing, or other activities. When students explain a problem they are having, the
teacher is often able to decide on a way to work through it. Graves (1983) suggests that
teachers balance the amount of their talk with the student's talk during the conference
and, at the end, reflect on what the student has taught them, what responsibilities the
student can take, and whether the student understands what to do next.

Checklists

Teachers can use checklists during specific observations or to track students' progress on
particular skills. For example, when students participate in writing conferences in
which they read their compositions to small groups of classmates and ask for suggestions
for improving their writing, teachers can check that students participate fully in the
group, share their writing with classmates, gracefully accept suggestions about improving their writing, and make substantive changes in their writing based on some of their
classmates' suggestions. Students can even help develop the checklists so they understand what types of behavior are expected of them.

Four checklists appear in Figure 2–14. The first is a "Weekly Reading-Writing
Activity Sheet" that students in middle and upper grades might complete each week to
monitor their reading and writing activities. Notice that students are directed to write
a letter to the teacher on the back of the sheet, reflecting on their work during that
week. Next is a "Response to Literature Checklist" that either the teacher or the
student might use to keep track of the response activities the student chooses to participate in after reading. The third checklist is an "Independent Reading Record" that
students keep as they read. Students list the title and author of each book they read,
the dates on which they read the book, the date of their conference with the teacher,
the type of response activity, and when the student shared the response activity with
the class. Fourth is a "Fables Unit Checklist" for use by third graders as they complete
activities in their fables unit. This checklist is clipped inside a unit folder, and as
students complete each assignment, they check the box in the right-hand column. At
the end of the unit, the folder with the checklist and all student materials is submitted
to the teacher. (Other checklists are presented when we discuss writing, spelling, and
handwriting.)

Weekly Reading–Writing Activity Sheet		
Name_____	Week_____	
Read independently	M T W Th F	Wrote in a journal	M T W Th F
Read in a guided reading group	M T W Th F	Wrote in a reading log	M T W Th F
Did a response activity	M T W Th F	Did a prewriting activity	M T W Th F
Listened to the teacher read aloud	M T W Th F	Wrote a rough draft	M T W Th F
Read during USSR time	M T W Th F	Went to a writing group	M T W Th F
Read to an adult	M T W Th F	Made revisions	M T W Th F
Read to other children	M T W Th F	Edited my own writing	M T W Th F
Read at the listening center	M T W Th F	Edited for a classmate	M T W Th F
Had a reading conference	M T W Th F	Had a writing conference	M T W Th F
Shared my reading with classmates	M T W Th F	Shared my writing with classmates	M T W Th F
Other		Other	
New words read this week		Spelling words needed this week	
Titles of books read		Titles of writings	
Write a letter to me on the back, thinking about the week and your reading and writing.			

FIGURE 2–14

Four Sample Assessment Checklists

Response to Literature Checklist	
Name_____	Grading Period 1 2 3 4
book jacket	point of view
book seller	portrait of character
cartoons	posters
character cluster	puppets
commercial or ad	quotable quotes
crossword puzzle	read other books
diorama	reading logs
dramatization	scripts
dress as character	simulated journals
exhibit	simulated letter
filmstrip	story rewrites
interview	travel brochure
letter to author	versions
map or diagram	5 Ws cluster
mobile	Win, Lose, or Draw
movie roll	word charts
mural	
newspaper article	
oral reading	
plot diagram	
poem	

FIGURE 2—14   *(continued)*

Interviews

Teachers can interview or talk with students about language to try to understand their perceptions and to clarify misunderstandings. Teachers can ask factual questions about language and language skills, but more valuable questions are metacognitive, focusing on how the students use language. Questions such as "Do you listen the same way to

Independent Reading Record				
Name_____			Grading Period 1 2 3 4	
Title/Author	Dates Read	Conference	Response	Sharing

Fables Unit Checklist

Name_____

1. I read *Fables* by Arnold Lobel. ☐
2. I wrote about 10 fables in my reading log. ☐
3. I did a project: ☐
   ☐ a story map
   ☐ puppets to retell a fable
   ☐ a mobile
   ☐ _____
4. I helped write our class fable ☐
5. I wrote a fable using the writing process ☐
   ☐ prewriting
   ☐ drafting
   ☐ revising
   ☐ editing
   ☐ sharing

FIGURE 2−14 *(continued)*

something that compares one thing to another (such as alligators and crocodiles) as you do to something that has a lot of descriptive words (such as what a swamp looks like)? Why or why not?" or "What do you do when you're writing and don't know how to spell a word? What else can you do?" These questions probe students' awareness of language processes and strategies for comprehending and producing language.

Language Samples

Teachers can collect students' oral and written language samples to use in assessing their progress. Oral language samples can be tape-recorded, and written language samples can be kept in folders. The teacher can compare samples from the first month of the school year to more recent samples to identify areas of growth, as well as areas that need instruction. When language samples are to be graded, students should be allowed to choose those to be assessed from the samples that have been collected.

Across-the-Curriculum Applications

A final approach to assessing students' progress in language arts is to examine how well students have applied their knowledge about listening, talking, reading, and writing to other areas of the curriculum. In fact, these applications are probably the best indicator of students' learning. As an example, students may score 100% on weekly spelling tests but continue to spell the same words incorrectly in science learning logs and research reports in social studies.

To assess students' language development systematically with alternative techniques, teachers should use at least three different evaluation approaches. Approaching an evaluation through at least three different viewpoints is called *triangulation*. In addition to tests, teachers can use these techniques: kid watching, anecdotal records, checklists, interviewing, tape-recording students' talk, writing samples, and across-the-curriculum applications. Using a variety of approaches enables teachers to be much more accurate in charting and assessing students' language growth.

❖ REVIEW

This chapter focuses on how teachers teach language arts. As Lefevre suggests, teachers need to provide opportunities for discovery; an example is a unit on mystery stories. The classroom environment is important in teaching, and elementary classrooms should be language-rich with a variety of literacy materials available. Through application of the characteristics of a literate environment and arrangement of the classroom, teachers can promote this language-rich setting.

Teachers facilitate students' learning in three ways: they provide scaffolds, models, and instruction. We have seen how teachers develop units, facilitate students' learning, and assess learning as exemplified in a second-grade weather unit.

Tests are only one way to assess students' learning; other ways are classroom observations, anecdotal records, conferences, checklists, interviews, language samples, and across-the-curriculum applications.

❖ EXTENSIONS

1. Visit an elementary classroom and note which characteristics of a language-rich classroom it exemplifies. What might the teacher change in the classroom to incorporate other characteristics?

2. Examine several language arts textbooks for the grade level at which you teach or expect to teach, using the guidelines in Figure 2–5. Evaluate the textbooks and consider how they should be used in teaching language arts.

3. Preview language arts software programs using the guidelines in Figure 2–7. Three highly rated programs you may want to preview are *Story Tree* (1984), *M-ss-ng l-nks: Young People's Literature* (1983), and *Jabbertalky* (1983). Also examine word-processing programs such as *The writing workshop* (1986), and *QUILL* (1983).

4. Choose a topic and develop a unit cluster like those illustrated in Figures 2–8 and 2–9.

5. Review at least six of the language arts journals and magazines listed in Figure 2–12. Summarize your review of each publication on an index card and include the following information:

   Title, mailing address, and sponsoring organization of the publication
   Number of issues published each year
   Cost of yearly subscription
   Types of articles in each issue
   Assessment of the journal and its value for elementary teachers

6. Interview an elementary teacher and ask about the kinds of assessment he or she uses.

7. Read Kitagawa's article (1989) about classroom observations of individual students, then make your own day-long observation of an elementary student.

❖ REFERENCES

Anno, M. (1983). *Anno's U.S.A.* New York: Philomel.

Applebee, A. N., & Langer, J. A. (1983). Instructional scaffolding: Reading and writing and natural language activities. *Language Arts, 60,* 168–175.

The Bank Street writer (1982). [Computer program]. San Rafael, CA: Broderbund Software.

Barber, B. (1982). Creating BYTES of language. *Language Arts, 59,* 472–475.

Baskwill, J., & Whitman, P. (1988). *Evaluation: Whole language, whole child.* New York: Scholastic.

Bruner, J. (1978). The role of dialogue in language acquisition. In A. Sinclair, R. J. Jarvelle, & W. J. M. Levelt (Eds.), *The child's concept of language.* New York: Springer-Verlag.

Burningham, J. (1985). *Opposites.* New York: Crown Books.

Carle, E. (1989). *Animals, animals.* New York: Philomel.

Carrick, C. (1978). *Octopus.* New York: Clarion Books.

Caselli, G. (1987). *The human body.* New York: Grosset & Dunlap.

Cazden, C. B. (1980). Peekaboo as an instructional model: Discourse development at home and at school. *Papers and Reports of Child Language Development, 17,* 1–29.

Cazden, C. B. (1983). Adult assistance to language development: Scaffolds, models, and direct instruction. In R. P. Parker & F. A. Davis (Eds.), *Developing literacy: Young children's use of language,* pp. 3–18. Newark, DE: International Reading Association.

Chomsky, C. (1984). Finding the best language arts software. *Classroom Computer Learning, 4,* 61–63.

Cleary, B. (1981). *Ramona Quimby, Age 8*. New York: Morrow.

Cole, J. (1973). *My puppy is born*. New York: Morrow.

Crews, D. (1982). *Carousel*. New York: Greenwillow.

Dahl, R. (1984). *Boy*. New York: Farrar, Straus & Giroux.

DeGroff, L. (1990). Is there a place for computers in whole language classrooms? *The Reading Teacher, 43,* 568–572.

Dickinson, D. K. (1986). Cooperation, collaboration, and a computer: Integrating a computer into a first-second grade writing program. *Research in the Teaching of English, 20,* 357–378.

Elkin, B. (1983). *Money*. Chicago: Children's Press.

Fleischman, P. (1988). *Joyful noise: Poems for two voices*. New York: Harper and Row.

Fleischman, S. (1986). *The whipping boy*. New York: Greenwillow.

Flood, J., & Lapp, D. (1989). Reporting reading progress: A comparison portfolio for parents. *The Reading Teacher, 42,* 508–514.

Fritz, J. (1976). *Will you sign here, John Hancock?* New York: Coward-McCann.

Genishi, C. (1988). Kindergartners and computers: A case study of six children. *The Elementary School Journal, 89,* 185–201.

Gibbons, G. (1982). *The post office book: Mail and how it moves*. New York: Harper and Row.

Goodall, J. S. (1986). *The story of a castle*. New York: Macmillan.

Goodall, J. S. (1988). *Little red riding hood*. New York: Macmillan.

Goodman, K. (1986). *What's whole in whole language?* Portsmouth, NH: Heinemann.

Goodman, K. S., Goodman, Y. M., & Hood, W. J. (Eds.). (1989). *The whole language evaluation book*. Portsmouth, NH: Heinemann.

Goodman, Y. M. (1978). Kid watching: An alternative to testing. *National Elementary Principals Journal, 57,* 41–45.

Goodman, Y. M., & Burke, C. L. (1972). *The reading miscue inventory manual*. New York: Richard C. Owen.

Graves, D. H. (1977). Research update: Language arts textbooks: A writing process evaluation. *Language Arts, 54,* 817–823.

Graves, D. H. (1983). *Writing: Teachers and children at work*. Portsmouth, NH: Heinemann.

Hall, N. (1987). *The emergence of literacy*. Portsmouth, NH: Heinemann.

Hamilton, V. (1974). *Paul Robeson: The life and times of a free black man*. New York: Harper and Row.

Hooper, M. (1985). *Seven eggs*. New York: Harper and Row.

Hopkins, L. B. (1976). *Good morning to you, valentine*. New York: Harcourt Brace Jovanovich.

Howe, D., & Howe, J. (1979). *Bunnicula*. New York: Atheneum.

Hyman, T. S. (1977). *The sleeping beauty*. Boston: Little, Brown.

Jabbertalky: The programmable word game (1983). [Computer program]. Sunnyvale, CA: Automated Simulations.

Kennedy, X. J., & Kennedy, D. M. (1982). *Knock at a star: A child's introduction to poetry*. Boston: Little, Brown.

Kitagawa, M. M. (1989). Observing Carlos: One day of language use in school. In G. S. Pinnell & M. L. Matlin (Eds.), *Teachers and research: Language learning in the classroom,* pp. 3–7. Newark, DE: International Reading Association.

Lasky, K. (1983). *Sugaring time*. New York: Macmillan.

Lefevre, C. A. (1970). *Linguistics, English, and the language arts*. Boston: Allyn and Bacon.

Lewis, C. S. (1950). *The lion, the witch, and the wardrobe*. New York: Macmillan.

Lindfors, J. W. (1989). The classroom: A good environment for language learning. In P. Rigg & V. G. Allen. (Eds.), *When they don't all speak English: Integrating the ESL student into the regular classroom,* pp. 39–54. Urbana, IL: National Council of Teachers of English.

Lobel, A. (1970). *Frog and toad are friends*. New York: Harper and Row.

Lobel, A. (1972). *Frog and toad together*. New York: Harper and Row.

Lobel, A. (1976). *Frog and toad all year*. New York: Harper and Row.

Lobel, A. (1979). *Days with frog and toad*. New York: Harper and Row.

Locker, T. (1987). *The boy who held back the sea*. New York: Dial.

Macaulay, D. (1977). *Castle*. Boston: Houghton Mifflin.

MacLachlan, P. (1985). *Sarah, plain and tall*. New York: Harper and Row.

Mayer, M. (1974). *Frog goes to dinner*. New York: Dial.

Mayers, F. C. (1986). *The National Air and Space Museum ABC*. New York: Abrams.

M-ss-ng l-nks: Young people's literature (1983). [Computer program]. Pleasantville, NY: Sunburst Communications.

Morrow, L. M. (1989). Designing the classroom to promote literacy development. In D. S. Strickland & L. M. Morrow (Eds.), *Emerging literacy: Young children learn to read and write*. Newark, DE: International Reading Association.

Parker, N. W. (1985). *Paul Revere's Ride*. New York: Greenwillow.

Paterson, K. (1977). *Bridge to Terabithia*. New York: Crowell.

Phenix, J., & Hannan, E. (1984). Word processing in the grade one classroom. *Language Arts, 61,* 804–812.

Prelutsky, J. (1983). *The Random House book of poetry for children*. New York: Random House.

Prelutsky, J. (1988). *Tyrannosaurus was a beast*. New York: Greenwillow.

QUILL (1983). [Computer program]. Lexington, MA: DC Heath.

Sendak, M. (1963). *Where the wild things are*. New York: Harper and Row.

Sharmat, M. W. (1974). *Nate the great goes undercover*. New York: Coward-McCann.

Smith, N. J. (1985). The word processing approach to language experience. *The Reading Teacher, 38,* 556–559.

Smith, P. L., & Tompkins, G. E. (1984). Selecting software for your LD students. *Academic Therapy, 20,* 221–224.

Sobol, D. J. (1963). *Encyclopedia Brown, boy detective*. New York: E. P. Dutton.

Spier, P. (1973). *The star-spangled banner*. New York: Doubleday.

Story tree (1984). [Computer program]. New York: Scholastic.

Taylor, R. (1980). *Computers in the schools: Tool, tutor, and tutee*. New York: Teachers College Press.

The writing workshop (1986). [Computer program]. St. Louis: Milliken.

Zaharias, J. A. (1983). Microcomputers in the language arts classroom: Promises and pitfalls. *Language Arts, 60,* 990–996.

Zalben, J. B. (1977). *Lewis Carroll's Jabberwocky*. New York: Warne.

3 WORDS: THE BUILDING BLOCKS OF LANGUAGE

HISTORY OF THE ENGLISH LANGUAGE

WORDS AND THEIR MEANINGS

HOW STUDENTS LEARN WORDS

TEACHING STUDENTS ABOUT WORDS

    Teaching Strategy
    Tying Word Study to Reading and Writing
    Tying Word Study to Literature and Content Areas
    Assessing Students' Use of Words

◆ WORDS ARE THE BUILDING BLOCKS OF LANGUAGE, AND IN THIS
chapter, we will focus on vocabulary and how to help students learn and use
words effectively. There are more than 750,000 words in the English language,
and elementary teachers introduce thousands of these words to students through
literature and content area units.

◆ AS YOU ARE READING, THINK ABOUT THESE QUESTIONS:

How does knowledge about the history of English help students understand the
meanings of words?

How do root words, prefixes, and suffixes affect the meaning of words?

What are homonyms, synonyms, and antonyms?

How do elementary students learn new words?

How can teachers facilitate students' learning?

Mark Twain said "the difference between the right word and the almost right word is the difference between lightning and the lightning bug." Learning about words and how to choose the right one to express the meaning you intend is what vocabulary is all about. Vocabulary is not decoding or word identification; rather, the focus is on meaning. Choosing the best word to express meaning is important to all language users. When we listen and read, we must understand the meaning that someone else intends, and when we talk and write, we must choose exactly the right word so that our audience will understand our message.

Words are the meaning-bearing units of language. Of the three-quarters of a million words in English, most people use only about 20,000 of them, and most of the words we commonly use come from a body of approximately 5000 to 7000 words (Klein, 1988). Our personal ownership of words is quite limited. We have overlapping but separate listening, talking, reading, and writing vocabularies. We may, for example, recognize a word such as *obfuscate* when listening or reading, but fewer of us would use the word in talking or writing. Our reading and listening vocabularies are more extensive than our talking and writing vocabularies, for many reasons. We may fear mispronouncing or misspelling a word, or we may fear what our friends will think if we use it in conversation. The words we use mark us in a number of ways: by our word choice, by our pronunciation, and how we string them together into sentences.

Words in our personal vocabularies reflect varying degrees of word knowledge. Klein (1988) divides our personal vocabularies, which he calls "dictionaries," into three levels: (1) the ownership dictionary of words we know and use competently; (2) the mid-level dictionary, which is accessible with contextual assistance; and (3) the low-level dictionary, composed of words we know marginally and, when we use them, risk making an error. We have each of the three dictionary levels in our heads, and when we learn a new word, it usually enters either the low- or mid-level dictionary. Then, after additional experiences or instruction, it is transferred into the ownership dictionary. Even though the number of words in the three dictionary categories grows, the number of categories does not.

❖ HISTORY OF THE ENGLISH LANGUAGE

Understanding the history of English and how words entered the language contributes greatly to understanding words and their meanings.[1] English is a historic language, and this fact accounts for word meanings and some spelling inconsistencies. We use some very different words for a single concept, and the history of English in general and the etymology of these words in particular explains the apparent duplications. Consider the variety of words related to *water*: aquatic, hydrant, aquamarine, waterfall, hydroelectric, watercress, watery, aquarium, waterproof, hydraulic, aqualung, and hydrogen, to name a few. These words have one of three root words that each mean water: *water* is English, of course, whereas *aqua* is Latin and *hydro* is Greek. Which root word was

[1]This section is adapted from Tompkins & Yaden, 1986.

Students learn many new words by reading.

used depends on the people who created and used the word, the purpose of the word, and when it entered English.

The development of the English language is divided into three periods: Old English, Middle English, and Modern English. The beginning and end of each period is marked by a significant event, such as an invasion or an invention.

Old English (450−1100). The recorded history of the English language begins in 449, when Germanic tribes, including the Angles and Saxons, invaded Britain. The invaders pushed the original inhabitants, the Celts, to the northern and western corners of the island. This annexation is romanticized in the King Arthur legends. Arthur is believed to have been a Celtic military leader who fought bravely against the German invaders.

The English language began as an intermingling of the dialects spoken by the Angles, Saxons, and other Germanic tribes in Britain. Many people assume that English is based on Latin, but it has Germanic roots and was brought to Britain by these invaders. Although 85 percent of Old English words are no longer used, many everyday words remain (e.g., *child, foot, hand, house, man, mother, old,* and *sun*). In contrast to Modern English, Old English had few loan words (words borrowed from another language and incorporated into English) and had a highly developed inflectional system for indicating number, gender, and verb tense. The Anglo-Saxons added affixes to existing words, including *be-, for-, -ly, -dom,* and *-hood.* They also invented vividly descriptive compound words. The Old English word for *music,* for example, was "ear-sport," *world* was "age of man," and *folly* was "wanwit." The folk epic *Beowulf,* the great literary work of the period, illustrates the poetic use of words; for instance, the sea is described as a "whale-path" and a "swan's road."

Through contact with other cultures, foreign words began to make their way into the predominantly Germanic word stock. The borrowed words came from two main sources: the Romans and the Vikings. A number of words were borrowed from Latin and incorporated into English. Contact between the Roman soldiers and traders and the Germanic tribes on the continent, before they had invaded England, contributed some words, including *cheese, copper, mile, street,* and *wine.* The missionaries who reintroduced Christianity to Britain in 597 also brought with them a number of religious words (e.g., *angel, candle, hymn*).

In 787, the Vikings from Denmark and other areas of Scandinavia began a series of raids against English villages, and for the next three centuries, they attacked, conquered, and occupied much of England. Their influence was so great that the Danish king Canute ruled England during the first part of the 11th century. The Vikings' contribution to the English language was significant. They provided the pronouns *they, their, them;* introduced the /g/ and /k/ sounds (e.g., *kid, get*); contributed most of our *sc-* and *sk-* words (e.g., *skin, sky*); and enriched our vocabulary with more than 500 everyday words, including *husband* and *window.*

In Old English, some consonant combinations were pronounced that are not heard today, including the /k/ in words like *knee.* The letter *f* represented both /f/ and /v/, resulting in the Modern English spelling pattern of *wolf* and *wolves.* The pronunciation of the vowel sounds was very different, too; for example, the Old English *stan* (*a* = *a* in *father*) has become our word *stone.*

The structure, spelling, and pronunciation of Old English were significantly different from Modern English; so much so that we would not be able to read an Old English text or understand someone speaking Old English. It was a highly inflected language with many different word endings, and the arrangement of words in sentences was different, too, with verbs often placed at the end of sentences. In many ways, Old English was more like Modern German than Modern English.

Middle English (1100–1500).   An event occurred in 1066 that changed the course of the English language and ushered in the Middle English period: the Norman Conquest. In that year, William the Conqueror crossed the English Channel from the French province of Normandy and defeated the English king, Harold, at the Battle of Hastings. William claimed the English throne and established a French court in London. This event had far-reaching consequences: for nearly 300 years, Norman-French was the official language in England, spoken by the nobility and upper classes, although the lower classes continued to speak English. By 1300, the use of Norman-French had declined, and before the end of the 14th century, English was restored as the official language of England. Chaucer's *Canterbury Tales,* written in the late 1300s, provides evidence that English was also replacing French as the preferred written language. Political, social, and economic changes contributed to this reversal.

The Middle English period was one of tremendous change. A large portion of the Old English vocabulary was lost as 10,000 new Norman-French loan words were added to the language, reflecting the Norman impact on English life and society (Baugh &

Cable, 1978). They included military words (*soldier, victory*), political words (*government, princess*), medical words (*physician, surgeon*), and words related to the arts (*comedy, music, poet*). Many of the new loan words duplicated Old English words. Typically, one word was eventually lost; if both words remained in the language, they developed slightly different meanings. Often it was the Old English word that disappeared. The words *hardy* (Old English) and *cordial* (French) were originally synonyms, both meaning "from the heart." In time they differentiated and now express different meanings.

Most of the Norman-French loan words were derived from Latin. In addition, a few Latin words (e.g., *individual, polite*) passed directly into English during this period. In contrast to the French loan words, Latin borrowings were more sophisticated words, used more often in writing than in speech. Also, several words (e.g., *dock, freight*) were borrowed from the Dutch during the Middle English period as a result of trade with the Low Countries.

During this period, there was a significant reduction in the use of inflections or word endings. Many irregular verbs were lost, and others developed regular past and past participle forms (e.g., *climb, talk*), although Modern English still retains some irregular verbs (e.g., *sing, fly*) that contribute to our usage problems. By 1000, -*s* had become the accepted plural marker, although the Old English plural form -*en* was used in some words; this artifact remains in a few plurals, such as *children*.

Modern English (1500–present).   The Modern English period is not characterized by invasions or other significant political events, but rather by the development of the printing press and the tremendous upswing in exploration, colonization, and trade with countries around the world. The introduction of the printing press in England by William Caxton in 1476 marks the dividing point between the Middle and Modern English periods. The printing press was a powerful force in standardizing English spelling as well as a practical means for providing increasing numbers of people with books. Until the invention of the printing press, English spelling kept pace with pronunciation, but the printing press served to standardize and fix spelling, and the lag between pronunciation and spelling began to widen. The tremendous increase in exploration, colonization, and trade with many different parts of the world resulted in a wide borrowing of words from more than 50 languages. Borrowings include *alcohol* (Arabic), *chocolate* (French), *cookie* (Dutch), *czar* (Russian), *hallelujah* (Hebrew), *hurricane* (Spanish), *kindergarten* (German), *smorgasbord* (Swedish), *tycoon* (Chinese), and *violin* (Italian).

Many Latin and Greek words were added to English during the Renaissance to increase the language's prestige; for example, *congratulate, democracy,* and *education* came from Latin, and *catastrophe, encyclopedia,* and *thermometer* came from Greek. Many modern Greek and Latin borrowings are scientific words (e.g., *aspirin, vaccinate*), and some of the very recently borrowed forms (e.g., *criterion, focus*) have retained their native plural forms, adding confusion about how to spell these forms in English. Also, some recent loan words from French have retained their native spelling and pronunciation, such as *hors d'oeuvre* and *cul-de-sac*.

Although vocabulary expansion has been great during the Modern English period, there have also been extensive sound changes. The short vowels have remained relatively stable, but there was a striking change in the pronunciation of long vowels. This change, known as the "Great Vowel Shift," has been characterized as "the most revolutionary and far-reaching sound change during the history of the language" (Alexander, 1962, p. 114). The change was gradual, occurring during the first century of this period. Because spelling had become fixed before the shift, the vowel letter symbols no longer corresponded to the sounds. To illustrate the change, the word *name* rhymed with *comma* during the Middle English period, but during the Great Vowel Shift, the Modern English pronunciation of *name* shifted to rhyme with *game* (Hook, 1975).

The Modern English period brought changes in syntax, particularly the disappearance of double negatives and double comparatives and superlatives. Eliminations came about slowly; for instance, Shakespeare still wrote, "the most unkindest cut of all." Also, the practice of using *-er* or *-est* to form comparatives and superlatives in shorter words and *more* or *most* with longer words was not standardized until after Shakespeare's time.

Learning about Word Histories.   The best source of information about word histories is an unabridged dictionary, which provides basic etymological information about words: the language the word was borrowed from, the form of the word in that language or the representation of the word in our alphabet, and the original meaning of the word. Etymologies are enclosed in square brackets and may appear at the beginning or the end of an entry. They are written in an abbreviated form to save space, and use abbreviations for language names such as *Ar* for *Arabic* and *L* for *Latin*. We will look at three etymologies for words derived from very different sources. Each etymology is from *The Random House Dictionary of the English Language* (Flexner, 1987); we translate and elaborate each etymology using a process we call *extrapolation*.

king   [bef. 900; ME, OE *cyng*]

Extrapolation: The word *king* is an Old English word originally spelled *cyng*. It was used in English before the year 900. In the Middle English period, the spelling changed to its current form.

kimono   [1885–1890; < Japn: clothing, garb, equiv. to *ki* wear + *mono* thing]

Extrapolation: Our word *kimono* comes from Japanese, and it entered English between 1885 and 1890. *Kimono* means clothing or garb, and it is equivalent to the Japanese words *ki,* meaning wear and *mono,* meaning thing.

thermometer   [1615–1625; thermo < Gr *thermos,*
hot + meter < Gr *metron,* measure]

Extrapolation: The first recorded use of the word *thermometer* in English was between 1615 and 1625. Our word was created from two Greek words meaning *hot* and *measure.*

Figure 3–1 lists books about the history of English that are appropriate for elementary students. The books include fascinating stories about how words grew and changed because of historical events and linguistic accidents.

❖ WORDS AND THEIR MEANINGS

Students' vocabularies grow at a rate of about 3000 words a year (Nagy & Herman, 1985). Through literature and content area study, students experiment with words and concepts, and their knowledge of words and meanings grows. Young children assume that every word has only one meaning, and words that sound alike, like *son* and *sun,* are confusing. Through continuing experiences with language, students become more sophisticated about words and their literal and figurative meanings. During the elementary grades, students learn about words and word parts, words that mean the same and the opposite of other words, words that sound alike, words with multiple meanings, the figurative language of idioms, and how words have been borrowed from languages around the world. They also learn about how words are created and have fun playing with words (Tompkins, 1990).

Adelson, L. (1972). *Dandelions don't bite: The story of words.* New York: Pantheon.

Arnold, O. (1979). *What's in a name: Famous brand names.* New York: Messner.

Artman, J. (1980). *Slanguage: Activities and ideas on the history and nature of language.* Carthage, IL: Good Apple.

Artman, J. (1983). *Slanguage II: Activities on words, their parts and their meanings.* Carthage, IL: Good Apple.

Asimov, I. (1961). *Words from myths.* Boston: Houghton Mifflin.

Asimov, I. (1968). *Words from history.* Boston: Houghton Mifflin.

Collis, H. (1987). *101 American English idioms.* Lincolnwood, IL: Passport.

Davidson, J. (1972). *Is that mother in the bottle? Where language came from and where it is going.* New York: Franklin Watts.

Epstein, S., & Epstein, B. (1964). *What's behind the word?* New York: Scholastic.

Fletcher, C. (1973). *One hundred keys: Names across the land.* Nashville, TN: Abingdon Press.

Funk, C. E. (1948). *A hog on ice and other curious expressions.* New York: Harper and Row.

Greenfeld, H. (1978). *Sumer is icumen in: Our ever-changing language.* New York: Crown Books.

Hazen, B. S. (1979). *Last, first, middle and nick: All about names.* Englewood Cliffs, NJ: Prentice-Hall.

Kaye, C. B. (1985). *Word works: Why the alphabet is a kid's best friend.* Boston: Little, Brown.

Kraske, R. (1975). *The story of the dictionary.* New York: Harcourt Brace Jovanovich.

Lambert, E. (1955). *Our language: The story of the words we use.* New York: Lothrop.

Lambert, E., & Pei, M. (1959). *The book of place-names.* New York: Lothrop.

McCrum, R., Cran, I., & MacNeil, R. (1986). *The story of English.* New York: Viking Press.

FIGURE 3–1

Books about the History of English for Elementary Students

Meltzer, M. (1984). *A book about names.* New York: Crowell.

Pickles, C., & Meynell, L. (1971). *The beginning of words: How English grew.* New York: Putnam.

Pizer, V. (1976). *Ink., Ark., and all that: How American places got their names.* New York: Putnam.

Pizer, V. (1981). *Take my word for it.* New York: Dodd, Mead.

Sacon, G. R. (1964). *Secrets in animal names.* Englewood Cliffs, NJ: Prentice-Hall.

Sarnoff, J., & Ruffins, R. (1981). *Words: A book about the origins of everyday words and phrases.* New York: Scribner.

Sorel, N. (1970). *Word people.* New York: American Heritage.

Sparke, W. (1966). *Story of the English language.* New York: Abelard-Schuman.

Sperling, S. (1979). *Poplollies and bellibones: A celebration of lost words.* New York: Penguin.

Steckler, A. (1979). *101 words and how they began.* Garden City, NY: Doubleday.

Steckler, A. (1981). *101 more words and how they began.* Garden City, NY: Doubleday.

Suid, M. (1983). *For the love of words.* Carthage, IL: Good Apple.

Terban, M. (1983). *In a pickle and other funny idioms.* Boston: Houghton Mifflin.

Weiss, A. E. (1980). *What's that you said: How words change.* New York: Harcourt Brace Jovanovich.

Wolk, A. (1980). *Everyday words from names of people and places.* New York: Elsevier/Nelson.

Zaslow, D. (1983). *What's in a word? Word history activity sheets.* Carthage, IL: Good Apple.

FIGURE 3–1　*(continued)*

Root Words and Affixes.　A *root word* is a morpheme, the basic part of a word to which affixes are added. Many words are developed from a single root word; for example, the Latin word *portare* (to carry) is the source of at least nine Modern English words: *deport, export, import, port, portable, porter, report, support,* and *transportation.* Latin is one source of English root words, and Greek and Old English are two other sources.

Some root words are whole words and others are parts of words. Some root words have become free morphemes and can be used as separate words, whereas others cannot. For instance, the word *act* comes from the Latin word *actus,* meaning *doing.* English uses part of the word and treats it as a root word that can be used independently, or in combination with affixes, as in *actor, activate, react,* and *enact.* In the words *alias, alien, unalienable,* and *alienate,* the root word *ali* comes from the Latin word *alius,* meaning *other;* it is not used as an independent root word in English. A list of root words appears in Figure 3–2.

Students can compile lists of words developed from the root words in Figure 3–2, and they can draw root word clusters to illustrate the relationship of the root word to the words developed from it. Figure 3–3 shows a root word cluster for the Greek root *graph,* meaning *to write.* Recognizing basic elements from word to word helps students cut down on the amount of memorizing necessary to learn meanings and spellings.

ann/enn (year): anniversary, annual, biennial, centennial, perennial
ast (star): aster, asterisk, astrology, astronaut, astronomy
auto (self): autobiography, automatic, automobile
bio (life): biography, biology, autobiography, biodegradable
cent (hundred): cent, centennial, centigrade, centipede, century
circ (around): circle, circular, circus, circumspect
corp (body): corporal, corporation, corps
cycl (wheel): bicycle, cycle, cyclist, cyclone, tricycle
dict (speak): contradict, dictate, dictator, predict, verdict
geo (earth): geography, geology, geometry
graph (write): biography, graphic, paragraph, phonograph, stenographer
gram (letter): diagram, grammar, monogram, telegram
grat (pleasing, thankful): congratulate, grateful, gratitude
jus/jud/jur (law, right): injury, judge, justice
man (hand): manacle, manual, manufacture, manuscript
mand (order): command, demand, mandate, remand
mar (sea): aquamarine, marine, maritime, submarine
meter (measure): barometer, centimeter, diameter, speedometer,
   thermometer
min (small): miniature, minimize, minor, minute
mort (death): immortal, mortal, mortality, mortician, post-mortem
ped/pod (foot): pedal, pedestrian, podiatry, tripod
phon (sound): earphone, microphone, phonics, phonograph, saxophone,
   symphony
photo (light): photograph, photographer, photosensitive, photosynthesis
quer/ques/quis (seek): query, question, inquisitive
rupt (break): abrupt, bankrupt, interrupt, rupture
scope (see): horoscope, kaleidoscope, microscope, periscope, telescope
struct (build): construction, indestructible, instruct
tele (far): telecast, telegram, telegraph, telephone, telescope, telethon,
   television
terr (land): terrace, terrain, terrarium, territory
tract (pull, drag): attraction, subtract, tractor
vict/vinc (conquer): convince, convict, evict, victor, victory
vis (see): television, visa, vision, visual
viv/vit (live): survive vitamin, vivid
volv (roll): involve, revolutionary, revolver

FIGURE 3–2

Teacher's Notebook Page: Root Words

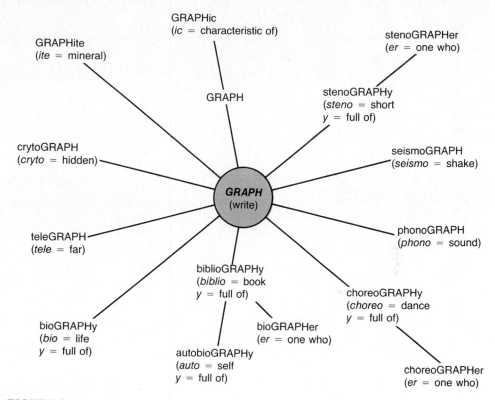

FIGURE 3—3

A Cluster for the Root Word **Graph**

There are two kinds of affixes. A *prefix* is essentially a bound morpheme added to the beginning of a root word; a *suffix* is a bound morpheme added to the end of a root word. Affixes, like root words, come from Old English, Latin, and Greek. They may change the part of speech of a word as well as its meaning, and some affixes have more than one form; for example, the prefixes *il-, im-,* and *ir-* are forms of the prefix *in-,* with the meanings of "in," "into," and "on," and are used with verbs and nouns. The prefixes *il-, im-, ir-,* and *ig-* are also forms of another prefix *in-,* with the meaning "not," and are used with adjectives. Both the *in-* prefixes are borrowed from Latin. The prefix *a-* and its alternate form *an-* are borrowed from Greek and also mean "not." Similarly, some suffixes have alternate forms; for example, the suffix *-ible* is an alternate form of *-able.*

Students can experiment with adding affixes to the root words in Figure 3—2 to create both real and invented words. Figure 3—4 shows a list of affixes. Examples of words that students have invented include *phonomatic* (makes sounds by itself), *mono-script* (written once), *jector* (hurler), *astrometer* (measures stars), and *solarscope* (sun-viewer) (Dale & O'Rourke, 1971, p. 12).

Synonyms and Antonyms. *Synonyms* are words that have the same or nearly the same meanings as other words. English has so many synonyms because so

Prefixes

a/an- (not): atheist, anaerobic
amphi- (both): amphibian
anti- (against): antiseptic
bi- (two, twice): bifocal, biannual
contra- (against): contradict
de- (away): detract
di- (two): dioxide
ex- (out): export
hemi- (half): hemisphere
il-/im-/in-/ir- (not): illegible,
    impolite, inexpensive, irrational
in- (in, into): include
inter- (between): intermission
kilo-/milli- (one thousand):
    kilometer, milligram
micro- (small): microfilm
mis- (wrong): mistake
mono- (one): monarch
multi- (many): multimillionaire
omni- (all): omnivorous
poly- (many): polygon
post- (after): postwar
pre-/pro- (before): precede,
    prologue
quad-/quart- (four): quadruple,
    quarter
re- (again): repay
retro- (back): retroactive
sol- (alone): solitary
sub- (under): submarine
super- (above): supermarket
trans- (across): transport
tri- (three): triangle
un- (not): unhappy

Suffixes

-able/-ible (worthy of, can be):
    lovable, audible
-ance/-ence (state or quality):
    annoyance, absence
-ant (one who): servant
-ard (one who is): coward
-ary/-ory (person, place):
    secretary, laboratory
-dom (state or quality): freedom
-ee (one who is): trustee
-er/-or/-ar (one who): teacher,
    actor, liar
-er/-or (action): robber
-ern (direction): northern
-et/-ette (small): booklet, dinette
-ful (full of): hopeful
-hood (state or quality): childhood
-ic (characterized by): angelic
-icle/-ucle (small): particle,
    molecule
-ify (to make): simplify
-ish (like): reddish
-ism (doctrine of): communism
-less (without): hopeless
-ling (young): duckling
-logy (the study of): zoology
-ly (in the manner of): slowly
-ment (state or quality): enjoyment
-ness (state or quality): kindness
-ship (state or, art or skill):
    friendship, seamanship
-sion/-tion (state or quality):
    tension, attraction
-ster (one who): gangster
-ure (state or quality): failure
-ward (direction): homeward
-y (full of): sleepy

FIGURE 3—4

Teacher's Notebook Page: Affixes

many words have been borrowed from other languages. Synonyms are useful because they provide options, allowing us to express ourselves with more exactness. Think of all the different synonyms for the word *cold: cool, chilly, frigid, icy, frosty, freezing,* and so on. Each word has a different shade of meaning: *cool* means "moderately cold"; *chilly* is "uncomfortably cold"; *frigid* is "intensely cold"; *icy* means "very cold"; *frosty* means "covered with frost"; and *freezing* is "so cold that water changes into ice." Our language would be limited if we could only say that we were cold.

The largest number of synonyms entered English during the Norman occupation of Britain. Compare these pairs of synonyms: *end–finish, clothing–garments, forgive–pardon, buy–purchase, deadly–mortal.* The first word in each pair comes from Old English; the second was borrowed from the Normans. The Old English words are more basic words, and the French loan words more sophisticated. Perhaps that is why both words in each pair have survived: they express slightly different meanings. Other pairs of synonyms come from different languages; for example: *comfortable* and *cozy—comfortable* is a Latin loan word, whereas *cozy* is probably of Scandinavian origin.

Antonyms are words that express the opposite meaning. Antonyms for *loud* include *soft, subdued, quiet, silent, inaudible, sedate, somber, dull,* and *colorless.* These words express shades of meaning just as synonyms do, and some opposites are more appropriate for one meaning of *loud* than for another. When *loud* means *gaudy,* for instance, appropriate opposites might be *somber, dull,* or *colorless.*

Dictionaries and thesauruses list synonyms and antonyms. A good thesaurus for students is *A First Thesaurus* (Wittels & Greisman, 1985), which includes more than 2000 entry words. Synonyms are printed in black ink for each entry word, and the antonyms follow in red ink.

Homonyms. *Homonyms,* words that have sound and spelling similarities, are divided into three categories: homophones, homographs, and homographic homophones. *Homophones* are words that sound alike but are spelled differently. Most homophones developed from entirely different root words, and it is only by accident that they have come to sound alike; for example, the homophones *right* and *write* entered English before 900 and were pronounced differently. *Right* was spelled *reht* or *riht* in Old English, and, during the Middle English period, the spelling was changed by French scribes to the current spelling. The verb *write* was spelled *writan* in Old English and *writen* in Middle English. *Write* is an irregular verb, suggesting its Old English heritage, and the silent *w* was pronounced hundreds of years ago. In contrast, a few words were derived from the same root words, such as *flea-flee, flower-flour, stationary-stationery,* and *metal-medal,* and the similar spelling has been retained to demonstrate the semantic relationships.

Homographs are words that are spelled the same but pronounced differently. Examples of homographs are *bow, close, lead, minute, record, read,* and *wind. Bow* is a homograph that has three unrelated meanings. The verb form meaning "to bend in respect" was spelled *bugan* in Old English; the noun form meaning "a gathering of ribbon" or "a weapon for propelling an arrow" is of Old English origin and was spelled *boga.* The other noun form of *bow* meaning "forward end of a ship" did not enter English until the 1600s from German.

Homographic homophones are words that are spelled and pronounced alike, such as *bark, bat, bill, box, fair, fly, hide, jet, mine, pen, ring, row, spell, toast,* and *yard.* Some are related words; others are linguistic accidents. The different meanings of *toast,* for example, came from the same Latin source word, *torrere* (to parch, bake). The derivation of the noun *toast* as heated and browned slices of bread is obvious; however, the relationship between the source word and *toast* as a verb, "drinking to someone's honor or health," is not immediately apparent. The connection is that toasted, spiced bread flavored the drinks used in making toasts. In contrast, *bat* is a linguistic accident: *bat* as a *cudgel* comes from the Old English word *batt;* the verb *to bat* is derived from the Old French word *batre;* and the nocturnal *bat* derives its name from an unknown Viking word and was spelled *bakke* in Middle English. Not only do the three forms of *bat* have unrelated etymologies, but they were borrowed from three different languages.

There are many books of homonyms for children, including Gwynne's *The King Who Rained* (1970), *A Chocolate Moose for Dinner* (1976), *The Sixteen Hand Horse* (1980), and *A Little Pigeon Toad* (1988); Maestro's *What's a Frank Frank?* (1984); *Homographic Homophones* (Hanson, 1973); and *Eight Ate: A Feast of Homonym Riddles* (Terban, 1982). Check Appendix C for additional trade books that can be used in teaching students about homonyms and other language concepts. Elementary students enjoy reading these books and making their own word books. Figure 3–5 shows a page from a second grader's homonym book.

Multiple Meanings.   Many words have more than one meaning. The word *bank,* for example, may refer to a piled-up mass of snow or clouds, the slope of land beside a lake or river, the slope of a road on a turn, the lateral tilting of an airplane in a turn, to cover a fire with ashes for slow burning, a business establishment that receives and lends money, a container in which money is saved, a supply for use in emergencies (e.g., *blood bank*), a place for storage (e.g., *computer's memory bank*), to count on, similar things arranged in a row (e.g., *a bank of elevators*), or to arrange things in a row. You may be surprised that there are at least 12 meanings for the common word *bank.* Why does this happen? The meanings of *bank* in this example come from three different sources. The first five meanings come from an old Norse (or Viking) word, and you will note that they are related—they all deal with something slanted or making a slanted motion. The next five meanings come from the Italian word *banca,* which originally meant "money changer's table." These meanings deal with financial banking except the tenth meaning, "to count on," which requires a bit more thought. We use the saying "to bank on" figuratively to mean "to depend on," but it began more literally from the actual counting of money on a table. The last two meanings come from the Old French word *banc,* meaning "a bench." Words acquired multiple meanings as society became more complex and finer shades of meaning were necessary; for example, the meanings of bank as "an emergency supply" and "a storage place" are fairly new. As with many words with multiple meanings, it is a linguistic accident that three original words from three languages, with related meanings, came to be spelled the same way.

Words assume additional meanings with an affix or with compounding (combining with another word). Consider the word *fire,* and the variety of words and phrases that

FIGURE 3–5

A Page from a Second Grader's Homonym Book

incorporate *fire: fire hydrant, firebomb, fireproof, fireplace, firearm, fire drill, under fire, set the world on fire, fire away,* and *open fire.* Students can compile a list of words or make a booklet illustrating the words; Figure 3–6 lists more than 100 *down* words that a sixth grade class compiled.

Idioms.   *Idioms* are groups of words, such as "spilled the beans," that have a special meaning. Idioms can be confusing to students because they must be interpreted figuratively rather than literally. The expression "spilling the beans" is thousands of years old, dating back to ancient Greece. Cox (1980) explains that at that time, many Greek men belonged to secret clubs, and when someone wanted to join the club, the members took a vote to decide whether or not to admit him. They wanted the vote to remain secret, so they voted by each placing a white or brown bean in a special jar. A white bean indicated a "yes" vote, and a brown bean was a "no" vote. The club leader would then count the beans, and if all the beans were white, the person was admitted to the club. The vote was kept secret to avoid hurting the person's feelings in case the members voted not to admit him to the club. Sometimes during the voting one member would accidentally (or not so accidentally) knock the jar over, spilling the beans, and the vote would no longer be a secret. The Greeks turned this real happening into a saying that we still use today. Another idiom with a different history but a similar meaning is "let the cat out of the bag." There are hundreds of idioms in English, and we use them every day to create word pictures that make language more colorful. Some examples are "out in left field," "a skeleton in the closet," "stick your neck out," "a chip off the old

downtown	climb down	reach down	downward
touchdown	down payment	write down	hunt down
get down	sit down	settle down	knock down
chow down	throw down	down it	breakdown
shake down	cut down	goose down	sundown
squat down	downhill	hop down	fall down
showdown	low down	hands down	tear down
lie down	slow down	downfall	turn down
quiet down	down right	close down	push down
shut down	beam down	run down	downstairs
shot down	downy	pin down	look down
cool down	downer	come down	inside down
crackdown	downslope	slam down	zip down
countdown	kickdown	slap down	pour down
pass down	stare down	hoe down	down pour
pass me down	boogy down	lock down	tape down
burn down	put down	water down	downgrade
downbeat	wrestle down	downturn	downstream
down to earth	flop down	stuff down	mow down
shimmey down	hung down	downcast	downhearted
downtrodden	chase down	hurl down	beat down

FIGURE 3—6

Sixth Graders' Class Collaboration List of 100 *Down* Words

block," and "cry over spilled milk." Some of these idioms are new, and others are hundreds or thousands of years old; some are American in origin, and others come from around the world.

Four excellent books of idioms for students are *Put Your Foot in Your Mouth and Other Silly Sayings* (Cox, 1980), *From the Horse's Mouth* (Nevin & Nevin, 1977), *Chin Music: Tall Talk and Other Talk* (Schwartz, 1979), and *In a Pickle and Other Funny Idioms* (Terban, 1983). Because idioms are figurative sayings, many children have difficulty learning them. It is crucial that children move beyond the literal meanings, thus learning flexibility in using language. One way for students to learn flexibility is to create idiom posters, as illustrated in Figure 3—7.

Borrowed Words.   The most common way of expanding vocabulary is to borrow words from other languages. This practice, which dates from Old English times, continues to the present day. Perhaps as many as 75 percent of our words have been borrowed from other languages and incorporated into English. Word borrowing has occurred during every period of language development, beginning when the Angles and Saxons borrowed over 400 words from the Romans. During the eighth and ninth centuries, the Vikings contributed approximately 900 words. The Norman conquerors introduced thousands of French words into English, reflecting every aspect of life: *adventure, fork, juggler,* and *quilt.* Later, during the Renaissance, when scholars trans-

FIGURE 3–7

A Fourth Grader's Idiom Poster

lated Greek and Latin classics into English, they recognized its limitations. They borrowed many words from Latin and Greek to enrich the language—for example, *chaos, encyclopedia, pneumonia,* and *skeleton.* More recently, words from at least 50 languages have been added to English through exploration, colonization, and trade. These are some of the loan words from other languages:

African (many languages):   banjo, cola, gumbo, safari, zombie

Arabic: alcohol, apricot, assassin, magazine

Australian/New Zealand (aboriginal):   kangaroo, kiwi

Celtic: walnut

Chinese: chop suey, kowtow, tea, wok

Czech: pistol, robot

Dutch: caboose, easel, pickle, waffle

Eskimo: igloo, parka

Finnish: sauna

French: ballet, beige, chauffeur

German: kindergarten, poodle, pretzel, waltz

Greek: atom, cyclone, hydrogen

Hawaiian: aloha, hula, lei, luau

Hebrew: cherub, kosher, rabbi

Hindi: dungaree, juggernaut, jungle, shampoo

Hungarian: goulash, paprika

Icelandic: geyser

Irish: bog, leprechaun, shamrock, slogan

Italian: broccoli, carnival, macaroni, opera, pizza

Japanese: honcho, judo, kimono, origami

Persian: bazaar, divan, khaki, shawl

Polish: mazurka, polka

Portuguese: cobra, coconut, molasses

Russian: czar, sputnik, steppe, troika, vodka

Scandinavian (Swedish, Norwegian, Danish):   egg, fiord, husband, ski, sky

Scottish: clan, golf, slogan

Spanish: alligator, guitar, mosquito, potato

Turkish: caviar, horde, khan, kiosk, yogurt

Yiddish: bagel, chutzpah, pastrami

(Tompkins & Yaden, 1986, p. 31)

Native Americans have also contributed a number of words to English. The early American colonists encountered many unfamiliar animals, plants, foods, and aspects of Indian life in America. They borrowed the Native American terms for these objects or events and tried to spell them phonetically. Native American loan words include *chipmunk, hickory, moccasin, moose, muskrat, opossum, papoose, pow-wow, raccoon, skunk, succotash, toboggan, tomahawk,* and *tepee.*

Other Sources of New Words.   New words continually appear in English, many of which are created to describe new inventions and scientific projects. Some of the newest words come from computer science and the space program. They are created in a variety of ways, including compounding, coining, and clipping.

Compounding means combining two existing words to create a new word. *Friendship* and *childhood* are two words that the Anglo-Saxons compounded more than a thousand years ago. Recent compoundings include *latchkey kids* and *software.* Compound words usually progress through three stages: they begin as separate words (e.g., *ice cream*), then are hyphenated (e.g., *baby-sit*), and finally are written as one word (e.g., *splashdown*). There are many exceptions to this rule, such as the compound words *post office* and *high school,* which have remained separate words. Other compound words use Greek and Latin elements, such as the scientific terms *stethoscope* and *television*.

Creative people have always coined new words. Lewis Carroll, author of *Alice in Wonderland* and *Through the Looking Glass,* is perhaps the best-known inventor of words. He called his new words *portmanteau words* (borrowing from the British word for a suitcase that opens into two halves) because they were created by blending two words into one. His most famous example, *chortle,* a blend of *snort* and *chuckle,* is from the poem "Jabberwocky," and Zalben's beautifully illustrated picture book version of *Jabberwocky* (1977) is popular with elementary students. Other examples of blended words include *brunch* (*breakfast* and *lunch*), *electrocute* (*electric* and *execute*), *guesstimate* (*guess* and *estimate*), and *smog* (*smoke* and *fog*).

Two other types of coined words are *trademarks* and *acronyms*. Examples of well-known trademarks and brand names include *Kleenex, Coca-Cola, Xerox,* and *nylon. Nylon,* for instance, was invented by scientists working in New York and London, and they named their product by combining *ny,* the abbreviation for *New York,* with *lon,* the first three letters of *London.* Acronyms, words formed by combining the initial letters of several words, include *radar, laser,* and *scuba. Scuba,* for example, was formed by combining the initial letters of *self-contained underwater breathing apparatus*.

Clipping is a process of shortening existing words; *bomb* is the shortened form of *bombard,* and *zoo* comes from *zoological park.* Most clipped words are only one syllable and are used in informal conversation. Although it is unlikely that your students will create new words that will eventually appear in the dictionary, students do create words to add pizzazz to their writing, and some terms created to fill a particular need become part of the everyday jargon in a classroom. For example, a group of third graders created the word *crocket* (*crocodile* + *rocket*) to describe the crocodile who became a rocket at the end of Dahl's *The Enormous Crocodile* (1978).

Authors also create new words in their stories, and students should be alert to the possibility of finding a created word when they read or listen to stories. Adams used *woggle* in *A Woggle of Witches* (1971), the Howes (1979) created *Bunnicula* to name their spooky young rabbit (*bunny* + *dracula*), and Horwitz describes the night as *bimulous* in *When the Sky Is Like Lace* (1975).

Sniglets are words that aren't in the dictionary, but, according to Rich Hall (1985), their creator, should be. One of his sniglets is *beavo,* a pencil covered with teeth marks. Several books of sniglets have been published, including one especially for children, *Sniglets for Kids* (Hall, 1985). Elementary students enjoy reading these books and creating their own words. To create a sniglet, they use affixes, compounding, coining, and clipping. A fifth grader's sniglet, *tappee,* is shown in Figure 3–8; the student used the Latin suffix *-ee,* meaning "one who."

❖ HOW STUDENTS LEARN WORDS

Students learn many, many words incidentally, through reading or content area study, and teachers supplement incidental learning through direct instruction. All the words students learn are not equally difficult or easy; the degree of difficulty depends on the

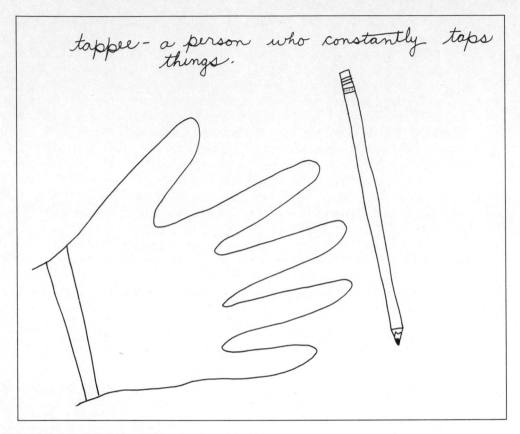

FIGURE 3–8

A Fifth Grader's Sniglet

relationship between the word and the student. Graves (1985) identifies four possible relationships:

1. Sight words—words that are in students' talking and listening vocabularies but that they don't know how to read
2. New words—words that are not in students' vocabularies, but for which they have concepts
3. New concepts—words that are not in students' vocabularies and for which they also don't have a concept
4. New meanings—words that are already in students' vocabularies with one or more meanings but for which additional meanings need to be learned

Probably the most difficult category of words for students to learn is the new concept words, because they must first learn the concepts and then attach word labels. Students may benefit from direct instruction on these words.

In inferring or learning the meanings of words independently when they read or listen to information presented orally, students use four strategies:

Phonics. Students use the knowledge of phoneme-grapheme relationships to pronounce an unknown word when reading, and often recognize the word's meaning when they hear it pronounced.

Structural analysis. Students analyze the word and use their knowledge of root words and affixes to figure out the meaning.

Context clues. Students use the surrounding information in the sentence to guess the meaning of the unknown word. Context clues take a variety of forms. Sometimes the word is defined in the sentence, and at other times synonyms or antonyms are used, or examples give students an idea of the meaning of the word. One way for students to understand how much the surrounding information in sentences supplies the meaning of unknown words is to use a nonsense word in a paragraph (Klein, 1988). For example, what word does *matto* stand for in this paragraph?

Mattos are made up of many bones. Your matto is made up of 206 bones. These bones give you your shape. Nothing can change your shape because you have a matto inside you. Some of the bones in your matto protect important parts inside you. Rib bones cover your heart and lungs and the skull protects your brain from injury.

The surrounding information in the sentences should help you determine that the nonsense word stands for *skeleton.*

Reference books. Students locate the unknown word in a dictionary or thesaurus and read the definition or synonyms and antonyms to determine the meaning.

❖ TEACHING STUDENTS ABOUT WORDS

The goal of vocabulary instruction is for students to learn how to learn new words, but traditional approaches, such as assigning students to look up the definitions of a list of words in a dictionary, often fail to produce in-depth understanding (Nagy, 1988). Carr and Wixon (1986) list four guidelines for effective instruction:

- Instruction should help students relate new words to their background knowledge.
- Instruction should help students develop ownership-level word knowledge.
- Instruction should provide for students' active involvement in learning new words.
- Instruction should develop students' strategies for learning new words independently.

Teaching Strategy

This teaching strategy can be used to teach a specific word or a group of related words. It is based on the strategy we discussed in Chapter 1 and embodies Carr and Wixon's characteristics of effective vocabulary instruction.

1.   Introduce the word (or group of words) and explain the meaning, tying the word to students' background knowledge.

2.   Use the word in context and consider possible strategies (e.g., phonics, structural analysis, context clues) to use in understanding the word's meaning. Also, identify the root word, talk about the etymology of the word, and consider related words or easily confused words, if appropriate.

3.   Discuss the word, bringing together all the information—semantic, structural, and contextual—presented earlier. If the word is one of a group of related words, use a semantic feature analysis matrix, as illustrated in Figure 3–9, to compare the word to other words. In semantic feature analysis, students compare a group of related words, such as different words for *house* grouped according to distinguishing characteristics.

4.   Review the words and strategies used in identifying the word. Students can add the word to vocabulary notebooks or make a word cluster (also called a *semantic map*). Figure 3–10 shows two types of word clusters. The first is a cluster for *maple sugar* that third graders made after reading *Sugaring Time* by Kathryn Lasky (1983). The second cluster on *reminiscent* is more structured. A small group of sev-

This student uses content area vocabulary in a meaningful way as he gives an oral report on the vulture's life cycle.

	for people	for animals	for storage	big/fancy	small	crude/rough	permanent	portable
house	+	−	−	O	O	O	+	−
shack	+	−	−	−	+	+	?	−
shed	−	−	+	−	+	+	?	−
barn	−	+	O	−	−	O	+	−
tent	+	−	−	−	O	O	−	+
mansion	+	−	−	+	−	−	+	−

FIGURE 3−9

A Semantic Feature Analysis on Houses
Nagy, 1988, p. 15

enth graders developed this cluster, considering the definition of the word; its history or etymology; part of speech; other related forms; word parts; and antonyms, synonyms, or homonyms. Clusters are particularly useful in helping students learn the meanings of new words (Heimlich & Pittelman, 1986).

5. Have students locate examples of the word in their reading or writing. Aim for three encounters that school day. Students need many experiences with a new word to make it a part of their vocabulary.

6. Provide opportunities for students to use the word in meaningful ways. They need to read the word; write the word in informal and formal writings; use the word in discussions, debates, and oral reports; and use the word in class, small group, and individual projects.

Tying Word Study to Reading and Writing

Teachers can directly teach students only a small number of the words they need to learn. Through the teaching strategy, students must learn how to learn other words independently. Students meet new words when they read, and they need to learn to use phonics, structural analysis, context clues, and reference books independently to learn other words. Reading, then, is probably the most important way a teacher can promote vocabulary growth (Nagy, 1988). Writing is also important, because after students meet words in reading, they interact with the words a second time by writing them, in learning logs or on word walls. Repeated exposure to words is crucial because students need to see and use the word many times before it becomes a part of their ownership dictionaries—words they understand and use competently.

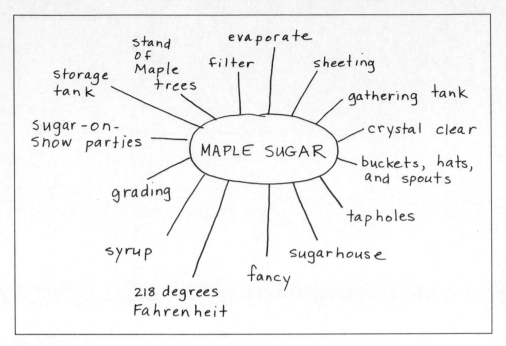

FIGURE 3–10

Word Clusters

Tying Word Study to Literature and Content Areas

When planning a literature or content area unit, teachers need to give attention to the theme-related words they want students to learn. For example, a unit on bears for kindergartners might include these words: *shaggy, fur, dangerous, tame, meat-eating, polar bear, grizzly bear, brown bear, claws, hind legs, hibernate, den,* and *cubs.* A unit on Martin Luther King for upper-grade students might include these words: *segregation, protest, sit-in, Nobel Peace Prize, Jim Crow laws, civil rights, boycott, Negro, prejudice, nonviolence, activist, assassinated,* and *martyr.* Whenever possible, students need to be involved in choosing some of the words for study, because the more they feel the need for individual words, the more likely they are to learn them. Words that are critical to understanding a concept or reading a selection independently should be taught; however, not all words can be directly taught because of time constraints and because students will infer the meanings of some words on their own. Students are introduced to the words through the various activities they are involved in: they meet the words in books they read, in films they view, and during oral presentations by the teacher. Teachers should use the instructional strategy for words they teach directly. As students interact with the words again and again, the words jockey for position, moving toward the ownership dictionary. According to Vygotsky's notion of "a zone of proximal development," teachers need to be alert to individual students and what words they are learning so they can provide instruction when students are most interested in learning more about the word.

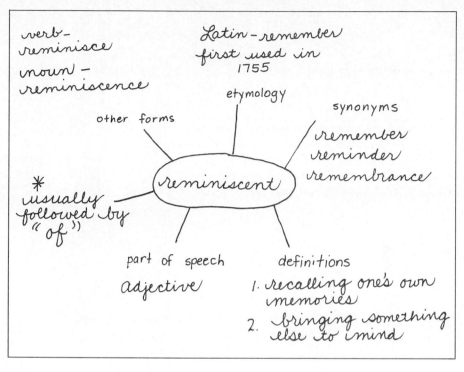

FIGURE 3–10 *(continued)*

Teachers can assess students' use of theme-related words in their learning logs.

❖ "PRO" FILE

WORD FAMILIES

"I don't teach vocabulary—at least not in the traditional way. Instead, my students are immersed in words through the books we read and the units we are studying. I know it sounds corny, but my students learn words because they are living them."

Carol Ochs, Fourth Grade Teacher,
Pioneer Intermediate School

PROCEDURE

Before I start a new literature unit, I read the books and highlight words that my students may need help with or that I want to use in vocabulary lessons. This gets me ready to teach. Then I hang a long sheet of butcher paper in the classroom—often from the ceiling to the floor. I call it a "word wall." As we read, I point out some words and my students spot others, and they write these words on the word wall. I ask students to write the words themselves because I want them to be involved in the activity. I also have them keep a reading log, a notebook with about 20 pages in it. They keep a list of words on one page in the log. Many of the words come from our word wall, but students also choose other words as they read.

Right now we're into a unit on children's author Chris Van Allsburg. In *The Garden of Abdul*

The most beneficial times for vocabulary instruction are during content area study, when students are reading literature, and when they are revising their writing, because these are times when students see a reason for learning the words. Exposure to words simply because they appear in the next unit in the teacher's manual or in a vocabulary workbook is rarely useful unless students feel a terrific need to expand their vocabulary. (Chapter 15 offers more information about tying vocabulary to literature and content area study.)

Gasazi (1979), I highlighted these words: *sinking (teeth into. . .), bolted, shadowed, bruised, detest, blurted, awesome,* and *incredible.* I explain most of the words informally as we come to them, and we add them to our word wall. The one word that I want to teach more formally is *incredible.* I look the word up in an unabridged dictionary, check its meaning and etymology, and make a list of related words. Then I decide how to present the lesson. For *incredible,* I start with the words *credit* and *credit card* because they are familiar. Then I make a cluster with the root word *cred-* in the middle (as shown). I draw out *credit, credit card,* and then add *incredible* from the story, and a few other related words. My students are amazed because they don't see a relationship among the words until we start talking about them. Then a light comes on! For the students who need to be challenged, I add the words *credulity* and *credulous* and talk about their meanings.

ASSESSMENT

I want my students to "own" these words. I use the words when I talk to students and notice when they use the words. I do give tests to check their knowledge of some words, but, more importantly, I check to see if students apply the words in their writing. Sometimes I ask students to highlight vocabulary words in their reading log entries or in their stories and reports. That's when I know my students "own" the words.

REFLECTIONS

I don't have students look up vocabulary words in the dictionary and copy the definitions into their reading logs. I tried it and it doesn't work. I also tried having students use the words in sentences, and that doesn't work either. Instead, we use the words every day—several times a day—but we use them as we talk and write about the story and beyond the story.

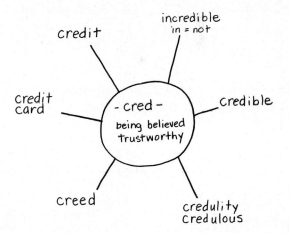

Assessing Students' Use of Words

Teachers can assess students' use of theme-related words in a variety of ways. They can listen while students talk during the unit, examine students' writing and other theme-related projects, and they can ask students to talk or write about the theme and what they have learned. Here are some specific strategies to determine whether students have learned and are applying new words:

- Check reading logs for theme-related words
- Use words in a reading conference and note the student's response
- Check learning logs and simulated journals for theme-related words
- Listen for vocabulary when students give an oral report
- Ask students to make a cluster or to freewrite about the theme or about specific words
- Ask students to brainstorm a list of words and phrases about the theme
- Check students' reports, biographies, stories or other formal writings for theme-related words
- Ask students to use theme-related words in writing a poem
- Ask students to write a letter to you, telling what they have learned in a unit

Teachers can also give a test on the vocabulary words, but this is probably the least effective strategy, because knowing the answer on a test does not indicate whether students have ownership of a word and are applying it in meaningful and genuine ways.

❖ REVIEW

Words are the building blocks of language because they carry meaning and are combined into sentences. The first half of this chapter focuses on words that elementary students learn. English is a historic language, and many of the confusing aspects of English can be explained within a historical context. Few words have only one meaning, and students in the elementary grades learn about multiple meanings as well as about root words and affixes; homonyms, synonyms, and antonyms; and figurative meanings of words, such as idioms.

The second half of the chapter focuses on how students learn new words and how teachers can facilitate that learning. Students learn approximately 3000 new words each year during the elementary grades, and they learn most of these words incidentally through reading and content area study. In learning a word, students must be able to recognize it as a sight word, understand the concept, and know the specific meaning (if the word has more than one). A teaching strategy based on the instructional model presented in Chapter 1 embodies the four guidelines for effective vocabulary instruction. This teaching strategy involves connecting the new word to students' background of experience, teaching students strategies for learning new words, and applying the new word through reading and writing.

❖ EXTENSIONS

1. Learn more about the history of English by reading one or more of the books listed in Figure 3–1.

2. Identify a literature or content area unit for a particular grade level, and choose the vocabulary you would teach in that unit. Which words do you think will be sight words, new words, new concepts, or new meanings for students?

3. Observe in an elementary classroom and note how vocabulary is taught both formally and informally. Or, interview an elementary teacher and ask how he or she teaches vocabulary. Compare the teacher's answers with the information in this chapter.

4. Plan and teach a unit on homonyms, synonyms, or antonyms using the teaching strategy in this chapter.

5. Think back to the discussion of language-rich classrooms in Chapter 2, and identify ten ways to facilitate students' incidental learning of vocabulary through the classroom environment.

❖ REFERENCES

Adams, A. (1971). *A woggle of witches*. New York: Scribner.

Alexander, H. (1962). *The story of our language*. Garden City, NY: Doubleday.

Baugh, A. C., & Cable, T. (1978). *The history of the English language* (3rd ed.). Englewood Cliffs, NJ: Prentice-Hall.

Carr, E., & Wixon, K. K. (1986). Guidelines for evaluating vocabulary instruction. *Journal of Reading, 29*, 588–595.

Cox, J. A. (1980). *Put your foot in your mouth and other silly sayings*. New York: Random House.

Dahl, R. (1978). *The enormous crocodile*. New York: Knopf.

Dale, E., & O'Rourke, J. (1971). *Techniques of teaching vocabulary*. Palo Alto, CA: Field Educational Publications.

Flexner, S. B. (1987). *The Random House dictionary of the English language* (2nd ed.). New York: Random House.

Graves, M. (1985). *A word is a word. . .or is it?* Portsmouth, NH: Heinemann.

Gwynne, F. (1970). *The king who rained*. New York: Windmill Books.

Gwynne, F. (1976). *A chocolate moose for dinner*. New York: Windmill Books.

Gwynne, F. (1980). *The sixteen hand horse*. New York: Prentice-Hall.

Gwynne, F. (1988). *A little pigeon toad*. New York: Simon & Schuster.

Hall, R. (1985). *Sniglets for kids*. Yellow Springs, OH: Antioch.

Hanson, J. (1973). *Homographic homophones*. Minneapolis, MN: Lerner.

Heimlich, J. E., & Pittelman, S. D. (1986). *Semantic mapping: Classroom applications*. Newark, DE: International Reading Association.

Hook, J. N. (1975). *History of the English language*. New York: Ronald Press.

Horwitz, E. L. (1975). *When the sky is like lace*. Philadelphia: Lippincott.

Howe, D., & Howe, J. (1979). *Bunnicula*. New York: Atheneum.

Klein, M. L. (1988). *Teaching reading comprehension and vocabulary: A guide for teachers*. Englewood Cliffs, NJ: Prentice-Hall.

Lasky, K. (1983). *Sugaring time*. New York: Macmillan.

Maestro, G. (1984). *What's a frank Frank? Tasty homograph riddles*. New York: Clarion Books.

Nagy, W. E. (1988). *Teaching vocabulary to improve reading comprehension*. Urbana, IL: ERIC Clearinghouse on Reading and Communication Skills and the National Council of Teachers of English and the International Reading Association.

Nagy, W. E., & Herman, P. (1985). Incidental vs. instructional approaches to increasing reading vocabulary. *Educational Perspectives, 23*, 16–21.

Nevin, A., & Nevin, D. (1977). *From the horse's mouth*. Englewood Cliffs, NJ: Prentice-Hall.

Schwartz, A. (1979). *Chin music: Tall talk and other talk*. Philadelphia: Lippincott.

Terban, M. (1982). *Eight ate: A feast of homonym riddles*. New York: Clarion Books.

Terban, M. (1983). *In a pickle and other funny idioms*. New York: Clarion Books.

Tompkins, G. E. (1990). *Teaching writing: Balancing process and product*. Columbus, OH: Merrill.

Tompkins, G. E., & Yaden, D. B., Jr. (1986). Answering students' questions about words. Urbana, IL: ERIC Clearinghouse on Reading and Communication Skills and the National Council of Teachers of English.

Van Allsburg, C. (1979). *The garden of Abdul Gasazi*. Boston: Houghton Mifflin.

Wittels, H., & Greisman, J. (1985). *A first thesaurus*. Racine, WI: Western.

Zalben, J. B. (1977). *Lewis Carroll's Jabberwocky*. New York: Harper and Row.

4 LISTENING TO LEARN

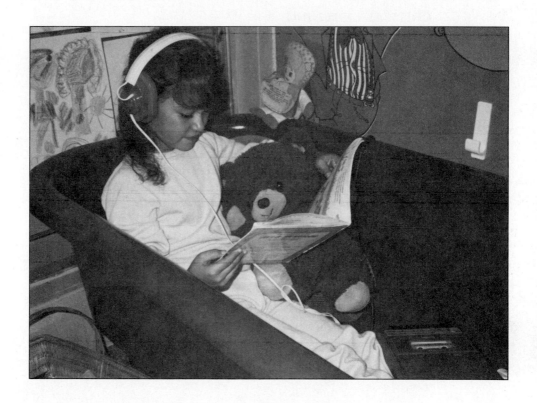

WHAT IS LISTENING?
The Listening Process
Purposes for Listening
The Need for Systematic Instruction

COMPREHENSIVE LISTENING
Strategies for Listening
Teaching Comprehensive Listening
Assessing Students' Comprehensive Listening

CRITICAL LISTENING
Persuasion and Propaganda
Teaching Critical Listening
Assessing Students' Critical Listening

APPRECIATIVE LISTENING
Reading Aloud to Students
Teaching Appreciative Listening

◆ **EVEN THOUGH LISTENING IS THE MOST-USED LANGUAGE ART, IT** is often neglected in elementary classrooms. Teachers often assume that students already know how to listen. Although it is true that students are experienced listeners, they still need to learn to become more effective listeners. In this chapter, we will discuss the listening process and three types of listening: comprehensive listening, critical listening, and appreciative listening.

◆ **AS YOU ARE READING, THINK ABOUT THESE QUESTIONS:**

What is the listening process?

Why is listening instruction needed in the elementary grades?

What are the different types of listening?

How can we teach each type of listening?

How can we assess students' listening?

L istening is the first language mode that children acquire, and it provides the basis for the other language arts (Lundsteen, 1979). Infants use listening to begin the process of learning to comprehend and produce language. From the beginning of their lives, they listen to sounds in their immediate environment, attend to speech sounds, and construct their knowledge of oral language. Listening is also important in learning to read. Children are introduced to reading by having stories read to them. When children are read to, they begin to see the connection between what they hear and what they see on the printed page. Reading and listening comprehension skills—main ideas, details, sequence, and so on—are similar in many ways (Sticht & James, 1984).

Listening also influences writing. Hansen explains, "A writing/reading program begins with listening, and listening holds the program together" (1987, p. 69). Writing begins as talk written down, and the stories students read become models for their writing. Listening is essential for students sharing their writing in conferences and receiving feedback on how to improve it. Inner listening, or "dialoguing" with oneself, also occurs as students write and revise their writing. Listening is "the most used and perhaps the most important of the language (and learning) arts" (Devine, 1982, p. 1).

Researchers have found that more of children's and adults' time is spent in listening than in the total time spent reading, writing, and talking. Figure 4−1 illustrates the amount of time we communicate in each language mode. Both children and adults spend approximately 50 percent of their communication time listening. Language researcher Walter Loban compares the four language modes this way: "We listen a book a day, we speak a book a week, we read a book a month, and we write a book a year" (cited in Erickson, 1985). Despite the importance of listening in our lives, listening has been called the "neglected" or "orphan" language art for 35 years or more (Anderson,

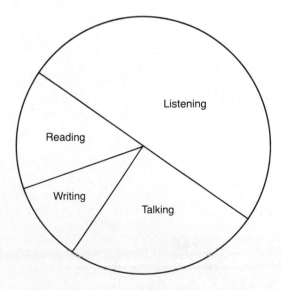

FIGURE 4−1

Percentage of Communication Time in Each Language Mode
Data from Rankin, 1926; Wilt, 1950; Werner, 1975.

1949). Little time has been devoted to listening instruction in most classrooms; listening is not stressed in language arts textbooks; and teachers often complain that they do not know how to teach listening (Devine, 1978; Landry, 1969; Wolvin & Coakley, 1985).

❖ WHAT IS LISTENING?

Listening is elusive because it occurs internally. Lundsteen (1979) describes listening as the "most mysterious" language process. In fact, teachers often do not know whether listening has occurred until they ask students to apply what they have listened to by answering questions, completing assignments, or taking tests. Even then, there is no guarantee that the students' responses indicate that they have listened, because they may have known the material before listening or learned it from someone else at about the same time.

The Listening Process

Listening is a highly complex, interactive process "by which spoken language is converted to meaning in the mind" (Lundsteen, 1979, p. 1). As this definition suggests, listening is more than just hearing, even though children and adults often use the two terms, *hearing* and *listening,* synonymously. Rather, hearing is an integral component, but only one component, of the listening process; it is thinking or converting to meaning what one hears that is the crucial part of the listening process.

Wolvin and Coakley (1985) describe three steps in the listening process: receiving, attending, and assigning meaning. In the first step, the listener receives the aural stimuli or the aural and visual stimuli presented by the speaker. Next, the listener focuses on selected stimuli while ignoring other distracting stimuli. Because so many stimuli surround students in the classroom, they must attend to the speaker's message, focusing on the most important information in that message. In the third step, the listener assigns meaning to, or understands, the speaker's message. Listeners assign meaning using assimilation and accommodation to fit the message into their existing cognitive structures or to create new structures if necessary. Responding or reacting to the message is not considered part of the listening process; the response occurs afterward, and it sets another communication process into action in which the listener becomes the message sender.

The second step of Wolvin and Coakley's listening process model may be called the "paying attention" component. Elementary teachers spend a great deal of instructional time reminding students to pay attention; unfortunately, however, children often do not understand the admonition. When asked to explain what "paying attention" means, some children equate it with physical behaviors such as not kicking their feet or cleaning off their desks. Learning to attend to the speaker's message is especially important because researchers have learned that students can listen to 250 words per minute, two to three times the normal rate of talking (Foulke, 1968). This differential allows one to time to tune in and out as well as to become distracted during listening.

Furthermore, the intensity of students' need to attend to the speaker's message varies with the purpose for listening. Some types of listening require more attentiveness than others. Effective listeners, for example, listen differently to directions on how to reach a friend's home than to a poem or story being read aloud.

Purposes for Listening

Why do we listen? Students often answer that question by explaining that they listen to learn or to avoid punishment (Tompkins, Friend, & Smith, 1984). It is unfortunate that some students have such a vague and limited view of the purposes for listening. Communication experts (Wolvin & Coakley, 1979, 1985) delineate five more specific purposes: discriminative listening, comprehensive listening, critical listening, appreciative listening, and therapeutic listening.

Discriminative Listening. People listen to distinguish sounds and to develop a sensitivity to nonverbal communication. Teaching discriminative listening involves one sort of activity in the primary grades and a different activity for older students. Having kindergarten and first grade students listen to tape-recorded animal sounds and common household noises is one discriminative listening activity. Most children are able to discriminate among sounds by the time they reach age five or six. In contrast, developing a sensitivity to the messages that people communicate nonverbally is a lifelong learning task.

Comprehensive Listening. People listen to understand a message, and this is the type of listening required in many instructional activities. Students need to determine the speaker's purpose and then organize the spoken information so as to remember it. Elementary students usually receive little instruction in comprehensive listening; rather, teachers assume that students simply know how to listen. Note-taking is typically the one comprehensive listening strategy taught in the elementary grades, although there are other strategies elementary students can learn and use.

Critical Listening. People listen first to comprehend and then to evaluate a message. Critical listening is an extension of comprehensive listening. As in comprehensive listening, listeners seek to understand a message, but then they must filter the message to detect propaganda devices and persuasive language. People listen critically when they listen to debates, commercials, political speeches, and other arguments.

Appreciative Listening. People listen to a speaker or reader for enjoyment. Listening to someone read literature or stories aloud or recite poems is a pleasurable activity. An important part of teaching listening in the elementary grades is to read aloud to students. Teachers can encourage and extend children's enjoyment of listening. Listening to classmates talk and share ideas is another component of appreciative listening. Students need to learn how to participate in conversations, discussions, and other talk activities, which we will discuss in Chapter 5.

Therapeutic Listening. People listen to allow a speaker to talk through a problem. Children, as well as adults, serve as sympathetic listeners for friends and family members. Although this type of listening is important, it is less appropriate for elementary students, so we will not discuss it in this chapter.

Our focus will be on the three listening purposes that are most appropriate for elementary students: *comprehensive listening*, or the type of listening required in many

DICTATED STORIES

"I integrate listening, talking, reading, and writing in my kindergarten classroom, but listening is the most basic one. That's where I start. Then I integrate the others."

Marie Whiteside, Kindergarten Teacher,
Norseman Elementary School

PROCEDURE

We're doing a thematic unit on the farm, and as part of the unit, I read *Who Took the Farmer's Hat?* (Nodset, 1963) to the class. It's a repetitive story about how some animals use the farmer's hat. First, we read the story for pleasure, but if my children really like it, that's just the beginning. And did they ever like it! It is so predictable that after a second reading, they were reading aloud with me. Next, the children dictate sentences about the events of the story, and we put them in sequence and place them in a pocket chart. We add pictures to illustrate each line, and the children are ready to read the chart.

At first I read each sentence aloud and they recite it, like an echo. After they are familiar with the words, we vary the way we read the chart. Sometimes we read it in unison; sometimes the boys and the girls alternate reading sentences; and sometimes individual children read the sen-

instructional activities; *critical listening,* or learning to detect propaganda devices and persuasive language; and *appreciative listening,* or listening to conversation and to literature read aloud for pleasure.

The Need for Systematic Instruction

Activities involving listening go on in every elementary classroom. Students listen to the teacher give directions and instruction, to tape-recorded stories at listening centers, to classmates during discussions, and to someone reading stories and poetry aloud. Since listening plays a significant role in these and other classroom activities, listening is not neglected. But whereas these activities provide opportunities for students to practice listening skills, they do *not* teach them how to be more effective listeners.

tences. Before long children are picking out words from the sentences and writing words and sentences from the chart or the book in their journals, reciting the entire story to anyone who will listen. That's where we are now. The children know the story well and want to make books with the sentences to take home and read to their moms and dads. This will be their 23rd book this school year! I write each sentence on a sheet of paper and duplicate the sheets. Then the children collect the sheets, illustrate them, compile the books, and add cardboard covers. Next they practice reading their books (sometimes it is really reciting or telling about the picture on each page) in class for several days before taking them home to share with their families.

ASSESSMENT

I'm a "kid-watcher"—I watch my children throughout the language arts activity and make mental notes about who asks me to reread the story, who volunteers sentences for the pocket chart, and who reads aloud the sentences on the chart. I also try to note which children are holding back, and I plan opportunities for the children who aren't actively participating to reread the book, act it out, and read the sentences on the chart in a small group setting. Once or twice a week, I transfer these mental notes to a checklist. I keep a list of the children's names on a clipboard in the classroom and add checkmarks and other comments next to each child's name to indicate how everyone is doing. The great thing about kindergarten is that everyone can be successful, and I watch my children and use checklists to make sure everyone is learning.

REFLECTION

Kindergarten used to be the "readiness" class, but now my children are using literature as the basis for listening, talking, reading, and writing. I'm excited about this new integrated approach because it works! They are quickly learning to use language to communicate. A number of the children in my class have been in the U.S. less than a year or come from homes in which parents speak little or no English. Even so, these children rapidly learn English through our listening, talking, reading, and writing activities.

Language arts educators have repeatedly cited the need for systematic instruction in listening (Devine, 1978; Lundsteen, 1979; Pearson & Fielding, 1982; Wolvin & Coakley, 1985). Most of what has traditionally been called "listening instruction" has been merely practice. When students listen to a story at a listening center and then answer questions about it, for example, teachers assume that the students know *how* to listen and will thus be able to answer the questions. But listening at a listening center is only a form of practice. Perhaps one reason listening has not been taught is simply that teachers do not know how to teach it. In a survey of elementary teachers enrolled in master's degree programs, only 17 percent recalled receiving any instruction in how to teach listening in their language arts methods class (Tompkins, Smith, & Friend, 1984). The teachers instead reported using practice activities instead of listening instruction.

In contrast to practice activities, listening instruction should teach students specific strategies to use when listening. Imagery, organization, and questions are examples of strategies that help students attend to the important information in a message and understand it more readily. Teachers have assumed that students acquire these strategies intuitively. Certainly some do; however, many students do not recognize that different listening purposes require different strategies. Many students have only one approach to listening, no matter what the purpose. They say they listen as hard as they can and try to remember everything. This strategy seems destined to fail for at least two reasons: (1) trying to remember everything places an impossible demand on short-term memory, and (2) many items in a message are not important enough to remember. Other students equate listening with intelligence, assuming that they "just aren't smart enough" if they are poor listeners.

❖ COMPREHENSIVE LISTENING

Comprehensive listening is listening to understand a message, and it is the most common type of listening in school. For example, a fifth grade teacher who discusses the causes of the American Revolution, a first grade teacher who explains how to dial 911 in an emergency, and an eighth grade teacher who discusses the greenhouse effect are providing information for students to relate to what they already know and remember.

Whether or not students comprehend and remember the message is determined by many factors. Some factors are operative before listening, others during and after. First, students need a background of prior knowledge about the content they are listening to. They must be able to relate what they are about to hear to what they already know, and speakers can help provide some of these links. Second, as they listen, students must use a strategy or other technique to help them remember. They need to organize and chunk the information they receive. They may want to take notes to help them remember. Then, after listening, students should somehow apply what they have heard so there is a reason to remember the information.

Strategies for Listening

Six listening strategies elementary students can learn and use are creating imagery, categorizing, asking questions, organizing, note-taking, and attention-directing.[1] These strategies are primarily aimed at comprehensive listening, but can also be used for other listening purposes. The purpose of each strategy is to help students organize and remember what they listen to.

Strategy #1: Forming a picture in your mind. Students can draw a mental picture while listening to help them remember. The imagery strategy is especially useful when a speaker's message has many visual images, details, or descriptive words, and when students are listening for enjoyment. Stories and pictures help teach students to create images, and students can draw or write about the mental pictures they create.

Strategy #2: Putting information into groups. Students can categorize so as to group or cluster information when the speaker's message contains many pieces of

[1]Adapted from Tompkins, Friend, & Smith, 1987.

information, comparisons, or contrasts. Students could use this strategy, for example. as they listen to a comparison of reptiles and amphibians. The teacher can make a two-column chart on the chalkboard, labeling one column *reptiles* and the other *amphibians*. Then together, teacher and students make notes in the columns while they listen or immediately after. Similarly, students can divide a sheet of paper into two columns and make notes themselves.

When students are listening to presentations that contain information on more than two or three categories, such as a presentation on the five basic food groups, drawing a cluster diagram on the chalkboard helps students classify what they are listening to. Students can also draw a cluster diagram on a sheet of paper and take notes about each food group by drawing lines from each food group and adding details. An example of a cluster diagram appears in Figure 4–2. More information about clustering is presented in Chapter 6.

Strategy #3: Asking questions. Students can ask questions to increase their understanding of a speaker's message. Two types of questions are helpful: students can ask the speaker to clarify information, or they can ask themselves questions to monitor their listening and understanding. Most students are familiar with asking questions of a speaker, but the idea of self-questions is usually new to them. Develop a list of self-questions similar to those that follow to help students understand the self-questioning procedure and how to monitor their understanding:

- Why am I listening to this message?
- Do I know what _____ means?
- Does this information make sense to me?

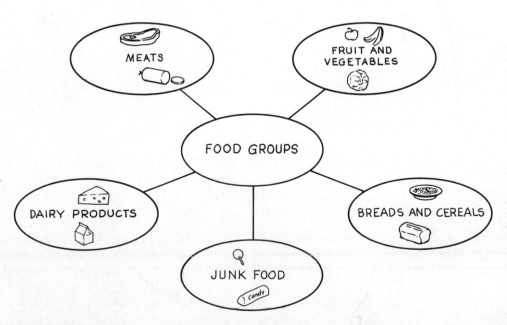

FIGURE 4–2

A Cluster Diagram on the Food Groups

Strategy #4: Discovering the plan. Speakers use one of several types of organization to structure a message. Five common organizational patterns are *description, sequence, comparison, cause and effect,* and *problem and solution.* Students can learn to recognize these patterns and use them to understand and remember a speaker's message more easily. They can develop graphic organizers for each of the five organizational patterns (Smith & Tompkins, 1988); sample organizers are shown in Figure 4–3. Graphic organizers help students visualize the organization of a message. Excerpts from social studies and science textbooks as well as from informational books can be used in teaching this strategy.

The design of a graphic organizer can be adapted to the information presented. Figure 4–4 shows three possible graphic organizers for the cause-and-effect pattern. Any of the three patterns might be used during a discussion on pollution. In talking

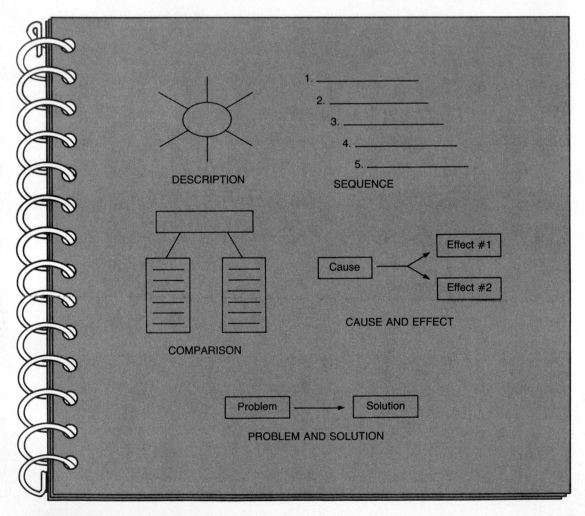

FIGURE 4–3

Teacher's Notebook Page: Graphic Organizers

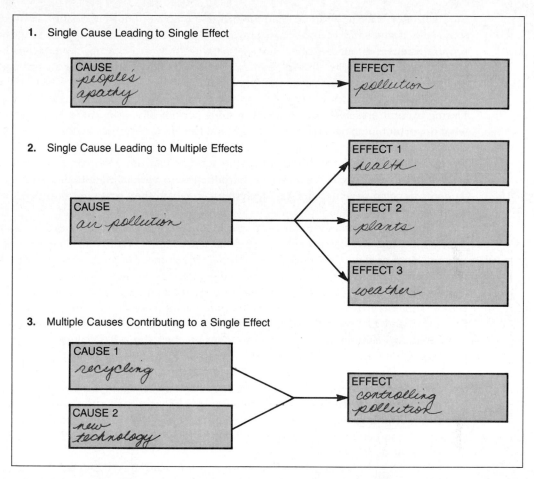

1. Single Cause Leading to Single Effect

   CAUSE
   people's apathy → EFFECT *pollution*

2. Single Cause Leading to Multiple Effects

   CAUSE
   air pollution →
   EFFECT 1 *health*
   EFFECT 2 *plants*
   EFFECT 3 *weather*

3. Multiple Causes Contributing to a Single Effect

   CAUSE 1 *recycling*
   CAUSE 2 *new technology* →
   EFFECT *controlling pollution*

FIGURE 4—4

Possible Graphic Organizers for Cause and Effect

about how people's apathy has allowed pollution to occur, the first organizer, single cause leading to single effect, might be used. Or, in explaining that air pollution has affected humans, plants, and the weather, the second pattern might be appropriate. If, instead, you were discussing that recycling and new technological developments are two ways of controlling pollution, the third graphic organizer in Figure 4—4 would be helpful.

Speakers often use certain words to signal the organizational patterns they are following. Signal words include *first, second, third, next, in contrast,* and *in summary.* Students can learn to attend to these signals to identify the organizational pattern the speaker is using as well as to better understand the message. For more information about organizational patterns and cue words to identify the pattern, see Chapter 8.

Strategy #5: Note-taking: Writing down important information. Note-taking helps students become more active listeners. Devine (1981) describes note-taking as "responding-with-pen-in-hand" (p. 156). Students' interest in note-taking begins with the realization that they cannot store unlimited amounts of information in their minds; they need some kind of external storage system. Many of the listening strategies require listeners to make written notes about what they are hearing. *Note-taking* is a general term to describe this strategy. Note-taking is often thought of as a listing or outline, but notes can also be written in clusters.

Teachers introduce note-taking by taking notes with the class on the chalkboard. During an oral presentation, the teacher stops periodically, asks students to identify what important information was presented, and lists their responses on the chalkboard. Teachers often begin by writing notes in a list format, but the notes can also be written in outline or cluster formats. Similarly, the teacher can use key words, phrases, or sentences in recording notes. After an introduction to various note-taking strategies, students develop personal note-taking systems in which they write notes in their own words and use a consistent format.

Upper-grade students might try a special kind of note-taking in which they divide their papers into two columns. They label the left column "note-taking" and the right column "note-making." They take notes in the left column, but more importantly, they think about the notes, make connections, and personalize the notes in the right column, "note-making" (Berthoff, 1981). Students can use this strategy when listening to oral presentations as well as when reading a content area textbook or an informational book. Students need to stop periodically and reflect on the notes they have taken. The "note-making" column should be more extensive then the other column. A sample note-taking and note-making sheet is presented in Figure 4–5. In this figure, a sixth grader is taking notes as she reads about illegal drugs.

Children's awareness of note-taking as a strategy "to help you remember what you are listening to" begins in the primary grades. Teachers should demonstrate the usefulness of note-taking on the chalkboard or on charts with kindergartners and first graders. Second and third graders then begin taking notes in their learning logs as a part of social studies and science classes.

Outlining is a useful note-taking strategy, but it has gained a bad reputation from misuse in secondary and college English classes (Devine, 1981). It may be preferable to use print materials to introduce outlining, because oral presentations are often less structured than print materials, and students must discover the speaker's plan in order to outline. Teachers who want to teach outlining through oral presentations, however, should begin with a simple organization of perhaps three main ideas with two subordinate ideas for each main idea. Teachers can also give students a partial outline to complete while they give an oral presentation.

The information in the notes students take depends on their purpose for listening. Thus, it is essential that students understand the purpose for listening before they begin to take notes. Some listening tasks require noting main ideas or details; other tasks require noting sequence, cause and effect, or comparisons.

Most language arts textbooks limit instruction in note-taking to taking notes from textbooks and reference materials (Tompkins, Smith, & Friend, 1984). Taking notes from a speaker, however, is an equally important strategy. When they are taking notes from a speaker, students cannot control the speed at which information is presented. They usually cannot relisten to a speaker to complete notes, and the structure of oral presentations is often not as formal as that of print materials. Students need to become

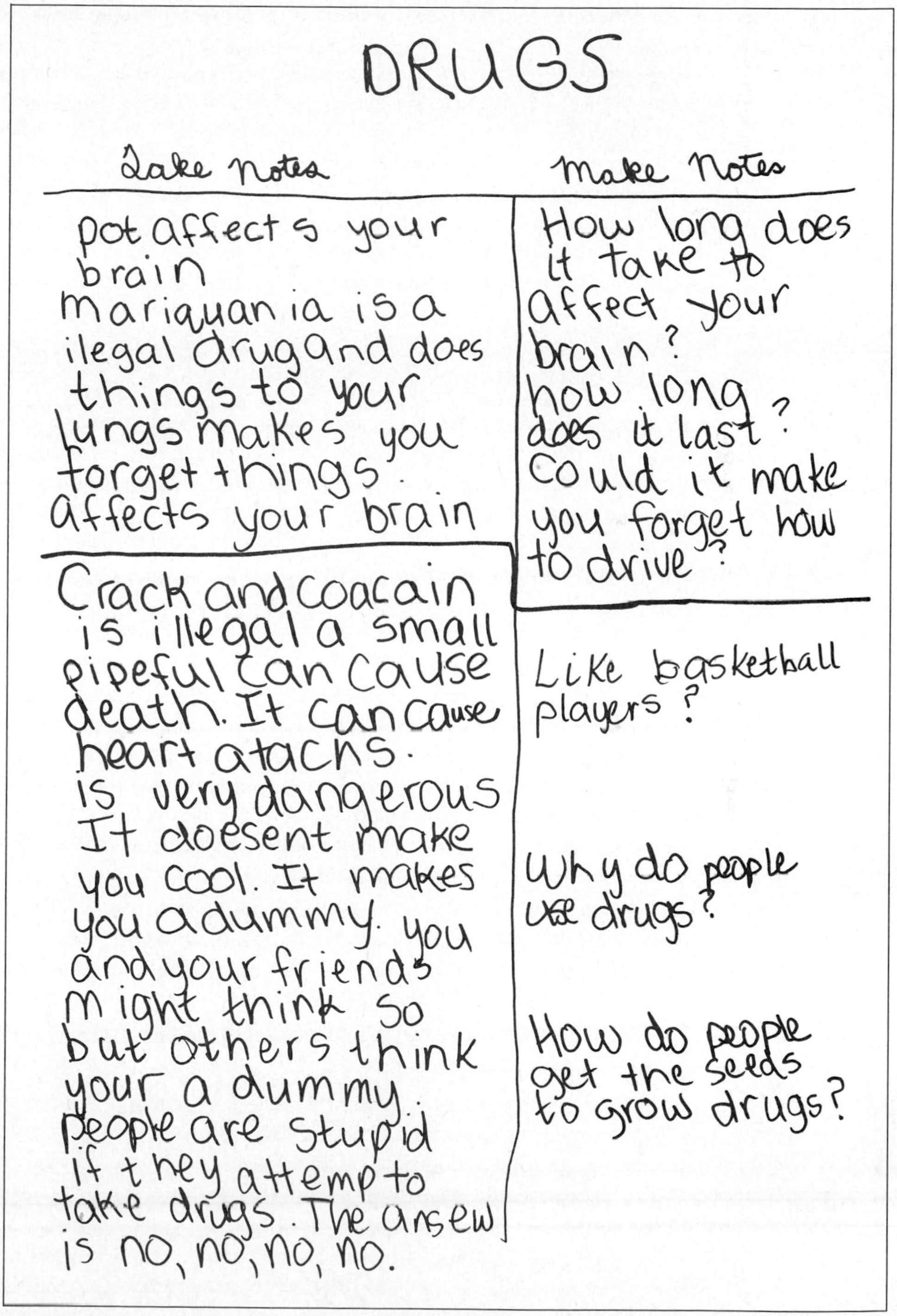

DRUGS

Take notes	Make Notes
pot affects your brain mariquania is a ilegal drug and does things to your lungs makes you forget things. Affects your brain	How long does it take to affect your brain? how long does it last? Could it make you forget how to drive?
Crack and coacain is illegal a small pipeful can cause death. It can cause heart atachs. Is very dangerous It doesent make you cool. It makes you a dummy. you and your friends might think so but others think your a dummy. People are stupid if they attempt to take drugs. The ansew is no, no, no, no.	Like basketball players? Why do people use drugs? How do people get the seeds to grow drugs?

FIGURE 4—5

A Fifth Grader's Note-taking and Note-making Sheet

aware of these differences so they can adapt their note-taking system to the presentation mode.

Strategy #6: Getting clues from the speaker. Speakers use both visual and verbal cues to convey their messages and direct their listeners' attention. Visual cues include gesturing, writing or underlining important information on the chalkboard, and changing facial expressions. Verbal cues include pausing, raising or lowering the voice, slowing down speech to stress key points, and repeating important information. Surprisingly, many students are not aware of these attention-directing behaviors, so teachers must point them out. Once students are aware of these cues, they can use them to increase their understanding of a message.

Teaching Comprehensive Listening

To understand a message they are listening to, students need to learn a strategic approach that involves activities before, during, and after listening. Students must learn to use each of the six listening strategies and apply them in comprehensive as well as critical and appreciative listening activities. You can use the following instructional strategy, developed from the instructional model presented in Chapter 1, to teach these listening strategies.

1. *Introduce the strategy.* Explain the listening strategy, how it is used, and the types of listening activities for which it is most effective. Develop a chart listing the characteristics or steps of the strategy; for example, the information about organizational patterns in Figure 4–3 can be listed in a chart for students to refer to.

2. *Demonstrate the strategy.* Demonstrate the strategy as you give an oral presentation or as students listen to a tape-recorded or film presentation. Stop the presentation periodically to talk aloud about what one does as one listens, asks oneself questions, and takes notes, and point out cues. After completing the activity, discuss your use of the strategy with students.

3. *Practice the strategy.* Have students model the strategy during other presentations. Stop the presentation periodically to ask students to describe how they are listening. After several large-group presentations, students can work in small groups and, later, individually practice the strategy.

4. *Review the strategy.* After each listening activity, have students explain the strategy and how they use it.

5. *Teach other strategies.* Present a variety of listening activities and have students experiment to determine if the strategy is effective or if a different strategy might be better. Introduce additional strategies to meet these other listening purposes. After presenting all six strategies and letting students practice them, continue to the next step.

6. *Apply the strategies.* After students develop a repertoire of the six listening strategies, they need to learn to select an appropriate strategy for specific listening purposes. The choice depends both on the listener's and the speaker's purpose. Although students must decide which strategy to use before they begin to listen, they

need to continue to monitor their selection during and after listening. Students can generate a list of questions to guide their selection of a strategy and monitor its effectiveness. Asking themselves questions like these before listening will help them select a listening strategy:

- What is the speaker's purpose?
- What is my purpose for listening?
- What am I going to do with what I listen to?
- Will I need to take notes?
- Which strategies could I use?
- Which one will I select?

These are possible questions to use during listening:

- Is my strategy still working?
- Am I putting information into groups?
- Is the speaker giving me cues about the organization of the message?
- Is the speaker giving me nonverbal cues, such as gestures and facial expressions?
- Is the speaker's voice giving me other cues?

These questions are appropriate after listening:

- Do I have questions for the speaker?
- Is any part of the message unclear?
- Are my notes complete?
- Did I make a good choice of strategies? Why or why not? (Tompkins, Friend, & Smith, 1987, p. 39)

Repeat the first five steps of this instructional strategy to teach students how to select an appropriate strategy for various listening activities.

Teachers' actions often determine whether students understand what they are listening to. Using a directed listening strategy with before, during, and after listening components is crucial. Before listening, teachers should make sure students have the necessary background information and then, when they present the new information, they link it to the background information. Teachers explain the purposes of the listening activity and suggest what type of strategy students can use to increase their understanding. While the students listen, teachers can draw graphic organizers on the chalkboard and add key words to help them organize information. This information can also provide the basis for the notes students take either during or after listening. Teachers should use both visual and verbal cues to direct students' attention. Finally, after students listen, teachers should provide opportunities to apply the new information.

Assessing Students' Comprehensive Listening

Teachers often use objective tests to measure students' comprehensive listening. If they have provided information about the causes of the American Revolution, how to dial 911 for an emergency, or the greenhouse effect, they can check students' understanding of the information and infer whether or not students listened. Teachers should also assess students' listening more directly. Specifically, they should check students' understanding of each of the six listening strategies and how they apply in listening activities. Asking students to reflect on and talk about the strategies they use and what they do before, during, and after listening provides insights into children's thinking in a way that objective tests cannot.

❖ CRITICAL LISTENING

Children, even primary-grade students, need to develop critical listening (and thinking) skills because they are exposed to many types of persuasion and propaganda. Peer pressure to dress, behave, and talk like their classmates exerts a strong pull on students. Interpreting books and films requires critical thinking and listening. And social studies and science lessons on topics such as pollution, political candidates, and drugs demand that students listen and think critically.

Television commercials are another form of persuasion and propaganda, and because many commercials are directed at children, it is essential that they listen critically and learn to judge the advertising claims. For example, do the jogging shoes actually help you to run faster? Will the breakfast cereal make you a better football player? Will a particular toy make you a more popular child?

Persuasion and Propaganda

There are three basic ways to persuade people. The first is by reason. People seek logical conclusions, whether from absolute facts or from strong possibilities; for example, people can be persuaded to practice more healthful living as the result of medical research. It is necessary, of course, to distinguish between reasonable arguments and unreasonable appeals. To suggest that diet pills will bring about exaggerated weight loss is an unreasonable appeal.

A second means of persuasion is an appeal to character. We can be persuaded by what another person recommends if we trust that person. Trust comes from personal knowledge or the reputation of the person who is trying to persuade. We must always question whether we can believe the persuader. We can believe what scientists say about the dangers of nuclear waste, but can we believe what a sports personality says about the effectiveness of a particular sports shoe?

The third way to persuade people is by appealing to their emotions. Emotional appeals can be as strong as intellectual appeals. We have strong feelings and concern for ourselves and other people and animals. Fear, peer acceptance, and freedom of expression are all strong feelings that influence our opinions and beliefs.

Any of the three types of appeals can be used to try to persuade someone. For example, when a child tries to persuade her parents that her bedtime should be delayed by 30 minutes, she might argue that neighbors allow their children to stay up later—an appeal to character. It is an appeal to reason when the argument focuses on the amount of sleep a ten-year-old needs. And when the child announces that she has the earliest bedtime of anyone in her class and it makes her feel like a baby, the appeal is to emotion. The same three appeals apply to in-school persuasion. To persuade classmates to read a particular book in a book report "commercial," a student might argue that they should read the book because it is short and interesting (reason); because it is hilarious and they'll laugh (emotion); or because it is the most popular book in the second grade and everyone else is reading it (character).

Children need to learn to become critical consumers of advertisements (Rudasill, 1986; Tutolo, 1981). Advertisers use appeals to reason, character, and emotion just as other persuaders do to promote products, ideas, and services; however, advertisers may also use *propaganda* to influence our beliefs and actions. Propaganda suggests something shady or underhanded. Like persuasion, propaganda is designed to influence people's beliefs and actions, but propagandists may use certain techniques to distort, conceal, and exaggerate. Two of these techniques are deceptive language and propaganda devices.

Deceptive Language.　People seeking to influence us often use words that evoke a variety of responses. They claim something is *improved, more natural,* or *50% better—loaded words* that are deceptive because they are suggestive. When a product is advertised as 50% better, for example, consumers need to ask, "50% better than what?" Advertisements rarely answer that question.

Students listen critically while classmates present puppet show "commercials" for their favorite Beverly Cleary books.

Doublespeak is another type of deceptive language characterized as evasive, euphemistic, confusing, and self-contradictory. Janitors may be called *maintenance engineers,* and repeats of television shows are termed *encore telecasts.* Lutz (1984) cited a number of kinds of doublespeak. Elementary students can easily understand two kinds, euphemisms and inflated language. Other kinds of doublespeak, such as jargon specific to particular groups, overwhelming an audience with words, and language that pretends to communicate but does not, are more appropriate for older students.

Euphemisms are words or phrases (for example, *passed away*) that are used to avoid a harsh or distasteful reality, often out of concern for someone's feelings rather than to deceive. *Inflated language* includes words intended to make the ordinary seem extraordinary—car mechanics become *automotive internists,* and used cars become *pre-owned* or *experienced cars.* Examples of deceptive language are listed in Figure 4–6. Children need to learn that people sometimes use words that only pretend to communicate; sometimes they use words to intentionally misrepresent, as when someone advertises a vinyl wallet as "genuine imitation leather" or a ring with a glass stone as a "faux diamond." Children need to be able to interpret deceptive language and to avoid using it themselves.

Propaganda Devices.   Advertisers use propaganda devices such as testimonials, the bandwagon effect, and rewards to sell products. Nine devices that elementary students can learn to identify are listed in Figure 4–7. Students can listen to commercials to find examples of each propaganda device and discuss the effect the device has on them. They can also investigate to see how the same devices vary in commercials directed toward youngsters, teenagers, and adults. For instance, a snack food commercial with a sticker or toy in the package will appeal to a youngster, and a videotape recorder advertisement offering a factory rebate will appeal to an adult. The propaganda device for both ads is the same: a reward! Propaganda devices can be used to sell ideas as well as products. Public service announcements about smoking or wearing seat belts, as well as political advertisements, endorsements, and speeches, use these devices.

When students locate advertisements and commercials they believe are misleading or deceptive, they can write letters of complaint to the following watchdog agencies:

Action for Children's Television
46 Austin St.
Newton, MA 02160

Children's Advertising
Review Unit
Council of Better Business
Bureaus
845 Third Ave.
New York, NY 10022

Federal Trade Commission
Pennsylvania Ave. at Sixth St. NW
Washington, DC 20580

Zillions Ad Complaints
256 Washington St.
Mt. Vernon, NY 10553

Students' letters should carefully describe the advertisement and explain what bothers them about it. They should also tell where and when they saw or heard the advertisement or commercial.

Loaded Words	
best buy	longer lasting
better than	lowest
carefree	maximum
discount	more natural
easier	more powerful
extra strong	new/newer
fortified	plus
fresh	stronger
guaranteed	ultra
improved	virtually

Doublespeak	Translations
bathroom tissue	toilet paper
civil disorder	riot
correctional facility	jail, prison
dentures	false teeth
disadvantaged	poor
encore telecast	re-run
funeral director	undertaker
genuine imitation leather	vinyl
inner city	slum, ghetto
Inoperative statement or misspeak	lie
memorial park	cemetery
mobile home	house trailer
nervous wetness	sweat
occasional irregularity	constipation
passed away	died
people expressways	sidewalks
personal preservation flotation device	life preserver
pre-owned or experienced	used
pupil station	student's desk
senior citizen	old person
terminal living	dying
urban transportation specialist	cab driver, bus driver

FIGURE 4–6

Examples of Deceptive Language
Lutz, n.d.

Teaching Critical Listening

The steps in teaching students to be critical listeners are similar to the steps in teaching listening strategies. In this instructional strategy, students view commercials to examine propaganda devices and persuasive language. Later they can create their own commercials and advertisements.

1. Glittering Generality

Generalities such as "motherhood," "justice," and "The American Way" are used to enhance the quality of a product or the character of a political figure. Propagandists select a generality so attractive that listeners do not challenge the speakers' real point. If a candidate for public office happens to be a mother, for example, the speaker may say, "Our civilization could not survive without mothers." The generalization is true, of course, and listeners may—if they are not careful—accept the candidate without asking these questions: Is she a mother? Is she a good mother? Does being a mother have anything to do with being a good candidate?

2. Testimonial

To convince people to purchase a product, an advertiser associates it with a popular personality such as an athlete or film star. For example, "Bozo Cereal must be good because Joe Footballstar eats it every morning." Similarly, film stars endorse candidates for political office and telethons to raise money for medical research and other causes. Consider these questions: Is the person familiar with the product being advertised? Does the person offering the testimonial have the expertise necessary to judge the quality of the product, event, or candidate?

3. Transfer

In this device, which is similar to the testimonial technique, the persuader tries to transfer the authority and prestige of some person or object to another person or object that will then be accepted. Good examples are found regularly in advertising: A film star is shown using Super Soap, and viewers are supposed to believe that they too may have healthy, youthful skin if they use the same soap. Likewise, politicians like to be seen with famous athletes or entertainers in hopes that the luster of the stars will rub off on them. This technique is also known as guilt or glory by association. Questions to determine the effect of this device are the same as for the testimonial technique.

4. Name-calling

Here advertisers try to pin a bad label on something they want listeners to dislike so that it will automatically be rejected or condemned. In a discussion of health insurance, for example, an opponent may call the sponsor of a bill a socialist. Whether or not the sponsor is a socialist does not matter to the name-caller; the purpose is to have any unpleasant associations of the term rub off on the victim. Listeners should ask themselves whether or not the label has any effect on the product.

5. Plain Folks

Assuming that most listeners favor common, ordinary people (rather than elitish, stuffed shirts), many politicians like to assume the appearance of common folk. One candidate, who really went to Harvard and wore $400 suits, campaigned in clothes from J.C. Penney's and spoke backcountry dialect. "Look at me, folks," the candidate wanted to say, "I'm just a regular country boy like you; I wouldn't sell you a bill of goods!" To determine the effect of this device, listeners should ask these questions: Is the person really the type of person he or she is portraying? Does the person really share the ideas of the people with whom he or she professes to identify?

6. Card Stacking

In presenting complex issues, the unscrupulous persuader often chooses only those items that favor one side of an issue. Any unfavorable facts are suppressed. To consider the argument objectively, listeners must seek additional information about other viewpoints.

7. Bandwagon

This technique appeals to many people's need to be a part of a group. Advertisers claim that everyone is using this product and you should, too. For example, "more physicians recommend this pill than any other." (Notice that the advertisement doesn't specify what "any other" is.) Questions to consider include the following: Does everyone really use this product? What is it better than? Why should I jump on the bandwagon?

8. Snob Appeal

In contrast to the plain folks device, persuaders use snob appeal to try to appeal to the people who want to become part of an elite or exclusive group. Advertisements for expensive clothes, cosmetics, and gourmet foods often use this technique. Listeners should consider these questions in evaluating the commercials and advertisements using this device: Is the product of high quality or does it have an expensive nametag? Is the product of higher quality than other non-snobbish brands?

9. Rewards

Increasingly, advertisers offer rewards for buying their products. For many years, snack food and cereal products offered toys and other gimmicks in their product packages. More often, adults are being lured by this device, too. Free gifts, rebates from manufacturers, low-cost financing, and other rewards are being offered for the purchase of expensive items such as appliances and automobiles. Listeners should consider the value of these rewards and whether they increase the cost of the product.

FIGURE 4–7

Propaganda Devices (Techniques 1–6 adapted from Devine, 1982, pp. 39–40.)

1. *Introduce commercials.* Talk about commercials and ask students about familiar commercials. Videotape some commercials and view them with students. Discuss the purpose of each commercial. Use these questions about commercials to probe students' thinking about persuasion and propaganda:

- What is the speaker's purpose?
- What are the speaker's credentials?
- Is there evidence of bias?
- Does the speaker use deceptive language?
- Does the speaker make sweeping generalizations or unsupported inferences?
- Do opinions predominate the talk?
- Does the speaker use any propaganda devices?
- Do you accept the message? (Devine, 1982, pp. 41–42)

2. *Explain deceptive language.* Present the terms *persuasion* and *propaganda*. Introduce the propaganda devices and view the commercials again to look for examples of each device. Introduce loaded words and doublespeak and view the commercials a third time to look for examples of deceptive language.

3. *Analyze deceptive language in commercials.* Have students work in small groups to critique a commercial as to the type of persuasion, propaganda devices, deceptive language. Students might also want to test the claims made in the commercial.

4. *Review concepts.* Review the concepts about persuasion, propaganda devices, and deceptive language introduced in the first three steps. It may be helpful for students to make charts about these concepts.

5. *Provide practice.* Present a new set of videotaped commercials for students to critique. Ask them to identify persuasion, propaganda devices, and deceptive language in the commercials.

6. *Create commercials.* Have students apply what they have learned about persuasion, propaganda devices, and deceptive language by creating their own products and writing and producing their own commercials to advertise them. Possible products include breakfast cereals, toys, beauty and diet products, and sports equipment, or students might create homework and house-sitting services to advertise. They can also choose community or environmental issues to campaign for or against. The storyboard for a commercial created by a group of fifth graders appears in Figure 4–8. As the students present the commercials, classmates act as critical listeners to detect persuasion, propaganda devices, loaded words, and doublespeak.

Using Advertisements. Students can use the same procedures and activities with advertisements they collect from magazines and product packages. Have children collect advertisements and display them on a bulletin board. Written advertisements also use deceptive language and propaganda devices. Students examine advertisements and then decide how the writer is trying to persuade them to purchase the

FIGURE 4–8

Fifth-graders' Storyboard for Their "Dream Date" Commercial

product. They can also compare the amount of text to the amount of pictures. Fox and Allen (1983) reported that children who examined advertisements found that, in contrast to advertisements for toys, cosmetics, and appliances, ads for cigarettes had comparatively little text and used pictures prominently. The students quickly speculated on the reasons for this approach.

Assessing Students' Critical Listening

Teachers can assess critical listening by having students view and critique commercials and other oral presentations after teaching them about persuasion, propaganda, and deceptive language. A second way to assess students' understanding is to have them develop their own commercials and advertisements. Critical listening goes beyond one unit, however, and is something that teachers should return to again and again during the school year.

❖ APPRECIATIVE LISTENING

Students are listening appreciatively when they listen for enjoyment. Appreciative listening includes listening to music, to a comedian tell jokes, to friends when they talk, to a storyteller, and to stories and poems read aloud. We will focus on reading stories aloud to students. When students listen to stories, they develop the ability to visualize, identify the speech rhythm, identify the speaker's style, interpret character from dialogue, recognize tone and mode, understand the effect of the speaker or reader's vocal qualities and physical action, and understand the effect of the audience on the listeners' responses (Wolvin & Coakley, 1979), as well as to gain an understanding of how authors structure stories and how the characters, plot, setting, and other elements are woven together.

Reading Aloud to Students

Sharing books orally is a valuable way to help students enjoy literature. Reading stories to children is an important component in most kindergarten and first grade classrooms. Unfortunately, teachers often think they need to read to children only until they learn to read for themselves; however, reading aloud and sharing the excitement of books, language, and reading should remain an important part of the language arts program at all grade levels. The common complaint is that there is not enough time in the school day to read to children, but reading a story or a chapter of a longer story aloud can take as little as 10 or 15 minutes a day. Many educators (Kimmel & Segel, 1983; Sims, 1977; Trelease, 1989) point out the necessity of finding time to read aloud so as to take advantage of the many benefits:

Stimulating children's interest in books and reading

Broadening children's reading interests and developing their taste for quality literature

Teachers should share stories by reading aloud to students every day.

Introducing children to the sounds of written language and expanding their vocabulary and sentence patterns

Sharing with children books that are "too good to miss"

Allowing children to listen to books that would be too difficult for them to read on their own or books that are "hard to get into"

Expanding children's background of experiences

Introducing children to concepts about written language, different genres of literature, poetry, and elements of story structure

Providing a pleasurable, shared experience

Modeling to children that adults read and enjoy reading to increase the likelihood that children will become lifelong readers

By reading aloud to students daily, you can introduce them to all types of literature and the enjoyment of reading. The guidelines for choosing books to read aloud are simple: choose books you like and that you think will appeal to your students. Trelease (1989) suggests four additional criteria of good read-aloud books: They should be fast-paced to hook children's interest as quickly as possible; contain well-developed characters; include easy-to-read dialogue; and keep long descriptive passages to a minimum. There are a number of annotated guidebooks to help teachers select books for reading aloud as well as for independent reading. Figure 4–9 lists these guides.

Books that have received awards or other acclaim from teachers, librarians, and children make good choices. Two of the most prestigious awards are the Caldecott and

Books

Bauer, C. F. (1983). *This way to books.* New York: Wilson.

Carroll, F. L. & Mecham, M. (Eds.). (1984). *Exciting, funny, scary, short, different, and sad books kids like about animals, science, sports, families, songs, and other things.* Chicago: American Library Association.

Christensen, J. (Ed.). (1983). *Your reading: A booklist for junior high and middle school students.* Urbana, IL: National Council of Teachers of English.

Freeman, J. (1984). *Books kids will sit still for.* Hagerstown, MD: Alleyside Press.

Kimmel, M. M. & Segel, E. (1983). *For reading out loud! A guide for sharing books with children.* New York: Delacorte.

Lipson, E. R. (1988). *The New York Times parents' guide to the best books for children.* New York: Random House.

McMullan, K. H. (1984). *How to choose good books for kids.* Reading, MA: Addison-Wesley.

Monson, D. L. (Ed.). (1985). *Adventuring with books: A booklist for pre-K–grade 6* (new ed.). Urbana, IL: National Council of Teachers of English.

Roser, N. & Frith, M. (Eds.). (1983). *Children's choices: Teaching with books children like.* Newark, DE: International Reading Association.

Stensland, A. L. (1979). *Literature by and about the American Indian: An annotated bibliography* (2nd ed.). Urbana, IL: National Council of Teachers of English.

Trelease, J. (1989). *The new read-aloud handbook.* New York: Penguin.

Tway, E. (Ed.). (1981). *Reading ladders for human relations* (6th ed.). Urbana, IL: National Council of Teachers of English.

Journals and Newsletters

CBC Features, The Children's Book Council, 67 Irving Place, New York, NY 10003.

The Horn Book, Park Square Building, 31 St. James Avenue, Boston, MA 02116.

Language Arts, National Council of Teachers of English, 1111 Kenyon Road, Urbana, IL 61801.

The New Advocate, Christopher-Gordon Publishers, P. O. Box 809, Needham Heights, MA 02194.

The Reading Teacher, International Reading Association, P. O. Box 8139, Newark, DE 19711.

FIGURE 4–9

Guides for Choosing Books to Read Aloud to Students

Newbery Awards, listed in Appendix B. Other lists of outstanding books are prepared annually by professional groups such as the National Council of Teachers of English and the National Council of Teachers of Social Studies. In many states, children read and vote on books to receive recognition, such as the Buckeye Book Award in Ohio and the Sequoia Book Award in Oklahoma. The International Reading Association sponsors a Children's Choices competition in which children read and select their favorite books; a list is published annually.

Teachers in many primary-grade classrooms read one story aloud as part of a literature or author unit and later during the day read informational books aloud as part of social studies or science units. Poems, too, are read aloud in connection with content area classes. It is not unusual for primary-grade students to listen to their teacher read aloud three or more stories and other books during the school day. If children are read to only once a day, they will listen to fewer than 200 books during the school year, and this is simply not enough! More than 40,000 books are available for children, and reading stories and other books aloud is an important way to share more of this literature with children. Students in middle and upper grades should also read and listen to chapter books and poems read aloud as part of literature or author units and informational books and magazine and newspaper articles in content area units.

Repeated Readings. Children, especially preschoolers and kindergartners, often beg to have a familiar book reread. Although it is important to share a wide variety of books with children, researchers have found that children benefit in specific ways from repeated readings (Yaden, 1988). Through repetition, students gain control over the parts of a story and are better able to synthesize the story parts into a whole. The quality of children's responses to a repeated story changes (Beaver, 1982), and children become more independent users of the classroom library center (Martinez & Teale, 1988).

Martinez and Roser (1985) examined young children's responses to stories and found that as stories become increasingly familiar, students' responses indicate a greater depth of understanding. They found that children talked almost twice as much about familiar books that had been reread many times as about unfamiliar books that had been read only once or twice. The form and focus of children's talk changed, too. While children tended to ask questions about unfamiliar stories, they made comments about familiar stories. Children's talk about unfamiliar stories focused on characters; the focus changed to details and word meanings when they talked about familiar stories. The researchers also found that children's comments after repeated readings were more probing and more specific, suggesting that they had greater insight into the story. Researchers investigating the value of repeated readings have focused mainly on preschool and primary-grade students, but rereading favorite stories may have similar benefits for older students as well.

Other Oral Presentation Modes. Stories can be shared with students through storytelling, readers' theater, and plays; these oral presentation modes will be discussed in Chapter 5. Students can also benefit from other forms of oral presentations, such as tape recordings of stories and filmstrip and film versions of stories. Audiovisual story presentations are available from Weston Woods (Weston, CT 06883), Random House/Miller Brody (400 Hahn Road, Westminster, MD 21157), Pied Piper (P.O. Box 320, Verdugo City, CA 91046), and other distributors.

Teaching Appreciative Listening

Teaching appreciative listening differs from teaching other kinds of listening because enjoyment is the goal. Rather than use the six-step teaching strategy, the directed reading lesson can be adapted for appreciative listening. Activities in this strategy are divided into three steps: before reading, during reading, and after reading.

Before Reading.   Teachers activate students' prior knowledge, provide neces-sary new information related to the story or the author, and interest students in the story. Teachers might discuss the topic or theme, show pictures, or share objects related to the story to draw on prior knowledge or to create new experiences. For example, teachers might talk about students' favorite games before reading Van Allsburg's jungle adventure game, *Jumanji* (1981).

Before beginning to read, teachers set the purpose for reading so that students have a reason for listening to the story.

During Reading.   Teachers read the story aloud, during which students should be actively involved with the story. One way to encourage active participation is to use the *Directed Reading Thinking Activity* (DRTA), a procedure developed by Russell Stauffer (1975) in which students make predictions about a story and then read or listen to the story to confirm or reject the predictions. DRTA involves three steps.

1.   *Predicting.* After showing students the cover of the book and reading the title, the teacher begins by asking students to make a prediction about the story us-ing questions like these:

What do you think a story with a title like this might be about?

What do you think might happen in this story?

Does this picture give you any ideas about what might happen in this story?

If necessary, the teacher reads the first paragraph or two to provide more in-formation for students to use in making their predictions. After a brief discussion in which all students commit themselves to one or another of the alternatives pre-sented, the teacher asks these questions:

Which of these ideas do you think would be the likely one?

Why do you think that idea is a good one?

2.   *Reasoning and predicting from succeeding pages.* After students set their purposes for listening, the teacher reads part of the story, and then students begin to confirm or reject their predictions by answering questions such as the following:

What do you think now?

What do you think will happen next?

What would happen if. . .?

Why do you think that idea is a good one?

The teacher continues reading the story aloud, stopping at key points to repeat this step.

3.   *Proving.* Students give reasons to support their predictions by answering further questions:

What in the story makes you think that?

Where in the story do you get information to support that idea?

The teacher can ask these "proving" questions during the reading or afterward. Note that this strategy can be used both when students are listening to the teacher read a story aloud or when they are reading the story themselves. Use the strategy only when students are reading or listening to an unfamiliar story so that the prediction actively involves them in the story.

Students keep a *reading log* in which they respond after the whole story or after each chapter is read aloud. Primary-grade students keep a reading log by writing the title and author of the story and drawing a picture related to the story. They can also add a few words or a sentence. During an author unit on Tomie de Paola, for instance, second graders, after hearing each de Paola story, record the title on a page in their notebooks, draw a picture related to the story, and write a sentence or two telling what they liked about the story, what it made them think of, or to summarize it. Middle- and upper-grade students write a response after each chapter, and they may add illustrations as well. (For more information about reading logs, see Chapter 6.) As an alternative to reading logs, students can discuss the events in the story, retell the story, or write a retelling of the story, either as a class or in small groups.

Two students present their filmstrip retelling a favorite story for an audience of their classmates.

After Reading.   Students share their reading log entries and, through discussion, relate the story to their lives and to other stories they have read. Discussion can be valuable when it leads students to think critically about the story; the focus of discussions should always be on higher level thinking skills, not factual recall questions.

Enjoyment is reason enough to read aloud to children; however, several kinds of activities extend children's interest in a story after reading. These activities, called *response to literature,* can be spontaneous expressions of interest and delight in a book as well as teacher-planned activities. Hickman (1980) cites the example of a kindergartner named Ben who spontaneously responded to a favorite story when his teacher shared *Pezzetino* (Lionni, 1975):

> Ben says, "I like *Pezzetino* because of all the colors 'n stuff, and the way it repeats. He keeps saying it. And there's marbelizing—see here? And this very last page. . ." Then Ben turns to the end of the book and holds up a picture for the group to see. "He cut paper. How many think he's a good cutter?" Ben conducts a vote, counting the raised hands that show a majority of the group believes Leo Lionni to be "a good cutter."
> (p. 525)

Ben's knowledge of the text and illustrations as well as his enjoyment are obvious. Through his comments and the class vote, Ben is involving his classmates in the story, and it seems likely that *Pezzetino* will be passed from student to student in the class. Spontaneous responses to literature, like Ben's, occur at all grade levels in supportive classrooms where students are invited to share their ideas and feelings.

Teacher-planned response activities include having students make puppets to use in retelling a favorite story, writing letters to authors, creating a mobile for a favorite story, and reading other books by the same author or on a similar theme, to name only a few possibilities. Figure 4–10 lists response to literature activities. These activities are equally useful with books students have listened to read aloud and with books they have read themselves.

The purpose of response to literature activities is for students to personalize and extend their reading. Having them enjoy reading and want to read is another goal. When researchers asked middle- and upper-grade students what they would like to do after reading a story, students responded that they preferred going to see a movie or play about the story, meeting the author, or listening to a recording of the author reading the story rather than participating in more traditional activities (Wiesenbanger & Bader, 1989). Traditional activities such as having students write a book report or answer factual recall test questions should not be an automatic follow-up to reading aloud because they may discourage interest in reading and literature. Instead, students should engage in activities that grow out of their enjoyment of a particular book.

Figure 4–11 (p. 136) illustrates how to use this teaching strategy with two stories, *Where the Wild Things Are* (Sendak, 1963) and *The Pied Piper of Hamelin* (Mayer, 1987). Sometimes teachers read a story aloud without going through all six steps. At times it is appropriate to just read the story aloud, but most of the time, students should be involved with activities related to the story before and after reading so they have the opportunity to understand and appreciate it.

Art Activities

Create a series of illustrations for a favorite book or story episode and compile the illustrations to form a wordless picture book.

Practice the illustration techniques (e.g., collage, styrofoam prints, watercolors, line drawing) used in a favorite book. Also, examine other books that use the same technique.

Create a collage to represent the theme of a favorite book.

Design a book jacket for a favorite book, laminate it, and place it on the book.

Construct a shoebox or other miniature scene of an episode from a favorite story.

Create a filmstrip to illustrate a favorite story.

Create a game based on a favorite story or series of stories. Possible game formats include card games, board games, word finds, crossword puzzles, and computer games.

Draw a map or make a relief map of a book's setting. Some stories, such as Lasky's *Beyond the Divide* (1983), include a map, usually on the book's end papers.

Create a mobile illustrating a favorite book.

Make a movie of a favorite book by drawing a series of pictures on a long strip of paper. Attach ends to rollers and place in a cardboard box.

Writing Activities

Assume the role of a book character and keep a simulated journal from that character's viewpoint.

Write a book review of a favorite book for the class newspaper.

Write a letter to a pen pal about a favorite book.

Create a poster to advertise a favorite book.

Write another episode for the characters in a favorite story.

Create a newspaper with news stories and advertisements based on characters and episodes from a favorite book.

Write a letter to the author of a favorite book. Check the guidelines for writing to children's authors presented in Chapter 6.

Write a simulated letter from one book character to another.

Select five "quotable quotes" from a favorite book and list them on a poster or in copybooks.

FIGURE 4–10

Types of Response Activities

Reading Activities

Research a favorite author and compile the information in a brief report to insert in the author's book.

Read other stories by the same author.

Read other stories with a similar theme.

Tape-record a favorite book or excerpts from a longer story to place in a listening center.

Read a favorite story to children in the primary grades.

Compare different versions of the same story.

Talk and Drama Activities

Give a readers theater presentation of a favorite story. See Chapter 5 for more information about readers theater.

Write a script and produce a play or puppet show about a favorite book.

Dress as a favorite book character and answer questions from classmates about the character and the story.

Retell a favorite story or episode from a longer story using puppets or other props. See Chapter 5 for information about retelling stories.

Give a chalk talk by sketching pictures on the chalkboard or on a large sheet of paper as the story is retold.

Discuss a favorite book informally with several classmates.

Tape-record a review of a favorite book using background music and sound effects.

Videotape a commercial for a favorite book.

Interview classmates about a favorite book.

Other Activities

Plan a special day to honor a favorite author with posters, publicity information from the author's publishers, letters to and from the author, a display of the author's books, and products from other activities listed above.

If possible, arrange to place a conference telephone call to the author or have the author visit the school on that day.

Conduct a class or school vote to determine students' 10 most popular books. Also, many states sponsor annual book awards for outstanding children's books such as Ohio's Buckeye Book Award and Oklahoma's Sequoia Book Award. Encourage students to read the books nominated for their state's award and to vote for their favorite books.

Cook a food described in a favorite book, such as gingerbread cookies after reading Galdone's *The gingerbread boy* (1975) or spaghetti after reading de Paola's *Strega Nona* (1975).

FIGURE 4–10 (*continued*)

Step	Where the Wild Things Are (Sendak, 1963)	The Pied Piper of Hamelin (Mayer, 1987)
Before Reading		
Initiating	Ask children if they have ever been sent to their rooms for misbehaving. What happens while you are in your room?	Ask students if they have heard the saying "A promise is a promise." What does it mean? Ask them if they keep all promises. When is it not necessary?
Structuring	Hang three large sheets of paper and label them *beginning, middle,* and *end.* Explain that the story is divided into three parts—beginning, middle, and end. After reading, students divide into groups to draw pictures of the three parts.	Explain that this story is a legend that may have some basis in fact. Review the characteristics of a legend and identify other familiar legends. Locate Hamelin (West Germany) on a world map.
During Reading		
Conceptualizing	Read the story aloud using DRTA.	Read the story aloud using DRTA, but have students write their predictions before sharing them orally.
After Reading		
Summarizing	Have students retell the story as a class collaboration with each child choosing one page to draw and dictate (or write) a retelling for. Compile the pages to make a book.	Discuss the story, focusing on the mayor's promise and the piper's retaliation when the promise was not kept.
Generalizing	Read the story *Hey, Al* (Yorinks, 1986) and compare the three parts and the fantasy in the middle part of the two stories.	Ask students to write in response to "A promise is a promise" or "The piper must be paid." What do these sayings mean in the story and today?
Applying	Dramatize the story after making costumes of the wild things from grocery sacks. Divide the dramatization into three acts—Act 1, The Beginning; Act 2, The Middle; and Act 3, The End.	Invite students to choose from these response activities: investigate the Pied Piper legend and its origin; read other legends; create a diorama about the story; in a small group, create a puppet show based on the legend and perform it for a second grade class; compile and illustrate a booklet of well-known sayings.

FIGURE 4–11

Teacher's Notebook Page: Using the Teaching Strategy

❖ REVIEW

Listening is the most basic and most used of the language modes. Despite its importance, listening instruction has been neglected in elementary classrooms; practice activities have often been substituted for instruction. The process of listening involves receiving, attending, and assigning meaning. Listening and hearing are not synonymous; rather, hearing is part of the listening process.

Students' need to attend to the speaker's message varies with the listening purpose. Comprehensive listening is the type of listening required in many instructional activities. Critical listening involves learning to detect propaganda devices and persuasive language. Appreciative listening is listening for enjoyment. Reading aloud is one important way to share literature with students.

❖ EXTENSIONS

1. Keep a record of how much time you spend listening, talking, reading, and writing for a day or two. Compare your time allotments with the chart in Figure 4–1. Also, record how much time students spend using each of the four language modes while you observe in an elementary classroom.

2. Visit a classroom and observe how listening is taught or practiced. Consider how practice activities might be changed into instructional activities.

3. Interview primary-, middle-, and upper-grade students about strategies they use while listening; ask questions such as these:

   • What is listening?
   • What is the difference between hearing and listening, or are they the same?
   • Why do people listen? Why else?
   • What do you do while you are listening?
   • What do you do to help you remember what you are listening to?
   • Do you always listen in the same way, or are there different ways to listen?
   • How do you know what is important in the message you are listening to?
   • What is the hardest thing about listening?
   • Are you a good listener? Why? Why not?

   Compare students' responses across grade levels. Are older students more aware of the listening process than younger students are? Can older students identify a greater variety of listening strategies than younger students can?

4. Plan and teach a lesson on one of the six comprehensive listening strategies discussed in this chapter.

5. Read one or more stories aloud to a group of students and involve them in several of the response activities listed in Figure 4–10. Also, use the Directed Listening Thinking Activity for students to make and confirm predictions for one of the stories.

6. Become a pen pal with several students and correspond about books their teacher is reading aloud to them. Read "Sixth Graders Write About Reading Literature" (Smith, 1982) for a description of a pen pal program.

7. After reading a story aloud to a small group of students, direct a reflective discussion. Be sure to choose a book that will stimulate discussion.

❖ **REFERENCES**

Anderson, H. (1949). Teaching the art of listening. *School Review, 57,* 63–67.

Beaver, J. M. (1982). *Say it!* over and over. *Language Arts, 59,* 143–148.

Berthoff, A. E. (1981). *The making of meaning.* Montclair, NJ: Boynton/Cook.

de Paola, T. (1975). *Strega nona.* Englewood Cliffs, NJ: Prentice-Hall.

Devine, T. G. (1978). Listening: What do we know after fifty years of theorizing? *Journal of Reading, 21,* 296–304.

Devine, T. G. (1981). *Teaching study skills: A guide for teachers.* Boston: Allyn and Bacon.

Devine, T. G. (1982). *Listening skills schoolwide: Activities and programs.* Urbana, IL: ERIC Clearinghouse on Reading and Communication Skills and the National Council of Teachers of English.

Erickson, A. (1985). Listening leads to reading. *Reading Today, 2,* 13.

Foulke, E. (1968). Listening comprehension as a function of word rate. *Journal of Communication, 18,* 198–206.

Fox, S. E. & Allen, V. G. (1983). *The language arts: An integrated approach.* New York: Holt, Rinehart & Winston.

Galdone, P. (1975). *The gingerbread boy.* New York: Seabury.

Hansen, J. (1987). *When writers read.* Portsmouth, NH: Heinemann.

Hickman, J. (1980). Children's response to literature: What happens in the classroom. *Language Arts, 57,* 524–529.

Kimmel, M. M. & Segel, E. (1983). *For reading aloud! A guide for sharing books with children.* New York: Delacorte.

Landry, D. (1969). The neglect of listening. *Elementary English, 46,* 599–605.

Lasky, K. (1983). *Beyond the divide.* New York: Macmillan.

Lionni, L. (1975). *Pezzetino.* New York: Pantheon.

Lundsteen, S. W. (1979). *Listening: Its impact on reading and the other language arts* (rev. ed.). Urbana, IL: National Council of Teachers of English.

Lutz, W. (1984). Notes toward a description of doublespeak. *Quarterly Review of Doublespeak, 10,* 1–2.

Lutz, W. (n.d.). *Some examples of doublespeak.* Unpublished manuscript, National Council of Teachers of English.

Martinez, M., & Roser, N. (1985). Read it again: The value of repeated readings during storytime. *The Reading Teacher, 38,* 782–786.

Martinez, M., & Teale, W. H. (1988). Reading in a kindergarten classroom library. *The Reading Teacher, 41,* 568–572.

Mayer, M. (1987). *The pied piper of Hamelin.* New York: Macmillan.

Nodset, J. L. (1963). *Who took the farmer's hat?* New York: Harper and Row.

Pearson, P. D., & Fielding, L. (1982). Research update: Listening comprehension. *Language Arts, 59,* 617–629.

Rankin, P. R. (1928). The importance of listening ability. *English Journal, 17,* 623–640.

Rudasill, L. (1986). Advertising gimmicks: Teaching critical thinking. In J. Golub (Ed.), *Activities to promote critical thinking* (Classroom practices in teaching English, 1986), pp. 127–129. Urbana, IL: National Council of Teachers of English.

Sendak, M. (1963). *Where the wild things are.* New York: Harper and Row.

Sims, R. (1977). Reading literature aloud. In B. E. Cullinan & C. W. Carmichael (Eds.), *Literature and young children* (pp. 108–119). Urbana, IL: National Council of Teachers of English.

Smith, L. B. (1982). Sixth graders write about reading literature. *Language Arts, 59,* 357–363.

Stauffer, R. G. (1975). *Directing the reading-thinking process.* New York: Harper and Row.

Sticht, T. G., & James, J. H. (1984). Listening and reading. In P. D. Pearson (Ed.), *Handbook of reading research,* pp. 293–318. New York: Longman.

Tompkins, G. E., Friend, M., & Smith, P. L. (1984). Children's metacognitive knowledge about listening. Presentation at the American Educational Research Association Convention, New Orleans, LA.

Tompkins, G. E., Friend, M., & Smith, P. L. (1987). Strategies for more effective listening. In C. R. Personke & D. D. Johnson (Eds.), *Language arts and the beginning teacher*

(Chapter 3). Englewood Cliffs, NJ: Prentice-Hall.

Tompkins, G. E., Smith, P. L., & Friend, M. (1984). Three dimensions of listening and listening instruction in the elementary school. Paper presented at the Southwestern Educational Research Association Annual Meeting, Dallas, TX.

Trelease, J. (1989). *The new read-aloud handbook*. New York: Penguin.

Tutolo, D. (1981). Critical listening/reading of advertisements. *Language Arts, 58,* 679–683.

Van Allsburg, C. (1981). *Jumanji*. Boston: Houghton Mifflin.

Werner, E. K. (1975). A study of communication time. Unpublished master's thesis, University of Maryland, College Park.

Wiesendanger, K. D., & Bader, L. (1989). Children's view of motivation. *The Reading Teacher, 42,* 345–347.

Wilt, M. E. (1950). A study of teacher awareness of listening as a factor in elementary education. *Journal of Educational Research, 43,* 626–636.

Wolvin, A. D. & Coakley, C. G. (1979). *Listening instruction* (TRIP Booklet). Urbana, IL: ERIC Clearinghouse on Reading and Communication Skills and the Speech Communication Association.

Yaden, D. (1988). Understanding stories through repeated read-alouds: How many does it take? *The Reading Teacher, 41,* 556–560.

Yorinks, A. (1986). *Hey, Al*. New York: Farrar, Straus and Giroux.

5 SUSTAINING TALK IN THE CLASSROOM

INFORMAL TALK ACTIVITIES
    Conversations
    Show-and-Tell
    Discussions

INTERPRETIVE TALK ACTIVITIES
    Storytelling
    Readers Theatre

MORE FORMAL TALK ACTIVITIES
    Oral Reports
    Interviews
    Debates

DRAMATIC ACTIVITIES
    Dramatic Play
    Role-playing
    Puppets and Other Props
    Scriptwriting and Theatrical Productions

◆   WE BELIEVE THAT TALK IS A POWERFUL WAY OF LEARNING AND
    should be a major part of the elementary school experience. In Chapter 5 we
    discuss informal talk, such as discussions and interpretive talk (including story-
    telling); more formal talk, such as interviews; and dramatic talk.

◆   AS YOU ARE READING, THINK ABOUT THESE QUESTIONS:

    Why is talk important in learning?

    In what types of talk activities do elementary students participate?

    How can talk activities be integrated into literature and content area units?

Talk is the primary expressive language mode (Stewig, 1983). Both children and adults use it more frequently than writing, and children learn to talk before they learn to read and write. Talk is also the communication mode that all peoples around the world develop. Stewig reports that of the 2,796 languages spoken today, only a fraction of them—approximately 153—have developed written forms.

When they come to school, most children are fluent in oral language. They have had four or five years of extensive practice talking and listening. Because students have acquired basic oral language competencies, teachers often assume they do not need to emphasize talk in the elementary school curriculum. Research shows, however, that students benefit from participating in both informal and formal talk activities through-out the school day and that language is necessary for learning (Cazden, 1986; Golub, 1988; Heath, 1983). Students converse in peer groups when they work on projects, tell and discuss stories with classmates, participate in role-play activities, give reports for social studies and science units, and debate current events. Many of these talk activities are integrated with other language modes and content area subjects. For instance, to give an oral report related to a science unit, students research the topic by reading informational books and interviewing persons in the community with expertise on the topic. Students take notes and write key information on clusters or notecards in prep-aration for giving the report. They may also construct charts, models, and other visuals to use with their reports.

Heath (1983) questioned whether talk in elementary classrooms is "talk about nothing" and concluded that children's talk is an essential part of the language arts curriculum and is necessary for academic success in all content areas. Quiet classrooms are often considered the most conducive to learning even though research shows that talk is a necessary ingredient for learning. Klein (1979) argues that "talk opportunities must be consciously structured into [the language arts] curriculum and done so in the most likely manner to encourage children to use talk in a wide variety of contexts and for a variety of purposes" (p. 656).

Halliday (1973) stresses that elementary students need to learn to control all seven of the language functions (discussed in Chapter 1) to become competent language users. In her research, however, Pinnell (1975) found that some of the language func-tions did not occur as frequently as might be expected in many classrooms. In this chapter, we will discuss the three types of talk activities that represent the language functions. The three types are informal conversations and discussions; more formal debates, oral reports, and interviews; and drama, including dramatic play, role-playing, and storytelling. These talk activities have several benefits: they expand children's oral language skills; they develop students' abilities to use talk for a variety of language functions; and they work to dispel the fear most adults have about speaking before a group.

❖ INFORMAL TALK ACTIVITIES

Conversation and discussion are social activities involving exchange of ideas, informa-tion, opinions, and feelings about people, places, things, and events. They are the most basic forms of talk and should be more than incidental activities. Conversations take place in the classroom, on the playground, in the media center, during lunch—anywhere, anytime. Discussions, in contrast, are more planned and often deal with specific topics. Reading Stanley's *The Conversation Club* (1983) is a good way to introduce conversation activities. The book emphasizes the need for participants to listen to each other and to take turns talking. Students may want to organize their own conversation club after listening to the story.

Conversations

Teachers can hold conversations with students at odd moments during the day and may need to plan some special times to talk with quiet children or children who need extra attention. Teachers may find it helpful to have a list of topics to which they can refer when they want to plan a special time for conversations. These are possible topics:

What do you do in your free time?

What books do you like best?

Do you have a hobby?

What sports do you play (or would like to play)?

What games are your favorites?

Do you have a pet? Tell me about it.

What kind of work do you think you will do when you finish school?

If you could live anywhere in the world, where would it be?

What do you like to do on the weekends?

Have you been to any museums?

Do you like to travel? Where have you been?

What do you like to do with your brothers or sisters?

What makes you happy (or unhappy)?

Holding conversations with their students enables teachers to make them feel important, find out about their interests, likes and dislikes, and become their friend. Shuy (1987) says conversation is often thwarted in elementary classrooms because of large class size and the mistaken assumption that silence facilitates learning. Teachers must make an extra effort to provide opportunities for socialization and talk.

Teachers often group students in pairs and small groups to work on reading and math assignments and for projects in other content areas. As they work collaboratively, students naturally converse with their classmates whether they were encouraged to talk or not. Golub (1988) explains that "students are *supposed* to talk with each other as they work together on various classroom projects and activities" (p. 1). Wilkinson (1984) makes several observations about children's language use in small-group situations. She found that in their conversations, students use language representing several different language functions. They ask and answer questions using informative language, make requests to satisfy their own needs using instrumental language, and use regulatory

Students participate in informal talk throughout the school day.

language to control classmates' behavior. Students also use interactional and personal language as they talk informally.

Wilkinson identifies three characteristics of effective speakers in peer group conversations. Although she focuses on students' use of one language function, instrumental language, her findings may be generalized to the wider context of peer group conversations. Wilkinson found that effective speakers' comments were (1) directly and clearly stated to particular students, (2) related to the task at hand, and (3) interpreted as being sincere by classmates.

Wilkinson recommends that teachers "listen in" on students' conversations to learn about students' language competencies and their understanding of an assignment as well as their ability to work in peer groups. Teachers can identify students who are not effective speakers and plan additional group activities to develop their conversational skills.

Show-and-Tell

A daily sharing time is a familiar ritual in many kindergarten and primary-grade classrooms. Children bring favorite objects to school and talk about them. This is a nice bridge between home and school, and the value of show-and-tell is that children have something familiar to talk about.

If sharing time becomes repetitive, children lose interest, so teachers must play an active role to make it a worthwhile activity. Teachers can, for example, discuss the roles and responsibilities of both speakers and listeners. A second grade class developed the list of responsibilities for speakers and listeners shown in Figure 5−1. This list, with minor variations, has been used with students in upper grades as well.

Some children need prompting even if they have been advised to plan in advance two or three things to say about the object they have brought to school. It is tempting

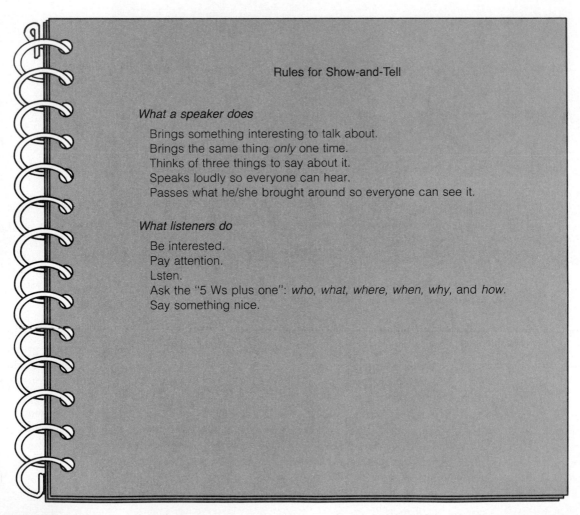

Rules for Show-and-Tell

What a speaker does

Brings something interesting to talk about.
Brings the same thing *only* one time.
Thinks of three things to say about it.
Speaks loudly so everyone can hear.
Passes what he/she brought around so everyone can see it.

What listeners do

Be interested.
Pay attention.
Lsten.
Ask the "5 Ws plus one": *who, what, where, when, why,* and *how.*
Say something nice.

FIGURE 5−1

Teacher's Notebook Page: Responsibilities of Speakers and Listeners for teachers to speed things up by asking questions and, without realizing it, to answer their own questions, especially for a very quiet child. Show-and-tell could go like this:

> *Teacher:* Jerry, what did you bring today?
>
> *Jerry:* (Holds up a stuffed bear.)
>
> *Teacher:* Is that a teddy bear?
>
> *Jerry:* Yeah.
>
> *Teacher:* Is it new?
>
> *Jerry:* (Shakes head yes.)
>
> *Teacher:* Can you tell us about your bear?
>
> *Jerry:* (Silence.)
>
> *Teacher:* Jerry, why don't you walk around and show your bear to everyone?

Jerry needed prompting, but the teacher in this example clearly dominated the conversation, and Jerry said only one word—"yeah." Two strategies may help. First, talk with children like Jerry and help them plan something to say. Second, invite listeners to ask the speakers the "5 Ws plus one" questions, also referred to as reporters' or journalists' questions: *what, who, when, where, why,* and *how.* It is crucial that the conversation be among the students!

Classmates should be the audience for show-and-tell activities, but often teachers become the focus (Cazden, 1988). To avoid this, teachers need to join the audience rather than direct the activity. They should also limit their comments and allow the student who is sharing to assume responsibility for the activity and the discussion that follows sharing. Student-sharers can ask three or four classmates for comments before choosing which student will share next. It is often difficult for teachers to share control of their classrooms, but students—even in kindergarten—are capable of handling the activity themselves.

Show-and-tell or sharing activities should continue throughout the elementary grades, because informal talk is a necessary part of classroom life (Camp & Tompkins, 1990). Many middle-grade teachers find the first few minutes of the day an appropriate time for sharing; often, the class becomes a more cohesive and caring group through sharing. Teachers of upper-grade students who change classes every 50 minutes must plan more carefully for sharing activities because of time constraints. Nonetheless, spending two or three minutes at the beginning of each class period in informal sharing, or planning a 50-minute, more formal sharing time every other week, will provide these needed opportunities.

Middle- and upper-grade students participate in sharing activities in much the same way as primary students do. Together students and teachers need to establish guidelines for sharing and discuss how students will prepare and present their show-and-tell. A brief oral presentation involves a process much like listening, reading, and writing do; a process of planning, presenting, and critiquing is recommended (Camp & Tompkins, 1990). Teachers should model a show-and-tell presentation for students by sharing hobbies or other interests.

Students first choose an object, experience, or current events topic to share and plan what information they will share about it. To encourage students to choose a meaningful topic for sharing, teachers can read *The Show-and-Tell War* (Smith, 1988). Students plan their presentation by deciding what they want to say, and clustering an effective planning strategy. In clustering, students draw a schematic diagram on a sheet of paper and list main ideas and details. They begin by writing the name of the topic in the center of the paper and drawing a circle around the word. Next, students draw lines or rays from the circle and list three, four, or five main ideas about the topic. They circle these words, then draw more lines from the circles and add details related to the main ideas. A sample cluster on porcelain dolls is presented in Figure 5–2. The main ideas and details are drawn out from the center. These clusters are used for gathering and organizing ideas during planning and as notes to refer to during the presentations.

Students' presentations are brief, usually lasting only a minute or two. They share their objects and experiences using the ideas gathered and organized during planning.

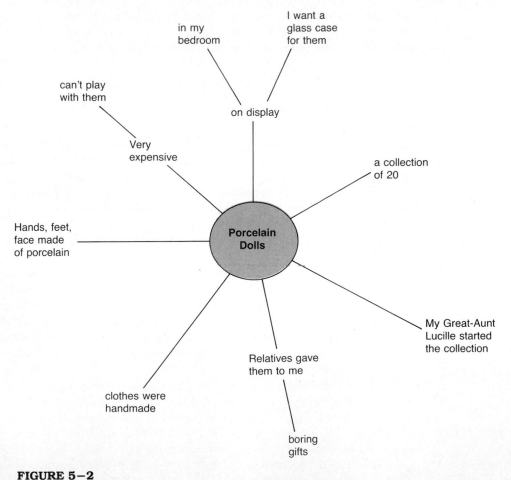

FIGURE 5–2

An Upper-Grade Student's Cluster for a Sharing Presentation

Students concentrate on speaking clearly and standing appropriately so as to not distract listeners. Older students who have not participated in sharing activities often find talking in front of their classmates intimidating. The planning step is crucial to a successful presentation. Other students should listen effectively by paying attention, asking pertinent questions, and responding to the speaker nonverbally. After the talk, listeners may ask questions to clarify and expand the speaker's comments.

The third component of show-and-tell is critiquing, when teachers and students discuss and critique the presentations using the guidelines in Figure 5–1. These guidelines can be converted into a checklist that both speakers and listeners can complete for each presentation. Through the checklists and discussion, students learn how to give interesting presentations and gain confidence in their ability to speak in front of a group.

Show-and-tell can evolve into an informal type of oral report for middle-grade students. When used effectively, older students gain valuable practice talking in an informal and nonthreatening situation. Beginning as a sharing activity, students' talk about a collection of shark's teeth, a program from an Ice Capades Show, a recently found snakeskin, or snapshots of a vacation at Yellowstone National Park can lead to informal dramatics, reading, and writing activities. One student may act out dances recalled from the Ice Capades Show; another student may point out the location of Yellowstone National Park on a map or check an almanac for more information about the park. A third student may write about the prized collection of shark's teeth and how they were collected. Experience plus oral rehearsal help students gear up for other language activities.

Discussions

Discussions are an effective means of helping students learn to express themselves in small groups or in whole class settings. They are usually more purposeful than conversations, and teachers often play an important role by asking questions and moderating the discussion. Dillon (1983) recommends that teachers ask questions "only when you are personally perplexed and you need the information in answer" (p. 21). This recommendation flies in the face of conventional practice in elementary classrooms. Most of the time, teachers ask questions at a rote-memory level for which they know the answer, to assess students' understanding.

Wilen (1986) reviewed the research about questioning strategies and offers these suggestions:

Ask carefully planned questions to organize and direct the lesson.

Ask single questions that are clearly phrased, rather than vaguely worded or multiple questions.

Ask questions in a planned sequence.

Ask factual questions to check basic understanding, but focus on higher-level questions that give students opportunities to think critically and creatively.

Ask questions to follow up students' responses.

Give students sufficient time to think about questions and plan their responses.

Encourage wide participation through interaction among students, drawing in nonvolunteers, and seating students in a circle.

Promote student involvement by having students create questions to ask, lead the discussion, and follow up ideas developed during the discussion.

Researchers have classified questions into cognitive levels. Bloom (1956) developed a scheme of six hierarchical classes, ranging from simple to complex intellectual abilities: knowledge, comprehension, application, analysis, synthesis, and evaluation. Similarly, Guilford (1956) identified five major groups of mental operations: cognition, memory, convergent thinking, divergent thinking, and evaluation. Gallagher and Aschner (1963) developed a four-point category system based on Guilford's model to investigate the interaction between teachers and students. The four categories can be used to classify questions as well: (1) cognitive memory, in which students recite facts or information remembered through rote; (2) convergent thinking, in which students analyze and integrate remembered information; (3) divergent thinking, in which students independently generate information or take a new direction; and (4) evaluative thinking, in which students choose among alternatives and make judgments. In the first two of these categories, there is one expected or "right" answer, and in the third and fourth categories, students' responses are more open-ended. Teachers can compare the questions they prepare for classroom discussions against these categories to gauge the level of mental operations they require of their students.

Discussions About Literature.   Discussions often accompany reading aloud to students or having them read silently. There are many books that stimulate discussions and talk activities for young children; for instance, Burningham's *Would You Rather. . .* (1979) invites primary-grade students to consider and talk about silly and absurd possibilities; older students are challenged to create stories for Van Allsburg's *The Mysteries of Harris Burdick* (1984). A list of books that encourage talk appears in Figure 5–3.

Middle- and upper-grade students often participate in discussions about the chapter-length books they are reading. Books such as *Tuck Everlasting* (Babbitt, 1975), *How to Eat Fried Worms* (Rockwell, 1975), and *The One-Eyed Cat* (Fox, 1984) are conducive to lively discussions. Too often, however, the teacher takes the role of leader rather than participant in discussions. Rather than asking questions to stimulate a deeper understanding of the text and students' responses to it, teachers often ask questions to assess comprehension. Higgins (quoted in Eeds & Wells, 1989) describes typical discussion groups this way: "What you most often get are gentle inquisitions, when what you really want are grand conversations" (p. 4).

To have "grand conversations," teachers must participate in discussions to learn rather than to judge. There are no right answers to most of the questions teachers and students ask; rather, participants use relevant personal experiences to reflect on their reading both critically and creatively. Students keep copies of the books they are reading handy to check specific incidents, ask questions, and support their comments. The group becomes a community of learners in these discussions, in which participants share personal responses to literature and create a social response.

Ahlberg, J. & Ahlberg, A. (1978). *Each peach pear plum: An "I spy" story.* New York: Scholastic.(P)

Anno, M. (1970). *Topsy turvies: Pictures to stretch the imagination.* New York: Walker. (P-M)

Baylor, B. (1974). *Everybody needs a rock.* New York: Atheneum. (M-U)

Baylor, B. (1977). *Guess who my favorite person is.* New York: Atheneum. (M-U)

Blume, J. (1974). *The pain and the great one.* New York: Bradbury Press. (M)

Brown, M. (1983). *Perfect pigs: An introduction to manners.* Boston: Little, Brown.(P)

Brown, M. W. (1949). *The important book.* New York: Harper and Row. (P-M)

Burningham, J. (1977). *Come away from the water, Shirley.* New York: Harper and Row. (M-U)

Burningham, J. (1979). *Would you rather . . .* New York: Crowell. (P)

Degan, B. (1983). *Jamberry.* New York: Harper and Row. (P)

Gardner, B. (1984). *The look again . . . and again, and again, and again book.* New York: Lothrop. (P)

Heide, F. P. (1971). *The shrinking of Treehorn.* New York: Holiday House. (M-U)

Hoban, T. (1971). *Look again!* New York: Macmillan. (P)

Hoguet, S. R. (1983). *I unpacked my grandmother's trunk: A picture book game.* New York: Dutton. (P-M)

Kroll, S. (1976). *The tyrannosaurus game.* New York: Holiday House. (P-M)

Martin, B. Jr., & Archambault, J. (1988). *Listen to the rain.* New York: Henry Holt. (P-M-U)

Martin, B. Jr., & Archambault, J. (1990). *Chicka chicka boom boom.* New York: Henry Holt. (P)

Numeroff, L. J. (1985). *If you give a mouse a cookie.* New York: Harper and Row. (P-M)

Scheer, J. (1964). *Rain makes applesauce.* New York: Holiday House. (M)

Silverstein, S. (1964). *The giving tree.* New York: Harper and Row. (M-U)

Strauss, J. (1984). *Imagine that!!! Exploring make-believe.* Chicago: Human Sciences Press. (P-M-U)

Van Allsburg, C. (1981). *Jumanji.* Boston: Houghton Mifflin. (P-M)

Van Allsburg, C. (1984). *The mysteries of Harris Burdick.* Boston: Houghton Mifflin. (M-U)

Wood, A. (1982). *Quick as a cricket.* London: Child's Play. (P-M)

Zolotow, C. (1967). *Summer is . . .* New York: Crowell. (P-M)

FIGURE 5—3

Books that Encourage Talk
P = primary grades (K–2)
M = middle grades (3–5)
U = upper grades (6–8)

The teacher can develop questions for discussion groups, or students can develop their own according to the guidelines mentioned earlier. Reardon (1988) reports that her third graders write their own questions, and the discussion group spends the first few minutes of group time considering the questions and deciding which ones to actually use. A fifth grader developed these questions for a discussion of *Do Bananas Chew Gum?* (Gilson, 1980):

> I wonder if Sam ever learned how to read. How could he learn?
>
> I wonder why Sam had a reading problem. What do you think? Why did people hate Alicia?
>
> I wonder why they called the book *Do Bananas Chew Gum?*
>
> What would you have called the book? Why?
>
> Do you think Alicia gets braces? Would you want braces?
>
> Do you think Sam has other friends besides Alicia and Wally? Who?
>
> I wonder if Sam ever gets fired from baby-sitting. Do you?
>
> Would you fire him? Why or why not? (Fiderer, 1988, pp. 60–61)

As the student developed the questions, she checked that they could not be answered with "yes" or "no" and that they required her classmates to give a personal opinion.

From their observational study of fifth and sixth graders conducting "grand conversations" about literature, Eeds and Wells (1989) found that, through talk, students extend their individual interpretations of their reading and even create a better understanding of it. They talk about their understanding of the story and can change their opinions after listening to classmates' alternative views. Students share personal stories related to their reading in poignant ways that trigger other students to identify with them. They are active readers who use prediction as they read. The students also gain insights about how authors use the elements of story structure to develop their message.

Content Area Discussions.   Other discussions grow out of content area study. Issues such as pollution, nuclear weapons, and apartheid are interesting, compelling topics for discussion. Students gather information for the discussion through reading textbooks, informational books, and newspapers and watching television news reports and films. As they participate in discussions—offering information, considering other points of view, searching for additional information to support opinions, and listening to alternative viewpoints—students learn social skills as well as content area information.

❖ INTERPRETIVE TALK ACTIVITIES

In interpretive talk activities, teachers and students do not create the material; rather, they interpret others' ideas and words (Busching, 1981). Two types of interpretive drama that involve students in interpreting literature are storytelling and readers theater.

Storytelling

Storytelling is an ancient art that is a valuable instructional tool. Not only should teachers share literature with their students using storytelling techniques, but students can and should tell stories, too. Storytelling is entertaining and stimulates children's imaginations. It expands their language abilities and helps them internalize the characteristics of stories (Morrow, 1985). Storytelling involves four steps: choosing a story, preparing to tell it, adding props, and telling the story.

Traditional stories, such as folktales, are often chosen for storytelling activities; however, any type of literature can be used. The most important consideration in choosing a story is to select a story you like and want to tell. Morrow (1979) lists other considerations:

The story has a simple, well-rounded plot.

The story has a clear beginning, middle, and end.

The story has an underlying theme.

The story has a small number of well-defined characters.

The story contains dialogue.

The story uses repetition.

The story uses colorful language or "catch phrases."

Figure 5–4 lists stories that contain many of these characteristics. Children can also create and tell stories to accompany wordless picture books. For example, Tomie de Paola's *Pancakes for Breakfast* (1978) is the charming story of a little old woman who tries to cook pancakes for breakfast but runs into a series of problems as she tries to assemble the ingredients. In the end, her neighbors invite her to their home for pancakes. The repetition of events in this story makes it easy for primary grade children to tell. For additional sources of stories, check Caroline Bauer's *Handbook for Storytellers* (1977).

It is not necessary to memorize a story to tell it effectively. Kingore (1982) lists the following six steps as preparation for storytelling:

1. Choose a story you really like.
2. Memorizing is not necessary. Just read the story a few times to get a "feel" for the sequence and major events in the story.
3. Plan interesting phrases or repeated phrases to enliven the language of your story.
4. Plan simple props or gestures to increase your audience's interest.
5. Prepare a brief introduction that relates the story to your audience's experiences.
6. Practice telling your story in front of a mirror. (p. 29)

This process can be abbreviated when very young children tell stories. They may choose a story they already know well and make props to guide the telling. (Try a set of puppets representing the main characters or a series of drawings.) They are then ready to tell their stories.

Several techniques can make the story come alive as it is told. Morrow (1979) describes three types of props that add variety and interest to stories:

Flannel board—place drawings or pictures cut from books and backed with flannel on the flannel board as the story is told.

Aardema, V. (1975). *Why mosquitoes buzz in people's ears.* New York: Dial. (M-U)

Andersen, H. C. (1965). *The nightingale.* New York: Harper. (U)

Brown, M. (1947). *Stone soup.* New York: Scribner. (P-M-U)

Brown, M. (1972). *The runaway bunny.* New York: Harper. (P)

Carle, E. (1970). *The very hungry caterpillar.* Cleveland: Collins-World. (P)

Flack, M. (1932). *Ask Mr. Bear.* New York: Macmillan. (P)

Gag, W. (1956). *Millions of cats.* New York: Coward McCann. (P)

Galdone, P. (1973). *The three billy goats Gruff.* Boston: Houghton Mifflin. (P)

Gipson, M. (1975). *Rip Van Winkle.* New York: Doubleday. (M-U)

Grimm, The Brothers. (1971). *The Bremen town musicians.* New York: Greenwillow. (M-U)

Hague, K., & Hague, M. (1980). *East of the sun and west of the moon.* New York: Harcourt. (U)

Hastings, S. (1985). *Sir Gawain and the loathly lady.* New York: Mulberry. (U)

Hyman, T. S. (1983). *Little red riding hood.* New York: Holiday House. (P-M-U)

Kellogg, S. (1973). *The island of the skog.* New York: Dial. (M)

Lionni, L. (1969). *Alexander and the wind-up mouse.* New York: Pantheon. (M)

Lobel, A. (1977). *How the rooster saved the day.* New York: Greenwillow. (M)

Low, J. (1980) *Mice twice.* New York: Atheneum. (M)

Martin, B., Jr., & Archambault, J. (1985). *The ghost-eye tree.* New York: Holt. (M-U)

Mayer, M. (1978). *Beauty and the beast.* New York: Macmillan. (U)

Numeroff, L. J. (1985). *If you give a mouse a cookie.* New York: Harper. (P-M-U)

Slobodkina, E. (1947). *Caps for sale.* New York: Scott. (P)

Steig, W. (1982). *Doctor DeSoto.* New York: Farrar. (M)

Still, J. (1977). *Jack and the wonder beans.* New York: Putnam. (M)

Thurber, J. (1974). *Many moons.* New York: Harcourt. (P-M-U)

Zemach, H., & Zemach, M. (1973). *Duffy and the devil.* New York: Farrar. (M-U)

Zemach, M. (1976). *It could always be worse.* New York: Farrar. (P-M-U)

FIGURE 5–4

Stories for Elementary Students to Tell

Puppets — use puppets representing the main characters to tell a story with dialogue. (For ideas on how to construct puppets, check the section in this chapter on puppets.)

Objects — use stuffed animals to represent animal characters or other small objects to represent important things in the story being told. Try, for instance, using a pile of caps in telling Slobodkina's *Caps for Sale* (1947) or a small gold ball for Thurber's *Many Moons* (1974).

Students tell the stories they have prepared to small groups of their classmates or to younger children. Try dividing the audience into small groups so that more students can tell stories at one time.

Readers Theater

Readers theater is "a formalized dramatic presentation of a script by a group of readers" (Busching, 1981, p. 330). Students each assume a role and read the character's lines in the script. The reader's responsibility is to interpret a story without using much action. Students may stand or sit, but must carry the whole communication of the plot, characterization, mood, and theme by using their voices, gestures, and facial expressions.

Readers theater avoids many of the restrictions inherent in theatrical productions. Students do not memorize their parts; elaborate props, costumes, and backdrops are not needed; and long, tedious hours are not spent rehearsing. Three steps in developing readers theater presentations are selecting a script, rehearsing the play, and staging the play.

Quality play scripts exhibit the same characteristics as do other types of fine literature. Manna (1984) lists five essential characteristics: an interesting story, a well-paced plot, recognizable and believable characters, plausible language, and a distinct style. The arrangement of the text on the page is also an important consideration when selecting a script. There should be a clear distinction between stage directions and dialogue through adequate spacing and by varying the print types and colors. This distinction is especially important for primary-grade students and for older students who are not familiar with the script format.

Readers theater is a relatively new idea, and the number of quality scripts available is limited, although more are being published each year. Play scripts in basal reading textbooks are another source of material for readers theater presentations. Some of the scripts currently available are Gackenback's *Hattie, Tom and the Chicken Witch* (1980), Dahl's *Charlie and the Chocolate Factory* (George, 1976), *Plays from African Folktales* (Korty, 1975), and Laurie's *Children's Plays from Beatrix Potter* (1980).

Students can also prepare their own scripts for readers theater from books of children's literature. Laughlin and Latrobe (1989) suggest that students begin by reading the entire book and thinking about its theme, characters, and plot. Next they choose a scene or scenes to script. Students make copies of the scene and use felt-tip pens to highlight the dialogue. They then adapt the scene by adding narrators' lines to bridge gaps, set the scene, and summarize. Students assume roles and read the script aloud, revising and experimenting with new text until they are satisfied with the script. The final version is typed, duplicated, and stapled into pamphlets. Some of the stories that Laughlin and Latrobe recommend are presented in Figure 5–5.

Begin by assigning readers for each character and a narrator, if the script calls for one. Read through the play once or twice, then stop to discuss the story. Busching (1981) recommends using the "5 Ws plus one" questions—*who, what, where, when, why,* and *how*—to probe students' understanding. Through this discussion, students gain a clearer understanding of the story and decide how to interpret their characters.

After students decide how to use their voice, gestures, and facial expressions to interpret the characters, they should read the script one or two more times, striving for accurate pronunciation, voice projection, and appropriate inflections. Obviously, less rehearsal is needed for an informal, in-class presentation than for a more formal production; nevertheless, interpretations should always be developed as fully as possible.

Atwater, R., & Atwater, F. (1938). *Mr. Popper's penguins*. Boston: Little, Brown. (M)

Babbitt, N. (1975). *Tuck everlasting*. New York: Farrar. (U)

Brittain, B. (1983). *The wish giver*. New York: Harper. (M-U)

Burch, R. (1980). *Ida Early comes over the mountain*. New York: Viking. (M)

Byars, B. (1981). *The Cybil war*. New York: Viking. (M-U)

Cleary, B. (1975). *Ramona and her father*. New York: Morrow. (M)

Cohen, B. (1974). *Thank you, Jackie Robinson*. New York: Lothrop. (M-U)

Fleischman, S. (1986). *The whipping boy*. New York: Greenwillow. (M-U)

Lewis, C. S. (1950). *The lion, the witch, and the wardrobe*. New York: Macmillan. (M-U)

MacLachlan, P. (1985). *Sarah, plain and tall*. New York: Harper. (M)

Milne, A. A. (1974). *Winnie-the-Pooh*. New York: Dutton. (P-M)

Rockwell, T. (1973). *How to eat fried worms*. New York: Watts. (M-U)

Sebestyen, O. (1979). *Words by heart*. Boston: Little, Brown. (U)

Stolz, M. (1960). *A dog on Barkham Street*. New York: Harper. (M)

Wallace, B. (1980). *A dog called Kitty*. New York: Holiday House. (M)

FIGURE 5–5

Stories that Can be Scripted for Readers Theater

Readers theater can be presented on a stage or in a corner of the classroom. Students stand or sit in a row and read their lines in the script. They must stay in position through the presentation or enter and leave according to the characters' appearances "on stage." If readers are sitting, they may stand to read their lines; if they are standing, they may step forward to read. The emphasis is not on production quality; rather, it is on the interpretive quality of the readers' voices and expressions. Costumes and props are unnecessary; however, adding a few enhances interest and enjoyment, as long as they do not interfere with the interpretive quality of the reading.

❖ MORE FORMAL TALK ACTIVITIES

For more formal talk activities, children use a process approach in which they prepare and organize their talks before giving them. These more formal, planned occasions grow out of informal talk. Three types are oral reports, interviews, and debates.

Oral Reports

Learning how to prepare and present an oral report is an important language skill for middle- and upper-grade students. But students are often simply assigned to give an oral report without any classroom preparation. Without guidance, they simply copy the report verbatim from an encyclopedia and then read it aloud. The result is that students learn to fear speaking in front of a group instead of building confidence in their oral language abilities.

We will focus on the steps in teaching students how to prepare and present two types of oral reports. The first type includes research reports on social studies or science topics, such as Native Americans, the solar system, or Canada. The second type includes book reviews, television shows, and movies. These oral reports have genuine language functions—to inform or to persuade.

Research Reports. Students can prepare and give research reports about topics they are studying in social studies, science, and other content areas. Giving a report orally helps students to learn about topics in specific content areas as well as to develop their communication abilities. Students need more than just an assignment to prepare a report for presentation on a particular date; they need to learn how to prepare and present research reports. The four steps in preparing reports are choosing a topic, gathering information, organizing information, and making the presentation.

The class begins by choosing a topic for the reports. For example, if a second grade class is studying the human body, then each student might select a different part of the body for a report. After students have chosen their topics, they need to inventory, or think over, what they know about the topic and decide what they need to learn about it. Students can learn to focus on the key points for their reports in several ways. One strategy is to create a cluster with the topic written and circled in the center of a piece of paper. The key points are drawn out from the topic like rays from the sun. Then students write the details on rays drawn from each main idea, as we mentioned in Chapter 4. (For more information about clustering, see Chapter 6.) Another strategy is a data chart, wherein the teacher provides a chart listing three or more key points to guide students as they gather information for their reports (McKenzie, 1979). Figure 5−6 shows a cluster and data chart for a report on a part of

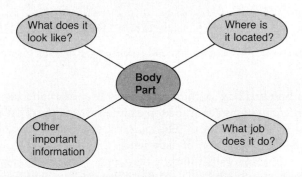

Human Body Report Data Chart				
Source of Information	What does it look like?	Where is it located?	What job does it do?	Other important information

FIGURE 5−6

A Cluster and Data Chart

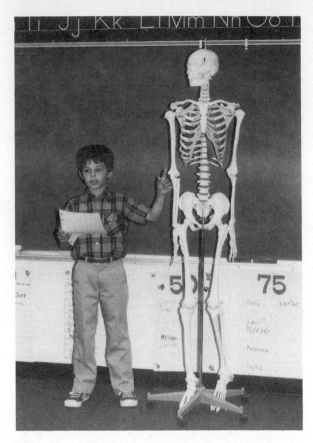

This student is presenting an oral report on the lungs to his classmates, using a skeleton as a prop.

the human body. A third strategy is brainstorming ideas for possible key points by asking questions about the topic prefaced with the "5 Ws plus one": *who, what, when, where, why,* and *how.* The number and complexity of the key points depend on students' age or level of experience.

Students gather information using a variety of reference materials, including, but not limited to, informational books, magazines, newspapers, encyclopedias, almanacs, and atlases. Encyclopedias are a valuable resource, but they are only one possible source, and other reference materials must be available. In addition to print sources, students can view filmstrips, films, and videotapes and can interview people in the community who have special expertise on the topic. For students who have had limited experience locating information in a library, a class trip to the school and public libraries to collect reference materials is useful.

Elementary students are not too young to understand what *plagiarism* is and why it is wrong. Even primary-grade students understand that they should not "borrow" items belonging to classmates and pretend they are theirs. Similarly, students should not "borrow" or "steal" someone's words, especially without asking permission or giving credit in the composition. Writing key words and phrases on clusters or data charts helps students learn to take notes without copying entire sentences and paragraphs from reference books.

The preliminary organization — deciding on the key points — completed in the first step gives direction for gathering the information. Now students review the information they have gathered and decide how best to present it so that the report will be both interesting and well organized. Students can transfer the "notes" they want to use for their reports from the cluster or data chart onto notecards. Only key words — not sentences or paragraphs — should be written on the cards.

Students may also develop visuals such as charts, diagrams, maps, pictures, models, and timelines. For example, the second graders who gave reports on parts of the body made drawings and clay models of the parts and used a large skeleton hanging in the classroom to show the location of the organ in the body. Visuals provide a "crutch" for the speaker and add an element of interest for the listeners.

The final step is to rehearse and then give the presentation. Students can rehearse several times by reviewing key points and reading over their notecards. They should not, however, read the report verbatim from the notecards. Students might want to choose a particularly interesting fact to begin the presentation.

Before the presentations begin, discuss the important things speakers should remember. For instance, speakers should talk loudly enough for all to hear, keep to the key points, refer to their notecards for important facts, and use the visuals they have prepared.

Through these four steps, elementary students can learn to prepare and present well-organized and interesting reports. The steps are summarized in Figure 5–7.

Book Talks. Students give oral reports to review books they have read or television shows and films they have viewed. Remember, however, that oral reports are only one way to respond to literature; other ideas for sharing and responding include informal dramatics, storytelling, art, and writing activities. The steps in preparing and presenting reviews are similar to those for informational reports:

1. Read or view the selection.
2. Select information for the report, including a brief summary of the selection and bibliographic information; comparisons to other selections (e.g., with similar themes, written by the same author, starring the same actor); strengths and weaknesses; and opinions and conclusions.
3. Record and organize the information on a cluster and then copy key words onto notecards.
4. Briefly rehearse the review.
5. Give the presentation, referring to the notecards but not reading them verbatim.

Interviews

Almost all children see interviews on television news programs and are familiar with the interviewing techniques reporters use. Interviewing is an exciting, real-life com-

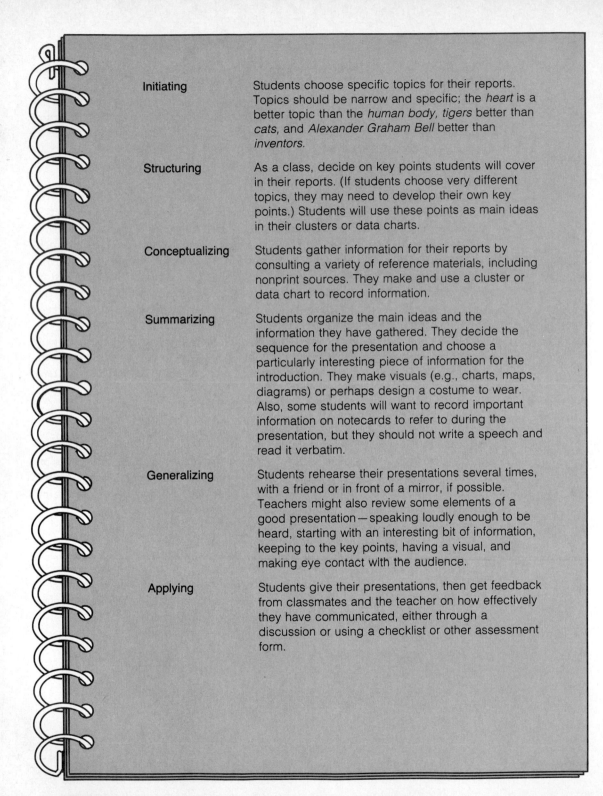

Initiating	Students choose specific topics for their reports. Topics should be narrow and specific; the *heart* is a better topic than the *human body*, *tigers* better than *cats*, and *Alexander Graham Bell* better than *inventors*.
Structuring	As a class, decide on key points students will cover in their reports. (If students choose very different topics, they may need to develop their own key points.) Students will use these points as main ideas in their clusters or data charts.
Conceptualizing	Students gather information for their reports by consulting a variety of reference materials, including nonprint sources. They make and use a cluster or data chart to record information.
Summarizing	Students organize the main ideas and the information they have gathered. They decide the sequence for the presentation and choose a particularly interesting piece of information for the introduction. They make visuals (e.g., charts, maps, diagrams) or perhaps design a costume to wear. Also, some students will want to record important information on notecards to refer to during the presentation, but they should not write a speech and read it verbatim.
Generalizing	Students rehearse their presentations several times, with a friend or in front of a mirror, if possible. Teachers might also review some elements of a good presentation—speaking loudly enough to be heard, starting with an interesting bit of information, keeping to the key points, having a visual, and making eye contact with the audience.
Applying	Students give their presentations, then get feedback from classmates and the teacher on how effectively they have communicated, either through a discussion or using a checklist or other assessment form.

FIGURE 5–7

Teacher's Notebook Page: Using the Teaching Strategy for Oral Reports

munication activity that helps students refine questioning skills and practice all four language modes—listening, talking, reading, and writing (Haley-James & Hodson, 1980).

Interviewing is an important language tool that can be integrated effectively with almost any area of the curriculum. Primary-grade students, for instance, can interview community helpers as part of a social studies unit on the community, and older students can interview long-time area residents about local history. Students can also interview people who live far away, such as a favorite author, legislator, or Olympic athlete, using a long-distance telephone conference call.

One way to introduce interviewing is to watch interviews conducted on a television newscast and discuss the purpose of the interview, what a reporter does before and after an interview, and what types of questions are asked. Interviewers use a variety of questions, some to elicit facts and others to probe for feelings and opinions, but all questions are open-ended. Rarely do they ask questions that require only a *yes* or *no* answer.

Interviewing involves far more than the actual interview. There are three steps in the interview process: planning the interview, conducting it, and sharing the results. The first step, planning, requires arranging for the interview and developing a list of questions to ask. The second step is the interview itself. Students conduct the interview by asking questions they have prepared in advance and taking notes or tape-recording the answers. In the third step, sharing the results, the interviewer prepares a report based on the information he or she has learned. The report can take many different forms, ranging from oral reports to class newspapers to published booklets. The activities in each of the three steps are outlined in Figure 5–8.

Teaching Students to Interview.   Students need to practice developing and asking questions before they interview people outside the classroom. One way to get this practice is to interview classmates. The proverbial "How I Spent My Summer Vacation" report that teachers have students give during the first few days of school can be turned into an interviewing opportunity. Have the class, as a group, brainstorm a list of possible questions, then pair students to interview each other about their summer activities. They can then report their interviews to the class. Other topics for class interviews include favorite films, hobbies, or games.

Next, invite someone, such as a police officer, the manager of a local fast-food restaurant, or a television news reporter, to visit the classroom and be interviewed. Have students follow the three-step interview process. Instruct them to prepare in advance for the interview by developing a list of questions and deciding who will greet the visitor and how the questions will be asked. After the interview, work together to prepare a class collaboration or group report about the interview to publish in the class or community newspaper.

A class interview is a useful practice activity for all students, but it is an especially valuable introduction to interviewing for kindergartners and first graders. After studying interviewing skills, for example, a class of first graders invited the local high school principal to visit their class to be interviewed. The principal, who had been blinded several years earlier, brought his guide dog with him. The children asked him questions about how visually impaired people manage everyday tasks as well as how he per-

Planning the Interview

Make arrangements for the interview.

Brainstorm a list of questions to ask the person being interviewed.

Write the questions on notecards, using one card for each question. Be sure the questions are open-ended, not *yes* or *no* questions.

Organize the notecards so you can ask related questions together.

Read over the questions, making sure they will elicit the information you are seeking.

Conducting the Interview

After a friendly greeting, explain the reason for the interview and begin asking the questions.

Allow the person you are interviewing to answer each question fully before you ask another question.

Ask follow-up questions about points that are not clear.

If the answer to one question brings up another question that has not been written down, do not hesitate to ask it.

Be polite and respectful of the answers and opinions of the person you are interviewing.

Take notes on the notecards or take notes and tape-record the interview.

Limit the time for the interview.

Thank the person for participating in the interview.

Sharing the Results

Read over the notes or listen to the tape recording of the interview.

Organize the information collected during the interview.

Share the results of the interview through an oral or written report, a newspaper article, or another type of presentation.

FIGURE 5–8

Steps in the Interview Process

formed his job as a principal. They also asked questions about his guide dog. After the interview, students drew pictures and wrote summaries of the interview. One first grader's report is shown in Figure 5–9.

To follow up an interview, children discuss what they have learned through the interview or dictate a report for the teacher to print on the chalkboard. Later, the report can be written on chart paper or photocopies of it can be made to which each child adds drawings.

Students can conduct interviews with family members and other members of the community on a variety of topics. One of the most interesting topics is community histories popularized by the Foxfire project (Wigginton, 1985). Cooper's *Who Put the*

Mr. Kirtley came down. We asked him questions. He answered them. He is blind. His dog's name is Milo.

FIGURE 5—9

A First Grader's Interview Summary
Tomara, age 7

Cannon in the Courthouse Square? A Guide to Uncovering the Past (1985) and Weitzman's *My Backyard History Book* (1975) are excellent books to use with students in planning a community history project. Students work individually or in small groups to interview long-time residents about the community's history, growth and changes, modes of dress, transportation, communication, types of work, and ways to have fun.

After gathering information through interviews, they write reports that are published in a class or community newspaper or in a book.

Debates

Debates are useful when the whole class is excited about an issue and most or all of the students have taken supporting or opposing positions. The class decides what the issue is, clarifies it, and identifies positions that support or oppose the issue. Students who wish to speak in favor of the issue move to a side of the room designated for supporters, and students who wish to speak against the issue move to the other side. Class members who have not formulated a position sit in the middle of the room. When anyone wishes to participate, he or she goes to the side of the room for the position he or she supports. After hearing arguments, students may change their minds and move to the opposite side of the room; if they are no longer certain what side they are on, they may take a seat in the middle. The teacher initiates the debate by asking someone from the supporting side of the issue to state that side. After the opening statement, the opposing side makes a statement. From then on, each side takes turns making statements. It is permissible to ask someone who has just made a statement a question before a side makes a return statement. Sixth graders who used this informal debate procedure in their social studies class enjoyed the experience and furthered their abilities to express themselves effectively.

A more formal type of debate is appropriate for students in the upper-elementary grades. Debates take the form of arguments between opposing sides of a proposition. A *proposition* is a debate subject that can be discussed from opposing points of view; for example:

> Resolved, that students should have a role in setting standards of behavior in classes and in disciplining those students who disrupt classes.

After determining the proposition, teams of two to four students each are designated to support the proposition (the affirmative team) or oppose it (the negative team). Depending on the number of members on each team, this is the order of debate:

1. The first and third statements support the proposition.
2. The second and fourth statements reject the proposition.
3. The first and third rebuttal statements are made by the affirmative team.
4. The second and fourth rebuttal statements are made by the negative team.

Each member makes both a statement about the proposition and a rebuttal statement to the opposite team. Normally there are as many rebuttal statements as there are statements about the proposition. Teachers may vary the procedure to fit the class and their purposes. Students can also choose judges to determine the winning team.

If judges evaluate the debates, let students decide the criteria for judging. Have them brainstorm questions that will form the basis for their criteria. Questions similar to the following might initiate the brainstorming sessions:

Did the speakers communicate their ideas to listeners?

Was a mastery of information evident in the presentations and rebuttals?

Was there evidence that the speakers knew the topic well?

Was the team courteous?

Did the team work cooperatively?

Did the second speaker on each team pick up and extend the statement of the first team member?

Students may want to interview the high school debating team for ideas on judging and presenting their topics. They might also enjoy attending a high school debate.

❖ DRAMATIC ACTIVITIES

Drama provides a medium for students to use language, both verbal and nonverbal, in a meaningful context. Drama is not only a powerful form of communication, but also a valuable way of knowing. When children participate in dramatic activities, they interact with classmates, share experiences, and explore their own understanding. According to Dorothy Heathcote, a highly acclaimed British drama teacher, drama "cracks the code" so the message can be understood (Wagner, 1976). Drama has this power because it involves both logical, left-brain and creative, right-brain thinking; it requires active experience (the basic, first way of learning); and integrates the four language modes. Recent research confirms that drama has a positive effect both on elementary students' oral language development and their literacy learning (Kardash & Wright, 1987; Wagner, 1988). Drama is often neglected, however, because some consider it a nonessential part of the language arts curriculum.

Dramatic activities range from young children's dramatic play to scripted plays that students produce. Students create imaginary worlds through their drama, and they increase their understanding of themselves and the world in which they live (Booth, 1985; Kukla, 1987). These activities can be grouped into four categories that are distinguishable from one another in three significant ways: spontaneity, process versus product orientation, and level of formality. The four categories are dramatic play, informal drama, interpretive drama, and theatrical productions.

Young children's natural, make-believe play activities are called *dramatic play*. This kind of drama is spontaneous, unrehearsed, process-oriented, and extremely informal.

Informal drama includes activities "in which students invent and enact dramatic situations" (NCTE, 1983, p. 370). Informal drama is the natural outgrowth of dramatic play. Like dramatic play, it is spontaneous, unrehearsed, process-oriented, and informal. Informal drama activities include dramatizing stories and role-playing.

Interpretive dramatic activities are those in which students interpret literature using voice, facial features, and gestures. Interpretive drama involves some rehearsal and is somewhat formal. It is a transition between informal drama and theatrical productions; examples include storytelling and readers theater. Participating in these ac-

❖ "PRO" FILE

DEBATES

"Debates are one way I encourage my students to become independent thinkers and to see another point of view."

Pat Daniel, Sixth Grade Teacher,
South Rock Creek School

PROCEDURE

We brainstorm possible debate topics, and the class votes to narrow our list: more sports for students, the Loch Ness Monster, soft drink machines for students, and women for president. My students enjoy defending answers, presenting logical reasons, or sharing their creative thought processes. I capitalize on the fact that they are entering a developmental stage ripe for questioning authority. Debates provide a supportive, appropriate environment for testing their ideas. Careful preparation allows students to build sound arguments and build confidence in expressing their opinions.

Students select the topic they want to debate. They divide into "pro" and "con" teams of three or four members each. Some groups have to choose numbers to form the teams; consequently, some students debated against the way they believed. The groups prepare for the debate by interviewing students, administrators, parents, and teachers; researching information in the library; and developing charts to present the data they

collect. I provide in-class time for the students to prepare. We talk about how to present information and how to be persuasive.

One debate is held each day. Each debate takes about 20 minutes, so all debates can be held within a week's time. Students arrange a podium in the front of the classroom; the podium divides the pro and con teams. Students hang their charts and other visuals on the wall behind the podium for easy reference. Another student is chosen as moderator, who opens and closes the debate. The moderator states the question in debate format; for example, "Should there be more sports for students at South Rock Creek School?" The first member of the pro team presents a prepared statement, referring to notecards. These remarks are followed by a response from the con team. Students alternate until each student has spoken once. Then comes the rebuttal—a time that students really need to think on their feet. The rebuttal is more freewheeling. I allow it to continue as long as someone has something to say—usually about ten minutes. Students have learned that comments such as "out of the ball park" or "you're wrong" are not polite. They quickly learn to substitute facts for emotional responses. The moderator closes with a statement such as "That concludes our debate."

ASSESSMENT

The students develop a list of criteria that the judges — three community members — use in assessing each student's performance in the debate and deciding the "winning" team. The winning team is the one that earns more overall points. The checklist for one debate is shown.

REFLECTIONS

I believe in using talk in my classroom, particularly debates. My students learn to take a stand and to marshall facts to support their position. They also learn about the power of language to solve real problems in their lives.

DEBATE

Resolved: there should be more sports for students at South Rock Creek School.

Rating Code:

1–5; 5 = highest, 1 = lowest

Pro	Appearance	Delivery	Factual information	Keeping to the point	Persuasiveness	Teamwork	Participation in rebuttal	Total
Sundee Aday	___	___	___	___	___	___	___	___
James Zientek	___	___	___	___	___	___	___	___
Jeremy Bailey	___	___	___	___	___	___	___	___
Kim Vassaur	___	___	___	___	___	___	___	___
							Total	___
Con								
Melody Brooks	___	___	___	___	___	___	___	___
Whitney Lawson	___	___	___	___	___	___	___	___
Darth Taylor	___	___	___	___	___	___	___	___
							Total	___

tivities refines students' concepts of "story," helps them learn the elements of story structure (e.g., characters, plot, and setting), and introduces them to script conventions.

Theatrical productions are polished performances of a play produced on a stage and before an audience. They require extensive rehearsal, are product-oriented, and are quite formal. Because the purpose of theatrical productions is the polished presentation, they are audience-centered rather than child-centered. They also require that students memorize lines rather than encourage them to be spontaneous and improvisational. They are not recommended for students in elementary grades unless students write the scripts themselves.

Again and again, educators caution that drama activities should be informal during the elementary years (Stewig, 1983; Wagner, 1976). The one exception is when students write their own play and puppet show scripts and want to perform them.

Dramatic Play

Playing in the housekeeping corner and putting on dress-up clothes—a bridal veil or a police officer's coat and hat—are familiar activities in preschool and kindergarten classrooms. Young children use these activities to reenact familiar, everyday activities and to pretend to be someone or something else. These *dramatic play* activities represent children's first attempt at drama (McCaslin, 1984).

A housekeeping corner is only one possible dramatic play center. Prop kits, which contain collections of materials for dramatic play, can be set out for children to experiment with. For example, a detective prop kit, with a Sherlock Holmes hat, raincoat, flashlight, magnifying glass, notepad, and pencil, becomes a popular center after children read Sharmat's *Nate the Great* series of easy-to-read mystery stories. Even middle-grade students are drawn to prop kit materials after reading Sobol's *Encyclopedia Brown* detective stories and writing their own mystery stories. A variety of prop kit ideas is offered in Figure 5–10. Many of the prop kits involve reading and writing materials, such as the notepad and pencil in the detective kit, menus in the restaurant kit, and a typewriter in the office kit. Thus, through dramatic play with these materials, young children are introduced to some of the functions of reading and writing.

Props for the kits can be collected, stored in boxes, and then used in social studies, science, math, or literature activities. They can also be used in conjunction with field trips and class visitors; for example, for a unit on community helpers, teachers could arrange a field trip to the post office and invite a mail carrier to the classroom to be interviewed. Then a mail carrier prop kit can be set up. With the information they have learned from the field trip, the in-class interview, and through books, children have many experiences to draw on when they experiment with the props.

Dramatic play has all the values of other types of informal drama (Schickedanz, 1978). Children have the opportunity to use talk in a meaningful context as well as to learn new vocabulary words. As with other talk activities, dramatic play helps children develop socialization skills. The children are integrating all the language modes— listening, talking, reading, and writing—through their play activities, and are also learning content area material.

Post Office Kit

mailboxes (use shoeboxes)
envelopes
stamps (use Christmas seals)
pens
string

wrapping paper
tape
packages
scale

package seals
address labels
cash register
money

Hairdresser Kit

hair rollers
brush and comb
mirror
empty shampoo bottle
towel

posters of hair styles
wig and wig stand
hairdryer (with cord cut off)
curling iron (with cord cut off)

ribbons, barrets, clips
appointment book
open/closed sign

Office Kit

typewriter
calculator
paper
notepads
transparent tape
stapler

hole punch
file folders
in/out boxes
pens and pencils
envelopes
stamps

telephone
message pad
rubber stamps
stamp pad

Medical Kit (doctor, nurse, paramedic)

white shirt/jacket
medical bag
stethoscope
hypodermic syringe (play)

thermometer
tweezers
bandages
prescription pad

prescription bottles and labels
walkie-talkie (for paramedics)

Grocery Store Kit

grocery cart
food packages
plastic fruit and artificial foods
price stickers

cash register
money
grocery bags
marking pen

FIGURE 5—10

Materials for Prop Kits

Restaurant Kit

tablecloth	napkins	apron for waitress
dishes	menus	vest for waiter
glasses	tray	hat and apron for chef
silverware	order pad and pencil	

Travel Agency Kit

travel posters	wallet with money and
travel brochures	credit cards
maps	cash register
airplane, train tickets	suitcases

Veterinarian Kit

white shirt/jacket	empty medicine bottles
stuffed animals	prescription labels
cages (cardboard	bandages
boxes)	popsicle stick splints
medical bag	hypodermic syringe
stethoscope	(play)

Library Kit

children's books and	book return box
magazines (with	sign for book fines
card pockets and	cash register
date due slips)	money
date stamp and stamp	
pad	
library cards	

Bank Kit

teller window (use a	roll papers for coins
puppet stage)	deposit slips
passbooks	money bags
checks	
money	

FIGURE 5–10   (*continued*)

Role-playing

Students assume the role of another person as they act out stories or reenact historical events. Through role-playing, children have the opportunity to step into someone else's shoes and view the world from another perspective.

    From their first experiences in dramatic play, students move into acting out stories, in which they combine retelling with drama. Choose familiar stories—folktales and fables—for students to act out using both dialogue and body movements. The stories listed in Figure 5–11 can be used for role-playing activities. Cumulative tales

Brown, M. (1947). *Stone soup*. New York: Scribner. (P-M)
Brown, M. W. (1972). *The runaway bunny*. New York: Harper and Row. (P)
Carle, E. (1970). *The very hungry caterpillar*. Cleveland: Collins-World.(P)
Flack, M. (1932). *Ask Mr. Bear*. New York: Macmillan. (P)
Gag, W. (1956). *Millions of cats*. New York: Coward McCann. (P)
Galdone, P. (1973). *The three billy goats Gruff*. Boston: Houghton Mifflin. (P)
Galdone, P. (1975). *The gingerbread boy*. New York: Seabury. (P)
Grimm, The Brothers. (1971). *The Bremen town musicians*. New York: Greenwillow. (P-M)
Johnson, O. (1955). *Harold and the purple crayon*. New York: Harper and Row. (See also other books in this series.)(P)
Kellogg, S. (1973). *The island of the skog*. New York: Dial. (P)
Low, J. (1980) *Mice twice*. New York: Atheneum. (P-M)
Slobodkina, E. (1947). *Caps for sale*. New York: Scott. (P)
Steig, W. (1982). *Doctor DeSoto*. New York: Farrar. (P)
Still, J. (1977). *Jack and the wonder beans*. New York: Putnam. (M)
Thurber, J. (1974). *Many moons*. New York: Harcourt. (P-M)
Turkle, B. (1976). *Deep in the forest*. New York: Dutton. (P-M)
Wildsmith, B. (1972). *The owl and the woodpecker*. New York: Watts. (P-M)
Zemach, H. & Zemach, M. (1973). *Duffy and the devil*. New York: Farrar. (P-M)
Zemach, M. (1976). *It could always be worse*. New York: Farrar. (P-M-U)

FIGURE 5–11

Stories for Role-playing Activities

such as *The Three Little Pigs* (Galdone, 1970) and *The Gingerbread Boy* (Galdone, 1975) are good for younger children to dramatize because they are repetitious (and predictable) in sequence, plot, and dialogue. Middle- and upper-grade students can act out favorite scenes from longer stories such as *The Wind in the Willows* (Grahame, 1961) and *Mrs. Frisby and the Rats of NIHM* (O'Brien, 1971). Students can also read biographies and dramatize events from these people's lives. *Columbus* (d'Aulaire & d'Aulaire, 1955) and *And Then What Happened, Paul Revere?* (Fritz, 1973) are two biographies that elementary students can dramatize.

Booth (Kukla, 1987) has developed an approach he calls *story-drama,* which expands story dramatizing into role-playing. After reading and discussing a story, students explore its issues, themes, and deeper meanings through drama. For example, after reading *The King's Fountain* (Alexander, 1971), the story of a king who takes away the water from the villagers so he can build a grand fountain, students think about surviving without water, how the villagers would react, and about the power and grandeur of kings. Working in small groups, students create the drama by dramatizing a problem from the story (e.g., the villagers' pleading with the king not to redirect the water). As they role-play, children participate in the story and explore situations different from their own lives. After role-playing the groups come together to share their experiences. As the teacher, Booth, too, assumes a role. After the dramatic activity, students reflect on the story, made richer and more memorable through drama.

These kindergarten students are role-playing a favorite story.

In role-playing, students take the role of another person—not roles in a story, but rather the roles people play in society. Role-playing is an educational experience designed to help students gain insights about how to handle real-life problems and understand historical and current events (Nelson, 1988). Heathcote has developed an innovative approach to role-playing to help students experience and better understand historical events (Wagner, 1976). Through a process she calls *funneling,* Heathcote chooses a dramatic focus from a general topic (e.g., Ancient Rome, the Civil War, the Pilgrims). She begins by thinking of all the aspects of the general topic and then decides on a dramatic focus—a particular critical moment. For example, using the topic of the Pilgrims, one possible focus is the night of December 20, 1620, eleven weeks after the Pilgrims set sail from England on the *Mayflower* and the night before the ship reached Plymouth.

The improvisation begins when students assume roles; the teacher becomes a character, too. As they begin to role-play the event, questions draw students' attention to certain features and probe their understanding. Questions about the Pilgrims might include:

Where are you?

After 11 weeks sailing the Atlantic Ocean, what will happen?

How are you feeling?

Why did you leave England?

What kind of life do you dream of in the new land?

Can you survive in this cold winter weather?

These questions also provide information by reminding students of the time of year, the problems they are having, and the length of the voyage.

Sometimes Heathcote stops students in the middle of role-playing and asks them to write what they are thinking and feeling. As part of the Pilgrim improvisation, students might be asked to write an entry in their simulated journals for December 20, 1620. (For more information on journals, see Chapter 6.) An example of a simulated journal entry written by a fourth-grade "Pilgrim" is shown in Figure 5–12. After the writing activity, students continue role-playing.

Heathcote uses drama to begin study on a topic rather than as a culminating activity in which students apply all they have learned, because she believes role-playing experiences stimulate children's curiosity and make them want to read books and learn more about a historical or current event. Whether you use role-playing as an introduction or as a conclusion, it is a valuable activity because students become immersed in the event. By reliving it, they are learning far more than mere facts.

Puppets and Other Props

Puppets have long been favorites of children. The delightful combinations of colorful language, novel body constructions, fantasy, and imaginative characters fascinate chil-

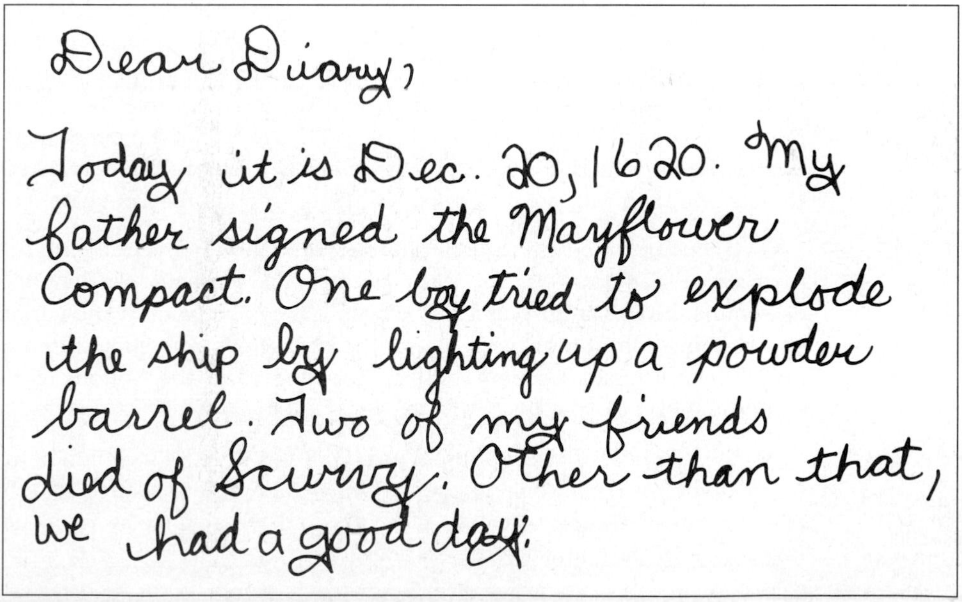

Dear Diary,

Today it is Dec. 20, 1620. My father signed the Mayflower Compact. One boy tried to explode the ship by lighting up a powder barrel. Two of my friends died of Scurvy. Other than that, we had a good day.

FIGURE 5–12

A Fourth Grade Pilgrim's Simulated Journal Entry for December 20, 1620
Stephanie, age 10

dren. Children can create puppet shows with commercially manufactured puppets, or they can construct their own. When children create their own puppets, the only limitations are students' imaginations, their ability to construct things, and the materials at hand. Puppets can be especially useful with shy students. Puppets can be used not only in all types of drama activities, but also as a novel way to introduce a language skill, such as quotation marks. Teachers can use puppets to improvise a dialogue, and then record it using quotation marks.

Simple puppets provide children with the opportunity to develop both creative and dramatic ability. The simpler the puppet, the more is left to the imagination of the audience and the puppeteer. Constructing elaborate puppets is beyond the resources of both teachers and students. The type of puppets the students make, however, depends on how they will be used. Students can construct puppets using all sorts of scrap materials. We will describe how to make eight types of hand and finger puppets; the eight types are illustrated in Figure 5–13.

Stick Puppets. Stick puppets are versatile and perhaps the easiest to make. Sticks, tongue depressors, dowels, and straws can be used. The rest of the puppet that is attached to the stick can be constructed from papier-maché, Styrofoam balls, pictures students have drawn, or pictures cut from magazines and mounted on cardboard. Students draw or paint the features on the materials they have selected for the head and body. Some puppets may need only a head; others may also need a body. Making stick puppets provides an opportunity to combine art and drama.

Paper Bag Puppets. This is another simple puppet to make. The paper bags should be the right size to fit students' hands. Paper lunch bags are a convenient size, although smaller bags are better for kindergartners. What characters they portray and what emphasis the students give the size of the character are the determining factors, however. The puppet's mouth can be placed at the fold of the paper bag. Paint on faces and clothes, add yarn for hair, and attach arms and legs. Students should choose ways to decorate their bag puppets to match the characters they develop.

Cylinder Puppets. Cylinder puppets are made from cardboard tubes from bathroom tissue, paper towels, and aluminum foil. The diameter and length of the cylinder determine the size of the puppet. The cylinders can be painted and various appendages and clothing can be attached. Again, the character's role should determine how the puppet is costumed. Students insert their fingers in the bottom of the cylinder to manipulate the puppet.

Sock Puppets. Sock puppets are quite versatile. A sock can be used as is, with button eyes, yarn hair, pipe cleaner antennae, and other features added. The sock can also be cut at the toe to create a mouth, and whatever else is needed to give the impression of the character can be added.

Cup Puppets. Even primary-grade students can make puppets from Styrofoam cups. They glue facial features, hair, wings, and other decorations on the cup. Pipe cleaners, toothpicks, and Q-tips tipped with glitter can easily be attached to Styrofoam cups. Then sticks or heavy-duty straws are attached to the inside of the cup as the handle.

FIGURE 5–13

Types of Puppets

 Paper Plate Puppets. Paper plates can be used for face puppets as well as for masks. Students add junk materials to decorate the puppets, then tape sticks or rulers to the back of the plates as handles.

 Finger Puppets. Students can make several different types of finger puppets. For one type, students can draw, color, and cut out small figures, then add tabs to either side of the figure and tape the tabs together to fit around the finger. Larger puppets can be taped to fit around the hand. For a second type of finger puppet, students can cut the finger section from a glove and add decoration. The pointed part that separates the compartments of an egg carton can also be used for a finger puppet.

Cloth Puppets.   If parents are available to assist with the sewing, students can make cloth puppets. Two pieces of cloth are sewn together on all sides except the bottom, then students personalize the puppets using scraps of fabric, lace, yarn, and other materials.

After students have created their puppets, they can perform the puppet show almost any place. They can make a stage from an empty appliance packing crate or an empty television cabinet. They can also drape blankets or cloths in front of classroom tables and desks. They might also turn a table on its side. There may be other class-room objects your students can use as makeshift stages.

Scriptwriting and Theatrical Productions

Scripts are a unique written language form that elementary students need opportuni-ties to explore. Scriptwriting often grows out of role-playing and storytelling. Soon students recognize the need to write notes when they prepare for plays, puppet shows, readers theater, and other dramatic productions. This need provides the impetus for introducing students to the unique dramatic conventions and for encouraging them to write scripts to present as theatrical productions.

Play Scripts.   Once students want to write scripts, they will recognize the need to add the structures unique to dramatic writing to their repertoire of written language conventions. Students begin by examining scripts. It is especially effective to have students compare narrative and script versions of the same story; for example, Richard George has adapted two of Roald Dahl's fantastic stories, *Charlie and the Chocolate Factory* (1976) and *James and the Giant Peach* (1982) into scripts. Then students discuss their observations and compile a list of the unique characteristics of scripts. An upper-grade class compiled the list of unique dramatic conventions presented in Figure 5–14.

The next step is to have students apply what they have learned about scripts by writing a class collaboration or group script. With the whole class, develop a script by adapting a familiar story. As the script is being written, refer to the chart of dramatic conventions and ask students to check that they are using these conventions. Collab-orative writing affords unique teaching opportunities and needed practice for students before they must write individually. After the script is completed, have students read it using readers theater procedures, or produce it as a puppet show or play.

Once students are aware of the dramatic conventions and have participated in writing a class collaboration script, they can write scripts individually or in small groups. Students often adapt familiar stories for their first scripts; later, they will want to create original scripts. "The Lonely Troll," a script written by a team of five upper-grade

---

Important Characteristics of Scripts

1. Scripts are divided into acts and scenes.
2. Scripts have these parts: (a) a list of characters (or cast); (b) the setting (at the beginning of each act or scene); (c) stage directions (written in parentheses); and (d) dialogue.
3. The dialogue carries the action.
4. Description and other information are set apart in the setting or in stage directions.
5. Stage directions give actors important information about how to act and how to feel.
6. The dialogue is written in a special way:

   CHARACTER'S NAME: Dialogue
7. Sometimes a narrator is used to quickly fill in parts of the story.

FIGURE 5—14

Dramatic Conventions Used in Scripts

students, appears in Figure 5—15 as an example of the type of scripts older students can compose. Although most of the scripts they write are narrative, students can also create scripts about famous people or historical events.

Film/Video Scripts. Students use a similar approach in writing scripts that will be filmed or videotaped, but they must now consider the visual component of the film as well as the written script. They often compose their scripts on storyboards, which focus their attention on how the story they are creating will be filmed (Cox, 1983, 1985). *Storyboards,* or sheets of paper divided into three sections, are used to sketch in scenes. Students place a series of three or four large squares in a row down the center of the paper, with space for dialogue and narration on the left and shooting directions on the right. Cox compares storyboards to road maps because they provide directions for filming the script. The scene renderings and the shooting directions help students tie the dialogue to the visual images that will appear on the film or videotape. Figure 5—16 shows a sample storyboard form with an excerpt from a fourth-grade class collaboration script.

The script can be produced several different ways—as a live-action play, as a puppet show, or through animation. After writing the script on the storyboards or transferring a previously written script to storyboards, students collect or construct the properties they will need to produce the script. As with other types of drama, the properties do not need to be extensive or elaborate—a simple backdrop and costumes will suffice. Students should also print the title and credits on large posters to appear at the beginning of the film. After several rehearsals, the script is filmed using a movie or video camera.

As video cameras and VCR playback systems become common equipment in elementary schools, we anticipate that they will be chosen more often than movie

The Lonely Troll

NARRATOR: Once upon a time, in a far, far away land, there was a troll named Pippin who lived all alone in his little corner of the woods. The troll hated all the creatures of the woods and was very lonely because he didn't have anyone to talk to since he scared everyone away. One day, a dwarf named Sam wandered into Pippin's yard and . . .

PIPPIN: Grrr. What are you doing here?

SAM: Ahhhhh! A troll! Please don't eat me!

PIPPIN: Why shouldn't I?

SAM: (Begging) Look, I'm all skin and bones. I won't make a good meal.

PIPPIN: You look fat enough for me. (Turns to audience) Do you think I should eat him? (Sam jumps off stage and hides in the audience.)

PIPPIN: Where did he go? (Pippin jumps off stage and looks for Sam. When he finds Sam, he takes him back on stage, laughing; then he ties Sam up.) Ha, ha, ha. Boy, that sure did tire me out. (Yawn) I'll take a nap. Then I'll eat him later. (Pippin falls asleep. Lights dim. Sam escapes and runs behind a tree. Lights return, and Pippin wakens.)

PIPPIN: (To audience) Where's my breakfast? (Sam peeps out from behind a tree and cautions the audience to be quiet.) Huh? Did someone say he was behind that tree? (Points to tree. Pippin walks around. Sam kicks him in the rear. Pippin falls and is knocked out.)

SAM: I must get out of here, and warn the queen about this short, small, mean, ugly troll. (Sam leaves. Curtains close.)

NARRATOR: So Sam went to tell Queen Muffy about the troll. Meanwhile, in the forest, Pippin awakens, and decides to set a trap for Sam. (Open curtains to forest scene, showing Pippin making a box trap.)

PIPPIN: Ha, ha, ha! That stupid dwarf will come back here looking for me. When he sees this ring, he'll take it. Then, I'll trap him! Ha, ha, ha, ha. (Pippin hides.)

NARRATOR: The dwarf finally reaches Queen Muffy's castle and hurries to tell her his story.

SAM: (Open curtains to Queen Muffy sitting on a throne, eating. Sam rushes in, out of breath.) I have some very important news for you. There's . . .

QUEEN: I don't have time for you.

SAM: But, I . . .

QUEEN: Come, come. Don't bother me with small things.

SAM: There's an ugly old . . .

QUEEN: You're wasting my time.

SAM: I just wanted to warn you, there's a big, ugly, mean . . .

FIGURE 5–15

A Script Written by a Group of Upper-Grade Students

Eighth graders: Raymond, Lisa, Jeff, Kathy, and Larry

QUEEN:	Hurry up.
SAM:	. . . man-eating . . .
QUEEN:	This had better be important.
SAM:	(Angry, he yells) THERE'S A TROLL IN THE FOREST!!!
QUEEN:	Who cares if there's a . . . a . . . (Screams) A TROLL!!!
SAM:	That's what I've been saying. A troll — in the forest.
QUEEN:	Then I must send out my faithful knight . . . Sir Skippy . . . to kill him. I shall offer a reward. (Queen exits.)
SAM:	A reward, huh? Hmmmm. I think I'll go out and get that troll myself — and collect that reward! (Close curtains.)
NARRATOR:	So Sam sets out to capture the troll, not knowing that Pippin set a trap out for him. (Open curtains to trap scene.)
SAM:	(Carries a huge net) Ohhh Mr. Troll. (He spots the ring and reaches for it.) Wow! A ring! (Pippin sneezes.) What was that? Aha! (Sam sees Pippin, and swings the net. Pippin dives for Sam and gets trapped in his own trap.)
SAM:	He's trapped! I did it! Oh boy, now I can get that reward. I get a hundred dollars . . . or maybe a thousand dollars . . . possibly a million.
SKIPPY:	(Comes in smiling) I am here to rid the forest of this mean, awful, ugly troll. I also want the reward. (Said in an evil way)
SAM:	The reward is mine. I caught him. It's all mine.
SKIPPY:	I want that reward, and I shall get it. (Takes sword) I will carve your throat if you don't hand him over. I'll kill him and take him to the queen, so she will see what a great warrior I am.
SAM:	You're going to kill him? I won't let you!
SKIPPY:	Do you think I'm stupid? I won't take a live troll to Queen Muffy.
SAM:	If you are going to kill him, I will release him. (Throws off box) Hey, Pippin, he's going to kill you. Run away, run for your life, and I shall protect you.
PIPPIN:	(Confused) You are trying to save me, after I tried to kill you?
SAM:	I don't want to see you hurt.
PIPPIN:	Then I will stay here and help you defeat Skippy.
SAM AND PIPPIN:	Friends, forever! (Skippy steps forward and swings at Pippin. Pippin ducks. Pippin and Sam give Skippy the Three Stooges treatment. Skippy is defeated.)
PIPPIN:	Leave my forest, now, Sir Skippy, before we kill you. (Skippy leaves.)
SAM:	Thank you, my friend. We will stay together always, and you will never be lonely again. (Close curtains.)
NARRATOR:	Pippin and Sam became best friends, and the queen never bothered them. They lived happily ever after.

FIGURE 5–15   *(continued)*

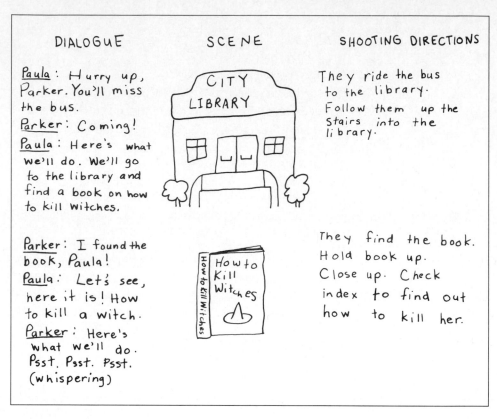

FIGURE 5–16

Excerpt from a Class Collaboration Storyboard Script
Fourth graders

cameras for filming student scripts. Video cameras and tapes are easier and less expensive to use than movie cameras and film, videotapes do not need to be developed as film does and can be reused, and the audio component can be recorded at the same time as the video. Many teachers prefer videotapes to movie films because they can tape rehearsals, which allows students to review their performances and make necessary changes before the final taping.

❖ REVIEW

Teachers need to sustain talk in the elementary classroom because talk has definite benefits for elementary students. Too often teachers assume that students already know how to talk and so concentrate on written language modes; instead, teachers should involve students in four types of talk activities: informal talk, interpretive talk, more formal talk, and dramatic talk. Informal talk activities such as conversation, show-and-tell, and discussion give students and teachers opportunities to socialize and talk in comfortable situations. Storytelling and readers theater are two interpretive talk activities in which students develop their concept of story and present a performance for an audience. Oral reports, book talks, interviews, and debates are more formal talk activities. Students learn a process approach to preparing and giving their talks through these activities. Dramatic talk activities include dramatic play, role-playing, and theatrical productions. Through drama, students explore another medium of expression and tap into a powerful way of knowing.

❖ EXTENSIONS

1. In an elementary classroom, observe what types of oral language activities students participate in and what language functions they use.

2. Observe a show-and-tell activity in a primary-grade classroom. What are the characteristics of students who are effective speakers? What questions could the teacher use to generate conversation from less verbal or shy students?

3. Plan and conduct a debate with a group of upper-grade students. Help them choose a topic from current events, school and community issues, or social studies units.

4. Stock a dramatic play center in a kindergarten or first grade classroom with one of the prop kits listed in Figure 5–10. Observe children over several days as they interact in the center and keep a log of the activities they participate in and how they use language in their play.

5. Plan and direct a role-playing activity with a group of students in conjunction with a social studies unit. Follow the guidelines in this chapter and integrate a writing activity with the role-playing (e.g., by having students keep a journal or writing a letter).

6. Assist a small group of middle- or upper-grade students as they prepare to tell stories to a class of primary-grade students. Help students use the four-step procedure discussed in this chapter.

7. Introduce scriptwriting to a group of middle- or upper-grade students by having them compile a list of the unique dramatic conventions used in scriptwriting, and then write a class collaboration script by adapting a familiar folktale.

❖ REFERENCES

Alexander, L. (1971). *The king's fountain*. New York: Dutton.

Babbitt, N. (1975). *Tuck everlasting*. New York: Farrar, Straus, & Giroux.

Bauer, C. F. (1977). *Handbook for storytellers*. Chicago: American Library Association.

Bloom, B. S. (1956). *Taxonomy of educational objectives, handbook I: Cognitive domain*. New York: McKay.

Booth, D. (1985). 'Imaginary gardens with real toads?': Reading and drama in education. *Theory into Practice, 24*, 193–198.

Brown, M., & Brown, L. K. (1984). *The bionic bunny show*. Boston: Little, Brown.

Burningham, J. (1979). *Would you rather. . . .* New York: Crowell.

Busching, B. A. (1981). Readers theatre: An education for language and life. *Language Arts, 58,* 330–338.

Camp, D. J., & Tompkins, G. E. (1990). Show-and-tell in middle school? *Middle School Journal, 21,* 18–20.

Cazden, C. B. (1986). Classroom discourse. In M. C. Wittrock (Ed.), *Handbook of research on teaching* (3rd ed.), pp. 432–463. New York: Macmillan.

Cazden, C. D. (1988). *Classroom discourse: The language of teaching and learning*. Portsmouth, NH: Heinemann.

Cooper, K. (1985). *Who put the cannon in the courthouse square? A guide to uncovering the past*. New York: Walker.

Cox, C. (1983). Young filmmakers speak the language of film. *Language Arts, 60,* 296–304, 372.

Cox, C. (1985). Filmmaking as a composing process. *Language Arts, 62,* 60–69.

Dahl, R. (1961). *James and the giant peach*. New York: Knopf.

Dahl, R. (1964). *Charlie and the chocolate factory*. New York: Knopf.

d'Aulaire, I. & d'Aulaire, E. P. (1955). *Columbus*. New York: Doubleday.

de Paola, Tomie. (1978). *Pancakes for breakfast*. New York: Harcourt Brace Jovanovich.

Dillon, J. T. (1983). *Teaching and the art of questioning* (Fastback No. 194). Bloomington, IN: Phi Delta Kappa.

Eeds, M., & Wells, D. (1989). Grand conversations: An exploration of meaning construction in literature study groups. *Research in the Teaching of English, 23,* 4–29.

Fiderer, A. (1988). Talking about books: Readers need readers. In J. Golub (Ed.), *Focus on collaborative learning* (Classroom Practices in Teaching English, 1988), pp. 59–65. Urbana, IL: National Council of Teachers of English.

Fox, P. (1984). *One-eyed cat*. New York: Bradbury.

Fritz, J. (1973). *And then what happened, Paul Revere?* New York: Coward.

Gackenback, D. (1980). *Hattie, Tom and the chicken witch*. New York: Harper and Row.

Galdone, P. (1970). *The three little pigs*. New York: Seabury.

Galdone, P. (1975). *The gingerbread boy*. New York: Seabury.

Gallagher, J. J., & Aschner, M. J. (1963). A preliminary report on analyses of classroom interaction. *Merrill-Palmer Quarterly, 9,* 183–194.

George, R. E. (1976). *Roald Dahl's Charlie and the chocolate factory*. New York: Knopf.

George, R. E. (1982). *Roald Dahl's James and the giant peach*. New York: Knopf.

Gilson, J. (1980). *Do bananas chew gum?* New York: Lothrop, Lee & Shepard.

Golub, J. (1988). Introduction. In J. Golub (Ed.), *Focus on collaborative learning* (Classroom Practices in Teaching English, 1988), pp. 1–2. Urbana, IL: National Council of Teachers of English.

Grahame, K. (1961). *The wind in the willows*. New York: Scribner.

Guilford, J. P. (1956). The structure of intellect. *Psychological Bulletin, 53,* 267–293.

Haley-James, S. M., & Hobson, C. D. (1980). Interviewing: A means of encouraging the drive to communicate. *Language Arts, 57,* 497–502.

Halliday, M. A. K. (1973). *Explorations in the functions of language*. London: Arnold.

Heath, S. B. (1983). Research currents: A lot of talk about nothing. *Language Arts, 60,* 999–1007.

Joint Committee on the Role of Drama in the Classroom. (1983). *Informal classroom drama*. Urbana, IL: NCTE.

Kardash, C. A. M., & Wright, L. (1987, Winter). Does creative drama benefit elementary school students: A meta-analysis. *Youth Theater Journal,* 11–18.

Kingore, B. W. (1982). Storytelling: A bridge from the university to the elementary school to the home. *Language Arts, 59,* 28–32.

Klein, M. L. (1979). Designing a talk environment for the classroom. *Language Arts, 56,* 647–656.

Korty, C. (1975). *Plays from African folktales*. New York: Scribner.

Kukla, K. (1987). David Booth: Drama as a way of knowing. *Language Arts, 64,* 73–78.

Laughlin, M. K., & Latrobe, K. H. (1989). *Readers theatre for children: Scripts and script development*. Englewood, CO: Libraries Unlimited.

Laurie, R. (1980). *Children's plays from Beatrix Potter*. New York: Warne.

Lionni, L. (1977). *A flea story*. New York: Pantheon.

Manna, A. L. (1984). Making language come alive through reading plays. *The Reading Teacher, 37*, 712–717.

McCaslin, N. (1984). *Creative dramatics in the classroom* (4th ed.) New York: Longman.

McKenzie, G. R. (1979). Data charts: A crutch for helping pupils organize reports. *Language Arts, 56*, 784–788.

Morrow, L. M. (1979). Exciting children about literature through creative storytelling techniques. *Language Arts, 56*, 236–243.

Morrow, L. M. (1985). Reading and retelling stories: Strategies for emergent readers. *The Reading Teacher, 38*, 870–875.

Nelson, P. A. (1988). Drama, doorway to the past. *Language Arts, 65*, 20–25.

O'Brien R. C. (1971). *Mrs. Frisby and the rats of NIHM*. New York: Atheneum.

Pinnell, G. S. (1975). Language in primary classrooms. *Theory into Practice, 14*, 318–327.

Reardon, S. J. (1988). The development of critical readers: A look into the classroom. *The New Advocate, 1*, 52–61.

Rockwell, T. (1973). *How to eat fried worms*. New York: Franklin Watts.

Roth, R. (1986). Practical use of language in school. *Language Arts, 63*, 134–142.

Schickedanz, J. (1978). 'You be the doctor and I'll be sick': Preschoolers learn the language arts through play. *Language Arts, 55*, 713–718.

Sharmat, M. W. (1977). *Nate the great and the phony clue*. New York: Coward.

Shuy, R. W. (1987). Research currents: Dialogue as the heart of learning. *Language Arts, 64*, 890–897.

Slobodkina, E. (1947). *Caps for sale*. New York: Scott.

Smith, J. (1988). *The show-and-tell war*. New York: Harper and Row.

Sobol, D. J. (1980). *Encyclopedia Brown carries on*. New York: Scholastic.

Stanley, D. (1983). *The conversation club*. New York: Macmillan.

Stewig, J. W. (1983). *Exploring language arts in the elementary classroom*. New York: Holt, Rinehart and Winston.

Stewig, J. W. (1983). *Informal drama in the elementary language arts program*. New York: Teachers College Press.

Thurber, J. (1974). *Many moons*. New York: Harcourt.

Van Allsburg, C. (1984). *The mysteries of Harris Burdick*. Boston: Houghton Mifflin.

Wagner, B. J. (1976). *Dorothy Heathcote: Drama as a learning medium*. Washington, DC: National Education Association.

Wagner, B. J. (1988). Research currents: Does classroom drama affect the arts of language? *Language Arts, 65*, 46–55.

Weitzman, D. (1975). *My backyard history book*. Boston: Little Brown.

Wilen, W. W. (1986). *Questioning skills for teachers* (2nd ed.). Washington, DC: National Education Association.

Wilkinson, L. C. (1984). Research currents: Peer group talk in elementary school. *Language Arts, 61*, 164–169.

6   INFORMAL WRITING

JOURNAL WRITING
  Personal Journals
  Dialogue Journals
  Writing Notebooks
  Learning Logs
  Simulated Journals
  Young Children's Journals
  Teaching Students to Write in Journals

INFORMAL WRITING STRATEGIES
  Brainstorming
  Clustering
  Freewriting
  Cubing
  Teaching Students to Use Informal Writing Strategies

STUDY SKILLS
  An Effective Study Strategy
  Taking Notes
  Summary Writing

◆ **IN THIS CHAPTER, YOU WILL LEARN ABOUT THREE TYPES OF** informal writing. One type of informal writing is journal writing, and there are many types of journal writing activities that elementary students can participate in. Informal writing strategies are a second type of informal writing. Students use brainstorming, clustering, freewriting, and other strategies to gather and organize ideas for writing. A third type of informal writing is note-taking and study skills, where students write informally to help them learn.

◆ **AS YOU ARE READING, THINK ABOUT THESE QUESTIONS:**
What kinds of journal writing activities are possible for elementary students?

How can journal writing help students learn?

What informal writing strategies can students use to gather and organize ideas for writing?

What study skills can elementary students use to help them learn?

Children's writing assumes many different forms, depending on the purpose and audience. Forms range from journals to newspapers, directions to poems, stories to research reports. Figure 6—1 lists a variety of writing forms appropriate for elementary students. Students' writing should not be limited to writing stories, poems, and a few other forms; instead, they need to experiment with a wide variety of writing forms and to explore their functions and formats. Writing forms can be used in creative as well as traditional ways—recipes are a good example. Most adults think of recipes as simply a list of ingredients and instructions for preparing a food, and they may question the appropriateness of having elementary students learn to write recipes. Older students who are learning to cook read recipes in cookbooks and copy or write food recipes, but kindergartners and primary-grade students can dictate humorous recipes that parents and teachers enjoy reading. Students can also write more creative and more interesting recipes; for instance, they can write a "recipe" for a war in conjunction with a social studies unit, which would probe students' understanding of the causes and events leading to wars. Students can also write recipes for success in a particular grade, which they can leave for the next year's class, or a recipe for being a best friend, a football player, or a hero. Here is a fourth grader's recipe for friendship:

5 1/3 c. love
1/2 t. anger
10 oz. happiness
2 c. smiles
2 T. sugar

Mix up slowly. Keep forever in a good heart. Remember to share with others.

Recipe-writing activities help students learn to write directions clearly and in sequence.

There are many ways to categorize writing forms. The traditional classifications are narration, description, exposition, and persuasion; however, this classification seems artificial when we consider that students use the forms for different purposes—to satisfy needs, maintain social relationships, express opinions, convey information, and entertain (Halliday, 1973, 1975). Students often combine two or more categories in a single piece of writing. Writing class newspapers, for instance, usually involves all four categories. Audiences vary, too; sometimes the audience is oneself, and other times it may be a trusted adult, classmates, or the community.

We use an arbitrary set of four writing categories in this textbook: informal writing, storywriting, informational writing, and poetry. This chapter focuses on *informal writing,* writing used to develop fluency and writing that students use as they learn. Informal writing is "rough draft" writing that has not been refined through a writing, revising, and rewriting process.

❖ JOURNAL WRITING

All kinds of people—artists, scientists, dancers, politicians, writers, assassins, and children—keep journals (Mallon, 1984). Usually, people record in their journals the everyday events of their lives and the issues that concern them. These journals, typ-

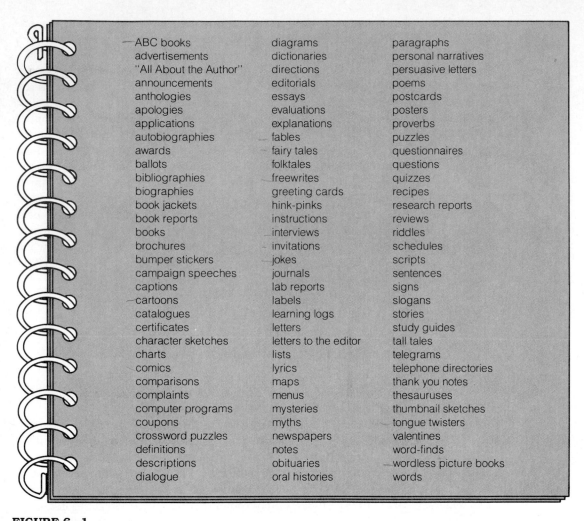

ABC books	diagrams	paragraphs
advertisements	dictionaries	personal narratives
"All About the Author"	directions	persuasive letters
announcements	editorials	poems
anthologies	essays	postcards
apologies	evaluations	posters
applications	explanations	proverbs
autobiographies	fables	puzzles
awards	fairy tales	questionnaires
ballots	folktales	questions
bibliographies	freewrites	quizzes
biographies	greeting cards	recipes
book jackets	hink-pinks	research reports
book reports	instructions	reviews
books	interviews	riddles
brochures	invitations	schedules
bumper stickers	jokes	scripts
campaign speeches	journals	sentences
captions	lab reports	signs
cartoons	labels	slogans
catalogues	learning logs	stories
certificates	letters	study guides
character sketches	letters to the editor	tall tales
charts	lists	telegrams
comics	lyrics	telephone directories
comparisons	maps	thank you notes
complaints	menus	thesauruses
computer programs	mysteries	thumbnail sketches
coupons	myths	tongue twisters
crossword puzzles	newspapers	valentines
definitions	notes	word-finds
descriptions	obituaries	wordless picture books
dialogue	oral histories	words

FIGURE 6–1

Teacher's Notebook Page: Possible Writing Forms

ically written in notebook form, are personal records, not intended for public display. Other journals might be termed "working" journals, in which writers record observations and other information to use for another purpose; for example, farmers might record weather or crop data or gardeners the blooming cycle of their plants.

Journals of some public figures have survived for hundreds of years and provide a fascinating glimpse of their authors and the times in which they lived. For example, the Renaissance genius Leonardo da Vinci recorded his daily activities, dreams, and plans for his painting and engineering projects in more than 40 notebooks. In the 1700s, Puritan theologian Jonathan Edwards documented his spiritual life in his journal. In the late 1700s, American explorers Meriwether Lewis and George Rogers Clark kept a journal of their travels across the North American continent, more for geographical than personal use. In the nineteenth century, the American writer Henry David Thoreau filled 39 notebooks with his essays. French author Victor Hugo carried a small pocket notebook to record ideas as they came to him—even at inopportune moments while talking with friends. American author F. Scott Fitzgerald filled his notebooks with snippets of overheard conversations, many of which he later used in *The Great Gatsby* and other novels. Anne Frank, who wrote while in hiding from the Nazis during World War II, is the best-known child diarist.[1]

Just as adults use them differently, journals may be used for a variety of purposes in elementary classrooms. For all types of journals, however, teachers should set aside specific periods for writing, daily or at least several times a week. Writing frequency varies according to the purpose of the journal. If students keep personal journals or reflect on what they are learning in learning logs, they may wish to record events daily. If they want to converse with the teacher in dialogue journals, write stories and poems in writing journals, or take the role of historical figures in simulated journals, they may wish to write two or three times a week. Young children often combine writing and drawing in their journals.

Tchudi and Tchudi (1984) suggest possible writing activities that explore students' experiences, investigate the world around them, and play with language:

Recording past experiences

Recording dreams

Analyzing opinions to better understand one's values and beliefs

Using the senses—seeing, hearing, feeling, smelling, tasting—to write more vividly

Recording impressions about people, places, and new experiences

Responding to newspaper/magazine articles, TV shows, or movies

Collecting examples of dialogues and dialects

Conducting a dialogue with oneself, friends, or historical personalities

Collecting words, puns, riddles, and other word plays

Copying quotes

Making lists of possible writing topics

Fulwiler (1985) shared excerpts from his daughter Megan's third-grade journal in *Language Arts,* demonstrating how she used writing for many of these functions. More recently, Megan Fulwiler (1986), now a teenager, reflected on her journal writing experience and her reasons for writing. Most importantly, Megan described her journal as "an extension of my mind" that she used to "work out my feelings, ask questions, and find answers and write down and organize all my floating thoughts" (p. 809). She noted that as time passed, her entries grew more personal and became a record of her growing up. As with Megan, journal writing gives students valuable writing practice. They gain

[1]The terms *diary* and *journal* are often used synonymously; diaries are sometimes considered the more personal and private of the two. Whether the records that children write are called diaries or journals is unimportant; for convenience, we use the term *journal* to refer to this type of informal writing.

Anderson, J. (1987). *Joshua's westward journal*. New York: Morrow. (M)

Blos, J. (1979). *A gathering of days: A New England girl's journal, 1830–1832*. New York: Scribner. (U)

Bourne, M. A. *Nabby Adams's diary*. New York: Coward. (U)

Cleary, B. (1983). *Dear M. Henshaw*. New York: Morrow. (M)

Crusoe, R. (1972). *My journals and sketchbooks*. New York: Harcourt. (U)

Fisher, L. E. (1972). *The death of evening star: Diary of a young New England whaler*. New York: Doubleday. (M-U)

Fitzhugh, L. (1964). *Harriet the spy*. New York: Harper. (M)

Frank, A. (1952). *Anne Frank: The diary of a young girl*. New York: Doubleday. (U)

George, J. C. (1959). *My side of the mountain*. New York: Dutton. (M-U)

Glaser, D. (1976). *The diary of Trilby Frost*. New York: Holiday House. (U)

Mazer, N. F. (1971). *I, Trissy*. New York: Delacorte. (U)

Oakley, G. (1987). *The diary of a church mouse*. New York: Atheneum. (M)

Orgel, D. B. (1978). *The devil in Vienna*. New York: Dial. (U)

Reig, J. (1978). *Diary of the boy king Tut-Ankh-Amen*. New York: Scribner. (M)

Sachs, M. (1975). *Dorrie's book*. New York: Doubleday. (M)

Wilder, L. E. (1962). *On the way home*. New York: Harper. (M)

Williams, V. B. (1981). *Three days on a river in a red canoe*. New York: Greenwillow. (P-M)

FIGURE 6–2

Stories in Which Characters Keep Journals
P = primary grades (K–2)
M = middle grades (3–5)
U = upper grades (6–8)

fluency and confidence that they can write. They can also experiment with writing conventions that must be considered in more public writing. If they decide to make an entry "public," students can later revise and edit their writing.

Characters in children's literature, such as Harriet in *Harriet the Spy* (Fitzhugh, 1964), Leigh in *Dear Mr. Henshaw* (Cleary, 1983), and Catherine Hall in *A Gathering of Days* (Blos, 1979), keep journals in which they record events, ideas, and dreams. Figure 6–2 is a list of stories in which characters keep journals. The characters demonstrate the process of journal writing and illustrate both the pleasures and difficulties of keeping a journal (Tway, 1981). A good way to introduce journal writing is by reading one of these books.

Personal Journals

Students can keep *personal journals* in which they recount events in their lives and write about topics of their choosing. An excerpt from a third grader's personal journal is presented in Figure 6–3. This excerpt shows the variety of topics students may

MondayOct.19

About a month ago I went to Pennsylvania to see my grandfather But I call him Papap I don't know why. He was in the hospital for kemothereipee treatment. Once we were there he cheered up. But now he dosn't feel good. He is still in the hospital. I think of him all the time.

Tuesday Oct.20

I am having a terrible day! First I had to go to G.T. lab. We have to do work there and we have homework Then I still have to do the same work in school that everybody does there and were gone all morning. Now I am stuck writing in this Journal. I am sick of it, every Tuesday it is like this cause on tuesday mornings is when we go to G.T. lab. I am still not finished with my work.

wednesday Oct. 21

You know I had a terrible day on Tuesday Well today I am having a good day. I have all my work finished.

Friday Oct.23

My mom is in Pennsylvania today because of that today is a desaster. First I have to get up at six thirty then I forget my lunchpail at home and at this rate I will never finish my work. I havn't seen or talked to my mom sinsed Wednesday and I hate it.

FIGURE 6–3

Entries from a Third Grader's Personal Journal

A student reflects on daily events while he writes in his personal journal.

choose to write about, as well as the depth of elementary students' feelings. It is normal for students to misspell a few words in their entries, as did this third grader; when students write in personal journals, the emphasis is on what they say, not how correctly they write.

It is often helpful to list possible journal writing topics on a chart in the classroom or on sheets of paper for students to clip inside their journal notebooks. Figure 6–4 shows a list of possible journal writing topics developed by a class of fourth and fifth graders. Students can add topics to their lists throughout the year, which may include more than 100 topics by the end of the school year. Students choose their own topics for personal journals. Although they can write about almost anything, some students will complain that they don't know what to write about, so a list of topics gives them a crutch. Referring students to the list or asking them to brainstorm a list of topics encourages them to become more independent writers and discourages them from becoming too dependent on teachers for writing topics.

Privacy becomes an important issue as students grow older. Most young children are willing to share what they have written, but by third or fourth grade, students grow less willing to read their journal entries aloud to the class, although they are usually willing to share the entries with a trusted teacher. Teachers must be scrupulous about respecting students' privacy and not insist that they share their writing when they are unwilling to do so. It is also important to talk with students about respecting each other's

my favorite place in town	if I had three wishes
boyfriends/girlfriends	my teacher
things that make me happy or sad	TV shows I watch
music	my favorite holiday
an imaginary planet	if I were stranded on an island
cars	what I want to be when I grow up
magazines I like to read	private thoughts
what if snow were hot	how to be a super hero
dreams I have	dinosaurs
cartoons	my mom/my dad
places I've been	my friends
favorite movies	my next vacation
rock stars	love
if I were a movie/rock star	if I were an animal or something
poems	else
pets	books I've read
football	favorite things to do
astronauts	my hobbies
the president	if I were a skydiver
jokes	when I get a car
motorcycles	if I had a lot of money
things that happen in my school	dolls
current events	if I were rich
things I do on weekends	wrestling and other sports
a soap opera with daily episodes	favorite colors
	questions answered with "never"

or ANYTHING else I want to write about

FIGURE 6—4

Possible Writing Topics
Fourth- and fifth-graders

privacy and not reading each other's journals. To protect students' privacy, many teachers keep personal journals on an out-of-the-way shelf when they are not in use.

When students share personal information with teachers through their journals, a second issue arises: teachers may learn details about students' problems and family life that they are not sure how to deal with. Entries about child abuse, suicide, or drug use may be the child's way of asking for help. Whereas teachers are not counselors, they do have a legal obligation to protect their students and to report possible problems to appropriate school personnel. Occasionally a student invents a personal problem in a journal entry as an attention-getting tactic; however, asking the student about the entry or having a school counselor do so will help to ensure that the student's safety is being fully considered.

Dialogue Journals

Another approach to journal writing is *dialogue journals,* in which students and teachers converse with each other through writing (Bode, 1989; Gambrell, 1985; Staton, 1980, 1987). These journals are interactive, conversational in tone, and provide the opportunity for real student-teacher communication—something that is often missing in elementary classrooms. Each day students write informally to the teacher about something of interest or concern, and the teacher responds. Students choose their own topics and usually control the direction the writing takes. Staton (1987) offers these suggestions for responding to students' writing and continuing the dialogue:

1. Acknowledge students' ideas and encourage them to continue to write about their interests.
2. Support students by complimenting them about behavior and school work.
3. Provide new information about topics, so that students will want to read your responses.
4. Write less than the students do.
5. Avoid unspecific comments like "good idea" or "very interesting."
6. Ask few questions; instead, encourage students to ask you questions.

Teachers' responses do not need to be lengthy; a sentence or two is often enough. Even so, it is time-consuming to respond to 25 or more journal entries every day. As an alternative, many teachers read and respond to students' journal entries on a rotating basis; they might respond to one group of students' writing one week and another group's the next week.

A series of entries from a dialogue journal appears in Figure 6–5. These entries were written between a learning disabled, second grade student and the student teacher working in her classroom. You will notice that this journal is not a series of teacher questions and student answers; instead the student and teacher are having a dialogue, or conversation, and the interchange is built on mutual trust and respect.

Dialogue journals can be effective in dealing with students who are misbehaving or having almost any type of problem in school (Staton, 1980). Teacher and student write back and forth about the problem and identify ways to solve it. In later entries, the student reflects on his or her progress toward solving the problem. The teacher responds to the student's message, asks clarifying questions, or offers sympathy and praise.

Kreeft (1984) believes the greatest value of dialogue journals is that they bridge the gap between talking and writing; they are written conversations. As Figure 6–5 shows, a second value is the strong bonds that develop between student and teacher through writing back and forth to each other.

Writing Notebooks

Writing notebooks are a specialized type of journal in which students record a variety of information about writing. They include ideas for writing, other content information,

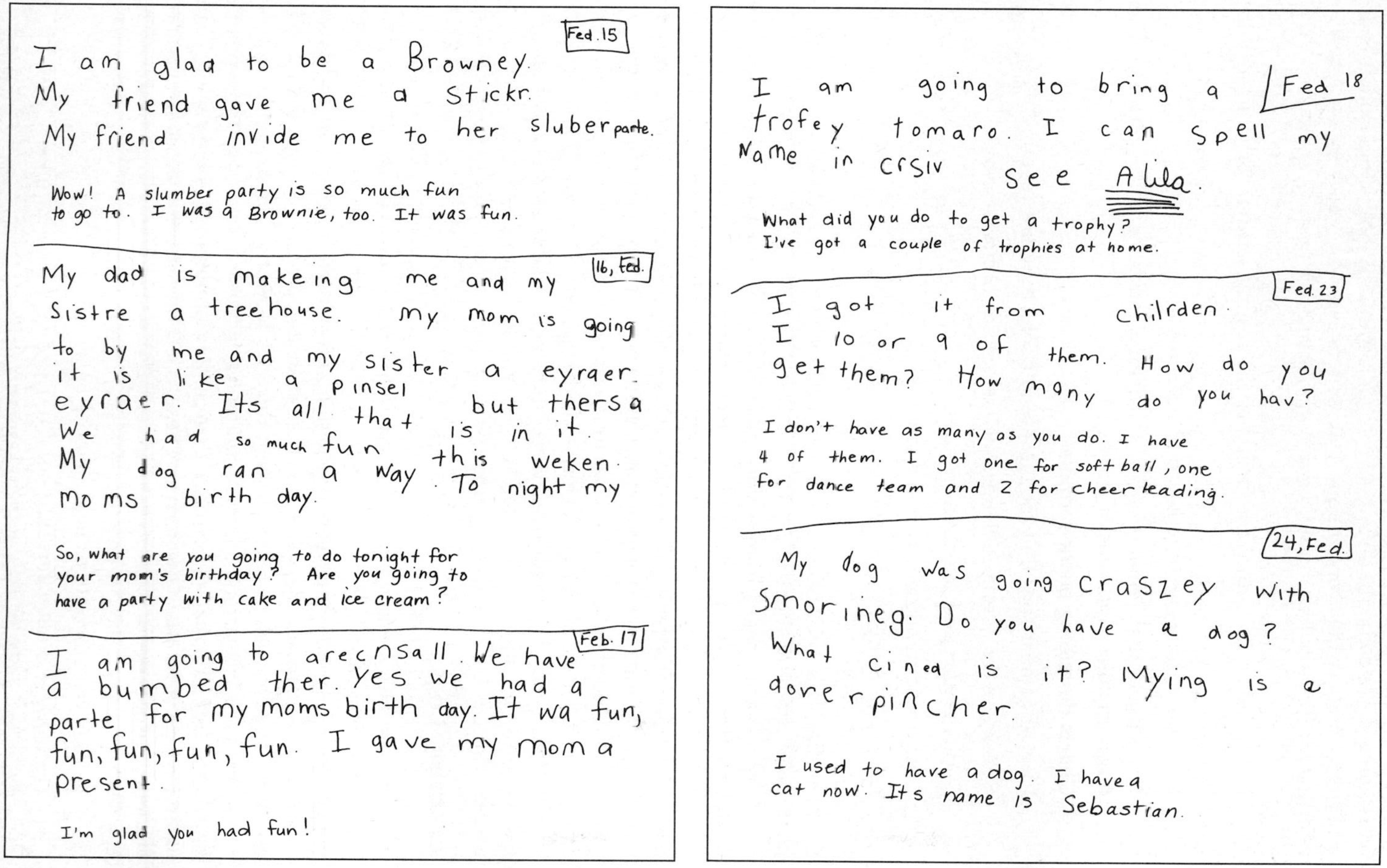
Fed. 15

I am glad to be a Browney.
My friend gave me a Stickr.
My friend invide me to her sluberparte.

Wow! A slumber party is so much fun to go to. I was a Brownie, too. It was fun.

16, Fed.

My dad is makeing me and my Sistre a treehouse. my mom is going to by me and my sister a eyraer. it is like a pinsel eyraer. Its all that is in it. but thersa We had so much fun My dog ran a way this weken. To night my moms birth day.

So, what are you going to do tonight for your mom's birthday? Are you going to have a party with cake and ice cream?

Feb. 17

I am going to arecnsall. We have a bumbed ther. Yes we had a parte for my moms birth day. It wa fun, fun, fun, fun, fun. I gave my mom a present.

I'm glad you had fun!

Fed 18

I am going to bring a trofey tomaro. I can spell my Name in crsiv see Alila.

What did you do to get a trophy? I've got a couple of trophies at home.

Fed. 23

I got it from children.
I 10 or 9 of them. How do you get them? How many do you hav?

I don't have as many as you do. I have 4 of them. I got one for softball, one for dance team and 2 for cheerleading.

24, Fed.

My dog was going craszey with Smorineg. Do you have a dog? What cined is it? Mying is a dorerpincher.

I used to have a dog. I have a cat now. It's name is Sebastian.

FIGURE 6–5

Entries from a Second Grader's Dialogue Journal

rules about using commas, and other mechanical information about punctuation, capitalization, and writing conventions that writers need to know to write well. Other
information students keep in writing notebooks include these examples:

> Lists of ideas for future compositions, interesting settings, or character descrip-
> tions
>
> Snippets of dialogue (overheard or invented)
>
> Notes about the elements of story structure, including characteristics of begin-
> nings, middles, and ends of stories
>
> Charts describing poetic formulas
>
> Lists of comparisons that they locate in books they are reading
>
> Synonyms for overused words, such as *said* or *pretty* or *nice*
>
> Capitalization and punctuation rules
>
> Lists of commonly misspelled words
>
> Lists of homonyms (e.g., *their-there-they're*)

By recording this information about writing in a journal notebook, students create a
permanent reference book.

Two sample pages from a fifth grader's writing notebook are shown in Figure
6–6. On the first page, the student lists synonyms for the overused word, *said,* collected
over several months from books she was reading and from a thesaurus. On the second
page, she organizes the words into five categories (ranging from *loud* to *soft*) that she
developed to locate the synonyms more easily.

Writing notebooks also function much like writing folders or portfolios in which
students write drafts of stories, poems, and other pieces of writing. Some students write
long stories in chapters or episodes, which they work on during daily journal writing or
free activity periods.

Learning Logs

Students can also use journals, called *learning logs,* to record or react to what they are
learning in language arts, science, math, or other content areas. Fulwiler (1987) explains, "When people write about something they learn it better" (p. 9). As students
write in these journals, they reflect on their learning, discover gaps in their knowledge,
and explore relationships between what they are learning and their past experiences.

One type of learning log is a *reading log,* which students use to respond to the
literature they are reading. Rather than simply summarize their reading, students
should relate it to their own lives. These questions suggest possible directions for
students' responses:

> Who is your favorite or least favorite character?
>
> Does one character remind you of a friend or family member?
>
> Does one character remind you of yourself?
>
> What event would you have handled differently if you were the character?

Words for *Said*

screamed	called	talked
remarked	screeched	giggled
insisted	hollered	warned
sighed	yelled	bellowed
answered	barked	ordered
cried	quoted	shrieked
pleaded	replied	whined
sobbed	wondered	mumbled
whimpered	moaned	responded
whispered	shouted	hissed
exclaimed	commanded	reminded
directed	raved	muttered
grumbled	questioned	murmured
bawled	argued	snapped
proclaimed	repeated	explained
bragged	laughed	

Words for *Said* Arranged According to Loudness

Loudest   *Softest*

yelled	snapped	questioned	whined	moaned
shouted	reminded	laughed	giggled	whispered
raved	called	answered	grumbled	muttered
bellowed	exclaimed	insisted	sighed	murmured
cried	commanded	wondered	sobbed	mumbled
hollered		pleaded		whimpered
screamed		replied		
screeched				
shrieked				

FIGURE 6–6

Entries from a Fifth Grader's Writing Notebook

Does the setting remind you of somewhere you have been?

What do you like best or least about the story?

How does this story make you feel?

What other stories that you have read does this story remind you of?

What would you change about this story, if you could?

Sample reading logs about *Bunnicula: A Rabbit-Tale of Mystery* (Howe & Howe, 1979) are shown in Figure 6–7. The picture entry was made by a second grader who listened to his teacher read the chapter book aloud; the handwritten entry was made by

When Bunicula bites a vegteble it turns white.

Chapter 1
"The Arrival"

I thought the part where Toby sat on Bunnicula at the movies and then popped out of his seat and shouted "I set on something!" was funny and sad. It was funny when Toby popped out of his seat but it was sad that Bunnicula got squished. And I already like it even though I've only heard one chapter and I think you would to! Oh ya, I forgot to tell about the note around Bunnicula's neck. But none of them could read because it was in a diffrent language, but Herold their dog could and it said "Take care of my baby." Next I think Chester the cat and Herold will get jellous and run away. Oh ya, Bunnicula is a rabbit.

FIGURE 6–7

Entries from Students' Reading Logs

a fourth grader who was reading the book himself. The fourth grader's entry is particularly interesting because he makes a prediction about what will happen in the next chapter.

In science, students can make daily records of the growth of seeds they plant or animals they are observing, such as mealworms, gerbils, or caterpillars. For instance, a second grade class observed caterpillars as they changed from caterpillars to chrysalides to butterflies over a period of four to six weeks. Students each kept a log with daily entries, in which they were to describe the changes they observed using shape, color, size, and other property words. Two pages from a second grader's log documenting the caterpillars' growth and change are presented in Figure 6–8. Older students also write lab reports in their logs. One fourth-grader's report for an experiment with hermit crabs is also presented in Figure 6–8. When students write in science logs, they are assuming the role of scientists, learning to make careful observations and to record them accurately.

Students can also use learning logs to write about what they are learning in math (Salem, 1982). They record explanations and examples of concepts presented in class and react to the mathematical concepts they are learning and any problems they may be having. Some upper-grade teachers allow students the last five minutes of math class to summarize the day's lesson and react to it in their learning logs. Through these

> Day 3
>
> The Caterpillars are
> 3 cm. They are Black
> and brown. they have
> littel Spikes on their
> Bodies. They have 9 legs.
> They have untanas on
> their heads.

> Day 25
>
> They are turning white.
> They are turning into
> Chrysalis and they
> are hanging from the
> roof.

FIGURE 6-8

Sample Entries from Students' Science Logs

activities, students practice taking notes, writing descriptions and directions, and other writing skills. They also learn how to reflect on and evaluate their own learning (Stanford, 1988).

Simulated Journals

In *simulated journals,* students assume the role of another person and write from that person's viewpoint. They can assume the role of a historical figure when they read biographies or study social studies units. When they read stories, they can assume the role of a character in the story. This activity gives students insight into other people's lives and into historical events. A look at a series of diary entries written by a fifth grader who has assumed the role of Betsy Ross shows how she carefully chose the dates for each entry and wove in factual information:

Lab Report

Do hermit crabs prefer a wet or dry habitat?

Materials
trough
trough cover
2 paper towels
water sprinkler

Procedures
1. Put one wet and one dry paper towel in the trough.
2. Place the hermit crab in the center of the trough and put on the cover.
3. Wait 60 seconds.
4. Open the cover and observe the location of the hermit crab.
5. Mark the location on the observation chart.
6. Do the experiment 6 times.

Observation Chart

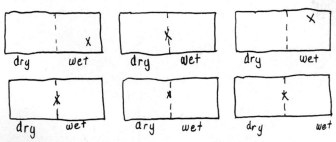

Results
Wet: 2
Dry: 0
center 4

Our hermit crab liked the center part best. 4 out of 6 times it stayed in the center. Then it liked the wet part next best. It didn't like the dry part at all.

FIGURE 6–8   (continued)

May 15, 1766

Dear Diary,

This morning at 5:00 I had to wake up my husband John to get up for work but he wouldn't wake up. I immediately called the doc. He came over as fast as he could. He asked me to leave the room so I did. An hour later he came out and told me he had passed away. I am so sad. I don't know what to do.

June 16, 1776

Dear Diary,

Today General Washington visited me about making a flag. I was so surprised. Me making a flag! I have made flags for the navy, but this is too much. But I said yes. He showed me a pattern of the flag he wanted. He also wanted six-pointed stars but I talked him into having five-pointed stars.

July 8, 1776

Dear Diary,

Today in front of Carpenter Hall the Declaration of Independence was read by Tom Jefferson. Well, I will tell you the whole story. I heard some yelling and shouting about liberty and everyone was gathering around Carpenter Hall. So I went to my next door neighbors to ask what was happening but Mistress Peters didn't know either so we both went down to Carpenter Hall. We saw firecrackers and heard a bell and the Declaration of Independence was being read aloud. When I heard this I knew a new country was born.

July 14, 1777

Dear Diary,

Today was a happy but scary day. Today the flag I made was adopted by Congress. I thought for sure that if England found out that a new flag was taking the old one's place something bad would happen. But I'm happy because I am the maker of the first American flag and I'm only 35 years old!

Young Children's Journals

Teachers have used journals effectively with preschoolers, kindergartners, and other young children who are emergent readers or who have not yet learned to read (Elliott, Nowosad, & Samuels, 1981; Hipple, 1985; Nathan, 1987). Young children's journal entries include drawings as well as some type of text. Some children write scribbles, random letters and numbers, simple captions, or extended texts using invented spelling. Their invented spellings often seem bizarre by adult standards, but are reasonable in terms of children's knowledge of phoneme-grapheme correspondences and spelling patterns. Other children want parents and teachers to take their dictation and write the text. After the text has been written, children can usually read it immediately, and they retain recognition of the words several days later.

Four kindergartners' journal entries are presented in Figure 6–9. In the top left journal entry, the child focuses on the illustration, drawing a detailed picture of a football game (note that the player in the middle right position has the ball), and adds five letters for the text so that his entry will have some writing. The top right entry is about a child's dog, and she writes a text vertically to accompany her illustration. She writes the first letter (or an important letter) in each word, except that she writes the

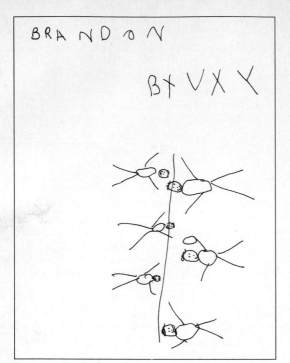

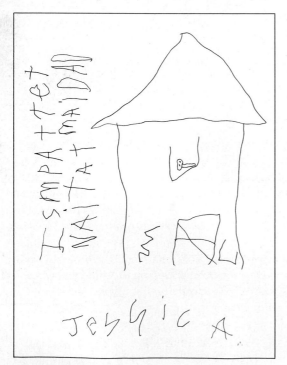

FIGURE 6–9

Entries from Young Children's Journals
Brandon, Becky, Jessica, and Marc, kindergartners

entire word *dog* because she knows how to spell it. The text is read this way: "My mother would like our black dog very much." The other two entries are more similar to personal journal entries because they describe events in the five-year-olds' lives. The entry on the bottom left reads "I spent the night at my dad's house"; the other entry reads "I'm going to be a phantom for Halloween," and the child has drawn a picture of himself in his Halloween costume.

Despite the variety of forms and purposes, journal writing helps elementary students discover the power of writing to record information and explore ideas. Students usually cherish their informal journals and are amazed by the amount of writing they contain.

Teaching Students to Write in Journals

Journals are typically written in notebooks. Spiral-bound notebooks are useful for long-term personal and dialogue journals and writing notebooks, and small booklets of paper stapled together are more often used for learning logs and simulated journals. Most teachers prefer to keep the journals in the classroom so they will be available for students to write in each day, but students might write in journals at home, as well.

Students usually write at a particular time each day. Many teachers have students make personal or dialogue journal entries while they take attendance or immediately after recess. Writing notebooks are often used during language arts class to record information about topics such as poetic forms or quotation marks. Learning logs and simulated journals can be written in as part of a daily assignment or as part of social studies or science class. For example, students may go over to an incubator of quail eggs, observe them, and then make an entry in their learning log during their language arts class. Students who are writing simulated journals as part of a social studies unit on the Crusades may make their entries during language arts class or during social studies class.

Introducing Students to Journal Writing. Teachers introduce students to journal writing by explaining the purpose of the journal-writing activity and writing a sample entry, often a class collaboration, on the chalkboard. This sample demonstrates that the writing is to be informal and that content is more important than mechanics. Then students make their own first entries, and several read their entries aloud. Sharing gives students who are still unclear about the activity additional models on which to base their own writing.

A similar introduction is necessary for each type of journal. Whereas all journals are informal writing activities, the purpose of the journal, the information in the entries, and the viewpoint of the writer vary according to the type.

Sustaining Journal Writing. Students write in journals on a regular schedule, usually daily. After students know how to write the appropriate type of entry, they can write independently. Some children prefer to write private journals, whereas others will volunteer to read their journal entries aloud each day no matter what type of journal they are writing. Young children should share their picture journal entries and talk about them. If the sharing becomes too time-consuming, several children can share each day. Teachers and classmates may offer compliments about the topic, word choice, humor, and so on.

JOURNALS

"We write every day and then the boys and girls share their journals in our circle. Sharing is the most important part of writing in my classroom."

Glenna Jarvis, Transitional First Grade Teacher
Western Hills Elementary School

PROCEDURE

My six-year-old children write in journals—one kind or another—every day. Sometimes they write about anything they want to. I usually start with these free-choice journals at the beginning of the school year. Later, they write about the stories we are reading or about what they are learning about in social studies or science.

This week the boys and girls are writing in bear-shaped booklets that I made to go along with our bear unit. Yesterday I read Freeman's *A Pocket for Corduroy* (1972), and we made a chart

If they wish, students can select entries from their journals to develop into polished compositions. Journal entries themselves are rarely revised and edited, however, because the emphasis is on writing fluency and self-expression rather than on correctness of spelling, punctuation, and other mechanical skills.

Students may continue to write in personal journals throughout the school year while their writing in other types of journals starts and stops with particular assignments. Students sometimes lose interest in personal journals, so many teachers find it useful to put the journals away for several weeks and substitute another type of journal or independent reading.

Assessing Students' Journals. Students can write in journals independently with little or no sharing with the teacher, or they can make daily entries that the teacher

of things my students would keep in their pockets. I see the ideas from the bear books I've read to them appear again and again in the children's writing. Several of the boys and girls even wrote in their journals about the stuff in their pockets.

Each morning as children finish writing in their journals, they leave their desks and come to sit on the carpet in our circle area. The first child to finish usually sits in our "author's chair" and gets to be the first one to share. As they share, boys and girls read or tell about their journal entries and then show them to the audience. Children in the audience raise their hands to offer comments and compliments. I always let the child who is sharing choose the children to offer comments and compliments. After three or four children have given compliments, the child who is sitting in the author's chair chooses the next boy or girl to share.

Sharing moves really quickly; the entire class can share in about 20 minutes, so I usually encourage everyone to share. If I'm pressed for time, I sometimes have half the children share in the morning and postpone the rest of sharing until afternoon. I've also tried having only five or six children share each day, but I prefer to have everyone be a part of the sharing every day so I know what every child is doing and what is happening in his or her life.

ASSESSMENT

Observing students as they share is probably the most important thing I do. I notice what topics they choose to write about, how they use drawing and writing to convey their message, and the confidence they have as they share their journals. I also look to see how they act when they are in the audience, the types of comments and compliments they offer, and how they respond to their classmates' journals. I participate in sharing every day and I watch and listen. I take a few minutes each day to update notes on index cards that I keep for each student in the class.

REFLECTIONS

My students are transitional first graders, and I try hard to tailor my program to meet their needs. They weren't "ready" for a traditional first grade program—for either academic or social reasons. Journal writing is the perfect activity for these students, because they are applying what they are learning about books, letters of the alphabet, and handwriting within a socialized and cooperative group setting.

monitors or reads regularly (Tway, 1984). Typically, students are accustomed to having teachers read all or most of their writing, but the quantity of writing students produce in journals is often too great for teachers to keep up with. Some teachers try to read all entries; others read selected entries and monitor remaining entries; still others rarely check students' journals. The three management approaches can be termed *private journals, monitored journals,* and *shared journals.* When students write private journals, they write primarily for themselves, and sharing with classmates or the teacher is voluntary—the teacher does not read the journals unless invited to. When students write monitored journals, they write primarily for themselves, but the teacher monitors the writing to ensure that entries are being made regularly. The teacher simply checks that entries have been made and does not read the entries unless they are specially marked "read me." Students write "shared" journals primarily for the teacher; the teacher regularly reads all entries, except those marked "private," and offers encouragement and suggestions.

Grading journal entries is a concern. Because the writing is informal and usually not revised and edited, teachers should not grade the quality of the entries. One option is to give points for each entry made, especially in personal journals. Some teachers grade the content in learning logs and simulated journals, though, because they can check to see if entries include particular pieces of information. For example, if students were writing simulated journals about the Crusades, they could be asked to include five pieces of historically accurate information in their entries. (It is helpful to ask students to identify the five pieces of information by underlining and numbering them.) Rough-draft journal entries should not be graded for mechanical correctness. Students need to complete the writing process (see Chapter 7) and revise and edit their entries if they are to be graded for mechanical correctness.

❖ INFORMAL WRITING STRATEGIES

When students make lists of ideas, organize information with a diagram, or write paragraphs to clarify their thinking, they are writing informally and using informal writing strategies.[2] This writing sometimes serves as prewriting and is expanded into more formal stories, reports, and poems; at other times it is more like taking notes or keeping a journal. As with journal writing, the strategies are informal, and the emphasis is on content, not mechanics. We will discuss four informal writing strategies— brainstorming, clustering, freewriting, and cubing—and appropriate places to use them.

Brainstorming

One good way to generate ideas is through *brainstorming,* a strategy that includes these steps:

1. Choose a topic.
2. Quickly list all words and phrases that come to mind in response to the topic.
3. Make no value judgments about items in the list; instead, look for unusual relationships among the items.

Students can brainstorm as a class, in small groups, or individually to help them discover what they already know about a topic. Brainstorming encourages the free flow of ideas. Introduce brainstorming with an activity for the whole class in which the teacher records students' ideas on the chalkboard or on a chart. After several whole-class brainstorming activities, students can brainstorm in small groups and, later, individually. By first using this strategy in a large group, students observe the process and learn how to use it before trying it independently. Brainstorming in small groups also

---

[2]This section is adapted from Tompkins and Camp (1988).

provides another rehearsal before students work independently. Even though brainstorming is a common strategy, it needs to be introduced and practiced several times before students feel comfortable with it.

Using Brainstorming in the Classroom.   Brainstorming can be used to generate ideas for writing; for example, students can use brainstorming to develop a list of the signs of spring to prepare for writing a poem, list the causes of the American Revolution before writing a chapter in a report, or list the characteristics of mysteries before writing their own. Brainstorming takes only a few minutes, but helps students generate ideas and words to use in writing.

Similarly, students can use brainstorming to identify a writing topic. For example, after reading Viorst's *Alexander and the Terrible, Horrible, No Good, Very Bad Day* (1972), students might be asked to write about a very bad, no good day they have had. They begin by listing some of their bad days, then choose from the list the most promising recollection for their topic. Or, after studying community helpers, students might brainstorm a list of all the helpers they have learned about and then select one helper to write about or to invite for an interview.

Students can also use brainstorming before they write in social studies, science, or other content area units. For example, on the day that a class of upper-grade students began a social studies unit on Egypt, the teacher asked them to brainstorm a list of all the words they knew about Egypt to put in their newly decorated "Egypt learning logs." The students suggested *mummy, Africa, Nile River, pyramids, slaves, tomb, hieroglyphics,* and *desert.* Students continued to add to their lists until, five weeks later, they contained over 100 words. The brainstormed list provided one measure of students' learning about Egypt, and students used the list for ideas for posters, journal entries, spelling words, acrostic poems, and research projects. Besides using the brainstormed list of words for many activities, the list itself was a piece of informal writing to help students learn, not a polished piece of writing that was graded by the teacher—the requirement was that students have a list of words about Egypt in their learning logs, and it was graded simply as done or not done.

Clustering

Another technique students can use to help them start writing is *clustering* (Rico, 1983). The process is similar to brainstorming, except that all the words generated are circled and linked to a nucleus word. The result is a weblike diagram rather than a list. Clustering includes the following steps:

1. Choose a topic.
2. Write the topic or nucleus word in a circle centered on a sheet of paper.
3. Draw rays from the circle and add main ideas.
4. Add branches with details and examples to complete each main idea.

Clustering is intended to capture as many associations as possible in a short time; ideas are triggered by associating one with another. This strategy helps students discover what they know about a topic.

Students and the teacher create a five-senses cluster.

The main ideas in a cluster are the same as main ideas in an outline (labeled with Roman numerals), and the details in a cluster are the same as details in an outline (labeled with uppercase letters). A biographical cluster is shown in Figure 6–10, with the same information in outline form. Although upper-grade students often feel outlining is a meaningless activity, they tend to enjoy clustering and recognize its usefulness in organizing ideas before writing. Outlining is a traditional prewriting activity that has outlived its usefulness. When required to have an outline as part of a high school or college writing assignment, many older students construct the outline after writing the composition. Whenever possible, students should use clustering rather than outlining to organize ideas before writing. When outlining must be taught, teachers should describe it as the formal rewriting of a cluster. Students first make a cluster as they gather and organize ideas for writing, then they can rewrite the cluster as an outline, sequencing the main ideas and details as they will appear in the composition.

Using Clusters in the Elementary Classroom.   Clusters take many different forms, depending on their purpose. A cluster for a story, for example, may include three rays—one for the beginning of the story, one for the middle, and one for the end. In contrast, a cluster for a research report on an animal might have five rays, one to answer each of these questions:

1.   What does the animal look like?
2.   Where does the animal live?
3.   What does the animal eat?
4.   How does the animal protect itself?
5.   What is special about the animal?

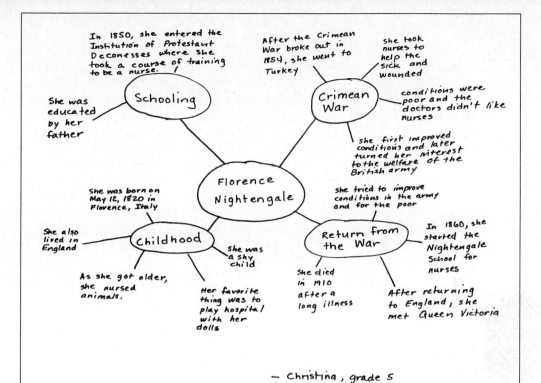

In 1850, she entered the Institution of Protestant Deconesses where she took a course of training to be a nurse.

After the Crimean War broke out in 1854, she went to Turkey

She took nurses to help the sick and wounded

She was educated by her father

Schooling

Crimean War

conditions were poor and the doctors didn't like nurses

she first improved conditions and later turned her interest to the welfare of the British army

Florence Nightengale

she tried to improve conditions in the army and for the poor

She was born on May 12, 1820 in Florence, Italy

She also lived in England

Childhood

She was a shy child

Return from the War

In 1860, she started the Nightengale School for nurses

As she got older, she nursed animals.

Her favorite thing was to play hospital with her dolls

She died in 1910 after a long illness

After returning to England, she met Queen Victoria

— Christina, grade 5

Florence Nightengale

I. Childhood
  A. She was born on May 12, 1820 in Florence, Italy.
  B. She also lived in England.
  C. She was a shy child.
  D. As she got older, she nursed animals.

II. Schooling
  A. She was educated by her father.
  B. In 1850, she entered the Institution of Protestant Deconesses where she took a course of training to be a nurse.

III. Crimean War
  A. After the Crimean War broke out in 1854, she went to Turkey.
  B. She took nurses to help the sick and wounded.
  C. Conditions were poor and the doctors didn't like the nurses.
  D. She first improved conditions and later turned her interest to the welfare of the British army.

IV. Return from the War
  A. She tried to improve conditions in the army and for the poor.
  B. In 1860, she started the Nightengale School for nurses.
  C. After returning to England, she met Queen Victoria.
  D. She died in 1910 after a long illness.

FIGURE 6–10

Biographical Information in a Cluster and in an Outline

A third type of cluster is a sensory cluster, in which each of the five senses is used as a main idea. Sensory clusters are useful for making abstract topics, such as the U.S. Constitution, more concrete. A fourth type of cluster is the "5 Ws plus one" cluster that journalists and student reporters use—the words *Who? What? Where? When? Why?* and *How?* are used as the main ideas. This type of cluster is useful for writing newspaper articles as well as for describing historical and autobiographical events. A fifth type of cluster is a biographical cluster, with information about a person's life and accomplishments. Figure 6–11 gives examples of five types of clusters.

These clusters are informal writing because students write for themselves. Students may develop a cluster to help them understand what they are learning or to use as background information in a writing activity. Sometimes the cluster is recopied as a piece of formal writing; for instance, the biographical cluster in Figure 6–11 was recopied on a large sheet of posterboard as a book report. The student added the title of the book, illustrations, and a quotation.

Freewriting

Freewriting is just what the name suggests—a technique in which students simply begin to write and let their thoughts flow from their minds to their pens without focusing on mechanics or revisions. Freewriting follows these steps:

1. Choose a topic.
2. Write for 5 to 10 minutes without pausing to think, to reread the writing, to make corrections, or for any other reason.
3. Write "I don't know what to write about" or a similar phrase over and over until a new idea comes.
4. *Optional:* At the end of the writing time, reread the writing and circle a specific and promising idea that can be expanded in another freewriting session.
5. *Optional:* Write again for another 5 to 10 minutes on the circled idea, without pausing for any reason.

Through freewriting, students can ramble on paper, generating words and ideas and developing writing fluency. This strategy, popularized by Peter Elbow (1973), is a way to help students focus on content rather than mechanics. Even by second or third grade, students have learned that many teachers emphasize correct spelling and careful handwriting more than the content of a composition. Elbow explains that focusing on mechanics makes writing "dead" because it does not allow students' natural voices to come through. Freewriting allows students to focus on content; later, if they choose, they can revise and polish their compositions using the writing process.

Student and adult writers often suffer from the "blank page syndrome," an inability to start writing—they look at the clean, blank sheet of paper and freeze. They discard sentence after sentence as they try to create a "perfect" first sentence—an imposing task for any writer! Freewriting is a good prescription for the blank-page syndrome because writers simply begin to write, with the confidence that after three or

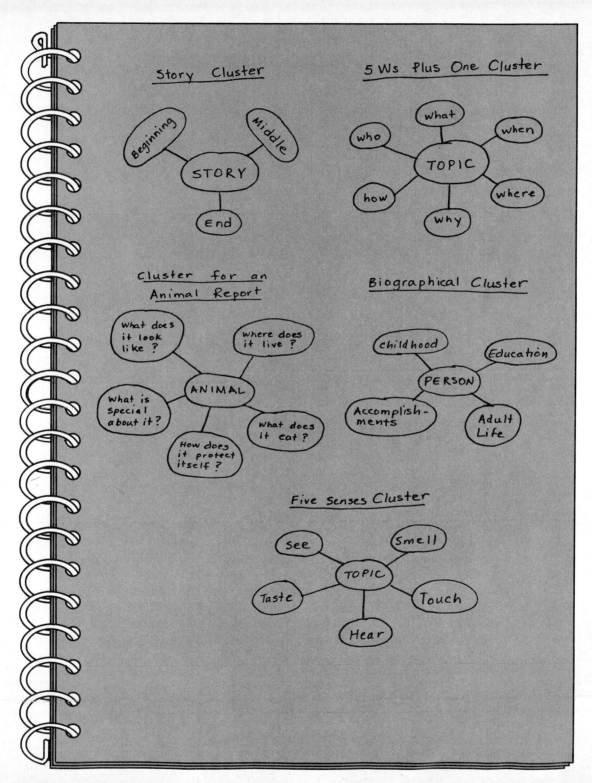

FIGURE 6–11

Teacher's Notebook Page: Five Types of Clusters

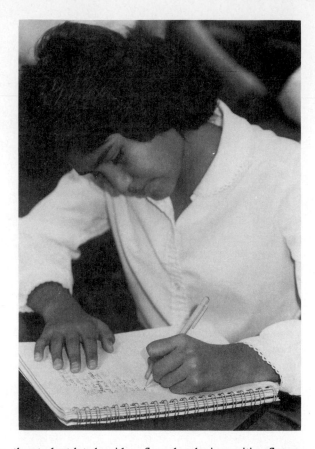

As she freewrites, the student lets her ideas flow, developing writing fluency.

four sentences, a usable, if not perfect, sentence will emerge (Elbow, 1981). Experienced writers often return to freewriting when they are stuck for ideas or words, knowing that freewriting gives them writing power.

Elbow developed two types of freewriting—unfocused and focused. In unfocused freewriting, students let their thoughts ramble from topic to topic. Freewriting can end after the first freewrite, or students can write a second, more focused, freewrite that develops and expands one of the ideas from the first attempt. If students are going to continue with a second freewrite, they reread what they have written and choose one idea to develop in the second try. Students should circle a word, phrase, or sentence in the first freewrite to specify the topic for the second freewrite, then write again for 5 to 10 minutes, following the guidelines for unfocused freewriting. This time students try to write on a single topic, probing as many dimensions of the topic as possible.

A set of unfocused and focused freewrites by a fifth grader is presented in Figure 6–12; the student writes about *A Family Apart* (Nixon 1987), a book about children of the Orphan Train that her class is reading. The first freewrite is general, about the

Unfocused Freewrite

The story starts in New York where a poor woman has six kids and the daughter Frances Mary finds out her brother Mike is a (copper stealer) and he gets caught by the police and he goes to court. His mother says she doesn't have a good home for them. She says she's going to put them on an orphan train so Frances Mary cuts her hair short and puts on boys' clothes because boys get adopted faster. And she wants to stay with her younger brother.

Focused Freewrite

Copper Stealer

In New York Mike and a bunch of his friends would hide in back alleys and when some wealthy men would walk by they would run and crash right into the group of men. They would reach and grab all the money out of the men's clothes. Then they would struggle away from the men and dart into another alley.

FIGURE 6–12

A Fifth Grader's Unfocused and Focused Freewriting on *A Family Apart* (Nixon, 1987)

beginning of the story, and the second is much more focused, about Mike, who is a copper stealer.

Using Freewriting in the Classroom.   Students freewrite for a variety of purposes. First, they can freewrite as they do in personal journal entries, letting their minds wander from topic to topic. This technique develops writing fluency; students are often amazed at how much they have written. When the timer rings, students ask, "Do we have to stop?"

Second, teachers can assign specific topics for students to explore in freewriting. Before starting a new unit of study, teachers might ask students to freewrite on the new topic to check their knowledge about the topic, to relate personal experiences about it, and to stimulate interest. For example, students can participate in the following freewrites in connection with current events, literature, social studies, and science units:

Freewrite on freedom or a geographic location before discussing a current events topic

Freewrite on the theme of friendship before reading *Bridge to Terabithia* (Paterson, 1977)

Freewrite on a trip students have taken before studying the Oregon Trail

Freewrite on snakes before studying reptiles

Freewrite on junk food before studying nutrition

After completing the unit, students freewrite again on the same topic, applying what they have learned, then compare the two freewrites as one measure of what they have learned in the unit.

Through this informal and unstructured writing, students collect ideas and words that may eventually be used in a polished composition. Even if the writing is never developed, however, the freewriting experience is valuable because students are developing writing fluency, learning a strategy to fall back on when they don't know how to start a writing assignment, and learning that they usually do have something to say on almost any topic. Students have their own reasons for liking to freewrite, as we see from these sixth graders' comments:

"The best thing about freewriting is that you can write things that are hard to say out loud and you can say what you feel." (Kathi, age 12)

"The best thing about freewriting is being able to show your feelings." (Bethany, age 11)

"The best thing about it is to let my mind go free and make it just dream on and I like that and I like telling about myself." (Beth, age 11)

"I think freewriting relaxes the mind." (Tami, age 12)

"I like it 'cause we can write down things and not have to write it correctly. But I wish we had more time to write." (Doug, age 12)

Clearly, these students enjoy freewriting and recognize its value as a writing strategy.

Cubing

When students want to explore a topic from several dimensions, *cubing* (Neeld, 1986) is a useful strategy. Cubing involves the following steps:

1. Choosing a topic
2. Examining it from all six sides of the cube and writing informally about each side
   - Describe (Describe its colors, shapes, and sizes.)
   - Compare (What is it similar to or different from?)
   - Associate (What does it make you think of?)
   - Analyze (Tell how it is made or what it is composed of.)
   - Apply (What can you do with it? How is it used?)
   - Argue for or against (Take a stand and list reasons for supporting it.)
3. Moving quickly (spending only 5 to 10 minutes on each side of the cube)

Students can brainstorm words, take notes, or freewrite about each side of the cube, or they can use a specially designed sheet of paper that can be cut and folded into a cube, as shown in Figure 6–13.

Cubing, a more complex informal strategy, requires students to be flexible and change their points of view as they examine a topic from the six sides of the cube. The strategy is more appropriate for older students. Because it is a more difficult strategy, begin by demonstrating cubing to the entire class and then have small groups of students cube a topic. A sixth grade class examined the topic of junk food by cubing; their

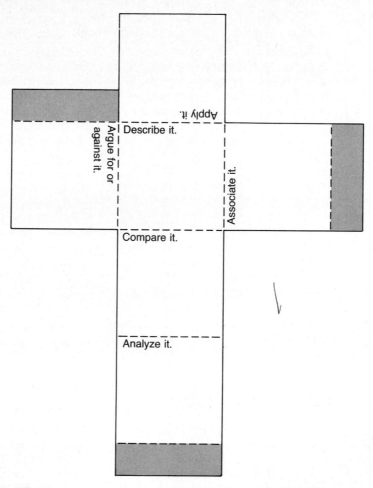

FIGURE 6–13

A Cubing Sheet

collaborative writing is shown in Figure 6–14. In this cubing, the students composed each paragraph together by first brainstorming a list of ideas. The teacher served as scribe and wrote their ideas on the chalkboard. Then students used the ideas to compose sentences for the paragraph they dictated to the teacher. As a last step, students refined the paragraph by checking the sequence of ideas, combining sentences, and choosing more appropriate vocabulary.

Using Cubing in the Classroom.   Middle- and upper-grade students divide into groups to cube a social studies topic, such as the Mississippi River, a book they have just read, or a scientific concept, such as gravity. They describe the topic, compare it to another, and focus on the topic from various points of view. This activity encourages students to become more flexible in their thinking and helps to expand their

Junk Food

1. **Describe it.**
Junk food is delicious! Some junk food is made of chocolate, like chocolate ice cream and brownies. Some junk food is salty, like potato chips and pretzels. Other junk food is usually sweet or sugary, like sugar cookies, sweet rolls, or soft drinks. Junk food packages are colorful and often show you what's inside to get your attention. Most of the packages are made of paper or plastic, and they make crinkly sounds.

2. **Compare it.**
Junk food tastes better than nutritious food, but nutritious food is better for you. Nutritious food is less sweet and salty. Parents would rather you eat nutritious food than junk food because nutritious food keeps you healthy, but kids would rather eat junk food because it tastes better and is more fun to eat.

3. **Associate it.**
Most often you eat junk food at get-togethers with friends. At parties, junk food such as chips and dip and soft drinks are served. At movies, you can buy popcorn, candy, nachos, and many other kinds of junk food. Other places where people get together and eat junk food are skating rinks, sporting events, and concerts.

4. **Analyze it.**
Junk food is not good to eat because of all the oils, sugar, salt and calories. Most of them have artificial colorings and flavorings. Many junk foods are low in vitamins and protein, but they have a high percentage of fats.

5. **Apply it.**
The most important thing you can do with junk food is to eat it. Some other uses are popcorn decorations at Christmas time, Halloween treats, and Easter candy. You can sell it to raise money for charities, clubs, and schools. Last year we sold junk food to raise money for the Statue of Liberty.

6. **Argue for or against it.**
We're for junk food because it tastes good. Even though it's not good for you, people like it and buy it. If there were no more junk food, a lot of people would be unemployed, such as dentists. Bakeries, convenience stores, fast food restaurants, grocery stores, and ice cream parlors would lose a lot of business if people didn't buy junk food. The Declaration of Independence guarantees our rights and freedoms, and Thomas Jefferson might have said, "Life, Liberty, and the Pursuit of Junk Food." We believe that he who wants something pleasing shall have it!

FIGURE 6–14

A Sixth Grade Collaborative Cubing on Junk Food
Tompkins & Camp, 1988, p. 213.

understanding of a topic. Whereas adults write all six sides of the cube individually, it is more reasonable for elementary students to work together in groups; each group can write one side of the cube. Students can write their side of the cube on a square piece of posterboard, and the squares can be taped together to create a cube. Students can also construct individual cubes and then share their writings.

Primary- and middle-grade teachers can adapt cubing for their students. After a second grade class takes a field trip to the zoo, for example, students may decide to make a class book about their trip. The teacher can guide students to think about the following questions, based on the six sides of the cube, do some research about zoos, and write their responses as chapters in the class book.

Describe: Describe the zoo.

Compare: Compare zoos to circuses or animals living in the wild.

Associate: What do sights, smells, and sounds of the zoo make you think of?

Analyze: How are zoos made?

Apply: Why do we have zoos?

Argue for or against: Are zoos good for animals or good for people?

Teaching Students to Use Informal Writing Strategies

Students need to learn how and when to use each of the informal writing strategies—brainstorming, clustering, freewriting, and cubing. They can use the strategies informally when they begin to discuss a topic, when they are listing facts, when they need information about a new concept, in response to reading, and in preparing to write. Teachers can help students apply the strategies by following certain steps.

1. Introduce the strategy. Introduce an informal writing strategy by demonstrating it through a whole class activity. It is best to use a familiar topic for students' first experience with the strategy, because it is difficult for them to focus on learning to use a strategy at the same time they are struggling with difficult content. Then review the steps in the strategy and work through the steps with the students, serving as a scribe and recording the writing on the chalkboard. After completing the steps, review the steps in the strategy again.

2. Apply the strategy. After introducing the strategy and working through the steps together as a class, have students practice using the strategy, first in small groups and, later, individually. The class and small group activities allow students to practice the strategy and clarify misconceptions before using it individually. Students who understand the strategy can quickly move on to use it in small groups, pairs, and individually, while students who need more support continue to work in a small group.

The four informal writing strategies can be used equally well in class, small group, or individual arrangements. For example, eighth graders can brainstorm about dreams before reading Martin Luther King's "I Have a Dream" speech as a class, in small groups, or individually. The arrangement for the brainstorming is not important and depends more on the classroom context and time constraints than on anything else. Similarly, kindergartners who are studying the color red can make a cluster of "red things" as a class, in a small group, or individually. Children can add words and pictures of red things to the cluster; the decision about how to arrange the activity depends on the students' independence and their previous experiences with clustering.

3. Learn when to use each strategy. Through a variety of experiences with the four strategies, students gain an intuitive awareness of the usefulness of each. It is best to talk about the strategies and ask students to choose which strategy to use, rather than tell them which to use for a specific writing activity. This practice helps students develop the ability to choose writing strategies, and to learn that brainstorming, for instance, is a good choice when they need to generate a list, whereas freewriting is more appropriate for exploring a topic.

After viewing a film about animals in the Arctic, for instance, the teacher may ask students to write informally about the film. They could use any of the four strategies; in a small group, students might brainstorm a list of concepts or facts from the film, or they might freewrite individually about what they learned. Together as a class, teacher and students might identify the main ideas in the film for a cluster, then students can complete the cluster individually by adding details. As another alternative, the class might do a cubing about Arctic animals using information from the film and other sources.

❖ STUDY SKILLS

Beginning in the middle grades, students read and learn from reading materials, and they are expected to make sense of and remember what they read. Students frequently complain that they have read the assigned materials but don't remember anything. To make sense of their reading, students need to be active readers, relating what they are reading to what they already know, and they need to be able to recognize main ideas.

In a recent study, older students were asked to read and remember everything they could about a selection, then to describe their study strategies. The results were disappointing: nearly half reported that they had read the material over a couple of times; seven percent mentioned remembering key words; and only two percent tried to visualize what they read or picked out the main idea of each paragraph. These responses suggest that many students have a limited repertoire of study strategies (Smith & Alvermann, 1981).

During the middle and upper grades, elementary students need to learn many types of study skills and strategies, including those that deal with organizing and retaining information, locating information, taking tests, and time management.

An Effective Study Strategy

The *SQ3R* strategy (Robinson, 1970) is a widely recommended systematic and effective study strategy. The formula is *S*urvey, *Q*uestion, *R*ead, *R*ecite and *R*eview.

1. *Survey.* Students skim through the reading material for a general idea or overview. Surveying allows readers to anticipate what ideas will be introduced in the material. Readers use headings to get an idea of the author's organization and the introduction and summary to survey the main ideas.

2. *Question.* Readers identify purposes to guide and organize their reading. One way to do this is to change headings and subheadings into questions.

If the material does not have these features, readers can use the introductions and summaries to develop questions. Another method is to identify key words or phrases. Readers should make note of their questions or key words.

3. *Read.* Students read to learn about the key words or to answer the questions they developed in the second step.

4. *Recite.* Students recite aloud what they learned about the key words or the answers to their questions. This step helps readers clarify their ideas. Students should always use their own words and think of examples to support their responses.

5. *Review.* For reinforcement, students review the assignment immediately after reading. Readers make notes during this step to help them remember the author's important ideas. They should reread any paragraphs that were unclear. Another review the next day also helps students remember better.

Taking Notes

Students can take notes in a variety of ways; we will focus on four techniques.

Questions and Answers. Students make a list of the questions they develop in the second step of the SQ3R strategy, using a sheet as shown in Figure 6–15. They write the questions in the left column; then, as they read or during the recite and review steps, students respond to each question in the right column. They can review their reading later by covering the right column and reciting answers to the questions.

Clusters. Students can make clusters to organize their note-taking. They use the key words they identified in the survey step to develop the cluster, then add details after reading. As an alternative, teachers can develop the cluster with circles for the main ideas and boxes for the details; students add the main ideas after they survey the reading material and fill in the details as they read. A cluster on personal computers with key words for the main ideas filled in and boxes for details to be completed after reading is shown in Figure 6–16.

Data Charts. Students can use data charts (McKenzie, 1979) to organize the information they will read. A data chart (Figure 6–17) is a matrix with two sets of key words or one set of key words and one set of questions. Students fill in the boxes in the matrix with details as they read. One set of key words represents the three geographic regions of the colonies—New England, Middle, and Southern. The other set of key words describes aspects of life in the colonies (questions could have been used instead of these key words). Teachers can make data charts for students to complete as they read or students can make their own charts after surveying the reading material.

Note-taking/Note-making. A more sophisticated form of note-taking is *note-taking/note-making* (Berthoff, 1981), in which students divide their paper into two columns—the left column for note-taking and the right one for note-making. Then they take notes in the left column. While and after taking notes, students reflect on their notes, and write comments in the right column, note-making. The right column is the

SQ3R Sheet

Question	Answer

FIGURE 6–15

SQ3R Question and Answer Sheet

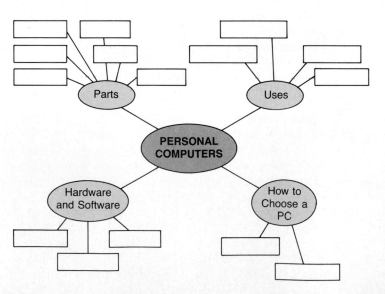

FIGURE 6–16

A Cluster on Personal Computers

	People	Society	Travel/ Communication	Economy	Government
New England Colonies					
Middle Colonies					
Southern Colonies					

FIGURE 6–17

A Data Chart on the American Colonies

more important because it is where students actively think about what they are learning and make connections to their own background of experiences, to events, to people, to things they have heard or read. They also note confusions, misunderstandings, and questions. When upper-grade students begin using this approach, they divide their papers in half, but with practice, they gradually increase the size of the especially important note-making column.

Students can use note-taking/note-making for almost any type of reading assignment. Students can take notes and make notes as they read a chapter book, a biography, a collection of poems, a content area textbook, a newspaper or magazine article, or an informational book.

Summary Writing

A *summary* is a statement of the main ideas gleaned from a selection rewritten in the student's own words. Teachers often ask upper-grade students to write summaries of their reading so that they will read more thoughtfully and reflect on their reading. When students don't know how to write a summary, however, they resort to copying a summary verbatim from another source. As with other types of informal writing, teachers need to teach students how to write a summary and model the procedure with the whole class and small groups.

Summary writing is an extension of note-taking because students take the notes they have compiled and rewrite the major points in their own words. (Steps in this procedure are adapted from Hayes [1989] and Manzo [1975].)

1. Read for information. Students read the selection, trying to remember all they can.

2. Brainstorm a list of details. When they have finished reading, students brainstorm a list of the details they remember. They divide a sheet of paper into two columns and write their brainstormed list in the left column; typically, the information is in fragments and in no particular sequence. Then students reread the list and make additions and corrections to the items.

3. Organize the information. Students reread the information in their lists looking for main ideas or categories, then write the categories in the right column and organize the information into the main idea categories. Some information may be deleted, and another reading of the selection may be necessary to organize the information. After the information has been classified, it is ready to be rewritten as a summary.

4. Write the summary. Students convert the main idea categories of information into sentences or, if possible, a single sentence. They can use sentence combining to combine short sentences or to embed ideas. (See Chapter 14 for more information about sentence combining.) As students write summary sentences, they leave out unimportant details, compress information by combining it, and add information so the summary makes sense (Hayes, 1989). After writing sentences for each category, they reread the sentences with an eye to revising to make the content easier to understand.

❖ REVIEW

Informal writing is writing that students do to develop writing fluency and to learn content area information more thoroughly. This type of writing is not developed or refined by the writing process. Three types of informal writing are journal writing, informal writing strategies, and note-taking. Students use journal writing to learn more about themselves, to practice writing, and to record the events in their lives. Literature also plays a role in journal writing. Students can read stories in which characters keep diaries and journals, and they can record their reactions to the stories they are reading in learning logs. Four types of informal writing strategies are brainstorming, clustering, freewriting, and cubing. Students use these strategies to gather and organize ideas, and other informal writing as part of some study skills; for example, note-taking figures in study strategies such as SQ3R, note-taking/note-making, and writing summaries.

❖ EXTENSIONS

1. Choose 15 of the writing forms in Figure 6–1 and plan how they could be incorporated at the grade level you teach or plan to teach. Consider ways to integrate them with other language arts activities or with social studies and other content area subjects.

2. Have students keep one of the six types of journals described in this chapter for three or four weeks.

3. Keep a personal journal in which you record experiences and feelings or a learning log in which you reflect on the material in this book as well as your teaching experiences for the remainder of the school term.

4. Have a small group of students participate in several unfocused and focused freewriting experiences. Explain that the goal of freewriting is to generate ideas and the words to express those ideas, and that correct spelling and careful handwriting are not important during freewriting. Later, students can polish one of their focused freewritings to share with classmates.

5. With a group of five classmates or a small group of upper-grade students, cube the topic of *birthdays*.

6. Use the SQ3R study strategy to read an informational book or an encyclopedia article on a topic such as whales or the moon and make a cluster with the information you learn.

❖ REFERENCES

Berthoff, A. E. (1981). *The making of meaning*. Montclair, NJ: Boynton/Cook.

Blos, J. (1979). *A gathering of days: A New England girl's journal, 1830–1832*. New York: Scribner.

Bode, B. A. (1989). Dialogue journal writing. *The Reading Teacher, 42*, 568–571.

Cleary, B. (1983). *Dear Mr. Henshaw*. New York: Morrow.

Elbow, P. (1973). *Writing without teachers*. London: Oxford University Press.

Elbow, P. (1981). *Writing with power*. New York: Oxford University Press.

Elliott, S., Nowosad, J., & Samuels, P. (1981). 'Me at home,' 'me at school': Using journals with pre-schoolers. *Language Arts, 58*, 688–691.

Fitzhugh, L. (1964). *Harriet the spy*. New York: Harper and Row.

Freeman, D. (1972). *A pocket for Corduroy*. New York: Viking.

Fulwiler, M. (1986). Still writing and learning, grade 10. *Language Arts, 63*, 809–812.

Fulwiler, T. (1985). Writing and learning, grade 3. *Language Arts, 62*, 55–59.

Fulwiler, T. (1987). *The journal book*. Portsmouth, NH: Boynton/Cook.

Gambrell, L. B. (1985). Dialogue journals: Reading-writing interaction. *The Reading Teacher, 38*, 512–515.

Halliday, M. A. K. (1973). *Explorations in the functions of language*. London: Edward Arnold.

Halliday, M. A. K. (1975). *Learning how to mean: Explorations in the development of language*. London: Edward Arnold.

Hayes, D. A. (1989). Helping students GRASP the knack of writing summaries. *Journal of Reading, 33*, 96–101.

Hipple, M. L. (1985). Journal writing in kindergarten. *Language Arts, 62*, 255–261.

Howe, D., & Howe, J. (1979). *Bunnicula: A rabbit-tale of mystery*. New York: Atheneum.

Kreeft, J. (1984). Dialogue writing—Bridge from talk to essay writing. *Language Arts, 61*, 141–150.

McKenzie, G. R. (1979). Data charts: A crutch for helping pupils organize reports. *Language Arts, 56*, 784–788.

Mallon, T. (1984). *A book of one's own: People and their diaries*. New York: Ticknor & Fields.

Manzo, A. V. (1975). Guided reading procedure. *Journal of Reading, 18*, 287–291.

Nathan, R. (1987). I have a loose tooth and other unphotographic events: Tales from a first grade journal. In T. Fulwiler (Ed.), *The journal book*, pp. 187–192. Portsmouth, NH: Boynton/Cook.

Neeld, E. C. (1986). *Writing*. Glenview, IL: Scott, Foresman.

Nixon, J. L. (1987). *A family apart*. New York: Bantam Books.

Paterson, K. (1977). *Bridge to Terabithia*. New York: Crowell.

Rico, G. L. (1983). *Writing the natural way.* Los Angeles: Tarcher.

Robinson, F. P. (1970). *Effective reading.* New York: Harper and Row.

Salem, J. (1982). Using writing in teaching mathematics. In M. Barr, P. D'Arcy, & M. K. Healy (Eds.), *What's going on? Language/learning episodes in British and American classrooms, grades 4–13,* pp. 123–134. Montclair, NJ: Boynton/Cook.

Smith, S. J., & Alvermann, D. E. (1981). Developing study-skilled readers. In E. K. Dishner, T. W. Bean, & J. E. Readence (Eds.), *Reading in the content areas: Improving classroom instruction.* Dubuque, IA: Kendall/Hunt.

Stanford, B. (1988). Writing reflectively. *Language Arts, 65,* 652–658.

Staton, J. (1980). Writing and counseling: Using a dialogue journal. *Language Arts, 57,* 514–518.

Staton, J. (1987). The power of responding in dialogue journals. In T. Fulwiler (Ed.), *The journal book,* pp. 47–63. Portsmouth, NH: Boynton/Cook.

Tchudi, S., & Tchudi, S. (1984). *The young writer's handbook: A practical guide for the beginner who is serious about writing.* New York: Scribner.

Tompkins, G. E., & Camp, D. E. (1988). Rx for writer's block. *Childhood Education, 64,* 209–214.

Tway, E. (1981). Come, write with me. *Language Arts, 58,* 805–810.

Tway, E. (1984). *Time for writing in the elementary school.* Urbana, IL: ERIC Clearinghouse on Reading and Communication Skills and the National Council of Teachers of English.

Viorst, J. (1972). *Alexander and the terrible, horrible, no good, very bad day.* New York: Atheneum.

7 THE WRITING PROCESS

PREWRITING
Choosing a Topic
Considering Function
Considering Audience
Considering Form
Prewriting Activities
Collaborative Compositions

DRAFTING
The Rough Draft
Writing Leads
Emphasis on Content

REVISING
Rereading the Rough Draft
Writing Groups
Students' Revisions

EDITING
Getting Distance
Proofreading
Correcting Errors

SHARING
Concept of Author
Ways to Share Writing
Responding to Student Writing

THE WRITING PROCESS IN ACTION
Introducing the Writing Process
Using the Writing Process in Elementary Classrooms
The Teacher's Role
Assessing Students' Writing

◆ THIS CHAPTER PRESENTS AN ALTERNATIVE APPROACH TO TEACH-
ing writing: the writing process. It is the same process that adult writers use. By
using the writing process, students learn how to write, not how to dislike writing.

◆ AS YOU ARE READING, THINK ABOUT THESE QUESTIONS:

What are the steps in the writing process?

How do elementary students learn to use the writing process?

What is the teacher's role?

When should students use the writing process?

M ost writing activities in the elementary grades fall under the rubric *creative writing*. Teachers select a creative topic, such as "If I were a leprechaun. . .," write it on the chalkboard, and direct students to write a story about being a leprechaun. They allow students 30 minutes to write a single-draft story, then collect the papers to grade—and are often disappointed with the results. Perhaps three or four students have written clever and creative stories; these papers are fun to read, and teachers feel gratified. Two or three students turn in papers of only several words or a single sentence. This is not surprising because these students never complete assignments. The teachers' biggest disappointment, however, is in the remaining 20 mediocre papers. These compositions include a few descriptive sentences, but overall, they lack interesting ideas and cannot be classified as stories.

Unsuccessful experiences with writing often lead teachers to believe their students cannot write, but the problem is not with the students; rather, it is with the traditional approach to writing. These students are not learning how to write, but are simply trying to perform their best on a difficult task that is unclear to them.

In recent years, because of the research about writing, the emphasis in writing instruction has shifted from product to process, and the teacher's role has shifted from merely assigning and assessing the product to working with students throughout the writing process. Figure 7–1 summarizes contrasts between the traditional and process approaches to teaching writing.

The writing process includes five stages: prewriting, drafting, revising, editing, and sharing. The key features of each stage are shown in Figure 7–2. The labeling and numbering of the stages should not be construed to suggest that this writing process is a linear series of neatly packaged categories. Research shows that the process is cyclical, involving recurring cycles, and labeling is only an aid to identifying and discussing the activities that represent each stage. In the classroom, the stages merge and cycle. Moreover, students personalize the process to meet their needs and vary the process according to the writing assignment.

❖ PREWRITING

Prewriting is the getting-ready-to-write stage. The traditional notion that writers have a topic completely thought-out and ready to flow onto the page is ridiculous. If writers wait for ideas to fully develop, they may wait forever. Instead, writers begin tentatively—talking, reading, writing—to see what they know and what direction they want to go.

Prewriting has probably been the most neglected stage in the writing process; however, it is as crucial to writers as a warm-up is to athletes. Murray (1982) believes that 70 percent or more of writing time should be spent in prewriting. During the prewriting stage, students

- Choose a topic
- Consider purpose, form, and audience
- Use informal writing strategies to generate and organize ideas
- Write a collaborative composition

	The Traditional Approach	The Process Approach
Topic Selection	A specific creative writing assignment is made by the teacher.	Students choose their own topics, or topics are drawn from content-area study.
Instruction	Teachers provide little or no instruction. Students are expected to write as best they can.	Teachers teach students about the writing process and about writing forms.
Focus	The focus is on the finished product.	The focus is on the process that students use when they write.
Ownership	Students write for the teacher and feel little ownership of their writing.	Students assume ownership of their writing.
Audience	The teacher is the primary audience.	Students write for genuine audiences.
Collaboration	There is little or no collaboration.	Students write collaboratively and share writing in groups.
Drafts	Students write single-draft compositions in which they must focus on content and mechanics at the same time.	Students write rough drafts to pour out ideas and then revise and edit these drafts before making final copies.
Mechanical Errors	Students are required to produce error-free compositions.	Students correct as many errors as possible during editing but a greater emphasis is on content than on mechanics.
Teacher's Role	The teacher assigns the composition and grades it after it is completed.	The teacher teaches about writing and provides feedback during revising and editing.
Time	Students complete most compositions in less than an hour.	Students may spend one, two, or three weeks working on a composition.
Assessment	The teacher assesses the quality of the composition after it is completed.	The teacher provides feedback while students are writing so they can use it to improve their writing. Assessment focuses on the process that writers use and the finished product.

FIGURE 7—1

The Traditional and Process Approaches to Writing

Stage 1: Prewriting

Students write on topics based on their own experiences.
Students engage in rehearsal activities before writing.
Students identify the audience to whom they will write.
Students identify the purpose of the writing activity.
Students choose an appropriate form for their compositions based on audience and
purpose.

Stage 2: Drafting

Students write a rough draft.
Students emphasize content rather than mechanics.

Stage 3: Revising

Students share their writing in writing groups.
Students participate constructively in discussions about classmates' writing.
Students make changes in their compositions to reflect the reactions and comments
of both teacher and classmates.
Between the first and final drafts, students make substantive rather than only minor
changes.

Stage 4: Editing

Students proofread their own compositions.
Students help proofread classmates' compositions.
Students increasingly identify and correct their own mechanical errors.

Stage 5: Sharing

Students publish their writing in an appropriate form.
Students share their finished writing with an appropriate audience.

FIGURE 7–2

Overview of the Writing Process Stages

Choosing a Topic

Choosing a topic for writing can be a stumbling block for students who have become
dependent on teachers to supply topics. Traditionally, teachers supplied topics by suggesting gimmicky story starters and relieving students of the "burden" of topic selection. Often, these "creative" topics stymied students, who were forced to write on topics
they knew little about or were not interested in. Graves (1976) calls the traditional
approach of supplying topics for students "writing welfare." Instead, students need to
take responsibility for choosing their own writing topics.

At first, dependent students will argue that they do not know what to write about;
however, teachers can help them brainstorm a list of three, four, or five topics, and then
identify the one topic they are most interested in and know the most about. Students

WRITERS' WORKSHOP

"My students are comfortable working in groups. They learn just as much from each other as they learn from me. That really surprised me, but it's true!"

Judy Reeves, Third Grade Teacher,
Western Hills Elementary School

PROCEDURE

Six third graders are meeting with me in a small group called a "Writers' Workshop." My purpose today is to touch base with these students about their new writing projects. Students are choosing their own topics and writing forms for this project. Jason eagerly tells us he is making a joke book, and he has already begun writing and illustrating his collection of favorite jokes. He's pleased with this opportunity to pursue a hobby. Trina wants to write a fairy tale, and she shows us a cluster she has made with ideas about the story. Lance is thinking about writing a Nintendo adventure story, but he says he isn't sure how to start. Group members encourage him to begin with one of his fantastic drawings. Nikki has just read a biography about Benjamin Franklin that she shares with us. She can't decide whether she should write a retelling of this biography or write her own autobiography. The students give her suggestions, but she hasn't decided yet. Eliza wants to write a letter to Beverly Cleary, her favorite author, and as her prewriting, she has

who feel they cannot generate any writing topics are often surprised that they have so many options available. Then, through prewriting activities, students talk, draw, read, and even write to develop information about their topics.

Asking students to choose their own topics for writing does not mean that teachers never give writing assignments; teachers do provide general guidelines. They may specify the writing form (journals, stories, poems, reports, and so on), and at other times, they may establish the function (for example, to share what students have learned about life in ancient Egypt), but students should choose their own specific content. For instance, students can demonstrate what they have learned about life in

made a list of the things she wants to include in her letter. Derek doesn't seem to have an idea yet, but Lance and Jason offer several suggestions.

Throughout this 20-minute meeting, my students are active group members. They take turns sharing ideas for their projects and talk about how they have developed their ideas, using writing process terminology such as "rough draft" and "clustering ideas." They are also supportive of their classmates. They listen thoughtfully and offer compliments and encouragement.

The group comes to an end with students each briefly explaining what they will do next. Those who are ready to prewrite or draft move back to their desks while I talk with Derek and Nikki, who are not sure what they want to write about. Nikki decides to try her hand at writing her autobiography, and she begins to draw a lifeline of her life. Derek decides to brainstorm a list of three possible topics and share them with me later today.

ASSESSMENT

My students use the writing process, and I confer with them during each stage. I want to see that they are on task. It is too easy for third graders to get sidetracked or bogged down with a problem that I or their classmates can solve.

I give my students contracts for each writing project. The contract lists the steps of the writing process and the activities students will complete in each step. My students staple the contracts inside the front cover of their writing folders and check off each activity as they complete it. This is how I keep track of each student and how they keep track of themselves. I ask them to confer with me during each step of the writing process, and I schedule time for the conferences three mornings a week. They confer with me at the beginning and at the end, before they are ready to share. I think touching base is important—having them tell me what their projects will be.

REFLECTIONS

I have been very pleased—maybe even amazed—at how well my third graders work in small groups and how responsible they have become. They are learning from each other and supporting each other as they learn. Cooperative learning really works! Besides conferences to touch base with students, we use conferences in this classroom when students want feedback on their writing, to teach language skills in minilessons, and to discuss authors we are studying.

ancient Egypt by writing a report on how people were mummified, a biography of Queen Nefertiti, an acrostic poem on the word *pyramid,* or a story set in ancient Egypt.

Considering Function

As students prepare to write, they need to think about their function or purpose for writing. Are they writing to entertain? To inform? To persuade? Halliday's (1973, 1975) seven language functions (see Chapter 1) apply to written as well as oral language; for example:

Instrumental language	Writing to satisfy needs, as in business letters
Regulatory language	Writing to control the behavior of others, as in directions and rules
Interactional language	Writing to establish and maintain social relationships, as in pen pal letters and dialogue journals
Personal language	Writing to express personal opinions, as in learning logs and letters to the editor
Imaginative language	Writing to express imagination and creativity, as in stories, poems, and scripts
Heuristic language	Writing to seek information and to find out about things, as in learning logs and interviews
Informative language	Writing to convey information, as in reports and biographies

Understanding the function of a piece of writing is important because function influences other decisions students make about audience and form.

Considering Audience

Students may write primarily for themselves, to express and clarify ideas and feelings, or they may write for others. Possible audiences include classmates, younger children, parents, foster grandparents, children's authors, and pen pals. Other audiences are more distant and less well known; for example, students write letters to businesses to request information, articles for the local newspaper, or stories and poems for publication in literary magazines.

Children's writing is influenced by their sense of audience. Britton, Burgess, Martin, McLeod, and Rosen (1975) define *sense of audience* as "the manner in which the writer expresses a relationship with the reader in respect to the writer's understanding" (pp. 65–66). When writing for others, students adapt to fit their audience just as they vary their speech to fit an audience. Students must be aware of their audience while writing to choose appropriately. Writing that students do simply to complete assignments often lacks a sense of audience because the student doesn't consider that factor.

Considering Form

One of the most important considerations is the form the writing will take: story? letter? poem? journal entry? A writing assignment could be handled in any one of these ways. As part of a science unit on hermit crabs, for instance, students could write a story about a hermit crab, draw a picture and label body parts, explain how hermit crabs obtain shells to live in, or keep a log of observations about the pet hermit crabs in the classroom. There is an almost endless variety of forms that children's writing may take. (A list of these forms was presented in Chapter 6.) Too often students' writing is limited to writing stories, poems, and reports; instead, they need to experiment with a wide variety of writing forms and explore the functions and formats.

Through reading and writing, students develop a strong sense of these forms and how they are structured. Langer (1985) found that by third grade, students responded in distinctly different ways to story and report writing assignments; they organized the writing differently and included varied kinds of information and elaboration. Similarly, Hidi and Hildyard (1983) found that elementary students could differentiate between stories and persuasive essays. Because children are clarifying the distinctions between various writing forms during the elementary grades, it is important that teachers use the correct terminology and not label all children's writing "stories."

Most writing forms look like the text on this page—block form, written from left to right and top to bottom, but some writing forms require a special arrangement on a page and others require special language patterns. Scripts, recipes, poems, and letters are four writing forms that have recognizable formats. Also, some writing forms use special language patterns. Many stories begin with "Once upon a time. . ."; letters require "Dear. . ." and "Sincerely." As children are introduced to these writing forms and have opportunities to experiment with them, they will learn about the unique requirements of the formats.

Teaching children about these three considerations—function, audience, and form—is an important component of writing instruction. Children need to learn to make decisions about the three considerations and to know the range of options available to writers.

Decisions about function, audience, and form influence each other. For example, if the function is to entertain, an appropriate form might be a story, poem, or script—and these three forms look very different on a piece of paper. Whereas a story is written in the traditional block format, scripts and poems have unique page arrangements. Scripts are written with the character's name and a colon, and the dialogue is set off. Action and dialogue, rather than description, carry the story line in a script. In contrast, poems have unique formatting considerations, and words are used judiciously. Each word and phrase is chosen to convey a maximum amount of information. Audience also plays an important role. Audiences for stories, scripts, and poems are often unknown or large, whereas audiences for letters are very specialized. A letter is usually written to a particular person, and although the function of a letter may be to request information or share personal information, it is customized according to audience. Children might share the same information with their pen pal and with their grandparents, but would present the information differently according to degree of familiarity or formality. Although these decisions may change as students write and revise, writers must begin with at least a tentative concept of function, audience, and form as they move into the drafting stage.

Prewriting Activities

Students engage in activities to gather and organize ideas for writing. These activities, which Graves (1983) calls "rehearsal," help students prepare for writing. There are two types of prewriting activities: background activities and informal writing strategies.

Background activities are the experiences that provide the knowledge students need for writing, because it is impossible to write well about a topic you don't know well. Rehearsal activities take many forms, including drawing, talking, reading, interviewing, informal drama, field trips, and other content area experiences.

Drawing. Drawing is the way young children gather and organize ideas for writing. Kindergarten and first grade teachers often notice that students draw before they write and, thinking that they are eating dessert before meat and vegetables, insist that they write first. But many young children cannot; when asked to write before drawing, they explain that they can't write yet because they don't know what to write until they see what they draw. Young children use drawing and other symbol systems as they grapple with the uniqueness of writing (Dyson, 1982, 1983, 1986).

Talking. Talk in the classroom is necessary to writing. Students talk with their classmates to share ideas about possible writing topics, try out ways to express an idea, and ask questions. They read and react to each other's writing. They also participate in class discussions about writing forms, elements of story structure, and other writing-related issues. Talk continues throughout the writing process as students discuss their compositions in conferences and proofread each other's writing.

Reading. Reading and writing are *symbiotic*—mutually beneficial processes. Through reading, children gather ideas for writing and investigate the structure of various written forms. Reading is a type of experience, and writers need a variety of experiences to draw on. Students often retell a favorite story in writing, write new adventures for favorite story characters, or experiment with repetition, onomatopoeia, or another poetic device used in a book they have read.

Informational books also provide raw material for writing. For example, if students are studying polar bears, they need to gather background information about the animal, its habitat, and predators, which they may use in writing a report. If they are interested in Olympic athletes, they may read biographies of Jesse Owens, Nadia Comaneci, Ray Leonard, Mary Lou Retton, and others, and then share what they learn by writing a collection of biographical sketches. (For more information about reading-writing connections, see Chapter 8.)

Interviews. Students can interview community members who have special knowledge about the topic they plan to write about. Interviewing involves three steps: planning the interview, conducting it, and sharing the results. In the first step, students arrange for the interview and develop a list of questions to ask during the interview. Next, students conduct the interview by asking questions they have prepared in advance and taking notes or tape-recording answers. Last, students share their information. Sharing can take many different forms, ranging from newspaper articles to reports to books.

Informal Drama. Children discover and shape ideas they will use in their writing through informal drama (Wagner, 1988). According to Mills (1983), having students role-play an experience gives energy and purpose to writing. Writing often grows out of dramatic play and role-playing stories. Children can learn to write directions by writing them for an obvious activity, such as making a peanut butter sandwich.

Typically, children omit crucial steps, such as opening the jar; however, if they write the directions after dramatizing the activity, the directions are better organized and more complete. Students can also assess the effectiveness of their written directions by having a classmate try to follow them; they can thus see what steps they have omitted.

Similarly, in social studies units and after reading stories, students can reenact events to bring an experience to life. Heathcote (Wagner, 1976, 1983) advocates an approach in which teachers choose a dramatic focus or a particular critical moment for students to reenact. The improvisation begins with students' assuming roles, and the teacher becomes a character, too. As they role-play the event, the teacher uses questions to draw students' attention to certain features and to prove their understanding. For example, after reading *Sarah Plain and Tall* (MacLachlan, 1985), children might reenact the day Sarah took the wagon to town. This is the critical moment in the story: Does Sarah like them and their prairie home well enough to stay? Through role-playing, students become immersed in the event, and by reliving it, they learn far more than mere facts.

Informal Writing Strategies. The second type of prewriting activities is informal writing strategies. Students use the informal writing strategies—brainstorming, clustering, freewriting, and cubing (discussed in Chapter 6)—to gather and organize information they learn through background experiences. They brainstorm lists of words and ideas, cluster main ideas and details, freewrite to discover what they know about a topic and what direction their writing might take, and cube a complex topic to consider it from several different dimensions. Many young children (and some older students) use drawing to gather and organize ideas for writing.

Collaborative Compositions

Another prewriting activity is to compose a collaborative or group composition. Writing a composition together with the teacher gives students an opportunity to rehearse before writing a similar composition independently. The teacher reviews concepts and clarifies misconceptions during the group composition, and students offer ideas for writing as well as suggestions for tackling common writing problems. The teacher also models or demonstrates the writing process and provides an opportunity for students to practice the process approach to writing in a supportive environment.

First, the teacher introduces the idea of writing a group composition and reviews the assignment. Students compose the class collaboration composition, moving through drafting, revising, editing, and sharing stages of the writing process. The teacher records students' dictation, noting any misunderstandings about the writing assignment or process. When necessary, the teacher reviews concepts and offers suggestions. Students first dictate a rough draft, which the teacher records on the chalkboard or on chart paper. Then teacher and students read the composition and identify ways to revise it. Some parts of the composition will need reworking, and other parts may be deleted or moved. More specific words will be substituted for less specific ones, and redundant words and sentences will be deleted. Students may also want to add new parts to the composition. After making the necessary content changes, students proofread the composition, checking for mechanical errors, paragraph breaks, and for sentences to combine. They correct errors and make changes. Then the teacher or a student copies the completed composition on chart paper or on a sheet of notebook paper. Copies can be duplicated and given to each student.

Fine (1987) explains how her middle-grade class of students with behavior disorders wrote a novel collaboratively. All of the students contributed to the writing and, through the experience, learned that they could write and that they had valuable contributions to make. Fine sums up the experience this way: "Collaboration is learning to learn and to work together . . . Collaboration is a great solution" (p. 487).

Collaborative compositions are an essential part of many writing experiences, especially when students are learning to use the writing process or a new writing form. Group compositions serve as a "dry run," during which students' questions and misconceptions can be clarified.

❖ DRAFTING

In the process approach to writing, students write and refine their compositions through a series of drafts. During the drafting stage, students focus on getting their ideas down on paper. Because writers do not begin writing with their compositions already composed in their minds, students begin with tentative ideas developed through prewriting activities. The drafting stage is the time to pour out ideas, with little concern about spelling, punctuation, and other mechanical errors.

The Rough Draft

Students should skip every other line when they write their rough draft so they will have space to make revisions. They should learn to use arrows to move sections of text, cross-outs to delete sections, and scissors and tape to cut apart and rearrange text just as adult writers do. They should write on only one side of a sheet of paper so they can cut it apart or rearrange it. As word processors become more accessible in elementary classrooms, revising, shifting, and deleting text will become much easier, but for the time being wide spacing is crucial. (Make small x's on every other line of children's papers as a reminder to skip lines when they draft their compositions.)

Students label their drafts by writing *Rough Draft* in ink at the top of the paper or by stamping them with a ROUGH DRAFT stamp. This label indicates to the writer, other students, parents, and administrators that the composition is a draft, in which the emphasis is on content, not mechanics, and explains why the teacher has not graded the paper or marked mechanical errors. Some students who are just learning the writing process and have been writing single-draft compositions secretly plan to continue to write this way and plan to make this rough draft their final draft if they write carefully. Stamping *Rough Draft* at the top of the paper obviates that possibility and emphasizes that writing involves more than one stage.

When drafting their compositions, students may need to modify earlier decisions about function, audience, and, especially, form; for example, a composition that began

This student uses information from a cluster in writing a rough draft.

as a story may be transformed into a report, letter, or a poem because the new format allows the student to communicate more effectively. The process of modifying earlier decisions continues into the revising stage.

Writing Leads

The lead or opening sentence or two of a composition is crucial. Think about the last time you went to a library to choose a novel to read. Several titles or book jackets may have caught your eye, but to make your selection, you opened the book and read the first paragraph or two. Which book did you choose? You chose the one that "hooked" you or "grabbed" your attention. The same is true for children's writing. Students who consider audience will want to grab that audience. Nothing is such a failure as a piece of writing that no one wants to read! Children use a variety of techniques to appeal to their audience, such as questions, facts, dialogue, brief stories, and problems.

Graves (1983) and Calkins (1986) recommend that students create several leads and try them out on classmates before choosing one. Writing leads gives students valuable knowledge about how to manipulate language and how to vary viewpoint or sequence.

Emphasis on Content

It is important in the rough draft stage not to emphasize correct spelling and neatness; in fact, pointing out mechanical errors during the drafting stage sends students a false message that mechanical correctness is more important than content (Sommers, 1982). Later, during editing, students can clean up mechanical errors and put their composition into a neat, final form.

❖ REVISING

During the revising stage, writers refine ideas in their compositions. Students often break the writing process cycle as soon as they complete a rough draft, believing that once they have jotted down their ideas, the writing task is complete. Experienced writers, however, know they must turn to others for reactions and revise on the basis of these comments. Revision is not just polishing; it is meeting the needs of readers by adding, substituting, deleting, and rearranging material. By definition, *revision* means *seeing again,* and in this stage writers see their compositions again with the help of classmates and teacher. Activities in the revising stage are

- Rereading the rough draft
- Sharing the rough draft in a writing group
- Revising on the basis of feedback from the writing group

Rereading the Rough Draft

Writers are the first to revise their compositions. Some revision occurs during drafting, when writers make choices and changes. After finishing the rough draft, writers need to distance themselves from the draft for a day or two, then reread the draft from a fresh perspective, as a reader might—not as a writer who knows what he or she intended to say. As they reread, students make changes—adding, substituting, deleting, and moving—and place question marks by sections they need help with, so they bring them up in their writing group.

Writing Groups

Students meet in writing groups[1] to share their compositions with small groups of classmates. Because writing cannot occur in a vacuum and must meet the needs of readers, feedback is crucial. Mohr (1984) identifies four general functions of writing groups: (1) to offer the writer choices; (2) to give the writer's responses, feelings, and thoughts; (3) to show different possibilities in revising; and (4) to speed up revising. Writing groups provide a "scaffold," or supportive environment, in which teachers and

---

[1]Adapted from Tompkins & Friend, 1988.

classmates talk about plans and strategies for writing and revising (Applebee & Langer, 1983; Calkins, 1983).

Writing groups can form spontaneously when several students have completed drafts and are ready to share their compositions, or can be formal groupings with identified leaders. Writing groups in a primary-grade classroom might form spontaneously when students finish writing and go to the reading rug and sit in a chair designated the "author's chair" (Graves & Hansen, 1983). As soon as a child with writing to share is sitting in the chair, others who are available to listen and respond go to sit in front of the author's chair. When three or four children have arrived for the writing group, the writer reads the writing and the other children listen and respond to it, offering compliments and relating this piece of writing to their own experiences and writing. Sometimes the teacher joins the listeners on the rug to participate in the writing group; if the teacher is involved in another activity, the children work independently. Writing groups in another primary-grade classroom might be more formal; reading groups may become writing groups when children have completed a rough draft and are ready to share their writing with classmates and teacher. The teacher participates in these groups, providing feedback along with the students. In a middle- or upper-grade classroom, groups might function independently. Four or five students are assigned to each group, and a list of groups and their members is posted in the classroom. The teacher puts a star by one student's name, and that student serves as a group leader. The leader changes every quarter.

Two students share their compositions, ask questions, and suggest ways to revise.

After writing group arrangements are established, students meet to share their writing through these activities:

- The writer reads the composition aloud to the group
- Listeners respond with compliments about the composition
- The writer asks listeners for assistance with trouble-spots
- Listeners offer comments and suggestions for improving the composition
- Each writer in the group repeats the process
- Writers identify two or three revisions they will make to improve their compositions

The Writer Reads.   Students take turns reading their compositions aloud to the group. Everyone listens politely, thinking about the compliments and suggestions they will make after the writer finishes reading. Only the writer should look at the composition, because when classmates and teacher look at it, they quickly notice and comment on mechanical errors, even though the emphasis during revising is on content. Listening to the writing without looking at it keeps the focus on content.

Listeners Offer Compliments.   After the reading, group members offer compliments, stating what they liked about the writing. These positive comments should be specific and focus on strengths. General remarks such as "I like it" or "It was good," even though positive, are not effective feedback. When teachers first introduce revision, they should model appropriate responses, because students will not know how to offer specific and meaningful comments. Working together, teacher and students brainstorm a list of acceptable comments and post it in the classroom for reference. Acceptable comments may focus on organization, leads, word choice, voice, sequence, dialogue, theme, and so on. Figure 7–3 lists sample compliments.

The Writer Asks Questions.   After a round of positive comments, writers ask for assistance with trouble-spots they have identified earlier when rereading their writing, or they may ask questions that reflect more general concerns about how well they are communicating. Admitting that they need help from their classmates is a major step in learning to revise. Sample questions to classmates also appear in Figure 7–3. The teacher can model some of these questions, prefacing them with "If I were the writer, I might ask. . ."; when students understand what is expected of them, they can brainstorm a list of questions to add to their list of compliments. Many students find it difficult to ask questions about their writing, but when they work with their writing to the extent that they ask questions, as in the examples above, they have become writers who look to their classmates for assistance.

Listeners Offer Suggestions.   Members of the writing group next ask questions about things that were unclear to them and make suggestions about how to revise the composition. Almost any writer resists constructive criticism, and it is especially difficult for elementary students to appreciate comments and suggestions. This approach is far more constructive than the traditional approach, however, in which the teacher grades the paper and covers it with comments and corrections. Students ask the

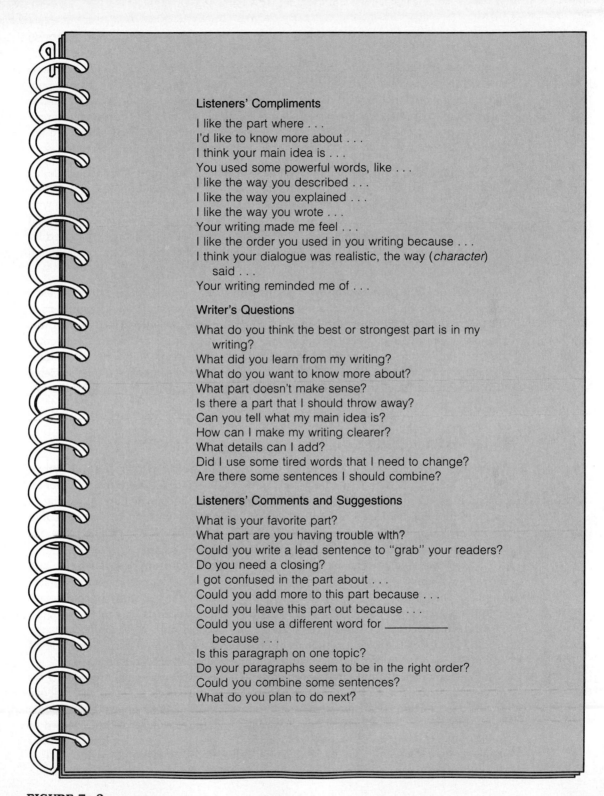

Listeners' Compliments

I like the part where . . .
I'd like to know more about . . .
I think your main idea is . . .
You used some powerful words, like . . .
I like the way you described . . .
I like the way you explained . . .
I like the way you wrote . . .
Your writing made me feel . . .
I like the order you used in you writing because . . .
I think your dialogue was realistic, the way (*character*)
    said . . .
Your writing reminded me of . . .

Writer's Questions

What do you think the best or strongest part is in my
    writing?
What did you learn from my writing?
What do you want to know more about?
What part doesn't make sense?
Is there a part that I should throw away?
Can you tell what my main idea is?
How can I make my writing clearer?
What details can I add?
Did I use some tired words that I need to change?
Are there some sentences I should combine?

Listeners' Comments and Suggestions

What is your favorite part?
What part are you having trouble with?
Could you write a lead sentence to "grab" your readers?
Do you need a closing?
I got confused in the part about . . .
Could you add more to this part because . . .
Could you leave this part out because . . .
Could you use a different word for _____
    because . . .
Is this paragraph on one topic?
Do your paragraphs seem to be in the right order?
Could you combine some sentences?
What do you plan to do next?

FIGURE 7–3

Teacher's Notebook Page: Writing Group Responses
Adapted from Tompkins & Friend, 1988.

same types of questions that adult writers ask. Figure 7–3 also lists sample questions that writing group members can use to make comments and suggestions. Here again, the teacher should model some of the questions, and when students understand what is expected of them, they can brainstorm a list of comments and suggestions. It is important to take time to teach students what kinds of comments and suggestions are acceptable so that they will word what they say in a helpful rather than hurtful way.

Repeat the Process. The feedback process is repeated for each student's composition. This is the appropriate time for teachers to provide input as well. They should react to the piece of writing as any other listener would—not error-hunting with red pen in hand (Sommers, 1982). In fact, most teachers prefer to listen to students read their compositions aloud rather than read them themselves and become frustrated by the numerous misspelled words and nearly illegible handwriting common in rough drafts.

Writers Plan for Revision. At the end of the writing group, students each make a commitment to revise their writing based on the comments and suggestions of the group members. The final decisions on what to revise always rest with the writers themselves, but with the understanding that their rough drafts are not perfect comes the realization that some revision will be necessary. When students verbalize their planned revisions, they are more likely to complete the revision stage. Some students also make notes for themselves about their revision plans. After the group disbands, students make the revisions.

Students' Revisions

In revising, students add words, substitute sentences, delete paragraphs, and move phrases. They cross out, draw arrows, and write in the space left between the double-spaced lines of their rough drafts. Students move back and forth into prewriting to gather additional information, into drafting to write a new paragraph, and back into revising to substitute an overused word. Messiness is inevitable, but despite the scribbles, students are usually able to decipher what they have written.

Students' changes can be classified as additions, substitutions, deletions, and movements, and the level of changes as a word, a phrase/clause, a sentence, a paragraph, or the entire text (Faigley & Witte, 1981). There is a hierarchy of complexity both in the four types of revisions and in the levels of revision, as illustrated in Figure 7–4. The least complex change is the addition of a word, and the most complex change is at the text level. Elementary students often focus at the word and phrase/clause level and make more additions and substitutions than deletions and movements.

Teachers can examine the types and levels of revisions students are making by examining their revised rough drafts; the revisions are another gauge of students' growth as writers. Teachers may want to share this hierarchy with upper-grade students so they know the available revision options and encourage them to keep a record of their revisions. Even though some revisions may be considered more sophisticated than others, students should make the change that is most effective for their writing—they should not move a paragraph when adding a sentence is the more effective revision.

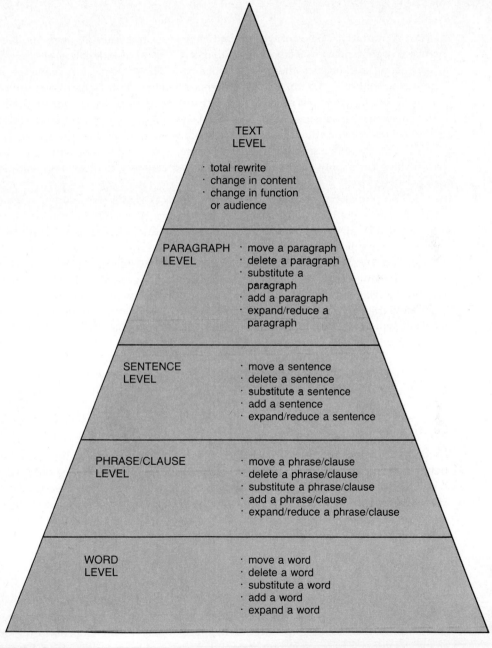

FIGURE 7–4

A Revision Hierarchy

❖ EDITING

Editing is putting the piece of writing into its final form. Until this stage, the focus has been on content; now the focus changes to mechanics, and students polish their writing by correcting spelling and other mechanical errors. The goal here is to make the writing "optimally readable" (Smith, 1982). Writers understand that if their compositions are not readable, they have written in vain, because their ideas will never be read.

Mechanics are the commonly accepted conventions of written Standard English. They include capitalization, punctuation, spelling, sentence structure, usage, and formatting considerations specific to poems, scripts, letters, and other writing forms. The use of these commonly accepted conventions is a courtesy to those who will read the composition.

The optimal time to teach mechanical skills is during the editing stage of the writing process, not by means of workbook exercises. When editing a composition that will be shared with a genuine audience, students are more interested in using mechanical skills correctly so they can communicate effectively.

In a study of two third grade classes, Calkins (1980) found that the students in the class who learned punctuation marks as a part of editing could define or explain more marks than the students in the other class who were taught punctuation skills in a traditional manner, with instruction and practice exercises on each punctuation mark. In other words, the results of this research, as well as other studies (Elley, Barham, Lamb, Wyllie, 1976; Bissex, 1980; Graves, 1983), suggest that a functional approach to teaching the mechanics of writing is more effective than practice exercises.

Students move through three activities in the editing stage: getting distance from the composition; proofreading to locate errors; and correcting errors.

Getting Distance

Students are more efficient editors if they set the composition aside for a few days before beginning to edit. After working so closely with a piece of writing during drafting and revising, they are too familiar with it to be able to locate many mechanical errors. With the distance gained by waiting a few days, children are better able to approach editing with a fresh perspective and gather the enthusiasm necessary to finish the writing process by making the paper optimally readable.

Proofreading

Students proofread their compositions to locate and mark possible errors. Proofreading is a unique type of reading in which students read slowly, word by word, hunting for errors rather than reading quickly for meaning (King, 1985). Concentrating on mechanics is difficult because of our natural inclination to read for meaning. Even experienced proofreaders often find themselves reading for meaning and thus overlooking errors that do not inhibit meaning. It is important, therefore, to take time to explain proofreading and demonstrate how it differs from regular reading.

To demonstrate proofreading, teachers take a piece of student writing and copy it on the chalkboard or display it on an overhead projector. The teacher reads it several times, each time hunting for a particular type of error. During each reading, the teacher reads the composition slowly, softly pronouncing each word and touching the word with a pencil or pen to focus attention on it. The teacher marks possible errors as they are located.

Errors are marked or corrected with special proofreader's marks. Students enjoy using these marks, the same ones that adult authors and editors use. Proofreader's marks that elementary students can learn to use in editing their writing are presented in Figure 7–5.

Editing checklists help students focus on particular categories of error. Teachers can develop checklists with two to six items appropriate for the grade level. A first grade checklist, for example, might include only two items—perhaps one about capital letters at the beginning of sentences and a second about periods at the end of sentences. In contrast, a middle-grade checklist might include items such as using commas in a series, paragraph indention, capitalizing proper nouns and adjectives, and spelling homonyms correctly. During the school year, teachers revise the checklist to focus attention on skills that have recently been taught. A sample third grade editing checklist is presented in Figure 7–6; the writer and a classmate work together as partners to edit their compositions. First, students proofread their own compositions, searching for errors in each category on the checklist and, after proofreading, check off each item. After

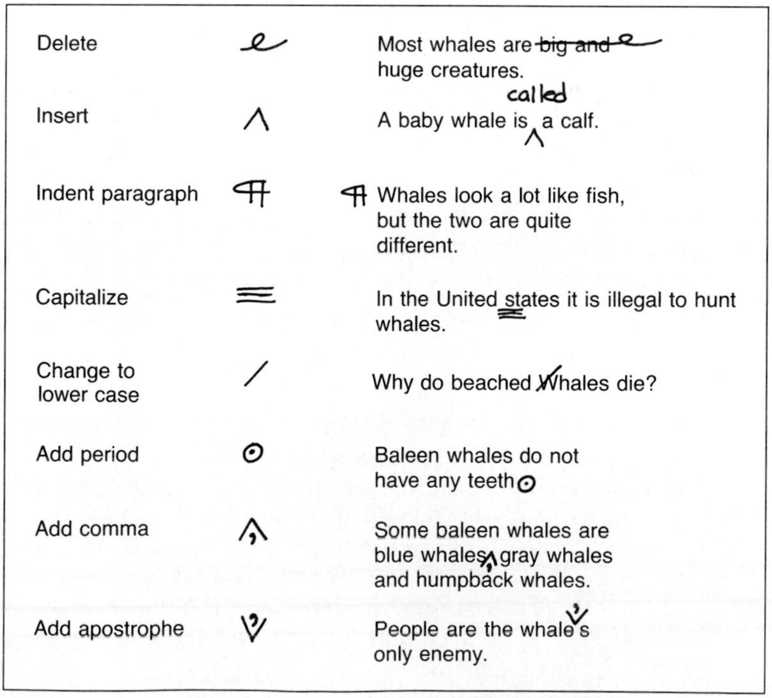

Delete	℮	Most whales are ~~big and~~ huge creatures.
Insert	∧	A baby whale is ∧ a calf. *called*
Indent paragraph	⊬	⊬ Whales look a lot like fish, but the two are quite different.
Capitalize	≡	In the United states it is illegal to hunt whales.
Change to lower case	/	Why do beached Whales die?
Add period	⊙	Baleen whales do not have any teeth⊙
Add comma	∧	Some baleen whales are blue whales∧ gray whales and humpback whales.
Add apostrophe	∨	People are the whale's only enemy.

FIGURE 7–5

Proofreader's Marks

EDITING CHECKLIST

Author   Editor

[ ]   [ ]   1. I have circled the words that might be misspelled.

[ ]   [ ]   2. I have checked that all sentences begin with capital
                               letters.

[ ]   [ ]   3. I have checked that all sentences end with
                               punctuation marks.

[ ]   [ ]   4. I have checked that all proper nouns begin with a
                               capital letter.

Signatures:

Author: _____ *Editor:* _____

FIGURE 7–6

A Third Grade Editing Checklist

completing the checklist, students sign their names and trade checklists and compositions. Now they become editors and complete each other's checklist. Having writer and
editor sign the checklist helps to impress on them the seriousness of the activity.

Correcting Errors

After students proofread their compositions and locate as many errors as possible, they
correct the errors individually or with their editor's assistance. Some errors are easy to
correct; some require use of a dictionary; others involve instruction from the teacher. It
is unrealistic to expect students to locate and correct every mechanical error in their
compositions—not even published books are error-free! Once in a while, students may
even change a correct spelling or punctuation mark and make it incorrect, but overall
they correct far more errors than they create.

Editing can end after students and their editors correct as many mechanical
errors as possible, or after students meet with the teacher in a conference for a final
editing. When mechanical correctness is crucial, this conference is important. Teachers
proofread the composition with the student, and they identify and make the remaining
corrections together, or the teacher makes checkmarks in the margin to note errors for
the student to correct independently.

Minilessons.   Many teachers use the editing stage as a time to informally assess students' mechanical and spelling skills and to give minilessons on a skill that a child or several children are having trouble with. The teacher notes which students are having difficulty with a particular skill—paragraphing, capitalizing proper nouns, or using the apostrophe in possessives—and conducts a brief minilesson using the students' writing instead of a language textbook. In this brief, five- to ten-minute lesson, the teacher reviews the particular skill and students practice the skill as they help to correct their classmates' writing. Then they may practice the skill a few more times on sentences they create or using text from their journals or another writing project. If additional work is needed, they might develop a lesson on it to teach to their classmates or students in another class. This procedure individualizes instruction and teaches the skill when learning it matters to students.

❖ SHARING

In the final stage of the writing process, *sharing,* students bring the composition to life by publishing their writing or sharing it orally with an appropriate audience. When they share their writing with real audiences of classmates, other students, parents, and the community, students come to think of themselves as authors.

Students sit in the "author's chair" to share writing with classmates.

Concept of Author

Most of the time children assume the role of "student" in school; however, they take more interest in a subject and learn more about it when they assume a more active role. The real-life role for writing is "author." Authors write for real purposes and for genuine audiences. In contrast, students often write so the teacher will have something to grade. Explaining that the writing process they are using is similar to what authors use is one way to help students think of themselves as authors.

Another way children move from the "student" to the "author" role is by developing the concept of an author. Graves and Hansen (1983) believe primary classrooms should have a special chair, designated the "author's chair," where whoever sits there—either teacher or child—is reading a book. At the beginning of the year, most of the books read from that chair are picture books; however, when children begin to write and construct their own books, they sit in that chair to share them. Sitting in the special author's chair and sharing their books makes children gradually realize that they are authors! Graves and Hansen describe children's transition from student to author in three steps:

1. *Replication: Authors write books.* After hearing many books read to them and reading books themselves, students develop the concept that authors are the people who write books.

2. *Transition: I am an author.* Sharing the books they have written with classmates from the author's chair helps students view themselves as authors.

3. *Option-awareness: If I wrote this published book now, I wouldn't write it this way.* Students learn that they have options when they write, and this awareness grows after experimenting with various writing functions, forms, and audiences.

In classrooms where reading, writing, and sharing writing are valued activities, students become authors. Often they recopy a story or other piece of writing into a stapled booklet or hardcover book, and these published books are added to the classroom or school library. Sometimes students form a classroom publishing company and add the name of the company and the year the book was made on the title page. In addition, students can add an "All About the Author" page with a photograph at the end of their books, just as information about the author is often included on book jackets of adult authors. A fifth grader's "All about the Author" page from a collection of poetry he wrote is presented in Figure 7−7. Notice that the student wrote about himself in the third person, as in adult biographical sketches.

Ways to Share Writing

Students read their writing to classmates or share it with larger audiences through hardcover books placed in the class or school library, class anthologies, letters, newspaper articles, plays, filmstrips and videotapes, or puppet shows. These and other ways to share children's writing are listed in Figure 7−8. Sharing enables students to communicate with genuine audiences who respond to their writing in meaningful ways. Sharing writing is a social activity that helps children develop sensitivity to an audience

All About the Author

Brian was born on August 22, 1976 in Woodward, Ok. He is going to be a USAF pilot and Army L.T., and a college graduate. He is also wanting to be a rockstar singer. He is going to write another book hopefully about the Air Force or Army. In his spare time he likes to run, ride his motorcycle, skate board, and play with his dogs. He also wrote "How the Hyena Got His Laugh."

FIGURE 7-7

A Fifth Grader's "All About the Author" Page

and confidence in themselves as authors. When students share writing, Dyson (1985) advises that teachers consider the social interpretations—students' behavior, teacher's behavior, and interaction between students and teacher—within the classroom context. Individual students will naturally interpret the sharing event differently. More than just providing the opportunity for students to share writing, teachers need to teach students how to respond to their classmates. Teachers themselves serve as a model for responding to students' writing without dominating the sharing.

Bookmaking. One of the most popular ways for children to share their writing is by making and binding books. Simple booklets can be made by folding a sheet of paper into quarters, like a greeting card. Students write the title on the front and use

Read writing aloud in class	Display poetry on a "poet-tree"
Submit to writing contests	Send to a pen pal
Display as a mobile	Make a hardbound book
Contribute to class anthology	Produce a roller movie
Contribute to the local newspaper	Display on a bulletin board
Place in the school library	Make a filmstrip
Make a shape book	Make a big book
Read the writing on a cassette tape	Design a poster
Submit to a literary magazine	Read to foster grandparents
Read at a school assembly	Share as a puppet show
Share in writing groups	Display at a public event
Share with parents and siblings	Read to children in other classes
Produce a videotape	

FIGURE 7—8

Twenty-five Ways to Share Writing

the three remaining sides for their compositions. They can also construct booklets by stapling sheets of writing paper together and adding construction paper covers. Sheets of wallpaper cut from old sample books also make good, sturdy covers. These stapled booklets can be cut into various shapes, too. Students can make more sophisticated books by covering cardboard covers with contact paper, wallpaper samples, or cloth. Pages are sewn or stapled together, and the first and last pages (endpapers) are glued to the cardboard covers to hold the book together. Directions for making one type of hardcover book are shown in Figure 7—9.

Magazines that Publish Student Writing. Students can also submit stories, poems, and other pieces of writing to magazines that publish children's writing. Some magazines also accept artwork to accompany the compositions. Figure 7—10 lists these magazines. Students should check a recent issue of the magazine or write to the editor for specific guidelines before submitting a contribution. These are general guidelines for submitting students' writing:

Read the information in the magazine about the types of contributions the editor wants to receive. Send the contribution to magazines that publish that type of writing.

Follow the information in the magazine in submitting the contribution.

Write a cover letter to send with the contribution, giving the author's name, address, telephone number, and age. Also state in the letter that the contribution is original.

Send a self-addressed, stamped envelope so the editor can return the contribution if it will not be published.

Keep a copy of the contribution in your files.

Expect to wait three months or more before learning whether the contribution has been accepted for publication.

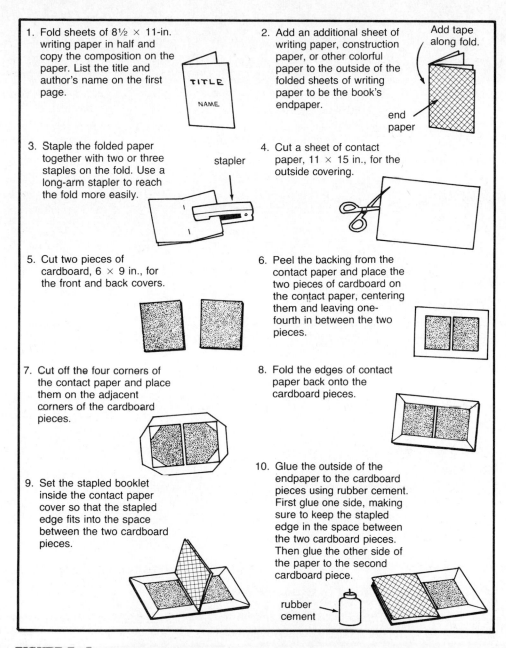

1. Fold sheets of 8½ × 11-in. writing paper in half and copy the composition on the paper. List the title and author's name on the first page.

2. Add an additional sheet of writing paper, construction paper, or other colorful paper to the outside of the folded sheets of writing paper to be the book's endpaper.

   Add tape along fold.

   end paper

3. Staple the folded paper together with two or three staples on the fold. Use a long-arm stapler to reach the fold more easily.

   stapler

4. Cut a sheet of contact paper, 11 × 15 in., for the outside covering.

5. Cut two pieces of cardboard, 6 × 9 in., for the front and back covers.

6. Peel the backing from the contact paper and place the two pieces of cardboard on the contact paper, centering them and leaving one-fourth in between the two pieces.

7. Cut off the four corners of the contact paper and place them on the adjacent corners of the cardboard pieces.

8. Fold the edges of contact paper back onto the cardboard pieces.

9. Set the stapled booklet inside the contact paper cover so that the stapled edge fits into the space between the two cardboard pieces.

10. Glue the outside of the endpaper to the cardboard pieces using rubber cement. First glue one side, making sure to keep the stapled edge in the space between the two cardboard pieces. Then glue the other side of the paper to the second cardboard piece.

    rubber cement

FIGURE 7–9

Directions for Making Hardcover Books

Children should be warned that competition is stiff in many publications and that their contributions may not be accepted even though they are well written. Children should not expect to receive monetary compensation for their writing; the honor is in seeing their name in print!

Magazine	Address	Ages	Types of Writing Accepted
American Girl	830 Third Avenue New York, NY 10022	12–14	Short stories, poems, and letters to the editor
Boys' Life	1325 Walnut Hill Lane Irving, TX 75602	all	Short stories, poems, and nonfiction
The Children's Album	P.O. Box 262 Manchester, CA 95459	all	Short stories, poems, and nonfiction
Children's Digest	P.O. Box 567 Indianapolis, IN 46206	8–10	Poetry, short stories, riddles, and jokes
Child Life	P.O. Box 567 Indianapolis, IN 46206	7–9	Short stories, poetry, riddles, jokes, and letters to the editor
Cricket	1058 8th Street LaSalle, IL 61301	6–12	Letters and Cricket League monthly; short story and poetry contests
FLIP Magazine (Future Literature in Progress)	The Art Center of Battle Creek 265 East Emmett Street Battle Creek, MI 49107	all	Poetry and short stories
Highlights for Children	803 Church Street Honesdale, PA 18431	5–10	Poetry, short stories, jokes, riddles, and letters to the editor
Jack and Jill	P.O. Box 567 Indianapolis, IN 46206	5–10	Short stories, poems, riddles, and letters to the editor
Kids Magazine	P.O. Box 3041 Grand Central Station New York, NY 10017	all	Short stories, reports, poems, cartoons, puzzles, and most other forms of writing

FIGURE 7–10

Magazines that Publish Children's Writing

Responding to Student Writing

The teacher's role should not be restricted to that of evaluator. Again and again researchers report that, although teachers are the most common audience for student writing, they are also one of the worst audiences, because they read with a red pen in their hands (Lundsteen, 1976). Teachers should instead read their students' writing for information, for enjoyment, and for all the other purposes that other readers do. Much of students' writing does not need to be assessed; it should simply be shared with the teacher as a "trusted adult" (Martin, D'Arcy, Newton, & Parker, 1976).

    If children use a process approach to writing, there is less chance they will plagiarize, because they will have developed their compositions, step by step, from pre-

Magazine	Address	Ages	Types of Writing Accepted
The McGuffey Writer	400A McGuffey Hall Miami University Oxford, OH 45056	all	Poetry, short stories, essays, and cartoons
Merlyn's Pen	P.O. Box 716 East Greenwich, RI 02818	12–14	Essays, poems, and short stories
Prism Magazine	1040 Bayview Drive, Suite 223 Ft. Lauderdale, FL 33304	10–14	Poetry, short stories
Scholastic Scope	50 West 44th Street New York, NY 10036	13–14	Poems, stories, plays
Scholastic Voice	50 West 44th Street New York, NY 10036	13–14	Short stories and poems; also writing contests
Spinoff (for gifted children)	P.O. Box 115 Sewell, NJ 08080	all	Stories, poems, essays, and word games
Stone Soup	Children's Art Foundation P.O. Box 83 Santa Cruz, CA 95063	all	Poetry, short stories, and book reports (books to be reviewed are provided by the magazine)
Wombat	365 Ashton Drive Athens, GA 30606	all	Short stories, poems, essays, puzzles, cartoons, and book reports
Young Author's Magazine	3015 Woodsdale Blvd. Lincoln, NB 68502	all	Short stories, essays, other nonfiction, poetry, and drama
Young World	P.O. Box 567 Indianapolis, IN 46206	10–14	Poetry, short stories, jokes, and letters to the editor

FIGURE 7–10 (*continued*)

writing and drafting to revising and editing. Nonetheless, at some time or other, most teachers fear that a composition they are reading is not the student's own work. Jackson, Tway, and Frager (1987) cite several reasons that children might plagiarize. First, some students may simply internalize a piece of writing through repeated readings so that, months or years later, they do not realize it is not their own work. Second, some students may plagiarize because of competition to succeed. Third, some students plagiarize by accident, not realizing the consequences of their actions. A final reason some students plagiarize is because they have not been taught to write by means of a process approach, so they may not know how to synthesize information for a report from published sources. The two best ways to avert having students copy work from another source and pass it off as their own are (1) to teach them the writing process and (2) to have students write at school rather than at home. Students who work at school and move through the various writing process activities know how to complete the writing project.

To measure students' growth in writing, it is not always necessary to assess finished products (Tway, 1980). Teachers make judgments about students' progress in other ways. One of the best ways is to observe students while they write and note whether they engage in prewriting activities, whether they focus on content rather than mechanics in their rough drafts, and whether they participate in writing groups.

When it is necessary to assess students' writing, teachers can judge whether students have completed all components of the writing project as well as the quality of the final product. (You will find information about assessing stories, poems, reports, and other forms of writing in the chapters that discuss these forms.)

❖ THE WRITING PROCESS IN ACTION

Although it may seem that the stages of the writing process are five separate ingredients that must be combined in sequence to complete a recipe, this is an oversimplification. In practice, writers move back and forth through the stages to develop, refine, and polish their compositions, and they participate in some activities, such as revising and editing, throughout the writing process (Hayes & Flower, 1980). Not all writing must go through all the stages. A journal entry, for example, may be abandoned after drafting, and editing receives less attention if a story will be shared orally as a puppet show.

Introducing the Writing Process

Introducing students to the writing process, whether first graders or eighth graders, and helping them learn the activities involved in each stage are crucial. The teacher explains the stages and has students develop a short composition as they practice each stage. The following guidelines may be useful.

1. *Teach the informal writing strategies before introducing the writing process.* There are so many things to explain about the writing process that students can get bogged down the first time they move through the five stages. One way to shorten the first writing process experience is to first teach students the informal writing strategies.

2. *Use the writing process terminology.* When introducing the process approach, teachers should use the names of the stages and the other terminology in this chapter. Even young children learn to use the terminology quickly and easily.

3. *Write class collaborations.* Too many teachers ignore the class collaboration step of the prewriting stage. Although students do not need to write class collaborations for every writing project, it is an important step here because the teacher models all the activities students will soon be doing individually. Teachers sometimes

omit this step because they worry they can't lead a class collaboration; this is a needless fear, as many students have good ideas and will be eager to share them.

4.   *Keep first writings short.* Students' first process writings should be short pieces—only one or two paragraphs—so they can move through the writing process rather quickly. A seven-page biography of Amelia Earhart is not a good first process writing because of the time and effort involved in gathering information, writing the rough draft, sharing it in writing groups, locating and correcting mechanical errors, and recopying the final draft. Personal narratives in which students write about an event in their own lives work well for the first writings.

5.   *Practice critiquing compositions as a class.* Working in writing groups teaches children new activities—giving compliments, asking writer-questions, and offering suggestions. Because these activities are unfamiliar to most students, introduce the activities and practice them as a class before having students work in writing groups. Read aloud a sample (and anonymous) composition and critique the composition together as a class. After listening to it read aloud, students offer compliments, the teacher role-plays the author and asks a question or two about trouble-spots, and then students make suggestions for improvement.

6.   *Begin with compliments in writing groups.* During the first two or three writing group sessions, teachers may have students shortcut the procedure and stop after complimenting the writer. When students feel comfortable giving compliments, you can add the next step, having the writer ask questions. Finally the remaining steps are added. Introducing writing group activities in a step-by-step approach gives students the opportunity to learn each activity.

7.   *Keep writing folders.* Keep students' writing in manila folders. They can put prewriting activities, informal writings, rough drafts, writing group notes, and editing checklists into this file. When a writing project is completed, all materials are organized, stapled together, and clipped to the final copy. Students prepare a new folder for the next writing project.

Learning the writing process takes time. Students need to work through the entire process again and again until the stages and activities become automatic. Then students can manipulate the activities to meet the different demands of particular writing projects and modify the process to accommodate their personal writing style.

Using the Writing Process in Elementary Classrooms

After students learn the stages of the writing process and some of the activities in each stage, they use this knowledge to write stories, poems, and many other forms of writing. It would be convenient if this five-stage model equated to prewriting on Monday, drafting on Tuesday, revising on Wednesday, editing on Thursday, and sharing on Friday, but it does not. In fact, it is difficult to predict how long a writing project will take because of the variations in how students write.

Students are engaged in various activities during each writing process stage. The activities vary according to the function, audience, and form of the writing. Activities in writing myths, animal reports, color poems, and business letters are outlined in Figure 7–11. When students write myths, for example, they read myths and analyze

	Write a Myth	Write an Animal Report	Write a Color Poem	Write a Business Letter
Function: **Form:** **Audience:**	Imaginative Story Classmates	Informative Report Younger children (books to be replaced in school library)	Imaginative Poem Classmates and family	Instrumental Business letter Unknown
Stage 1 **Prewriting**	Read myths. Analyze characteristics of myths. Brainstorm a list of characteristics. Write a collaborative myth.	Design research questions. Gather and organize information on a cluster. Interview an expert and add information to cluster.	Review the form of a color poem. Read examples of color poems written by students. Write a collaborative color poem.	Review the form of a business letter. Brainstorm a list of the information to include in the letter.
Stage 2 **Drafting**	Write a rough draft of the myth.	Write a rough draft of the report.	Write a rough draft of the color poem, beginning each line or stanza with a color.	Write a rough draft of the letter.
Stage 3 **Revising**	Share the rough draft in a writing group. Listeners offer compliments and suggestions.	Share the rough draft in a writing group. Listeners offer compliments and suggestions.	Share the rough draft in a writing group. Listeners offer compliments and suggestions.	Share the rough draft in a writing group. Listeners offer compliments and suggestions.

Ask questions about the content and form of the myth. Make revisions based on classmates' suggestions.	Ask questions about the completeness of the information in the report. Make revisions based on classmates' suggestions.	Ask questions about the content and form of the poem. Make revisions based on classmates' suggestions.	Ask questions about the completeness of the information in the letter and appropriateness of language. Make revisions based on classmates' suggestions.
Stage 4 Editing Proofread with a classmate and the teacher to locate and correct errors.	Proofread with a classmate and the teacher to locate and correct errors. Add a bibliography.	Proofread with a classmate and the teacher to locate and correct errors.	Proofread with a classmate and the teacher to locate and correct mechanical and formatting errors.
Stage 5 Sharing Recopy the myth and share with classmates. Alternative: Videotape a dramatic presentation of the myth.	Construct a hardbound book. Recopy the report in the book. Share the book with younger children and add to the school library.	Recopy the poem and add to a personal anthology. Share with classmates.	Recopy the letter. Address the envelope. Mail the letter.

FIGURE 7–11

An Analysis of Four Writing Projects

what constitutes a myth. They record what they have learned in a list of characteristics and refer to the list to write a class collaboration myth. These activities represent the prewriting stage of gathering ideas. During the drafting stage, students write a rough draft of their myth. In revising, they meet in writing groups to share their myths and get feedback on how to improve them. Then students make revisions based on the feedback they receive. Students may move on to the editing stage or may do more prewriting, drafting, or meet again in a writing group for additional feedback. When they move into editing, students proofread their myths with a classmate and correct as many mechanical errors as possible before meeting with the teacher for a final editing. Students complete the writing process by recopying the myth into a hardbound book and reading the myth to students in another class. As an alternative, a small group of students might prepare and videotape a dramatic presentation of the myth and show it to students in other classes.

Similar activities are shown in Figure 7–11 for three other writing projects. Students may use brainstorming for one writing project, clustering in another, or, in yet another project, review the format of a business letter, but all are prewriting activities because they prepare students to write. Variation in each stage results from differences in the function, audience, and form of the project.

The Teacher's Role

The teacher's role in the writing process varies according to the stage. Simpson (1986) describes teachers' roles as forming a partnership with students, instructing, listening, encouraging, challenging, and responding. Figure 7–12 features a list of questions teachers can use to monitor their behavior as their roles shift during the writing process; we will examine those roles in each stage of the process.

Prewriting. During prewriting, teachers make plans for the writing project, provide necessary background experiences, and arrange for rehearsal activities. They also teach students about informal writing strategies or about the writing form (e.g., biographies) that students will write. Teachers also provide a scaffold for students through class collaborations.

Drafting. Teachers provide support and encouragement as students pour out their ideas during drafting. They confer with students as they search for words to express themselves, to clarify their thinking, and to search for voice. It is important in this stage not to emphasize correct spelling and neatness. In fact, when teachers point out mechanical errors during the drafting stage, they send a false message that mechanical correctness is more important than content.

Revising. During the revising stage, the teacher is a reader and reactor just as students are, responding, as Sommers suggests, "as any reader would, registering questions, reflecting befuddlement, and noting places where we are puzzled about the meaning" (1982, p. 155). Teachers participate in writing groups and conferences and

Prewriting

The teacher:

Provides background experiences so students will have the prerequisite knowledge to write about the topic

Allows students to participate in decisions about topic, function, audience, and form

Defines the writing project clearly and specifies how it will be assessed

Teaches information about the writing form

Provides opportunities for students to participate in idea gathering and organizing activities

Writes a class collaboration with students

Drafting

The teacher:

Provides support, encouragement, and feedback

Emphasizes content over mechanics

Teaches students how to draft

Encourages students to cycle back to prewriting to gather more ideas or ahead to revise when needed

Revising

The teacher:

Organizes writing groups

Teaches students how to function in writing groups

Participates in a writing group as any listener and reactor would

Provides feedback about the content of the writing and makes suggestions for revision

Insists that students make some revisions

Encourages students to cycle back to prewriting or drafting when necessary

Editing

The teacher:

Teaches students how to edit with partners

Prepares editing checklists for students

Assists students in locating and correcting mechanical errors

Diagnoses students' errors and provides appropriate instruction

Corrects any remaining errors that students cannot correct

Sharing

The teacher:

Arranges for genuine audiences for student writing

Does not serve only as a judge when receiving student writing

FIGURE 7—12

Teacher's Notebook Page: The Teacher's Role in the Writing Process

model appropriate responses, admiring students' efforts and seeing potential as well as providing feedback about how to improve writing. Teachers offer suggestions in this stage rather than at the end of the process because students still have the opportunity to benefit from the suggestions and incorporate changes into their writing.

Editing. It is unrealistic to expect students to locate and correct every mechanical error in their compositions during editing, so many teachers find it more practical to focus on particular categories of error in each composition. In a conference, they can quickly review a particular problem area, such as quotation marks, and help the student make the necessary corrections. This minilesson procedure individualizes instruction, and during the school year, teachers review the mechanical skills each student needs. If correctness is crucial, teachers can make the corrections or put checkmarks in the margin to note remaining errors so that students can complete the correcting.

Sharing. Teachers need to make sure students have genuine audiences to share their writing with. Sending letters to pen pals, reading student-written picture books to a kindergarten class, compiling a class anthology, and submitting a newspaper article to the local newspaper all require behind-the-scenes work by the teacher. Most importantly, teachers should enjoy students' writing as other audiences do, not simply serve as an evaluator.

Assessing Students' Writing

By observing students while they are writing, teachers can note how students move through the writing process stages, from gathering and organizing ideas during prewriting, to pouring out and shaping ideas during drafting, to meeting in writing groups to get feedback and making substantive changes during revising, to proofreading and correcting mechanical errors in editing, and to publishing and sharing their writing in the last stage (McKenzie & Tompkins, 1984). Figure 7–13 lists several characteristic activities in each stage of the writing process. Teachers can observe students while they write and participate in other writing process-related activities and place checkmarks and add comments as necessary for each observed activity. Students can also use the checklist for self-assessment to help make them aware of the activities in the writing process.

The writing process checklist can also be adapted for various types of writing projects. If students are writing autobiographies, for example, the checklist can include items in the prewriting stage about developing a lifeline and clustering ideas for each chapter topic. The sharing stage can include items such as adding a table of contents, an illustration for each chapter, and sharing the complete autobiography with at least two other people. (Checklists adapted from the process writing checklist for an autobiography project and other types of writing are presented in Chapters 9, 10, and 11.)

	Dates					
Student: _____						
Prewriting Can the student identify the specific audience to whom he/she will write?						
Does this awareness affect the choices the student makes as he/she writes?						
Can the student identify the purpose of the writing activity?						
Does the student write on a topic that grows out of his/her own experience?						
Does the student engage in rehearsal activities before writing?						
Drafting Does the student write rough drafts?						
Does the student place a greater emphasis on content than on mechanics in the rough drafts?						
Revising Does the student share his/her writing in conferences?						
Does the student participate in discussions about classmates' writing?						
In revising, does the student make changes to reflect the reactions and comments of both teacher and classmates?						
Between first and final drafts, does the student make substantive or only minor changes?						
Editing Does the student proofread his/her own papers?						
Does the student help proofread classmates' papers?						
Does the student increasingly identify his/her mechanical errors?						
Sharing Does the student publish his/her writing in an appropriate form?						
Does the student share this finished writing with an appropriate audience?						

FIGURE 7–13

A Writing Process Checklist

❖ REVIEW

The writing process involves five interrelated stages that both students and adult authors work through. In prewriting, students consider function, audience, and form and participate in activities to gather and organize ideas. Students write a rough draft, with emphasis on content rather than mechanics. Next, in the revising stage, students refine the content of their compositions in writing groups. After revising, students edit to identify and correct spelling, capitalization, and punctuation errors. In the last stage, students publish and share their writing. In contrast to the traditional approach to writing, the emphasis in the writing process is on the *process* students use when they write, not on the finished product. After students learn about each stage of the writing process, they use it to write stories, reports, poems, and other forms of writing. Teachers become facilitators or partners and their role varies according to the stage of the process.

❖ EXTENSIONS

1. Observe students using the writing process in an elementary classroom. In what types of prewriting, drafting, revising, editing, and sharing activities are they involved?

2. Interview students who use a process approach to writing and other students who use a traditional approach. Ask questions similar to the following and compare the students' answers:

   • How do you choose a topic for writing?
   • How do you get started writing?
   • Do you ask your classmates or the teacher to read your writing?
   • What do you do when you are having a problem while writing?
   • What is easiest about writing for you?
   • What is hardest about writing for you?
   • What is the most important thing to remember when you are writing?
   • What happens to your writing after you finish it?
   • What kinds of writing (e.g., stories, poems, reports) do you like best?

3. Sit in on a writing conference in which students share their writing and ask classmates for feedback in revising their compositions. Make a list of the students' questions and comments. What conclusions can you draw about their interactions with each other? You might want to compare your findings with those reported in "Talking about writing: The language of writing groups" (Gere & Abbott, 1985).

4. Examine language arts textbooks to see how they approach writing. Do they use the process approach? Do some steps in the writing process lend themselves to the textbook format better than others?

5. Reflect on your own writing process. Do you write single-draft papers, or do you write a series of drafts and refine them? Do you ask friends to read and react to your writing or to help you proofread your writing? Write a two- to three-page paper comparing your writing process to the process described in this chapter. How might you modify your own writing process in light of the information in this chapter?

❖ REFERENCES

Applebee, A. L., & Langer, J. A. (1983). Instructional scaffolding: Reading and writing and natural language activities. *Language Arts, 60,* 168–175.

Bissex, G. L. (1980). *Gyns at wrk: A child learns to write and read.* Cambridge, MA: Harvard University Press.

Britton, J., Burgess, T., Martin, N., McLeod, A., & Rosen, H. (1975). *The development of writing abilities (11–18).* London: Schools Council Publications.

Calkins, L. M. (1980). When children want to punctuate: Basic skills belong in context. *Language Arts, 57,* 567–573.

Calkins, L. M. (1983). *Lessons from a child: On the teaching and learning of writing.* Portsmouth, NH: Heinemann.

Calkins, L. M. (1986). *The art of teaching writing.* Portsmouth, NH: Heinemann.

Dyson, A. H. (1982). The emergence of visible language: Interrelationships between drawing and early writing. *Visible Language, 6,* 360–381.

Dyson, A. H. (1983). Early writing as drawing: The developmental gap between speaking and writing. Presentation at the Annual Meeting of the American Educational Research Association, Montreal, CA.

Dyson, A. H. (1985). Second graders sharing writing: The multiple social realities of a literacy event. *Written Communication, 2,* 189–215.

Dyson, A. H. (1986). The imaginary worlds of childhood: A multimedia presentation. *Language Arts, 63,* 799–808.

Elley, W. B., Barham, I. H., Lamb, H., & Wyllie, M. (1976). The role of grammar in a secondary school English curriculum. *Research in the Teaching of English, 10,* 5–21.

Faigley, L., & Witte, S. (1981). Analyzing revision. *College Composition and Communication, 32,* 400–410.

Fine, E. S. (1987). Marbles lost, marbles found. Collaborative production of text. *Language Arts, 64,* 474–487.

Gere, A. R., & Abbott, R. D. (1985). Talking about writing: The language of writing groups. *Research in the Teaching of English, 19,* 362–381.

Graves, D. H. (1976). Let's get rid of the welfare mess in the teaching of writing. *Language Arts, 53,* 645–651.

Graves, D. H. (1983). *Writing: Teachers and children at work.* Exeter, NH: Heinemann.

Graves, D. H., & Hansen, J. (1983). The author's chair. *Language Arts, 60,* 176–183.

Halliday, M. A. K. (1973). *Explorations in the functions of language.* London: Edward Arnold.

Halliday, M. A. K. (1975). *Learning how to mean: Explorations in the development of language.* London: Edward Arnold.

Hayes, J. R., & Flower, L. S. (1980). Identifying the organization of writing processes. In L. W. Gregg & E. R. Steinberg (Eds.), *Cognitive processes in writing,* pp. 3–30. Hillsdale, NJ: Erlbaum.

Hidi, S., & Hildyard, A. (1983). The comparison of oral and written productions in two discourse modes. *Discourse Processes, 6,* 91–105.

Jackson, L. A., Tway, E., & Frager, A. (1987). Dear teacher, Johnny copied. *The Reading Teacher, 41,* 22–25.

King, M. (1985). Proofreading is not reading. *Teaching English in the two-year college, 12,* 108–112.

Langer, J. A. (1985). Children's sense of genre. *Written Communication, 2,* 157–187.

Lundsteen, S. W. (Ed.). (1976). *Help for the teacher of written composition: New directions in research.* Urbana, IL: National Conference on Research in English and ERIC Clearinghouse on Reading and Communication Skills.

MacLachlan, P. (1985). *Sarah, plain and tall.* New York: Harper and Row.

Martin, N., D'Arcy, P., Newton, B., & Parker, R. (1976). *Writing and learning across the curriculum 11–16.* London: Schools Council Publications.

McKenzie, L., & Tompkins, G. E. (1984). Evaluating students' writing: A process approach. *Journal of Teaching Writing, 3,* 201–212.

Mills, B. S. (1983). Imagination: The connection between writing and play. *Educational Leadership 41,* 50–53.

Mohr, M. M. (1984). *Revision: The rhythm of meaning.* Upper Montclair, NJ: Boynton/Cook.

Murray, D. H. (1982). *Learning by teaching.* Montclair, NJ: Boynton/Cook.

Simpson, M. K. (1986). What am I supposed to do while they're writing? *Language Arts, 63,* 680–684.

Smith, F. (1982). *Writing and the writer.* New York: Holt, Rinehart and Winston.

Sommers, N. (1982). Responding to student writing. *College Composition and Communication, 33,* 148–156.

Tompkins, G. E., & Friend, M. (1988). After your students write: What's next? *Teaching Exceptional Children, 20,* 4–9.

Tway, E. (1980). Teacher responses to children's writing. *Language Arts, 57,* 763–772.

Wagner, B. J. (1976). *Dorothy Heathcote: Drama as a learning medium.* Washington, DC: National Education Association.

Wagner, B. J. (1983). The expanding circle of informal classroom drama. In B. A. Busching and J. I. Schwartz (Eds.), *Integrating the language arts in the elementary school,* pp. 155–163. Urbana, IL: National Council of Teachers of English.

Wagner, B. J. (1988). Does classroom drama affect the arts of language? *Language Arts, 65,* 46–55.

8 READING AND WRITING CONNECTIONS

THE READING AND WRITING PROCESSES
    The Reading Process
    Comparing the Two Processes
    Benefits of Connecting Reading and Writing

MAKING THE CONNECTION WITH YOUNG CHILDREN
    Assisted Reading
    Language Experience Approach
    Big Books

MAKING THE CONNECTION WITH AUTHORS

MAKING THE CONNECTION WITH STORIES
    Directed Reading-Thinking Activity
    Predictable Books
    Wordless Books
    Pattern Books
    Basal Reader Stories

MAKING THE CONNECTION WITH INFORMATIONAL BOOKS
    Expository Text Structures
    KWL Strategy

◆ IN THIS CHAPTER, WE WILL EXPLORE CONNECTIONS BETWEEN reading and writing and suggest ways to integrate reading and writing in elementary classrooms.

◆ AS YOU ARE READING, THINK ABOUT THESE QUESTIONS:

How are the reading and writing processes similar?

How can teachers help young children make the connection between reading and writing?

How do students connect reading and writing as they learn about authors?

What are some ways to integrate reading and writing stories?

What are some ways to integrate reading and writing informational books?

In the past decade there has been a significant shift in thinking about reading and writing. It used to be that reading and writing were thought of as the flip sides of a coin—they were opposites; a reader decoded or deciphered written language and a writer encoded or produced written language. Then researchers began to note similarities between the two processes and talked of reading and writing as parallel processes. Reading was described as a process much like the writing process, and readers and writers used strategies for making meaning from the text. The important connection was that the goal of both reading and writing is to make meaning. Teachers were encouraged to have students write about their reading and read their own writing. Reading and writing should be taught together, teachers were told, not reading in the morning and writing in the afternoon (Anderson et al., 1985). We now know that interrelationships or interactions between the two language processes exist, and reading and writing can be described as essentially similar processes of meaning construction.

❖ THE READING AND WRITING PROCESSES

Reading and writing are both transactive processes (Harste, Woodward, & Burke, 1984; Rosenblatt, 1978). In Chapter 7, we described the writing process as a recursive process involving a variety of activities as students gather and organize ideas, draft their compositions, revise and edit the drafts, and, finally, publish and share their writings. Reading involves a similar process of several steps during which readers construct meaning through their interaction with text or reading materials. The term *text* includes all reading materials—stories, maps, newspapers, cereal boxes, textbooks, and so on; it is not limited to basal reader textbooks.

The Reading Process

Reading is a sociopsycholinguistic process like writing. It can be described as a *transaction* or interaction between the mind of the reader and the language of the text in a particular situational and social context (Weaver, 1988). Meaning is constructed when the reader transacts with the text. Comprehension does not go from the page to the reader; instead, it is a complex negotiation between text and reader that is shaped by the immediate situational context and broader sociolinguistic contexts. The immediate situational context includes the reader's knowledge about the topic, purpose for reading, and other factors related to the immediate environment. Broader sociolinguistic contexts include the language community the reader belongs to and how closely it matches the language used in the text, the reader's culturally based expectations about reading, and the reader's own expectations about reading based on previous experiences. This description of reading is presented schematically in Figure 8–1.

Readers begin the reading process by activating their prior knowledge or schemata about the text. The title, an illustration, something someone says about the text, the topic, or something else may trigger this activation, but for the reader to make meaning from the text, a schema in the mind must be activated. Then readers sample the text, recognizing some words and decoding others using phonics and context cues.

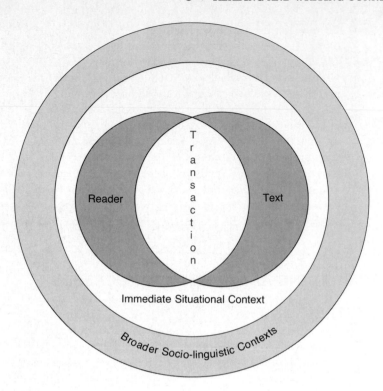

FIGURE 8–1

The Reading Process
Weaver, 1988, p. 30.

(It is not necessary for readers to recognize every word or to look at every letter in a word to decode it.) From this sampling, readers construct personal meaning using the text as a blueprint. This is the transaction between the text and the reader's mind. As readers construct meaning, they continue reading, and as long as what they are reading fits the meaning they are constructing, the transaction continues. When something doesn't make sense, readers slow down, back up, and reread until they are making meaning again. After reading, the construction of meaning from the text is extended. Readers compare, interpret, and evaluate their understanding through talk, writing, reading, and projects. Rosenblatt (1978) explains that as students write about reading, they unravel their thinking so that we can see how they understand and, at the same time, help them elaborate and clarify their responses.

Teaching Strategy.   The instructional strategy developed in Chapter 1 can be used to teach reading, based on the reading process and the types of activities readers engage in.

Step 1: *Introducing the text.* Teachers introduce the text so that students make connections between their background of experiences and the text they will read or that will be read to them. These are ways to introduce the text:

- Relate the text to a thematic unit being studied.
- Talk about the title.
- Relate the text to others by the same author or students' other reading.
- Brainstorm a list of words related to the title, topic, theme, or characters.
- Freewrite about the topic or theme.
- Make predictions about the text based on the title, the cover illustration, or the first paragraph.

For instance, to introduce a picturebook version of *The Pied Piper of Hamelin* (Mayer, 1987), teachers might:

- Invite students who are familiar with the story to talk about it
- Compare the story to other legends students are familiar with
- Show the illustration on the cover of the book and ask students to predict what might happen in the story
- Brainstorm a list of words related to the story

Step 2: *Reading the text.* Students read the text in one of four ways.

Guided reading: Students read the text silently with the teacher's guidance. Teachers may meet with small groups for guided reading, or the entire class may read together.

Reading aloud: Students listen to the teacher read the text, or they may listen to the text read aloud at a listening center.

Shared reading: Students follow along in the text as the teacher reads it or as it is read together as a class. Shared reading is possible if there are multiple copies of the text, or if the text is displayed on a chart, with an enlarged copy of a book, or using sentence strips.

Independent reading: Students read the text independently. One type of independent reading is Uninterrupted Sustained Silent Reading (USSR) or Drop Everything And Read (DEAR) time. Students and teacher each choose something to read, then everyone reads silently without interruption for a specified period (Berglund & Johns, 1983). Independent reading lasts for about five to ten minutes in primary-grade classrooms and up to 20 minutes a day in upper-grade classrooms. This activity gives students the opportunity to transfer and apply isolated skills in a pleasurable, independent reading experience. These are guidelines for independent reading:

- Students choose reading materials and read silently.
- The teacher also reads, allowing no interruptions.
- A timer is used.
- Students do not write book reports, and no records are kept as to what they read.
- After the timer rings, students may briefly share what they were reading.

Independent reading allows students to practice reading skills, develop responsibility in selecting their own reading materials, learn content area information, and receive a positive message about reading. Some researchers believe independent reading improves students' reading skills, while others argue that it does not; nevertheless, there is agreement that students learn that reading can be an enjoyable activity through daily independent reading. With any of the reading approaches, questions or discussion may arise, or can be postponed until after reading.

Step 3: *Exploring the text.* Students make tentative and exploratory comments while reading (or immediately after reading), either by talking about the story or writing in a reading log. According to Davala (1987), when logs become a regular part of classroom activities, students take an active part in their own learning, and they " 'tune in' to the curriculum when they explore it personally" (p. 179). As students make connections between their own experiences and events in the story, they create mental images, anticipate what will happen next, construct a reaction, and value the story. When students read *The Pied Piper of Hamelin,* for example, they often ask whether the event really happened. They also talk about the corrupt mayor and compare him to today's politicians.

Teachers also focus on vocabulary, and they may ask students to brainstorm a list of words from the story and then sort the words into categories; for example, *burrowing, mimicking, vermin,* and *filthy* in *The Pied Piper of Hamelin* all relate to the rats. Then students may write reactions to the story or freewrite in response to one of these lines from the story: "A promise is a promise" or "The piper must be paid."

Step 4: *Responding to the text.* Students build on the exploratory responses they make while reading to create a more extended (and often more formal) response. This response may take many forms; a list of response activities is presented in Figure 8–2. Examples of response activities related to *The Pied Piper of Hamelin* include these:

Write a retelling of the story

Compare the version they are reading to other versions of the story or to other legends

Dramatize the story

Paint a mural of the story

Create puppets or flannel board figures and retell the story

Research the legend of the Pied Piper

Interview a public health official to learn why rats are harmful

Make a diorama of an event in the story

Compare the Pied Piper to another legendary character, such as Johnny Appleseed or Paul Bunyan

Dress a doll as the Piper

Comparing the Two Processes

The reading and writing processes have comparable *before, during,* and *after* activities. As shown in Figure 8–2, reading and writing activities at each of the three stages are

WHAT READERS DO	WHAT WRITERS DO
Before	
Readers use knowledge about	Writers use knowledge about
• the topic	• the topic
• syntax	• syntax
• phonology	• phonology
Readers bring expectations cued by	Writers bring expectations cued by
• previous reading experiences	• previous writing experiences
• format of the text	• previous reading experiences
• purpose for reading	• purpose for writing
• audience for reading	• audience for writing
During	
Readers read to	Writers prewrite and draft to
• predict outcomes	• gather ideas
• monitor predictions	• organize ideas
• create meaning	• write a rough draft
Readers reread to	Writers revise and edit to
• discuss text	• discuss text
• interpret meaning	• interpret meaning
• clarify meaning	• clarify meaning
• examine the impact of words, sentences, and paragraphs to the whole text	• examine the impact of words, sentences, and paragraphs to the whole text
• make notes	• identify and correct mechanical errors
After	
Readers	Writers
• respond in many ways	• get response from readers
• reflect on the reading	• give response to readers
• feel success	• feel success
• want to read again	• want to write again

FIGURE 8–2

A Comparison of the Reading and Writing Processes
Adapted from Butler & Turbill, 1984.

similar, and in both reading and writing, the goal is to construct meaning. Notice the activities listed for rereading and revising in the *during* stage, for example. Fitzgerald (1989) analyzed these two activities and concluded that they draw on similar processes of author-reader-text interactions. Similar analyses can be made for other activities, as well.

Tierney (1983) explains that reading and writing are multidimensional and involve concurrent, complex transactions between writers, between writers as readers, between readers, and between readers as writers. Writers participate in several types of reading activities. They read other authors' works for ideas and to learn about the structure of stories, but they also read and reread their own work—to problem-solve, discover, monitor, and clarify. The quality of these reading experiences seems closely tied to success in writing. "Readers as writers" is a newer idea, but readers are involved in many of the same activities that writers use. They generate ideas, organize, monitor, problem-solve, and revise. Smith (1983) believes that reading influences writing skills because readers unconsciously "read like writers":

> To read like a writer we engage with the author in what the author is writing. We can anticipate what the author will say, so that the author is in effect writing on our behalf, not showing how something is done but doing it with us. . . . Bit by bit, one thing at a time, but enormous numbers of things over the passage of time, the learner learns through reading like a writer to write like a writer. (pp. 563–564)

Also, both reading and writing are recursive, cycling back through various parts of the process, and, just as writers compose text, readers compose their meaning.

Teachers can help students appreciate the similarities between reading and writing in many ways. Tierney (1983) explains: "What we need are reading teachers who act as if their students were developing writers and writing teachers who act as if their students were readers" (p. 151). These are some ways to point out the relationships between reading and writing:

Help writers assume alternative points of view as potential readers.

Help readers consider the writer's purpose and viewpoint.

Point out that reading is much like composing, so that students will view reading as a process, much like the writing process.

Talk with students about the reading and writing processes.

Talk with students about reading and writing strategies.

Readers and writers use a number of strategies for constructing meaning as they interact with print. As readers, we use a variety of problem-solving strategies to make decisions about an author's meaning and to construct meaning for ourselves. As writers we also use problem-solving strategies to decide what our readers need as we construct meaning for them and for ourselves. Comparing reading to writing, Tierney and Pearson (1983) described reading as a composing process because readers compose and refine meaning through reading much as writers do.

Langer (1986) followed this line of thinking in identifying four strategies that both readers and writers use to interact with text. The first strategy is generating ideas: both readers and writers generate ideas as they get started, as they become aware of important ideas and experiences, and as they begin to plan and organize the information. Formulating meaning is the second strategy—the essence of both reading and writing. Readers and writers formulate meaning by developing the message, considering audience, drawing on personal experience, choosing language, linking concepts, summarizing, and paraphrasing. Assessing is the next strategy. In both reading and writing, students review, react, and monitor their understanding of the message and the text itself. The fourth strategy is revising, wherein both readers and writers reconsider and restructure the message, recognize when meaning has broken down, and take appropriate action to change the text to improve understanding.

Langer's research will have a great impact on reading and writing instruction because she has documented that readers and writers use the same four major groups of literacy strategies. Through Langer's work we see how readers use a strategy, such as revision, that is often thought of as part of the writing process. Readers use revision, but they use it differently than writers do.

Benefits of Connecting Reading and Writing

Researchers have linked reading and writing, but what about the practical benefits of connecting reading and writing? Tierney and Leys (1986) analyzed research on the reading-writing connection and found these benefits:

Some reading experiences contribute to students' writing performance.

Some writing experiences contribute to students' reading performance.

Writers acquire values and behaviors from reading and readers acquire values and behaviors from writing.

Successful writers integrate reading into their writing experience and successful readers integrate writing into their reading experience.

❖ MAKING THE CONNECTION WITH YOUNG CHILDREN

Young children's introduction to reading and writing begins before they come to school. Parents and other caregivers read to young children, and they observe adults reading. They learn to read signs in their community. Children experiment with writing and have parents write for them. They also observe adults writing. When young children come to kindergarten, their understandings about reading and writing expand quickly through the language-rich classroom environment and teacher-led demonstrations of reading and writing (Noyce & Christie, 1989). Three types of teacher-led demonstrations of literacy are assisted reading, the language experience approach, and big books.

Assisted Reading

Assisted Reading is a technique that parents and teachers can use to introduce young children to reading (Hoskisson, 1974, 1975a, 1975b, 1977; Hoskisson & Krohm, 1974; Hoskisson, Sherman, & Smith, 1974). Adults read to young children and allow them to handle books. Children learn that books have front and back parts and top and bottom dimensions, and they discover that readers begin at the front of the book and turn pages toward the back. They learn this by holding books while listening to stories, by playing with books, and by trying out the behaviors they have experienced while being read to.

Pictures also play an important role in books read to young children because they provide contextual situations that bridge the gap between children's actual experiences and the abstract language presented by authors. Pictures provide the context, the visual images that help children relate what they know to what is presented in the story. Eventually children will be able to supply their own context to the stories they read, but in the beginning, pictures bridge the gap from the abstract to the real.

As children learn that pictures relate the meaning of the story to their own experiences, they begin to attend to the words they hear and consider the meaning again. Before long they can "read" a book by using the pictures as prompts in retelling the story. Most parents have succumbed to the temptation to skip pages of a story they have read innumerable times, only to have children correct them. Although parents tend to call this memorization, children store the meaning of the story rather than memorize exact words; skipping any part disrupts this meaning and results in the corrective feedback they give their errant parents.

1. *Reading to children.* The first stage in assisted reading is to read to children and have them repeat each phrase or sentence. At first most children's attention will not be on the lines of print as they repeat the words. They may be looking around the room, at the pictures in the book, or at other parts of the book. To direct their attention to the lines of print, the reader points to the words on each line as they are read. This allows children to see that lines of print are read from left to right, not randomly. Many different books are read and reread during this stage. Rereading is important because the visual images of the words must be seen and read many times to ensure their recognition in other stories. Later, one repetition of a word may be sufficient for subsequent recognition of the word in context.

2. *Repeated reading.* When children begin to notice that some words occur repeatedly, from story to story, they enter the second stage of assisted reading. In this stage, the reader reads and children repeat or echo the words; however, the reader does not read the words the children seem to recognize. The reader omits those words, and children fill them in. The fluency, or flow, of the reading should not be interrupted. If fluency is not maintained during this stage, children will not grasp the meaning of the passage, because the syntactic and semantic cues that come from a smooth flow of language will not be evident to them.

3. *Shared reading.* The transition to stage three occurs when children begin to ask the reader to let them read the words themselves. Stage three may be initiated in this manner by the child, or it may be introduced by the person assisting the child. When children know enough words to do the initial reading themselves, they read and the person assisting supplies any unknown words. It is important to assist children so that the fluency of the reading is not disrupted. In stage three, children do the major portion of the reading, but they tire more easily because they are struggling to use all the information they have acquired about written language. Children at this stage need constant encouragement; they must not feel a sense of frustration or failure. Moving to independent reading is a gradual process.

Language Experience Approach

The *language experience approach* (LEA) to beginning reading instruction is based on children's language and experiences (Ashton-Warner, 1965; Lee & Allen, 1963;

Stauffer, 1970). According to this method, students dictate about their experiences, either as a group or individually, the teacher does the writing, and the text they develop becomes the reading material. Because the language comes from the children themselves and the content is based on their experiences, students are usually able to read the text easily. Reading and writing are connected as students are actively involved in reading what they have written.

Step 1: Provide the experience. A meaningful experience is identified to serve as the stimulus for the writing. For group writing, it can be an experience shared in school, a book read aloud, a field trip, or some other experience, such as having a pet or playing in the snow, that all students are familiar with. For individual writing, the stimulus can be any experience that is important for the particular student.

Step 2: Discuss the experience. Students and teacher discuss the experience prior to writing. The purpose of discussion is to review the experience so that students' dictation will be more interesting and complete. Teachers might begin the discussion with an open-ended question, such as "what are you going to write about?" As students talk about their experiences, they clarify and organize ideas, use more specific vocabulary, and extend their understanding.

Step 3: Record the dictation. Teachers write down the student's dictation. Texts for individual students are written on sheets of writing paper or in small booklets, and group texts are written on chart paper. Teachers print neatly, spell words correctly, and preserve students' language as much as possible. It is a great temptation to change the student's language to the teachers' own, in either word choice or grammar, but editing should be kept to a minimum so that students do not get the impression that their language is inferior or inadequate.

For individual texts, teachers continue to take the student's dictation and write until the student finishes or hesitates. If the student hesitates, the teacher rereads what has been written and encourages the student to continue. For group texts, students take turns dictating sentences, and after writing each sentence, the teacher rereads it.

It is interesting that, as students become familiar with dictating to the teacher, they learn to pace their dictation to the teacher's writing speed. At first, students dictate as they think of ideas, but with experience, they watch as the teacher writes and supply the text word by word.

Step 4: Read the text. After the text has been dictated, the teacher reads it aloud, pointing to each word. This reading reminds the student of the content of the text and demonstrates how to read it aloud with appropriate intonation. Then students join in the reading. After reading group texts together, individual students can take turns rereading. Group texts can also be copied so each student has a copy to read independently.

Step 5: Extend the text. After dictating, reading, and rereading their texts, students can extend the experience in several ways; these are possibilities:

- Add illustrations to their writing.
- Read their texts to classmates from the author's chair.
- Take their texts home to share with family members.
- Add this text to a collection of their writings.
- Pick out words from their texts that they would like to learn to read.

The language experience approach is an effective beginning reading method. Even students who have not been successful with other types of reading activities can read what they have dictated. There is a drawback, however; teachers provide a "perfect" model when they take children's dictation—they write neatly and spell words correctly. After language experience activities, some young children are not eager to do their own writing. They prefer their teacher's "perfect" writing to their own childlike writing. To avoid this problem, young children should be doing their own writing in personal journals and responding to literature activities at the same time they are participating in language experience activities so they will learn that sometimes they do their own writing and at other times the teacher takes their dictation.

Despite the differences, the language experience approach and process writing are compatible and can be used together to help kindergartners experiment with print. Karnowski (1989) points out that the two approaches are alike in several ways. Students are actively involved in creating their own text in both LEA and process writing. Reading and writing are presented as meaningful, functional, and genuine in both, and the two approaches stress the meaning-making nature of communication. Karnowski suggests that LEA can be modified to make it more like process writing:

1. Prewriting: Students gather ideas for writing through experiences, talk, and art.

2. Drafting: Students dictate the LEA text, which the teacher records. This writing is a first draft.

3. Revising: Students and teacher read and reread the LEA text. They talk about the writing and make one or more changes.

4. Editing: Student and teacher reread the revised text and check that spelling, punctuation, capital letters, and other mechanical considerations are correct. Then students recopy the text in a book format.

5. Sharing: Students share the text with classmates from the author's chair, and the text can be used for other reading activities. With these modifications, students can learn that reading and writing are whole processes.

Big Books

Big books are greatly enlarged picture books that teachers use in shared reading, most commonly with primary-grade students. According to this technique, developed in New Zealand, teachers enlarge a picture book, place it on an easel or chart rack where all the students can see it, and read it with small groups of students or the whole class (Holdaway, 1979). Any type of picture book may be turned into a big book, but predictable books, nursery rhymes, songs, and poems are most popular. Teachers can purchase these books from educational publishers (such as Scholastic or the Wright Group), and some publishers of basal reading textbooks have developed big books to supplement their programs. Teachers can also make big books themselves by printing the text of a picture book on large sheets of posterboard and adding illustrations. The steps in making a big book are listed in Figure 8–3. Heald-Taylor (1987) lists these types of big books that teachers can make:

Replica book—an exact copy of a picture book

Newly illustrated book—a familiar book with new illustrations

Adapted book—a new version of a familiar picture book

Original book—an original book composed by students or the teacher

With the big book on a chart stand or easel, the teacher reads it aloud, pointing to every word. Before long, students are joining in the reading. Then the teacher rereads the story, inviting students to help with the reading. The next time the book is read, the teacher reads to the point that the text becomes predictable, such as the last word of a sentence or the beginning of a refrain, and the students supply the missing text. Having students supply missing text is important because it leads to independent reading. When students have become familiar with the text, they are invited to read the big book independently (Slaughter, 1983).

Students can also make big books of familiar stories to retell and of original stories that they compose. First, students choose a familiar story and write a retelling of it, or

FIGURE 8–3

Steps in Making a Big Book

1. Choose a picture book, short story, nursery rhyme, song, or poem to enlarge.

2. Collect materials, including sheets of posterboard or chart paper, pens, crayons, paints, or other art materials.

3. Print the text of the story, nursery rhyme, song, or poem on the sheets of paper, dividing the text evenly across the pages of the book and leaving at least half the page for the illustration.

4. Add illustrations, which can be done freehand or by children. Teachers can also use opaque projectors to reproduce the illustrations.

5. Add a title page with names of authors, illustrations, and copyright. When students adapt books, that should also be stated on the title page.

6. Design a cover.

7. Put the pages into sequence.

8. Bind the book together with metal rings, yarn, or other clips.

A first grade class made a big book with their retelling of *Corduroy*.

they write an original story. Next, they divide the text page by page and prepare illustrations. Then they write the text on large sheets of posterboard and add the illustrations. They make the title page and cover and compile the pages, and teachers can use the book with young children just as they would use commercially produced big books and big books they made themselves.

Teachers can use big books for a variety of reading and writing activities. Students identify individual letters and words, and the teacher uses words from the stories to analyze phonetic principles. Students can predict vocabulary words and events from the story and develop comprehension skills. Trachtenburg and Ferruggia (1989) used big books with their class of transitional first graders (students with skills too advanced to warrant kindergarten retention, but not strong enough for success in first grade) and found that making and reading big books dramatically improved students' reading scores on standardized achievement tests. The teachers reported that students' self-concepts as readers were decidedly improved as well.

❖ MAKING THE CONNECTION WITH AUTHORS

In reading stories, poems, and informational books, students become curious about the people who write and illustrate books. Units that focus on particular authors and illustrators will further their interest. One way that students learn about authors and illus-

Students talked with Caldecott-winning author and illustrator Gail Haley when she visited their school.

trators is by reading about them. A number of biographies and autobiographies of well-known authors and illustrators, including Beatrix Potter (Aldis, 1969), Jean Fritz (1982), and Tomie de Paola (1989) are available for elementary students. Students can also read profiles of favorite authors in books such as Hopkins's *Books Are by People* (1969) and *More Books Are by More People* (1974). Filmstrips, videotapes, and other audiovisual materials about authors and illustrators are becoming increasingly available. Figure 8–4 lists books and audiovisual materials about authors. In addition, students can read journal articles to learn about favorite writers. Many articles profiling authors and illustrators have been published in *Language Arts, Horn Book,* and other journals, which teachers can clip and file. A last source of information is the publicity brochures that teachers or students can request from publishers and that are usually free of charge.

A second way to learn about authors and illustrators is by writing them letters. Students can share their ideas and feelings about the books they are reading, ask how a particular character was developed, or why the illustrator used a particular art medium. (We will discuss writing letters to authors in greater detail in Chapter 10.)

A third way children can learn about authors is by meeting them in person. Authors and illustrators often make public appearances at libraries, bookstores, and schools. Students also meet authors at young authors' conferences, often held in schools as the culminating event for a year's work in writing, or in libraries to spotlight an

Books

Aldis, D. (1969). *Nothing is impossible: The story of Beatrix Potter*. New York: Atheneum. (M)

Blair, G. (1981). *Laura Ingalls Wilder*. New York: Putnam. (P–M)

Blegvad, E. (1979). *Self-portrait: Erik Blegvad*. Reading, MA: Addison-Wesley. (P–M–U)

Boston, L. M. (1979). *Perverse and foolish: A memoir of childhood and youth*. New York: Atheneum. (U)

Cleary, B. (1988). *A girl from Yamhill: A memoir*. New York: Morrow. (M–U)

Dahl, R. (1984). *Boy: Tales of childhood*. New York: Farrar. (M–U)

de Paola, T. (1989). *The art lesson*. New York: Putnam. (P)

Duncan, L. (1982). *Chapters: My growth as a writer*. Boston: Little, Brown. (U)

Fritz, J. (1982). *Homesick: My own story*. New York: Putnam. (M–U)

Goodall, J. S. (1981). *Before the war, 1908–1939. An autobiography in pictures*. New York: Atheneum. (wordless picture book)(M–U)

Henry, M. (1980). *The illustrated Marguerite Henry*. Chicago: Rand McNally. (M–U)

Lewis, C. S. (1985). *Letters to children*. New York: Macmillan. (M–U)

Hyman, T. S. (1981). *Self-portrait: Trina Schart Hyman*. Reading, MA: Addison-Wesley. (P–M–U)

Naylor, P. R. (1978). *How I came to be a writer*. New York: Atheneum. (U)

Peet, B. (1989). *Bill Peet: An Autobiography*. Houghton Mifflin. (M).

Singer, I. B. (1969). *A day of pleasure: Stories of a boy growing up in Warsaw*. New York: Farrar. (U)

Yates, E. (1981). *My diary—My world*. New York: Westminister. (M–U)

Zemach, M. (1978). *Self-portrait: Margot Zemach*. Reading, MA: Addison-Wesley. (P–M–U)

Collections of Profile Articles

Commire, A. (1971–1985). *Something about the author* (38 volumes). Chicago: Gale Research. (M–U)

Gallo, D. R. (1990). *Speaking for ourselves: Autobiographical sketches by notable authors of books for young adults*. Urbana, IL: National Council of Teachers of English. (U)

Hoffman, M., & Samuels, E. (Eds.). (1972). *Authors and illustrators of children's books*. New York: Bowker. (M–U)

Hopkins, L. B. (1969). *Books are by people: Interviews with 104 authors and illustrators of books for young children*. New York: Citation. (M–U)

Hopkins, L. B. (1974). *More books by more people: Interviews with 65 authors of books for children*. New York: Citation. (M–U)

Jones, C., & Way, O. R. (1976). *British children's authors: Interviews at home*. Chicago: American Library Association. (M–U)

Weiss, M. J. (Ed.). (1979). *From writers to students: The pleasures and pains of writing*. Newark, DE: International Reading Association. (U)

Wintle, J., & Fischer, E. (1975). *The pied pipers: Interviews with the influential creators of children's literature*. London: Paddington Press. (M–U)

FIGURE 8—4

Books and Audiovisual Materials About Children's Authors and Illustrators

Audiovisual Materials

"Bill Peet in his studio," Houghton Mifflin (videotape).

"The case of a Model-A Ford and the man in the snorkel under the hood: Donald J. Sobol," Random House (sound filmstrip).

"Charlotte Zolotow: The grower," Random House (sound filmstrip).

"David Macaulay in his studio," Houghton Mifflin (videotape).

"Edward Ardizzone," Weston Woods (film).

"Ezra Jack Keats," Weston Woods (film).

"First choice: Authors and books," set of nine sound filmstrips from Pied Piper featuring Judy Blume, Clyde Bulla, Beverly Cleary, John D. Fitzgerald, Sid Fleischman, Virginia Hamilton, Marguerite Henry, E. L. Konigsburg, and Theodore Taylor.

"First choice: Poets and poetry," set of five sound filmstrips from Pied Piper featuring Nikki Giovanni, Karla Kuskin, Myra Cohn Livingston, David McCord, and Eve Merriam.

"Gail E. Haley: Wood and linoleum illustration," Weston Woods (sound filmstrip).

"James Daugherty," Weston Woods (film).

"Laurant de Brunhoff: Daydreamer," Random House (sound filmstrip).

"Maurice Sendak," Weston Woods (film).

"Meet Stan and Jan Berenstain," Random House (sound filmstrip).

"Meet the Author," a collection of 12 sound filmstrips or videotapes from Random House featuring well-known authors such as L. Frank Baum, Dr. Seuss, and Charlotte Zolotow.

"Meet the Newbery author," collection of 22 individual sound filmstrips from Random House featuring Lloyd Alexander, William H. Armstrong, Natalie Babbitt, Carol Ryrie Brink, Betsy Byars, Beverly Cleary, James Lincoln and Christopher Collier, Susan Cooper, Eleanor Estes, Jean Craighead George, Bette Green, Virginia Hamilton, Marguerite Henry, Jamake Highwater, Madeleine L'Engle, Arnold Lobel, Scott O'Dell, Katherine Paterson, Isaac Bashevis Singer, Laura Ingalls Wilder, Elizabeth Yates, and Laurence Yep.

"Mr. Shepard and Mr. Milne," Weston Woods (film).

"Poetry explained by Karla Kuskin," Weston Woods (sound filmstrip).

"Robert McCloskey," Weston Woods (film).

"Steven Kellogg: How a picture book is made," Weston Woods (sound filmstrip).

"Tomi Ungerer: Storyteller," Weston Woods (film).

"A visit with Scott O'Dell," Houghton Mifflin (videotape).

"Who's Dr. Seuss? Meet Ted Geisel," Random House (sound filmstrip).

Addresses for Audiovisual Manufacturers

Houghton Mifflin Co.
2 Park Street
Boston, MA 02108

Random House
School Division
400 Hahn Road
Westminister, MD 21157

Weston Woods
Weston, CT 06883

Pied Piper
P.O. Box 320
Verdugo City, CA 91046

FIGURE 8—4   (*continued*)

P = primary grades (K–2)
M = middle grades (3–5)
U = upper grades (6–8)

❖ "PRO" FILE

THE AUTHOR'S CORNER

"I have an author's corner in my classroom because it changes my students' attitudes about reading and writing. I want them to see a real purpose for becoming literate. Getting good grades is not reason enough for many children to learn."

Pat Bishop, Fourth Grade Teacher,
Heaton Elementary School

PROCEDURE

I have set up an author's corner in our classroom, and during the first semester, each student makes and binds a book. Then, during the second semester, they make many, many more. I begin talking about making books on the first day of school and show three or four sample books that my students have made in previous years. Later during the first week, the first book we make is a class collaboration, one of those writing activities in which every student contributes a page. I demonstrate how to make a hardcover book and the care and pride that goes along with it. Students often do their work quickly and hand it in to the teacher without any pride of ownership; that's something that making books changes.

author and his or her books. Students are usually selected to attend the special conference on the basis of their interest or expertise in writing and share their writing and listen to the guest author talk about his or her work. Special-interest sessions help students hone their writing skills or experiment with new techniques. The conferences give students recognition for their work and emphasize the importance of writing. They also stimulate community interest in writing. Special sessions for parents and teachers are often included to teach parents how to encourage their children's writing and to introduce teachers to new strategies for teaching writing.

Then, whenever we are doing a writing activity, I'll just mention that if students have a particularly good piece, they may want to make it into a book. Not every student makes a hardbound book from the same writing activity; instead, two or three students are always making a book.

We use the writing process to make books. Students begin by prewriting about personal experiences, in response to a book, or as part of social studies or science. They write rough drafts and meet in writing groups to share their writing. A classmate will comment that this writing is so good it should be made into a book, and that's usually when students first decide to turn their writing into books. Then students carefully revise and edit their writing and recopy it into the book they have made. Our books aren't elaborate—we use cardboard for the covers and colored tape for the binding. Students draw a picture or decorate the covers with contact paper. Then they use press-on letters for the title and author.

ASSESSMENT

My goal is for every student to make a book, and as they do, they add their name to our Author's Chart. Around the outside of the chart I've made a collage of pictures of authors my students love—such as Beverly Cleary, Tomie de Paola, and Steven Kellogg—and after students read their book aloud to the class, they sign their name to the list. I've made it sort of a ritual—a rite of passage— from student to author. Then students read their books to their family, to students in another class, to the principal, to other groups of children—to whomever will listen. We keep the book in our classroom library all year, but the author can check it out whenever he or she wants to.

Toward the end of the first semester, I check the list to see which students haven't written a book yet (usually five or six children) and work with them as a group to select something they have already written or a topic for a new piece. Then these students serve as a writing group to support and encourage each other to make their books. I talk with the students to get to know them better as readers and writers. I also gauge their language arts skills and their confidence. It's often a lack of confidence that keeps them from publishing a book sooner.

REFLECTIONS

I want my students to think of themselves as authors, not students. When they are authors, they look at reading and writing differently. They are members of the "literacy club"; that's what Frank Smith (1988) calls it. I want all my students to become part of this club, and publishing their own books does it. It literally changes their lives.

❖ MAKING THE CONNECTION WITH STORIES

Teachers are increasingly using trade books either in conjunction with or instead of basal readers. Tunnell and Jacobs (1989) reviewed the research on the literature-based approach to literacy and concluded that students were at least as successful with trade books as with basal readers, and many studies showed trade books to be superior to basal readers. As students read more and more trade books, it is important that teachers find ways to connect reading and writing. The directed reading-thinking strategy is a useful instructional technique, and three types of trade books that can be used to connect reading and writing are predictable books, wordless picture books, and pattern books. Another way to connect reading and writing is to use writing to extend basal reader stories.

Directed Reading-Thinking Activity

In the *Directed Reading-Thinking Activity* (DRTA) (Stauffer, 1975), students make predictions about a story and then read to confirm or reject their predictions. The procedure involves three steps, presented in Figure 8–5, and works best with stories in which characters must make difficult choices or solve complex problems. There is little point in making predictions in response to questions with obvious answers.

This procedure can be easily adapted for writing by having students write their predictions before sharing them orally (Tompkins, 1990). A group of fourth and fifth graders in a reading lab class listened to Lionni's *Tico and the Golden Wings* (1964), a fable about a bird named Tico who was born without wings. He was, however, a happy bird, because he had friends who took care of him. One day a wishingbird granted Tico's wish for wings, and he received wings covered with golden feathers. After his jealous friends abandoned him, Tico traveled around the world, giving away his golden feathers to people who needed help. Black feathers grew on his wings in place of the golden feathers, and when he was all black again, Tico's friends welcomed him.

The teacher began by reading the title and showing the cover of the picture book. She asked, "What do you think the story will be about?" and the students wrote the following responses:

> Tico will probably have them at the first of the story and then lose them at the end.
>
> Tico might have regular wings at first and then something drastic might happen and he would get gold wings.
>
> He'll have them at the beginning and he keeps them forever.
>
> Tico was just a normal bird and then one day his wings turned to gold.

Soon Tico is given the opportunity to make a wish, and the teacher asked, "What do you think Tico will wish for?" Students predicted:

> Tico wants wings so he can fly like the other birds.
>
> Tico wishes for golden wings and to be able to fly from tree to tree and soar through the sky like other birds.

Later, after Tico gets the golden wings, he meets a poor man with a sick daughter, and the teacher asked, "How do you think Tico will help the poor man and his sick daughter?" Students answered:

Step 1: Predicting

After showing students the cover of the book and reading the title, the teacher begins by asking students to make a prediction about the story, using questions such as:

- What do you think a story with a title like this might be about?
- What do you think might happen in this story?
- Does this picture give you any ideas about what might happen in this story?

The teacher or students may read the first paragraph or two of the story, if necessary, to provide more information to use in making predictions. Then students write a brief response and read their responses aloud. After sharing their responses, the teacher asks these questions:

- Which of these ideas do you think would be the likely one?
- Why do you think that idea is a good one?

Step 2: Reasoning and Predicting from Succeeding Pages

After setting their purpose for reading or listening, the students or teacher read part of the story, and students begin to confirm or reject their predictions. At crucial points in the story, the teacher asks questions such as:

- What do you think now?
- What do you think will happen next?
- What would happen if . . . ?
- Why do you think that idea is a good one?

Students write brief responses and read them aloud. Then the students or the teacher continue reading the story.

Step 3: Proving

Students give reasons to support their predictions by writing answers to questions such as:

- What in the story makes you think that?
- Where in the story do you get information to support that idea?

The teacher can ask these "proving" questions during the story or after it has been read.

FIGURE 8–5

Teacher's Notebook Page: Steps in the Directed Reading-Thinking Activity

Tico would fly to town and get the medicine.

He would call for that wishingbird and ask her.

Tico will pick one of his golden feathers off and give it to the man.

After Tico gives away all of his golden feathers, the teacher asked, "Will Tico's friends welcome him back now?" and students wrote:

Yes, because he don't have golden wings no more.

Yes, because he is just like the other birds now.

Yes, because his friends won't think he's trying to be better than them.

Yes, they will because he is different on the outside but still the same on the inside.

After reading the end of the story, students were asked, "Did you like the story? Why or why not?" Before beginning an oral discussion of the story, they reflected:

Yes, because it told about Tico's ups and his downs.

Yes, I did because it was interesting.

Yes, because it was a very exciting book.

Yes, because Tico was a smart bird to give his golden wings to the poor people so he can be the same as the other birds.

I liked it because Tico was a likable bird.

After students wrote each response, they read them aloud to the group before the teacher continued reading. Then students had a purpose for listening: to learn if their predictions were correct. Through this activity, students engaged with the text, anticipated story events, and constructed meaning and an emotional response.

A warning is in order: teachers should not interrupt a story too often, because this procedure can become tedious for students who are comprehending and making their own predictions (Corcoran, 1987). The process is more useful with less capable readers who need help making connections or for students who are reading a complex piece of literature. For the remedial readers who used DRTA with *Tico and the Golden Wings,* the procedure encouraged them to probe their thoughts more deeply than if they had simply listened to the story read aloud.

Predictable Books

Predicting is a strategy we use in all aspects of our lives. In reading, we predict what the author will say next and how he or she will say it. Readers globally predict the next event in a story at the same time they make a more local prediction about the next sentence. They may also predict how the author will use language in the rest of a sentence and what letters are likely to be in the rest of a word. Prediction is an important reading strategy for all kinds of books, but some books are especially easy to predict because they contain repetitive phrases or sentences, repetitive sentences in a cumulative structure, or sequential events that make them easier to read. These *predictable books* are a valuable tool for beginning readers because the repetitive patterns enable children to predict the next sentence or episode in the story (Bridge, 1979; Rhodes, 1981; Tompkins & Webeler, 1983; Heald-Taylor, 1987).

A list of predictable books appropriate for beginning readers, arranged in three categories, is presented in Figure 8–6. Books in the first category, repetitive sentences, include phrases or sentences that are repeated throughout the story. An example is Gag's *Millions of Cats* (1956), in which the refrain "Cats here, Cats there, Cats and kittens everywhere, Hundreds of cats, Thousands of cats, Millions and billions and trillions of cats" is repeated again and again. The second category, repetitive sentences in a cumulative structure, includes books in which phrases or sentences are repeated and expanded in each episode. In *The Gingerbread Boy* (Galdone, 1975), for instance, the gingerbread boy repeats and expands his boast as he meets each character. Books in the third category, sequential patterns, use cultural sequences, such as letters of the alphabet, numbers, and days of the week, to structure the story; for example, *The Very Hungry Caterpillar* (Carle, 1969) combines the number and day of the week sequences. Children may also use rhyme to anticipate events in reading; many of the Dr. Seuss stories use rhyme extensively to make them predictable.

Predictable books are excellent reading materials for young children because they are able to gain reading "independence" quickly. In two related studies, Bridge and her colleagues (1982, 1983) found that first graders learn sight words more easily with predictable picture books than with traditional basal reading textbooks. Also, after reading predictable books, these students were more likely to use both phonics and context clues to identify unfamiliar words, while students reading in basal readers depended on phonics alone.

Teachers often choose predictable books to make into big books for shared reading because of their repetitions (Heald-Taylor, 1987). Teachers read the selection aloud to students, then reread it many times, with teacher or a student tracking the text with a pointer. One of several procedures can be used to share the text:

Unison—teacher and students read the story together as a group, in unison.

Repetition—the teacher reads the story one sentence at a time, and students repeat the sentence in unison.

Refrain—the teacher reads the story, but students read the refrain or repeated text.

Cloze—the teacher reads most of text, but pauses for students to fill in missing words or phrases that are highly predictable (Heald-Taylor, 1987).

Connecting to Writing. Not only are predictable books useful as reading material for young children, but they also provide patterns for their writing. Children often create their own books following the repetitive sentence patterns, cumulative

---

Repetitive Sentences

Balian, L. (1972). *Where in the world is Henry?* Nashville, TN: Abingdon.
Brown, M. W. (1947). *Goodnight moon.* New York: Harper and Row.
Brown, R. (1981). *A dark, dark tale.* New York: Dial.
Cauley, L. B. (1982). *The cock, the mouse, and the little red hen.* New York: Putnam.
Charlip, R. (1969). *What good luck! What bad luck!* New York: Scholastic.
Gag, W. (1956). *Millions of cats.* New York: Coward-McCann.
Galdone, P. (1973). *The little red hen.* New York: Seabury.
Galdone, P. (1973). *The three billy goats Gruff.* Boston: Houghton Mifflin.
Ginsburg, M. (1972). *The chick and the duckling.* New York: Macmillan.
Hill, E. (1980). *Where's Spot?* New York: Putnam.
Hutchins, P. (1972). *Good-night, owl!* New York: Macmillan.
Martin, B. (1983). *Brown bear, brown bear, what do you see?* New York: Holt, Rinehart and Winston.
Nelson, J. (1989). *There's a dragon in my wagon.* Cleveland: Modern Curriculum Press.
Peek, M. (1981). *Roll over!* Boston: Houghton Mifflin.
Tafuri, N. (1984). *Have you seen my duckling?* New York: Greenwillow.
Viorst, J. (1972). *Alexander and the terrible, horrible, no good, very bad day.* New York: Atheneum.

Repetitive Sentences in a Cumulative Structure

Bolton, F. (1986). *The greedy goat.* New York: Scholastic.
Brett, J. (1989). *The mitten.* New York: Putnam.
Carle, E. (1971). *Do you want to be my friend?* New York: Crowell.
Ets, M. H. (1972). *Elephant in a well.* New York: Viking.

FIGURE 8–6

Predictable Books for Primary Grade Students

story episode structures, and other sequential patterns they have learned. An excerpt from a first grader's predictable story appears in Figure 8–7.

Wordless Books

Another way to connect reading and writing is with *wordless picture books,* in which, as the name suggests, the story is told entirely through pictures. Few words other than the title appear in the book. Well-known illustrators, including Mitsumasa Anno, Tomie de Paola, Fernando Krahn, John Goodall, and others have created a number of these marvelous stories. For instance, de Paola's *Pancakes for Breakfast* (1978) is a charming story of a little old woman who tries to cook pancakes for breakfast, but runs into a series of problems as she assembles the ingredients; in the end, her neighbors invite her to their home for pancakes. The book encourages young children to tell the story and

Flack, M. (1932). *Ask Mr. Bear*. New York: Macmillan.
Fox, H. (1986). *Hattie and the fox*. New York: Bradbury.
Fox, H. (1989). *Shoes from grandpa*. New York: Orchard Books.
Galdone, P. (1975). *The gingerbread boy*. New York: Seabury.
Hutchins, P. (1968). *Rosie's walk*. New York: Macmillan.
Kellogg, S. (1974). *There was an old woman*. New York: Parents.
Peppe, R. (1970). *The house that Jack built*. New York: Delacorte.
Tolstoi, A. (1968). *The great big enormous turnip*. New York: Watts.
Westcott, N. B. (1980). *I know an old lady who swallowed a fly*. Boston: Little,
    Brown.
Zemach, H. (1969). *The judge*. New York: Farrar, Straus & Giroux.
Zemach, H., & Zemach, M. (1966). *Mommy, buy me a china doll*. Chicago: Follett.
Zemach, M. (1983). *The little red hen*. New York: Farrar, Straus & Giroux.

Sequential Patterns

Alain. (1964). *One, two, three, going to sea*. New York: Scholastic.
Baskin, L. (1972). *Hosie's alphabet*. New York: Viking.
Carle, E. (1969). *The very hungry caterpillar*. Cleveland: Collins-World.
Carle, E. (1977). *The grouchy ladybug*. New York: Crowell.
Carle, E. (1987). *A house for a hermit crab*. Saxonville, MA: Picture Book Studio.
Domanska, J. (1985). *Busy Monday morning*. New York: Greenwillow.
Keats, E. J. (1973). *Over in the meadow*. New York: Scholastic.
Mack, S. (1974). *10 bears in my bed*. New York: Pantheon.
Martin, B. (1970). *Monday, Monday, I like Monday*. New York: Holt, Rinehart and
    Winston.
Schulevitz, U. (1967). *One Monday morning*. New York: Scribner.
Sendak, M. (1975). *Seven little monsters*. New York: Harper and Row.

FIGURE 8–6   *(continued)*

to talk about it, as well as introduces them to some of the elements of stories. The rustic New England setting and the repetition of events are essential to the story's success. Young children may begin by pointing out familiar objects in the pictures and follow along as the teacher tells the story. Soon, however, they are telling the story themselves, using "book language" such as dialogue and alliteration. Cooking pancakes is a natural follow-up activity. Figure 8–8 lists wordless picture books.

Teachers typically use these books with young children because even nonreaders can enjoy and understand many of them. Students can tell the story for a small group of classmates, role-play the story, and dictate or write their own versions. Many wordless picture books have sophisticated story lines, however, often presented on several levels of understanding, which are more appropriate for older students. For example, Goodall's *Above and Below Stairs* (1983) compares the lifestyle of English lords and peasants during the Middle Ages. This book is a useful resource for a unit on medieval life for upper-grade students, but hardly appropriate for primary-grade students, even though it has no words.

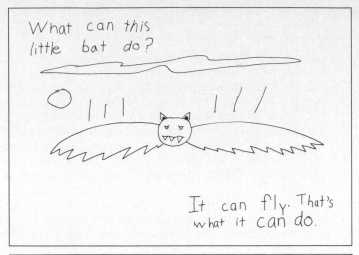

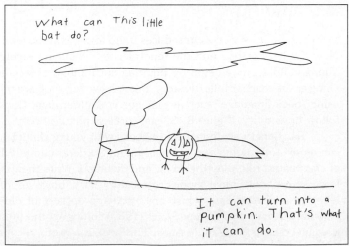

FIGURE 8—7

An Excerpt from a First Grader's Predictable Book
Shawn

Alexander, M. (1968). *Out! out! out!* New York: Dial. (P)
Alexander, M. (1970). *Bobo's dream.* New York: Dial. (P)
Anno, M. (1983). *Anno's USA.* New York: Philomel. (M–U)
Aruego, J. (1971). *Look what I can do.* New York: Scribner. (P)
Bang, M. (1980). *The grey lady and the strawberry snatcher.* New York: Four Winds. (P–M–U)
Briggs, R. (1980). *The snowman.* New York: Random House. (P)
Carle, E. (1971). *Do you want to be my friend?* New York: Crowell. (P)
Carroll, R. (1965). *What whiskers did.* New York: Walck. (P)
Day, A. (1985). *Good dog, Carl.* New York: Green Tiger Press. (M)
deGroat, D. (1977). *Alligator's toothache.* New York: Crown. (P–M)
de Paola, T. (1979). *Flicks.* New York: Harcourt Brace Jovanovich. (P)
de Paola, T. (1981). *The hunter and the animals: A wordless picture book.* New York: Holiday House. (P–M)
de Paola, T. (1983). *Sing, Pierrot, sing.* New York: Harcourt Brace Jovanovich. (M–U)
Goodall, J. S. (1975). *Creepy castle.* New York: Macmillan. (M)
Goodall, J. S. (1979). *The story of an English village.* New York: Atheneum. (M–U)
Goodall, J. S. (1980). *Paddy's new hat.* New York: Atheneum. (M)
Goodall, J. S. (1983). *Above and below stairs.* New York: Atheneum. (U)
Goodall, J. S. (1988). *Little Red Riding Hood.* New York: McElderry Books. (P–M)
Henstra, F. (1983). *Mighty mizzling mouse.* New York: Lippincott. (P–M)
Hoban, T. (1971). *Look again.* New York: Macmillan. (P)
Krahn, F. (1970). *A flying saucer full of spaghetti.* New York: Dutton. (P–M)
Krahn, F. (1977). *The mystery of the giant footprints.* New York: Dutton. (P–M)
Krahn, F. (1978). *The great ape.* New York: Penguin. (P–M–U)
Mayer, M. (1967). *A boy, a dog, and a frog.* New York: Dial. (P–M)
Mayer, M. (1974). *Frog goes to dinner.* New York: Dial. (P–M–U)
Spier, P. (1982). *Rain.* New York: Doubleday. (P–M)
Turkle, B. (1976). *Deep in the forest.* New York: Dutton. (P–M)
Winters, P. (1976). *The bear and the fly.* New York: Crown. (P–M–U)
Winters, P. (1980). *Sir Andrew.* New York: Crown. (P–M)
Young, E. (1984). *The other bone.* New York: Harper and Row. (P–M)

FIGURE 8–8

Wordless Picture Books

The Writing Connection.   Wordless picture books can be used for a variety of writing activities (Abrahamson, 1981; D'Angelo, 1979; Degler, 1979). Students can write dialogue for the characters using cartoonlike balloons, or write their own versions of the story. These books are also especially valuable for teaching point of view; because there is no text to "bias" the reader, students can tell, dictate, or write the story from different viewpoints more easily. This is seven-year-old Whitney's dictated retelling of Mayer's hilarious *Frog Goes to Dinner* (1974), in which a frog travels to a fancy restaurant hiding in the pocket of a boy's jacket:

I Am the Frog

Once there was this boy. His family was going to dinner. They had a dog named Jerry and a turtle. His name was Jeff. And they had a frog which was me! Then the boy takes me to dinner. I jumped out of the boy's pocket. I flew out to the man that was playing the saxophone. And boy WAS he mad! And boy, did I get in trouble! The other musicians fell into the drum. Then I jumped into some salad. And the girl who was served the salad screamed! She screamed so loud that I almost popped my ears! And I jumped right in a man's cup. When the man was about to get a drink, I kissed him. Then the man who served the dinner got mad. We had to leave.

Whitney's retelling is especially interesting because she retold the story from the frog's point of view.

Even though these books are wordless, they are also a valuable tool in teaching reading (McGee & Tompkins, 1983). Students dictate a story to accompany a wordless picture book; the teacher records the story, page by page, and clips the text to each page of the book. Then students read and reread the story. This approach works well even with older students who are experiencing reading difficulties.

Pattern Books

Many stories have a pattern or format that students can adapt for stories they write. For example, after reading Viorst's *Alexander and the Terrible, Horrible, No Good, Very Bad Day* (1972), students are eager to write about their own worst days or—for a change—about their wonderful, fantastic, really rad days. Students use the writing process as they draft and refine their writing. They use the pattern book as the skeleton for their stories, but adapt the format as necessary. Books that students can use as models for writing are listed in Figure 8–9.

Basal Reader Stories

Instead of doing workbook pages before and after reading a selection in a basal reader, students can keep a reading log and write about the stories they read. They can brainstorm lists of words or cluster the main ideas from the story. They can also respond to the reading through a variety of talk, drama, reading, and writing activities (Buckley, 1986). What is important is that students connect the basal reader stories to real world reading and writing so they see a reason to learn language skills. These are some activities through which students can respond to reading:

Brainstorming—students brainstorm a list of words related to the topic or theme of a story, then use the words in a freewrite.

Writing class collaboration stories—students choose a favorite story and retell it; each student retells one page, and after the pages are completed, they compile them to form a book that can be placed in the class library.

Barrett, J. (1978). *Cloudy with a chance of meatballs.* New York: Macmillan.
Students write a sequel to Barrett's book describing other mishaps in the crazy town of Chewandswallow.

Barrett, J. (1983). *A snake is totally tail.* New York: Atheneum.
Students write a book with sentences following Barrett's pattern.

Baylor, B. (1974). *Everybody needs a rock.* New York: Scribner.
Students write a sequel, "Everybody Needs a Friend" or "Everybody Needs a Book," with a list of rules for selecting a friend or a book as Baylor did.

Baylor, B. (1977). *Guess who my favorite person is.* New York: Atheneum.
Students choose a favorite person to write about following Baylor's style.

Baylor, B. (1986). *I'm in charge of celebrations.* New York: Scribner.
Students create their own celebrations and write about them, or about Thanksgiving, the 4th of July, and other well-known celebrations.

Brown, M. W. (1949). *The important book.* New York: Harper and Row.
Students follow Brown's pattern and write about families, community helpers, historical figures, U.S. states, or modes of transportation.

Burningham, J. (1978). *Would you rather . . .* New York: Crowell.
Students write books with a series of "Would you rather . . ." choices.

Carle, E. (1973). *Have you seen my cat?* New York: Philomel.
Students choose another topic such as dinosaurs, dogs, or boats and write a "Have You Seen My_____?" book.

Charlip, R. (1964). *Fortunately.* New York: Four Winds.
Students use Charlip's pattern to write their own lucky-unlucky story.

Degen, B. (1983). *Jamberry.* New York: Harper and Row.
Students write their own book using invented "berry" words.

Goss, J. L., & Harste, J. C. (1981). *It didn't frighten me.* New York: Scholastic.
Students follow Goss and Harste's pattern in writing a book about what doesn't frighten them.

Hill, E. (1980). *Where's Spot?* New York: Putnam.
Students construct their own movable books.

Hoberman, M. A. (1978). *A house is a house for me.* New York: Viking.
Students write their own book about houses.

Kellogg, S. (1987). *Aster Aardvark's alphabet adventures.* New York: Morrow.
Students write an alliterative ABC book following Kellogg's pattern.

Krauss, R. (1952). *A hole is to dig.* New York: Harper and Row.
Students create their own book of definitions following the pattern of Krauss's book.

Lobel, A. (1984). *The rose in my garden.* New York: Morrow.
Students follow Lobel's pattern and write their own cumulative story.

Martin, Jr., B. (1983). *Brown bear, brown bear, what do you see?* New York: Holt.
Students choose other animals and follow Martin's pattern in their own book.

Martin, Jr., B., & Archambault, J. (1988). *Listen to the rain.* New York: Henry Holt.
Students paint a word picture for another type of weather or for dogs, dinosaurs, Halloween, or some other concept.

FIGURE 8–9

Books that Provide Models for Students' Writing

Numeroff, L. J. (1985). *If you give a mouse a cookie.* New York: Harper and Row.
Students write their own circle story about giving a cat, a teacher, or themselves a cookie.

Parker, N. W. (1985). *Paul Revere's ride.* New York: Greenwillow.
Students make a picture book illustrating a poem or song with one line or stanza on each page.

Spier, P. (1982). *Rain.* New York: Doubleday.
Students add words to this wordless book or create their own wordless storybook.

Van Allsburg, C. (1984). *The mysteries of Harris Burdick.* Boston: Houghton Mifflin.
Students select an illustration from Van Allsburg's book to write about, or make their own collection of fantastic illustrations for classmates to turn into stories.

Viorst, J. (1972). *Alexander and the terrible, horrible, no good, very bad day.* New York: Atheneum.
Students write about a terrible, horrible, no good, very bad day or about a wonderful, spectacular, fantastic, very rad day.

Wood, A. (1982). *Quick as a cricket.* London: Child's Play.
Students collect comparisons and compile them in a book.

Wood, A. (1985). *King Bidgood's in the bathtub.* New York: Harcourt Brace Jovanovich.
Students follow Wood's pattern to write a hilarious story about someone who won't get out of bed or won't get off a motorcycle.

FIGURE 8–9   (*continued*)

Writing simulated journals—after reading a story, students assume the persona of a story character and write a journal from that person's viewpoint.

Comparing a story to other versions of a story—after reading a basal reader version of a well-known story, students read other versions of the story in trade books and compare the different versions. There are many versions available, for example, of "The Hare and the Tortoise," "Cinderella," and other folktales.

Drawing a wordless picture book—students choose a favorite story, draw a series of pictures to illustrate it, and compile the pictures to make a wordless picture book.

Writing dialogue—students rewrite an excerpt from a script in narrative form.

Retelling stories from different viewpoints—students retell stories from the viewpoint of another character; the retellings can be oral, tape-recorded, or written.

Research and informational writing—students choose a subject (e.g., Alaska, rabbits) from one of the informational selections in the textbook, research the topic, and write a concept book or brief report on it.

Writing simulated letters—students write simulated letters from one character to another, then classmates who have also read the story answer the letters.

Developing timelines—students choose a person profiled in a biographical or autobiographical selection in the textbook and develop a timeline of the person's life; they also highlight the part of the timeline discussed in the selection.

❖ MAKING THE CONNECTION WITH INFORMATIONAL BOOKS

Many forms of writing are organized or structured in particular ways. Many students are familiar with elements of story structure, such as characters and plot, through telling and reading stories as well as watching them on television. They write poems such as haiku and cinquain, which follow syllable-counting formulas, and read and write biographies, which usually follow a chronological sequence.

Informational books are trade books that deal with careers, animals, countries, planets, human body, Indians, and other nonfiction topics, social studies and other content area textbooks, and encyclopedias. They are also called *expository texts*. Reading educators have examined content area materials for elementary and high school levels to devise ways to help students comprehend the materials more easily. They have identified a number of patterns or structures used in these texts, called *expository text structures*.

Expository Text Structures

Five of the most common organizational patterns are description, sequence, comparison, cause and effect, and problem and solution (Niles, 1974; Meyer & Freedle, 1984). Figure 8–10 describes these patterns and presents sample passages and cue words that signal use of each pattern.

Description. In this organizational pattern, the writer describes a topic by listing characteristics, features, and examples. Phrases such as *for example* and *characteristics are* cue this structure. When students delineate any topic, such as the Mississippi River, eagles, or Alaska, they use description.

Sequence. The writer lists items or events in numerical or chronological order. Cue words include *first, second, third, next, then,* and *finally.* Directions for completing a math problem, stages in an animal's life cycle, and events in a biography are often written in the sequence pattern.

Comparison. The writer explains how two or more things are alike or different. *Different, in contrast, alike, same as,* and *on the other hand* are cue words and phrases that signal this structure. When students compare and contrast book and movie versions of a story, reptiles and amphibians, or life in ancient Greece with life in ancient Egypt, they use this organizational pattern.

Pattern	Description	Cue Words	Graphic Organizer	Sample Passage
Description	The author describes a topic by listing characteristics, features, and examples.	for example characteristics are		The Olympic symbol consists of five interlocking rings. The rings represent the five continents—Africa, Asia, Europe, North America, and South America—from which athletes come to compete in the games. The rings are colored black, blue, green, red, and yellow. At least one of these colors is found in the flag of every country sending athletes to compete in the Olympic games.
Sequence	The author lists items or events in numerical or chronological order.	first, second, third next then finally	1. 2. 3. 4. 5.	The Olympic games began as athletic festivals to honor the Greek gods. The most important festival was held in the valley of Olympia to honor Zeus, the king of the gods. It was this festival that became the Olympic games in 776 B.C. These games were ended in A.D. 394 by the Roman Emperor who ruled Greece. No Olympic games were held for more than 1,500 years. Then the modern Olympics began in 1896. Almost 300 male athletes competed in the first modern Olympics. In the games held in 1900, female athletes were allowed to compete. The games have continued every four years since 1896 except during World War II, and they will most likely continue for many years to come.
Comparison	The author explains how two or more things are alike and/or how they are different.	different in contrast alike same as on the other hand	Alike · Different	The modern Olympics is very unlike the ancient Olympic games. Individual events are different. While there were no swimming races in the ancient games, for example, there were chariot races. There were no female contestants and all athletes competed in the nude. Of course, the ancient and modern Olympics are also alike in many ways. Some events, such as the javelin and discus throws, are the same. Some people say that cheating, professionalism, and nationalism in the modern games are a disgrace to the Olympic tradition. But according to the ancient Greek writers, there were many cases of cheating, nationalism, and professionalism in their Olympics, too.

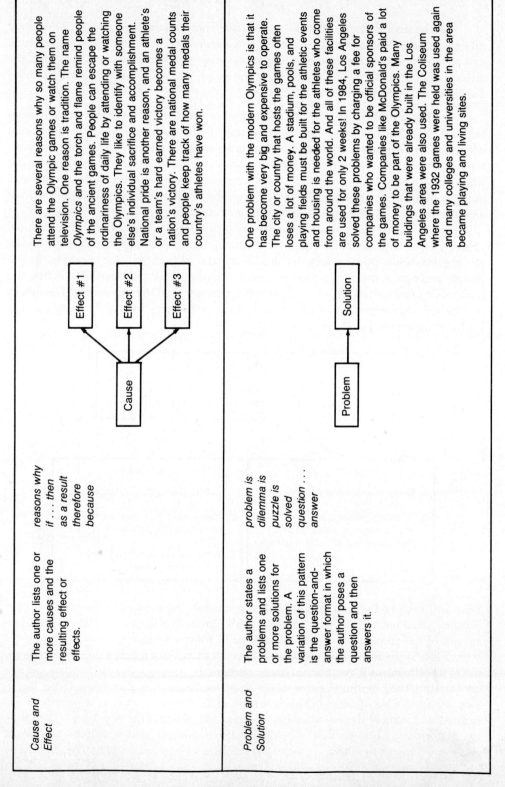

Cause and Effect	The author lists one or more causes and the resulting effect or effects.	*reasons why* *if . . . then* *as a result* *therefore* *because*	

There are several reasons why so many people attend the Olympic games or watch them on television. One reason is tradition. The name *Olympics* and the torch and flame remind people of the ancient games. People can escape the ordinariness of daily life by attending or watching the Olympics. They like to identify with someone else's individual sacrifice and accomplishment. National pride is another reason, and an athlete's or a team's hard earned victory becomes a nation's victory. There are national medal counts and people keep track of how many medals their country's athletes have won.

Problem and Solution	The author states a problem and lists one or more solutions for the problem. A variation of this pattern is the question-and-answer format in which the author poses a question and then answers it.	*problem is* *dilemma is* *puzzle is solved* *question . . . answer*	

One problem with the modern Olympics is that it has become very big and expensive to operate. The city or country that hosts the games often loses a lot of money. A stadium, pools, and playing fields must be built for the athletic events and housing is needed for the athletes who come from around the world. And all of these facilities are used for only 2 weeks! In 1984, Los Angeles solved these problems by charging a fee for companies who wanted to be official sponsors of the games. Companies like McDonald's paid a lot of money to be part of the Olympics. Many buildings that were already built in the Los Angeles area were also used. The Coliseum where the 1932 games were held was used again and many colleges and universities in the area became playing and living sites.

FIGURE 8–10

The Five Expository Text Structures

Adapted from McGee & Richgels, 1985; Smith & Tompkins, 1988.

Cause and Effect.   The writer explains one or more causes and the resulting effect or effects. *Reasons why, if . . . then, as a result, therefore,* and *because* are words and phrases that cue this structure. Explanations of why dinosaurs became extinct, the effects of pollution on the environment, or the causes of the Civil War are written using the cause and effect pattern.

Problem and Solution.   In this expository structure, the writer states a problem and offers one or more solutions. A variation is the question and answer format, in which the writer poses a question and then answers it. Cue words and phrases include *the problem is, the puzzle is, solve,* and *question . . . answer.* Students use this structure when they write about why money was invented, saving endangered animals, and building dams to stop flooding. They often use the problem-solution pattern in writing advertisements and other persuasive writing as well.

These organizational patterns correspond to the traditional organization of main ideas (or topic sentences) and details within paragraphs. The main idea is embodied in the organizational pattern and the details are the elaboration; for example, in the sample passage of the comparison pattern in Figure 8–10, the main idea is that the modern Olympic games are very different from the ancient Olympic games. The details are the specific comparisons and contrasts. We can diagram the main idea and details for the comparison as follows:

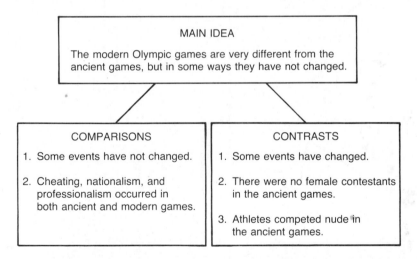

Diagrams called *graphic organizers* can help students organize ideas for the other four organizational patterns as well (Piccolo, 1987; Smith & Tompkins, 1988). Sample diagrams of the graphic organizers also appear in Figure 8–10.

Most of the research on expository text structures has focused on older students' use of these patterns in reading; however, elementary students also use the patterns and cue words in their writing (Langer, 1986; Raphael, Englert, & Kirschner, 1989; Tompkins, 1990). A class of second graders examined the five expository text structures and learned that authors use cue words as a secret code to signal the structures. Then they read informational books that used each of the expository text structures, and wrote paragraphs to use the patterns themselves. Working in small groups, they developed graphic organizers and wrote paragraphs to exemplify each of the five organizational patterns. The graphic organizers and paragraphs are presented in Figure 8–11; the secret code (or cue) words in each paragraph appear in boldface type.

Teaching Students about Expository Text Structures.   Students can learn to recognize the five organizational patterns and use them to improve their reading comprehension as well as to organize their writing (Flood, Lapp, & Farnan, 1986; McGee & Richgels, 1985; Piccolo, 1987). The steps in the teaching strategy are as follows.

1.   Introduce an organizational pattern to students. Explain the pattern and when writers use it; note cue words that signal the pattern; then, share an example of the pattern and describe the graphic organizer for that pattern.

2.   Analyze examples of the pattern in informational books, not in stories. Figure 8–12 lists books that illustrate each of the five expository text structures. Sometimes the pattern is signaled clearly by means of titles, topic sentences, and cue words, and sometimes it is not. Students learn to identify cue words, and they talk about why writers may or may not explicitly signal the structure. They also diagram the structure using a graphic organizer.

3.   Write paragraphs using the pattern. The first writing activity may be a whole class activity; later, students can write paragraphs in small groups and individually. For prewriting activities, students choose a topic, gather information, and organize it using a graphic organizer. Next they write a rough draft of the paragraph, inserting cue words to signal the structure. Then they revise, edit, and write a final copy of the paragraph.

4.   Explain the patterns. Students share the paragraphs they have written and explain how they have used the particular organizational pattern in their writing.

These students are analyzing the structure of the informational material they are reading.

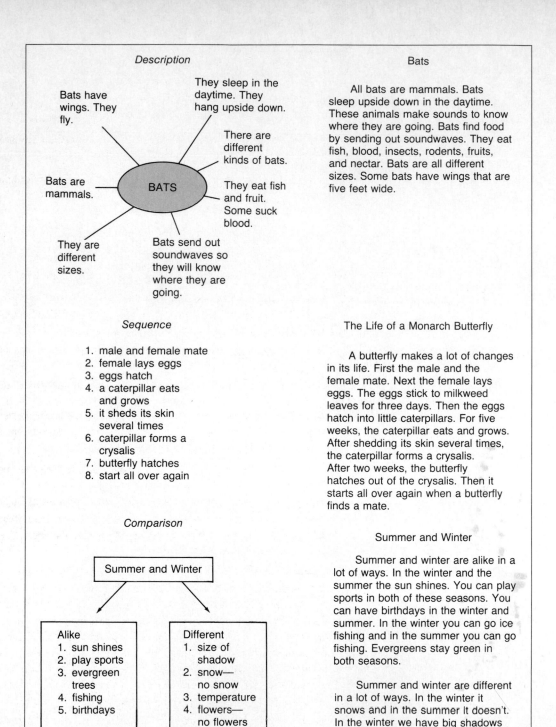

Description

Bats have wings. They fly.

They sleep in the daytime. They hang upside down.

There are different kinds of bats.

Bats are mammals.

BATS

They eat fish and fruit. Some suck blood.

They are different sizes.

Bats send out soundwaves so they will know where they are going.

Bats

All bats are mammals. Bats sleep upside down in the daytime. These animals make sounds to know where they are going. Bats find food by sending out soundwaves. They eat fish, blood, insects, rodents, fruits, and nectar. Bats are all different sizes. Some bats have wings that are five feet wide.

Sequence

1. male and female mate
2. female lays eggs
3. eggs hatch
4. a caterpillar eats and grows
5. it sheds its skin several times
6. caterpillar forms a crysalis
7. butterfly hatches
8. start all over again

The Life of a Monarch Butterfly

A butterfly makes a lot of changes in its life. First the male and the female mate. Next the female lays eggs. The eggs stick to milkweed leaves for three days. Then the eggs hatch into little caterpillars. For five weeks, the caterpillar eats and grows. After shedding its skin several times, the caterpillar forms a crysalis. After two weeks, the butterfly hatches out of the crysalis. Then it starts all over again when a butterfly finds a mate.

Comparison

Summer and Winter

Alike
1. sun shines
2. play sports
3. evergreen trees
4. fishing
5. birthdays

Different
1. size of shadow
2. snow— no snow
3. temperature
4. flowers— no flowers

Summer and Winter

Summer and winter are alike in a lot of ways. In the winter and the summer the sun shines. You can play sports in both of these seasons. You can have birthdays in the winter and summer. In the winter you can go ice fishing and in the summer you can go fishing. Evergreens stay green in both seasons.

Summer and winter are different in a lot of ways. In the winter it snows and in the summer it doesn't. In the winter we have big shadows and in the summer we have little shadows. Summer is hot and winter is cold.

FIGURE 8–11

Second Graders' Graphic Organizers and Paragraphs Illustrating the Five Expository Text Structures

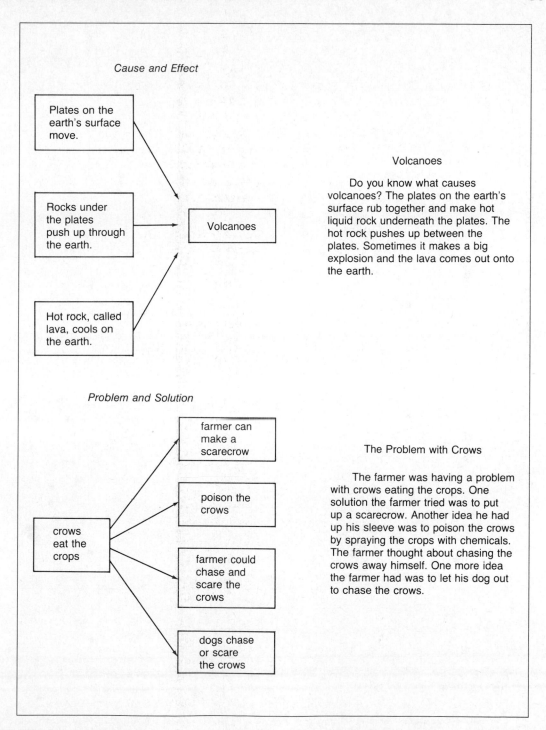

Cause and Effect

Plates on the earth's surface move.

Rocks under the plates push up through the earth.

Hot rock, called lava, cools on the earth.

Volcanoes

Volcanoes

Do you know what causes volcanoes? The plates on the earth's surface rub together and make hot liquid rock underneath the plates. The hot rock pushes up between the plates. Sometimes it makes a big explosion and the lava comes out onto the earth.

Problem and Solution

farmer can make a scarecrow

poison the crows

farmer could chase and scare the crows

dogs chase or scare the crows

crows eat the crops

The Problem with Crows

The farmer was having a problem with crows eating the crops. One solution the farmer tried was to put up a scarecrow. Another idea he had up his sleeve was to poison the crows by spraying the crops with chemicals. The farmer thought about chasing the crows away himself. One more idea the farmer had was to let his dog out to chase the crows.

FIGURE 8−11 (*continued*)

Description

Balestrino, P. (1971). *The skeleton inside you.* New York: Crowell. (P)
Branley, F. M. (1986). *What the moon is like.* New York: Harper and Row. (M)
Hansen, R., & Bell, R. A. (1985). *My first book of space.* New York: Simon and Schuster. (M)
Parish, P. (1974). *Dinosaur time.* New York: Harper and Row. (P)

Sequence

Carrick, C. (1978). *Octopus.* New York: Clarion. (M)
Cole, J. (1973). *My puppy is born.* New York: Morrow. (P–M)
Gibbons, G. (1985). *Lights! camera! action!* New York: Crowell. (M)
Jaspersohn, W. (1988). *Ice cream.* New York: Macmillan. (M–U)
Lasky, K. (1983). *Sugaring time.* New York: Macmillan. (M–U)
Macaulay, D. (1977). *Castle.* Boston: Houghton Mifflin. (M–U)

Comparison

Gibbons, G. (1984). *Fire! Fire!* New York: Harper and Row. (P–M)
Lasker, J. (1976). *Merry ever after: The story of two medieval weddings.* New York: Viking.
    (M–U)
Rowan, J. P. (1985). *Butterflies and moths* (A new true book). Chicago: Children's Press. (M)

Cause and Effect

Branley, F. M. (1985). *Flash, crash, rumble, and roll.* New York: Harper and Row. (P–M)
Branley, F. M. (1985). *Volcanoes.* New York: Harper and Row. (P–M)
Branley, F. M. (1986). *What makes day and night?* New York: Harper and Row. (P–M)
Selsam, M. E. (1981). *Where do they go? Insects in winter.* New York: Scholastic. (P–M)
Showers, P. (1985). *What happens to a hamburger?* New York: Harper and Row. (P–M)

Problem and Solution

Cole, J. (1983). *Cars and how they go.* New York: Harper and Row. (P–M)
Gibbons, G. (1980). *Locks and keys.* New York: Crowell. (M–U)
Horwitz, J. (1984). *Night markets: Bringing food to a city.* New York: Harper and Row. (M–U)
Showers, P. (1980). *No measles, no mumps for me.* New York: Crowell. (P–M)
Simon, S. (1984). *The dinosaur is the biggest animal that ever lived and other wrong ideas
    you thought were true.* New York: Harper and Row. (P–M)

Combination

Aliki. (1981). *Digging up dinosaurs.* New York: Harper and Row. (M)
de Paola, T. (1978). *The popcorn book.* New York: Holiday House. (P–M)
Podendorf, I. (1982). *Jungles* (A new true book). Chicago: Children's Press. (M)
Sabin, F. (1982). *Amazing world of ants.* Manwah, NJ: Troll. (M)
Simon, S. (1985). *Meet the computer.* New York: Harper and Row. (M–U)
Venutra, P., & Ceserani, G. P. (1985). *In search of Tutankhamun.* Morristown, NJ: Silver
    Burdett. (U)

FIGURE 8–12

Informational Books Representing the Expository Text Structures

5.   Repeat the first four steps in the teaching strategy for each of the five expository text structures.

6.   Choose the most appropriate pattern. After students learn to use each of the five patterns, they need to learn to choose the most appropriate pattern to communicate effectively. Students can experiment to discover the appropriateness of various patterns by writing paragraphs about one set of information using different

organizational patterns. For example, information about igloos might be written as a description, as a comparison to Indian teepees, or as a solution to a housing problem in the Arctic.

KWL Strategy

Another way to help students take an active role in reading and writing informational books is the *KWL Strategy* (Ogle, 1986, 1989)—KWL stands for Know, Want to Know, and Learned. Teachers use this three-step strategy to help students prepare to read, read, and understand informational texts.

1. *Before reading.* To begin, the teacher asks students to brainstorm what they know about a topic and records the information in the "K" or "What We Know" column on a class chart, as shown in Figure 8–13. As students suggest information and as conflicts and confusions arise, the teacher adds questions in the "W" or "What We Want to Find Out" column. Then students complete the "K" and "W" columns on individual charts like the one in Figure 8–13. (Teachers can omit individual charts when working with young children.) Brainstorming information in the "K" column helps students activate prior knowledge, and developing questions in the "W" column provides students with specific purposes for reading. Next, teachers ask students to look for ways to chunk or categorize the information they brainstormed and for information they expect to find in the text they will read. For example, second graders making a KWL chart on penguins might identify these categories: what they look like, where they live, how they move, and what their families are like. Older students might use categories such as appearance, habitat, enemies, and classification.

2. *During reading.* Students read actively, looking for new information and for answers to questions in the "W" column. Depending on the length and complexity of the material, students can read the complete piece, or it can be broken into parts. As students read, they can take notes about what they are learning on their KWL charts, or they can recall the information after reading.

3. *After reading.* Students reflect on what they have learned and complete the "L" or "What We Learned" column of the class chart. Then they complete the "L" column on their individual charts. Students can also add additional information to the categories section of the charts to reflect the types of information the author included in the informational text.

The KWL strategy is useful for helping students gain more from an individual reading assignment, such as if a second grade class were reading a book about penguins. It can also be used during a unit of study in social studies, science, or another content area. Students begin by completing the "K" and "W" columns and the categories sections at the beginning of the unit, then add to the chart throughout the two, three, or four weeks of the unit. At the end of the unit, students complete the chart and share what they have learned. Students are thus better prepared to learn, to organize their learning, to clarify misconceptions, and to appreciate their learning.

K What we know	W What we want to find out	L What we learned

Categories of information we expect to use

A.

B.

C.

D.

FIGURE 8—13

Teacher's Notebook Page: K-W-L Chart

Ogle, 1986, p. 565

❖ REVIEW

Research shows that students learn to read and write better when the two processes are connected. Shanahan (1988) has developed seven instructional principles for relating reading and writing so that students develop a clear conception of literacy:

1. Teach both reading and writing daily.

2. Introduce reading and writing in kindergarten.

3. Instruction should reflect the developmental nature of the reading-writing relationship.

4. Make the reading-writing connection explicit to students.

5. Instruction should emphasize both process and product relations.

6. Emphasize the communicative functions of reading and writing.

7. Teach reading and writing in meaningful contexts.

The reading-writing connections discussed in this chapter embody these seven principles, as we have seen in making the reading-writing connection with young children, with authors, with stories, and with informational books.

❖ EXTENSIONS

1. Use the assisted reading strategy with a young child who is just learning to read or with an older child who is having difficulty learning to read. Read with the child over a two- or three-week period, moving from stage 1 to stage 2 or 3, if possible. Keep a journal to document the child's progress and what books you use.

2. Share a predictable book with a class of kindergartners or first graders, then make a big book retelling the story using the language experience approach.

3. Examine 20 wordless picture books and develop a card file that includes information about the story line, the illustrations, the author/illustrator, and related activities.

4. Plan and teach a reading lesson using a basal reader series and incorporate one or more of the reading-writing connection activities suggested in this chapter instead of workbook pages.

5. Use the KWL strategy to teach a content area lesson.

6. Observe in an elementary classroom and identify the ways reading and writing are connected and other ways the connection might be strengthened.

❖ REFERENCES

Abrahamson, R. F. (1981). An update on wordless picture books with an annotated bibliography. *The Reading Teacher, 32,* 417–421.

Aldis, D. (1969). *Nothing is impossible: The story of Beatrix Potter.* New York: Atheneum.

Anderson, R. C., Hiebert, E. C., Scott, J. A., & Wilkinson, I. A. G. (1985). *Becoming a nation of readers: The report of the Commission on Reading.* Washington, D.C.: National Institute of Education.

Ashton-Warner, S. (1965). *Teacher.* New York: Simon and Schuster.

Berglund, R. L., & Johns, J. L. (1983). A primer on uninterrupted sustained silent reading. *The Reading Teacher, 36,* 534–539.

Bridge, C. A. (1979). Predictable materials for beginning readers. *Language Arts, 56,* 503–507.

Bridge, C. A., & Burton, B. (1982). Teaching sight vocabulary through patterned language materials. In J. A. Niles & L. A. Harris (Eds.), *New inquiries in reading research and instruction* (Thirty-first yearbook of the National Reading Conference), pp. 119–123. Rochester, NY: National Reading Conference.

Bridge, C. A., Winograd, P. N., & Haley, D. (1983). Using predictable materials vs. preprimers to teach beginning sight words. *The Reading Teacher, 36,* 884–891.

Buckley, M. H. (1986). When teachers decide to integrate the language arts. *Language Arts, 63,* 369–377.

Butler, A., & Turbill, J. (1984). *Towards a reading-writing classroom.* Portsmouth, NH: Heinemann.

Carle, E. (1969). *The very hungry caterpillar.* New York: Philomel.

Cleary, B. (1983). *Dear Mr. Henshaw.* New York: Morrow.

Corcoran, B. (1987). Teachers creating readers. In B. Corcoran & E. Evans (Eds.), *Readers, texts, teachers,* pp. 41–74. Upper Montclair, NJ: Boynton/Cook.

D'Angelo, K. (1979). Wordless picture books: Also for the writer. *Language Arts, 56,* 813–814, 835.

Davala, V. (1987). Respecting opinions: Learning logs in middle school. In T. Fulwiler (Ed.), *The journal book,* pp. 179–186. Portsmouth, NH: Boynton/Cook.

Degler, L. S. (1979). Putting words into wordless books. *The Reading Teacher, 30,* 399–402.

de Paola, T. (1978). *Pancakes for breakfast.* New York: Harcourt Brace Jovanovich.

de Paola, T. (1989). *The art lesson.* New York: Putnam.

Fitzgerald, J. (1989). Enhancing two related thought processes: Revision in writing and critical thinking. *The Reading Teacher, 43,* 42–48.

Flood, J., Lapp, D., & Farnan, N. (1986). A reading-writing procedure that teaches expository paragraph structure. *The Reading Teacher, 39,* 556–562.

Fritz, J. (1982). *Homesick: My own story.* New York: Putnam.

Gag, W. (1956). *Millions of cats.* New York: Coward-McCann.

Galdone, P. (1975). *The gingerbread boy.* New York: Seabury.

Goodall, J. S. (1983). *Above and below stairs.* New York: Atheneum.

Harste, J. C., Woodward, V. A., & Burke, C. L. (1984). Examining our assumptions: A transactional view of literacy and learning. *Research in the Teaching of English, 18,* 84–108.

Heald-Taylor, G. (1987). How to use predictable books for K–2 language arts instruction. *The Reading Teacher, 40,* 656–661.

Holdaway, D. (1979). *The foundations of literacy.* Sydney, Australia: Ashton Scholastic.

Hopkins, L. B. (1969). *Books are by people.* New York: Citation.

Hopkins, L. B. (1974). *More books are by more people.* New York: Citation.

Hoskisson, K. (1974). Should parents teach their children to read? *Elementary English, 51,* 295–299.

Hoskisson, K. (1975a). The many facets of assisted reading. *Elementary English, 52,* 312–315.

Hoskisson, K. (1975b). Successive approximation and beginning reading. *Elementary School Journal, 75,* 442–451.

Hoskisson, K. (1977). Reading readiness: Three viewpoints. *Elementary School Journal, 78,* 44–52.

Hoskisson, K., & Krohm, B. (1974). Reading by immersion: Assisted reading. *Elementary English, 51,* 832–836.

Hoskisson, K., Sherman, T., & Smith, L. (1974). Assisted reading and parent involvement. *The Reading Teacher, 27,* 710–714.

Karnowski, L. (1989). Using LEA with process writing. *The Reading Teacher, 42,* 462–465.

Langer, J. (1986). Reading, writing, and understanding: An analysis of the construction of meaning. *Written Communication, 3,* 219–267.

Lee, D. M., & Allen, R. V. (1963). *Learning to read through experience* (2nd ed.). New York: Meredith.

Lionni, L. (1964). *Tico and the golden wings.* New York: Knopf.

McGee, L. M., & Richgels, D. J. (1985). Teaching expository text structure to elementary students. *The Reading Teacher, 38,* 739–748.

McGee, L. M., & Tompkins, G. E. (1983). Wordless picture books are for older readers, too. *Journal of Reading, 27,* 120–123.

Mayer, M. (1974). *Frog goes to dinner.* New York: Dial.

Mayer, M. (1987). *The pied piper of Hamelin.* New York: Macmillan.

Meyer, B. J., & Freedle, R. O. (1984). Effects of discourse type on recall. *American Educational Research Journal, 21,* 121–143.

Niles, O. S. (1974). Organization perceived. In H. L. Herber (Ed.), *Perspectives in reading: Developing study skills in secondary schools.* Newark, DE: International Reading Association.

Noyce, R. M., & Christie, J. F. (1989). *Integrating reading and writing instruction in grades K–8.* Boston: Allyn and Bacon.

Ogle, D. M. (1986), K-W-L: A teaching model that develops active reading of expository text. *The Reading Teacher, 39,* 564–570.

Ogle, D. M. (1989). The know, want to know, learn strategy. In K. D. Muth (Ed.), *Children's comprehension of text: Research into practice,* pp. 205–223. Newark, DE: International Reading Association.

Piccolo, J. A. (1987). Expository text structures: Teaching and learning strategies. *The Reading Teacher, 40,* 838–847.

Raphael, T. E., Englert, C. S., & Kirschner, B. W. (1989). Acquisition of expository writing skills.

In J. M. Mason (Ed.), *Reading and writing connections,* pp. 261–290. Boston: Allyn & Bacon.

Rhodes, L. K. (1981). I can read! Predictable books as resources for reading and writing instruction. *The Reading Teacher, 34,* 511–518.

Rosenblatt, L. (1978). *The reader, the text, the poem: The transactional theory of literary work.* Carbondale: Southern Illinois University Press.

Shanahan, T. (1988). The reading-writing relationship: Seven instructional principles. *The Reading Teacher, 41,* 636–647.

Slaughter, J. P. (1983). Big books for little kids: Another fad or a new approach for teaching beginning reading? *The Reading Teacher, 36,* 758–762.

Smith, F. (1983). Reading like a writer. *Language Arts, 60,* 553–564.

Smith, F. (1988). *Joining the literacy club: Further essays into education.* Portsmouth, NH: Heinemann.

Smith, P. L., & Tompkins, G. E. (1988). Structured notetaking: A new strategy for content area readers. *The Journal of Reading, 32,* 46–53.

Stauffer, R. G. (1970). *The language experience approach to the teaching of reading.* New York: Harper.

Stauffer, R. G. (1975). *Directing the reading-thinking process.* New York: Harper.

Tierney, R. J. (1983). Writer-reader transactions: Defining the dimensions of negotiation. In P. L. Stock (Ed.), *Forum: Essays on theory and practice in the teaching of writing,* pp. 147–151. Upper Montclair, NJ: Boynton/Cook.

Tierney, R. J., & Leys, M. (1986). What is the value of connecting reading and writing? In P. L. Stock (Ed.), *Convergences: Transactions in reading and writing,* pp. 15–29. Urbana, IL: National Council of Teachers of English.

Tierney, R. J., & Pearson, P. D. (1983). Toward a composing model of reading. *Language Arts, 60,* 568–580.

Tompkins, G. E. (1990). *Teaching writing: Balancing process and product.* Columbus, OH: Merrill.

Tompkins, G. E., & Webeler, M. B. (1983). What will happen next? Using predictable books with young children. *The Reading Teacher, 36,* 498–502.

Trachtenburg, R., & Ferruggia, A. (1989). Big books from little voices: Reaching high risk beginning readers. *The Reading Teacher, 42,* 284–289.

Tunnell, M. O., & Jacobs, J. S. (1989). Using "real" books: Research findings on literature-based reading instruction. *The Reading Teacher, 42,* 470–477.

Viorst, J. (1972). *Alexander and the terrible, horrible, no good, very bad day.* New York: Atheneum.

Weaver, C. (1988). *Reading process and practice: From socio-psycholinguistics to whole language.* Portsmouth, NH: Heinemann.

9 READING AND WRITING STORIES

ELEMENTS OF STORY STRUCTURE
Beginning-Middle-End
Repetition
Plot
Setting
Characters
Theme
Point of View

TEACHING STUDENTS TO WRITE STORIES
Part 1: Preparing to Teach
Part 2: Teaching an Element of Story Structure
Assessing Students' Stories

STORY GENRE
Folktales
Fables
Myths
Hero Stories
Fantasies

◆ IN THIS CHAPTER, OUR FOCUS IS ON STORIES AND HOW CHIL-
dren expand their concepts of story. We explore the organizational patterns of
stories and discuss how to teach students to write stories.

◆ AS YOU ARE READING, THINK ABOUT THESE QUESTIONS:

What are the elements of story structure?

Which stories illustrate these elements?

How do elementary students learn about these patterns?

What other organizational patterns are used in stories?

Young children have a rudimentary awareness, called *concept of story* or *story schema,* of what makes a story. Children's concept of story includes information about the elements of story structure, such as characters, plot, and setting, as well as information about the conventions authors use. This knowledge is usually intuitive; that is, children are not conscious of what they know. Golden (1984) describes children's concept of story as "a mental representation of story structure, essentially an outline of the basic story elements and their organization" (p. 578).

Researchers have documented that children's concept of story begins in the preschool years, and that children as young as two-and-a-half have a rudimentary sense of story (Applebee, 1978, 1980; Pitcher & Prelinger, 1963). Children acquire this concept of story gradually, through listening to stories read to them, by reading stories themselves, and by telling and writing stories. Not surprisingly, older children have a better understanding of story structure and conventions than do younger children. Similarly, the stories older children tell and write are increasingly more complex; the plot structures are more tightly organized, and the characters are more fully developed. Yet, Applebee (1980) found that by the time children begin kindergarten, they have already developed a concept of what a story is, and these expectations guide them in responding to stories and telling their own stories. He found, for example, that kindergartners could use three story markers: the convention "Once upon a time. . ." to begin a story; the past tense in telling a story; and formal endings such as "The End" or "and they lived happily ever after."

Concept of story plays an important role in students' ability to comprehend and recall information from the stories they read (Mandler & Johnson, 1977; Rumelhart, 1975; Stein & Glenn, 1979), but it is just as important in writing (Golden, 1984). Just as they draw on their concept of story in reading, students use this knowledge in writing stories. Researchers have identified five types of activities that help students develop and refine their concept of story and prepare them to better comprehend stories they read and create the stories they write.

1. *Read stories.* Reading stories is the most basic way to help children develop a concept of story. By listening to and reading stories, students internalize the structure of stories and assimilate the sophisticated language structures authors use.

2. *Talk about stories.* Students should talk about stories they read, and teachers often ask questions to stimulate talk. Recent research suggests that questions that focus on the structure of stories are more effective for comprehension than traditional questions about main ideas and details.

3. *Retell stories.* Retelling a story provides interaction between teller and listener, opportunities for active engagement with literature, and the transformation of story meanings. Unfortunately, many teachers see retelling stories as a time-consuming frill; however, researchers have documented the educational value of the activity.

4. *Examine the structure of stories.* Stories are organized in predictable ways, and research demonstrates that students' comprehension and production of stories improves when they understand the organization. Several strategies have been rec-

A student shares her retelling of the beginning, middle, and end of a story with her classmates.

ommended for teaching students about story structure (Gordon & Braun, 1982; Fitzgerald & Spiegel, 1983; Spiegel & Fitzgerald, 1986; Tompkins & McGee, 1989); these are common features of the strategies:

- The teacher presents an element of story structure, often using a chart to summarize important information.
- Students read stories exemplifying this element.
- Students discuss how the element is used in the stories.
- Students participate in activities to reinforce their understanding.
- Students write stories incorporating the element being studied.

5. *Write stories.* Writing is a valuable way of learning, and by writing stories, children apply their expanding knowledge of stories—of the structural elements as well as of the creative ideas.

❖ ELEMENTS OF STORY STRUCTURE

Stories have unique elements of structure that distinguish them from other forms of writing. In fact, the structure of stories is quite complex—characters, plot, setting, and other elements interact with each other to produce a story. Authors manipulate the elements to make their stories complex and interesting. We will focus on seven elements of story structure—beginning-middle-end, repetition, plot, setting, characters, theme, and point of view—and illustrate each element with familiar and award-winning trade books.

Beginning-Middle-End

The most basic element of story structure is the division of the main events of a story into three parts: the *beginning, middle,* and *end.* Upper-grade students may substitute the terms *introduction, development* or *complication,* and *resolution.* No matter what we call the three parts, their functions remain the same. In *The Tale of Peter Rabbit* (Potter, 1902), for instance, one can easily pick out the three story parts: as the story begins, Mrs. Rabbit sends her children out to play after warning them not to go into Mr. McGregor's garden; in the middle, Peter goes to Mr. McGregor's garden and is almost caught; then Peter finds his way out of the garden and gets home safely—the end of the story. A cluster for *The Tale of Peter Rabbit* appears in Figure 9–1.

Authors include specific types of information in each of the three story parts. In the beginning, they introduce the characters, describe the setting, and present a problem. Together, the characters, setting, and events develop the plot and sustain the theme through the story. In the middle, authors add to events they presented in the

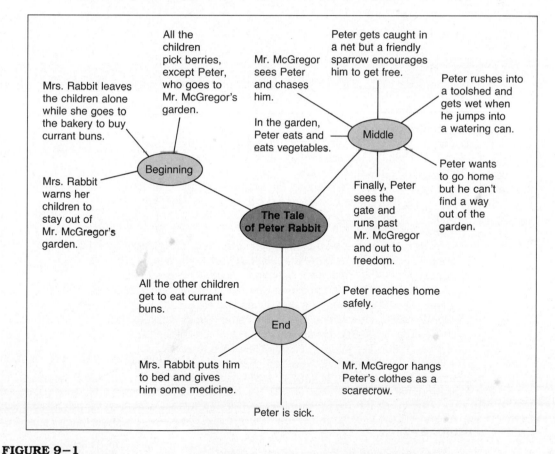

FIGURE 9–1

A Beginning-Middle-End Cluster for *The Tale of Peter Rabbit* beginning, with each event preparing readers for what will follow. Conflict heightens as the characters face roadblocks that keep them from solving their problems. How the characters tackle these problems adds suspense to keep readers interested. In the end, authors reconcile all that has happened in the story, and readers learn whether or not the characters' struggles are successful.

Almost any story can be divided into these three parts. Short stories with clearly identifiable beginnings, middles, and ends are listed in Figure 9–2.

Repetition

Authors use *repetition* to make the plot more complex and the story more interesting. In Galdone's retelling of *Henny Penny* (1968), for instance, as she travels to tell the king that the sky is falling, the hen meets a series of animals—Cocky Locky, Ducky Lucky, Goosey Loosey, Turkey Lurkey, and Foxy Loxy—who join her on the trip to the king's palace. The repetition in this story involves presenting new characters, each with a

---

Andersen, H. C. (1979). *The ugly duckling.* New York: Harcourt Brace Jovanovich. (P–M)

Bunting, E. (1987). *Ghost's hour, spook's hour.* Boston: Houghton Mifflin (P)

Gag, W. (1956). *Millions of cats.* New York: Coward. (P)

Gallo, D. R. (Ed.). (1984). *Sixteen short stories by outstanding writers for young adults.* New York: Dell. (U)

Howe, J. (1988). *Rip Van Winkle.* Boston: Little, Brown. (M–U)

Huck, C. (1989). *Princess Furball.* New York: Greenwillow. (M–U)

Hyman, T. S. (1983). *Little red riding hood.* New York: Holiday House. (P)

Kellogg, S. (1973). *The island of the skog.* New York: Dial. (P–M)

Locker, T. (1987). *The boy who held back the sea.* New York: Dial. (M–U)

London, J. (1960). *To build a fire. The call of the wild and other selected stories.* New York: Signet. (U)

Mayer, M. (1987). *The pied piper of Hamelin.* New York: Macmillan. (M)

Potter, B. (1902). *The tale of Peter Rabbit.* New York: Warne. (P)

Rogasky, B. (1982). *Rapunzel.* New York: Holiday House. (M–U)

Schulevitz, U. (1978). *The treasure.* New York: Farrar, Straus & Giroux. (M)

Sendak, M. (1963). *Where the wild things are.* New York: Harper and Row. (P)

Steig, W. (1986). *Brave Irene.* New York: Farrar, Straus & Giroux. (M)

Van Allsburg, C. (1981). *Jumanji.* Boston: Houghton Mifflin. (M)

Yolen, J. (1986). *The sleeping beauty.* New York: Knopf. (M–U)

Yorinks, A. (1986). *Hey, Al.* New York: Farrar, Straus & Giroux. (P)

Zemach, H., & Zemach, M. (1973). *Duffy and the devil.* New York: Farrar, Straus & Giroux. (P–M)

FIGURE 9–2

Short Stories that Illustrate Beginning-Middle-End
P = primary grades (K–2)
M = middle grades (3–5)
U = upper grades (6–8)

rhyming name, and repeating the hen's warning that "The sky is falling." A variation of the beginning-middle-end cluster in Figure 9–1 can be used to chart repetition stories (Tompkins & McGee, 1989). A cluster for *Henny Penny* is presented in Figure 9–3, in which the *middle* ray is divided into two parts—one for repeated events and one for repeated dialogue.

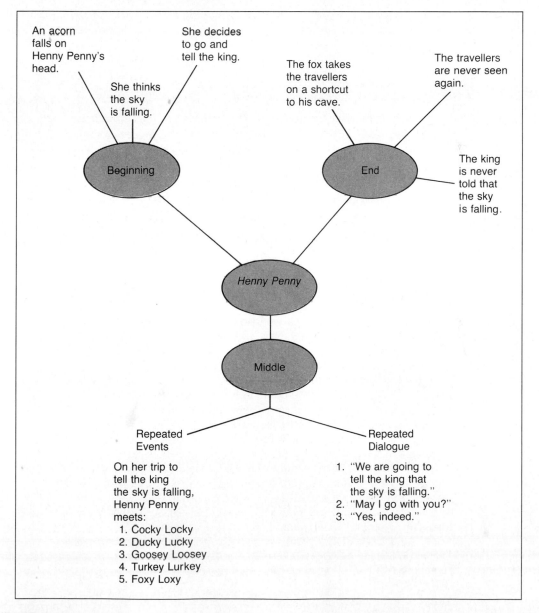

FIGURE 9–3

A Repetition Cluster for *Henny Penny*

Many traditional stories or folktales, such as *Henny Penny, The Gingerbread Boy* (Galdone, 1975), and *The Little Red Hen* (Galdone, 1973), have both repeated events and repeated dialogue. Other stories repeat either the events or the words. Stories that use repetition are listed in Figure 9–4. Many of these traditional stories or folktales began as oral stories, retold by traveling minstrels. Just as repetition made the stories easier for storytellers to remember, this element of story structure is particularly effective for students in the primary grades because the repetition helps them predict the events and words in the stories (Tompkins & Webeler, 1983; Blackburn, 1985; Tompkins & McGee, 1989).

Plot

Plot is the sequence of events involving characters in conflict situations. A story's plot is based on the goals of one or more characters and the processes they go through to attain these goals (Lukens, 1986). The main characters want to achieve a goal, and other characters are introduced to oppose or prevent the main characters from being successful. The story events are put in motion by characters as they attempt to overcome conflict, reach their goals, and solve their problems.

Brown, R. (1985). *The big sneeze.* New York: Lothrop, Lee & Shepard. (P–M)
Burningham, J. (1975). *Mr. Gumpy's outing.* New York: Holt, Rinehart and Winston. (P)
Cauley, L. B. (1988). *The pancake boy.* New York: Putnam. (P)
Ets, M. H. (1973). *Elephant in a well.* New York: Viking. (P)
Flack, M. (1958). *Ask Mr. Bear.* New York: Macmillan. (P)
Fox, M. (1989). *Shoes from grandpa.* New York: Orchard Books. (P–M)
Galdone, P. (1973). *The little red hen.* New York: Seabury. (P–M)
Galdone, P. (1973). *The three billy goats Gruff.* Boston: Houghton Mifflin. (P)
Galdone, P. (1975). *The gingerbread boy.* New York: Seabury. (P)
Hailey, G. E. (1970). *A story a story.* New York: Atheneum. (P–M)
Kellogg, S. (1985). *Chicken little.* New York: Morrow. (P)
Kent, J. (1971). *The fat cat.* New York: Scholastic. (P–M)
McGovern, A. (1967). *Too much noise.* New York: Scholastic. (P)
Plume, I. (1980). *The Bremen town musicians.* New York: Watts. (P–M)
Tolstoy, A. (1969). *The great big enormous turnip.* New York: Watts. (P–M)
Tresselt, A. (1964). *The mitten.* New York: Lothrop. (P)
Westcott, N. B. (1988). *The lady with the alligator purse.* Boston: Little, Brown. (P)
Wildsmith, B. (1985). *Give a dog a bone.* New York: Pantheon. (P)
Wood, A., and Wood, D. (1985). *King Bidgood's in the bathtub.* San Diego: Harcourt Brace Jovanovich. (P–M)
Zemach, M. (1976). *It could always be worse.* New York: Farrar, Straus & Giroux. (P–M)

FIGURE 9–4

Stories that Illustrate Repetition

Conflict is the tension or opposition between forces in the plot, and it is introduced to interest readers enough to continue reading the story. Conflict usually takes one of four forms:

1. Conflict between a character and nature
2. Conflict between a character and society
3. Conflict between characters
4. Conflict within a character (Lukens, 1986)

We find conflict between a character and nature in stories in which severe weather plays an important role, as in *Julie of the Wolves* (George, 1972), and in stories set in isolated geographic locations, such as *Island of the Blue Dolphins* (O'Dell, 1960), in which the Indian girl Karana struggles to survive alone on a Pacific island. In some stories, a character's activities and beliefs differ from those of other members of the society, and the differences cause conflict between that character and the local society. One example of this type of conflict is *The Witch of Blackbird Pond* (Speare, 1958) in which Kit Tyler is accused of being a witch because she continues activities in a New England Puritan community that were acceptable in the Caribbean community where she grew up. Conflict between characters is a common type of conflict in children's literature. In *Tales of a Fourth Grade Nothing* (Blume, 1972), for instance, the never-ending conflict between Peter and his little brother Fudge is what makes the story interesting. The fourth type of conflict is conflict within a character, and stories such as *Ira Sleeps Over* (Waber, 1972) and *The Summer of the Swans* (Byar, 1970) are examples. In *Ira Sleeps Over,* six-year-old Ira must decide whether to take his teddy bear with him when he goes next door to spend the night with a friend, and in *The Summer of the Swans,* Sara feels guilty when her mentally retarded brother wanders off and is lost. Figure 9–5 lists stories representing the four conflict situations.

Authors develop plot through the introduction, development, and resolution of the conflict. Plot development can be broken into four steps:

1. A problem that introduces conflict is presented at the beginning of a story.
2. Characters face roadblocks in attempting to solve the problem.
3. The high point in the action occurs when the problem is about to be solved; this high point separates the middle and end of the story.
4. The problem is solved and the roadblocks are overcome at the end of the story.

The problem is introduced at the beginning of the story, and the main character is faced with trying to solve it. The problem determines the conflict. The problem in *The Ugly Duckling* (Mayer, 1987), is that the big, gray duckling does not fit in with the other ducklings, and conflict develops between the ugly duckling and the other ducks. (This is an example of conflict between characters.)

After the problem has been introduced, authors use conflict to throw roadblocks in the way of an easy solution. As characters remove one roadblock, the author devises another to further thwart the characters. Postponing the solution by introducing road-

---

Conflict Between a Character and Nature

Ardizzone, E. (1971). *Little Tim and the brave sea captain.* New York: Scholastic.
  (P)
George, J. C. (1972). *Julie of the wolves.* New York: Harper and Row. (M–U)
O'Dell, S. (1960). *Island of the blue dolphins.* Boston: Houghton Mifflin. (M–U)
Sperry, A. (1968). *Call it courage.* New York: Macmillan. (U)

Conflict Between a Character and Society

Hickman, J. (1978). *Zoar blue.* New York: Macmillan. (U)
Kellogg, S. (1973). *The island of the skog.* New York: Dial. (P–M)
O'Brien, R. C. (1971). *Mrs. Frisby and the rats of NIMH.* New York: Atheneum. (M)
Speare, E. G. (1958). *The witch of Blackbird Pond.* Boston: Houghton Mifflin.
  (M–U)

Conflict Between Characters

Blume, J. (1972). *Tales of a fourth grade nothing.* New York: Dutton. (M)
Hoban, R. (1970). *A bargain for Frances.* New York: Scholastic. (P)
Raskin, E. (1978). *The westing game.* New York: Dutton. (U)
Zelinsky, P. O. (1986). *Rumpelstiltskin.* New York: Dutton. (P–M)

Conflict Within a Character

Byars, B. (1970). *The summer of the swans.* New York: Viking. (M)
Fritz, J. (1958). *The cabin faced west.* New York: Coward-McCann. (M)
Taylor, T. (1969). *The cay.* New York: Doubleday. (U)
Waber, B. (1972). *Ira sleeps over.* Boston: Houghton Mifflin. (P)

FIGURE 9–5

Stories that Illustrate the Four Types of Conflict

blocks is the core of plot development. Stories may contain any number of roadblocks, but many children's stories contain three, four, or five.

The first conflict in *The Ugly Duckling* comes in the yard when the ducks, the other animals, and even the woman who feeds the ducks make fun of him. The conflict is so great that the duckling goes out into the world. Next, conflict comes from the wild ducks and other animals who scorn him, too. Third, the duckling spends a miserable, cold winter in the marsh.

The high point of the action occurs when the solution of the problem hangs in the balance. Tension is high, and readers continue reading to learn whether the main characters will solve the problem. With *The Ugly Duckling*, readers experience some relief that the duckling has survived the winter, but tension continues because he is an outcast. Then the swan flies to a garden pond and sees three beautiful swans. He flies near to them even though he expects to be scorned.

At the end of the story, the problem is solved and the goal is achieved. When the swan joins the other three swans at the garden pond, they welcome him. The swan looks at his reflection in the water and realizes that he is no longer an ugly duckling. Children from the nearby farm come to feed the swans and praise the new swan's beauty. The newly arrived swan is happy at last!

We can diagram or chart the plot of a story. A basic plot diagram, shaped somewhat like a mountain, appears in Figure 9–6, with the four steps of plot development— introduction of the problem, roadblocks, high point in the action, and solution— marked on the diagram. Information about any story's plot can be added to this diagram; as an example, a plot diagram of *The Ugly Duckling* is shown in Figure 9–7.

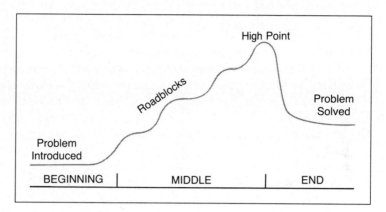

FIGURE 9–6

A Basic Plot Diagram

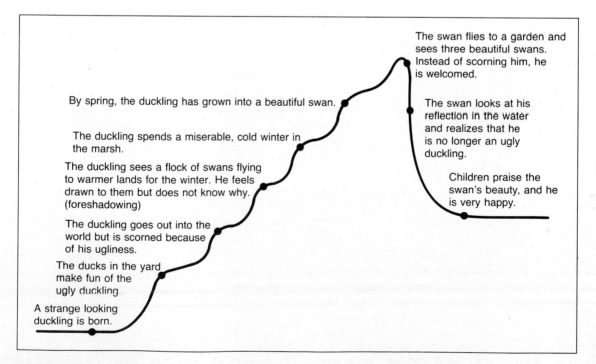

FIGURE 9–7

A Plot Diagram of *The Ugly Duckling*

Setting

A setting that is barely sketched is a *backdrop setting*. The setting in many folktales, for example, is relatively unimportant and may simply use the convention, "Once upon a time. . ." to set the stage. In other stories, however, the setting is elaborated and integral to the story's effectiveness—an *integral setting* (Lukens, 1986). The importance of the setting to plot and character development determines how much attention writers give to describing it. Some stories could take place anywhere and require little description; in others, however, the setting must be specific, and authors must take care to ensure the authenticity of the historical period or geographic location.

Of the elements of story structure, setting is the one most people feel comfortable with—it is simply where the story takes place. Certainly location is an important dimension of setting, but there are three other dimensions as well: weather, time, and time period.

Location is an important dimension of setting in many stories. The Boston Commons in *Make Way for Ducklings* (McCloskey, 1969), the Alaskan North Slope in *Julie of the Wolves* (George, 1972), and New York City's Metropolitan Museum of Art in *From the Mixed-up Files of Mrs. Basil E. Frankweiler* (Konigsburg, 1983) are integral to the stories' effectiveness. The settings are artfully described and add something unique to the story. In contrast, many stories take place in predictable settings that do not contribute to the story's effectiveness.

Weather is a second dimension of setting and, like location, is crucial in some stories. For example, a rainstorm is essential to the plot development in both *Bridge to Terabithia* (Paterson, 1977) and *Sam, Bangs, and Moonshine* (Ness, 1966). At other times, the author may not even mention the weather because it has no impact on the story. Many stories take place on warm, sunny days. Think about the impact weather can have on a story; for example, what might have happened if a snowstorm had prevented Little Red Riding Hood from reaching her grandmother's house?

The third dimension, *time,* includes both time of day and the passage of time. Most stories ignore time of day, except Halloween or ghost stories, which typically take place after dark. In stories that take place at night, such as the folktale *The Teeny-Tiny Woman* (Galdone, 1984), time is a more important dimension than in stories that take place during the day, because events that happen at night seem scarier than those that happen during the day.

Many short stories span a brief period of time, often less than a day, and sometimes less than an hour. In *Jumanji* (Van Allsburg, 1981), for instance, Peter and Judy's bizarre adventure, during which their house is overtaken by an exotic jungle, lasts only the several hours their parents are at the opera. Other stories, such as *Charlotte's Web* (White, 1952) and *The Ugly Duckling* (Mayer, 1987), span a long enough period for the main character to grow to maturity.

The fourth dimension of setting is *time period,* an important element in stories set in the past or future. If *The Witch of Blackbird Pond* (Speare, 1958) and *Beyond the Divide* (Lasky, 1983) were set in different eras, for example, they would lose much of their impact. Today, few people would believe that Kit Tyler is a witch, and travel across the U.S. would not be nearly so difficult with today's modern conveniences. In stories such as *A Wrinkle in Time* (L'Engle, 1962) that take place in the future, things are possible that are not possible today. A list of stories with integral settings is shown in Figure 9—8; these stories illustrate the four dimensions of setting—location, weather, time, and time period.

Characters

Characters are the people or personified animals who are involved in the story. Characters are often the most important element of story structure because the experience the author creates is centered around a character or group of characters. Usually, one fully rounded and two or three supporting characters are introduced and developed in a story. Fully developed main characters have all the characteristics of real people. A list of fully developed main characters in children's stories is presented in Figure 9—9.

Supporting characters may be individualized, but they will be portrayed much less vividly than the main character. The extent to which supporting characters are developed depends on the author's purpose and the needs of the story. In *Queenie Peavy* (Burch, 1966), for instance, Queenie is the main character, whom we get to know as a real person. She pretends that she is tough, as when the other children taunt her that her father is in the chain gang, but actually Queenie is a sensitive girl who wants a family to care for her. In contrast, the author tells us little about the supporting

---

Andersen, H. C. (1979). *The ugly duckling.* New York: Harcourt Brace Jovanovich. (P–M)

Babbitt, N. (1975). *Tuck everlasting.* New York: Farrar, Straus & Giroux. (M–U)

Cauley, L. B. (1984). *The town mouse and the country mouse.* New York: Putnam. (P–M)

Fritz, J. (1982). *Homesick: My own story.* New York: Putnam. (M–U)

Galdone, P. (1984). *The teeny-tiny woman.* New York: Clarion. (P)

George, J. C. (1972). *Julie of the wolves.* New York: Harper and Row. (M–U)

Hodges, Margaret. (1984). *Saint George and the dragon.* Boston: Little, Brown. (M–U)

Konigsburg, E. L. (1983). *From the mixed-up files of Mrs. Basil E. Frankweiler.* New York: Atheneum. (M)

Lasky, K. (1983). *Beyond the divide.* New York: Macmillan. (M–U)

L'Engle, M. (1962). *A wrinkle in time.* New York: Farrar, Straus & Giroux. (U)

McCloskey, R. (1969). *Make way for ducklings.* New York: Viking. (P)

Ness, E. (1966). *Sam, Bangs and moonshine.* New York: Holt. (P)

Paterson, K. (1977). *Bridge to Terabithia.* New York: Crowell. (M–U)

Speare, E. (1958). *The witch of Blackbird Pond.* Boston: Houghton Mifflin. (M–U)

Van Allsburg, C. (1981). *Jumanji.* Boston: Houghton Mifflin. (P–M)

White, E. B. (1952). *Charlotte's web.* New York: Harper and Row. (M)

Wilder, L. I. (1971). *The long winter.* New York: Harper and Row. (M)

FIGURE 9—8

Stories with Integral Settings

Character	Story
Queenie	Burch, R. (1966). *Queenie Peavy.* New York: Viking. (U)
Ramona	Cleary, B. (1981). *Ramona Quimby, age 8.* New York: Morrow. (M)
Leigh	Cleary, B. (1983). *Dear Mr. Henshaw.* New York: Morrow. (M)
Harriet	Fitzhugh, L. (1964). *Harriet the spy.* New York: Harper and Row. (M)
Johnny	Forbes, E. (1974). *Johnny Tremain.* Boston: Houghton Mifflin. (U)
Sam	George, J. C. (1959). *My side of the mountain.* New York: Dutton. (U)
Patty	Greene, B. (1973). *Summer of my German soldier.* New York: Dial. (U)
Beth	Greene, B. (1974). *Philip Hall likes me. I reckon maybe.* New York: Dial. (U)
Frances	Hoban, R. (1976). *Best friends for Frances.* New York: Harper and Row. (P)
Alex	Jukes, M. (1984). *Like Jake and me.* New York: Knopf. (P–M)
Frog, Toad	Lobel, A. (1970). *Frog and toad are friends.* New York: Harper and Row. (P)
Anastasia	Lowry, L. (1979). *Anastasia Krupnik.* Boston: Houghton Mifflin. (M)
Sarah	MacLachlan, P. (1985). *Sarah, plain and tall.* New York: Harper and Row. (M)
Karana	O'Dell, S. (1960). *Island of the blue dolphins.* Boston: Houghton Mifflin. (M–U)
Gilly	Paterson, K. (1978). *The great Gilly Hopkins.* New York: Crowell. (M–U)
Peter	Potter, B. (1902). *The tale of Peter Rabbit.* New York: Warne. (P)
Matt	Speare, E. (1983). *The sign of the beaver.* Boston: Houghton Mifflin. (M–U)
Mafatu	Sperry, A. (1968). *Call it courage.* New York: Macmillan. (U)
Irene	Steig, W. (1986). *Brave Irene.* New York: Farrar, Straus & Giroux. (P–M)
Cassie	Taylor, M. (1976). *Roll of thunder, hear my cry.* New York: Dial. (U)

FIGURE 9–9

Stories with Fully Developed Characters

characters in the story: Queenie's parents, her neighbors, and her classmates and teachers. The story focuses on Queenie and how this lonely 13-year-old copes with times that have "turned off hard" in the 1930s.

Authors must determine how to develop and present characters to involve readers in the experiences they are writing about. They develop characters in four ways: through appearance, action, dialogue, and monologue.

Appearance.   Authors describe how their characters look as the story develops; however, they generally provide some physical description when they introduce characters. Readers learn about characters by the description of their facial features, body shapes, habits of dress, mannerisms, and gestures. Dahl (1961) vividly describes James's two wicked aunts in *James and the Giant Peach*:

> Aunt Sponge was enormously fat and very short. She had small piggy eyes, a sunken mouth, and one of those white flabby faces that looked exactly as though it had been boiled. She was like a great white soggy overboiled cabbage. Aunt Spiker, on the other hand, was lean and tall and bony, and she wore steel-rimmed spectacles that fixed onto the end of her nose with a clip. She had a screeching voice and long wet narrow lips, and whenever she got angry or excited, little flecks of spit would come shooting out of her mouth as she talked. (p. 7)

Dahl's descriptions bring these two despicable characters vividly to life. He has carefully chosen the specific details to influence readers to appreciate James's dismay at having to live with these two aunts.

Action.   What a character does is the best way to know about that character. In Byars's story about three unwanted children, *The Pinballs* (1977), fifteen-year-old Carlie is described as "as hard to crack as a coconut" (p. 4), and her dialogue is harsh and sarcastic; however, Carlie's actions belie these other ways of knowing about her. She demonstrates through her actions that she cares about her two fellow-pinballs and the foster family who cares for them; for example, she gets Harvey a puppy as a birthday present and sneaks it into the hospital.

Dialogue.   Another important technique authors use to develop their characters is dialogue. What characters say is important, but so is how they speak. The level of formality of the characters' language is determined by the social situation. A character might speak less formally with friends than with respected elders or characters in positions of authority. The geographic location of the story and the characters' socio-economic status also determine how characters speak; for example, in *Roll of Thunder, Hear My Cry* (Taylor, 1976), Cassie and her family speak Black English, and in *Ida Early Comes over the Mountain* (Burch, 1980), Ida's speech is characteristic of rural Georgia, and she says, "Howdy-do?" and "Yes, sir-ee." Even in animal stories such as *Rabbit Hill* (Lawson, 1972), dialect is important. Uncle Analdas from Danbury speaks a rural dialect, in contrast to the "proper" standard English spoken by the animals on the hill.

Monologue.   Authors also provide insight into the characters by revealing their thoughts. In *Anastasia Krupnik* (Lowry, 1979), for example, Lowry shares ten-year-old

Anastasia's thinking with us. Anastasia has enjoyed being an only child and is upset that her mother is pregnant. To deal with Anastasia's feelings of sibling rivalry, her parents suggest that she choose a name for the new baby, and Anastasia agrees; through monologue, readers learn why Anastasia has agreed to choose the name—she will pick the most awful name she can think of for the baby. Lowry also has Anastasia keep a journal in which she lists things she likes and hates, another reflection of her thinking.

Theme

Theme is a story's underlying meaning. Themes embody general truths about society or human nature and usually deal with the characters' emotions and values. Themes can be stated either explicitly or implicitly. *Explicit themes* are stated openly and clearly in the story. Lukens (1986) uses *Charlotte's Web* to point out how friendship is expressed as an explicit theme:

> Charlotte has encouraged, protected, and mothered Wilbur, bargained and sacrificed for him, and Wilbur, the grateful receiver, realizes that "Friendship is one of the most satisfying things in the world." And Charlotte says later, "By helping you perhaps I was trying to lift up my life a little. Anyone's life can stand a little of that." Because these quoted sentences are exact statements from the text they are called explicit themes. (p. 102)

Implicit themes are implied in the story rather than explicitly stated in the text. Implicit themes are developed as the characters attempt to overcome the obstacles that

Children respond to stories with a friendship theme.

would prevent them from reaching their goal. Plot and character development are interwoven with theme as the writer prepares the characters for the resolution of the complications introduced into their lives. Theme emerges through the thoughts, speech, and actions of the characters as they seek to resolve their conflicts. Lukens also uses *Charlotte's Web* to illustrate implicit themes:

> Charlotte's selflessness—working late at night to finish a new word, expending her last energies for her friend—is evidence that friendship is giving oneself. Wilbur's protection of Charlotte's egg sac, his sacrifice of first turn at the slops, and his devotion to Charlotte's babies—giving without any need to stay even or to pay back—leads us to another theme: True friendship is naturally reciprocal. As the two become fond of each other, still another theme emerges: One's best friend can do no wrong. In fact, a best friend is sensational! Both Charlotte and Wilbur believe in these ideas; their experiences verify them. (p. 112)

Friendship is also one theme in *Bridge to Terabithia* (Paterson, 1977), but it is implied through Jess's and Leslie's enduring friendship rather than explicitly stated in the text.

Authors convey theme through the characters' actions, dialogue, and monologue rather than by moralizing. A list of stories with explicit and implicit themes is shown in Figure 9–10.

Andersen, H. C. (1965). *The nightingale.* New York: Harper and Row. (M–U)
Bunting, E. (1987). *Ghost's hour, spook's hour.* Boston: Houghton Mifflin. (P)
Cooney, B. (1958). *Chanticleer and the fox.* New York: Crowell. (P–M)
Galdone, P. (1968). *Henny Penny.* New York: Clarion. (P)
Greene, B. (1973). *Summer of my German soldier.* New York: Dial. (U)
Lawson, R. (1972). *Rabbit hill.* New York: Viking. (M)
L'Engle, M. (1962). *A wrinkle in time.* New York: Farrar, Straus & Giroux. (U)
Lewis, C. S. (1981). *The lion, the witch and the wardrobe.* New York: Macmillan. (M–U)
Lionni, L. (1985). *Frederick's fables.* New York: Pantheon. (P–M)
Lobel, A. (1970). *Frog and toad are friends.* New York: Harper and Row. (P)
Locker, T. (1987). *The boy who held back the sea.* New York: Dial. (U)
Mayer, M. (1987). *The pied piper of Hamelin.* New York: Macmillan. (M)
Neville, E. (1963). *It's like this cat.* New York: Harper and Row. (U)
Piper, W. (1954). *The little engine that could.* New York: Platt and Munk. (P)
Steig, W. (1982). *Doctor De Soto.* New York: Farrar, Straus & Giroux. (P)
Van Allsburg, C. (1985). *The polar express.* Boston: Houghton Mifflin. (M–U)
Westcott, N. B. (1984). *The emperor's new clothes.* Boston: Little, Brown. (P–M)
White, E. B. (1952). *Charlotte's web.* New York: Harper and Row. (M)
Yep, L. (1977). *Child of the owl.* New York: Harper and Row. (M–U)
Yorinks, A. (1986). *Hey, Al.* New York: Farrar, Straus & Giroux. (P)

FIGURE 9–10

Stories that Illustrate Implicit and Explicit Themes

Point of View

People see others and the world from different points of view. Listening to several people recount an event they have witnessed proves the impact of viewpoint. The focus of the narrator determines to a great extent readers' understanding of a story—characters and events—and whether readers believe what they are being told. Student authors must decide who will tell their stories and follow that viewpoint consistently in the stories they write. Four points of view are first-person viewpoint, omniscient viewpoint, limited omniscient viewpoint, and objective viewpoint (Lukens, 1986). A list of stories written from each point of view is presented in Figure 9–11.

First-person Viewpoint. Authors use the first-person viewpoint when they tell the story through the eyes of one character using the first-person pronoun "I." This point of view is used so the reader can live the story as the narrator tells it. The narrator, usually the main character, speaks as an eyewitness and a participant in the events. For example, in *The Slave Dancer* (Fox, 1973), Jessie tells the story of his kidnapping and frightful voyage on a slave ship, and in *Alexander and the Terrible, Horrible, No Good,*

First-person Viewpoint

Greene, B. (1974). *Philip Hall likes me. I reckon maybe.* New York: Dial. (M–U)
Howe, D., & Howe, J. (1979). *Bunnicula.* New York: Atheneum. (M)
MacLachlan, P. (1985). *Sarah, plain and tall.* New York: Harper and Row. (M)
Viorst, J. (1977). *Alexander and the terrible, horrible, no good, very bad day.* New York: Atheneum. (P)

Omniscient Viewpoint

Babbitt, N. (1975). *Tuck everlasting.* New York: Farrar, Straus & Giroux. (M–U)
Grahame, K. (1961). *The wind in the willows.* New York: Scribner. (M)
Lewis, C. S. (1981). *The lion, the witch and the wardrobe.* New York: Macmillan. (M–U)
Steig, W. (1982). *Doctor De Soto.* New York: Farrar, Straus & Giroux. (P)

Limited Omniscient Viewpoint

Burch, R. (1966). *Queenie Peavy.* New York: Dell. (U)
Cleary, B. (1981). *Ramona Quimby, age 8.* New York: Morrow. (M)
Lionni, L. (1969). *Alexander and the wind-up mouse.* New York: Pantheon. (P)
Lowry, L. (1979). *Anastasia Krupnik.* Boston: Houghton Mifflin. (M)

Objective Viewpoint

Brown, M. (1954). *Cinderella.* New York: Scribner. (P)
Lobel, A. (1972). *Frog and toad together.* New York: Harper and Row. (P)
Wells, R. (1973). *Benjamin and Tulip.* New York: Dial. (P)
Zemach, M. (1983). *The little red hen.* New York: Farrar, Straus & Giroux. (P)

FIGURE 9–11

Stories that Illustrate the Four Viewpoints

Very Bad Day (Viorst, 1977), Alexander tells about a day everything seemed to go wrong for him. One limitation to this viewpoint is that the narrator must remain an eyewitness.

Omniscient Viewpoint. The author who uses the omniscient viewpoint is godlike, seeing all and knowing all. The author tells readers about the thought processes of each character without worrying about how the information is obtained. *Doctor De Soto* (Steig, 1982), a story about a mouse dentist who outwits a fox with a toothache, is written from the omniscient viewpoint. Steig lets readers know that the fox is thinking about eating the dentist as soon as his toothache is cured and that the mouse dentist is aware of the fox's thoughts and plans a clever trick.

Limited Omniscient Viewpoint. Authors use the limited omniscient point of view to overhear the thoughts of one of the characters without being all-knowing and all-seeing. The story is told in third person, and the author concentrates on the thoughts, feelings, and significant past experiences of the main character or another important character. Burch uses the limited omniscient viewpoint in *Queenie Peavy* (1966), and Queenie is the character Burch concentrates on, showing why she has a chip on her shoulder and how she overcomes it.

Objective Viewpoint. Authors use the objective viewpoint as though they were making a film of the story and can only learn what is visible and audible and what others say about the characters and situations. Readers are eyewitnesses to the story and are confined to the immediate scene. A limitation of this viewpoint is that the author cannot probe very deeply into characters. *Cinderella* (Galdone, 1978) and *The Little Red Hen* (Zemach, 1983) are examples of stories told from the objective viewpoint; the authors focus on recounting events rather than on developing the personalities of the characters.

These seven elements are the building blocks of stories. With this structure, authors—both children and adults—can let their creativity flow and combine ideas with structure to craft a good story.

❖ TEACHING STUDENTS TO WRITE STORIES

During the preschool years, children develop a concept of story by listening to stories read aloud and telling stories. With this introduction, elementary students are ready to learn more about how stories are organized and how authors use the elements of story structure. Students use this knowledge to compose the stories they write as well as to comprehend stories they read.

Our teaching strategy builds on students' concept of story by examining the elements of story structure in connection with a literature program and then having students apply the elements in writing stories. The reader-writer connection is crucial: as readers, students consider how the author used a particular structure and its impact on themselves as readers; then, as writers, they experiment with structure and consider the impact on their classmates who read the stories.

This teaching strategy has two components: preparing to teach and teaching students about the elements of story structure. Before introducing an element, teachers prepare by learning about the element, collecting stories that exemplify the element, and developing a set of instructional materials. In the second component, teachers introduce students to an element of story structure. Students read stories and analyze how authors use the element in the story. Next, they participate in activities, such as retelling stories and drawing clusters, in which they investigate how authors used the element in particular stories. With this background of experiences, students write collaborative and individual stories applying what they have learned about the element.

Part 1: Preparing to Teach

1. *Learn about the element.* Review the information about the particular element of story structure in this chapter and in other reference books, such as *A Critical Handbook of Children's Literature* (Lukens, 1986).

2. *Collect stories that illustrate the element.* Collect as many stories as possible; folktales, other short stories, and novels can be used as examples. It is helpful to collect multiple copies of books that students will read independently. Stories can also be tape-recorded for students to listen to at a listening center. Also identify stories in basal reader textbooks that illustrate specific elements of story structure.

3. *Analyze the element in stories.* Read the stories to learn how authors use the element in constructing their stories. Take notes about how authors use the element in particular stories to aid in teaching.

4. *Develop charts.* Develop one or more charts for presenting the information to students. The charts should define the element and list its characteristics. Figure 9–12 shows charts that can be developed for each element of story structure. Leave space on the charts for students to add information about the element in their own words. Develop and laminate the charts, and add children's words in grease pencil. The charts can thus be personalized for each group of students.

Part 2: Teaching an Element of Story Structure

1. *Introduce the element.* Introduce the element of story structure and display charts defining and/or listing the characteristics of the element. Next, read several stories that illustrate the element to students or have them read the stories themselves. After reading, discuss the story to probe students' awareness of how the author used the element in constructing the story.

2. *Analyze the element in stories.* Have students read or listen to one or more stories that illustrate the element. After reading, students analyze how the author used the element in each story. Questions that can be used in discussing each element of story structure are presented in Appendix D. As students talk about the stories they have read, they tie their analyses to the definition and characteristics of the element presented in the first step. Students can also make their own copies of the chart to put in their writer's notebooks.

A student learns about story structure by reading a story and analyzing the author's use of the element.

3. *Participate in application activities.* Students participate in application activities in which they investigate how authors use the element in particular stories. Possible activities include retelling stories orally, with drawings, and in writing; dramatizing stories with puppets and other informal techniques; and drawing clusters to graphically display the structure of stories. Ten application activities to use with this teaching strategy follow.

Class collaboration retelling of stories. Choose a favorite story that students have read or listened to several times and have each student draw or write a retelling of a page or short part of the story. Collect the children's contributions and compile them to make a class book. Younger students can draw pictures and dictate their retellings, which the teacher prints in large type. These pictures and text can be attached to sheets of posterboard to make a big book that students can read together.

Retelling and telling stories. Students can retell familiar stories to small groups of classmates using simple hand or finger puppets or pictures on a flannel board. Similarly, students can create their own stories to tell. A gingerbread

Chart 1	Chart 2	Chart 3
Stories	**Beginnings of Stories**	**Middles of Stories**
Stories have three parts:	Writers put these things in the beginning of a story.	Writers put these things in the middle of a story.
1. A beginning	1.	1.
2. A middle	2.	2.
3. An end	3.	3.
		4.
		5.

Chart 4	Chart 5	Chart 6
Ends of Stories	**Repetition**	**Conflict**
Writers put these things in the end of a story.	Writers sometimes repeat words and events in stories:	Conflict is the problem that characters face in the story. There are four kinds of conflict:
1.	1. Sometimes words are said over and over.	1. Conflict between a character and nature
2.	2. Some events happen over and over.	2. Conflict between a character and society
3.		3. Conflict between characters
		4. Conflict within a character

FIGURE 9–12

Charts for the Elements of Story Structure

Chart 7

Plot

Plot is the sequence of events in a story. It has four parts:

1. A problem: The problem introduces conflict at the beginning of the story.

2. Roadblocks: Characters face roadblocks as they try to solve the problem in the middle of the story.

3. The High Point: The high point in the action occurs when the problem is about to be solved. It separates the middle and the end.

4. The Solution: The problem is solved and the road-blocks are overcome at the end of the story.

Chart 8

Setting

The setting is where and when the story takes place.

1. Location: Stories can take place anywhere.

2. Weather: Stories take place in different kinds of weather.

3. Time of Day: Stories take place during the day or at night.

4. Time Period: Stories take place in the past, at the current time, or in the future.

Chart 9

Characters

Writers develop characters in four ways:

1. Appearance: How characters look

2. Action: What characters do

3. Dialogue: What characters say

4. Monologue: What characters think

Chart 10

Theme

Theme is the underlying meaning of a story.

1. Explicit themes are stated clearly in the story.

2. Implicit themes are suggested by the characters, action and monologue

Chart 11

Point of View

Writers tell the story according to one of four viewpoints:

1. First-Person Viewpoint: The writer tells the story through the eyes of one character using "I."

2. Omniscient Viewpoint: The writer sees all and knows all about each character.

3. Limited Omniscient Viewpoint: The writer focuses on one character and tells that character's thoughts and feelings.

4. Objective Viewpoint: The writer focuses on the events of the story without telling what the characters are thinking and feeling.

FIGURE 9–12 (*continued*)

boy might become a gingerbread bunny that runs away with a basket of Easter eggs, or Peter might make a second trip to Mr. McGregor's garden.

Retelling stories with pictures. Students can retell a favorite story by drawing a series of pictures and compiling them to make a wordless picture book. Young children can make a booklet by folding one sheet of drawing paper in quarters like a greeting card. They write the title of the book on the front side and draw illustrations to represent the beginning, middle, and end of the story on the three remaining sides. A sample four-sided booklet is shown in Figure 9–13. Older students can produce a "film" of a favorite story by drawing a series of pictures on a long sheet of butcher paper and scrolling the pictures on a screen made from a cardboard box. Students can also draw pictures to retell a story on a filmstrip. (Filmstrip kits with blank film and colored pens are available from school supply stores.)

Retelling stories in writing. Students can write retellings of favorite stories in their own words. Predictable books—stories with repetition—are often the easiest to retell. Students don't copy the text out of a book; rather, they retell a

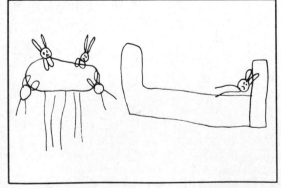

FIGURE 9–13

A Four-sided Booklet Retelling *The Tale of Peter Rabbit*

story they know well in their own words. After writing, students can point out how they used in their retelling the element of story structure they are studying. They can point out the conflict situation, point of view, repeated words, or the beginning-middle-end parts. This activity is a good confidence-builder for students who can't seem to continue a story to its conclusion; using a story they are familiar with tends to make them more successful.

Dramatizing stories. Students can dramatize favorite stories or use puppets to retell a story. The dramatizations should be informal; fancy props are unnecessary and students should not memorize or read dialogue.

Drawing story clusters and other diagrams. Students can draw beginning-middle-end story clusters, repetition clusters, and plot diagrams for stories they have read.

Comparing different versions of stories. Students can compare different versions of folktales such as "The Hare and the Tortoise," "The Gingerbread Boy," and "Cinderella." Students can compare the beginning-middle-end of each version. One version of "The Hare and the Tortoise," for example, has a much longer beginning because the author describes the elaborate plans for the race, whereas other versions have a brief beginning. Students can also compare the events in each story; for example, the characters the Gingerbread Boy runs past vary in different versions, and in one version of "Cinderella," the heroine attends the ball twice.

Creating character clusters. Students can complete a character cluster for a fully developed main character, as shown in Figure 9–14. This character cluster describes Rumpelstiltskin from Zelinsky's (1986) retelling of the Grimms' folktale. Rumpelstiltskin, the name of the character, is the nucleus word for the cluster, and the four ways authors develop characters—*appearance, action, dialogue,* and *monologue*—are the main ideas for the rays. Students add details about the character to each main idea, as the cluster illustrates.

Writing dialogue. Students can choose an excerpt from a favorite story and create a script with dialogue. They then read the script to classmates as a readers theater presentation. Also, students can draw comic strips for an excerpt from a story and add dialogue. They can try varying the register of the language, from informal to very formal or from standard to nonstandard English, to appreciate the power of language.

Retelling stories from different points of view. Students need to experiment with point of view to understand how the author's viewpoint can slant a story. To demonstrate how point of view changes according to the viewpoint of the narrator, read *The Pain and the Great One* (Blume, 1974) to students. In this book, the same brief story is told twice, first from the viewpoint of "the great one," an eight-year-old girl, and then from the viewpoint of "the pain," her six-year-old brother. Even children in the primary grades are struck by how different the two versions are and how the narrator filters the information. Another way to demonstrate the impact of different viewpoints is for students to retell or rewrite a familiar story, such as *Little Red Riding Hood* (Hyman,

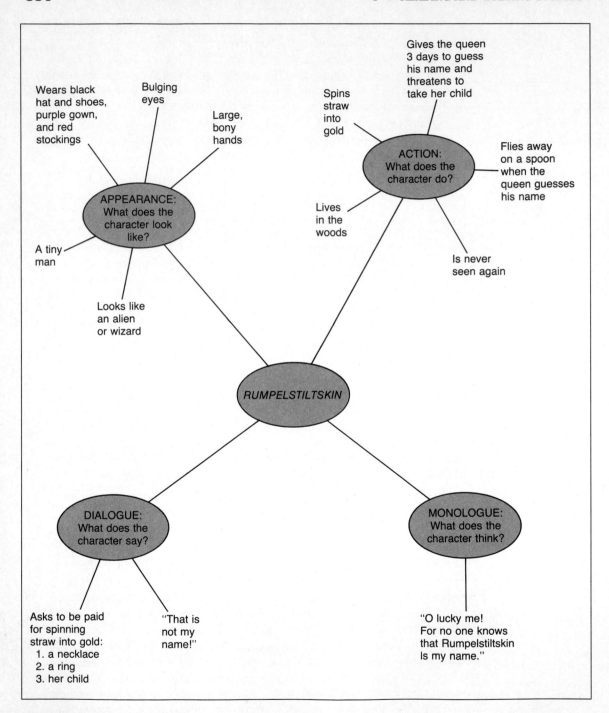

FIGURE 9—14

A Character Cluster of Rumpelstiltskin

1983), from specific points of view—through the eyes of Little Red Riding Hood, her sick, old grandmother, the hungry wolf, or the hunter.

As they shift the point of view, students learn that they can change some aspects of a story but not others. To help them appreciate how these changes affect a story, have them take a story such as *The Lion, the Witch and the Wardrobe* (Lewis, 1981), which is told from the omniscient viewpoint, and retell short episodes from the viewpoints of each character as well as from the four viewpoints. The omniscient viewpoint is a good one to start with because the readers learn all. As students shift to other points of view, they must decide what to leave out according to the new perspective. They must decide whether to tell the story in first or third person and what kinds of information about the characters they are permitted to share.

4. *Review the element.* Review the characteristics of the element under study, using the charts introduced in the first step. Ask students to restate the definition and characteristics of the element in their own words, using one book they have read to illustrate the characteristics.

5. *Write a class collaboration story.* Have students apply what they have learned about the element of story structure by writing a class (or group) collaboration story. A collaborative story provides students with a rehearsal before they write stories independently. Review the element of story structure and refer to the chart presented in the first step as the story is being written. Encourage students to offer ideas for the story and explain how to incorporate the element into the story. Follow the writing process stages by writing a rough draft on the chalkboard, chart paper, or using an overhead projector. Then students revise the story, working both to improve the content as well as to check that the particular element of story structure has been incorporated. Next, edit the story and make a final copy to be shared with all class members.

6. *Write individual stories.* Have students write individual stories incorporating the element and other elements of story structure they have already learned. Students use the process approach, in which they move through the drafting, revising, editing, and publishing stages of the writing process. The activities in the first five steps of this instructional strategy constitute the prewriting stage; now, students complete the remaining stages of the writing process. First, they write rough drafts of their stories and meet in writing groups to share their writing. Writing group members focus their comments on both the content of the story and how effectively the writer has used the story structure element. Next, they revise, using the feedback they receive. Before completing the revising stage, students can complete a "Revision Checklist" in which they doublecheck their story to be sure they have applied the element. A sample revision checklist for plot is presented in Figure 9–15. The first two questions in the checklist require students to focus on the conflict situation in their story and their overall development, the two most important components of plot. The third question focuses on a trouble-spot for many students—roadblocks that complicate the plot—and asks students to count their roadblocks and add more if they don't have at least three. After editing their stories and correcting as many mechanical errors as possible, students recopy the stories and share them with an appropriate audience.

REVISION CHECKLIST ON PLOT

Name _____

Story _____

1. Which type of conflict did you use in your story?

2. Draw a plot diagram of your story.

3. How many roadblocks are in your story? _____

   Circle each of the roadblocks on your plot diagram with a colored pencil.

REMEMBER!
YOU MUST HAVE AT LEAST 3 ROADBLOCKS IN YOUR STORY.

FIGURE 9–15

A Revision Checklist

Assessing Students' Stories

Assessing the stories students write with this approach involves far more than simply judging the quality of the finished stories. Any assessment should also take into account students' activities and learning as they study the element of story structure as well as the activities they engage in while writing and refining their stories. Teachers should consider four components in assessing students' stories: (1) students' study of the element of story structure; (2) their knowledge about and application of the element in writing; (3) their use of the writing process; and (4) the quality of the finished stories.

These are ways to assess the first component, students' participation in the study of the element:

- Did the student read stories illustrating the element?
- Did the student participate in discussions analyzing how the element was used in particular stories?
- Did the student participate in one or more application activities?

The second component is knowledge about the element and application of the element in their stories. Determining whether students learned about the element and applied what they learned in their stories is crucial in assessing students' stories. Consider the following points:

- Can the student define or identify the characteristics of the element?
- Can the student explain how the element was used in a particular story?
- Did the student apply the element in the story he or she has written?

The third component is students' use of the process approach to write stories. Learning about the element is prewriting; after they learn about the element, students draft, revise, edit, and share their stories as they do with other types of writing. Assess students' use of the writing process by observing them as they write and asking these questions:

- Did the student write a rough draft?
- Did the student participate in a writing group?
- Did the student revise the story according to feedback received from the writing group?
- Did the student complete a revision checklist?
- Did the student proofread the story and correct as many mechanical errors as possible?
- Did the student share the story?

The fourth component, the quality of the story, is difficult to measure, but is often described as its creativeness or inventiveness. A second aspect of quality is organization. Students who write high quality and interesting stories use the elements of story structure to their advantage. Ask these questions to assess the quality of children's stories:

- Is the story interesting?
- Is the story well organized?

These four components and the questions that refer to them will help in assessing students' stories, but remember that grading students' stories reflects more than simply the quality of the finished product; any assessment should reflect all components of students' involvement with stories.

❖ "PRO" FILE

READER RESPONSE GROUPS

"There's so much to do with a chapter book like The Sign of the Beaver. *I use it to teach about characters and to connect with our social studies unit on Indians."*

Kathy Brown, Fourth Grade Teacher,
Jackson Elementary School

PROCEDURE

My class is reading *The Sign of the Beaver* by Elizabeth George Speare (1983). I have copies for each student, and we're reading it together in groups—two or three short chapters each day. Students are already sitting in groups, so that makes the logistics easier. Each group has a leader, and when I want to share something about a chapter, I give the information to the leader, who shares it with the group. I move from group to group to keep tabs on their progress, but the groups operate without me.

Students read each group of chapters silently and then write in their reading logs. They write reactions to their reading, not just a summary. They also write questions to use in the group discussion. After everyone in the group finishes, the leader starts the discussion with a question or by asking a student to read his or her reading log entry. Students take turns talking about the chapter and sharing their ideas, comments, and questions. I take a few minutes at the end of the discussion to bring the class together so that each group can share something or make a prediction about what will happen in the next chapter.

I'm focusing on one element of story structure—character—in this story. Students are examining how Mrs. Speare develops Matt's character. Before beginning the story, I told the students a bit about Matt, the twelve-year-old main character. I asked them to write in their reading logs and predict what they thought this boy living in the Maine wilderness in 1769 would be like and what might happen to him in the story. Every two or three days, we talk again about Matt, and how Mrs. Speare has unveiled more about this character through appearance, action, dialogue, and monologue. Students add new information that they have read to the character cluster chart hanging on the wall. The cluster has Matt's name in the middle and rays for "What he looks like," "What he does," "What he says," and "What he thinks" and students add information to each ray.

After reading ten chapters, my students were surprised to find that Mrs. Speare tells about Matt primarily through his actions. The only fact students have learned about his appearance is that he wore boots, until his disastrous attempt to get honey from a beehive, and now he wears moccasins that a friendly Beaver Indian gave him.

After we finish reading the story, each student will do a response activity. We've started a list of activities to choose from. I know what kinds of activities I want them to do: read informational books about Maine, write a poem about Matt, make a map of the area in Maine where the story takes place, research Indians of the New England area, read another book by Mrs. Speare, write a sequel about life after Matt's parents arrive, and so on. But I'd rather have the students suggest these topics themselves. Whenever someone asks a question about the Indians or colonial life, I grab the idea and announce that this student has identified a great response activity and add it to our list. I plan to have 25 to 40 ideas for the students to pick from, and they suggest other ideas, too.

ASSESSMENT

I keep tabs on how each group is doing as I move around the room. Sometimes I hear what is happening in the group beside or behind me. I also read the students' logs, and I'll be able to assess their understanding through their projects.

REFLECTIONS

I'm learning how to make connections between the different areas of the curriculum, and through *The Sign of the Beaver* I'm connecting language arts and social studies. The students learn more and enjoy it more. It makes so much sense, I just wonder why I didn't think of it sooner.

❖ STORY GENRE

Just as students read and examine stories to learn about beginning-middle-end and the other elements of story structure, they read *genre* stories to learn about these unique forms. Examples of story genres are folktales, fables, myths, fantasies, and hero stories. After reading and discussing these stories, students apply what they have learned to writing their own stories, using the teaching strategy in this chapter. As children examine the structure and unique forms of these stories, they become better readers and writers (Bosma, 1987).

Folktales

Folktales, including fairy tales, are relatively short stories that originated as part of the oral tradition. Well-known folktales include *Cinderella* (Galdone, 1978), *Anansi the Spider* (McDermott, 1972), *Little Red Riding Hood* (Hyman, 1983), *Rapunzel* (Rogasky, 1982), and *Duffy and the Devil* (Zemach & Zemach, 1973). These stories come from different countries: *Cinderella* is a French tale, *Anansi the Spider* is African, *Little Red Riding Hood* and *Rapunzel* are German, and *Duffy and the Devil* is a Cornish version of the German tale *Rumpelstiltskin*.

Folktales have a number of distinctive characteristics:

The story is often introduced with the words "Once upon a time."

The settings are not worked out in any detail; they are usually generalized and could be located anywhere.

The plot structure is simple and straightforward.

The problem usually revolves around a journey from home to perform some tasks, a journey that involves a confrontation with a monster, the miraculous change from a harsh home to a secure home, or a wise character-foolish character confrontation.

Characters are portrayed in one dimension: They are either good or bad, stupid or clever, industrious or lazy.

The ending is positive, and everyone "lives happily ever after."

Bettelheim (1976) argued that from the experience of literature, children gain access to "deeper meaning" in life, and the degree of meaning should be appropriate for their stage of development. He believed that folktales help children learn more about possible solutions to problems than they can learn from other types of stories. Folktales convey the advantages of moral behavior through characters and experiences that children can relate to.

Reading folktales is the first step in the teaching strategy. After reading, students examine the stories to learn their characteristics and develop a chart listing the characteristics they have identified. Next, students participate in a variety of activities to dramatize and retell favorite folktales. Then they apply what they have learned by writing their own folktales. This summary of the teaching strategy discussed earlier can be used to involve students in each type of genre stories.

Fables

Fables are brief narratives intended to teach a moral. The story itself teaches a lesson, and the author usually states the moral at the end of the fable. These are characteristics of fables:

> They are short, often less than a page long.
>
> The characters are usually animals.
>
> The characters are one-dimensional, either strong or weak, wise or foolish.
>
> The backdrop setting is barely described.
>
> Fables involve only one event.
>
> The conflict situation is conflict between characters.
>
> The theme is usually stated as a moral at the end of the story.

Our best known fables, including "The Hare and the Tortoise" and "The Ant and the Grasshopper," were written by a Greek slave, Aesop, in the sixth century B.C. Collections of Aesop's fables for elementary students include *Twelve Tales from Aesop* (Carle, 1980), *Aesop's Fables* (Hague, 1985), *Once Upon a Wood: Ten Tales from Aesop* (Rice, 1979), and *Doctor Coyote: A Native American Aesop's Fables* (Bierhorst, 1987). Also, Lobel (1980) wrote 20 original fables in Aesop's style with short narratives and clearly stated morals.

Other well-known fables include *Once a Mouse,* an Indian fable retold by Brown (1961), Hans Christian Andersen's *The Emperor's New Clothes* (Westcott, 1984) and *The Ugly Duckling* (Cauley, 1979), *Doctor De Soto* (Steig, 1982), and Chaucer's *Chanticleer and the Fox* (Cooney, 1958). These fables are longer than Aesop's and their morals are implied rather than clearly stated in the text.

After students read fables, they choose a moral and construct a brief story to illustrate it, following the instructional strategy we have discussed. This is a sixth-grader's fable with a modern setting.

The Peacock and the Mouse

The peacock was a very boastful bird who bragged and spread his feathers whenever he did something. He gave a report in front of our Language Arts class and bragged about it for three weeks.

The mouse was very quiet and never bragged. She was just a quiet person who did her work.

Well, it turned out at the end of the year the mouse's average was an A + and the Peacock's was a D −.

MORAL: Boastful people don't always come out on top.

Myths

People around the world have created myths to explain the origin of the world, how human beings came into existence, their relationship to gods, and how the sun and moon originated. Other myths were created to explain the seasons, physical features of the earth, and characteristics of animals and constellations. Myths explained many phenomena that have more recently been explained scientifically. *Gods, Stars, and Computers: Fact and Fancy in Myth and Science* (Weiss, 1980) provides an interesting comparison of ancient beliefs and scientific facts for middle- and upper-grade students. Characteristics of myths include these:

Myths explain creations.

Characters are often heroes with supernatural powers.

The setting is backdrop and barely sketched.

Magical powers are required.

Myths about different cultures have been compiled for children and provide a valuable way to tie literature and writing with history. The D'Aulaires have chronicled Greek myths (1980) and Norse myths (1967), and other myths have been compiled from Native American, Greek, Egyptian, African, and other cultures. One example is *A Story, A Story* (Haley, 1970), an African explanation of how stories were hidden from humans, which appeals to primary students because of its repetition.

Students' myths usually explain how animals acquired their physical characteristics, modeled on Kipling's *Just So Stories* (1987). Many picture book versions of the *Just So Stories* are now available and popular with middle-grade students. Native American myths, such as *The Fire Bringer* (Hodges, 1972), tell how fire and other natural phenomena came to be. Children read and examine myths, compare myths from various cultures, and write their own myths. Here is a seventh-grade class collaboration myth about the origin of the sun and moon.

Suntaria and Lunaria: Rulers of the Earth

Long ago when gods still ruled the earth, there lived two brothers, Suntaria and Lunaria. Both brothers were wise and powerful men. People from all over the earth sought their wisdom and counsel. Each man, in his own way, was good and just, yet the two were as different as gold and coal. Suntaria was large and strong with blue eyes and brilliantly golden hair. Lunaria's hair and eyes were the blackest black.

One day Zeus, looking down from Mount Olympus, decided that Earth needed a ruler—someone to watch over his people whenever he became too tired or too busy to do his job. His eyes fell upon Suntaria and Lunaria. Both men were wise and honest. Both men would be good rulers. Which man would be the first ruler of the earth?

Zeus decided there was only one fair way to solve his problem. He sent his messenger, Postlet, down to earth with ballots instructing the mortals to vote for a king. There were only two names on the ballot—Suntaria and Lunaria.

Each mortal voted and after the ballots were placed in a secure box, Postlet returned them to Zeus. For seven years Zeus and Postlet counted and recounted the ballots. Each time they came up with the same results: 50% of the votes were for Suntaria and

50% were for Lunaria. There was only one thing Zeus could do. He declared that both men would rule over the earth.

This is how it was, and this is how it is. Suntaria still spreads his warm golden rays to rule over our days. At night he steps down from his throne, and Lunaria's dark, soft night watches and protects us while we dream.

It is interesting to compare this myth to the sun and moon myths told by aboriginal Australians, Native Americans, Nigerians, and Polynesians collected in *Legends of the Sun and Moon* (Hadley & Hadley, 1983).

Hero Stories

Two types of hero stories are epics and legends. *Epics* are long narratives or cycles of stories written about a hero such as Odysseus, Robin Hood, and King Arthur. They may be written in prose or poetry, and they deal with heroic actions and those who share the adventure or oppose the hero. Some elements of a myth may be present in the epic, but the story centers on a human hero rather than on the gods. An epic hero is strongly nationalistic, embodying the ideals of courage, sagacity, beauty, and other characteristics representing the code of chivalry.

Legends are stories from the past that are thought to have some basis in history but are not verifiable. They may have elements of other literary forms such as myths and epics. The hero or main character (e.g., Johnny Appleseed or Davy Crockett) does something important enough to be remembered in story. The tall tales of Paul Bunyan, Mike Fink, John Henry, Casey Jones, and Pecos Bill are legends created when the American West was settled.

Some hero stories appropriate for primary- and middle-grade students include *Fin M'Coul: The Giant of Knockmany Hill* (de Paola, 1981), *Saint George and the Dragon* (Hodges, 1984), *John Henry: An American Legend* (Keats, 1965), *The Pied Piper of Hamelin* (Mayer, 1987), and *American Tall Tales* (Stoutenburg, 1966). Many more hero stories have been written for older students, such as *The Children's Homer: The Adventures of Odysseus and the Tales of Troy* (Colum, 1962), *Sir Gawain and the Green Knight* (Hastings, 1981), *Beowulf* (Keeping, 1982), *The Merry Adventures of Robin Hood* (Pyle, 1952), and *The Sword and the Circle: King Arthur and the Knights of the Round Table* (Sutcliff, 1981). After students read hero stories, they can create puppets of a favorite hero and tell their heroes' stories, rewrite excerpts of the stories, or write their own hero stories.

Fantasies

In fantasies, authors create another world for their characters, and readers must believe this other world exists. Fantasies can range from personified animals that talk to science fiction set in the future. Examples include *The House at Pooh Corner* (Milne, 1956), *The Lion, the Witch and the Wardrobe* (Lewis, 1981) and other stories in the Narnia series, and *The Borrowers* (Norton, 1981). To enjoy these stories, readers must suspend disbelief. Characteristics of fantasies include these:

> The events in the story are fantastic; things happen that could not happen in today's world.
>
> The setting is realistic.
>
> Main characters are people or personified animals, and many have magical qualities.
>
> Themes often deal with conflict between good and evil.
>
> In science fiction, characters use scientific processes to resolve the conflict.

Other fantasies that are appropriate for elementary students include *Jumanji* (Van Allsburg, 1981), *The Wizard of Oz* (Baum, 1982), *A Wrinkle in Time* (L'Engle, 1962), and *The Wish Giver* (Brittain, 1983). After reading and examining the characteristics of fantasies, children write class collaboration and individual stories, incorporating as many of the characteristics as they can.

❖ REVIEW

The seven elements of story structure—beginning-middle-end, repetition, plot, setting, characters, theme, and point of view—and five types of genre stories—folktales, fables, myths, hero stories, and fantasies—are appropriate for teaching students about story structure. Students read stories, examine how authors use the elements, and apply what they have learned by writing stories using the process approach.

Learning about story structure not only influences students' ability to comprehend and recall stories, but enhances their abilities to compose stories. When students develop an explicit concept of story, they are more capable of writing interesting and well-structured stories.

❖ EXTENSIONS

1. Compile a list of books to use in teaching stories at the grade level you teach or plan to teach. Write a brief summary for each book, commenting specifically on the element of story structure or genre that the book exemplifies.

2. Construct a set of charts to use in teaching the elements of story structure, as shown in Figure 9–12.

3. Interview several students about their concept of stories and how they write them. Ask questions such as these:

   • Tell me about a story you have read that is really a good one.
   • What things do authors include in stories to make them good?
   • Do you like to write stories?
   • Tell me about some of the stories you have written.
   • Tell me some of the things you think about while you are writing a story.

- What do you include in stories you write to make them good?
- What have your teachers taught you about writing stories?
- What would you like to learn about so you can be a better writer?

4. Teach one of the elements of story structure or a story genre to a small group of students. Use the instructional strategy presented in this chapter.

5. Collect samples of children's stories and examine them to see how students use the elements of story structure.

❖ REFERENCES

Applebee, A. N. (1978). *The child's concept of story: Ages 2 to 17*. Chicago: The University of Chicago Press.

Applebee, A. N. (1980). Children's narratives: New directions. *The Reading Teacher, 34*, 137–142.

Baum, L. F. (1982). *The Wizard of Oz*. New York: Holt, Rinehart and Winston.

Bettelheim, B. (1976). *The uses of enchantment: The meaning and importance of fairy tales*. New York: Random House.

Bierhorst, J. (1987). *Doctor coyote: A native American Aesop's fables*. (Trans.). New York: Macmillan.

Blackburn, E. (1985). Stories never end. In J. Hansen, J. Newkirk, & D. Graves (Eds.), *Breaking ground: Teachers relate reading and writing in the elementary school*, pp. 3–13. Portsmouth, NH: Heinemann.

Blume, J. (1972). *Tales of a fourth grade nothing*. New York: Dutton.

Blume, J. (1974). *The pain and the great one*. New York: Bradbury.

Bosma, B. (1987). *Fairy tales, fables, legends, and myths: Using folk literature in your classroom*. New York: Teachers College Press.

Brittain, B. (1983). *The wish giver*. New York: Harper and Row.

Brown, M. (1961). *Once a mouse*. New York: Scribner.

Burch, R. (1966). *Queenie Peavy*. New York: Viking.

Burch, R. (1980). *Ida Early comes over the mountain*. New York: Viking.

Byars, B. (1970). *The summer of the swans*. New York: Viking.

Byars, B. (1977). *The pinballs*. New York: Harper and Row.

Carle, E. (1980). *Twelve tales from Aesop*. New York: Philomel.

Cauley, L. B. (1979). *The ugly duckling*. New York: Harcourt Brace Jovanovich.

Colum, P. (1962). *The children's Homer: The adventures of Odysseus and the tales of Troy*. New York: Macmillan.

Cooney, B. (1958). *Chanticleer and the fox*. New York: Crowell.

Dahl, R. (1961). *James and the giant peach*. New York: Knopf.

D'Aulaire, I., & D'Aulaire, P. E. (1967). *Norse gods and giants*. New York: Doubleday.

D'Aulaire, I., & D'Aulaire, P. E. (1980). *D'Aulaires' book of Greek myths*. New York: Doubleday.

de Paola, T. (1981). *Fin M'Coul: The giant of Knockmany Hill*. New York: Holiday House.

Fitzgerald, J., & Spiegel, D. L. (1983). Enhancing children's reading comprehension through instruction in narrative structure. *Journal of Reading Behavior, 15*, 1–17.

Fox, P. (1973). *The slave dancer*. New York: Bradbury.

Galdone, P. (1968). *Henny Penny*. New York: Seabury.

Galdone, P. (1973). *The little red hen*. New York: Seabury.

Galdone, P. (1975). *The gingerbread boy*. New York: Seabury.

Galdone, P. (1978). *Cinderella*. New York: McGraw-Hill.

Galdone, P. (1984). *The teeny-tiny woman*. New York: Clarion.

George, J. C. (1972). *Julie of the wolves*. New York: Harper and Row.

Golden, J. M. (1984). Children's concept of story in reading and writing. *The Reading Teacher, 37*, 578–584.

Gordon, C. J., & Braun, C. (1982). Story schemata: Metatextual aid to reading and writing. In J. A. Niles & L. A. Harris (Eds.), *New inquiries in reading: Research and instruction.* Rochester, NY: National Reading Conference.

Hadley, E., & Hadley, T. (1983). *Legends of the sun and moon.* Cambridge, England: Cambridge University Press.

Hague, M. (1985). *Aesop's fables.* New York: Holt, Rinehart and Winston.

Haley, G. (1970). *A story, a story.* New York: Atheneum.

Hastings, S. (1981). *Sir Gawain and the green knight.* New York: Lothrop.

Hodges, M. (1972). *The fire bringer: A Paiute Indian legend.* Boston: Little, Brown.

Hodges, M. (1984). *Saint George and the dragon.* Boston: Little, Brown.

Hyman, T. S. (1983). *Little red riding hood.* New York: Holiday House.

Keats, E. J. (1965). *John Henry: An American legend.* New York: Pantheon.

Keeping, C. (1982). *Beowulf.* Oxford, England: Oxford University Press.

Kipling, R. (1987). *Just so stories.* Harmondsworth, England: Penguin.

Konigsburg, E. L. (1983). *From the mixed-up files of Mrs. Basil E. Frankweiler.* New York: Atheneum.

Lasky, K. (1983). *Beyond the divide.* New York: Macmillan.

Lawson, R. (1972). *Rabbit hill.* New York: Penguin.

L'Engle, M. (1962). *A wrinkle in time.* New York: Farrar, Straus & Giroux.

Lewis, C. S. (1981). *The lion, the witch and the wardrobe.* New York: Macmillan.

Lobel, A. (1980). *Fables.* New York: Harper and Row.

Lowry, L. (1979). *Anastasia Krupnik.* Boston: Houghton Mifflin.

Lukens, R. J. (1986). *A critical handbook of children's literature* (3rd ed.). Glenview, IL: Scott, Foresman.

Mandler, J. M., & Johnson, N. S. (1977). Remembrance of things parsed: Story structure and recall. *Cognitive Psychology, 9,* 111–115.

Mayer, M. (1987). *The pied piper of Hamelin.* New York: Macmillan.

Mayer, M. (1987). *The ugly duckling.* New York: Macmillan.

McCloskey, R. (1969). *Make way for ducklings.* New York: Viking.

McDermott, G. (1972). *Anansi the spider: A tale from Ashante.* New York: Holt, Rinehart and Winston.

Milne, A. A. (1956). *The house at Pooh Corner.* New York: Dutton.

Ness, E. (1966). *Sam, Bangs and moonshine.* New York: Holt, Rinehart and Winston.

Norton, M. (1981). *The borrowers.* New York: Harcourt Brace Jovanovich.

O'Dell, S. (1960). *Island of the blue dolphins.* Boston: Houghton Mifflin.

Paterson, K. (1977). *Bridge to Terabithia.* New York: Crowell.

Pitcher, E. G., & Prelinger, E. (1963). *Children tell stories: An analysis of fantasy.* New York: International Universities Press.

Potter, B. (1902). *The tale of Peter Rabbit.* New York: Warne.

Pyle, H. (1952). *The merry adventures of Robin Hood.* New York: Grosset & Dunlap.

Rice, E. (1979). *Once upon a wood: Ten tales from Aesop.* New York: Greenwillow.

Rogaski, B. (1982). *Rapunzel.* New York: Holiday House.

Rumelhart, D. (1975). Notes on a schema for stories. In D. G. Bobrow (Ed.), *Representation and understanding: Studies in cognitive science.* New York: Academic Press.

Speare, E. G. (1958). *The witch of Blackbird Pond.* Boston: Houghton Mifflin.

Speare, E. G. (1983). *The sign of the beaver.* Boston: Houghton Mifflin.

Spiegel, D. L., & Fitzgerald, J. (1986). Improving reading comprehension through instruction about story parts. *The Reading Teacher, 39,* 676–682.

Steig, W. (1982). *Doctor De Soto.* New York: Farrar, Straus & Giroux.

Stein, N. L., & Glenn, C. G. (1979). An analysis of story comprehension in elementary school children. In R. O. Freedle (Ed.), *New Directions in Discourse Processing.* Norwood, NJ: Ablex.

Stoutenburg, A. (1966). *American tall tales.* New York: Viking.

Sutcliff, R. (1981). *The sword and the circle: King Arthur and the knights of the round table.* New York: Dutton.

Taylor, M. C. (1976). *Roll of thunder, hear my cry.* New York: Dial.

Tompkins, G. E., & McGee, L. M. (1989). In K. D. Muth-Glynn (Ed.), *Children's comprehension of narrative and expository text: Research into practice*. Newark, DE: International Reading Association.

Tompkins, G. E., & Webeler, M. B. (1983). What will happen next? Using predictable books with young children. *The Reading Teacher, 36,* 498–502.

Van Allsburg, C. (1981). *Jumanji*. Boston: Houghton Mifflin.

Viorst, J. (1977). *Alexander and the terrible, horrible, no good, very bad day*. New York: Atheneum.

Waber, B. (1972). *Ira sleeps over*. Boston: Houghton Mifflin.

Weiss, M. E. (1980). *Gods, stars, and computers: Fact and fancy in myth and science*. New York: Doubleday.

Westcott, N. B. (1984). *The emperor's new clothes*. Boston: Little, Brown.

White, E. B. (1952). *Charlotte's web*. New York: Harper and Row.

Zelinsky. P. O. (1986). *Rumpelstiltskin*. New York: Dutton.

Zemach, H., & Zemach, M. (1973). *Duffy and the devil*. New York: Farrar, Straus & Giroux.

Zemach, M. (1983). *The little red hen*. New York: Farrar, Straus & Giroux.

10 READING AND WRITING INFORMATION

RESEARCH REPORTS
    Young Children's Reports
    Collaborative Reports
    Individual Reports
    Teaching Students to Write Research Reports

NEWSPAPERS
    Organization of a Newspaper Article
    Class Newspapers
    Simulated Newspapers
    Teaching Students to Write Newspapers

LETTERS
    Friendly Letters
    Business Letters
    Simulated Letters
    Teaching Students to Write Letters

LIFE-STORIES
    Autobiography
    Biography
    Teaching Students to Write Life-stories

◆ IN CHAPTER 10, WE DISCUSS FOUR TYPES OF INFORMATIONAL
    reading and writing: research reports, newspapers, letters, and life-stories.

◆ AS YOU ARE READING, THINK ABOUT THESE QUESTIONS:
    How can teachers help students connect the reading and writing of information?
    How do elementary students write research reports?
    How are written reports similar to oral reports?
    How do elementary students write class newspapers?
    What biographies and autobiographies can elementary students read?
    How do elementary students write life-stories about themselves and others?

$\mathbf{A}$uthors write informative texts to share information with their readers. The information might be about whales, how a road is built, Alaska, tearing down the Berlin Wall, the Revolutionary War, or Helen Keller's life. Science, geography, history, current events, and biography are all informational writing. Britton (1970) says this type of writing is intended "to interact with people and things and to make the wheels of the world, for good or ill, go round" (p. 8).

Students read informational books to learn about social studies and science concepts, then they write their own reports, often in book format, to share what they have learned. Students read about current events in newspapers and share their own current events in class newspapers. Informational books and newspapers are written for wide, and often unknown, audiences. In contrast, letters are written to a specific audience. When students write letters, they share information, experiences, and feelings in personal letters and share or seek information in business letters. Autobiographies and biographies are special types of informational writing in which writers combine information with narration to write life-stories about themselves and others.

❖ RESEARCH REPORTS

Often, students are not exposed to research reports until they are faced with writing a term paper in high school, and they are overwhelmed with learning how to take notes on notecards, how to organize and write the paper, and how to compile a bibliography. There is no reason to postpone report writing until students reach high school. Students in the elementary grades can search for answers to questions that interest them and write both class collaboration and individual reports (Krogness, 1987; Queenan, 1986). Early, successful experiences with report writing teach students how to write research reports as well as about content areas.

Young Children's Reports

Contrary to the popular assumption that young children's first writing is narrative, educators have found that kindergartners and first graders write many nonnarrative compositions in which they provide information about familiar topics, including "Signs of Fall," or directions for familiar activities, such as "How to Feed Your Pet" (Bonin, 1988; Sowers, 1985). Many of these writings might be termed "All about . . ." books, and others are informational pieces that children dictate for the teacher to record. These two types introduce young children to informational writing.

In young children's "All about . . ." books, they write an entire booklet on a single topic. Usually one piece of information and an illustration appear on each page. A second grader wrote an "All about . . ." book, "Snowy Thoughts" (shown in Figure 10—1) as part of a unit on the four seasons. John-David omitted some capital letters and punctuation marks and used invented spelling for a few words in his book, but the information can be easily deciphered.

Young children can dictate reports to their teacher, who serves as scribe to record them. After listening to a guest speaker, viewing a film, or reading several books about

FIGURE 10–1

A Second Grader's "All about . . ." Book

Our Report about Police Officers

Page 1: Police officers help people who are in trouble. They are nice to kids. They are only mean to robbers and bad people. Police officers make people obey the laws. They give tickets to people who drive cars too fast.

Page 2: Men and women can be police officers. They wear blue uniforms like Officer Jerry's. But sometimes police officers wear regular clothes when they work undercover. They wear badges on their uniforms and on their hats. Officer Jerry's badge number is 3407. Police officers have guns, handcuffs, whistles, sticks, and two-way radios. They have to carry all these things.

Page 3: Police officers drive police cars with flashing lights and loud sirens. The cars have radios so the officers can talk to other police officers at the police station. Sometimes they ride on police motorcycles or on police horses or in police helicopters or in police boats.

Page 4: Police officers work at police stations. The jail for the bad people that they catch is right next door. One police officer sits at the radio to talk to the police officers who are driving their cars. The police chief works at the police station, too.

Page 5: Police officers are your friends. They want to help you so you shouldn't be afraid of them. You can ask them if you need some help.

Page 6: How We Learned about Police Officers for Our Report

   1. We read these books:
      Police by Ray Broekel
      What Do They Do? Policemen and Firemen by Carla Greene

   2. We interviewed Officer Jerry.

   3. We visited the police station.

FIGURE 10–2

Kindergartners' Report about Police Officers

a particular topic, kindergartners and first graders can dictate brief reports. A class of kindergartners compiled the book-length report on police officers in Figure 10–2. The teacher read two books aloud to the students and Officer Jerry visited the classroom and talked to the students about his job. The students also took a field trip to the police station. The teacher took photos of Officer Jerry, his police car, and the police station to illustrate the report. With this background, the students and the teacher together developed a cluster with these five main ideas: what police officers do, what equipment police officers have, how police officers travel, where police officers work, and police officers are your friends. The students added details to each main idea until each main idea developed into one page of the report. The background of experiences and the clustering activity prepared students to compose their report. After students completed the report, included a bibliography called "How We Learned about Police Officers for Our Report," and inserted the photographs, it was ceremoniously presented to the school library to be enjoyed by all students in the school.

Collaborative Reports

A successful first report writing experience for middle- and upper-grade students is a class collaboration research report. Small groups of students work together to write sections of the report, which are then compiled. Students benefit from writing a group report first because they learn the steps in writing a research report, with the group as a scaffold or support system, before tackling individual reports. Also, working in groups lets them share the laborious parts of the work.

A group of four fourth graders wrote a collaborative report on hermit crabs. The students sat together at one table and watched hermit crabs in a terrarium. They cared for the crustaceans for two weeks and made notes of their observations in learning logs. After this period, the students were bursting with questions about the hermit crabs and were eager for answers. They wanted to know about the crabs' natural habitat and what the best habitat was for them in the classroom, how they breathed air, why they lived in "borrowed" shells, why one pincer was bigger than the other, and so on. Their teacher provided some answers and directed them to books that would provide additional information. As they collected information, they created a cluster that they taped to the table next to the terrarium. The cluster became inadequate for reporting information, so they decided to share their knowledge by writing a book titled "The Encyclopedia about Hermit Crabs." This book and the cluster used in gathering information appear in Figure 10–3.

The students decided to share the work of writing the book, and they chose four main ideas, one for each to write: what hermit crabs look like, how they act, where they really live, and what they eat. One student wrote each section and returned to the group to share the rough draft. The students gave each other suggestions and made revisions based on the suggestions. Next, they edited their report with the teacher and added an introduction, conclusion, and bibliography. Finally, they recopied their report and added illustrations in a cloth-bound book, which they read to each class in the school before adding it to the school library.

Individual Reports

Toby Fulwiler (1985) recommends that students do "authentic" research, in which they explore topics that interest them or hunt for answers to questions that puzzle them. When students become immersed in content area study, questions arise that they want to explore. A fourth grade class that was studying dinosaurs quickly asked more questions than the teacher could answer. The teacher encouraged them to search for answers in the books they had checked out of the school and community libraries. When they located answers to their questions, the students were eager to share their new knowledge and decided to write reports and publish them as books.

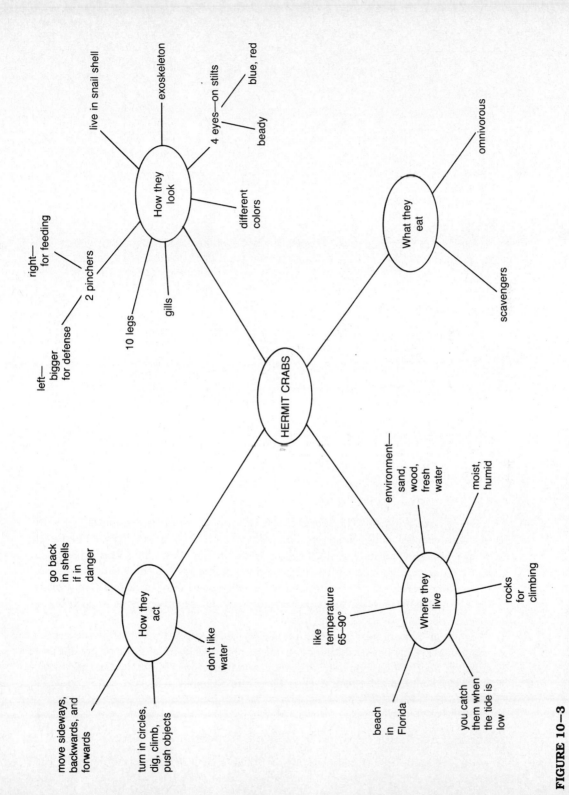

FIGURE 10–3

Fourth Graders' Cluster and Collaborative Report on Hermit Crabs

---

The Encyclopedia About Hermit Crabs

How They Look

Hermit crabs are very much like regular crabs but hermit crabs transfer shells. They have gills. Why? Because they are born in water and when they mature they come to land and kill snails so they can have a shell. They have two beady eyes that look like they are on stilts. Their body is a sight! Their shell looks like a rock. Really it is an exoskeleton which means the skeleton is on the outside. They have two pincers. The left one is bigger so it is used for defense. The right one is for feeding. They also have ten legs.

Where They Live

Hermit crabs live mostly on beaches in Florida where the weather is 65°–90°. They live in fresh water. They like humid weather and places that have sand, wood, and rocks (for climbing on). The best time to catch hermit crabs is a low tide.

What They Eat

Hermit crabs are omnivorous scavengers which means they eat just about anything. They even eat leftovers.

How They Act

Hermit crabs are very unusual. They go back into their shell if they think there is danger. They are funny because they walk sideways, forwards, and backwards. They can go in circles. They can also get up when they get upside down. And that's how they act.

FIGURE 10–3 (*continued*)

One fourth grader's "The World of the Dinosaurs" report is presented in Figure 10–4. Each chapter focuses on a question he examined. The first chapter, "The Death Star," answered his question about how the dinosaurs died out. The second chapter, to answer his question about whether the dinosaurs all lived at the same time, focuses on the three time periods. In the third chapter, he described the pterodactyl, an unusual flying lizard that lived when the dinosaurs did. He chose this topic after locating an interesting book about these flying lizards.

Students can organize reports in a variety of formats—formats they see used in informational books. One possibility is a question-answer format; another possibility is an alphabet book. One group of fourth grade students wrote "The ABC Nintendo Book of Strategies" with one page for each letter of the alphabet. The "G" page appears in Figure 10–5.

Teaching Students to Write Research Reports

To write a research report, either as a class collaboration or individually, students use a process approach. They search for answers to questions about a topic, then compose

The World of the Dinosaurs

Chapter 1
The Death Star

Over the years, scientists have noticed that almost all stars have a sister star. But what about the sun? Scientists have found out that the sun does have a sister star. It's darker than the sun, and it takes 28 million years to orbit around our solar system. They named it Nemesis after the Greek god of revenge. When Nemesis reaches its closest point to the sun, it makes the asteroid belt go beserk! Asteroids and comets were flying everywhere! The earth was a disaster! Scientists have studied and found out that if a comet or an asteroid hit the earth it would be like dropping an atomic bomb (or a thousand billion tons of dynamite) on the earth. Whenever that happens, almost everything on the face of the earth is destroyed. The next time Nemesis reaches its closest point to the sun will be in about fifteen million years.

Chapter 2
The Three Periods: Triassic, Jurassic, and Cretaceous

There were three periods when the dinosaurs came, and then they were just wiped off the face of the earth. It may have been the Death Star. Whatever the reason, nobody knows. The three periods were the Triassic, Jurassic, and the Cretaceous.

Most of the smaller animals like Orniholestes and Hysilophodon came in the Triassic Period. They were mostly plant eaters.

Most of the flying dinosaurs like Pteradactyl and Pteranadon came in the Jurassic Period. A number of the big plant eaters like Brontosaurus and Brachiosaurus also came in that period. A lot of sea reptiles came in that time, too.

The bigger dinosaurs like Tyrannosaurus Rex and Trachodon came in the Cretaceous Period. Most of these were meat eaters.

Chapter 3
Pterodactyl: The Flying Lizard

The Pterodactyl is a flying lizard that lived millions of years ago when the dinosaurs lived. Pterodactyl means "flying lizard." It was huge animal. It had skin stretched between the hind limb and a long digit of the forelimb. It didn't have any feathers. Some had a wingspan of 20 feet. Some paleontologists think Pterodactyl slept like a bat, upside down, because of the shape of its wings. It had a long beak and very sharp teeth. When it would hunt for food, it would fly close to the water and look for fish. When it saw one, it would dive in and get it. It also had sharp claws that helped it grab things. The Pterodactyl had a strange looking tail. It was long with a ball shape at the end. Some people say it really looked like a flying lizard.

FIGURE 10—4

A Fourth Grader's Dinosaur Report

G   is   for   Godzilla

*In Godzilla you breathe fire to kill other monsters.
You can change into Mothra which is a giant butterfly. You try to transport to other planets and defeat
the main boss of that planet. To breathe fire you
press select.*

FIGURE 10—5

The G Page from "The ABC Nintendo Book of Strategies"

a report to share what they have learned. Designing questions and gathering information is the prewriting stage; they complete the stages by drafting, revising, editing, and publishing their reports.

Writing Class Collaboration Reports. To apply the process approach in writing class collaboration reports, students follow six steps.

1. *Choose a topic.* The first step is to choose a topic, which should be something students are studying or want to study. Almost any social studies, science, or current events topic that can be subdivided into four to ten parts works well for class collaboration reports. Some possible general topics are oceans, dinosaurs, the solar system, the human body, continents, life in the Middle Ages, and transportation.

From these general topics, they choose specific topics for small groups or pairs of students to research. For a report on the continents, students choose which continent they will research; for a unit on the solar system, they choose a planet. For a unit such as dinosaurs or the Middle Ages, students may not be able to identify the specific topic they will research until they have learned more and designed research questions.

2. *Design research questions.* Research questions emerge as students study a topic. They brainstorm a list of questions on a chart posted in the classroom and add to the list as other questions arise. If they are planning a report on the human body, for example, the small groups that are studying each organ may decide to research the same three, four, or five questions: "What does the organ look like?" "What job does the organ do?" and "Where is the organ located in the human body?" (Elementary students who research the human body often want to include a question as to

whether a person can live without the organ; this interest probably reflects the current attention in the news media to organ transplants.)

Students studying a unit such as the Middle Ages might brainstorm the following questions about life in that era: "What did the people wear?" "What did they eat?" "What were their communities like?" "What kind of entertainment did people enjoy?" "What kinds of occupations?" "How did people protect themselves?" "What kinds of transportation did people use?" Each small group selects one of the questions as the specific topic for its report and chooses questions related to the specific topic.

To provide a rehearsal before students research and write their section of the report, the teacher and students may work through the procedure using a research question that no one chose. Together as a class, students gather information, organize it, and write the section of the report using the drafting, revising, and editing stages of the writing process.

3. *Gather and organize information.* Students work in small groups or pairs to search for answers to their research questions. The questions provide the structure for data collection, because students are seeking answers to specific questions, not just randomly writing down information. Students can use clusters or data charts to record the information they gather. The research questions are the same for each data collection instrument. On a cluster, students add information as details to each main idea ray; if they are working with data charts, they record information from the first source in the first row under the appropriate questions, from the second

A student reads an informational book to gather information for a report he will write.

source in the second row, and so on. These two instruments are effective because they organize the data collection question by question and limit the amount of information that can be gathered from any source. Students list their sources of information for clusters and data charts on the back of the paper.

Students gather information from a variety of reference materials, including trade books, textbooks, encyclopedias, magazines, films, videotapes, filmstrips, field trips, interviews, demonstrations, and observations. Teachers often require that students consult two or three different sources and that no more than one source be an encyclopedia.

Report writing has been equated with copying facts out of an encyclopedia, but even elementary students are not too young to understand what plagiarism is and why it is wrong. Even primary-grade students realize they should not "borrow" items belonging to classmates and pretend the items are theirs. Similarly, students should not "borrow" someone else's words, especially without giving credit in the composition. The format of clusters and data charts makes it easier for students to take notes without plagiarizing.

After students gather information, they read it over to check that they have answered their research questions fully and to delete unnecessary or redundant information. Next, they consider how they will sequence the information in their rough drafts. Some students tentatively number the research questions in the order they plan to use them in their composition. They also identify a piece of information that is especially interesting to use as the lead-in to the section.

4. *Draft the sections of the report.* Students write their report sections using the process approach to writing. They write the rough draft, skipping every other line to allow space for revising and editing. Because students are working in pairs or small groups, one student can be the scribe to write the draft while the other students in the group dictate the sentences, using information from a cluster or data chart. Next, they share their draft with students from other small groups and revise it on the basis of feedback they receive. Last, students proofread and correct mechanical errors.

5. *Compile the sections.* Students compile their completed sections of the research report and, as a class, write the introduction, conclusion, and bibliography to add to the report. A list at the end of the report should identify the authors of each section. After all the parts are compiled, the entire report is read aloud so students can catch inconsistencies or redundant passages.

6. *Publish the report.* The last step in writing a class collaboration research report is to publish it. A final copy is made with all the parts of the report in the correct sequence. If the report has been written on a microcomputer, it is easy to print out the final copy; otherwise, the report can be typed or recopied by hand. Copies are made for each student, and special bound copies can be constructed for the class or school library.

Writing Individual Reports.   Writing an individual report is similar to writing a collaborative report. Students continue to design research questions, gather information to answer the questions, and compile what they have learned in a report. Writing individually demands two significant changes: (1) students must narrow their topics and (2) must assume the entire responsibility for writing the report.

1. *Choose and narrow a topic.* Students choose topics for research reports from a content area, hobbies, or other interests. After choosing a general topic, such as cats or the human body, they need to narrow the topic so that it is manageable. The broad topic of cats might be narrowed to pet cats or tigers, and the human body to one organ or system.

2. *Design research questions.* Students design research questions by brainstorming a list of questions in a learning log. They review the list, combine some questions, delete others, and finally arrive at four to six questions that are worthy of answering. When they begin their research, they may add new questions and delete others if they reach a dead end.

3. *Gather and organize information.* As in collaborative reports, students use clusters or data charts to gather and organize information. Data charts, with their rectangular spaces for writing information, serve as a transition for upper-grade students between clusters and notecards.

4. *Draft the report.* Students write a rough draft from the information they have gathered. Each research question can become a paragraph, a section, or a chapter in the report.

5. *Revise and edit the report.* Students meet in writing groups to share their rough drafts and make revisions based on the feedback they receive from their classmates. After they revise, students use an editing checklist to proofread their reports and identify and correct mechanical errors.

6. *Publish the report.* Students recopy their reports in books and add bibliographic information. Research reports can also be published in several other ways; for example, as a filmstrip or video presentation, as a series of illustrated charts or dioramas, or as a dramatization.

Assessing Students' Research Reports. Students need to know the requirements for the research project and how they will be assessed or graded. Many teachers distribute a checklist of requirements for the project before students begin working, so they know what is expected of them and can assume responsibility for completing each step of the assignment. The checklist for an individual research report might include these observation behaviors and products:

- Choose a narrow topic.
- Identify four or five research questions.
- Use a cluster to gather information to answer the questions.
- Write a rough draft with a section or chapter to answer each question.
- Meet in writing groups to share your report.
- Make at least three changes in your rough draft.
- Complete an editing checklist with a partner.

COLLABORATIVE CLASS BOOKS

"We write class books. That's how I teach my students about reading and writing. We make 20 to 30 books each year, and that's quite an addition to our class library!"

Mary Ann Comeau, Second Grade Teacher,
Western Hills Elementary School

PROCEDURE

Last week I read Maurice Sendak's book *Chicken Soup with Rice* (1962) in connection with our unit on the seasons and months of the year. Before I finished reading the book, several students were already asking to make a class book and thinking up sentences for it. The students recognized that Sendak arranged the book with one page for each month of the year, so we arranged our book the same way. We created the formula we would use for each page:

In month, we . . . .
And. . .
Then we. . .
And eat. . .

After reading Sendak's book several more times, students divided into small groups to write the book, make the cover, title page, table of contents, and "All About the Authors" page. Students worked for several days, then we met again as a whole class writing group to share their rough drafts. The students took turns sharing their

- Add a bibliography.
- Write the final copy of the report.
- Share the report with someone.

The checklist can be simpler or more complex depending on students' ages and experiences. Students staple the checklist to the inside cover of the folder in which they keep all the work for the project and check off each requirement as they complete it.

work, and their classmates offered compliments about the work as well as suggestions for revisions. It was at this stage that we realized our book had a name: "Hot Dogs and Chili." It comes from the January page:

In January it snows and blows
And we get to go outside
And we get to make snowballs.
Then we go inside the house
And eat a hot dog with chili
While we're warming up.

After my students made their revisions, I met with them to edit their writing to correct spelling and other errors. Then they recopied and illustrated their pages. (My students do all their recopying themselves.) Finally, we compiled the book. For this book, I laminated each page because I knew it was going to get a lot of wear, and I used three metal rings to bind it together. We read the book ourselves and then visited other classes to share our new book with them. My students often check out the book and take it home to share with their parents.

ASSESSMENT

I want every student in my class to be involved in our class book projects. For our "Hot Dogs and Chili" book, I divided the class into 15 teams—a team for each month of the year, a team to make the cover, a team to make the title page and table of contents, and another team to write the "All About the Authors" page. After we make a book, we have a ritual: one at a time, each student comes to sign his or her name on the authors' page, which follows the title page in the book. This is the acknowledgement of everyone's contribution, and students who have not contributed to making the book do not sign. This ritual helps me keep track of how my students are working together and their contributions to the project, and gives them a sense of pride and accomplishment.

REFLECTIONS

I can always tell which books will be made into class books—and they are the books the students like best. When they're already composing text for our class book before I finish reading the book aloud, I know I've got a winner. I began having students make books to enlarge our class library with books they could read easily, but now I recognize other benefits as well. My students think of themselves as authors, they gain valuable reading practice, and they learn the content area material we're studying better.

A checklist enables students to monitor their own work and learn that writing is a process, not just a final product.

After completing the project, students submit their folders to the teacher for assessment. The teacher considers all the requirements on the checklist in determining the student's grade. If the checklist has ten requirements, each requirement might be worth ten points, and the grading can be done objectively on an 100-point scale. Thus, if the student's project is complete with all required materials, the student scores 100, or a grade of A. Points can be subtracted for work that is sloppy or incomplete.

❖ NEWSPAPERS

Newspapers are one of the richest and least expensive sources of reading material and information about writing. Newspapers use language for several different functions—to inform and to persuade as well as to entertain. To appeal to all segments of their huge and diverse audiences, newspapers contain many different types of information:

General news or current events

Sports news

Comics and cartoons

Women's news

Human relations/Guidance articles

Arts features

Advertisements

Weather information

Opinions

Business news

Youth/Teen features

Society news

Human interest features

Leisure/Recreation information

Real estate listings

Legal notices

Organization of a Newspaper Article

Students can investigate the kinds of information in each category of newspaper articles. For instance, a weather forecast includes different kinds of information and is written in a different way than a sports article or a news article. Most news articles are written to answer the 5 *W*s plus one questions.

Class Newspapers

After students have investigated newspapers and the types of information in each category of articles, they apply what they have learned by writing their own class newspapers. A class newspaper, *The Goggles Gazette,* produced by a class of third, fourth, and fifth graders, is shown in Figure 10–6. Students wrote articles, revised and edited them, and then recopied them on paper cut into column-sized sheets. The teacher and student editorial staff reviewed the articles and selected those to put into the newspaper. They chose articles about news events as well as puzzles and riddles that would appeal to their audience. They also decided to include a letter the class had received from Patricia Lee Gauch, an author of children's books who had recently visited the class. Then the teacher and another group of students decided on the arrangement of articles and glued them to sheets of paper. The teacher had the newspaper duplicated, and the distribution staff collated and stapled the copies and distributed them to each student in the class and to the other classes in the school. Although it is nice to have the articles typed, it is not necessary, as the newspaper in Figure 10–6 illustrates. Students can recopy their own articles neatly.

Kindergarten teachers often ask students to dictate accounts of the week's events to form a one-page class newspaper that students take home to inform their parents about what is going on in the classroom. The teacher and the children decide together what important events to write about, and the teacher records the children's dictation on the chalkboard. Next, the teacher reads the rough draft with the children and encourages them to suggest changes, additions, and deletions to improve the article. After the children are satisfied with their articles, the teacher copies them onto paper and duplicates it for the children to take home. A class newspaper is an excellent way to keep parents informed about what is happening in the classroom, introduces young children to another form and function of written language, and helps them learn to use the writing process to communicate effectively.

Simulated Newspapers

Students can write simulated newspapers in connection with units in other content areas, applying what they have learned about historical events and personalities. In connection with a unit on the American Revolution, a fifth grade class produced a simulated newspaper as it might have been published in Boston on April 20, 1775, the day after the battles of Lexington and Concord. Figure 10–7 illustrates the first two pages of this newspaper.

Simulated newspapers contain the same categories of articles as real newspapers—current events, weather, advertisements, editorials, and sports news; the change is that they reflect the era in which they are supposed to have been written. Students have to consider, for example, whether a Revolutionary War newspaper might include football game scores or a satellite weather map.

Teaching Students to Write Newspapers

Students learn to write newspaper articles using a process approach. They learn about the format of newspaper articles and then apply what they have learned by writing a class newspaper or simulated newspapers.

1. *Read to learn about the format of newspaper articles.* Students learn about the types of newspaper articles by reading and examining newspapers. Have students bring in newspapers or order a class set of your local newspaper or *USA Today*. Working in pairs or small groups, students investigate the parts of a newspaper,

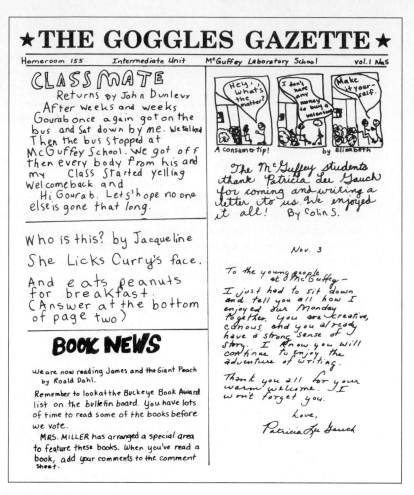

FIGURE 10–6

A Middle-Grade Class Newspaper

list the categories they discover on a chart, and cite examples of each category to add to the chart. Upper-grade students might cite editorials, letters to the editor, syndicated columns, and editorial cartoons as examples of opinion articles. After they learn about the structure of newspaper articles, students are ready to write their own.

2. *Plan the newspaper and the articles each student will write.* Certain decisions must be made before starting to write the newspaper. For example, students need to choose a name for the newspaper, decide what categories of articles to include, identify the audience, and develop a timeline for its production.

After making these decisions, students write articles for the various categories they will include in the newspaper. All students act as reporters. Students can be

FIGURE 10−6 (continued)

assigned to write specific articles, but it is often more effective to have them sign up for the articles they wish to contribute.

3. *Gather and organize information for the articles.* Students use informal writing strategies, such as brainstorming and clustering, to gather and organize information for their articles. The "5 Ws Plus One" cluster discussed in Chapter 6 is the most effective approach to news articles. Students write the topic of the article in the center circle and then draw out *who, what, when, where, why,* and *how* rays to complete the cluster.

4. *Write articles using the writing process.* Students use the process approach to write their articles; after completing their rough drafts, they meet in writing groups to revise and edit. After the articles have been completed, they can be typed

REVOLUTIONARY TIMES

SUMMER QUARTERLY 1775   LEXINGTON, MASS.   3¢

LOCAL PATRIOTS WARN OF BRITISH ONSLAUGHT

On 17 April William Dawes rode to Lexington to warn the colonists there that the British would soon be coming from Boston. The route which they would be traveling by was not yet known.

The following day, 18 April, Boston's Minutemen realized the British were leaving by boat. With that knowledge, Paul Revere, a local silversmith, crossed the Charles River in a rowboat. By wrapping the oars with cloth he was able to pass the armed English transport which was anchored in the river.

At Lexington, Revere was met by William Dawes and Dr. Sam Prescott. Together they set off toward Concord.

During the trip to Concord, they were stopped by British patrols. Revere and Dawes were captured, but Prescott escaped and made it to Concord.

While Revere and Dawes were being escorted to Lexington by the British patrols, along with other prisoners, a volley of gunfire was heard. Revere told the colonists it was a signal to the colonists.

The prisoners were then released, but their horses were taken by the patrols.

BUNKER HILL CLOSEUP

I'm at Bunker Hill. As I got up this morning, it looked like it was going to be a boring day. We were behind the earthworks, then the British soldiers arrived. General William said, "Don't fire until you see the whites of their eyes." Then the British soldiers arrived. As the British got closer and closer, we got more and more nervous. I heard a voice yell "fire!" The Battle had begun. Guns fired, when the smoke cleared I could see many British soldiers dead. I was standing by my best friend John Wilson. Then I heard a big boom! Part of the earthwork collapsed. My friend was down for two minutes. I knew he was dead, but I kept fighting. I was shot in the shoulder. While I was being carried to a safer place, the blood was seeping out. I could still hear the guns firing. The sick wagon came to pick me up for the long and ruff journey home.

NEW MEMBERS JOIN CONGRESS

On 10 May, 56 delegates of the Continental Congress met to vote three new delegates who were John Hancock, Benjamin Franklin, and Thomas Jefferson. Some of the wisest men voted George Washington Commander in Chief of Continental Army. The Congress said they would take on duties of a government, uniting the colonies for the war effort.

WOMEN CONTRIBUTE TO BATTLES

The women of the surrounding colonies have had to consistently manage the men's trades as well as their own households. This is due to the fact that the men are engaged in the battle against Britain. While worried about their husbands' welfare, the women have many new responsibilities. But because of their determination to do their part, they have so far kept up their towns, businesses, and farms.

Along with the pressures of new trades and responsibilities, the women have had to contribute their personal possessions to supply the Continental Army with needed provisions. Clothing, food, water, pewter pots and pans, and dishes have all helped the army's success. The women are playing a very important role in fighting the battles.

ACTION AT BREEDS HILL

The battle of Bunker Hill is actually being fought at Breed's Hill. 1,000 Redcoats led by Gen. Howe and Gen. Pigot marched up the hill. When the British were within 40 paces, Americans opened fire. Possibly 1,000 Britains are lost and 440 Americans are dead. It could be the bloodiest encounter of the war.

LETTERS TO THE EDITOR

Dear Editor

I think I or anyone else important should have warned the colonists. Paul Revere is just a silversmith. William Dawes is a smuggler. I am a captain of an army. If somebody more organized warned us we would have been more successful in the Battle of Lexington. We also would have been more alert. Captains are important people not silversmiths or smugglers. William Dawes should be sent to gaol.

Signed, Captain Williams

Dear Editor

Why did the Battle of Bunker Hill start? The British commander decided it was time for action. So the British marched up the hill on 17 June 1775. The American's were behind their earthworks and fired their muskets and killed some of the British. The British won, but I believe it was a victory to the Americans. We killed half of the British army. Very few Americans got killed. We showed the British that we had strength and that we were brave.

Molly Cline

Did You Know?

Did you know, out of all the colors that you can think of black draws more sunlight. You can tell by laying an assortment of cloth on the ground of all different colors. Be sure you lay them apart. Put some black with the colors. Come back in about one hour and feel them. That's how you can tell.

Benjamin Franklin

In the Battle of Bunker Hill 10 very important soldiers died. Let's remember them.

An Interview with G. Washington

When did you observe your soldiers at their best?

I observed my army at their best when they had a conflict on a public common.

Were you pleased with the results of your army's efforts?

My army was not very disciplined, but they sometimes fought as a team and won a great deal.

Were you mad at your army for not working as a team?

I was not mad, but probably the most embarrassed general in the army.

I met George Washington at the 2 Star Inn. We talked over some glasses of ale. We had a long and cheerful talk.

Was the Lexington Battle Worth it?

The Lexington Battle I know was very important. The battle was fought so Americans could have their rights.

My husband Thomas Madden was 1 out of the 49 American soldiers that were killed. I loved my husband. He was a strong, brave man. He went out on the battle field and fought the Lobster Backs to get our freedom. He never even got to see our little girl Mary.

I asked myself was it worth losing my husband and gaining freedom? I guess it was really worth it. At least now I know my baby will grow up and be free from the king.

Martha Madden

PEOPLE CONFUSED ABOUT BUNKER HILL

It was 17 June when the battle began. Thoughts about King George are half and half. Some think that he is an intelligent person but others are still very angry at him.

Most of the other colonists thought that Bunker Hill would be a good risk. Even with this difference of opinion, the colonists no longer doubted that the Americans must break all ties with Great Britain. General Washington is working hard to turn the volunteers into a efficient fighting force.

Rumor has it Washington is planning to drive the British out of Boston forever!!

LOCAL NEWS

George Adams can walk again after his leg got wounded in the Battle of Bunker Hill.

Kristie and Bill Stockup had twins. The babies and mother died. Bill killed himself.

Peter's Cafe is open now on Elm Road by Linda Cowitt's house.

Linda Cowitt is opening a store by Peter's Cafe on Elm Road.

Foy Hunting was held on 20 May by John Clark on his plantation.

Greg Blame has opened a war supplies store by Steve's Black Carriage Store and his store is called Greg's War Supplies.

HORSE KILLS LOCAL MAN

On Tuesday 5 July Tom Haley was killed by a horse. Tom was behind his horse putting medicine on the horse's leg. Tom's brother Jason witnessed the scene of the tragedy. Jason said all of the sudden the horse kicked him in the jaw. The horse was real sick and needed medicine thats probably why it started kicking. Tom's funeral will be 8 July, Saturday.

NEW SCHOOL THREATENED

The G. W. Honeywitt School of Concord opened on 7 September 1774. George Windsor Honeywitt, a former student of the British Conservatory of London, is the headmaster. Twenty students successfully completed their first year.

Honewitt is teaching the students about unfair taxes and unreasonable acts passed by Parliament.

After receiving recent threats from British officers, Mr. Honeywitt is concerned that his school may be destroyed.

Honeywitt, although fearful of the threats, takes pride in his new school, and because of his patriotism, continues to educate his students in the ways of the colonial patriots.

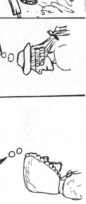

WIGS

New powdered or non-powdered men's or women's wigs just came in. You can find these wigs at Lucy's wig shop.

HENRY,
WHERE'S MY LEB POT?

I MADE BULLITS OF IT, HONEY.

THE WAR HAS BEGUN!

HELP!

DOG—MAN'S BEST FRIEND

It started when Paul Revere said, "Put two lanterns in the church steeple, the sounds of bells might alert the British." After a few long nights of watching from a nearby hill, Paul Revere noticed the lanterns were finally lit. Revere then went home, got his jacket and said good-bye to his wife and children. He took out the door and apparently was followed by his dog. Rever told the dog to return home but the dog would not go. Lucky for Revere his dog was with him as he later discovered he had forgotten his spurs. He tied a note to his dog telling his wife to get his spurs, fasten them to the dog's neck and send the dog back to him. The dog went home and returned with the spurs. Revere took the spurs, got on his horse and was on his mission. He warned the colonists of the British arrival. Revere did his job well.

BOONE AND THE WILDERNESS ROAD

On 16 March 1775 Daniel Boone and a group of pioneers set out to settle Kentucky. Problems arose along the way. Some problems were Indians and wild animal attacks. Other problems were getting wagons and herds through the long travel. With these problems a road was built.

After the road was built Daniel Boone returned to North Carolina. He gather his relatives and neighbors to make a party. They had a rough and difficult trip. Daniel Boone and the pioneers finally settled. People from all around started settling in Kentucky.

ENTERTAINMENT

Picnic - 15 August Village Commons

Horse race on 2 July was held by Clark Stone. Twenty people came and afterwards they ate cake and drank lemonade.

Climbing greased poles. Running after a greased pig is some of the activities. There are also Music and contests. The prices are 5¢ for adults and 3¢ for children.

30 August ballroom of Black Horse New York held by Clint Adams - noon

WEATHER

This summer's weather has been primarily mild, sunny, and calm. The evenings have been warm and partly cloudy. The expected weather for August and September will be mostly sunny with a greater chance of rain. Farmers be sure to plant early this fall.

FASHION

Fashions – A new fashion has just arrived from France. Hats that look like bonnets with lace strings that you can tie around your neck. They also have pocket-hoop farthingales to make your dress stick out. You can get the set at Southern Belle and at Jan's Tailor Shop.

SHOES

Women's shoes – Women wear shoes that look like sandals and high heels. You can find them at the Shoe Shop.

New leather shoes have just arrived from France. These shoes have gold or silver buckles. The colors are brown, dark blue, and black. You can find the shoes at Mr. Brown's shoe shop.

Inventions

Bow Beater
by George Herald

A new egg beater has been made. It is a bow drill mixed with an egg beater to make a bow beater. To see how you can build your own, come to the farm by the courthouse.

Benjamin Franklin invented a chair with a table hooked onto it. It looks like this.

A student clips newspaper articles to use in examining their characteristics.

or recopied neatly by hand. Word-processing programs such as *The Newsroom* (1984) help simplify formatting the newspaper.

    5. *Compile the newspaper from articles and illustrations.* The editorial staff meets to make final decisions about which articles to include in this issue of the newspaper and what additional work needs to be done. After the articles are selected, they must be arranged on sheets of paper, using either traditional cut-and-paste layouts or a word-processing program. Then the newspaper is duplicated and distributed.

    Assessing Students' Newspaper Articles.   As with other types of projects, students need to know the requirements for the newspaper project and how they will be assessed before beginning to work. Again, a checklist approach. The checklist might require the following components:

- Cut out samples of five kinds of newspaper articles and paste them in your learning log.

- Make a "5Ws Plus One" cluster for your article.

- Write one article for the newspaper.

- Participate in a writing group to revise your article.

- Make at least 2 revisions.

- Edit your article with a classmate.

- Draw an illustration to go with your article.

- Write 3 possible titles for your article.

- Type or recopy your article for the newspaper.

Students keep the checklist in their project folders and check off each item as they complete it. At the end of the project, students submit their folders to be assessed or graded.

❖ LETTERS

Letters are a way of talking to people who live too far away to visit. Audience and function are important considerations, but form is also important in letter writing. Although letters may be personal, they involve a genuine audience of one or more persons. Students have the opportunity not only to sharpen their writing skills through letter writing, but also to increase their awareness of audience. Because letters are written to communicate with a specific and important audience, students take more care to think through what they want to say; to use spelling, capitalization, and punctuation conventions correctly; and to write legibly.

Elementary students' letters are typically classified as friendly or business letters. Formats for friendly and business letters are shown in Figure 10–8; choice of format depends on the function of the letter. Friendly letters might be informal, chatty letters to pen pals or thank-you notes to a television newscaster who has visited the classroom. When students write to General Mills requesting information about the nutritional content of breakfast cereals or letters to the President expressing an opinion about current events, they use the more formal, business letter style. Before students write either type of letter, they need to learn how to format them.

Friendly and business letter formats are accepted writing conventions, and most teachers simply explain the formats to students and prepare a set of charts to illustrate them. Attention to format should not suggest, however, that form is more important than content; rather, it should highlight formatting considerations of letter writing that elementary students are typically unfamiliar with.

Friendly Letters

Children write friendly letters to classmates, friends who live out of town, relatives, and pen pals. Students may want to keep a list of addresses of people to write friendly letters to on a special page in their journals or in address booklets. In these casual letters, they share news about events in their lives and ask questions to learn more

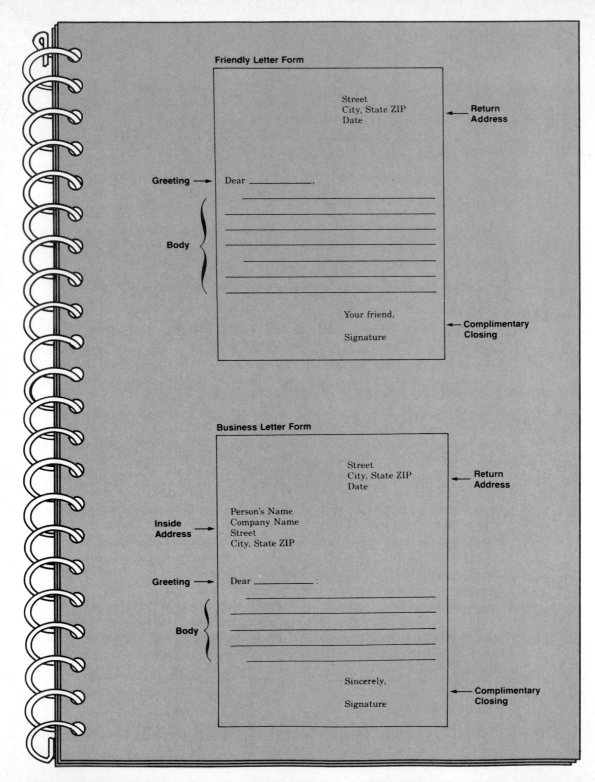

FIGURE 10–8

Teacher's Notebook Page: Forms for Friendly and Business Letters

about the person they are writing to and to encourage that person to write back. Receiving mail is the real reward for letter writing!

After introducing the friendly letter format, students need to choose a "real" someone to write to. Writing authentic letters that will be delivered is much more valuable than writing practice letters to be graded by the teacher. Students may draw names and write letters to classmates, to pen pals from another class in the same or another school, or to friends and relatives.

Students use the writing process in letter writing. In the prewriting stage, they decide what to include in their letters. Brainstorming and clustering are effective strategies to help students choose information to include and questions to ask. Figure 10–9 shows a cluster with four rays developed by a third grade class for pen pal letters. As a class, the students brainstormed a list of possible topics and finally decided on the four main idea rays (me and my family, my school, my hobbies, and questions for my pen pal). Then students completed the clusters by adding details to each main idea. Their rough drafts incorporated the information from one ray into the first paragraph, information from a second ray into the second paragraph, and so on for the body of the letters. After writing their rough drafts, students met in writing groups to revise content and edited to correct mechanical errors, first with a classmate and later with the teacher. Next, they recopied their final drafts, addressed envelopes, and mailed them. A sample letter is also presented in Figure 10–9. Comparing each paragraph of the letter with the cluster reveals that using the cluster helped the student write a well-organized and interesting letter that was packed with information.

Pen Pal Letters. Teachers can arrange for their students to exchange letters with students in another class by contacting a teacher in a nearby school, through local educational associations, or by answering advertisements in educational magazines.

Individual students can also arrange for pen pals by contacting one of the following organizations:

International Friendship League
22 Batterymarch
Boston, MA 02109

League of Friendship
PO Box 509
Mt. Vernon, OH 43050

Student Letter Exchange
910 Fourth Street SE
Austin, MN 55912

World Pen Pals
1690 Como Avenue
St. Paul, MN 55108

Students should write to one of the organizations, describing their interests and including name, address, age, and sex. They should ask if a fee is required and enclose a self-addressed, stamped envelope (identified by the acronym SASE) for a reply.

Another possible arrangement is to have an elementary class become pen pals with college students in a language arts methods class. Over a semester, the elementary students and preservice teachers can write back and forth to each other four, five, or six times, and perhaps can even meet each other at the end of the semester. The children have the opportunity to be pen pals with college students, and the college students have the opportunity to get to know an elementary student and examine the student's writing. In a recent study (Greenlee, Hiebert, Bridge, & Winograd, 1986), a class of

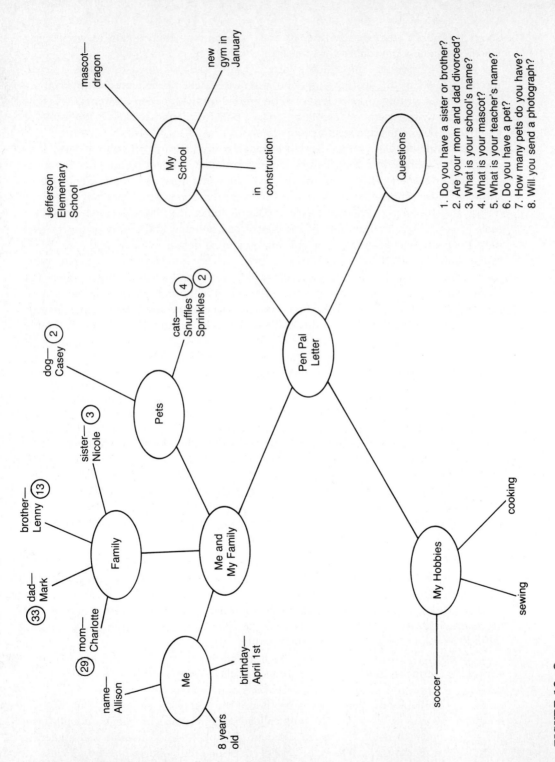

FIGURE 10–9

A Third Grader's Cluster and Pen Pal Letter

December 10

Dear Annie,

    I'm your pen pal now. My name is Allison and I'm 8 years old. My birthday is on April 1st.

    I go to Jefferson Elementary School. Our mascot is a dragon. We are in construction because we're going to have a new gym in January.

    My hobbies are soccer, sewing, and cooking. I play soccer, sewing I do in free time, and I cook dinner sometimes.

    My pets are two cats and a dog. The dog's name is Casey and he's a boy. He is two years old. The cat is a girl and her name is Snuffles. She is four years old. The kitten is a girl and her name is Sprinkles. She is two months old.

    My dad's name is Mark and my mon's name is Charlotte. Her birthday is the day after Mother's Day. My brother's name is Lenny. He is 13 years old. My sister's name is Nicole. She is 3 years old.

    I have some questions for you. Do you have a sister or a brother? Are your mom and dad divorced? Mine aren't. What is your school's name? What is your mascot? What is your teacher's name? Do you have a pet? How many pets do you have? Will you send me a photograph of yourself?

Your friend,
Allison

FIGURE 10–9 (*continued*)

second graders became pen pals with a class of college students who were majoring in elementary education. The researchers investigated whether having a genuine audience would influence the quality of the letters the students wrote. They compared the second graders' letters to letters written by a control group who wrote letters to imaginary audiences and received traditional teacher comments on their letters. The researchers found that the students who wrote to pen pals wrote longer and more complex letters once they received responses to their letters. The results of this study emphasize the importance of providing real audiences for student writing.

    Courtesy Letters. Invitations and thank-you notes are two other types of friendly letters that elementary students write. They may write to parents to invite them to an after-school program, to the class across the hall to visit a classroom exhibit, or to invite a community person to be interviewed as part of a content area unit. Similarly, children write letters to thank people who have been helpful.

    Letters to Authors and Illustrators. Students write letters to favorite authors and illustrators to share their ideas and feelings about the books they read. They ask questions about how a particular character was developed or why the illustrator used a certain art medium. Students also describe the books they have written. A first grader's letter to Dr. Seuss is presented in Figure 10–10. Most authors and illustrators reply to children's letters when possible; however, they receive thousands of letters from children every year and cannot be pen pals with students.

    Beverly Cleary's award-winning book, *Dear Mr. Henshaw* (1983), offers a worthwhile lesson about what students (and their teachers) can realistically expect from

Dear Dr. Seuss,
I like the SLEEP Book
Becos it is contagus
Amd the illustrations
Are the best of all.
I hav fourde Books
of yours and I have
rede them all.
              Love, Sara

FIGURE 10–10

A First Grader's Letter to Dr. Seuss

authors and illustrators. The following guidelines are suggested when writing to authors and illustrators:

- Follow the correct letter format with return address, greeting, body, closing, and signature.
- Use the process approach to write, revise, and edit the letter. Be sure to proofread and correct errors.
- Recopy the letter so it will be neat and easy to read.
- Write the return address on both envelope and letter.

- Include a stamped, self-addressed envelope for a reply.
- Be polite in the letter; use the words "please" and "thank you."
- Write genuine letters to share thoughts and feelings about the author's writing or the illustrator's artwork. Students should only write to authors and illustrators whose work they are familiar with.

Avoid these pitfalls:

- Do not include a long list of questions to be answered.
- Do not ask personal questions, such as how much money he or she earns.
- Do not ask for advice on how to become a better writer or artist.
- Do not send stories for the author or artwork for the illustrator to critique.
- Do not ask for free books, because authors/illustrators do not have copies of their books to give away.

Send letters to the author/illustrator in care of the publisher. The publisher's name appears on the book's title page; the address usually appears on the copyright page, the page following the title page. If you cannot find the complete mailing address, check *Books in Print* or *Literary Market Place,* reference books that are available in most public libraries. (The suggestions in this list are adapted from Cleary [1983, 1985].)

Young Children's Letters.   Young children can write individual letters, as the first grader's letter to Dr. Seuss in Figure 10–10 illustrates. They prewrite as older students do, by brainstorming or clustering possible ideas before writing. A quick review of how to begin and end letters is also helpful. In contrast with older children's letters, kindergartners and first graders' letters may involve only a single draft, since invented spellings and the artwork may carry much of the message.

Primary-grade students can also compose class collaboration letters. The children brainstorm ideas, which the teacher records on a large chart. After the letter is finished, children add their signatures. They might write collaborative letters to thank community persons who have visited the class, to invite another class to attend a puppet show, or to compliment a favorite author. Class collaboration letters can also serve as pen pal letters to another class.

Two books are useful in introducing young children to letter writing: *The Jolly Postman or Other People's Letters* (Ahlberg & Ahlberg, 1986) is a fantastic storylike introduction to the reasons people write letters, and *Arthur's Pen Pal* (Hoban, 1982) is a delightful way to explain what it means to be a pen pal.

Business Letters

Students write business letters to seek information, to complain and compliment, and to transact business. They use this more formal letter style to communicate with businesses, local newspapers, and governmental agencies. Students may write to businesses to order products, to ask questions, and to complain about or compliment specific products; they write letters to the editors of local newspapers and magazines to comment on articles and to express their opinions. It is important that students support their comments and opinions with facts if they hope to have their letters published. Students can also write to local, state, and national government officials to express concerns, make suggestions, or to seek information.

Addresses of local elected officials are listed in the telephone directory, and addresses of state officials are available in the reference section of the public library. Here are the addresses of the President and U.S. senators and representatives:

President's name, The White House, Washington, DC 20500

Senator's name, Senate Office Building, Washington, DC 20510

Representative's name, House of Representatives Office Building, Washington, DC 20515

Students may also write other types of business letters to request information and free materials. One source of free materials is *Free Stuff for Kids* (Lansky, 1990), which lists more than 250 free or inexpensive materials that elementary students can write for and is updated yearly. Children can also write to NASA, the National Wildlife Federation, publishers, state tourism bureaus, and other businesses to request materials.

Simulated Letters

Students can also write simulated letters, in which they assume the identity of a historical or literary figure. They can write letters as though they were Davy Crockett or another of the men defending the Alamo, or Thomas Edison, inventor of the electric light. Students can write from one book character to another; for example, after reading *Sarah, Plain and Tall* (MacLachlan, 1985), students can assume the persona of Sarah and write a letter to her brother William, as this third grader did in this letter:

Dear William,

I'm having fun here. There was a very big storm here. It was so big it looked like the sea. Sometimes I am very lonesome for home but sometimes it is very fun here in Ohio. We swam in the cow pond and I taught Caleb how to swim. They were afraid I would leave. Maggie and Matthew brought some chickens.

Love,
Sarah

Even though these letters are never mailed, they provide an opportunity for students to focus on a specific audience. After they write their original letters, students can exchange letters among classmates and reply to the letters.

Teaching Students to Write Letters

Students use the process approach to write both friendly and business letters.

1. *Gather and organize information for the letter.* Students participate in prewriting activities, such as brainstorming or clustering, to decide what information to

include in their letters. If they are writing friendly letters, particularly to pen pals, they also identify several questions to include.

2. *Review the friendly or business letter form.* Before writing the rough drafts of their letters, students review the friendly or business letter form.

3. *Write the letters using a process approach.* Students write a rough draft, incorporating the information developed during prewriting and following either the friendly or business letter style. Next, students meet in a writing group to share their rough drafts, receive compliments, and get feedback. They make changes based on the feedback and edit their letters with a partner, proofreading to identify errors and correcting as many as possible. They also make sure they have used the appropriate letter format. After making all the mechanical corrections, students recopy their letters and address envelopes. The crucial last step is to mail the letters.

Assessing Students' Letters.   Traditionally, students wrote letters and turned them in for the teacher to grade. The letters were returned to the students after they were graded, but they were never mailed. Educators now recognize the importance of having an audience for student writing, and research suggests that students write better when they know their writing will be read by someone other than the teacher. Whereas it is often necessary to assess student writing, it would be inappropriate for the teacher to put a grade on the letter if it is going to be mailed to someone. Teachers can instead develop a checklist for evaluating students' letters without marking on them.

A third grade teacher developed the checklist in Figure 10–11, which identifies specific behaviors and measurable products. The teacher shares the checklist with students before they begin to write so they know what is expected of them and how they will be graded. At an evaluation conference before the letters were mailed, the teacher reviewed the checklist with each student. The letters were mailed without evaluative comments or grades written on them, but the completed checklist went into students' writing folders. A grading scale can be developed from the checklist; for example, points can be awarded for each checkmark in the *yes* column or five checkmarks can be determined to equal a grade of A, four checkmarks a B, and so on.

❖ LIFE-STORIES

Elementary students enjoy sharing information about their lives and learning about the lives of well-known personalities. As they read life-stories written for young people, students examine their structure and use the books as models for their own writing. Life-stories combine expository writing with some elements of narration.

Authors use several different approaches in writing autobiographies and biographies (Fleming & McGinnis, 1985). The most common approach is historical; the writer focuses on dates and events and presents them chronologically. Many autobiographies and biographies that span the person's entire life follow this pattern.

A second pattern is the sociological approach, wherein the writer describes life during a historical period, providing information about family life, food, clothing, ed-

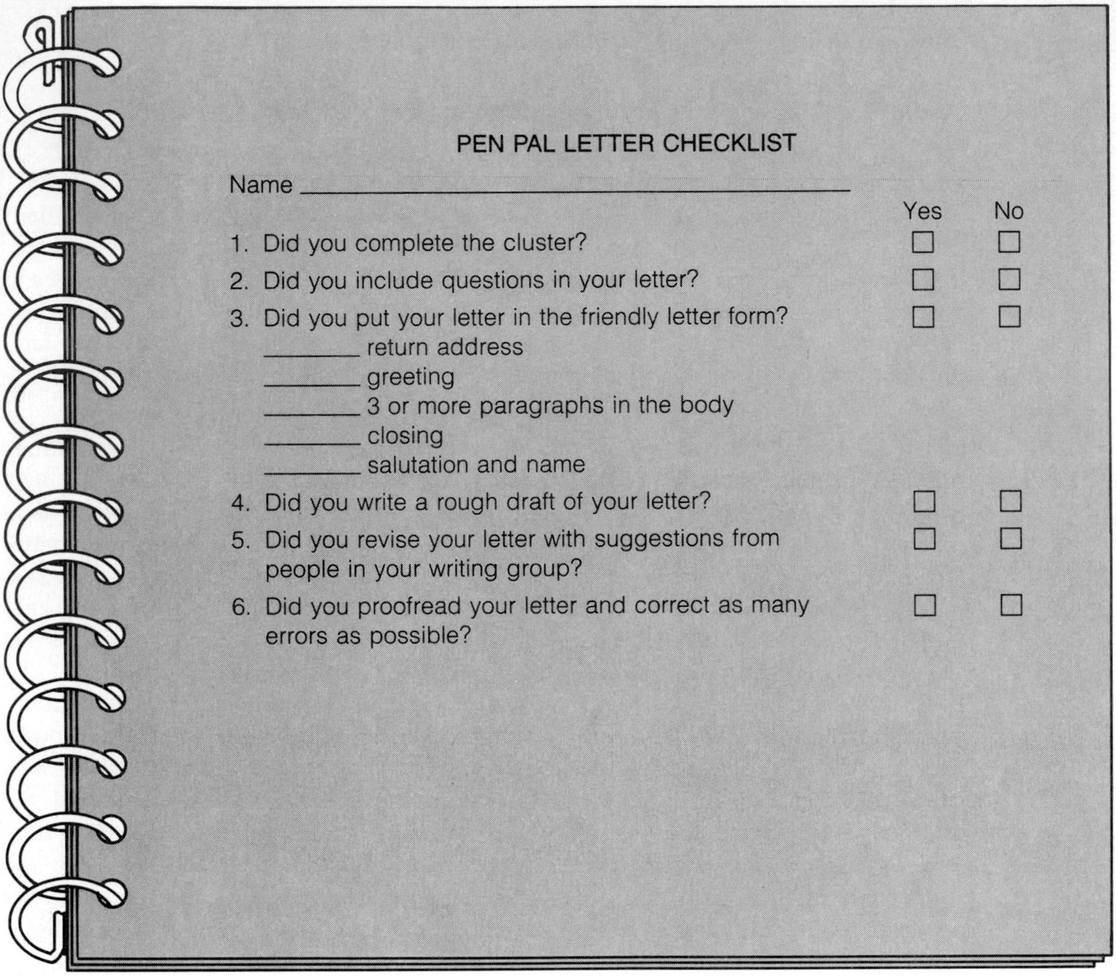

PEN PAL LETTER CHECKLIST

Name _____

		Yes	No
1.	Did you complete the cluster?	☐	☐
2.	Did you include questions in your letter?	☐	☐
3.	Did you put your letter in the friendly letter form?	☐	☐

_____ return address
_____ greeting
_____ 3 or more paragraphs in the body
_____ closing
_____ salutation and name

		Yes	No
4.	Did you write a rough draft of your letter?	☐	☐
5.	Did you revise your letter with suggestions from people in your writing group?	☐	☐
6.	Did you proofread your letter and correct as many errors as possible?	☐	☐

FIGURE 10–11

Teacher's Notebook Page: A Checklist for Assessing Students' Pen Pal Letters

ucation, economics, transportation, and so on. For instance, *Worlds Apart: The Autobiography of a Dancer from Brooklyn* (Maiorano, 1980) describes the author's childhood in an impoverished New York City neighborhood and how he escapes it through a career with the Metropolitan Opera Company.

A third approach is psychological: the writer focuses on conflicts the central figure faces. Conflicts may be with oneself, others, nature, or society. (We have already discussed conflict in Chapter 7.) The psychological approach has many elements in common with stories and is most often used in shorter autobiographies and biographies that revolve around particular events or phases. An example is the single event biography, *And Then What Happened, Paul Revere?* (Fritz, 1973), in which Paul Revere faces a conflict with the British army.

Autobiography

When students write an autobiography, they relive and document their lives, usually in a chronological order. They describe the memorable events that are necessary to know them. A second grader's autobiography is shown in Figure 10–12. In six chapters, Eddie describes himself and his family, his pets, his "favorites" and hobbies, and vacations to a Texas town. Autobiographical writing grows out of children's personal journal entries and "All about Me" books that they write in kindergarten and first grade. Their primary source of information for writing is their own experiences.

"All about Me" Books. Children in kindergarten and first grade often compile "All about Me" books. These first autobiographies usually list information such as the child's birthday, family members, friends, and favorite activities, with drawings as well as text. Figure 10–13 shows two pages from a first grader's "All about Me" book. To write these books, the children and the teacher decide on a topic for each page and, after brainstorming possible ideas for the topic, children draw a picture and write about it. Children may also need to ask their parents for information about their birth and events during their preschool years.

Biography

A biography is an account of a person's life written by someone else, and writers try to make the account as accurate and authentic as possible. Writers consult a variety of sources of information to research a biography. The best source, of course, is the biography's subject, and writers can learn many things about the person through an interview. Other primary sources include diaries and letters, photographs, mementos, historical records, and recollections of people who know the person. Secondary sources are books, newspapers, and films written by someone other than the biographical subject.

Biographies are categorized as contemporary or historical. Contemporary biographies are written about a living person, especially someone the writer can interview. Historical biographies are about persons who are no longer alive, and the information must come from secondary sources.

Contemporary Biographies. Students write biographies about living people they know personally as well as about famous personalities. In contrast to the primary sources of information available for gathering information about local people, students may have to depend on secondary sources (e.g., books, newspapers, letters) for information about well-known and geographically more distant persons. Sometimes, however, students can write letters to well-known personalities or perhaps arrange conference telephone calls.

Historical Biographies. Whereas biographies are based on known facts, some parts of historical biographies must necessarily be fictionalized. Dialogue and other details about daily life, for example, must often be invented after careful research of the period. In *The Double Life of Pocahontas* (Fritz, 1983), for instance, the author had to take what sketchy facts are known about Pocahontas and make some reasonable guesses to fill in the missing ones. To give one example, historians know that Pocahontas was a young woman when she died in 1617, but they are unsure how old she was

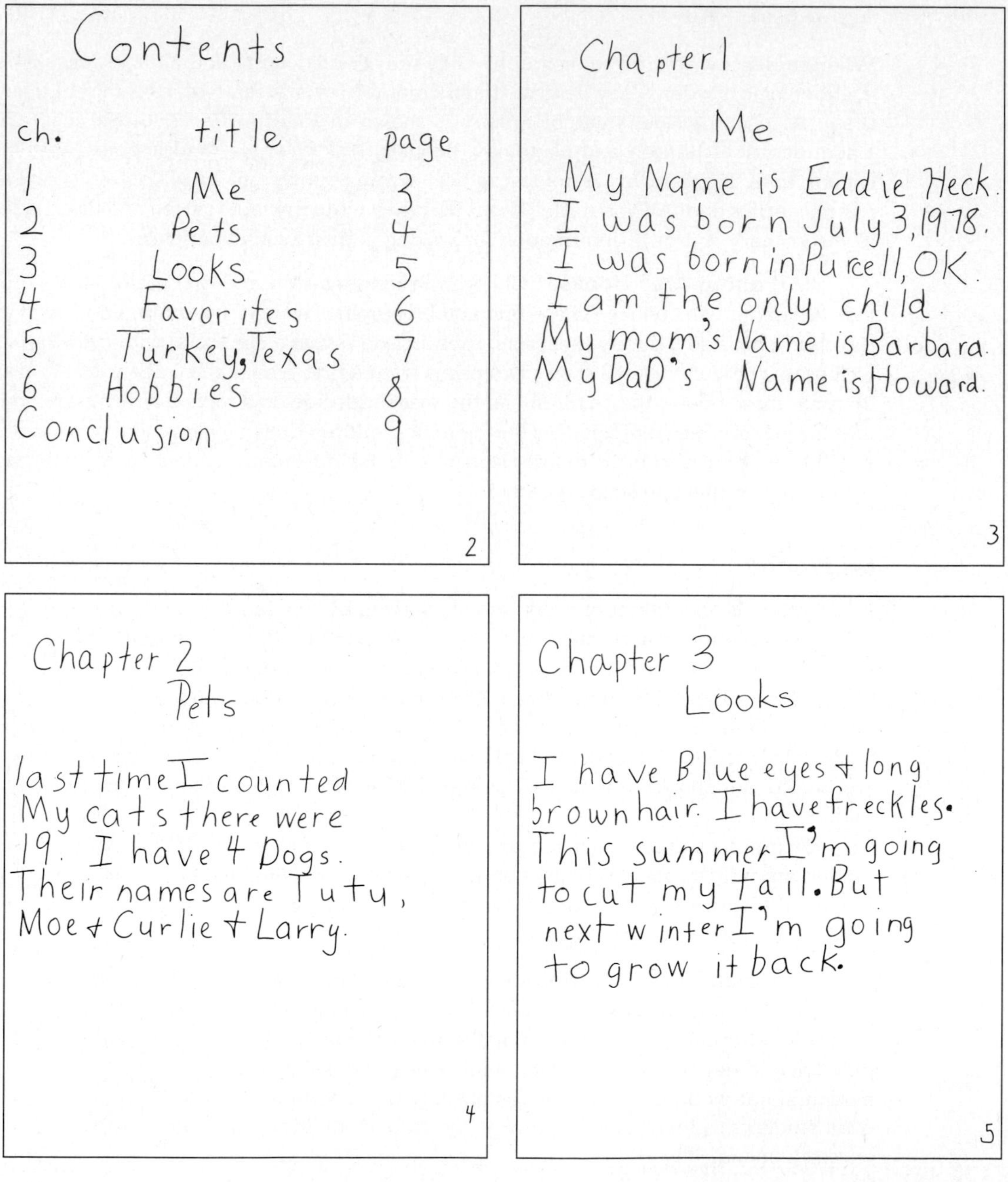

Contents

ch.	title	page
1	Me	3
2	Pets	4
3	Looks	5
4	Favorites	6
5	Turkey, Texas	7
6	Hobbies	8
Conclusion		9

2

Chapter1

Me

My Name is Eddie Heck.
I was born July 3, 1978.
I was born in Purcell, OK.
I am the only child.
My mom's Name is Barbara.
My DaD's Name is Howard.

3

Chapter 2

Pets

last time I counted
My cats there were
19. I have 4 Dogs.
Their names are Tutu,
Moe + Curlie + Larry.

4

Chapter 3

Looks

I have Blue eyes + long
brown hair. I have freckles.
This summer I'm going
to cut my tail. But
next winter I'm going
to grow it back.

5

FIGURE 10–12

A Second Grader's Autobiography

Chapter 4

Favorites

My favorite president is Georrge Washington. My favorite pet is a Dog. My favorite thing is my Bike. My favorite toy is G.I. LoE. My favorite color is black. My favorite Game is NINJA.

6

Chapter 5

Turkey, Texas

I went to Turkey, Texas for My first time at 2½ yrs. old. I liked it so much we have gone ever since. I went to see BoB Wills and his Texas Play Boys but BoB Wills is dead now.

7

Chapter 6

Hobbies

My favorite hobbies are inventing games. I've invented these games: NINJA & Goldtar defender of The Universe. These are Games that some times I play by my self and some times I play with my friends.

8

Conclusion

The day after school is out I'm going to Dog-Patch, Arkansas to see Daisy Mae and Mammy Yoakum. I may go to Six Flags this summer. I may also go to Frontier City. I will be looking forward to school starting.

9

FIGURE 10–12 *(continued)*

I have 3 best friends. they are very nice to do things with me. My friends names are Randy, Kasey, and Kimberly. I go to Randy's house every morning. Her mom baby sits me.

FIGURE 10—13

Two Pages from a First Grader's "All about Me" Book

when John Smith and the other English settlers arrived in Virginia in 1607. Fritz chose to make her eleven years old when the settlers arrived.

When children write historical biographies, they will have to make some of the same types of reasonable guesses that Fritz did. In the following biography of Daniel Boone, a third grader added details and dialogue to complete his report:

> *Daniel Boone was born in 1734 in Omley, Pennsylvania. When Daniel grew up, he hunted a lot. He began his journey to Kentucky to hunt for game.*
>
> *Every day, Daniel tried to hunt for game in Kentucky. In the morning, he would catch two or three deers. At night, he wouldn't hunt because all the animals would be hiding. Daniel wouldn't give up hunting for game in Kentucky.*
>
> *Finally, he decided to travel through Kentucky. Soon Indians took their meat and furs away. Would Daniel and his family survive?*
>
> *One day when Daniel was walking to his fellow friend's fort, he looked all around. Indians were surrounding him. One Indian called Chief Blackfish said, "Take me to your men. If you do, I will not hurt you or them. If you don't, I will kill you and your friends." Daniel was trapped. When they were walking to the fort, Daniel ran inside. Just then, gunshots were fired. They were at war. Soon the war was over. Daniel's people had won.*
>
> *Daniel died in 1820 at the age of 85. Daniel Boone is remembered for opening the land of Kentucky for white men to hunt in and fighting for Kentucky.*

This is my Grammy's house. I have my own room in it. Sometimes I sleep on the love seat. I like to see papa. Sometimes my papa takes me fishing. I love to go fishing. My Grammy makes me feel special.

FIGURE 10—13   (*continued*)

When students study someone else's life in preparation for writing a biography, they need to become personally involved in the project (Zarnowski, 1988). There are several ways to engage students in biographical study; that is, to help them walk in the subject's footsteps. For contemporary biographies, meeting and interviewing the person is the best way; for other projects, students read books about the person, view films and videos, dramatize events from the person's life, and write about the persons they are studying. An especially valuable activity is simulated journals, in which students assume the role of the person they are studying and write journal entries just as that person might have. (See Chapter 6 for more information about simulated journals.)

Teaching Students to Write Life-stories

Students learn to write life-stories through a process approach. The instructional strategy is similar for writing autobiographies and biographies, but the two forms are different and should be taught separately.

1. *Read to learn about the format and unique conventions.* Others' autobiographies and biographies can serve as models for the life-stories students write. Many autobiographies of scientists, entertainers, sports figures, and others are available for upper-grade students, but, unfortunately, only a few autobiographies have been written for younger children. A list of suggested autobiographies appears in Figure 10—14; some are entire-life and others are shorter-event types. When students read

Autobiographies

Ali, M. (with R. Durham). (1976). *The greatest: Muhammad Ali.* New York:
    Ballantine. (M–U)
Begley, K. A. (1977). *Deadline.* New York: Putnam. (U)
Bulla, C. R. (1985). *A grain of wheat: A writer begins.* New York: Godine. (U)
Chukosky, K. (1976). *The silver crest: My Russian boyhood* (B. Stillman, Trans.).
    New York: Holt, Rinehart and Winston. (U)
Collins, M. (1976). *Flying to the moon and other strange places.* New York: Farrar,
    Straus & Giroux. (M–U)
de Paola, T. (1989). *The art lesson.* New York: Putnam. (P–M)
Fisher, L. E. (1972). *The death of evening star: Diary of a young New England
    whaler.* New York: Doubleday. (U)
Fritz, J. (1982). *Homesick: My own story.* New York: Putnam. (M–U)
Gish, L. (1988). *An actor's life for me.* New York: Viking. (U)
Goodall, J. (1988). *My life with the chimpanzees.* New York: Simon and Schuster.
Hamill, D. (with E. Clairmont). (1983). *Dorothy Hamill: On and off the ice.* New
    York: Knopf. (M)
James, N. (1979). *Alone around the world.* New York: Coward-McCann. (U)
Jenner, B. (with R. S. Kiliper). (1980). *The Olympics and me.* New York:
    Doubleday. (M)
Keller, H. (1980). *The story of my life.* New York: Watermill Press. (M–U)
Maiorano, R. (1980). *Worlds apart: The autobiography of a dancer from Brooklyn.*
    New York: Coward-McCann. (U)
Nuynh, Q. N. (1982). *The land I lost: Adventures of a boy in Vietnam.* New York:
    Harper and Row. (M–U)
O'Kelley, M. L. (1983). *From the hills of Georgia: An autobiography in paintings.*
    Boston: Little, Brown. (P–M–U)
Peet, B. (1989). *An autobiography.* Boston: Houghton Mifflin. (M)
Rudolph, W. (1977). *Wilma: The story of Wilma Rudolph.* New York: New
    American Library. (U)
Schulz, C. M. (with R. S. Kiliper). (1980). *Charlie Brown, Snoopy and me: And all
    the other Peanuts characters.* New York: Doubleday. (M–U)
Singer, I. B. (1969). *A day of pleasure: Stories of a boy growing up in Warsaw.*
    New York: Farrar, Straus & Giroux. (U)
Sullivan, T., & Gill, D. (1975). *If you could see what I hear.* New York: Harper and
    Row. (U)

FIGURE 10–14

Recommended Life-Stories for Elementary Students

P = primary grades (K–2)
M = middle grades (3–5)
U = upper grades (6–8)

Biographies

Adler, D. A. (1989). *A picture book of Martin Luther King.* New York: Holiday House. (See other biographies by the same author.) (P–M)

Aliki. (1988). *The many lives of Benjamin Franklin.* New York: Simon and Schuster. (See other biographies by the same author.) (M)

Blassingame, W. (1979). *Thor Heyerdahl: Viking scientist.* New York: Elsevier/ Nelson. (M–U)

Burleigh, R. (1985). *A man named Thoreau.* New York: Atheneum. (U)

D'Aulaire, I., & D'Aulaire, E. P. (1936). *George Washington.* New York: Doubleday. (See other biographies by the same authors.) (P–M)

Dobrin, A. (1975). *I am a stranger on Earth: The story of Vincent Van Gogh.* New York: Warne. (M–U)

Felton, H. W. (1976). *Deborah Sampson: Soldier of the revolution.* New York: Dodd, Mead. (M)

Freedman, R. (1987). *Lincoln: A photobiography.* New York: Clarion. (M–U)

Fritz, J. (1973). *And then what happened, Paul Revere?* New York: Coward-McCann. (See other biographies by the same author.) (P–M)

Giff, P. R. (1987). *Laura Ingalls Wilder.* New York: Viking. (M)

Greenberg, K. E. (1986). *Michael J. Fox.* Minneapolis: Lerner. (M)

Greenfield, E. (1977). *Mary McLeod Bethune.* New York: Crowell. (P–M)

Hamilton, V. (1974). *Paul Robeson: The life and times of a free black man.* New York: Harper and Row. (U)

Jakes, J. (1986). *Susanna of the Alamo: A true story.* New York: Harcourt Brace Jovanovich. (M)

Mitchell, B. (1986). *Click: A story about George Eastman.* Minneapolis: Carolrhoda Books. (M)

Peterson, H. S. (1967). *Abigail Adams. "Dear partner."* Champaign, IL: Garrard. (M)

Provensen, A., & Provensen, M. (1984). *Leonardo da Vinci.* New York: Viking. (A moveable book) (M–U)

Quackenbush, R. (1981). *Ahoy! Ahoy! are you there? A story of Alexander Graham Bell.* Englewood Cliffs, NJ: Prentice-Hall. (See other biographies by the same author.) (P–M)

Stanley, D. (1986). *Peter the great.* New York: Four Winds. (P–M)

FIGURE 10–14 (*continued*)

autobiographies, they should note which events the narrator focuses on, how the narrator presents information and feelings, and what the narrator's viewpoint is.

Biographies of well-known people such as explorers, kings and queens, scientists, sports figures, artists, and movie stars, as well as "common" people who have endured hardship and shown exceptional courage, are available for elementary students to read. Figure 10–14 also lists biographies. Biographers Jean Fritz and the D'Aulaires have written many excellent biographies for primary and middle-grade students, some of which are noted in the list, and numerous authors have written biographies for older students. Students' autobiographies and biographies from previous years are another source of books for your class to read. Students can often be persuaded to bring their prized life-stories back the following year to share with your students.

2. *Gather information for the life-story.* Students gather information about themselves or about the person they will write about in several different ways. Students are the best source of information about their own life, but they may need to get information from parents and other family members. Parents often share information from baby books and photo albums, and older brothers and sisters can share their remembrances. Another strategy students can use to gather information for an autobiography is to collect objects that symbolize their life and hang them on a "lifeline" clothesline or put them in a life-box made from a shoebox (Fleming, 1985). They can then write briefly about each object, explaining what it is and how it relates to their lives. They can also decorate the box with words and pictures clipped from magazines to create an autobiographical collage.

For biographical writing, students can interview their subject, either in person or by telephone and letter. To write a historical biography, students read books to learn about the person and the time period in which he or she lived. Other sources of information are films, videotapes, and newspaper and magazine articles. Students also need to keep a record of their sources for the bibliography they will include with their biographies.

Lifelines.   Students sequence the information they gather, either about their life or someone else's, on a lifeline or timeline. This activity helps students identify and sequence milestones and other events. They can use the information on the lifeline to identify topics for the life-story.

3.   *Organize the information for the life-story.* Students select from their lifelines the topics they will write about and develop a cluster with each topic as a main idea. They add details from the information they have gathered; if they do not have four or five details for each topic, they can search for additional information. When students aren't sure if they have enough information, they can cluster the topic using the "5Ws Plus One" questions (who, what, when, where, why, and how) and try to answer the six questions. If they can complete the cluster, they are ready to write; if they cannot, they need to gather additional information. After developing the cluster, students decide on the sequence of topics and add an introduction and conclusion.

4.   *Write the life-story using the writing process.* Students use their clusters to write their rough drafts. The main ideas become topic sentences for paragraphs, and details are expanded into sentences. After they write the rough draft, students meet in writing groups to get feedback on their writing, then make revisions. Next, they edit and recopy. They add drawings, photographs, or other memorabilia. Students also add a bibliography to a biography, listing their sources of information. Besides making the final copy of their life-stories, students can share what they have learned in other ways. They might dress up as the subject of their biography and tell the person's story or let classmates interview them.

This middle-grade class is planning a TV show during which students will dress up as well-known historical figures.

Assessing Students' Life-stories.   Students need to know the requirements for their autobiography or biography project and how they will be assessed or graded. A checklist for an autobiography might include the following components:

- Make a lifeline showing at least one important event for each year of your life.
- Draw a cluster showing at least three main-idea topics and at least five details for each topic.
- Write a rough draft with an introduction, three or more chapters, and a conclusion.
- Meet in a writing group to share your autobiography.
- Make at least three changes in your rough draft.
- Complete an editing checklist with a partner.
- Write a final copy with photos or drawings as illustrations.
- Add an "All about the Author" page.
- Compile your autobiography as a book.
- Decorate the cover.

The checklist for a biography might list the following requirements:

- Learn about the person's life from at least three sources (and no more than one encyclopedia).
- Make a lifeline listing at least ten important events.
- Write at least ten simulated journal entries as the person you are studying.

- Make a cluster with at least three main-idea topics and at least five details for each topic.

- Write a rough draft with at least three chapters and a bibliography.

- Meet in a writing group to share your biography.

- Make at least three changes in your rough draft.

- Complete an editing checklist with a partner.

- Recopy the biography.

- Add an "All about the Author" page.

Students keep the checklist in their project folders and check off each item as it is completed; at the end of the project, they submit the folders to be assessed or graded. Teachers can award credit for each item on the checklist, as we discussed regarding research reports. This approach helps students assume greater responsibility for their own learning and gives them a better understanding of why they receive a particular grade.

❖ REVIEW

Informative writing conveys information. Four types of informative writing are research reports, newspapers, letters, and life-stories. Students read informative books in social studies, science, and other content areas and apply what they have learned in writing research reports. Young children's reports are often written as "All about . . ." books, and older students write collaborative and individual reports. Students read newspaper articles, learn the structures of the articles, and write their own newspapers, either to share current events or as simulated newspapers.

Two types of letters that elementary students write are friendly letters to pen pals and to favorite authors, and business letters to request information, to complain and compliment, and to transact business.

Autobiographies and biographies are life-stories. Students read life-stories to learn about this writing form, then they write their own. Students use the writing process in all four types of informative writing, to draft, refine, and polish. After writing, it is crucial to share the compositions with genuine audiences.

❖ EXTENSIONS

1. Follow the guidelines in this chapter to write a class collaboration report on a social studies topic, such as modes of transportation, types of houses, or the countries in Europe, or on a science topic, such as the solar system or the human body.

2. Choose a topic related to teaching language arts in the elementary school, such as journals, writing across the curriculum, the writing process, or the uses of drama. Research the topic following the guidelines in this chapter and write an "All about . . ." book or report.

3. Write and publish a class newspaper according to the guidelines in this chapter, or write and publish a simulated newspaper in conjunction with a social studies unit.

4. Have students interview a community leader and then write a collaborative biography.

5. Arrange for a group of students to write friendly letters to pen pals in another school. Review the friendly letter form and how to address an envelope. Use the writing process in which students draft, revise, and edit their letters before mailing them.

6. Have a small group of students develop a lifeline for a historical character or other famous person, choose several events from the lifeline to write about, and compile the writings to form a biography.

7. Read one of the biographies or autobiographies listed in Figure 10–14. Then develop a lifeline or a cluster about the subject's life (similar to the cluster about Florence Nightingale in Chapter 6).

❖ REFERENCES

Ahlberg, J., & Ahlberg, A. (1986). *The jolly postman or other people's letters*. Boston: Little, Brown.

Bonin, S. (1988). Beyond storyland: Young writers can tell it other ways. In T. Newkirk & N. Atwell (Eds.), *Understanding writing* (2nd ed.), pp. 47–51. Portsmouth, NH: Heinemann.

Britton, J. (1970). *Language and learning*. New York: Penguin Books.

Cleary, B. (1983). *Dear Mr. Henshaw*. New York: Morrow.

Cleary, B. (1985). Dear author, answer this letter now . . . *Instructor, 95*, 22–23, 25.

Fleming, M. (1985). Writing assignments focusing on autobiographical and biographical topics. In M. Fleming, & J. McGinnis (Eds.), *Portraits: Biography and autobiography in the secondary school*, pp. 95–97. Urbana, IL: National Council of Teachers of English.

Fleming, M., & McGinnis J. (Eds.). (1985). *Portraits: Biography and autobiography in the secondary school*. Urbana, IL: National Council of Teachers of English.

Fritz, J. (1973). *And then what happened, Paul Revere?* New York: Putnam.

Fritz, J. (1983). *The double life of Pocahontas*. New York: Putnam.

Fulwiler, T. (1985). Research writing. In M. Schwartz (Ed.), *Writing for many roles*, pp. 207–230. Upper Montclair, NJ: Boynton/Cook.

Greenlee, M. E., Hiebert, E. H., Bridge, C. A., & Winograd, P. N. (1986). The effects of different audiences on young writers' letter writing. In J. A. Niles & R. V. Lalik (Eds.), *Solving problems in literacy: Learners, teachers, and researchers*, pp. 281–289. Rochester, NY: National Reading Conference.

Hoban, L. (1982). *Arthur's pen pal*. New York: Harper and Row.

Krogness, M. M. (1987). Folklore: A matter of the heart and the heart of the matter. *Language Arts, 64*, 808–818.

Lansky, B. (1990). *Free stuff for kids*. New York: Simon and Schuster.

MacLachlan, P. (1985). *Sarah, plain and tall*. New York: Harper and Row.

Maiorano, R. (1980). *Worlds apart: The autobiography of a dancer from Brooklyn*. New York: Coward-McCann.

The newsroom (1984). [Computer program]. New York: Scholastic.

Queenan, M. (1986). Finding grain in the marble. *Language Arts, 63*, 666–673.

Sowers, S. (1985). The story and the 'all about' book. In J. Hansen, T. Newkirk, & D. Graves (Eds.), *Breaking ground: Teachers relate reading and writing in the elementary school*, pp. 73–82. Portsmouth, NH: Heinemann.

Zarnowski, M. (1988, February). The middle school student as biographer. *Middle School Journal, 19*, 25–27.

11 READING AND WRITING POETRY

SHARING POETRY
   Children's Favorite Poems
   Ways to Share Poetry

PLAYING WITH WORDS
   Inventing New Words
   Laughing with Language
   Creating Word Pictures
   Experimenting with Rhyme

WRITING POETRY
   Formula Poems
   Free-form Poems
   Syllable- and Word-count Poems
   Rhymed Verse Forms
   Model Poems
   Teaching Students to Write Poems
   Assessing Students' Poems

POETIC DEVICES
   Comparison
   Alliteration
   Onomatopoeia
   Repetition
   Rhyme

◆ IN THIS CHAPTER, WE SUGGEST WAYS TO INVOLVE ELEMENTARY
students with poetry. As students read and write poetry, they play with words
and learn about poetic devices.

◆ AS YOU ARE READING, THINK ABOUT THESE QUESTIONS:

What poems do students like best?

How can teachers share poetry with students?

How can students experiment with words?

What types of poems can elementary students write?

How do teachers teach students to write poems?

What poetic devices can elementary students use in their writing?

This is a golden era of poetry for children. Today more poets are writing for children, and more books of poetry for children are being published than ever before. No longer is poetry confined to rhyming verse about daffodils, clouds, and love. Recently published poems about dinosaurs, Halloween, chocolate, and insects are very popular with children.

Children, too, are writing poetry as never before. The current attention on the writing process and publishing students' writing makes poetry a natural choice. Poems are usually short and can easily be revised and edited. They lend themselves to anthologies more readily than stories and other longer forms of writing. Too often children write only haiku and other syllable-counting formula poems. Instead, through a variety of poetry writing activities, students can paint word pictures, make comparisons, and express themselves in imaginative and poignant ways.

❖ SHARING POETRY

Children grow rather naturally into poetry. The Opies (1959) have verified what we know from observing children: children have a natural affinity to verse, songs, riddles, jokes, chants, and puns. Preschoolers are introduced to poetry when their parents repeat Mother Goose rhymes, read *The House at Pooh Corner* (Milne, 1956) and the Dr. Seuss stories, and sing little songs to them. During the elementary grades, youngsters often create jump-rope rhymes and other ditties on the playground.

Children's Favorite Poems

Poems for children assume many different forms. The most common type of poetry is *rhymed verse,* such as Robert Louis Stevenson's "Where Go the Boats?", Vachel Lindsay's "The Little Turtle," and "Mummy Slept Late and Daddy Fixed Breakfast" by John Ciardi. Poems that tell a story are *narrative poems;* examples are Clement Moore's "The Night Before Christmas," "The Pied Piper of Hamelin" by Robert Browning, and Henry Wadsworth Longfellow's "The Song of Hiawatha." A Japanese form, haiku, is popular in anthologies of poetry for children. *Haiku* is a three-line poem that contains just 17 syllables. Because of its brevity, it has been considered an appropriate form of poetry for children to read and write. *Free verse* has lines that do not rhyme, and rhythm is less important than in other types of poetry. Images take on greater importance in free form verse. Langston Hughes's "Subway Rush Hour" and "This Is Just to Say" by William Carlos Williams are two examples of free verse. Other forms of poetry include *limericks,* a short five-line rhymed verse form popularized by Edward Lear, and *concrete poems,* poems arranged on the page to create a picture or image. Figure 11–1 lists books of poetry for elementary students.

Many poets are writing for children today, among them, Arnold Adoff, Byrd Baylor, Gwendolyn Brooks, John Ciardi, Aileen Fisher, Karla Kuskin, Myra Cohn Livingston, David McCord, Eve Merriam, Lilian Moore, Mary O'Neill, Jack Prelutsky, and Shel Silverstein. Thumbnail sketches of six contemporary children's poets are

Adoff, A. (Ed.). (1974). *My black me: A beginning book on black poetry.* New York: Dutton.

Arwood, A. (1971). *Haiku: The mood of earth.* New York: Scribner.

Dunning, S., Lueders, E., & Smith, H. (Eds.). (1966). *Reflections on a gift of watermelon pickle . . . and other modern verse.* Glenview, IL: Scott, Foresman.

Fleischman, P. (1988). *Joyful noise: Poems for two voices.* New York: Harper and Row.

Froman, R. (1974). *Seeing things: A book of poems.* New York: Crowell.

Hopkins, L. B. (Ed.). (1976). *Good morning to you, valentine.* New York: Harcourt Brace Jovanovich. (See books for other holidays compiled by the same editor.)

Jones, H. (Ed.). (1971). *The trees stand shining: Poetry of the North American Indians.* New York: Dial.

Kennedy, X. J., & Kennedy, D. M. (Eds.). (1982). *Knock at a star: A children's introduction to poetry.* Boston: Little, Brown.

Kuskin, K. (1980). *Dogs and dragons, trees and dreams.* New York: Harper and Row.

Lattick, N. (Ed.). (1968). *Piping down the valleys wild.* New York: Dell.

Livingston, M. C. (1976). *4-way stop and other poems.* New York: Atheneum.

Livingston, M. C. (1982). *A circle of seasons.* New York: Holiday House.

McCord, D. (1974). *One at a time.* Boston: Little, Brown.

O'Neill, M. (1966). *Words, words, words.* Garden City, NY: Doubleday.

Prelutsky, J. (1983). *The Random House book of poetry for children.* New York: Random House.

Prelutsky, J. (1984). *The new kid on the block.* New York: Greenwillow.

Prelutsky, J. (1988). *Tyrannosaurus was a beast.* New York: Greenwillow.

Rothenberg, J. (1972). *Shaking the pumpkin: Traditional poetry of the Indian North Americans.* Garden City, NY: Doubleday.

Silverstein, S. (1974). *Where the sidewalk ends: The poems and drawings of Shel Silverstein.* New York: Harper and Row.

Viorst, J. (1981). *If I were in charge of the world and other worries.* New York: Atheneum.

FIGURE 11–1

Poetry Collections Appropriate for Elementary Students

presented in Figure 11–2. Children are just as interested in learning about favorite poets as they are in learning about story authors. When children view poets and other writers as real people, people they can relate to and who enjoy the same things they do, they begin to see themselves as poets—a necessary criterion for successful writing. Information about poets is available from many of the sources about authors listed in Chapter 8. Inviting poets to visit the classroom to share their poetry is one of the most valuable poetry experiences for children. For example, Chapman (1985) shares what happened when poet Arnold Adoff visited her classroom, and Parker (1981) relates a visit by Karla Kuskin.

Arnold Adoff

I am the darker brother (1968)
Black out loud (1970)
Ma nDa la (1971)
Black is brown is tan (1973)
Make a circle keep us in: Poems for a good day (1975)

Arnold Adoff grew up in New York City, and he taught at a public school in Harlem for 12 years. During his teaching, Adoff was frustrated by the lack of materials about black culture and began to collect the work of black writers to use with his students. His writing focuses on black life; however, Adoff says he sees himself as a student rather than an expert on black culture. Several of his books of poetry and a biography, *Malcolm X* (1970), have been chosen as American Library Association Notable Books. He is married to award-winning children's author Virginia Hamilton, and they live in Yellow Springs, Ohio.

Karla Kuskin

Roar and more (1956)
Any me I want to be (1972)
Near the window tree (1975)
Dogs and dragons, trees and dreams (1980)

Karla Kuskin is a native New Yorker who wrote and published her first book, *Roar and more,* as a class assignment while a student at Yale University. Kuskin writes both humorous picture books for preschoolers and books of poetry for older children. Her poems are often short, with a gentle rhythm and whimsical tone; "Knitted Things" is a good example. She says she writes from her memories of childhood, and she is especially successful in capturing the essence of childhood experiences in poems such as "I Woke Up This Morning." Kuskin discusses how she writes poetry on "Poetry Explained by Karla Kuskin," a sound filmstrip available from Weston Woods.

Myra Cohn Livingston

Whispers and other poems (1958)
Wide awake and other poems (1959)
What a wonderful bird the frog are (1973)
A circle of seasons (1982)

Myra Cohn Livingston was born in Omaha, Nebraska, and began writing poems and stories as soon as she could read. She had a special interest in both writing and music. As a teenager, she played the French horn in the California Junior Symphony and wrote for her high school newspaper. Livingston wrote her first book of poems, *Whispers and other poems,* while she was in college, but it was not published until 12 years later. Since then, she has written nearly 30 books of poetry. Today Livingston lives in Beverly Hills, California. She teaches creative writing at the University of California and has written a book on teaching children to write poetry, *When you are alone/It keeps you capone* (1974), based on her work with teachers.

FIGURE 11–2

Thumbnail Sketches of Six Contemporary Children's Poets

David McCord

Far and few (1952)
Take sky (1962)
All day long (1966)
Everytime I climb a tree (1967)
Once at a time: Collected poems for the young (1977)

David McCord was born in New York City and grew up there and in Oregon. After completing undergraduate studies in physics and graduate studies in English at Harvard University, McCord became a professional fund raiser for the Harvard Fund Council. He began writing poetry when he was 15, and as an adult, turned his attention to writing poetry for children. During his long career, he has composed more than 400 poems for children. McCord is called "an acrobat with language" and uses surprising rhythm, sound effects, and word play in his poetry. In 1977, David McCord was the first recipient of the National Council of Teachers of English Award for Excellence in Poetry for Children.

Jack Prelutsky

Circus (1974)
Nightmares: Poems to trouble your sleep (1976)
It's Halloween (1977)
The snopp on the sidewalk and other poems (1977)
The Random House book of poetry for children (1983)

Jack Prelutsky was born in New York City. His career has included singing and acting jobs as well as writing poetry. He has sung with opera companies in Boston and Seattle and has written more than 30 books of poetry. His poetry is delightful nonsense in rhymed, rhythmic verse, and his poems are often about imaginary animals, like "The Snopp on the Sidewalk." His nonsense verse has definite child-appeal. Jack Prelutsky now makes his home in Albuquerque, New Mexico, and travels around the country to visit libraries and schools and share his poems with children.

Shel Silverstein

The giving tree (1964)
Where the sidewalk ends (1974)
The missing piece (1976)
The light in the attic (1981)

Shel Silverstein was born in Chicago, but now divides his time among homes in Greenwich Village, Key West, and a houseboat in Sausalito, California. Silverstein began to write and draw when he was a teenager and, when he served in the U.S. armed forces in the 1950s, was a cartoonist for the military newspaper, *Stars and Stripes*. Silverstein never planned to write or draw for children, but friends convinced him that his work had appeal for children as well as adults. He says he hopes readers will experience "a personal sense of discovery" when they read his poems. Silverstein has other interests in addition to writing poetry; he is a folksinger, lyricist, and playwright.

FIGURE 11–2   *(continued)*

In addition to poetry written specifically for children, some poetry written for adults can be used effectively with elementary students, especially at upper-grade levels. Apseloff (1979) explains that poems written for adults use more sophisticated language and imagery and provide children with an early introduction to poems and poets they will undoubtedly study later. For instance, elementary students will enjoy Shakespeare's "The Witches' Song" from *Macbeth* and Carl Sandburg's "Fog." A list of poems written for adults that may be appropriate with some elementary students is shown in Figure 11–3.

Children have definite preferences about which poems they like best, just as adults do. Fisher and Natarella (1982) surveyed the poetry preferences of first, second, and third graders; Terry (1974) investigated fourth, fifth, and sixth graders' preferences; and Kutiper (1985) researched seventh, eighth, and ninth graders' preferences. The results of the three studies are important for teachers to consider when they select poems. The most popular forms of poetry were limericks and narrative poems; least popular were haiku and free verse. In addition, children preferred funny poems, poems about animals, and poems about familiar experiences. The most important elements were rhyme, rhythm, and sound. Primary-grade students preferred traditional poetry, middle graders preferred modern poetry, and upper-grade students preferred rhyming verse. The ten best-liked poems for each grade group are ranked in Figure 11–4. The researchers found that children in all three studies liked poetry, enjoyed listening to poetry read aloud, and could give reasons why they liked or disliked particular poems.

Ways to Share Poetry

Sharing poetry is simple: teachers should choose poems they like and share them with students. It is an easy task to browse through an anthology of poems, find a favorite poem, read it silently several times, and then share it with students. In her poem, "How to Eat a Poem" (1966), Eve Merriam provides useful advice: she compares reading a poem to eating a piece of fruit and advises to bite right in and let the juice run down your chin. Poetry sharing does not need to be scheduled for a particular time of day. First thing in the morning or right after lunch are good times, but because poems can be shared quickly, they can be tied in with almost any activity. Often poems are coordinated with a holiday, a social studies unit, a story being read to the class, or even when a language skill is being taught. These are guidelines for sharing poetry with children:

> Read or recite only poems that are personal favorites. Students can tell when a teacher does not care for a poem.
>
> Rehearse the poem several times to get the feel of the words and rhythm. Decide where to pause and which words or phrases to accent.
>
> Start a collection of favorite poems. Jot them down on notecards and have a poem ready to share during a free moment.
>
> Keep a collection of poetry books in the classroom for children to browse through. Students may want to use bookmarks to mark favorite poems to share or add to their copybooks. (See Chapter 14 for more information on copybooks.)

Poet	Poems and/or Books of Poetry
William Blake	"The Lamb," "The Tyger," "The Piper," and other selections from *Songs of experience* and *Songs of innocence*. Compare with Nancy Willard's *A visit to William Blake's inn: Poems for innocent and experienced travelers* (Harcourt Brace Jovanovich, 1981).
Emily Dickinson	"I'm nobody! Who are you?," "There is no frigate like a book," and other favorite poems from *I'm nobody! Who are you? Poems of Emily Dickinson for children* (Stemmer House, 1978).
T. S. Eliot	Poems about cats from *Old possum's book of practical cats* (Harcourt Brace Jovanovich, 1967).
Robert Frost	"The Pasture," "Birches," "Fire and Ice," "Stopping by Woods on a Snowy Evening," and other favorites are included in *The poetry of Robert Frost,* edited by E. C. Latham (Holt, 1969). Also check the picture book version of *Stopping by woods on snowy evening,* illustrated by Susan Jeffers (Dutton, 1978).
Langston Hughes	"Dreams," "City," "April Rain Song," and other selections are included in *The dream keeper and other poems* (Knopf, 1960). Also, Lee Bennett Hopkins has compiled a collection of Hughes' poetry for young people: *Don't you turn back: Poems by Langston Hughes* (Knopf, 1969).
D. H. Lawrence	William Cole has prepared a selection of Lawrence's poetry suitable for upper grade students: *D. H. Lawrence: Poems selected for young people* (Knopf, 1967). Also, Alice and Martin Provensen have illustrated a collection of D. H. Lawrence's poems for students, *Birds, beasts and the third thing: Poems by D. H. Lawrence* (Viking, 1982).
Carl Sandburg	"Fog," "Daybreak," "Buffalo Dusk," and other poems for elementary students are included in *Wind song* (Harcourt Brace Jovanovich, 1960), *Chicago poems* (Harcourt Brace Jovanovich, 1944) and other books of Sandburg's poetry. Also, see Lee Bennett Hopkins' collection of Sandburg's poems: *Rainbows are made: Poems by Carl Sandburg* (Harcourt Brace Jovanovich, 1982).
Walt Whitman	Elementary students will enjoy "I Hear America Singing," "I Believe in a Leaf of Grass," and other selections from *Leaves of grass* (Doubleday, 1926).

FIGURE 11–3

Adult Poems Appropriate for Elementary Students

First, Second, and Third Graders' Favorite Poems

Rank	Title	Author
1	"The Young Lady of Lynn"	Unknown
2	"The Little Turtle"	Vachel Lindsay
3	"Bad Boy"	Lois Lenski
4	"Little Miss Muffet"	Paul Dehn
5	"Cat"	Eleanor Farjeon
6	"Adventures of Isabel"	Ogden Nash
7	"Mummy Slept Late and Daddy Fixed Breakfast"	John Ciardi
8	"The Lurpp Is on the Loose"	Jack Prelutsky
9	"A Bookworm of Curious Breed"	Ann Hoberman
10	"The Owl and the Pussy-cat"	Edward Lear

Fourth, Fifth, and Sixth Graders' Favorite Poems

Rank	Title	Author
1	"Mummy Slept Late and Daddy Fixed Breakfast"	John Ciardi
2	"Fire! Fire!"	Unknown
3	"There was an old man of Blackheath"	Unknown
4	"Little Miss Muffet"	Paul Dehn
5	"There once was an old kangaroo"	Edward S. Mullins
6	"There was a young lady of Niger"	Unknown
7	"Hughbert and the Glue"	Karla Kuskin
8	"Betty Barter"	Unknown
9	"Lone Dog"	Irene Rutherford McLeod
10	"Eletelephony"	Laura E. Richards

Seventh, Eighth, and Ninth Graders' Favorite Poems

Rank	Title	Author
1	"Sick"	Shel Silverstein
2	"Oh, Teddy Bear"	Jack Prelutsky
3	"Mother Doesn't Want a Dog"	Judith Viorst
4	"Mummy Slept Late and Daddy Fixed Breakfast"	John Ciardi
5	"The Unicorn"	Shel Silverstein
6	"Why Nobody Pets the Lion at the Zoo"	John Ciardi
7	"Homework"	Jane Yolen
8	"Dreams"	Langston Hughes
9	"Questions"	Marci Ridlon
10	"Willie Ate a Worm Today"	Jack Prelutsky

FIGURE 11—4

Children's Poetry Preferences
Fisher & Natarella, 1982, p. 344; Terry, 1974, p. 15; Kutiper, 1985, p. 51.

Students enjoy sharing favorite poems with classmates.

Set up a listening center with records or audiocassettes of poems. Students may also want to record their favorite poems for the listening center.

Poetry is meant to be shared orally, not silently. Do not ask students to read poems silently.

Have children become the primary readers and sharers of poetry as quickly as possible. Try group poetry reading or reciting and choral reading activities.

Do not assign children to memorize a particular poem, but encourage children who are interested in learning a favorite poem to share with class members.

Do not ask students to analyze the meaning of a poem or its rhyme scheme. Many students stop enjoying poetry when teachers require them to analyze poems.

Choral Reading.   There are many ways to share poetry with children and to involve them in sharing poetry with their classmates. *Choral reading,* in which children take turns reading a poem together, is one way. Active participation with poetry helps students learn to appreciate the sounds, feelings, and magic of poetry.

There are a number of things to consider when selecting and preparing a selection for presentation. First, how will four of the basic elements of oral language enhance the interpretation? The relevant elements are *tempo* (how fast or slow to read the lines), *rhythm* (which words to stress or say loudest), *pitch* (when to raise or lower the voice), and *juncture* (when and how long to pause) (Stewig, 1981). When students select a poem to prepare for presentation, they will need to consider these four elements and experiment with each element to create the desired interpretation. Teachers copy the poem on a large chart or on a transparency so that students can underline particular words and use arrows or other marks to indicate the tempo, rhythm, pitch, and juncture they have decided on for their choral reading. This procedure is similar to that used by composers to mark tempo and other considerations on their musical scores.

The second consideration concerns how to arrange the poem for choral reading. Students may read the poem aloud together or in small groups, or individual students can read particular lines or stanzas. Four possible arrangements are echoic, refrain, antiphonal, and cumulative.

> Echoic—The leader reads each line and the group repeats it.
>
> Refrain—The leader reads the main part of the poem, and the group reads the refrain or chorus in unison.
>
> Antiphonal—The class divides into two or more groups, and each group reads one part of the poem.
>
> Cumulative—A cumulative effect is created by adding voices as the poem is read. One student or one group reads the first line or stanza, and another student or group joins in as each line or stanza is read (Stewig, 1981).

The choral arrangement can easily be marked on the copy of the poem along with the information about tempo, rhythm, pitch, and juncture.

Two books of award-winning poems written for choral reading are *I Am Phoenix* (Fleischman, 1985), a collection of poems about birds, and *Joyful Noise* (Fleischman, 1988), a collection of poems about insects. Many other poems are appropriate for choral reading; try, for example, Shel Silverstein's "Boa Constrictor," "Full of the Moon" by Karla Kuskin, Laura E. Richards's "Eletelephony," and "Catch a Little Rhyme" by Eve Merriam. Many of the poems in the books listed in Figure 11–2 can also be used in choral reading interpretations.

Compiling Collections of Poems.   Some students enjoy compiling anthologies of their favorite poems. The activity often begins quite naturally when students read poems. They copy favorite poems to keep, and soon they are stapling their collections together to make books. Copying poems can also be a worthwhile handwriting activity, because students are copying something meaningful to them, not just words or sentences from a workbook. Poet and anthologist Lee Bennett Hopkins (1972) suggests setting up a dead tree branch or an artificial Christmas tree in the classroom as a "poetree" on which students can hang copies of their favorite poems for their classmates to read and enjoy.

Other Activities.   Informal drama, art, and music activities can also accompany favorite poems. For instance, students can role-play Kuskin's "I Woke Up This Morning" or construct monster puppets for the Lurpp creature in Prelutsky's "The Lurpp Is on the Loose." Students may also compile picture book versions of narrative poems, such as Ciardi's "Mummy Slept Late and Daddy Cooked Breakfast," or they may make filmstrip versions of a poem using a filmstrip kit. Several frames from a filmstrip illustrating "Mummy Slept Late . . ." are presented in Figure 11–5.

Daddy fixed the breakfast.
He made us each a waffle.
It looked like gravel pudding.
It tasted something awful.

"Ha, ha," he said, "I'll try again.
This time I'll get it right."

But what *I* got was in between
Bituminous and anthracite.

"A little too well done? Oh well,
I'll have to start all over."
That time what landed on my plate
Looked like a manhole cover.

I tried to cut it with a fork:
The fork gave off a spark.

I tried a knife and twisted it

Into a question mark.

I tried it with a hack-saw.

I tried it with a torch.

It didn't even make a dent.
It didn't even scorch.

The next time Dad gets breakfast
When Mummy's sleeping late,
I think I'll skip the waffles.
I'd sooner eat the plate.

FIGURE 11–5

Excerpt from a Filmstrip Illustrating "Mummy Slept Late and Daddy Fixed Breakfast"

Children may also compile a book of poems and illustrate them with photographs. In *A Song in Stone: City Poems* (1983), Lee Bennett Hopkins compiled a collection of city poems and Anna Held Audette selected black and white photographs to illustrate each one. Children can create a similar type of book, and photocopies can be made so each child will have a personal copy.

❖ PLAYING WITH WORDS

As students experiment or play with words, they invent new words, laugh with language, create word pictures, and experiment with rhyme. These types of activities provide the background of experiences children need for writing poetry. Although these activities are not poetry, students gain confidence and flexibility in using words to write poetry. Figure 11—6 lists word play books that elementary students enjoy.

Inventing New Words

Authors sometimes create new words in their stories; Adams used *woggle* in *A Woggle of Witches* (1971), Horwitz described the night as *bimulous* in *When the Sky Is Like Lace* (1975), and Van Allsburg named his jungle adventure game *Jumanji* (1981). Students should be alert to the possibility of finding a new word when they read or listen to stories.

Laughing with Language

As children learn that words have the power to amuse, they enjoy reading, telling, and writing riddles and jokes. Linda Gibson Geller (1985) has researched children's humorous language and identified two stages of riddle play that elementary students move through. Primary-grade children experiment with the riddle form and its content, and middle- and upper-grade students explore the paradoxical constructions in riddles. Riddles are written in a question-answer format, but young children at first may only ask questions, or ask questions and offer unrelated answers. With more experience, students both provide questions and give related answers, and their answers may be either descriptive or nonsensical. An example of a descriptive answer is *Why did the turtle go out of his shell? Because he was getting too big for it;* a nonsensical answer involving an invented word for this riddle, *Why did the cat want to catch a snake?* is *Because he wanted to turn into a rattlecat* (Geller, 1981, p. 672). Many primary-grade students' riddles seem foolish by adult standards, but word play is an important precursor to creating true riddles.

Riddles depend on manipulating words with multiple meanings or similar sounds and using metaphors. The Opies (1959) identified five riddle strategies used by elementary students:

1. Using multiple referents for a noun: What has an eye but cannot see? (A needle)

2. Combining literal and figurative interpretations for a single phrase: Why did the moron throw the clock out the window? (Because he wanted to see time fly)

3. Shifting word boundaries to suggest another meaning: Why did the cookie cry? (Because its mother was a wafer/away for/so long)

4. Separating a word into syllables to suggest another meaning: When is a door not a door? (When it's ajar/a jar/)

5. Creating a metaphor: What are polka dots on your face? (Pimples)

Children begin riddle play by telling familiar riddles and reading riddles written by others. Several excellent books of riddles to share with elementary students are *Tyrannosaurus Wrecks: A Book of Dinosaur Riddles* (Sterne, 1979), *What Do You Call*

Barcheck, L. (1976). *Snake in, snake out.* New York: Crowell. (M)
Barrett, J. (1983). *A snake is totally tail.* New York: Atheneum. (P–M)
Bayer, J. (1984). *A my name is Alice.* New York: Dial. (P–M)
Brown, M. (1983). *What do you call a dumb bunny? And other rabbit riddles, games, jokes, and cartoons.* Boston: Little, Brown. (P–M)
Cox, J. A. (1980). *Put your foot in your mouth and other silly sayings.* New York: Random House. (P–M)
Degen, B. (1983). *Jamberry.* New York: Harper and Row. (P)
Eiting, M., & Folsom, M. (1980). *Q is for duck: An alphabet guessing game.* New York: Clarion. (P–M)
Esbensen, B. J. (1986). *Words with wrinkled knees.* New York: Crowell. (M–U)
Funk, C. E. (1948). *A hog on ice and other curious expressions.* New York: Harper and Row. (U)
Gwynne, F. (1970). *The king who rained.* New York: Dutton. (M–U)
Gwynne, F. (1976). *A chocolate moose for dinner.* New York: Dutton. (M–U)
Gwynne, F. (1980). *The sixteen hand horse.* New York: Prentice-Hall. (M–U)
Gwynne, F. (1988). *A little pigeon toad.* New York: Simon & Schuster. (M–U)
Hall, F., & Friends. *Sniglets for kids.* Yellow Springs, OH: Antioch. (M–U)
Hanson, J. (1972). *Homographic homophones.* Fly *and* fly *and other words that look and sound the same but are as different in meaning as* bat *and* bat. Minneapolis: Lerner. (M)
Hanson, J. (1972). *Homographs:* Bow *and* bow *and other words that look the same but sound as different as* sow *and* sow. Minneapolis: Lerner. (M)
Houget, S. R. (1983). *I unpacked my grandmother's trunk: A picture book game.* New York: Dutton. (P–M)

FIGURE 11–6

Word Play Books for Elementary Students
P = primary grades (K–2)
M = middle grades (3–5)
U = upper grades (6–8)

a *Dumb Bunny? And Other Rabbit Riddles, Games, Jokes, and Cartoons* (Brown, 1983), and *Eight Ate: A Feast of Homonym Riddles* (Terban, 1982). Soon children are composing their own by adapting riddles they have read; others turn jokes into riddles. An excellent book for helping children write riddles is *Fiddle with a Riddle: Write Your Own Riddles* (Bernstein, 1979).

Larissa, a third grader, wrote this riddle using two meanings for Milky Way: *Why did the astronaut go to the Milky Way? Because he wanted a Milky Way Bar.* Terry, a fifth grader, wrote this riddle using the homophones *hair* and *hare: What is gray and jumpy and on your head? A gray hare!* The juxtaposition of words is important in many jokes and riddles.

Creating Word Pictures

In the primary grades, children learn to place words in horizontal lines from left to right and top to bottom across a sheet of paper just as the lines on this page are printed;

Hunt, B. K. (1975). *Your ant is a which: Fun with homophones.* New York: Harcourt Brace Jovanovich. (P–M)

Juster, N. (1982). *Otter nonsense.* New York: Philomel. (P–M)

Kellogg, S. (1987). *Aster Aardvark's alphabet adventures.* New York: Morrow. (P–M)

Maestro, G. (1984). *What's a frank Frank? Tasty homograph riddles.* New York: Clarion. (P–M)

Perl, L. (1988). *Don't sing before breakfast, don't sing in the moonlight.* New York: Random House. (M–U)

Schwartz, A. (1973). *Tomfoolery: Trickery and foolery with words.* Philadelphia: Lippincott. (M–U)

Schwartz, A. (1982). *The cat's elbow and other secret languages.* New York: Farrar. (M–U)

Sterne, N. (1979). *Tyrannosaurus wrecks: A book of dinosaur riddles.* New York: Crowell. (M)

Tallon, R. (1979). *Zoophabets.* New York: Scholastic. (P–M)

Terban, M. (1982). *Eight ate: A feast of homonym riddles.* New York: Clarion. (P–M)

Terban, M. (1983). *In a pickle and other funny idioms.* New York: Clarion. (M)

Terban, M. (1985). *Too hot to hoot: Funny palindrome riddles.* New York: Clarion. (M–U)

Tobias, H., & Baskin, L. (1972). *Hosie's alphabet.* New York: Viking. (M–U)

Van Allsburg, C. (1987). *The z was zapped.* Boston: Houghton Mifflin. (M)

Zalben, J. B. (1977). *Lewis Carroll's Jabberwocky.* New York: Warne. (M–U)

FIGURE 11–6   (*continued*)

however, they can break this pattern and create word pictures by placing words as they would draw lines in a drawing. These word pictures can be single-word pictures or a string of words or a sentence arranged in a picture.

Word Pictures.   Students use words instead of lines to draw a picture, as the *rabbit* picture in Figure 11–7 illustrates. Students first draw a picture with lines, then place a second sheet of paper over the drawing and replace all or most of the lines with repeated words.

Descriptive Words.   Students write descriptive words so that the arrangement, size, and intensity of the letters in the word illustrate the meaning. The word *nervous* is written concretely in Figure 11–7. Students can also write the names of objects and animals, such as *bird,* concretely, illustrating features of the named item through the style of the letters.

Sentence Pictures.   Students can compose a descriptive phrase or sentence and write it in the shape of an object, as the ice cream cone in Figure 11–7 illustrates. An asterisk indicates where to start reading the sentence picture.

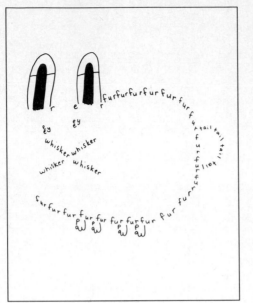

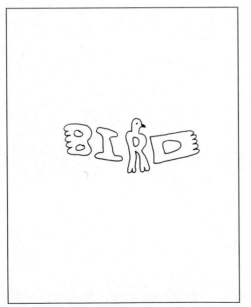

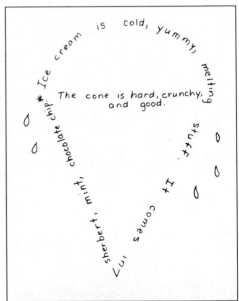

FIGURE 11—7

Students' Word Pictures

Experimenting with Rhyme

Because of their experience with Dr. Seuss stories, finger plays, and nursery rhymes, kindergartners and first graders enjoy creating rhymes. Unfortunately, many children equate poetry with rhyme, and their dependence on rhyme thwarts their attempts to write poetry. Nonetheless, rhyme is a special kind of word play that children enjoy. A small group of first graders created their own version of *Oh, A-hunting We Will Go* (Langstaff, 1974). After reading the book, they identified the refrain (lines 1, 2, and 5) and added their own rhyming couplets. For example:

> *Oh, a-hunting we will go,*
> *a-hunting we will go.*
> *We'll catch a little bear*
> *and curl his hair,*
> *and never let him go.*
> *Oh, a-hunting we will go,*
> *a-hunting we will go.*
> *We'll catch a little mole*
> *and put him in a hole,*
> *and never let him go.*
> *Oh, a-hunting we will go,*
> *a-hunting we will go.*
> *We'll catch a little snake*
> *and hit him with a rake,*
> *and never let him go.*
> *Oh, a-hunting we will go,*
> *a-hunting we will go.*
> *We'll catch a little bug*
> *and give him a big hug*
> *and never let him go.*
> *Oh, a-hunting we will go,*
> *a-hunting we will go.*
> *We'll catch a little bunny*
> *and fill her full of honey,*
> *and never let her go.*
> *Oh, we'll put them in a ring*
> *and listen to them sing*
> *and then we'll let them go.*

The first graders wrote this collaboration with the teacher taking dictation on a large chart. After the rough draft was written, students reread it, checking the rhymes and changing a word here or there. Then each student chose one stanza to copy and illustrate. The pages were collected and compiled to make a book. Students shared the book with their classmates, with each student reading his or her "own" page.

Hink-pinks. *Hink-pinks* are short rhymes that either take the form of an answer to a riddle or describe something. Hink-pinks are composed with two one-syllable rhyming words; they are called *hinky-pinkies* when two two-syllable words are used, and *hinkity-pinkities* with two three-syllable words (Geller, 1981). Two examples of these rhymes are:

> *Ghost*
> *White*
> *Fright*
> *—Marshall, grade 6*
>
> *What do you call an astronaut?*
> *A sky guy.*
> *—Tara, grade 6*

❖ WRITING POETRY

Elementary students can have successful experiences writing poetry if they use poetic formulas. They can write formula poems by beginning each line with particular words, as is the case with color poems; count syllables for haiku; or create word pictures in concrete poems. Writing quickly and under guidelines, children can use the writing process to revise, edit, and share their writing without a time-consuming process of

Students write and illustrate poems using formulas such as "I wish. . . ."

making changes, correcting errors, and recopying. Poetry also allows students more freedom in punctuation, capitalization, and page arrangement.

Many types of poetry do not use rhyme, but rhyme is the sticking-point for many would-be poets. In searching for a rhyming word, children often create inane verse; for example:

> *I see a funny little goat*
> *Wearing a blue sailor's coat*
> *Sitting in an old motorboat.*

Whereas children should not be forbidden to write rhyming poetry, rhyme should never be imposed as a criterion for acceptable poetry. Children may use rhyme when it fits naturally into their writing. When children write poetry during the elementary grades, they are searching for their own voices, and they need freedom to do that. Freed from the pressure to create rhyming poetry or from other constraints, children create sensitive word pictures, vivid images, and unique comparisons, as we see in the poems throughout this chapter.

Five types of poetic forms are formula poems, free form poems, syllable- and word-count poems, rhymed poems, and model poems. Elementary students' poems illustrate each poetic form. Kindergartners' and first graders' poems may seem little more than lists of sentences compared to the more sophisticated poems of older students, but the range of poems effectively shows how elementary and middle-grade students grow in their ability to write poetry through these writing activities.

5 types of poetic forms

Formula Poems

The poetic forms may seem like recipes, but they are not intended to be followed rigidly. Rather, they provide a scaffold, organization, or skeleton for students' poems. After collecting words, images, and comparisons through brainstorming, clustering, freewriting, or another prewriting strategy, students craft their poems, choosing words and arranging them to create a message. Meaning is always most important, and form follows the search for meaning. Perhaps a better description is that children "dig for poems" (Valentine, 1986) through words, ideas, poetic forms, rhyme, rhythm, and conventions. Poet Kenneth Koch (1970), working with students in the elementary grades, developed some simple formulas that make it easy for nearly every child to become a successful poet. These formulas call for students to begin every line the same way or to insert a particular kind of word in every line. The formulas use repetition, a stylistic device that is more effective for young poets than rhyme. Some forms may seem more like sentences than poems, but the dividing line between poetry and prose is a blurry one, and these poetry experiences help children move toward poetic expression.

"I wish . . ." Poems. Children begin each line of their poems with the words "I wish," and complete the line with a wish (Koch, 1970). In a second grade class collaboration, children simply listed their wishes.

Our Wishes

I wish I had all the money in the world.
I wish I was a star fallen down from Mars.
I wish I were a butterfly.
I wish I were a teddy bear.
I wish I had a cat.
I wish I were a pink rose.
I wish it wouldn't rain today.
I wish I didn't have to wash a dish.
I wish I had a flying carpet.
I wish I could go to Disney World.
I wish school was out.
I wish I could go outside and play.

After this experience, students choose one of their wishes and expand on the idea in another poem. Brandi expanded her wish this way:

I Wish

I wish I were a teddy bear
Who sat on a beautiful bed
Who got a hug every night
By a little girl or boy
Maybe tonight I'll get my wish
And wake up on a little girl's bed
And then I'll be as happy as can be.

Color Poems.   Students begin each line of their poems with a color. They can repeat the same color in each line or choose a different color (Koch, 1970); for example, a class of seventh graders writes about yellow.

Yellow is shiny galoshes
splashing through mud puddles.
Yellow is a street lamp
beaming through a dark, black night.
Yellow is the egg yolk
bubbling in a frying pan.
Yellow is the lemon cake
that makes you pucker your lips.
Yellow is the sunset
and the warm summer breeze.
Yellow is the tingling in your mouth
after a lemon drop melts.

Students can also write more complex poems by expanding each idea into a stanza, as this poem about black illustrates.

Black

*Black is a deep hole
sitting in the ground
waiting for animals
that live inside.*

*Black is a beautiful horse
standing on a high hill
with the wind
swirling its mane.*

*Black is a winter night sky
without stars
to keep it
company.*

*Black is a panther
creeping around a jungle
searching for
its prey.*

Hailstones and Halibut Bones (O'Neill, 1961) is another source of color poems; however, O'Neill uses rhyme as a poetic device, and it is important to emphasize that students' poems need not rhyme.

Writing color poems can be coordinated with teaching young children to read and write color words. Instead of having kindergartners and first graders read worksheets and color pictures the designated colors, students can create color poems in booklets of paper stapled together. They write and illustrate one line of the poem on each page.

Five Senses Poems.   Students write about a topic using each of the five senses. Sense poems are usually five lines long, with one line for each sense, as this poem written by a sixth grader demonstrates.

Being Heartbroken

*Sounds like thunder and lightning
Looks like a carrot going through a blender
Tastes like sour milk
Feels like a splinter in your finger
Smells like a dead fish
It must be horrible!*

It is often helpful to have students develop a five senses cluster and collect ideas for each sense. Students select from the cluster the most vivid or strongest idea for each sense to use in a line of the poem.

"If I were . . ." Poems.   Children write about how they would feel and what they would do if they were something else—a Tyrannosaurus Rex, a hamburger, or the sunshine (Koch, 1970). They begin each poem with "If I were" and tell what it would be like to be that thing; for example, seven-year-old Robbie writes about what he would do if he were a dinosaur.

> If I were a Tyrannosaurus Rex
> I would terrorize other dinosaurs
> And eat them up for supper.

Students use personification in composing "If I were . . ." poems, explore ideas and feelings, and consider the world from a different vantage point.

"I used to . . ./But now . . ." Poems.   In these contrast poems, students begin the first line (and every odd-numbered line) with "I used to" and the second line (and every even-numbered line) with "But now" (Koch, 1970). Students can use this formula to explore ways they have changed as well as how things change. Two third grade students wrote

> I used to be a kernel
> but now I am a crunchy,
> tasty, buttery cloud
> popped by Orville Redenbacher.

A fifth grade teacher adapted this formula for a social studies class, and her students wrote a class collaboration "I used to think . . ./But now I know . . ." poem using the information they had learned during a unit on the American Revolution. Here is their poem.

On the American Revolution

> I USED TO THINK that Florida was one of the thirteen colonies,
> BUT NOW I KNOW it belonged to Spain.
> I USED TO THINK the War for Independence was one big battle,
> BUT NOW I KNOW it was made up of many battles.
> I USED TO THINK that Americans and British fought the same way,
> BUT NOW I KNOW they had different military styles.
> I USED TO THINK when the War for Independence ended, our troubles were over,
> BUT NOW I KNOW we still had trouble with Britain.
> I USED TO THINK that the Constitution was our first set of rules,
> BUT NOW I KNOW that the Articles of Confederation were.
> I USED TO THINK that the United States was founded all at once,
> BUT NOW I KNOW it grew little by little.
> I USED TO THINK that war was exciting and glamorous,
> BUT NOW I KNOW that it was not that way at all.

Lie Poems.   Children write a poem in which nothing is true or with a lie in each line (Koch, 1970). These "lies" are imaginary or make-believe, such as "I live on Pluto," rather than a real lie, such as whether a child has set the table for dinner. Sixth graders collaborated on this lie poem.

The Whole Truth and Nothing But the Truth

The world is a square, purple desert.
The year is 2000 in black oil Oklahoma.
I can fly in the blue sky on the beach.
Alaska is as hot as the Amazon River is pink.
I'm 556 blue years old.
My brother is sailing on 50 maroon yachts.
I can fly in two silver boats inside a ham.
My room is a small fuchsia morgue.
I drink fluorescent pink Scope inside my locker.
Our yellow polka-dotted school is as tiny as a Georgia peanut.

When the students revised their poem, they added a color word to each line of their lies poem to create interest. This is a good way to combine two different kinds of formula poems! Note that lie poems are more appropriate for older students who understand the difference between lies they aren't supposed to tell and the imaginary lies in these poems.

". . . is" Poems. In these description or definition poems, students describe what something is or what something or someone means to them. To begin, the teacher or students identify a topic to fill in the blank, such as *anger, a friend, liberty,* or *fear,* then students start each line with ". . . is" and describe or define that thing. A group of second graders wrote the following poem as a part of their weather unit. Before discussing what causes thunder, they brainstormed a list of possible explanations for this phenomenon.

Thunder is . . .

Thunder is someone bowling.
Thunder is a hot cloud bumping against a cold cloud.
Thunder is someone playing basketball.
Thunder is dynamite blasting.
Thunder is a Brontosaurus sneezing.
Thunder is people moving their furniture.
Thunder is a giant laughing.
Thunder is elephants playing.
Thunder is an army tank.
Thunder is Bugs Bunny chewing his carrots.

Students often write powerful poems using this formula, when they move beyond the cute "Happiness is . . ." and "Love is . . ." patterns.

Preposition Poems. Students begin each line of preposition poems with a preposition, and a delightful poetic rewording of lines often results in the attempt. Seventh grader Mike wrote this preposition poem about a movie superhero.

Superman

Within the city
In a phone booth
Into his clothes
Like a bird
In the sky
Through the walls
Until the crime
Among us
is defeated!

It is helpful for children to brainstorm a list of prepositions to refer to when they write preposition poems. Students may find that they need to ignore the formula for a line or two to give the content of their poems top priority, or they may mistakenly begin a line with an infinitive verb (e.g., *to say*) rather than a preposition. These forms provide a structure or skeleton for students' writing that should be adapted as necessary.

Free-form Poems

In free-form poems, children choose words to describe something and put them together to express a thought or tell a story, without concern for rhyme or other arrangements. The number of words per line and use of punctuation vary. In the following poem, an eighth grader poignantly describes his topic concisely, using only 15 well-chosen words.

Loneliness

A lifetime
Of broken dreams
And promises
Lost love
Hurt
My heart
Cries
In silence

Students can use one of several methods for writing free-form poems. They can select words and phrases from brainstormed lists and clusters, or they can write a paragraph and then "unwrite" it to create the poem by deleting unnecessary words. They arrange the remaining words to look like a poem.

Concrete Poems.   Students create concrete poems through art and the careful arrangement of words on a page. Words, phrases, and sentences can be written in the shape of an object, or word pictures can be inserted within poems written left to right and top to bottom. Concrete poems are extensions of the word pictures discussed earlier. Two concrete poems are shown in Figure 11–8. In "Ants," the words *ants, cake,* and *frosting* create the image of a familiar picnic scene, and in "Cemetery," repetition and form create a reflection of peace. Three books of concrete poems for students are *Concrete Is Not Always Hard* (Pilon, 1972), *Seeing Things* (Froman, 1974), and *Walking Talking Words* (Sherman, 1980).

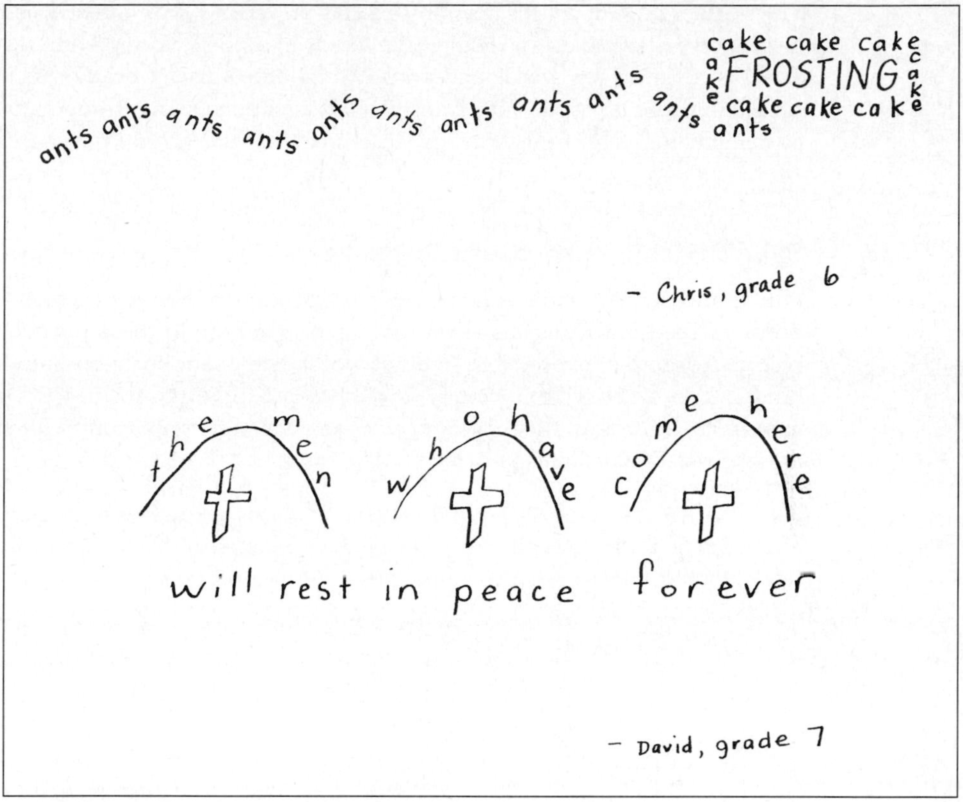

ants ants ants ants ants ants ants ants ants ants ants
cake cake cake
FROSTING
cake cake cake
ants

— Chris, grade 6

the men who have come here
will rest in peace forever

— David, grade 7

FIGURE 11–8

Students' Concrete Poems

Found Poems.   Students create poems by culling words from other sources, such as newspaper articles, songs, and stories. A seventh grader "found" this poem in an article about racecar driver Richard Petty.

Fast Moving

Moving down the track,
faster than fast, is Richard Petty
seven-time winner of
the crowned jewel
Daytona 500.
At 210 mph—dangerous—
pushing his engine to the limit.
Other NASCARs running fast
but Richard Petty takes the lead
at last.
Running across the line
with good time.

The student developed this poem by circling powerful words and phrases in the 33-line newspaper article and rearranging the words in a poetic form. After reading over the draft, he deleted two words and added three others that were not in the newspaper article but that he needed for transitions. Found poems give students the opportunity to manipulate words and sentence structures they don't write themselves.

Syllable- and Word-count Poems

Haiku and other syllable- and word-count poems provide a structure that helps students succeed in writing; however, the need to adhere to these poems' formulas may restrict freedom of expression. In other words, the poetic structure may both help and hinder. The exact syllable counts force students to search for just the right words to express their ideas and feelings and provide a valuable opportunity for students to use thesauruses and dictionaries.

Haiku.   The most familiar syllable-counting poem is *haiku* (high KOO), a Japanese poetic form consisting of 17 syllables arranged in three lines of five, seven, and five syllables. Haiku poems deal with nature and present a single clear image. It is a concise form, much like a telegram. A fourth grader wrote this haiku poem about a spider web she saw one morning.

> *Spider web shining*
> *Tangled on the grass with dew*
> *Waiting quietly.*

Books of haiku to share with students include *My Own Rhythm: An Approach to Haiku* (Atwood, 1973), *Haiku: The Mood of the Earth* (Atwood, 1971), *In a Spring Garden* (Lewis, 1965), *Cricket Songs* (Behn, 1964), and *More Cricket Songs* (Behn, 1971). The photographs and artwork in these trade books may give students ideas for illustrating their haiku poems. Lewis (1968, 1970) has written about the lives of two of the greatest Japanese haiku poets, Issa and Basho; he provides biographical information as well as a collection of poems.

Tanka.   Tanka (TANK ah) is a Japanese verse form containing 31 syllables arranged in five lines, 5−7−5−7−7. This form is similar to haiku except with two additional lines of seven syllables each. Amy wrote this tanka poem about stars that was published in her middle school anthology.

> *The summer dancers*
> *Dancing in the midnight sky,*
> *Waltzing and dreaming.*
> *Stars glistening in the night sky.*
> *Wish upon a shooting star.*

Even though one line is a syllable short and another is a syllable long in this poem, it illustrates the beauty of this syllable-counting form.

Cinquain.   A cinquain (SIN cane) is a five-line poem containing 22 syllables in a 2–4–6–8–2 syllable pattern. Cinquain poems often describe something, but they may also tell a story. Have students ask themselves what their subject looks like, smells like, sounds like, and tastes like and record their ideas using a five-senses cluster. The formula is as follows.

Line 1: a one-word subject with two syllables

Line 2: four syllables describing the subject

Line 3: six syllables showing action

Line 4: four syllables expressing a feeling or observation about the subject

Line 5: two syllables describing or renaming the subject

Here is a cinquain poem written by an upper-grade student.

Wrestling
skinny, fat
coaching, arguing, pinning
trying hard to win
tournament

If you compare this poem to the cinquain formula, you'll notice that some lines are short a syllable or two. The student bent some of the guidelines in choosing words to create a powerful image of wrestling; however, the message of the poem is always more important than adhering to the formula.

An alternate cinquain form contains five lines, but instead of following a syllable count, each line has a specified number of words. The first line contains a one-word title; the second line has two words that describe the title; the third line has three words that express action; the fourth line has four words that express feelings; and the fifth line contains a two-word synonym for the title.

Diamante.   Tiedt (1970) invented the diamante (dee ah MAHN tay), a seven-line contrast poem written in the shape of a diamond. This poetic form helps students apply their knowledge of opposites and parts of speech. The formula is as follows.

Line 1: one noun as the subject

Line 2: two adjectives describing the subject

Line 3: three participles (ending in *-ing*) telling about the subject

Line 4: four nouns (the first two related to the subject and the second two re-lated to the opposite)

Line 5: three participles telling about the opposite

Line 6: two adjectives describing the opposite

Line 7: one noun that is the opposite of the subject

The poem is written in the shape of a diamond.

```
                          noun
                  adjective  adjective
         participle  participle  participle
     noun        noun        noun        noun
         participle  participle  participle
                  adjective  adjective
                          noun
```

A third grade class wrote this diamante poem about the stages of life.

> *BABY*
> *wrinkled tiny*
> *crying wetting sleeping*
> *rattles diapers money house*
> *caring working loving*
> *smart helpful*
> *ADULT*

Notice that the students created a contrast between *baby,* the subject represented by the noun in the first line, and *adult,* the opposite in the last line. This contrast gives students the opportunity to play with words and apply their understanding of opposites. The third word, *money,* in the fourth line begins the transition from *baby* to its opposite, *adult.*

Rhymed Verse Forms

Several rhymed verse forms such as clerihews and limericks can be used effectively with middle- and upper-grade students. It is important that teachers try to prevent the forms and rhyme schemes from restricting students' creative and imaginative expression.

Limericks. The *limerick* is a form of light verse that uses both rhyme and rhythm. The poem consists of five lines; the first, second, and fifth lines rhyme, while the third and fourth lines rhyme with each other and are shorter than the other three. The rhyme scheme is a-a-b-b-a, and a limerick is arranged this way.

Line		Rhyme
1	_____	a
2	_____	a
3	_____	b
4	_____	b
5	_____	a

The last line often contains a funny or surprise ending, as in this limerick written by an eighth grader.

There once was a frog named Pete
Who did nothing but sit and eat.
He examined each fly
With so careful an eye
And then said, "You're dead meat."

Writing limericks can be a challenging assignment for many upper-grade students, but middle-grade students can also be successful with this poetic form, especially if they write a class collaboration.

Limericks are believed to have originated in the city of Limerick, Ireland, and were first popularized over a century ago by Edward Lear (1812–1888). Poet X. J. Kennedy (1982) described limericks as the most popular type of poem in the English language today. Introduce students to limericks by reading aloud some of Lear's verses so that students can appreciate the rhythm of the verse. One fine edition of Lear's limericks is *How Pleasant to Know Mr. Lear!* (Livingston, 1982). Another popular book is *They've Discovered a Head in the Box of Bread and Other Laughable Limericks* (Brewton & Blackburn, 1978). Arnold Lobel has also written a book of unique pig limericks, *Pigericks* (1983). After reading Lobel's pigericks, students will want to write "birdericks" or "fishericks."

Clerihews. *Clerihews* (KLER i hyoo), four-line rhymed verses that describe a person, are named for Edmund Clerihew Bentley (1875–1956), a British detective writer who invented the form. The formula is as follows.

Line 1:   the person's name

Line 2:   last word rhymes with last word in first line

Lines 3 and 4:   last words in these lines rhyme with each other

Clerihews can be written about anyone—historical figures, characters in stories, and even the students themselves. A sixth grader named Heather wrote this clerihew about Albert Einstein.

Albert Einstein
His genius did shine.
Of relativity and energy did he dream
And scientists today hold him in high esteem.

Model Poems

Students can model their poems on poems composed by adult poets. Koch suggested this approach in *Rose, Where Did You Get That Red* (1973); students read a poem and write their own, using the theme expressed in the model poem.

Apologies.   Using William Carlos Williams's "This Is Just to Say" as the model, children write a poem in which they apologize for something they are secretly glad they did (Koch, 1973). Middle- and upper-grade students are familiar with offering apologies and enjoy writing humorous apologies to inanimate things. A seventh grader named Jeff, for example, wrote this apology to his dad.

The Truck

Dad,
I'm sorry
that I took
the truck
out for
a spin.
I knew it
was wrong.
But . . .
the exhilarating
motion was
AWESOME!

Apology poems don't have to be humorous; they may be sensitive, genuine apologies, as a seventh grader's poem demonstrates.

Open Up

I didn't
open my
immature eyes
to see
the pain
within you
a death
had caused.
Forgive me,
I misunderstood
your anguished
broken heart.

Invitations.   Students write poems in which they invite someone to a magical, beautiful place full of sounds and colors and where all kinds of marvelous things happen. The model is Shakespeare's "Come Unto These Yellow Sands" (Koch, 1973). Guidelines for writing an invitation poem are that it must be an invitation to a magical place and include sound or color words. The following example of an invitation poem written by seventh grader Nikki follows these two guidelines.

The Golden Shore

Come unto the golden shore
Where days are filled with laughter,
And nights filled with whispering winds.
Where sunflowers and sun
Are filled with love.
Come take my hand
As we walk into the sun.

Prayers from the Ark.   Students write a poem or prayer from the viewpoint of an animal, following the model poems in Carmen Bernos de Gasztold's *Prayers from the Ark* (1965). Gasztold was a French nun during World War II, and, in her poems, she assumed the persona of the animals on Noah's ark as they prayed to God, questioning their existence and thanking Him for His mercies. Children can write similar poems in which they assume the persona of an animal. Sixth grader Davis assumes the persona of a monkey for his prayer.

Dear Lord,
I forgive you for making my face so ugly.
I thank you for giving me hands.
Thank you for placing the trees so high away
from my enemies.
I almost forgot,
Bless you for last month's big crop of bananas.

If I Were in Charge of the World.   Students write poems in which they describe what they would do if they were in charge of the world. Judith Viorst's "If I Were in Charge of the World" (1981) is the model for this poetic form. Children are eager to share ideas about how they would change the world, as this fourth grade's collaborative poem illustrates.

If I Were In Charge of the World

If I were in charge of the world
School would be for one month,
Movies and videogames would be free, and
Foods would be McCalorieless at McDonalds.
Poor people would have a home,
Bubble gum would cost a penny, and
Kids would have cars to drive.
Parents wouldn't argue,
Christmas would be in July and December, and
We would never have bedtimes.
A kid would be president,
I'd meet my long lost cousin, and
Candybars would be vegetables.
I would own the mall,
People would have as much money as they wanted, and
There would be no drugs.

Teaching Students to Write Poems

Before students write poems, teachers need to provide them with an "enlightened" view of poetry. Children often have misconceptions that interfere with their ability to write poems. Many students think poems must rhyme and, in their search for rhymes, create inane verse.

Introducing Students to Poetry.   Children need to have a concept of poetry before writing poems. One way to expand students' knowledge about poetry is to share a variety of poems written by children and adults.

Another way to introduce poetry is to read excerpts from the first chapter of *Anastasia Krupnik* (Lowry, 1979), in which ten-year-old Anastasia, the main character, is excited when her teacher, Mrs. Westvessel, announces that the class will write poems. Anastasia works at home for eight nights to write a poem. Lowry does an excellent job of describing how writers search long and hard for words to express meaning and the delight that comes when they realize their poems are finished. Then Anastasia and her classmates bring their poems to class to read aloud; one student reads his four-line rhymed verse.

> *I have a dog whose name is Spot.*
> *He likes to eat and drink a lot.*
> *When I put water in his dish,*
> *He laps it up just like a fish. (p. 10)*

Anastasia is not impressed. She knows the child who wrote the poem has a dog named Sputnik, not Spot! But Mrs. Westvessel gives it an A and hangs it on the bulletin board. Soon it is Anastasia's turn, and she is nervous because her poem is very different. She reads her poem about tiny creatures that move about in tidepools at night:

> *hush   hush   the sea-soft night is aswim*
> *with wrinklesquirm creatures*
> 　　　　　　　　　　　　　*listen(!)*
> *to them   move   smooth   in the moistly dark*
> *here in the   whisperwarm wet. (pp. 11–12)*

In this free-form poem without rhyme or capital letters, Anastasia has created a marvelous picture with invented words. Regrettably, Mrs. Westvessel has an antiquated view that poems should be about only serious subjects, be composed of rhyming sentences, and use conventional capitalization and punctuation. She doesn't understand Anastasia's poem, and gives Anastasia an F because she didn't follow directions.

Although this first chapter presents a depressing picture of elementary teachers and their lack of knowledge about poetry, it is a dramatic introduction about what poetry is and what it is not. After reading excerpts from the chapter, develop a chart with your students comparing what poetry is in Mrs. Westvessel's class and what poetry is in your class. A class of upper-grade students developed the chart in Figure 11–9.

Teaching Students to Write Poems Following a Poetic Form.   After the teacher introduces students to an "enlightened" view of poetry, they are ready to write. Beginning with formula poems (e.g., "I wish . . ." poems and color poems) will probably make the writing easier for young children or for students who have had little or no experience with poetry. Steps for writing any type of poetry are as follows.

1.   *Explain the poetic form.* The teacher describes the poetic form and explains what is included in each line or stanza. Displaying a chart that describes the

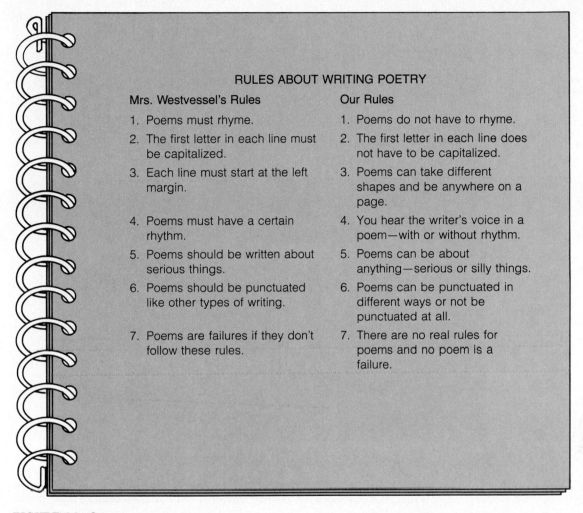

RULES ABOUT WRITING POETRY

Mrs. Westvessel's Rules

1. Poems must rhyme.

2. The first letter in each line must be capitalized.

3. Each line must start at the left margin.

4. Poems must have a certain rhythm.

5. Poems should be written about serious things.

6. Poems should be punctuated like other types of writing.

7. Poems are failures if they don't follow these rules.

Our Rules

1. Poems do not have to rhyme.

2. The first letter in each line does not have to be capitalized.

3. Poems can take different shapes and be anywhere on a page.

4. You hear the writer's voice in a poem—with or without rhythm.

5. Poems can be about anything—serious or silly things.

6. Poems can be punctuated in different ways or not be punctuated at all.

7. There are no real rules for poems and no poem is a failure.

FIGURE 11–9

Teacher's Notebook Page: Guidelines for Writing Poems

form or having students write a brief description of the poetic form in their writers' notebooks helps them remember it.

2. *Share examples written by children.* The teacher reads other children's poems that adhere to the form. You can share poems from this chapter along with additional poems written by your students. Point out how the writer of each poem used the form. Then you can share examples written by adults.

3. *Review the poetic form.* After explaining the poetic form and sharing poems, review the form and read one or two more poems that follow it. Have students explain how the poems fit the form, or have them freewrite about the poetic form to check their understanding.

Poetry, whether written for or by children, should be shared orally.

4. *Write class collaboration poems.* Students write a class collaboration poem before writing individual poems. Each contributes a line for a class collaboration "I wish . . ." poem or a couplet for an "I used to/But now" poem. To write other types of poems, such as concrete poems, students can work together by suggesting ideas and words. They dictate the poem to the teacher, who records it on the chalkboard or on chart paper. Older students work in small groups to create poems. Through collaborative poems, students review the form and gather ideas to use later in writing their own poems. The teacher should compliment students when they play with words or use poetic devices. Students also need information about how to arrange the poem on the page, how to decide about capital letters and punctuation marks, and why it may be necessary to "unwrite" and delete some words.

5. *Write individual poems using the writing process.* The first four steps are prewriting experiences that prepare students to write their own poems following the poetic form they have been taught. Students write rough drafts, meet in writing groups to receive feedback, make revisions based on this feedback, and then edit their poems with a classmate and with the teacher. Students then share their poems.

They can keep their poems in a poetry notebook, or make filmstrips and oral presentations.

Teachers often simply explain several poetic forms and then allow students to choose a form and write a poem. This approach ignores the teaching component; it's back to the "assign and do" syndrome. Instead, students need to experiment with each poetic form. After these preliminary experiences, they can apply what they have learned and write poems that adhere to any of the forms they have learned. Class collaborations are crucial because they are a practice run for children who are not sure what to do. The five minutes it takes to write a class collaboration poem can be the difference between success and failure for would-be poets.

Assessing Students' Poems

The poetic formulas discussed in this chapter provide options for students as they experiment with ways to express their thoughts. Although children experiment with a variety of forms during the elementary grades, it is not necessary to test their knowledge of particular forms. Knowing that a haiku is a Japanese poetic form composed of 17 syllables arranged in three lines will not make a child a poet. Descriptions of the forms should instead be posted in the classroom or added to writers' notebooks for students to refer to as they write.

Assessing the quality of students' poems is especially difficult, because poems are creative combinations of word play, poetic forms, and poetic devices. Instead of trying to give a grade for quality, students may be assessed on other criteria:

- Has the student used the formula presented in class?
- Has the student used the process approach in writing, revising, and editing the poem?
- Has the student used word play or a poetic device in the poem?

Teachers might also ask students to assess their own progress in writing poems. Students keep copies of their poems in their writing folders or poetry booklets so they can review and assess their own work. If a grade for quality is absolutely necessary, students should choose several of the poems in their writing folders for the teacher to evaluate.

❖ POETIC DEVICES

Good poets choose words carefully (Kennedy, 1982). They create powerful images when they use unexpected comparisons, repeat sounds within a line or stanza, imitate sounds, repeat words and phrases, and choose rhyming words. These techniques are *poetic devices,* and students need to learn about the devices so they can use them in their writing. The terminology is also helpful in writing groups, so that students can compliment classmates on the use of a device or suggest that they try a particular device when they revise their writing.

SHARING MODEL POEMS

"My seventh graders think they don't like poetry. Then we read lots of poems by Shel Silverstein, Jack Prelutsky, and others, and the students discover that poetry can be fun!"

Sandy Harris, Seventh Grade Teacher,
Anadarko Middle School

PROCEDURE

I start by bringing at least 50 books of poetry into the classroom. I share my favorites, and soon the students bring their favorites to read aloud to the class. The seventh graders invite each other to comment on the poetry they read aloud.

I start the year with a unit on poetry because I can demonstrate the writing process without getting bogged down in extensive revision and editing work, as often happens with longer compositions. The experience my students have reading and sharing poetry and discussing their favorites is reflected in the comments I hear them making in writing groups.

I've taken many of my ideas from Kenneth Koch's *Rose, Where Did You Get That Red?* (1973). One poetry writing activity my students enjoy is creating "model" poems; for example, I read

Comparison

One way to describe something is to compare it to something else. Students can compare images, feelings, and actions to other things using two types of comparisons, similes and metaphors. A *simile* is an explicit comparison of one thing to another—a statement that one thing is like something else. Similes are signaled by the use of *like* or *as . . . as*. In contrast, a *metaphor* compares two things by implying that one is something else, without using *like* or *as*. Differentiating between the two terms is less

William Blake's "The Tyger," and my students try their hands at writing poems in which they speak directly to an animal. Like Blake, they try to create strong images. One of my students wrote this poem in which he talks to an eagle:

> Eagle, is it the color you see
> from the sky, or is it the movement
> that catches your eye?
> Eagle, at what moment do you know
> as you dive from the sky,
> precisely when something will die?
> Eagle, do you have fear
> while you dive and peal,
> or might your nerves be made of steel?
> Eagle, what are your thoughts,
> as your claws and beak
> prepare the main course?
> Eagle, do you know
> as you perch majestically on the tree,
> that you represent our country's liberty?

After drafting their poems, students refine them in writing groups, then they meet with me for editing. Finally, students recopy their poems. For this activity, I'm working with the art teacher and my students will make papier-mâché animals to accompany their poems.

ASSESSMENT

Before writing these "Talk to the Animals" poems, the students and I make a checklist of the components they should include. In these poems, they were to (1) speak directly to an animal, (2) ask the animal a question in each stanza, and (3) create a strong visual image in each stanza. Almost every student is successful using this approach. I think identifying the criteria before they begin and the writing groups make the difference. In writing groups, students check each poem against the criteria and offer suggestions to authors on how to revise their poems if they don't meet the criteria.

REFLECTIONS

By observing the poems my students choose to share, I get a clearer idea of their preferences. By beginning from a base that is popular with the students, I can extend their appreciation to more sophisticated poetry—even Blake and Shakespeare. I begin with their choices and before long, my students—even the jocks—are reading poetry and enjoying it. Then when the students write poems, I use models and other formulas so they can be successful. The formulas provide the skeleton so students can concentrate on creating images and interesting words. I deemphasize rhyme because it often gets in the way when my students write.

important than using comparisons to make writing more vivid; for example, children can compare anger to a thunderstorm. Using a simile, they might say: *Anger is like a thunderstorm, screaming with thunder-feelings and lightning words.* Or, as a metaphor, they might say: *Anger is a volcano, erupting with poisonous words and hot-lava actions.*

Students begin by learning traditional comparisons and idioms and to avoid stale comparisons, such as "high as a kite," "butterflies in your stomach," and "soft as a feather." Then they invent fresh, unexpected comparisons. Sixth grader Amanda uses a combination of expected and unexpected comparisons in this poem.

People

People are like birds
who are constantly getting their feathers ruffled.
People are like alligators
who find pleasure in evil cleverness.
People are like bees
who are always busy.
People are like penguins
who want to have fun.
People are like platypuses—
unexplainable!

Alliteration

Alliteration is the repetition of the same initial consonant sound in consecutive words or in words in close proximity to one another. Repeating the same initial sound makes poetry fun to read, and children enjoy reading and reciting alliterative verses like *A My Name Is Alice* (Bayer, 1984) and *The Z Was Zapped* (Van Allsburg, 1987). After reading one of these books, children can create their own versions. A fourth grade class created its own version of Van Allsburg's book, which they called "The Z was Zipped." Students divided into pairs, and each pair composed two pages for the class book. Students illustrated their letter on the front of the paper and wrote a sentence on the back to describe their illustration, following Van Allsburg's pattern. Two pages from the book are shown in Figure 11–10. Before reading the sentences, examine the illustrations and try to guess the sentences. These are the students' alliterative sentences:

The D got dunked by the duck.
The T was totally terrified.

Tongue twisters are an exaggerated type of alliteration in which every word (or almost every word) in the twister begins with the same letter. Dr. Seuss has compiled an easy-to-read collection of tongue twisters in *Oh Say Can You Say?* (1979) for primary-grade students. Schwartz's *A Twister of Twists, a Tangler of Tongues* (1972) and Kellogg's *Aster Aardvark's Alphabet Adventures* (1987) are two good books of tongue twisters for middle- and upper-grade students. Practice with tongue twisters and alliterative books increases children's awareness of the poetic device in poems they read and write. Few students consciously think about adding an alliteration to a poem they are writing, but they get high praise in writing groups when classmates notice an alliteration and compliment the writer on it.

Onomatopoeia

Onomatopoeia is a device in which poets use sound words to make their writing more sensory and more vivid. Sound words (e.g., *crash, slurp, varoom, me-e-e-ow*) sound like their meanings. Students can compile a list of sound words they find in stories and

FIGURE 11—10

Two Pages from "The Z was Zipped"

poems and display the list on a classroom chart or in their writer's notebooks to refer to when they write their own poems.

Spier has compiled two books of sound words; *Gobble Growl Grunt* (1971) is about animal sounds, and *Crash! Bang! Boom!* (1972) is about the sounds people and machines make. Students can use these books to select sound words for their writing. Comic strips are another good source of sound words; children collect frames from comic strips with sound words to add to a classroom chart.

In *Wishes, Lies and Dreams* (1970), Koch recommends having children write noise poems that include a noise or sound word in each line. These first poems often sound contrived (e.g., *A dog barks "bow-wow"*), but the experience helps children learn to use onomatopoeia, as this poem dictated by a kindergartner illustrates.

Elephant Noses

Elephant noses
Elephant noses
Elephants have big noses
Big noses
Big noses
Elephants have big noses
through which they drink
SCHLURRP

Repetition

Repetition of words and phrases is another device writers use to structure their writing as well as to add interest. Poe's use of the word *nevermore* in "The Raven" is one example, as is the gingerbread boy's boastful refrain in "The Gingerbread Boy." In this riddle, fourth grader Bonnie uses a refrain effectively.

A Man

I am a little man standing all alone
In the deep, dark wood.
I am standing on one foot
In the deep, dark wood.
Tell me quickly, if you can,
What to call this little man
Standing all alone
In the deep, dark wood.
Who am I?
(Answer: a mushroom)

Rhyme

Although rhyme is an important element of many types of poetry, it can be a sticking point for many young poets. When rhyme comes naturally, it adds a delightful quality to children's writing, but when it is equated with poetry, it gets in the way of word play and vivid images. The following three-line poem shows fifth grader Roy's effective use of rhyme.

Thoughts After a 40-Mile Bike Ride

My feet
And seat
Are beat.

❖ REVIEW

Elementary students enjoy reading and writing poems. Research indicates that they like humorous and narrative poems best. Word play is an excellent introduction to poetry; students can invent new words, laugh with language, create word pictures, and experiment with rhyme. Five types of poems that elementary students can write successfully are formula, free form, syllable- and word-count, rhymed, and model poems. An instructional strategy based on the model presented in Chapter 1 can be used to teach students to write poems. Comparison, alliteration, onomatopoeia, repetition, and rhyme are poetic devices that children should become familiar with.

❖ EXTENSIONS

1. Invite a small group of students to study a favorite poet. Students can read the poet's work and learn about his or her life. They may also want to arrange a conference telephone call or write letters to the poet. (Note: You can arrange for a conference call by contacting the poet's publisher and renting a special telephone from the telephone company.)

2. Share poetry with a group of students and encourage students to respond through choral reading, dramatization, compiling a picture book version of the poem, or creating a filmstrip.

3. Copy favorite poems on index cards and compile a collection of poems appropriate for the grade level you teach or plan to teach.

4. Plan and teach a lesson on word play to a group of elementary students.

5. Make a set of charts listing the formulas for poetic forms to use in teaching students to write poetry.

6. Teach a small group of students to write several types of poems using the instructional strategy and student examples presented in this chapter, then have students compile their poems in a class anthology or in hardbound books.

❖ REFERENCES

Adams, A. (1971). *A woggle of witches.* New York: Scribner.

Apseloff, M. (1979). Old wine in new bottles: Adult poetry for children. *Children's Literature in Education, 10,* 194–202.

Atwood, S. (1971). *Haiku: The mood of the Earth.* New York: Scribner.

Atwood, S. (1973). *My own rhythm: An approach to haiku.* New York: Scribner.

Bayer, J. (1984). *A my name is Alice.* New York: Dial.

Behn, H. (1964). *Cricket songs.* New York: Harcourt Brace Jovanovich.

Behn, H. (1971). *More cricket songs.* New York: Harcourt Brace Jovanovich.

Bernstein, J. E. (1979). *Fiddle with a riddle: Write your own riddles.* New York: Dutton.

Brewton, J. E., & Blackburn, L. A. (1978). *They've discovered a head in the box of bread and other laughable limericks.* New York: Crowell.

Brown, M. (1983). *What do you call a dumb bunny? And other rabbit riddles, games, jokes, and cartoons.* Boston: Little, Brown.

Chapman, D. L. (1985). Poet to poet: An author responds to child writers. *Language Arts, 62,* 235–242.

de Gasztold, C. B. (1965). *Prayers from the ark.* New York: Penguin Books.

Fisher, C. J., & Natarella, M. A. (1982). Young children's preferences in poetry: A national survey of first, second and third graders. *Research in the Teaching of English, 16,* 339–354.

Fleischman, P. (1985). *I am phoenix: Poems for two voices.* New York: Harper and Row.

Fleischman, P. (1988). *Joyful noise: Poems for two voices.* New York: Harper and Row.

Froman, R. (1974). *Seeing things: A book of poems.* New York: Crowell.

Geller, L. G. (1981). Riddling: A playful way to explore language. *Language Arts, 58,* 669–674.

Geller, L. G. (1985). *Word play and language learning for children.* Urbana, IL: National Council of Teachers of English.

Hall, R., & Friends. (1985). *Sniglets for kids.* Yellow Springs, OH: Antioch.

Hopkins, L. B. (1972). *Pass the poetry, please! Using poetry in pre-kindergarten-six classrooms.* New York: Citation Press.

Hopkins, L. B. (1983). *A song in stone: City poems.* New York: Crowell.

Horwitz, E. L. (1975). *When the sky is like lace.* Philadelphia: Lippincott.

Kellogg, S. (1987). *Aster Aardvark's alphabet adventures.* New York: Morrow.

Kennedy, X. J., & Kennedy, D. M. (1982). *Knock at a star: A child's introduction to poetry.* Boston: Little, Brown.

Koch, K. (1970). *Wishes, lies, and dreams.* New York: Vintage.

Koch, K. (1973). *Rose, where did you get that red?* New York: Vintage.

Kutiper, K. (1985). *A survey of the poetry preferences of seventh, eighth, and ninth graders.* Unpublished doctoral dissertation, University of Houston.

Langstaff, J. (1974). *Oh, a-hunting we will go.* New York: Atheneum.

Lewis, R. (Ed.). (1965). *In a spring garden.* New York: Dial.

Lewis, R. (1968). *Of this world: A poet's life in poetry.* New York: Dial.

Lewis, R. (1970). *The way of silence: The prose and poetry of Basho.* New York: Dial.

Livingston, M. C. (Ed.). (1982). *How pleasant to know Mr. Lear!* New York: Holiday House.

Lobel, A. (1983). *Pigericks: A book of pig limericks.* New York: Harper and Row.

Lowry, L. (1979). *Anastasia Krupnik.* Boston: Houghton Mifflin.

Merriam, E. (1966). *It doesn't always have to rhyme.* New York: Atheneum.

Milne, A. A. (1956). *The house at Pooh corner.* New York: Dutton.

O'Neill M. (1961). *Hailstones and halibut bones: Adventures in color.* Garden City, NJ: Doubleday.

Opie, I., & Opie, P. (1959). *The lore and language of school children.* Oxford, England: Oxford University Press.

Parker, M. K. (1981). A visit from a poet. *Language Arts, 58,* 448–451.

Pilon, B. (1972). *Concrete is not always hard.* Middletown, CT; Xerox Educational Publications.

Schwartz, A. (1972). *A twister of twists, a tangler of tongues.* New York: Harper and Row.

Seuss, Dr. (1979). *Oh say can you say?* New York: Beginner Books.

Sherman, I. (1980). *Walking talking words.* New York: Harcourt Brace Jovanovich.

Spier, P. (1971). *Gobble growl grunt.* New York: Doubleday.

Spier, P. (1972). *Crash! Bang! Boom!* New York: Doubleday.

Sterne, N. (1979). *Tyrannosaurus wrecks: A book of dinosaur riddles.* NY: Crowell.

Stewig, J. W. (1981). Choral speaking: Who has the time? Why take the time? *Childhood Education, 57,* 25–29.

Terban, M. (1982). *Eight ate: A feast of homonym riddles.* New York: Clarion.

Terry, A. (1974). *Children's poetry preferences: A national survey of upper elementary grades* (NCTE Research Report No. 16). Urbana, IL: National Council of Teachers of English.

Tiedt, I. (1970). Exploring poetry patterns. *Elementary English, 45,* 1082–1084.

Valentine, S. L. (1986). Beginning poets dig for poems. *Language Arts, 63,* 246–252.

Van Allsburg, C. (1981). *Jumanji.* Boston: Houghton Mifflin.

Van Allsburg, C. (1987). *The z was zapped.* Boston: Houghton Mifflin.

Viorst, J. (1981). *If I were in charge of the world and other worries.* New York: Atheneum.

12 WRITERS' TOOLS: SPELLING

THE ALPHABETIC PRINCIPLE
Spelling Rules
Lexical Spelling

CHILDREN'S INVENTED SPELLINGS
Stages of Invented Spelling
Middle- and Upper-grade Students' Spelling Errors
Analyzing Children's Stage of Spelling Development

TEACHING SPELLING IN THE ELEMENTARY GRADES
The Contract Spelling Approach
The Spelling Textbook Approach
Developing a Spelling Conscience
Learning to Use a Dictionary
Assessing Students' Progress in Spelling

◆ **IN THIS CHAPTER, WE DESCRIBE SPELLING AS A TOOL THAT** writers need for communicating with their readers. We examine the nature of English spelling, how children learn to spell, and how to teach spelling.

◆ **AS YOU ARE READING, THINK ABOUT THESE QUESTIONS:**

Is English spelling regular or irregular?

What is invented spelling?

How do elementary students learn to spell?

How do teachers teach spelling?

| arctic | consciousness | embarrass | grammar | ingenious |
| liquefy | marshmallow | occasion | professor | souvenir |

Which of these words are spelled correctly? Which are misspelled? If you're like most people, you may be confused about one or more of these words. They're all spelled correctly, but it's not hard to be unsure, especially if you expect pronunciation to determine spelling. English is not a purely phonetic language, and many words, such as *souvenir,* continue to reflect their origins in other languages.

Spelling is a tool for writers that allows them to communicate effectively and efficiently with readers. As Graves (1983) explains,

> Spelling is for writing. Children may achieve high scores on phonic inventories, or weekly spelling tests. But the ultimate test is what the child does under "game conditions," within the process of moving toward meaning. (pp. 193–194)

Spelling is too often treated as a separate subject in elementary classrooms; the end goal of spelling instruction is to spell a list of words correctly on Friday's test. <u>Students need instead to learn to spell words correctly</u> so that others <u>can read their writing</u>. English *X* spelling is complex, and attempts to teach spelling through weekly spelling lists have not been notably successful. Some students don't learn to spell the words correctly for the tests, and others spell the words correctly on the test, but continue to misspell them in their writing. Questions arise about the nature of English spelling, how children learn to spell, and how to teach spelling.

❖ THE ALPHABETIC PRINCIPLE

The *alphabetic principle* suggests a one-to-one correspondence between a language's phonemes or sounds and graphemes or letters such that each letter consistently represents one sound. English, however, does not have this correspondence. The 26 letters represent approximately 44 phonemes. Moreover, three letters—*c, q,* and *x*—are superfluous because they do not represent unique phonemes; for instance, the letter *c* can be used to represent either /k/ as in *cat* or /s/ as in *decide,* and it can be joined with *h* to represent the digraph /ch/. To further complicate the problem, there are more than 500 spellings to present the 44 phonemes. According to Horn (1957), long *e* is spelled 14 different ways in common words! This situation is known as "lack of fit." Appendix D lists common spelling options.

The reasons for lack of fit can be found by examining events in the history of the English language (Tompkins & Yaden, 1986). As we discussed in Chapter 3, approximately 75 percent of English words have been borrowed from languages around the world, and many of the words, especially the more recently acquired (e.g., *souvenir* was borrowed from French in the middle 1700s and literally means "to remember"), have retained their native spellings. Spellings of other words have been tinkered with by linguists. More than four hundred years ago, for instance, in an effort to relate the word *island* to its supposed French or Latin origin, the unnecessary and unpronounced *s* was added. *Island* (spelled *ilond* in the Middle Ages) is a native English word, however, and the spelling change sends a false message about its etymology.

The controversy about whether English spelling is regular or irregular has been waged for years. Linguists have recently begun to examine the deeper, underlying structure of language and have been able to account for many of the seeming irregularities in English. They suggest that English spelling is indeed regular, not at the phoneme-grapheme level, but at a deeper, more abstract level. Because of the number of available spelling options for many phonemes, it is helpful to develop a set of spelling option charts to display in the classroom. Write a phoneme (e.g., long e) at the top of a chart and ask students to list possible spelling options for the phoneme (e.g., e as in *be*, ee as in *tree, ea* as in *sea, ie* as in *chief,* and eo as in *people*). Compiling the list of spelling options and sample words can continue as a year-long activity, and students can add words to the charts as they find them in reading and writing activities.

An understanding of morphology can be a big help to students. Knowing that there is some system to the way words are spelled and how to change a word from one part of speech to another will help them express themselves in writing. The reason we learn to spell words, after all, is to express ourselves and to communicate with others through writing.

Spelling Rules

Because so many words have been borrowed from other languages, most spelling rules have exceptions. A classic long vowel rule, "when two vowels go walking, the first one does the talking," is not particularly useful (Grief, 1981). Commonly used exceptions are *said, air,* and *head.* Some rules are regular, however, and only rules that apply to a majority of words and have few exceptions should be taught. According to Horn (1960), only six types of rules are regular enough to be useful:

1. Rules for adding suffixes
2. That letter *q* is followed by *u*
3. That words do not end in *v*
4. That proper nouns and most adjectives formed from them begin with a capital letter
5. Rules for using periods in abbreviations
6. Rules for using an apostrophe in possessives and contractions

A list of these rules is presented in Figure 12–1. As students become aware of the regularities in the English spelling system, they can learn and apply the rules in their spelling. Have students verify the usefulness of each rule they learn by listing words from their reading and writing that follow the rule as well as any exceptions they find.

Lexical Spelling

English spelling often appears to be irregular, if not chaotic, when considered on the basis of phoneme-grapheme correspondences alone. Transformational linguists (e.g.,

1. Some rules governing the addition of suffixes and inflected endings include the following:

   a. Words ending in silent *e* drop the *e* when adding a suffix or ending beginning with a vowel and keep the *e* when adding a suffix or ending beginning with a consonant.

bake	manage
baking	managing
baker	management

   b. When a root word ends in *y* preceded by a consonant, the *y* is changed to *i* in adding suffixes and endings unless the ending or suffix begins with *i*.

fly	study
flies	studying
flying	studious
	studies

   c. When a root word ends in *y* preceded by a vowel, the root word is not changed when adding suffixes or endings.

play	monkey
playful	monkeys

   d. When a one-syllable word ends in a consonant with one vowel before it, the consonant is doubled before adding a suffix or ending beginning with a vowel.

run	ship
running	shipping
	shipment

   e. In words of more than one syllable, the final consonant is doubled before adding a suffix or ending if (a) the last syllable is accented, (b) the last syllable ends in a consonant with one vowel before it, and (c) the suffix or ending begins with a vowel.

begin	admit
beginning	admittance

2. The letter *q* is always followed by *u* in common English words.

queen	quiet

3. No English words end in *v*.

love	glove

4. Proper nouns and most adjectives formed from proper nouns should begin with capital letters.

America	American

5. Most abbreviations end with a period.

etc.	Nov.

FIGURE 12–1

Spelling Rules with Few Exceptions
Allred, 1977, pp. 27–28.

6. The apostrophe is used to show the omission of letters in contractions.

    don't   haven't

7. The apostrophe is used to indicate the possessive form of nouns but not pronouns.

    boy's   its
    dog's   theirs

8. When adding *s* to words to form plurals or to change the tense of verbs, *es* must be added to words ending with the hissing sounds (*x, s, sh, ch*).

    glass   watch
    glasses   watches

9. When *s* is added to words ending in a single *f,* the *f* is changed to *v* and *es* is added.

    half   shelf
    halves   shelves

10. When *ei* or *ie* are to be used, *i* usually comes before *e* except after *c* or when sounded like *a.* (Note these exceptions: leisure, neither, seize, and weird.)

    believe   neighbor
    relieve   weigh

FIGURE 12–1   (*continued*)

Noam Chomsky, 1965; Chomsky & Halle, 1968) began several decades ago to take a more careful look at the role phonology plays in English. They found that our spelling system's regularity is not at the phonological level, but at a deeper, lexical base level and that morphological aspects of English spelling indicate greater regularity than might otherwise be expected if phoneme-grapheme correspondences are considered alone. Certain nonphonetic aspects in spelling pertain to a deeper level of representation that considers the lexical nature of the word.

Tying the spelling system too closely to pronunciation raises some problems, because pronunciation shifts occur in English words when suffixes are added to them (C. Chomsky, 1970). Each added suffix and each pronunciation shift creates a new word, and a new spelling of the derived word would be necessary if spellings were created solely on the basis of the phoneme-grapheme correspondences. The word pairs *nation-national, major-majority,* and *sane-sanity,* for example, illustrate the shift from the long vowel sound /ey/ to /ae/. If you were to spell by pronunciation, the shift in the vowel sound would signal a change in spelling; thus, one lexical entry or spelling would be created for *nation* and another for *national.* Shifts in vowel sounds would result in many new entry words and would mask the underlying lexical relationships between the word pairs.

Vowel alternations are common in English. The same principles that govern the /ey/ to /ae/ alternation also govern other vowel alternations, such as the /iy/ to /e/ shift in *extreme-extremity* and the /ay/ to /i/ alternation in *wide-width.* Examples of vowel alternations are listed in Figure 12–2. These pairs, though phonemically different, are

FIGURE 12–2

Vowel and Consonant Alternations
Adapted from C. Chomsky, 1970.

Vowel Alternations

Alternations	Sample Word Pairs
/ā/→/ă/	courageous-courage
	explain-explanation
	major-majority
	nation-national
	nature-natural
	sane-sanity
/ē/→/ĕ/	convene-convention
	extreme-extremity
	precede-precedent
/ī/→/ĭ/	expedite-expeditious
	preside-president
	revise-revision
	sign-signature
	wide-width
/ō/→/ŏ/	compose-composition
	democratic-democracy
	phone-phonic
	photograph-photography

Consonant Alternations

/k/→/s/	medicate-medicine
	critical-criticize
	romantic-romanticize
/g/→/j/	sagacity-sage
	prodigal-prodigious
/d/→/j/	grade-gradual
	mode-modular
/t/ → /sh/	resident-residential
	expedite-expeditious
/t/ → /ch/	fact-factual
	quest-question
	right-righteous
/z/→/zh/	revise-revision
/s/→/z/	sign-resign
	gymnastics-gymnasium

variant forms of the same word. If the dictionary had just one spelling, a lexical spelling, vowel and pronunciation shifts would be the result of rules of pronunciation. Lexical spelling, therefore, operates at a deeper level than the surface level phoneme-grapheme correspondences.

Other surface phonemic variations are better represented by phonological rules. These rules operate on lexical spellings, which are able to preserve underlying relationships in words that a phonemic representation would fail to capture. English has a number of consonant alternations, such as the /k/ to /s/ shift in *medicate-medicine,* which are not expressed in the lexical spelling. A list of consonant alternations also appears in Figure 12–2. As you examine this list, note the influence of the vowels in the affixes on the consonants nearest to them; for example, in *medicate-medicine,* the shift from *a* to *i* in the suffixes results in the /k/ to /s/ consonant alternation.

Carol Chomsky makes the point "that the orthography bears an *indirect* rather than a direct relation to pronunciation. The direct correlation is to lexical spelling, a level of linguistic processing that is beneath the surface, related to pronunciation by regular phonological rules that are part of the child's normal linguistic equipment" (1970, p. 298). An example of this dependence can be observed in the addition of suffixes to root words. The root *cour-* needs to have a suffix, such as *-age* or *-ageous,* added before the pronunciation can be determined. Students need to be aware of the spelling of words with close phoneme-grapheme correspondences and those that are systematic in terms of lexical spellings with vowel and consonant alternations. As students examine relations among words according to their lexical spellings, they are adding cognitive categories and discovering new relationships among the categories. Teachers can help students realize that spelling is systematic and that many spelling errors can be avoided if they will look for relationships among words. Linguists' suggestion that orthography has a lexical base and is more regular than was supposed has helped spelling researchers move beyond the notion that phoneme-grapheme correspondences were the basic unit of study in spelling. The view that words, not phoneme-grapheme correspondences, are the appropriate unit of analysis for studying orthography helped them realize that "*both* phonological and morphological relationships play fundamental roles in establishing the spelling patterns within words" (Hodges, 1982, p. 286).

❖ CHILDREN'S INVENTED SPELLINGS

As young children begin to write, they create unique spellings based on their knowledge of English orthography. Charles Read (1971, 1975, 1986), one of the first researchers to study preschoolers' efforts to spell words, discovered that they used their knowledge of phonology to invent spellings. These children used letter names to spell words such as U (*you*), ME (*me*), and R (*are*), and they used consonant sounds rather consistently: GRL, (*girl*), TIGR (*tiger*), and NIT (*night*). The preschoolers used several unusual but phonetically based spelling patterns to represent affricates. They spelled *tr* with *chr* (e.g., CHRIBLES for *troubles*), *dr* with *jr* (e.g., JRAGIN for *dragon*), and substituted *d* for *t* (e.g., PREDE for *pretty*). Words with long vowels were spelled using letter names: MI (*my*), LADE (*lady*), and FEL (*feel*). The children used several ingenious strategies to spell words with short vowels. The three-, four-, and five-year-olds rather consistently selected letters to represent short vowels on the basis of place of articulation in the mouth. Short *i* was represented with *e* as in FES (*fish*), short *e* with *a* as in LAFFT (*left*), and short *o* with *i* as in CLIK (*clock*). These spellings may seem odd to adults, but are based on phonetic relationships. The children often omitted nasals within words (e.g., ED for *end*) and substituted -*eg* or -*ig* for -*ing* (e.g., CUMIG for *coming* and GOWEG for *going*). Also, they often ignored the vowel in unaccented syllables, as in AFTR (*after*) and MUTHR (*mother*).

These children had clearly developed some strategies for their spellings based on their knowledge of the phonological system and of letter names, their judgments of phonetic similarities and differences, and their ability to abstract phonetic information from letter names. Read suggested that, from among the many phonetic properties in the phonological system, children abstract away certain phonetic details and preserve others in their invented spellings.

Based on Read's seminal work, other researchers began to systematically study the development of children's spelling abilities. Henderson and his colleagues (Beers & Henderson, 1977; Gentry, 1978, 1981; Templeton, 1979; Zutell, 1979) have studied the manner in which children proceed developmentally from invented spelling to correct spelling. This research puts spelling into a developmental framework that is more closely akin to the pyscho- and sociolinguistic view of language learning, which stresses that students construct their own knowledge of language systems, including the orthographic system.

Stages of Invented Spelling

Researchers have found that, whereas all children do not invent spellings in exactly the same way or at the same speed, they do develop spelling strategies in roughly the same sequence (Henderson, 1980a). For example, a four-year-old child might use the random series of letters *btBpa* to spell the word *monster*. Months later, the child might use *MTR,* an abbreviated spelling that uses letters to represent sounds, to spell *monster*. In first grade, the child might spell monster as *MOSTR* and represent all the essential sound features of the word. By second grade, the child might write *MONSTUR,* a spelling that is not correct by adult standards but does adhere to the basic conventions of our spelling system. In time the child learns that *er* is the most likely spelling for the /r/ sound and spells the word correctly (Gentry, 1982b).

Based on observations of children's spellings, researchers have identified five stages that children move through on their way to becoming conventional spellers, and at each stage they use different types of strategies (Bean & Bouffler, 1987). The stages are precommunicative spelling, semiphonetic spelling, phonetic spelling, transitional spelling, and correct spelling (Gentry, 1978, 1981, 1982a, 1982b, 1987).

Stage 1: Precommunicative Spelling.   In this stage, children string scribbles, letters, and letterlike forms together, but they do not associate the marks they make with any specific phonemes. Precommunicative spelling represents a natural, early expression of the alphabet and other concepts about writing. Children may write from left to right, right to left, top to bottom, or randomly across the page. Some precommunicative spellers have a large repertoire of letter forms to use in writing, and

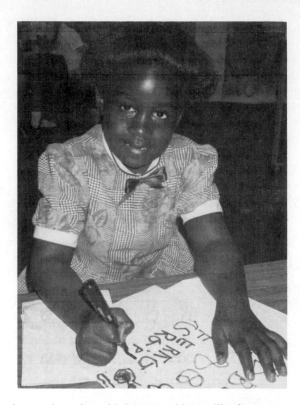

This kindergartner is experimenting with letters and letter–like forms.

others repeat a small number of letters over and over. Children may use both upper-
and lowercase letters, but they show a distinct preference for uppercase letters. At this
stage, children have not discovered how spelling works or the alphabetic principle that
letters represent sounds in words. This stage is typical of preschoolers, ages three to
five.

   Stage 2: Semiphonetic Spelling.   At this stage, children begin to represent
phonemes in words with letters, indicating that they have a rudimentary understanding
of the alphabetic principle, that a link exists between letters and sounds. Spellings are
quite abbreviated, and children use only one, two, or three letters to represent an entire
word. Examples of Stage 2 spelling are DA (*day*), KLZ (*closed*), and SM (*swimming*). As
these examples illustrate, semiphonetic spellers use a letter-name strategy to determine
which letters to use to spell a word, and their spellings represent some sound features
of words while ignoring other equally important features. Semiphonetic spellers include
five- and six-year-old children.

   Stage 3: Phonetic Spelling.   In this third stage, children's understanding of
the alphabetic principle is further refined. They continue to use letter names to represent sounds, but they also use consonant and vowels sounds at this stage. Examples
of Stage 3 spelling are LIV (*live*), DRAS (*dress*), and PEKT (*peeked*). As these examples show, children choose letters on the basis of sound alone, without considering

acceptable English letter sequences (e.g., using -*t* rather than -*ed* as a past tense marker in *peeked*) or other spelling conventions. These spellings do not resemble English words, and although spelling does not look like adult spelling, it can be deciphered. The major achievement of this stage is that, for the first time, children represent *all* essential sound features in the words they are spelling. Henderson (1980b) explains that words are "bewilderingly homographic" at this stage because children spell on the basis of sound alone; for example, *bat, bet,* and *bait* might all be spelled BAT (Read, 1971). Phonetic spellers are typically about six years old.

Stage 4: Transitional Spelling. Transitional spellers come close to the correct spellings of English words. They spell many words correctly, but continue to misspell words with irregular spellings. Examples of Stage 4 spelling are HUOSE (*house*), TRUBAL (*trouble*), EAGUL (*eagle*), and AFTERNEWN (*afternoon*). This stage is characterized by children's growing ability to represent the features of English orthography. First, they include a vowel in every syllable (as the *trouble* and *eagle* spellings show). Next, they demonstrate knowledge of vowel patterns even though they might make a faulty decision about which marker to use. For example, *toad* is often spelled TODE when children choose the wrong vowel marker, or TAOD when the two vowels are reversed. Also, transitional spellers use common letter patterns in their spelling, such as YOUNIGHTED for *united* and HIGHCKED for *hiked*. In this stage, children use conventional alternatives for representing sounds, and although they continue to misspell words according to adult standards, transitional spelling resembles English orthography and can easily be read. As the examples show, children stop relying entirely on phonological information and begin to use visual clues and morphological information as well. Transitional spellers are generally around seven and eight years old.

Stage 5: Correct Spelling. As the name implies, children spell many, many words correctly at this stage, but not all. They have mastered the basic principles of English orthography, and this achievement indicates that children are ready for formal spelling instruction (Gentry, 1981; 1982a). Children typically reach Stage 5 and are ready for formal spelling instruction by the age of eight or nine. During the next four or five years, children learn to control homonyms (e.g., *road-rode*), contractions, consonant doubling and adding affixes (e.g., *runing/running*), and vowel and consonant alternations. They also learn to spell most common irregularly spelled words. Spellers also learn about spelling alternatives—different ways to spell the same sound. The characteristics of each of the five stages of invented spelling are summarized in Figure 12–3.

In a short period of three or four years, young children move from precommunicative spelling to correct spelling. This learning happens informally rather than through direct instruction; when formal spelling instruction begins before children have reached the fifth stage, their natural development is interrupted. Typically, children are advised to sound out words or to memorize spellings. Sounding out is a stage children naturally progress through in the developmental sequence. If instruction interrupts their progress at that point, they are less likely to generalize the morphemic component of spelling. Similarly, the fourth and fifth stages are cut short when children memorize words.

Stage 1: Precommunicative Spelling

Child uses scribbles, letter-like forms, letters, and sometimes numbers to
    represent a message.
Child may write from left-to-right, right-to-left, top-to-bottom, or randomly on the
    page.
Child shows no understanding of phoneme-grapheme correspondences.
Child may repeat a few letters again and again or use most of the letters of the
    alphabet.
Child frequently mixes upper and lower case letters but shows a preference for
    upper case letters.

Stage 2: Semiphonetic Spelling

Child becomes aware of the alphabetic principle that letters are used to represent
    sounds.
Child uses abbreviated one, two, or three letter spelling to represent an entire
    word.
Child uses letter-name strategy to spell words.

Stage 3: Phoentic Spelling

Child represent all essential sound features of a word in spelling.
Child develops particular spellings for long and short vowels, plural and past
    tense markers and other aspects of spelling.
Child chooses letters on the basis of sound without regard for English letter
    sequences or other conventions.

Stage 4: Transitional Spelling

Child adheres to basic conventions of English orthography.
Child begins to use morphological and visual information in addition to phonetic
    information.
Child may include all appropriate letters in a word but reverse some of them.
Child uses alternate spellings for the same sound in different words, but only
    partially understands the conditions governing their use.
Child uses a high percentage of correctly spelled words.

Stage 5: Correct Spelling

Child applies the basic rules of the English orthographic system.
Child extends knowledge of word structure including the spelling of affixes,
    contractions, compound words, and homonyms.
Child demonstrates growing accuracy in using silent consonants and doubling
    consonants before adding suffixes.
Child recognizes when a word doesn't "look right" and can consider alternate
    spellings for the same sound.
Child learns irregular spelling patterns.
Child learns consonant and vowel alternations and other morphological structures.
Child knows how to spell a large number of words.

FIGURE 12–3

Characteristics of the Invented Spelling Stages
Adapted from Gentry, 1982, pp. 192–200.

Movement through these stages depends on immersion in a written language environment with daily opportunities to read and write. Teachers should also deemphasize standard spelling until students reach the correct stage and should tolerate children's invented spellings—even celebrate nonstandard spellings. Teachers can use these "mistakes" to identify the stage of invented spelling the child is in and to determine when the child has reached Stage 5 and is ready for formal spelling instruction.

Middle- and Upper-Grade Students' Spelling Errors

Researchers are continuing to study children's spelling development beyond age eight. Hitchcock (1989) studied children's spellings in grades two through six and classified the errors these older, correct-stage spellers continue to make. The categories are listed in Figure 12–4 in order of frequency. The most frequently occurring category is phonetic, in which students spell words as they pronounce them. That students continue to misspell words by spelling them phonetically is not surprising, because teachers and parents often encourage students to sound out the spelling when children ask how to spell an unknown word. This category and several others, such as homonyms, are characteristic of the third stage of invented spelling, phonetic spelling. The other categories represent spelling errors that are characteristic of the transitional stage of invented spelling. When Taylor and Kidder (1988) examined children's misspellings across the elementary grades, they concluded that deleting letters in words (*hoping* for *hopping* and *spose* for *suppose*) was the most frequent spelling error.

Other research has focused on the relationship between reading and spelling (Anderson, 1985). Researchers have examined the spelling strategies of poor readers in fourth through sixth grade and found that these students were likely to use a sounding-out strategy. Good readers, on the other hand, used a variety of spelling strategies, including visual information, knowledge about root words and affixes, and analogy to known words (Barron, 1980; Marsh et al., 1980). Frith (1980) concluded that older students who are good readers and spellers make spelling errors characteristic of the transitional stage, whereas students who are poor readers and spellers make spelling errors characteristic of the semiphonetic and phonetic stages. It seems reasonable that further research will identify several additional stages beyond the fifth one to more accurately describe children's spelling development through eighth grade.

The press and concerned parent groups periodically raise the question of whether elementary students learn to spell. There seems to be a public perception that today's children cannot spell. Researchers who are examining the types of errors students make have noted that the *number* of misspellings increases in grades one through four, as students write longer, but that the *percentage* of errors decreases. The percentage continues to decline in the upper grades, although some students continue to make errors (Taylor & Kidder, 1988). The Educational Testing Service (Applebee, Langer, & Mullis, 1987) reported on the frequency of spelling errors in formal writing assessments. Nine-year-olds averaged 92 percent correct spelling; 13-year-olds spelled 97 percent of words correctly, and 17-year-olds scored 98 percent. Stewig (1987) reported that the fourth graders in his study spelled 98 to 99 percent of words correctly. This data suggests that by third grade, most students are correct spellers, making 10 percent or fewer errors.

Category	Description	Sample
Phonetic	Students spell the word as it sounds.	*doter* for *daughter*
Omission of pronounced letter	Students omit a letter that is pronounced.	*aross* for *across*
Vowel pattern rule	Students use wrong vowel digraph or misuse silent *e*.	*speach* for *speech*
Reversal of a letter	Students reverse letters in words.	*croner* for *corner*
Vowel substitution	Students substitute one vowel for another, use incorrect vowel to represent the schwa sound, or substitute a vowel for a consonant.	*jab* for *job* *anemals* for *animals* *firet* for *first*
Homonym	Students use wrong homonym for the meaning intended.	*peace* for *piece*
Pronunciation	Students shorten or lengthen words, substitute graphemes, or shorten suffixes.	*spose* for *suppose*
Insertion of a letter	Students insert a letter which is not needed.	*ulgly* for *ugly*
Semiphonetic	Students use several letters chosen phonetically, to represent a word.	*peda* for *party*

FIGURE 12–4

Categories of Spelling Errors Made by Correct Stage Spellers
Hitchcock, 1989, pp. 100–101

Analyzing Children's Stage of Spelling Development

Teachers can analyze spelling errors in children's compositions by classifying the errors according to the five stages of spelling development. This analysis will provide information about the child's current level of spelling development and the kinds of errors the child makes. Knowing the stage of a student's spelling development will suggest an appropriate type of spelling instruction. Children who are not yet at the correct stage of spelling development—that is, who do not spell approximately 90 to 95 percent of words correctly and whose errors are not mostly at the transitional level—do not benefit from formal spelling instruction. Instead, early instruction interferes with spelling development because children move from phonetic spelling to memorizing spelling words without learning visual and morphological strategies.

A composition written by Marc, a first grader, is presented in Figure 12–5. He reverses *b* and *s*, and these two reversals make his writing more difficult to decipher. Here is a translation of Marc's composition:

Double consonants	Students double a consonant when it is not needed or fail to double a consonant when needed.	*untill* for *until* *peper* for *pepper*
Consonant substitution	Students substitute one consonant for another or substitute a consonant for a vowel.	*swin* for *swim* *fell* for *feel*
Compounding	Students separate compound words or combine words that are not compound words.	*a way* for *away* *alot* for *a lot*
Plurals, possessives, and contractions	Students omit an apostrophe in possessives and contractions and add an apostrophe in plurals.	*moms* for *mom's* *make's* for *makes* *wont* for *won't*
Affixes	Students use the wrong prefix or suffix.	*sking* for *skiing* *dissappeared* for *disappeared*
Omission of a silent letter	Students omit silent letters that are not heard in the pronunciation of the word.	*bome* for *bomb*

FIGURE 12–4   (*continued*)

Today a person at home called us and said that a bomb was in our school and made us go outside and made us wait a half of an hour and it made us waste our time on learning. The end.

Marc was writing about a traumatic event, and it was appropriate that he used invented spelling in his composition. Primary-grade students should feel free to write using invented spelling, and correct spelling is appropriate only if the composition will "go public." Prematurely differentiating between "child" and "adult" spelling interferes with children's natural spelling development and makes them dependent on adults to supply the "adult" spelling.

Spelling can be categorized by means of a chart, such as that illustrated in Figure 12–6, to gauge students' stage of spelling development and to anticipate upcoming changes in their spelling strategies. Write the stages of spelling development across the top of the chart, and list each word in the student's composition under one of the categories, ignoring proper nouns, capitalization errors, and poorly formed or reversed letters. Because a quick review of Marc's writing revealed no precommunicative spellings, this category was not included in the analysis.

Perhaps the most interesting thing about Marc's writing is that he spelled 56 percent of the words correctly. Only one word, *kod* (called), is categorized as semiphonetic, and it is classified this way because the spelling is extremely abbreviated, with

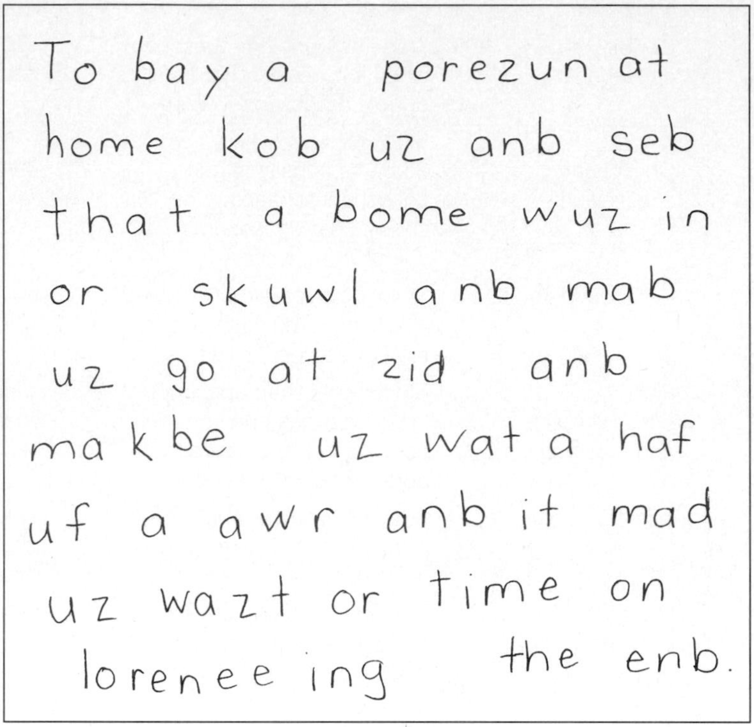

To bay a   porezun at
home kob uz anb seb
that a bome wuz in
or   skuwl anb mab
uz go at zid   anb
makbe   uz wat a haf
uf a awr anb it mad
uz wazt or time on
   loreneeing   the enb.

FIGURE 12–5

A First Grader's Composition Using Invented Spelling

only the first and last sounds represented. The 12 words categorized as phonetic are words in which it appears his spelling represents only the sounds heard; unpronounced letters, such as the final *e* in *made* and the *i* in *wait,* are not represented. Marc pronounces *our* as though it were a homophone for *or,* so *or* is a reasonable phonetic spelling. Homophone errors are phonological, because the child focuses on sound, not on meaning.

The words categorized as transitional illustrate the use of some type of spelling strategy other than sound. In *bome* (*bomb*), for example, Marc applies the final *e* rule he recently learned, even though it isn't appropriate in this word. In time he will learn to spell the word with an unpronounced *b* and that this *b* is needed because *bomb* is a newer, shortened form of *bombard,* in which the *b* in the middle of the word is pronounced. The *b* remains in *bomb* because of the etymology of the word. The word *makde* is especially interesting. Marc pronounced the word "maked," and the *de* is a reversal of letters, a common characteristic of transitional spelling. Transitional spellers often spell *girl* as *gril* and *friend* as *freind.* That *made,* not *maked,* is the past tense of *make* is a grammatical error and unimportant in determining the stage of spelling development. *Loreneeing* (*learning*) is categorized as transitional because Marc added long vowel markers (an *e* after *lor* and *ee* after *n*). Because the spelling is based on his pronunciation of *learning,* the long vowel markers and the correct spelling of the suffix *-ing* signal a transitional spelling. Categorizing spelling errors in a child's composition

Semiphonetic	Phonetic	Transitional	Correct
kod	sed	poresun	today
	wus	bome	a
	or	skuwl	at
	mad	makde	home
	at sid	loreneeing	us
	wat		and
	haf		that
	uf		a
	awr		in
	mad		and
	wast		us
	or		go
			and
			us
			a
			a
			and
			it
			us
			time
			on
			the
			end
Total Words 1	12	5	23
Percent 3	29	12	56

FIGURE 12–6

Analysis of Marc's Invented Spellings

and computing the percentage of errors in each category is a useful tool for diagnosing the level of spelling development and readiness for spelling instruction.

From the spelling in Marc's composition, he might be classified as a phonetic speller who is moving toward the transitional stage. Marc's paper in Figure 12–5 was written in January of his first grade year, and he is making expected progress in spelling. During the next few months, he will begin to notice that his spelling doesn't look right (e.g., *sed* for *said, uf* for *of*) and will note visual features of words. He will apply the vowel rules he is learning more effectively, particularly the final *e* (*mad* will become *made, sid* will become *side,* and *wast* will become *waste*).

Marc is not ready for formal spelling instruction, in which he would memorize correct spellings of words, because he has not yet internalized the visual and morpho- logical spelling strategies of the transitional stage. Also, Marc will probably self-correct the two letter reversals through daily writing experiences, as long as he is not placed under great pressure to form the letters correctly.

APPLIED SPELLING

"I tell my students to 'think it out' when they ask how to spell unfamiliar words. I used to say 'sound it out,' but then they wrote too many spellings that were phonetically correct but not really correct."

Judy Kenney, Fifth Grade Teacher,
Jackson Elementary School

PROCEDURE

I teach my students to think out the spellings for unfamiliar words. They need to consider the phonetic aspects of the word, but then they must go beyond to consider what the word looks like, its etymology, root words and affixes, and related words. Even though my students are

fifth graders, I encourage them to use invented spelling when they write; the invented spellings become placeholders. When they edit their writing later, they can check the correct spelling of the word.

We have just finished reading *Bridge to Terabithia* (Paterson, 1977), and my students are doing projects related to the book. Carlos and Will are making puppets to use in retelling the story, Annie is making a poster about the story, Elizabeth and Michelle are making a Venn diagram to compare Leslie and Jess, and the other students are involved in their own reading, writing, listening, and talking projects. Elena and Hua are designing the bulletin board for our display of the finished projects.

Students who are doing projects that involve writing use the process approach. They use invented spellings in their rough drafts and correct them during the editing stage. I tell my students I want them to make lots of corrections during editing, because that's a sign of a good writer. Many students think a paper that needs no editorial changes is a good paper.

I make up their spelling lists with words they misspell in their writing. I put together a list of 35 words each week. I'd call some of the words easy, even though a few students keep missing them, and I include a few that are challenging. On Monday they take a pretest on all 35 words. They immediately correct their pretests and choose ten of the words they missed for their personal lists. Then they make two copies of their lists, one for me and one for them. They practice the words for about five minutes each day using a simple strategy in which they look at the word, spell it aloud, copy it, write it from memory, and then write it again. On Friday, we have the final test. I read aloud all 35 words, but students write only their own ten words. This system took a lit-

tle work, but now my students number their papers according to the list so they know they have to spell words numbered 2, 17, 24, and so on.

ASSESSMENT

I give grades on the weekly spelling tests and check that students continue to spell those words from the weekly lists correctly in their written work. Students also make personal dictionaries with the words they correct during editing so they have the words to use again. Also, I examine invented spellings to see what strategies students are using to create the spellings and then I teach skills that particular students need in minilessons.

REFLECTIONS

I used to use a textbook for spelling instruction. We spent 30 minutes each day on it, and most students did well on the weekly tests. The difference now is that I see my students applying the spelling in their writing. We spend less time on spelling now, and the results are better.

I try to expand my students' horizons about spelling: I encourage them to think out spellings rather than just sound out spellings, to use invented spellings on rough drafts, and to correct spelling errors during the editing stage of the writing process. Another way I've expanded their view is to focus on using these spelling strategies on all written projects. Students' spelling on mobiles and on murals counts just as much as spelling on reports and stories.

❖ TEACHING SPELLING IN THE ELEMENTARY GRADES

After students have reached the correct stage of spelling development and spell 90 to 95 percent of words correctly, they are ready for formal spelling instruction. Providing opportunities for students to read and write each day is prerequisite to any spelling program. Spelling is a writer's tool best learned through writing (Bean & Bouffler, 1987). Students who write daily and use invented spellings will move naturally toward correct spelling. When they write, children guess at spellings using their knowledge of letter names and sounds. They gradually recognize that the words they are reading and writing are spelled the same way each time. When students recognize that words have consistent spellings, they are ready to be helped in a direct way. Teachers can then begin to point out conventions of the spelling system.

Emphasis on correct spelling, like handwriting and other mechanics, belongs in the editing stage of the writing process. As children write and revise their rough drafts, they should be encouraged not to worry about correct spelling and to invent spelling as needed. Stopping to ask a classmate or the teacher how to spell a word, or checking a spelling in a dictionary while pouring out ideas in a rough draft, interrupts the writer's train of thought. Through the process approach, children recognize spelling for what it is—a courtesy to the reader. As they write, revise, edit, and share their writing with genuine audiences, students will begin to learn that they need to spell correctly so that their audience will be able to read their compositions.

Reading also plays an enormous role in learning to spell. During reading, students store the words that they can recall on sight. The ability to recall how words look helps students decide when a spelling is or is not correct. If a word does not look right, they must check the spelling. When they decide a word does not look right, they can either rewrite the word several different ways until it does look right, or they can ask the teacher or a classmate who knows the spelling.

There are two basic approaches to teaching spelling. One is *contract spelling;* students choose which words they want to learn to spell according to the words they need for their writing and for content area study. The second approach is based on spelling *textbooks,* and the methods of teaching emphasize phoneme-grapheme correspondences. Some textbooks also emphasize morphology, and students study words in terms of root words, prefixes, and suffixes.

The Contract Spelling Approach

Research on children's invented spelling suggests that spelling is best learned through writing and that spelling instruction should be individualized so that children can learn to spell the words they need for their writing. In the contract approach, students choose words from their writing to learn to spell, and, because they are using the words in their writing and want to learn them, they remember how to spell them more easily. Students develop individual contracts with the teacher to learn specific words during the week. Contract spelling places more responsibility on students for their own learning, and when students have responsibility, they tend to perform better.

Developing the Word List.   Contract spelling begins with the development of a weekly word list from which teachers and students select. Words for the master list are drawn from all the words students needed in their writing activities during the previous week and words related to content area units or seasonal words. To accumulate words for the list, students can keep a sheet of paper taped to their desks, and teachers can record the words students need help with on the slips of paper. Or, teachers can write the needed words on slips of paper, which students return to a box on the teacher's desk after they are used. The list may include 30, 40, or even 50 words at the middle and upper grades.

The master word list also provides an opportunity to point out aspects of orthography. Students can look for phoneme-grapheme correspondences and develop lists of words to discover which letters most frequently represent each phoneme and whether the letters are in the initial, medial, or final positions. Students can also examine inflectional endings and the rules that operate on them as the words occur in sentences. In addition, students can examine the words for applications of the spelling rules with few exceptions.

Pretest. The master list of words serves as the pretest at the beginning of the week, and students try to spell as many of the master words as they can. From the words that each student misspells, he or she chooses words to study during the week, and these words become each student's spelling contract. After students have corrected their own pretests, they complete a spelling contract similar to the form shown in Figure 12–7. Students circle the words they spelled correctly on the pretest and transfer this information to the word list by circling the number of each correctly spelled word. Then they draw a box around the number of each word they plan to learn that week. If the word list and spelling contract are on the same form, students have less trouble keeping track of their work.

The master word list used for the pretest includes words at several levels of difficulty because of the students' different spelling needs. Because of the range of words on the master word list, students will be able to select words at their own level for their spelling contracts. They will need to experiment to determine the appropriate difficulty level for them and the number of words they can learn each week. Good spellers will be able to learn both more difficult words and a greater number of words each week than poor spellers will. Five words a week will be an achievement for some students, whereas others may be able to learn ten or 15 words.

Negotiating the Spelling Contract. Students negotiate with the teacher for the number of words they believe they can learn in one week. This number includes the words they spelled correctly plus additional words they misspelled on the pretest that they think they can learn. The negotiations help students learn to be realistic about their spelling ability.

Word Study. Students spend approximately five to ten minutes studying the words each day during the week. Instead of busywork activities such as using their spelling words in sentences or gluing yarn in the shape of the words, research shows it is more effective for students to learn and use a systematic strategy for practicing spelling words. The strategy should focus on the whole word rather than breaking it apart into sounds or syllables, and it should include visual, auditory, and kinesthetic components. An eight-step strategy that meets these two criteria is as follows.

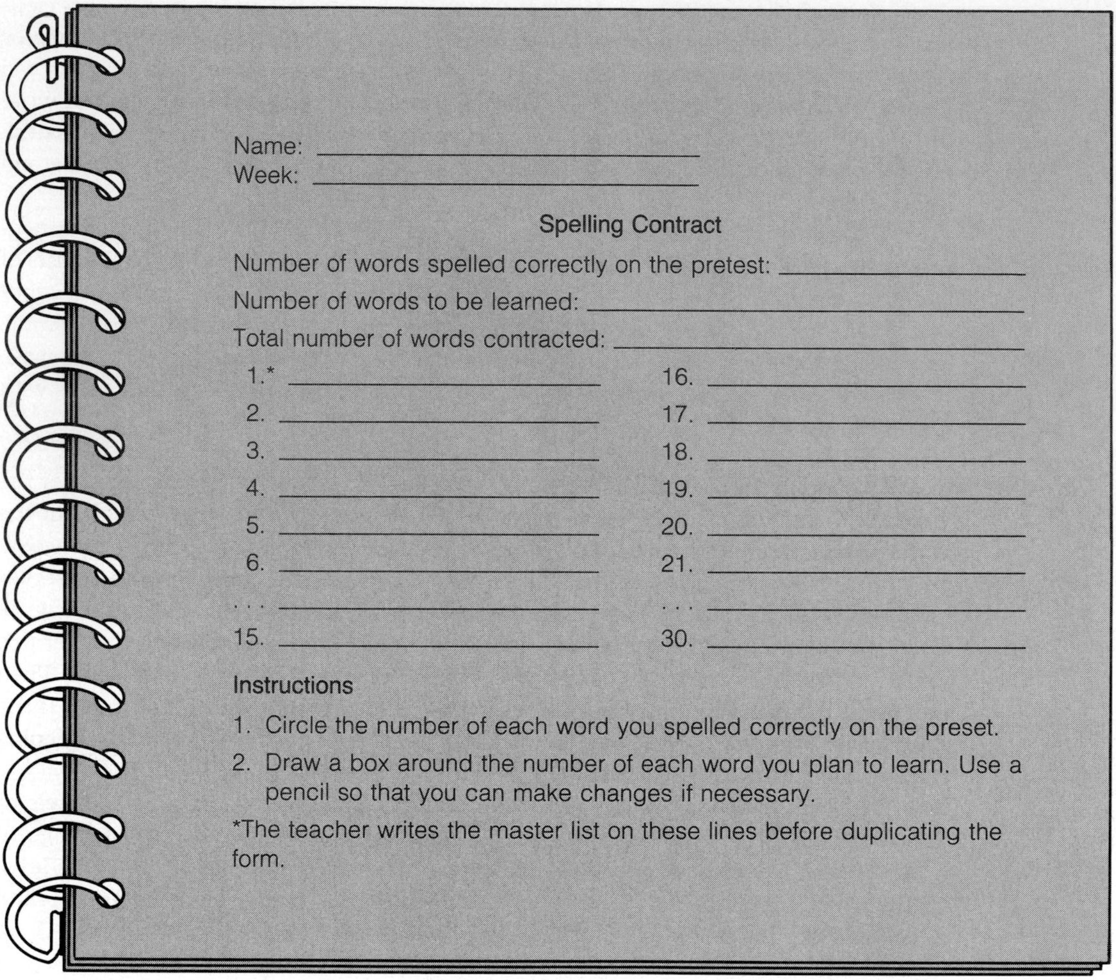

Name: _____
Week: _____

Spelling Contract

Number of words spelled correctly on the pretest: _____

Number of words to be learned: _____

Total number of words contracted: _____

1.* _____	16. _____
2. _____	17. _____
3. _____	18. _____
4. _____	19. _____
5. _____	20. _____
6. _____	21. _____
. . . _____	. . . _____
15. _____	30. _____

Instructions

1. Circle the number of each word you spelled correctly on the preset.

2. Draw a box around the number of each word you plan to learn. Use a pencil so that you can make changes if necessary.

*The teacher writes the master list on these lines before duplicating the form.

FIGURE 12–7

Teacher's Notebook Page: Spelling Contract and Word List

1. Look at the word and say it.

2. Read each letter in the word.

3. Close your eyes and spell the word to yourself.

4. Look at the word. Did you spell it correctly?

5. Copy the word from your list.

6. Cover the word and write it again.

7. Look at the word. Did you write it correctly?

8. If you made any mistakes, repeat the steps. (Cook et al., 1984, p. 1)

Weekly Final Test. A final test is administered at the end of the week on the words the students have contracted to learn. The teacher reads the master list, and students write only those words they have contracted to learn. To make it easier to administer the test, students first list the numbers of the words they have contracted to spell on their test papers; they can locate the numbers of their contracted spelling words on their spelling contracts.

Follow-up. Any words that students misspell should be included on their lists for the following week. Students should also list these problem words in a special spelling log notebook and try to determine why the words are difficult for them.

The Spelling Textbook Approach

The spelling textbook approach is the traditional way to help students learn to spell. There is little variation in the content of the textbooks and in the methods suggested for teaching the words. Typically, the textbook is arranged in week-long units, with lists of

A student corrects his own pretest to identify what words he already knows how to spell and what words he needs to study.

ten to twenty words around which a variety of practice activities are planned. Researchers have made five recommendations regarding use of the textbook approach. The recommendations deal with study and testing procedures, unit arrangements, the word list, instructional strategy, and time allocation.

Study and Testing Procedures. Most spelling textbooks use a variation of the *test-study-test* plan, in which students are given a pretest on Monday, encouraged to study during the week the words they missed, and are retested on Friday. Some teachers omit the pretest and use a study-test plan in which students study all words, even those they already know; other teachers add a midweek trial test (test-study-test-study-test plan). Researchers have found that the pretest is a critical component in the study procedure. The pretest helps to identify words that students already know how to spell. By eliminating those words, students can direct their study toward the words that are difficult for them. Students need immediate feedback about their efforts to learn to spell. According to Horn (1947), the best way to improve students' spelling is to have them correct their own pretests and trial tests to receive immediate feedback.

pretests are very important

Unit Arrangement. Spelling textbooks use a weekly plan that includes lessons for each of the five days. On Monday, the words in the new unit are introduced, and, typically, students copy the word list and sometimes use the words to write sentences or to fill in blanks to complete a paragraph. On Tuesday, spellers usually have a set of exercises that provides practice for an aspect of word structure, such as phoneme-grapheme correspondences, spelling patterns, or root words and affixes. In many programs, Wednesday is the day for the trial test, and some programs also include additional word study activities. Spelling textbooks provide a variety of activities for Thursday, ranging from grammar, dictionary, and handwriting activities to enrichment word activities. Friday is reserved for the final spelling test. A sample textbook unit appears in Figure 12–8.

The Word List. Spelling lists usually include the most frequently used words. Spelling textbooks for the elementary grades present at least 3000 words, and researchers have found that these 3000 most frequently used words account for more than 97 percent of all the words children and adults use in writing. Even more interesting, the three most frequently used words—*I, and, the*—account for 10 percent of all words written, and the 100 most frequently used words represent more than 50 percent of all the words written (E. Horn, 1926). Thus, a relatively small number of words accounts for an amazingly large percentage of words students use in their writing. Figure 12–9, p. 462, lists the 100 most frequently used words.

The words in each unit are often grouped according to spelling patterns or phonetic generalizations; that is, all the words in one spelling list may follow a vowel rule (e.g., *i-e*) or a spelling pattern (e.g., *-igh*). Researchers question this approach; Johnson, Langford, and Quorn (1981) found that "the effectiveness of teaching spelling via phonic generalizations is highly questionable" (p. 586). Students often memorize the rule or spelling pattern and score perfectly on the spelling test, but later are unable to choose among spelling options in their writing. For example, after learning the *i-e* vowel rule and the *-igh* spelling pattern in isolation, students are often stumped about how to spell a word such as *light*. They have learned two spelling options for /ay/, *i-e* and *-igh*, and *lite* is an option, one they often see in their environment. Instead of organizing words according to phonetic generalizations and spelling rules, many educators recommend that teachers simply point out the rules whenever they occur.

The Instructional Strategy. Students need a systematic and efficient strategy for learning to spell words. The strategy should focus on the whole word rather than breaking it apart into sounds or syllables, and it should include visual, auditory, and kinesthetic components, as does the strategy outlined for contract spelling. Similar strategies are presented in most spelling textbooks. Research indicates that a whole-word approach to spelling instruction is more successful than phonetic or syllable approaches (T. Horn, 1969).

Time Allocation. Assignments in spelling textbooks often require at least 30 minutes per day to complete, totaling two hours per week of spelling instruction. Research indicates that only 60 to 75 minutes per week should be spent on spelling instruction, however, and greater periods of time do not result in increased spelling ability (Johnson et al., 1981). Many of the activities in spelling textbooks involve language arts skills that are not directly related to learning to spell (Graves, 1977). If these activities, which often duplicate other language arts activities, were eliminated and students were to focus for 15 minutes each day on practicing their spelling words using the instructional strategy, they could learn to spell more quickly and more easily.

A checklist for assessing spelling textbooks according to these five criteria and researchers' recommendations is presented in Figure 12–10, p. 463.

Developing a Spelling Conscience

Spelling involves more than just learning to spell specific words, whether they are drawn from children's writing or from words listed in spelling textbooks. Hillerich (1977) believes that students need to develop a *spelling conscience*—a positive attitude toward spelling and a concern for using standard spelling. Two dimensions of a spelling conscience are understanding that standard spelling is a courtesy to readers and developing the ability to proofread to spot and correct misspellings.

Students in the middle and upper grades need to learn that it is unrealistic to expect readers to try to decipher numerous misspelled words. This dimension of a spelling conscience develops as students write frequently and for varied audiences. Writing for a variety of audiences helps students acquire a concept of audience and a realization that readers will read their writing. As students move from writing for self to writing that communicates, they internalize this concept. Teachers help students recognize the purpose of standard spelling by providing meaningful writing activities directed to a variety of genuine audiences. The second dimension, proofreading for spelling errors, is an essential part of the writing process. As discussed in Chapter 7, proofreading is part of the editing stage, and it should be introduced in kindergarten and first grade rather than postponed to the middle grades. Young children and their teachers proofread class collaboration and dictated stories together, and students can be encouraged to read over their own compositions and make necessary corrections as soon as they begin writing. With this introduction, students accept proofreading as a

/ôr/

OUR WORDS

sport   pour   score
order   or   poor
storm   corner   sore
forget   snore   course
horn   fort   fourth

_____

PATTERN POWER

Say each spelling word.

1. Write the three spelling words in which /ôr/ as in **born** is spelled **ore.**

_____

2. Write the eight spelling words in which /ôr/ is spelled **or.**

_____

3. Write the three spelling words in which /ôr/ is spelled **our.**

_____

4. Write the spelling word in which /ôr/ is spelled **oor.**

_____

In most words, /ôr/ as in born is spelled or, ore, or our.

90

MEANING MASTERY

Mr. Gibben has a very unusual store. Use the spelling words below to complete this paragraph about his strange shop.

sore   order   sport   corner   storm   horn

Mr. Gibben owns an odd store just around the (1) _____. He has everything you can think of. If you like to play music, you can buy a (2) _____. If your back is (3) _____, you can buy something to make it feel better. You can buy equipment for any kind of (4) _____ you want to play. You can even buy a coat to keep you warm in a snow (5) _____. If you want something he does not have, Mr. Gibben will (6) _____ it for you.

DICTIONARY SKILLS

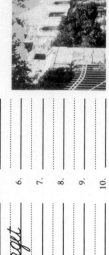

Pretend *forget* and *snore* are guide words on a dictionary page. Write in alphabetical order the ten spelling words that would appear on this page. Be sure to include the guide words. The first one is done for you.

1. _forget_   6. _____
2. _____   7. _____
3. _____   8. _____
4. _____   9. _____
5. _____   10. _____

WORD BUILDING

You can make new words by adding -**ly** at the end of some base words. Add the suffix -**ly** to each base word below. Write the new words. The first one is done for you.

1. loud   *loudly*
2. poor
3. proud
4. order
5. high
6. deep
7. even
8. certain

sport
order
storm
forget
horn
pour
or
corner
snore
fort
score
poor
sore
course
fourth

WRITING ACTIVITIES

Write two sentences using spelling words to describe what is happening in the picture to the right.

92

HANDWRITING PRACTICE

A. Practice writing **our** and **ore**. Be sure the **o** is closed at the top. Be sure the **u** is pointed at the top, so it does not look like an **n**.

our   ore

B. Now practice writing these sentences.

1. *The fourth score is yours.*

2. *Of course I snore.*

CHALLENGE WORDS

Use the challenge words to complete each sentence below.

fifty   forty   age   thirty   twenty

1. If you want to know a person's _____, ask, "How old are you?"
2. There are _____ states in the United States.
3. Two times ten is _____.
4. April and June each has _____ days.
5. Halfway between thirty and fifty is _____.

93

FIGURE 12–8

Sample Unit from a Third-Grade Spelling Textbook
Cook, Esposito, Gabrielson, & Turner, 1984, pp. 90–93.

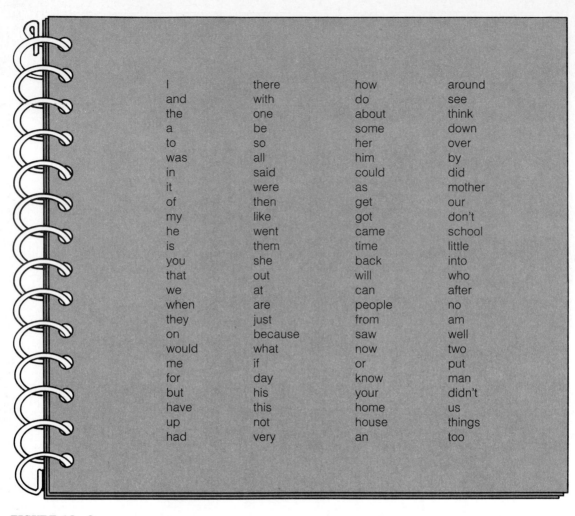

FIGURE 12–9

Teacher's Notebook Page: The 100 Most Frequently Used Words
Hillerich, 1978, p. xiii.

natural part of both spelling and writing, and together with their growing awareness of audience, will appreciate the importance of proofreading to correct misspellings and other mechanical errors.

Learning to Use a Dictionary

Students need to learn to locate the spellings for unknown words in the dictionary. Of the approximately 450,000 entry words in an unabridged dictionary, students typically learn to spell 3000 by the end of eighth grade—leaving 447,000 words unaccounted for! Obviously, students must learn how to locate the spellings of many of these additional words. Whereas it is relatively easy to find a "known" word in the dictionary, it

---

SPELLING TEXTBOOK ASSESSMENT

Textbook _____

Publisher _____

Grade Level _____ Reviewer _____

Study and Testing Procedures

____ Does the textbook use a test-study-test plan (or a variation of that plan)?
____ Do students take a pretest before studying the list of spelling words?
____ Do students correct their own pretests and trial tests?
____ Do students study all words in the list or only those that they do not know how to spell?

Unit Arrangement

____ Does the textbook use a five-day approach?
____ Do the activities focus on learning to spell the words or on related activities such as grammar, dictionary skills, or handwriting?

Spelling Words

____ How are the spelling words selected?
____ Are the spelling words grouped according to spelling patterns or phonetic generalizations?

Instructional Strategy

____ Does the textbook present a systematic and efficient strategy for learning to spell words?
____ Does the strategy focus on whole words rather than breaking words apart into sounds or syllables?
____ Does the strategy include visual, auditory, and kinesthetic components?

Time

____ How much time is required for students to complete the assignments in the textbook?

FIGURE 12–10

Checklist for Assessing Spelling Textbooks

is much harder to locate an unfamiliar word, and students need to learn what to do when they do not know how to spell a word. One approach is to consider spelling options and predict possible spellings for unknown words, then check the predicted spelling by consulting a dictionary. This strategy involves six steps:

1. Identify root words and affixes.

2. Consider related words (e.g., medicine-medical).

3. Determine the sounds in the word.

4. Generate a list of spelling options.

5. Select the most likely alternatives.

6. Consult a dictionary to check the correct spelling.

The fourth step is undoubtedly the most difficult. Using knowledge of both phonology and morphology, students develop a list of possible spellings. Phoneme-grapheme relationships may rate primary consideration in generating spelling options for some words; root words and affixes or related words may be more important in determining how other words are spelled.

Assessing Students' Progress in Spelling

Grades on weekly spelling tests are the traditional measure of progress in spelling. Both contract spelling and the textbook approach provide teachers with a convenient way to assess students, based on the number of words they spell correctly on weekly tests. This method of assessing student progress is somewhat deceptive, however, because the goal of spelling instruction is not simply to spell words correctly on weekly tests but to use the words, correctly spelled, in writing. Grades on weekly spelling tests are meaningless unless students can use the words in their writing. Samples of student writing should be collected periodically to determine whether words that were spelled correctly on tests

A student notes her spelling errors and categorizes them to determine patterns of error.

are being spelled correctly in writing assignments. If students are not applying in their writing what they have learned through the weekly spelling instruction, they may not have learned to spell the words after all. Students sometimes memorize the words or the spelling pattern for the tests without really learning to spell the words.

When students perform poorly on spelling tests, consider whether faulty pronunciation or poor handwriting is to blame. Ask students to pronounce words they habitually misspell to see if pronunciation or dialect differences may be contributing to spelling problems. Students need to recognize when pronunciation does not always predict spelling. In some parts of the U.S., people pronounce the words *pin* and *pen* as though they were spelled with the same vowel. Sometimes we pronounce *better* as though it were spelled *bedder* and *going* as though it were spelled *goin'*. Ask students to spell orally the words they spell incorrectly in their writing to see whether handwriting difficulties are contributing to spelling problems. Sometimes a lesson on how to connect two cursive letters (e.g., *br*) or a reminder about the importance of legible handwriting will solve the problem.

In addition to the grades on weekly spelling tests, it is essential that teachers keep anecdotal information and samples of children's writing to monitor their overall progress in learning to spell. Teachers need to examine error patterns and spelling strategies in these samples. Checking to see if students have spelled their spelling words correctly in writing samples provides one type of information, and examining writing samples for error patterns and spelling strategies provides an additional type of information. Fewer misspellings do not necessarily indicate progress, because to learn to spell, students must experiment with spellings of unfamiliar words, which will result in errors from time to time. Students often misspell a word by misapplying a newly learned spelling pattern. The word *extension* is a good example. Middle-grade students spell the word *extenshun,* then change their spelling to *extention* after they learn the suffix *-tion*. Although they are still misspelling the word, they have moved from using sound-symbol correspondences to using a spelling pattern—from a less sophisticated to a more sophisticated spelling strategy.

Students' behavior as they proofread and edit their compositions also provides evidence of progress in spelling. They should become increasingly able to spot misspelled words in their compositions and to locate the spelling of unknown words in a dictionary. It is easy for teachers to calculate the number of spelling errors students have identified in proofreading their compositions and to chart students' progress in learning to spot errors. Locating errors is the first step in proofreading; correcting the errors is the second step. It is fairly easy for students to correct the spelling of known words, but to correct unknown words, they must consider spelling options and predict possible spellings before they can locate the words in a dictionary. Teachers can also document students' growth in locating unfamiliar words in a dictionary by observing their behavior when they edit their compositions.

Teachers should collect writing samples to document children's spelling competence. Teachers can note primary-grade students' progression through the stages of invented spelling by analyzing writing samples against the checklist in Figure 12–3 to determine a general stage of development. A checklist incorporating the list of categories of errors made by correct spellers in the middle and upper grades is shown in Figure 12–4. A sample checklist is presented in Figure 12–11. Teachers and students can use this checklist to analyze students' spelling errors and plan for instruction.

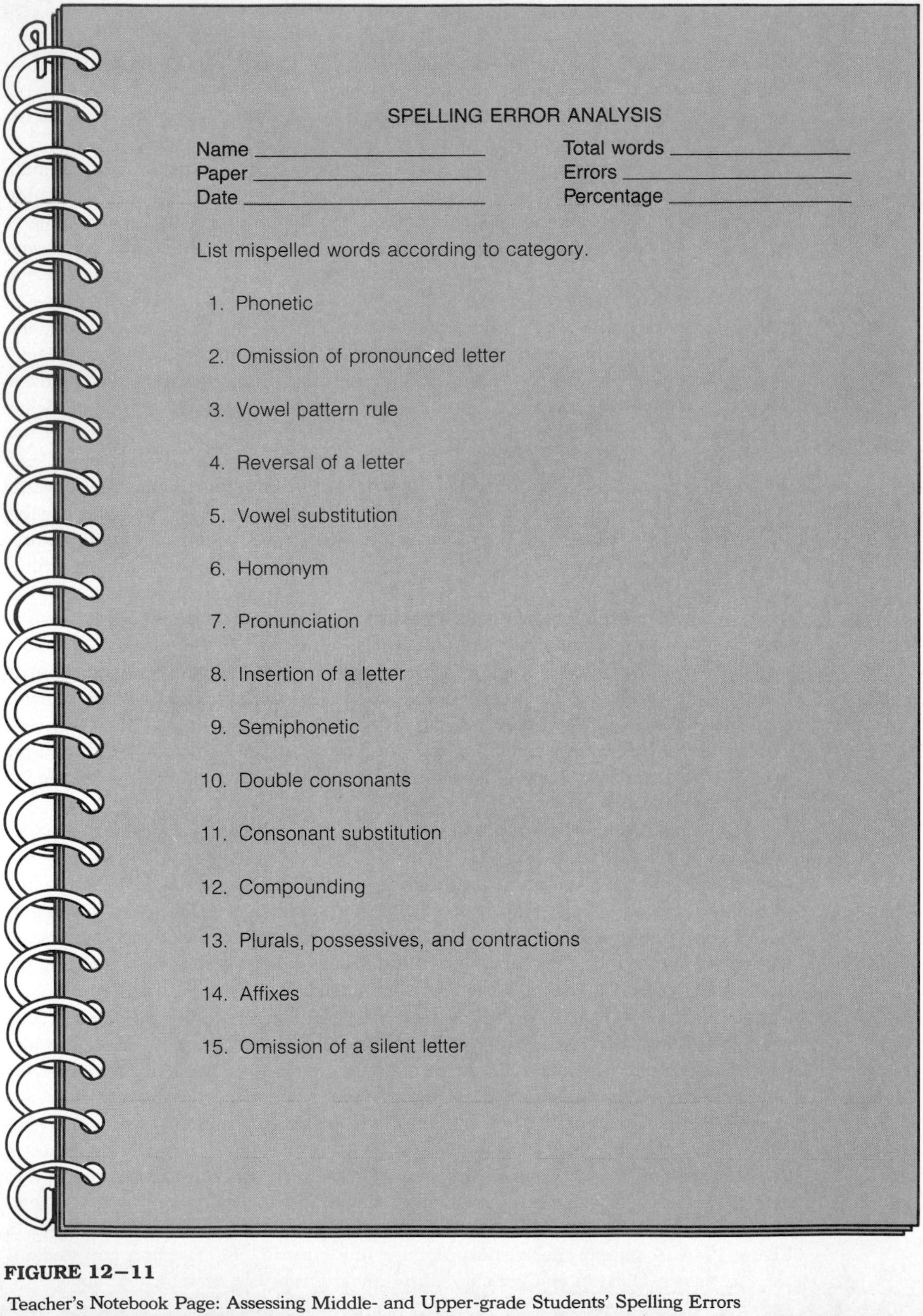

SPELLING ERROR ANALYSIS

Name _____   Total words _____

Paper _____   Errors _____

Date _____   Percentage _____

List mispelled words according to category.

1. Phonetic

2. Omission of pronounced letter

3. Vowel pattern rule

4. Reversal of a letter

5. Vowel substitution

6. Homonym

7. Pronunciation

8. Insertion of a letter

9. Semiphonetic

10. Double consonants

11. Consonant substitution

12. Compounding

13. Plurals, possessives, and contractions

14. Affixes

15. Omission of a silent letter

FIGURE 12–11

Teacher's Notebook Page: Assessing Middle- and Upper-grade Students' Spelling Errors

❖ REVIEW

The alphabetic principle suggests a one-to-one correspondence between phonemes and graphemes, but English does not have this correspondence. English is a historic rather than a phonetic language, and events in the development of the language and borrowing of words from other languages explain many of the seeming inconsistencies.

When young children begin to write, they create invented spellings based on their knowledge of English orthography. Researchers have documented that students move through a sequence of five stages in learning to spell during the elementary grades. When students reach the fifth stage, Correct Spelling, and spell at least 90 percent of the words in their compositions correctly, they are ready for formal spelling instruction.

There are two basic approaches to teaching spelling: contract spelling and the textbook approach. Contract spelling, in which students choose their spelling words from the words they need to spell in their writing projects and for content area study, is the recommended approach. In addition to a formal spelling program, students should read widely, write daily, and connect their spelling words to content area study.

❖ EXTENSIONS

1. Examine several spelling textbooks at the grade level you teach or expect to teach and evaluate them using the checklist in Figure 12–10. How well do the textbooks adhere to the research findings about how spelling should be taught?

2. Observe how spelling is taught in a classroom where the textbook approach is used and in another class in which contract spelling is used. Compare the two approaches. If possible, assist in teaching a lesson in each classroom.

3. Collect samples of a student's writing and analyze the spelling as shown in Figures 12–6 and 12–11.

4. Interview a middle- or upper-grade student about spelling. Ask questions such as these:
   - Who do you know who is a good speller? Why is he/she a good speller?
   - Are you a good speller? Why? Why not?
   - What do you do when you do not know how to spell a word? What else do you do?
   - How would you help a classmate who did not know how to spell a word?
   - Are some words harder for you to spell than other words? Which words?
   - What rules about how to spell words have you learned?
   - Do you think that "sound it out" is a good way to try to figure out the spelling of a word you do not know? Why or why not?
   - Do you use a dictionary to look up the spelling of words you do not know how to spell?
   - Do you have a list of words to learn to spell each week?
   - How do you study these words?

5. Help students proofread their writing and identify possible misspelled words. Watch what strategies students use to identify and correct misspelled words.

6. Students ask many questions about the seeming inconsistencies of English words and their spellings. For example, first graders often ask why there are silent e's. Consult *Answering Students' Questions About Words* (Tompkins & Yaden, 1986) to find answers to students' questions. Use the answers and activities suggested in the book to prepare and teach a spelling lesson to a small group of students.

❖ REFERENCES

Allred, R. A. (1977). *Spelling: An application of research findings*. Washington, DC: National Education Association.

Anderson, K. F. (1985). The development of spelling ability and linguistic strategies. *The Reading Teacher, 39,* 140–147.

Applebee, A. N., Langer, J. A., & Mullis, I. V. S. (1987). *Grammar, punctuation, and spelling: Controlling the conventions of written English at ages 9, 13, and 17* (Report No. 15-W-03). Princeton, NJ: Educational Testing Service.

Barron, R. W. (1980). Visual and phonological strategies in reading and spelling. In U. Frith (Ed.), *Cognitive processes in learning to spell*. London: Academic Press.

Bean, W., & Bouffler, C. (1987). *Spell by writing*. Rozelle, New South Wales (Australia): Primary English Teaching Association.

Beers, J. W., & Henderson, E. H. (1977). A study of developing orthographic concepts among first graders. *Research in the Teaching of English, 11,* 133–148.

Chomsky, C. (1970). Reading, writing, and phonology. *Harvard Educational Review, 40,* 287–309.

Chomsky, N. (1965). *Aspects of the theory of syntax*. Cambridge, MA: M.I.T. Press.

Chomsky, N., & Halle, M. (1968). *The sound pattern of English*. New York: Harper and Row.

Cook, G. E., Esposito, M., Gabrielson, T., & Turner, G. (1984). *Spelling for word mastery*. Columbus, OH: Merrill.

Dale, E., & O'Rourke, J. (1971). *Techniques of teaching vocabulary*. Palo Alto, CA: Field Educational Publications.

Frith, U. (1980). Unexpected spelling problems. In U. Frith (Ed.), *Cognitive processes in learning to spell*. London: Academic Press.

Gentry, J. R. (1978). Early spelling strategies. *Elementary School Journal, 79,* 88–92.

Gentry, J. R. (1981). Learning to spell developmentally. *The Reading Teacher, 34,* 378–381.

Gentry, J. R. (1982a). An analysis of developmental spellings in *Gnys at wrk. The Reading Teacher, 36,* 192–200.

Gentry, J. R. (1982b). Developmental spelling: Assessment. *Diagnostique, 8,* 52–61.

Gentry, J. R. (1987). *Spel. . .is a four-letter word*. Portsmouth, NH: Heinemann.

Graves, D. H. (1977). Research update: Spelling texts and structural analysis methods. *Language Arts, 54,* 86–90.

Graves, D. H. (1983). *Writing: Teachers and students at work*. Portsmouth, NH: Heinemann.

Grief, I. P. (1981). "When two vowels go walking," they should get lost. *The Reading Teacher, 34,* 460–461.

Henderson, E. H. (1980a). Developmental concepts of word. In E. H. Henderson & J. W. Beers (Eds.), *Developmental and cognitive aspects of learning to spell: A reflection of word knowledge,* pp. 1–14. Newark, DE: International Reading Association.

Henderson, E. H. (1980b). Word knowledge and reading disability. In E. H. Henderson & J. W. Beers (Eds.), *Developmental and cognitive aspects of learning to spell: A reflection of word knowledge,* pp. 138–148. Newark, DE: International Reading Association.

Hillerich, R. L. (1977). Let's teach spelling—Not phonetic misspelling. *Language Arts, 54,* 301–307.

Hillerich, R. L. (1978). *A writing vocabulary for elementary children*. Springfield, IL: Thomas.

Hitchcock, M. E. (1989). *Elementary students' invented spellings at the correct stage of spelling development*. Unpublished doctoral dissertation, Norman, OK: University of Oklahoma.

Hodges, R. E. (1982). Research update: On the development of spelling ability. *Language Arts, 59,* 284–290.

Horn, E. (1926). *A basic writing vocabulary*. Iowa City: University of Iowa Press.

Horn, E. (1957). Phonetics and spelling. *Elementary School Journal, 57,* 233–235, 246.

Horn, E. (1960). Spelling. In C. W. Harris (Ed.), *Encyclopedia of educational research* (3rd ed.), pp. 1337–1354. New York: Macmillan.

Horn, T. D. (1947). The effect of the corrected test on learning to spell. *Elementary School Journal, 47,* 277–285.

Horn, T. D. (1969). Spelling. In R. L. Ebel (Ed.), *Encyclopedia of educational research* (4th ed.), pp. 1282–1299. New York: Macmillan.

Johnson, T. D., Langford, K. G., & Quorn, K. C. (1981). Characteristics of an effective spelling program. *Language Arts, 58,* 581–588.

Marsh, G., Friedman, M., Desberg, P., & Welsh, V. (1981). The development of strategies in spelling. In U. Frith (Ed.), *Cognitive processes in learning to spell.* London: Academic Press.

Paterson, K. (1977). *Bridge to Terabithia.* New York: Crowell.

Read, C. (1971). Pre-school children's knowledge of English phonology. *Harvard Educational Review, 41,* 1–34.

Read, C. (1975). *Children's categorization of speech sounds in English* (NCTE Research Report No. 17). Urbana, IL: National Council of Teachers of English.

Read, C. (1986). *Children's creative spelling.* London: Routledge & Kegan Paul.

Stewig, J. W. (1987). Students' spelling errors. *Clearing House, 61,* 34–37.

Taylor, K. K., & Kidder, E. B. (1988). The development of spelling skills: From first grade through eighth grade. *Written Communication, 5,* 222–244.

Templeton, S. (1979). Spelling first, sound later: The relationship between orthography and higher order phonological knowledge in older students. *Research in the Teaching of English, 13,* 255–265.

Tompkins, G. E., & Yaden, D. B. (1986). *Answering students' questions about words.* Urbana, IL: ERIC Clearinghouse on Reading and Communication Skills and National Council of Teachers of English.

Zutell, J. (1979). Spelling strategies of primary school children and their relationship to Piaget's concept of decentration. *Research in the Teaching of English, 13,* 69–79.

13 WRITERS' TOOLS: HANDWRITING

◆   IN THIS CHAPTER, WE DISCUSS HANDWRITING AS A FUNCTIONAL
support skill for writing.

◆   AS YOU ARE READING, THINK ABOUT THESE QUESTIONS:

What are the handwriting forms that elementary students learn to use?

How does handwriting develop during the elementary grades?

What special adaptions are necessary for left-handed writers?

How do teachers teach handwriting?

How do elementary students learn to diagnose and correct their handwriting problems?

Like spelling, handwriting is a functional support skill for writing. Graves (1983) explains further:

> Children win prizes for fine script, parents and teachers nod approval for a crisp, well-crafted page, a good impression is made on a job application blank . . . all important elements, but they pale next to the *substance* they carry. (p. 171)

It is important to distinguish between *writing* and *handwriting*. Writing is the substance of a composition; handwriting is the formation of alphabetic symbols on paper. Students need to develop a legible and fluent style of handwriting so they will be able to fully participate in all written language activities.

Most teachers spend a great deal of time insisting that students perfect their handwriting until it closely approximates the samples in handwriting textbooks. The goal in handwriting instruction, however, is to help students develop legible forms to communicate effectively through writing. The two most important criteria in determining quality in handwriting are *legibility* (the writing can be easily and quickly read), and *fluency* (the writing can be easily and quickly written).

Handwriting is a motor skill, not an art form! Even though a few students take great pleasure in developing flawless handwriting skills, most students feel that handwriting instruction is boring and unnecessary. It is imperative, therefore, to recognize the functional purpose of handwriting and convey the importance of developing legible handwriting to your students. Writing for genuine audiences is the best way to convey the importance of legibility. A letter sent to a favorite author that is returned by the post office because the address is not decipherable or a child's published, hardcover book that sits unread on the library shelf because the handwriting is illegible makes clear the importance of legibility. Illegible writing means a failure to communicate, a harsh lesson for a writer!

❖ HANDWRITING FORMS

Two forms of handwriting are currently used in elementary schools: *manuscript,* or printing, and *cursive,* or connected writing, illustrated in Figure 13−1. Typically, students in the primary grades learn and use the manuscript form and switch to cursive handwriting in the middle grades, usually in second or third grade (Koenke, 1986). In the middle and upper grades, students use both handwriting forms.

Manuscript Handwriting

Until the 1920s, students learned only cursive handwriting. Marjorie Wise is credited with introducing the manuscript form for primary-grade students in 1921 (Hildreth, 1960). Manuscript handwriting is considered superior to the cursive form for young children because they seem to lack the necessary fine motor control and eye-hand coordination for cursive handwriting. In addition, manuscript handwriting is similar to the type style in primary level reading textbooks. Only two lower case letters, *a* and *g,*

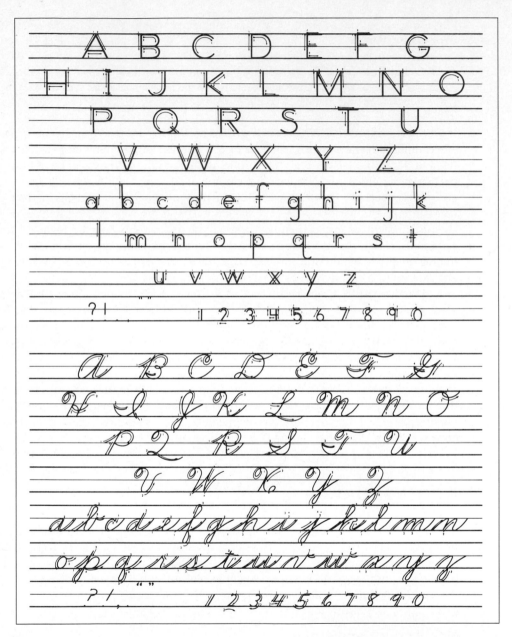

FIGURE 13–1

Manuscript and Cursive Handwriting Forms
Barbe et al., 1984.

are different in typed and handwritten forms. The similarity is assumed to facilitate young children's introduction to reading and writing.

Barbe and Milone (1980) suggested several additional reasons that students in the primary grades should learn manuscript before cursive handwriting. First, manuscript handwriting is easier to learn. Studies show that young children can copy letters and words written in the manuscript form more easily than when they are written in the cursive form. Also, young children can form the vertical and horizontal lines and circles of manuscript handwriting more easily than the cursive strokes. Furthermore, manuscript handwriting is more legible than cursive handwriting. Because it is easier to read, signs and advertisements are printed in letter forms closely approximating manuscript handwriting. Finally, people are often requested to print when completing applications and other forms. For these reasons, manuscript handwriting has become the preferred handwriting form for young children as well as a necessary handwriting skill for older children and adults.

Children's use of the manuscript form often disappears in the middle grades after they have learned cursive handwriting. It is essential that middle- and upper-grade teachers learn and use the manuscript form with their students so that manuscript handwriting remains an option. Second and third graders learn cursive handwriting, a new form, just when they are becoming proficient in the manuscript form, so it is not surprising that some students want to switch back and forth between the two. The need to develop greater writing speed is given as the reason for the quick transfer to cursive handwriting, but research does not show that one form can be written more quickly than the other.

There have also been criticisms of the manuscript form. A major complaint is the reversal problem caused by some similar lower-case letters; *b* and *d* are particularly confusing for young children. Other detractors argue that using both the manuscript and cursive forms in the elementary grades requires teaching students two totally different kinds of handwriting within the span of several years. They also complain that the "circle and sticks" style of manuscript handwriting requires frequent stops and starts, inhibiting a smooth and rhythmic flow of writing.

Cursive Handwriting

When most people think of handwriting, the cursive or connected form comes to mind. The letters in cursive handwriting are joined together to form a word with one continuous movement. Children often view cursive handwriting as the "grown up" type. Primary-grade students often attempt to imitate this form by connecting the manuscript letters in their names and other words before they are taught how to form and join the letters. Awareness of cursive handwriting and interest in imitating it are indicators that students are ready for instruction.

D'Nealian Handwriting

A new manuscript and cursive handwriting style, D'Nealian, was developed in 1968 by Donald Neal Thurber, a teacher in Michigan. The D'Nealian handwriting forms are shown in Figure 13–2. In the D'Nealian manuscript form, letters are slanted and formed with a continuous stroke; in the cursive form, the letters are simplified, without the flourishes of traditional cursive. Both forms were designed to increase legibility and fluency and to ease the transition from manuscript to cursive handwriting.

Thurber's purpose in developing the D'Nealian style was to ameliorate some of the problems associated with the traditional manuscript form (Thurber, 1981). D'Nealian manuscript uses the same basic letter forms students will need for cursive handwriting as well as the slant and rhythm required for cursive. Another advantage of the D'Nealian style is that the transition from manuscript to cursive involves adding only connective strokes to most manuscript letters. Only five letters—*f, r, s, v,* and *z*—have a different shape in the cursive form. Figure 13–3 shows the transition from D'Nealian manuscript to cursive handwriting. Research is currently under way to compare the effectiveness of the D'Nealian style with the traditional handwriting forms.

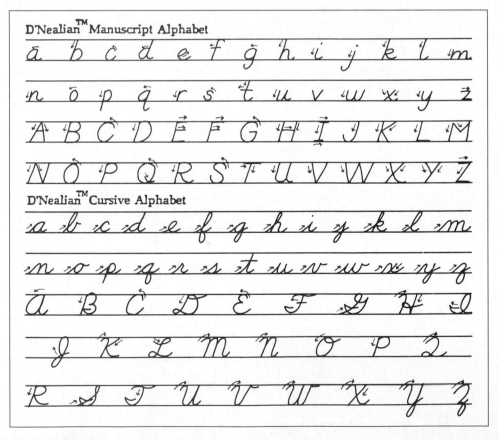

FIGURE 13–2

D'Nealian Manuscript and Cursive Handwriting Forms
Thurber, 1981.

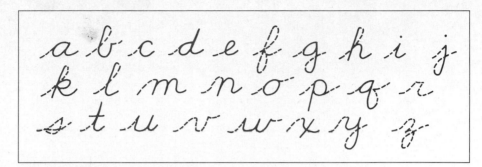

FIGURE 13–3

Transition to the Cursive Form Using the D'Nealian Style
Thurber, 1981.

❖ CHILDREN'S HANDWRITING DEVELOPMENT

During the elementary grades, children grow from using scribbles and letterlike forms in kindergarten to learning the manuscript handwriting form in the primary grades and the cursive form beginning in the middle grades. Students in the middle and upper grades use both forms interchangeably for a variety of handwriting tasks.

Handwriting Before First Grade

Children's handwriting grows out of their drawing activities. Young children observe words all around them in their environment: *McDonald's, Coke, STOP.* They also observe parents and teachers writing messages. From this early interest in written words and communicating through writing, three-, four-, and five-year-olds begin to write letterlike forms and scribbles. In kindergarten, children watch the teacher transcribe experience stories and begin to copy their names and familiar words. Once they are familiar with most of the letters, they use invented spelling to express themselves in writing. Through this drawing-reading-writing-handwriting connection, youngsters discover that they can experiment with letters and words and communicate through written language. Handwriting becomes the functional tool for this written communication.

Young children enter kindergarten with different backgrounds of handwriting experience. Some five-year-olds have never held a pencil, and many others have written cursivelike scribbles or manuscript letterlike forms. Some preschoolers have learned to print their names and some other letters. Handwriting in kindergarten typically includes three types of activities: stimulating children's interest in writing, developing their ability to hold writing instruments, and refining their fine motor control.

Stimulating Interest in Writing. Adults can be influential role models in stimulating interest in writing. Parents can encourage interest at home through their own writing activities, such as writing letters, telephone messages, and grocery lists.

Forming letters in shaving cream is a good way for young children to practice fine motor skills.

They can also provide paper, pencils, and pens so children can imitate their parents' writing. At school, picture journals and experience stories stimulate interest in writing.

Developing the Ability to Hold Writing Instruments. Students develop the ability to hold a pencil or other writing instrument by modeling parents and teachers and through numerous opportunities to experiment with pencils, pens, paint brushes, crayons, and other writing instruments.

Refining Motor Skills. Young children develop and refine their fine motor skills through a variety of motor activities and experiences with manipulative materials. Possible activities include building with blocks, stringing beads, completing parquetry designs and puzzles, drawing, cutting, pasting, and other art activities.

Handwriting instruction in kindergarten usually focuses on teaching children to form upper- and lowercase letters and to print their names. Many kindergarten teachers use a multisensory approach: students trace letters in shaving cream, sand, and fingerpaint; glue popcorn in the shape of letters; and arrange blocks or pipe cleaners to form letters. Children learn to print their names through similar multisensory activities and through daily practice writing their names on attendance sheets, experience stories, paintings, and other papers.

Handwriting must be linked with writing at all grade levels, even in kindergarten. Young children write labels, draw and write stories, keep journals, and write other messages (Klein & Schickedanz, 1980). The more they write, the greater their need becomes for instruction in handwriting. Writers need to know how to grip a pencil, how to form letters, and how to space between letters and words. Instruction is necessary so students will not learn bad habits that later must be broken. Students often devise their own rather bizarre way to form a letter, and these bad habits will cause problems when they need to develop greater writing speed.

Handwriting in the Primary Grades

Formal handwriting instruction begins in first grade. Students learn how to form manuscript letters, how to space between them, and to develop skills related to the six elements of legibility. Researchers have found that primary-grade students have more difficulty forming the lowercase than the uppercase letters, and by third grade, some students still have difficulty forming *r, u, h,* and *t* (Stennett, Smithe, & Hardy, 1972).

A common handwriting activity requires students to copy short writing samples from the chalkboard, but this type of activity is not recommended. For one thing, young children have great difficulty with far-to-near copying (Lamme, 1979); a piece of writing should be placed close to the child for copying. Children can recopy their own compositions, language experience stories, and self-selected writing samples; other types of copying should be avoided. It is far better for children to create their own writing than to copy words and sentences they may not even be able to read!

Writing Instruments and Paper. Special pencils and handwriting paper are often provided for handwriting instruction. Kindergartners and first graders commonly use "fat" beginner pencils, because it has been assumed that these pencils are easier for young children to hold; however, most children prefer to use regular-sized pencils that older students and adults use. Moreover, regular pencils have erasers! Research now indicates that beginner pencils are not better than regular-sized pencils for young children (Lamme & Ayris, 1983). Likewise, there is no evidence that specially shaped pencils and little writing aids that slip onto pencils to improve children's grip are effective.

Many types of paper, both lined and unlined, are used in elementary classrooms. Paper companies manufacture paper lined in a range of sizes. Typically, paper is lined at two-inch intervals for kindergartners, ⅞-inch intervals for first graders, ¾-inch intervals for second graders, ½-inch intervals for third graders, and ⅜-inch intervals for older students. Lined paper for first and second graders has an added midline, often dotted, to guide students in forming lowercase letters. Sometimes a line appears below the baseline to guide placement of letters such as lowercase *g, p, q,* and *y* that have "tails" that drop below the baseline. The few research studies that have examined the value of lined paper in general and paper lined at these specific intervals offer conflicting results. One recent study suggests that younger children's handwriting is more legible when they use unlined paper and older children's is better when they use lined paper (Lindsay & McLennan, 1983). Most teachers seem to prefer that students use lined paper for handwriting activities, but students easily adjust to whichever type of writing paper is available. Children often use rulers to line their paper when they are given unlined paper, and, likewise, they ignore the lines on lined paper if they interfere with their drawing or writing.

Transition to Cursive Handwriting

Students' introduction to cursive handwriting typically occurs in the second semester of second grade or the first semester of third grade. Parents and students often attach great importance to the transition from manuscript to cursive, thus adding unnecessary pressure for the students. The time of transition is usually dictated by tradition rather than by sound educational theory. All students in a school or school district are usually introduced to cursive handwriting at the same time, regardless of their readiness to make the change.

Some students indicate an early interest in cursive handwriting by trying to connect manuscript letters or by having their parents demonstrate how to write their names in the cursive form. Because of individual differences in motor skills and levels of interest in cursive writing, it is better to introduce some students to cursive handwriting in first or second grade and to provide other students with additional opportunities to refine their manuscript skills. These students can then learn cursive handwriting in third or fourth grade.

The transition to cursive handwriting requires a full semester of instruction. Before students learn to form the cursive letters, they must learn to identify them. First, students learn to recognize the upper- and lowercase cursive letters. Flash cards and bingo and lotto games are useful for teaching cursive letter recognition. Next, students learn to read words and sentences written in the cursive form.

Invariably, the first thing students want to write in cursive handwriting is their own names. With individual and small group instruction, your students can quickly learn to write their names and then progress to learning the basic strokes in forming cursive letters.

The practice of changing to cursive handwriting only a year or two after children learn the manuscript form is receiving increasing criticism. The argument has been that students need to learn cursive handwriting as early as possible because of their increasing need for handwriting speed. Because of its continuous flow, cursive handwriting was thought to be faster to write than manuscript; however, research suggests that manuscript handwriting can be written as quickly as cursive handwriting (Jackson, 1971). The controversy over the benefits of the two forms and the best time to introduce cursive handwriting is likely to continue.

Handwriting in the Middle and Upper Grades

Students are introduced to the cursive handwriting form in second and third grades. Usually, the basic strokes that make up the letters (e.g., slant stroke, undercurve, downcurve) are taught first. Next, the lowercase letters are taught in isolation and then the connecting strokes are introduced. Uppercase letters are taught later because they are used far less often and are more difficult to form.

Which cursive letters are most difficult? According to the results of a study that examined sixth graders' handwriting, the lowercase *r* is the most troublesome letter. The other lowercase letters students frequently form incorrectly are *h, k, p,* and *z.* The least difficult lowercase letters are *a, b, c, i, l, m, n, u, v,* and *x* (Horton, 1970).

After students have learned both manuscript and cursive handwriting, they need to review both forms periodically. By this time, too, they have firmly established handwriting habits, both good and bad. At the middle- and upper-grade levels, emphasis is on helping students diagnose and correct their handwriting trouble-spots so they can develop a legible and fluent handwriting style. Older students both simplify their letter forms as well as add unique flourishes to their handwriting to develop their own "trademark" styles.

Private and Public Handwriting. Teachers often insist that students demonstrate their best handwriting every time they pick up a pencil or pen. This requirement is unrealistic; certainly there are times when handwriting is important, but, at other times, speed or other considerations outweigh neatness. Children need to learn to recognize two types of writing occasions, *private* and *public*. Legibility counts in public writing, but when students make notes for themselves or write a rough draft of a composition, they are doing private writing, and should decide for themselves whether neatness is important.

Left-handed Writers

Approximately 10 percent of the American population is left-handed, and there may be two or three left-handed students in most classrooms. Until recently, teachers insisted that left-handed students use their right hands for handwriting because left-handed writers were thought to have inferior handwriting skills. Parents and teachers are more realistic now and accept children's natural tendencies for left- or right-handedness. In fact, research has shown that there is no significant difference in the quality or speed of left- or right-handed students' writing (Groff, 1963).

Handedness. Most young children develop *handedness,* the preference for using either the right or left hand for fine motor activities, before entering kindergarten or first grade. Teachers must help those few students who have not already developed handedness to choose and consistently use one hand for handwriting and other fine motor activities. Your role consists of observing the student's behavior and hand preference in play, art, writing, and playground activities. Over a period of days or weeks, observe and note which hand the child uses in these activities:

Building with blocks

Catching balls

Cutting with scissors

Holding a paintbrush

Holding a pencil or crayon

Manipulating clay

Manipulating puzzle pieces

Pasting

Pouring water or sand

Stringing beads

Throwing balls

Teachers need to make special adaptations for left-handed writers.

During the observation period, teachers may find that a child who has not established hand preference uses both hands interchangeably; for example, a child may first reach for several blocks with one hand and then reach for the next block with the alternate hand. During drawing activities, the child will sometimes switch hands every few minutes. Consult the child's parents and ask them to observe and monitor the child's behavior at home, noting hand preferences when they eat, brush teeth, turn on the television, open doors, and so on. The teacher, the child, and the child's parents should then confer, and, based on the results of joint observations, the handedness of family members, and the child's wishes, a tentative decision about hand preference can be made. At school, teacher and child will work closely together so the child will only use the chosen hand. As long as the child continues to use both hands interchangeably, neither hand will develop the prerequisite fine motor control for handwriting, and teachers should postpone handwriting instruction until the child develops a dominant hand.

Teaching Left-handed Students.   Teaching handwriting to left-handed students is not simply the reverse of teaching handwriting to right-handed students (Howell, 1978). Left-handed students have unique handwriting problems, and special adaptations of procedures for teaching right-handed students are necessary. In fact, many of the problems that left-handed students have can be made worse by using the procedures designed for right-handed writers (Harrison, 1981). The special adjustments are necessary to allow left-handed students to write legibly, fluently, and with less fatigue.

The basic difference between right- and left-handed writers is physical orientation. Right-handed students pull their hands and arms toward their bodies as they write, whereas left-handed writers must push away. As left-handed students write, they move their left hands across what they have just written, often covering it. Many children adopt a "hook" position to avoid covering and smudging what they have written.

Because of their different physical orientation, left-handed writers need to make three major types of adjustments: how they grip their pens or pencils, how they position the writing paper on their desks, and how they slant their writing (Howell, 1978).

First, left-handed writers should hold pencils or pens an inch or more farther back from the tip than right-handed writers do. This change helps them see what they have just written and avoid smearing their writing. Left-handed writers need to work to avoid "hooking" their wrists. Have them keep their wrists straight and elbows close to their bodies to avoid the awkward hooked position. Practicing handwriting on the chalkboard is one way to help them develop a more natural style.

Next, left-handed students should tilt their writing papers slightly to the right, in contrast to right-handed students, who tilt their papers to the left. Sometimes it is helpful to place a piece of masking tape on the student's desk to indicate the proper amount of tilt.

Third, whereas right-handed students are encouraged to slant their cursive letters to the right, left-handed writers often write vertically or even slant their letters slightly backward. Some handwriting programs recommend that left-handed writers slant their cursive letters slightly to the right as right-handed students do, but others advise teachers to permit any slant between vertical and 45 degrees to the left of vertical. These and other special adaptations are summarized in Figure 13–4.

---

1. Group left-handed students together for handwriting instruction.
2. Provide a left-handed person to serve as the model if you are not left-handed. Perhaps another teacher, parent, or an older student could come to the classroom to assist left-handed students.
3. Direct students to hold their pencils farther back from the point than right-handed students do.
4. Encourage students to practice handwriting skills at the chalkboard.
5. Have students tilt their papers to the right, rather than to the left, as right-handed students do.
6. Encourage students to slant their cursive letters slightly to the right, but allow them to form them vertically or even with a slight backhand slant.
7. Encourage students to eliminate excessive loops and flourishes from their writing to increase handwriting speed.

FIGURE 13–4

Special Adaptations for Left-Handed Writers

Left-handed writers need special support, and one way to provide support is by grouping left-handed students together for handwriting instruction. Right-handed teachers should consider asking a left-handed teacher, parent, or an older student to come into the classroom to work with left-handed writers. It is important to carefully monitor left-handed students while they are developing handwriting skills, because bad habits such as "hooking" are difficult to break.

❖ TEACHING HANDWRITING IN THE ELEMENTARY GRADES

Handwriting is best taught in separate periods of direct instruction and teacher-supervised practice. As soon as skills are taught, they should be applied in real-life writing activities. Busywork assignments, such as copying lists of words and sentences from the chalkboard, lack educational significance. Moreover, students may develop poor handwriting habits or learn to form letters incorrectly if they practice without direct supervision. It is much more difficult to correct bad habits and errors in letter formation than to teach handwriting correctly in the first place.

Handwriting instruction and practice periods should be brief; 15- to 20-minute periods of instruction several times a week are more effective than a single lengthy period weekly or monthly. Regular periods of handwriting instruction are necessary when teaching the manuscript form in kindergarten and first grade and the cursive form in second or third grade. In the middle and upper grades, instruction depends on specific handwriting problems that students demonstrate and periodic reviews of both handwriting forms.

Teaching Strategy

The teaching strategy presented in Chapter 1 can be adapted to teach the manuscript and cursive handwriting forms. The adaptation is multisensory, with visual, auditory, and kinesthetic components, and is based on research in the field of handwriting (Askov & Greff, 1975; Furner, 1969; Hirsch & Niedermeyer, 1973). The five steps of the strategy follow.

1. The teacher demonstrates a specific handwriting skill while students observe. During the demonstration, the teacher describes the steps involved in executing it.

2. Students describe the skill and the steps for executing it as the teacher or a classmate demonstrates the skill again.

3. The teacher reviews the specific handwriting skill, summarizing the steps involved in executing the skill.

4. Students practice the skill using pencils, pens, or other writing instruments. As they practice the skill, students softly repeat the steps involved in executing it, and the teacher circulates, providing assistance as needed.

5.   Students apply the skill they have learned in their writing. To check that they have learned the specific skill, students can review their writing over a period of several days and mark examples of correct use.

An example of applying this strategy in teaching manuscript letter formation is shown in Figure 13–5.

The Teacher's Role

As in most language arts activities, the teacher plays a crucial role in handwriting instruction. The teacher *teaches* the handwriting skill and then *supervises* as students practice it. Research has shown the importance of the teachers' active involvement in handwriting instruction and practice.

One aspect of the teacher's role is particularly interesting. To save time, teachers often print or write handwriting samples in advance on practice sheets. Then they distribute the sheets and ask students to practice a handwriting skill by copying the model they have written. Researchers have found, however, that *moving* models, that is, observing the teacher write the handwriting sample, are of far greater value than copying models that have already been written (Wright & Wright, 1980). Moving models are possible when the teacher circulates around the classroom, stopping to demonstrate a skill for one student and moving to assist another; circling incorrectly

The best way for students to practice handwriting is to apply what they have learned in real-life writing activities.

1. *Initiating*

   Demonstrate the formation of a single letter or family of letters (e.g., the manuscript circle letters—*O, o, C, c, a, e, Q*) on the chalkboard while explaining how the letter is formed.

2. *Structuring and Conceptualizing*

   Have students describe how the letter is formed while you or a student forms the letter on the chalkboard. At first you may need to ask questions to direct students' descriptions. Possible questions include:

   > How many strokes are used in making the letter?
   > Which stroke comes first?
   > Where do you begin the stroke?
   > In which direction do you go?
   > What size will the letter be?
   > Where does the stroke stop?
   > Which stroke comes next?

   Students will quickly learn the appropriate terminology such as *baseline, left-right, slant line, counterclockwise,* and so on to describe how the letters are formed.

3. *Summarizing*

   Review the formation of the letter or letter family with students while demonstrating how to form the letter on the chalkboard.

4. *Generalizing*

   Have the students print the letter at the chalkboard, in sand, and with a variety of other materials such as clay, shaving cream, fingerpaint, pudding, and pipecleaners. As students form the letter, they should softly describe the formation process to themselves.

   Have students practice writing the letter on paper with the accompanying verbal descriptions.

   Circulate among students providing assistance and encouragement. Demonstrate and describe the correct formation of the letter as the students observe.

5. *Applying*

   After practicing the letter or family of letters, have students apply what they have learned in authentic writing activities. This is the crucial step!

FIGURE 13—5

Teacher's Notebook Page: Using the Teaching Strategy to Teach Letter Formation

formed letters and marking other errors with a red pen on completed handwriting sheets is of little value. As in the writing process, the teacher's assistance is far more worthwhile while the student is producing handwriting, not after it has been completed.

Practice Activities

As Graves (1983) said, "handwriting is for writing" (p. 171), and for the most meaningful transfer of skills, students should be involved in writing for various purposes and for genuine audiences. Students apply their handwriting skills whenever they write, and the best way to practice handwriting is through writing.

In addition to the writing activities discussed in previous chapters, students at all grade levels can use copybooks to compile a collection of favorite poems, quotes, and excerpts from stories.[1] Students choose poems, quotations, paragraphs from stories, riddles, or other short pieces of writing they would like to write and save in their copybooks (spiral-bound notebooks or bound blank books). Usually students make one or two entries each week in either manuscript or cursive handwriting. Students can concentrate on their handwriting when they make entries in their books, because they do not have to worry about creating content at the same time. Examples of students' copybook entries are shown in Figure 13–6. Copybooks are especially beneficial because they provide a meaningful context for handwriting practice. Instead of writing rows of letters and isolated words, students are immersed in language and literature. For many students, copybooks become valued, personal anthologies of favorite literary selections.

Students can practice specific letter formations using salt or sand trays or using shaving cream or finger paint. Using these materials heightens students' tactile responses and makes handwriting practice fun to do. Teachers need to supervise students to be sure they are forming the letters correctly.

Another activity, "Let's Go on a Bear Hunt" (Tompkins, 1980), adapts the familiar language game to practice basic manuscript letter strokes. (See Appendix E.)

❖ ASSESSING STUDENTS' HANDWRITING

The goal of handwriting instruction is for students to develop legible handwriting. To reach this goal, students must first understand what qualities or elements determine legibility and then analyze their own handwriting according to these elements.

Elements of Legibility

The six elements of legible and fluent handwriting are letter formation, size and proportion, spacing, slant, alignment, and line quality (Barbe, Lucas, Wasylyk, Hackney, & Braun, 1984).

---

[1]The authors are grateful to Janet Kretchmer, principal and teacher at the McGuffey Foundation School, Oxford, Ohio, for this activity idea.

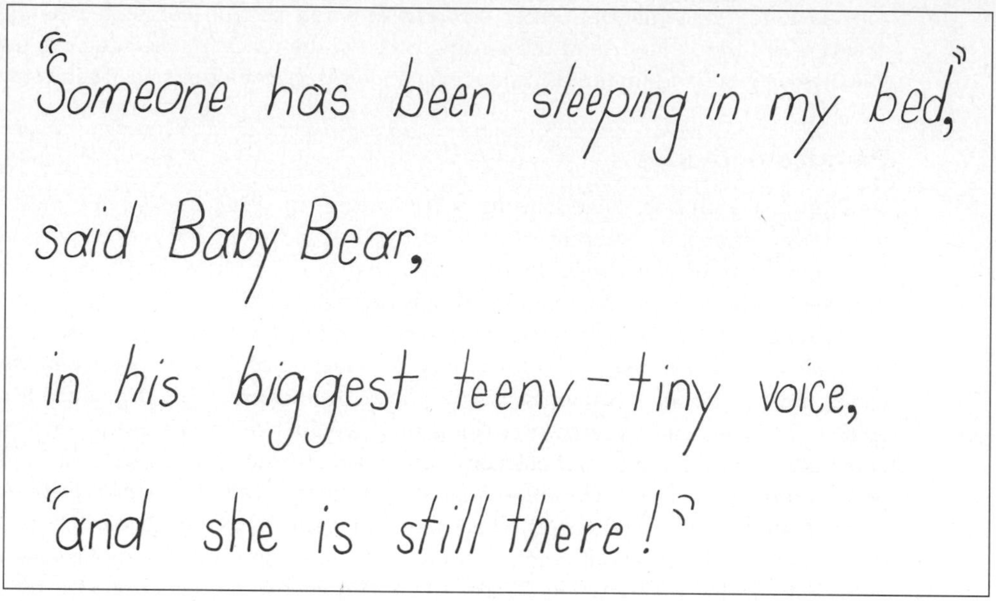

Someone has been sleeping in my bed,

said Baby Bear,

in his biggest teeny-tiny voice,

"and she is still there!"

Jennifer, age 6

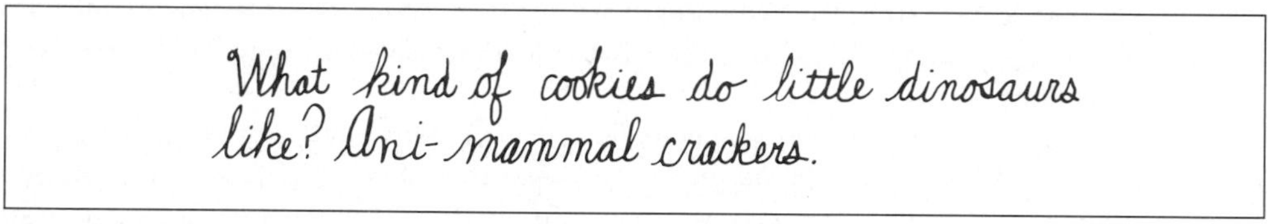

What kind of cookies do little dinosaurs
like? Ani-mammal crackers.

Aaron, age 9

FIGURE 13–6

Entries from Students' Copybooks from Galdone's *The Three Bears* (1972) and Sterne's *Tyrannosaurus Wrecks: A Book of Dinosaur Riddles* (1979)

Letter Formation.   Letters are formed with specific strokes. Letters in manuscript handwriting are composed of vertical, horizontal, and slanted lines plus circles or parts of circles. The letter *b,* for example, is composed of a vertical line and a circle, and *M* is composed of vertical and slanted lines. The cursive letters are composed of slanted lines, loops, and curved lines. The lowercase cursive letters *e* and *ℓ* , for instance, are composed of a slant stroke, a loop, and an undercurve stroke. An additional component in cursive handwriting is the connecting strokes used to join letters.

Size and Proportion.   Through the elementary grades, students' handwriting becomes smaller, and the proportional size of upper- to lowercase letters increases. Uppercase manuscript letters are twice the size of lowercase letters. When second and third grade students first begin cursive handwriting, the proportional size of letters remains 2:1; later, the proportion of uppercase to lowercase cursive letters increases to

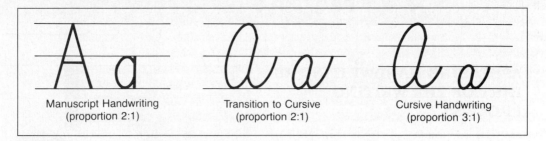

FIGURE 13–7

Size and Proportion of Elementary Students' Handwriting

3:1 for middle- and upper-grade students. The three sizes are illustrated in Figure 13–7.

Spacing.   Students must leave adequate space between letters in words and between words in sentences if their handwriting is to be read easily. Spacing between words in manuscript handwriting should equal one lowercase letter o, and spacing between sentences should equal two lowercase o's. The most important aspect of spacing within words in cursive handwriting is consistency. To correctly space between words, the writer should make the beginning stroke of the new word directly below the end stroke of the preceding word. Spacing between sentences should equal one uppercase letter O, and spacing between paragraphs should equal two uppercase letter O's.

Slant.   Letters should be consistently parallel. Letters in manuscript handwriting are vertical, and in the cursive form, letters slant slightly to the right. To ensure the correct slant, right-handed students tilt their papers to the left, and left-handed students tilt their papers to the right.

Alignment.   For proper alignment in both manuscript and cursive handwriting, all letters are uniform in size and consistently touch the baseline.

Line Quality.   Students should write at a consistent speed and hold their writing instruments correctly and in a relaxed manner to make steady, unwavering lines of even thickness.

Correct letter formation and spacing receive the major focus in handwriting instruction during the elementary grades. Although the other four elements usually receive less attention, they, too, are important in developing legible and fluent handwriting.

Diagnosing and Correcting Handwriting Problems

Students can refer to the characteristics of the six elements of legibility to diagnose their handwriting problems. Primary-grade students, for example, can check to see if they have formed a particular letter correctly, if the round parts of letters are joined neatly, or if slanted letters are joined in sharp points. Older students can examine a piece of handwriting to see if their letters are consistently parallel or if the letters touch the

ASSESSING HANDWRITING AS PART OF THE WRITING PROCESS

"I'd like to say that my second graders' handwriting doesn't concern me. I'd like to, but I can't. My students print well, but I have to plan time to review skills and constantly stress the importance of legible handwriting."

Gordon Martindale, Second Grade Teacher
Columbia Elementary School

PROCEDURE

I teach handwriting as part of the writing process. Before my students start to make the final copies of their writing projects, I take 10 to 15 minutes for a handwriting minilesson on a skill that my students need, such as connecting letter strokes, spacing between letters and words, or touching the base line consistently. This week my students are writing reports on the planets in the solar system that they will copy into hard-bound books. Because grades often speak louder than I do, I will use these published books as an oppor-

tunity to critique students' handwriting and assign handwriting grades.

After the minilesson, I remind the students about the importance of legible handwriting, and then they begin writing the final copies of their reports. I circulate among them, observing as they practice the handwriting skill that I've reviewed. I offer positive comments to students and provide additional instruction to students who need it. Through this observation, I also note other handwriting skills that individual students need help with or skills for future handwriting minilessons. I use those little yellow notes with the sticky back to take notes about particular students' handwriting. Later, I add these notes to students' language arts portfolios so that I can refer to them during conferences that I hold with each student.

After their books are published and shared in this class and with their sixth-grade reading buddies, I ask them to review their handwriting according to the elements of legibility that I've taught. This is a good time for thinking about handwriting because my students can see that the quality of their handwriting can affect how well the 6th grade readers understand and enjoy their stories. Legible handwriting becomes part of the overall goal of successful communication with an audience, not just an exercise.

Then I hold brief conferences with each student and we talk about his or her handwriting. Through our discussion and my notes, we make a list of two or three strengths and weaknesses which I add to the student's language arts portfolio. This list provides a handwriting focus for the student on the next writing project. We also decide on a handwriting grade which I record in my grade book.

ASSESSMENT

Handwriting isn't the most exciting part of the language arts curriculum in second grade. It's just one of those things that has to be done, and I teach handwriting as a means to an end—as a tool for writers. In order to adequately assess my students' progress, I like to collect three or four different kinds of information, and to assess their handwriting, I collect four types of information: (1) handwriting samples, (2) anecdotal and observational notes, (3) notes about conferences I have with students, and (4) grades. I keep all of this information in students' language arts portfolios, and it makes the job of assigning grades more objective.

REFLECTIONS

In this school, we don't introduce cursive handwriting until third grade, and I support this decision. Because my students don't have to learn a whole new handwriting form, I'm able to stress fluency, and during second grade, my students finally come to see handwriting as a tool for writers. This happens as they become more fluent writers and through writing real books that their classmates are eager to read.

I've found that this approach works, and it works better than using a handwriting workbook or dittos. This way students' handwriting on their book projects and other writing assignments is easy to read because I teach at that teachable moment. I'm able to individualize instruction and show my students why they need to learn these skills. My students are learning to analyze their handwriting and identify their own strengths and weaknesses even though they are only eight years old! Teaching handwriting through the writing process makes a difference in my classroom.

baseline consistently. A sample checklist for evaluating manuscript handwriting is shown in Figure 13–8. Checklists can also be developed for cursive handwriting. It is important to involve students in developing the checklists so they can appreciate the need to make their handwriting more legible.

Another reason students need to diagnose and correct their handwriting problems is because handwriting quality influences teacher evaluation and grading. Markham (1976) found that both student teachers and experienced classroom teachers consistently graded papers with better handwriting higher than papers with poor handwriting, regardless of the quality of the content. Students in the elementary grades are not too young to learn that poor quality or illegible handwriting may lead to lower grades.

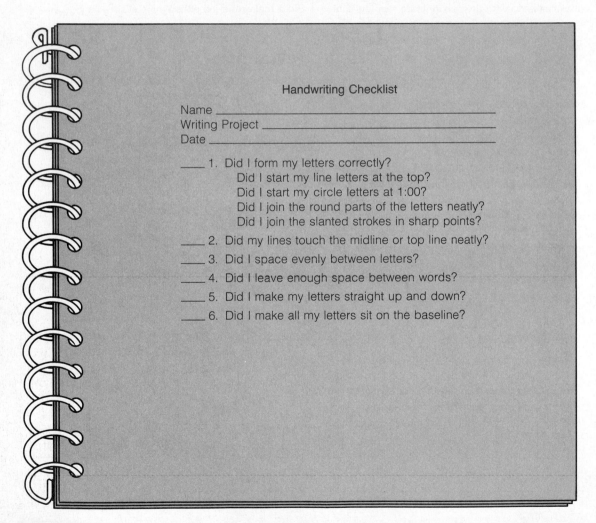

Handwriting Checklist

Name _____
Writing Project _____
Date _____

____ 1. Did I form my letters correctly?
        Did I start my line letters at the top?
        Did I start my circle letters at 1:00?
        Did I join the round parts of the letters neatly?
        Did I join the slanted strokes in sharp points?

____ 2. Did my lines touch the midline or top line neatly?

____ 3. Did I space evenly between letters?

____ 4. Did I leave enough space between words?

____ 5. Did I make my letters straight up and down?

____ 6. Did I make all my letters sit on the baseline?

FIGURE 13–8

Teacher's Notebook Page: A Checklist for Manuscript Handwriting

❖ REVIEW

Handwriting is a functional, support skill for writing, not an art form. Two forms of handwriting are taught in the elementary grades. Manuscript handwriting is the print form, and cursive writing is a connected, flowing form. A new handwriting style, D'Nealian, has been developed to ameliorate some of the problems associated with manuscript handwriting.

Children's handwriting grows out of their drawing. In the primary grades, students learn the manuscript form; in second or third grade, they are introduced to cursive handwriting. Critics argue that it is unrealistic to expect students to master two handwriting forms in such a short time span. Teachers often have two or three left-handed writers in their class and must make adaptions for these students.

A teaching strategy based on the model introduced in Chapter 1 can be used to teach manuscript and cursive handwriting. The most crucial step is the last one, in which students apply the skills in genuine writing activities. The elements of legible handwriting are letter formation, size and proportion, spacing, slant, alignment, and line quality. Students learn to assess their own handwriting according to the six elements. One strategy for helping students identify their handwriting problems is to use checklists based on the elements of legibility.

❖ EXTENSIONS

1. Practice forming the manuscript and cursive letters shown in Figures 13–1 and 13–2 until your handwriting approximates the models. Practicing these handwriting forms will prepare you for working with elementary students. Be sure, though, to take note of the manuscript and/or cursive handwriting forms displayed in the classroom before beginning to work with students, because schools use several different handwriting programs. The programs are similar, but some students, especially younger children, are quick to point out when you are not forming a letter correctly!

2. Observe in a primary-grade classroom where the D'Nealian handwriting program is used. Talk with teachers and students about this innovative form. How do the students like it? Do the teachers believe it ameliorates some of the problems with manuscript handwriting and the transition to cursive, as Thurber claims?

3. Practice manuscript and cursive handwriting skills with a small group of middle- or upper-grade students using copybooks. Supply students with small notebooks and have them copy favorite poems, quotations, excerpts from stories they are reading, and other short pieces of writing. Meet with students weekly for several weeks as they work in their copybooks.

4. Practice manuscript handwriting skills with a small group of kindergartners or first graders using the "Let's Go on a Bear Hunt" activity in Appendix E.

5. Work with a small group of students to develop a checklist similar to that in Figure 13–8 to evaluate their handwriting. After developing the checklist, have students evaluate their handwriting and set goals for improving both legibility and fluency.

6. Observe a left-handed writer and compare this student to right-handed writers in the same classroom. How does the left-handed student's handwriting differ from right-handed students'? What types of special adaptions has the teacher made for teaching the left-handed student?

❖ REFERENCES

Askov, E., & Greff, K. N. (1975). Handwriting: Copying versus tracing as the most effective type of practice. *Journal of Educational Research, 69,* 96–98.

Barbe, W. B., Lucas, V. H., Wasylyk, T. M., Hackney, C. S., & Braun, L. A. (1984). *Zaner-Bloser creative growth in handwriting* (Grades K–8). Columbus, OH: Zaner-Bloser.

Barbe, W. B., & Milone, M. N., Jr. (1980). *Why manuscript writing should come before cursive writing* (Zaner-Bloser Professional Pamphlet No. 11). Columbus, OH: Zaner-Bloser.

Furner, B. A. (1969). Recommended instructional procedures in a method emphasizing the perceptual-motor nature of learning in handwriting. *Elementary English, 46,* 1021–1030.

Galdone, P. (1972). *The three bears.* New York: Houghton Mifflin.

Graves, D. H. (1983). *Writing: Teachers and children at work.* Exeter, NH: Heinemann.

Groff, P. J. (1963). Who writes faster? *Education, 83,* 367–369.

Harrison, S. (1981). Open letter from a left-handed teacher: Some sinistral ideas on the teaching of handwriting. *Teaching Exceptional Children, 13,* 116–120.

Hildreth, G. (1960). Manuscript writing after sixty years. *Elementary English, 37,* 3–13.

Hirsch, E., & Niedermeyer, F. C. (1973). The effects of tracing prompts and discrimination training on kindergarten handwriting performance. *Journal of Educational Research, 67,* 81–83.

Horton, L. W. (1970). Illegibilities in the cursive handwriting of sixth graders. *Elementary School Journal, 70,* 446–450.

Howell, H. (1978). Write on, you sinistrals! *Language Arts, 55,* 852–856.

Jackson, A. D. (1971). A comparison of speed of legibility of manuscript and cursive handwriting of intermediate grade pupils. Unpublished doctoral dissertation, University of Arizona. *Dissertation Abstracts, 31* (1971), 4384A.

Klein, A., & Schickedanz, J. (1980). Preschoolers write messages and receive their favorite books. *Language Arts, 57,* 742–749.

Koenke, K. (1986). Handwriting instruction: What do we know? *The Reading Teacher, 40,* 214–216.

Lamme, L. L. (1979). Handwriting in an early childhood curriculum. *Young Children, 35,* 20–27.

Lamme, L. L., & Ayris, B. M. (1983). Is the handwriting of beginning writers influenced by writing tools? *Journal of Research and Development in Education, 17,* 32–38.

Lindsay, G. A., & McLennan, D. (1983). Lined paper: Its effects on the legibility and creativity of young children's writing. *British Journal of Educational Psychology, 53,* 364–368.

Markham, L. R. (1976). Influences of handwriting quality on teacher evaluation of written work. *American Educational Research Journal, 13,* 277–283.

Stennett, R. G., Smithe, P. C., & Hardy, M. (1972). Developmental trends in letter-printing skill. *Perceptual and Motor Skills, 34,* 183–186.

Sterne, N. (1979). *Tyrannosaurus wrecks: A book of dinosaur riddles.* New York: Crowell.

Thurber, D. N. (1981). *D'Nealian handwriting* (Grades K–8). Glenview, IL: Scott, Foresman.

Tompkins, G. E. (1980). Let's go on a bear hunt! A fresh approach to penmanship drill. *Language Arts, 57,* 782–786.

Wright, C. D., & Wright, J. P. (1980). Handwriting: The effectiveness of copying from moving versus still models. *Journal of Educational Research, 74,* 95–98.

14 WRITERS' TOOLS: GRAMMAR

THE CONTROVERSY ABOUT TEACHING GRAMMAR

TYPES OF GRAMMAR
    Traditional Grammar
    Structural Grammar
    Transformational Grammar

TEACHING GRAMMAR
    Teaching Strategy
    Assessing Students' Knowledge about Grammar

LEARNING GRAMMAR THROUGH WRITING

◆ IN CHAPTER 14, WE FOCUS ON GRAMMAR, THE THIRD TOOL FOR
writers. Grammar is an issue that divides the teaching profession. We take the
position that instruction should be tied to writing and how authors use sentences
to communicate effectively.

◆ AS YOU ARE READING, THINK ABOUT THESE QUESTIONS:
    What is grammar?
    Why is the teaching of grammar controversial?
    How can teachers tie grammar instruction to literature and writing?
    Why is grammar a writer's tool?

Grammar is probably the most controversial area of language arts. Suhor (1987) calls it one of the "orthodoxies" that divides language arts educators. Teachers, parents, and the community disagree about the content of grammar instruction, how to teach it, and when to begin teaching it. Some people believe that formal instruction in grammar is unnecessary—if not harmful—during the elementary grades; others believe that grammar instruction should be the central emphasis of language arts instruction. Before getting into the controversy, let's clarify terms. *Grammar* is the description of the structure of a language. It involves principles of word and sentence formation. In contrast, *usage* is "correctness," or using the appropriate word in a sentence—the socially preferred way of using language within a dialect. *My friend, she; the man brung;* or *hisself* are examples of standard English usage errors that elementary students sometimes make. Fraser and Hodson (1978) explain the distinction between grammar and usage this way: "Grammar is the rationale of a language; usage is its etiquette" (p. 52).

Children learn the structure of the English language—its grammar—intuitively as they learned to talk; the process is an unconscious one. They have almost completed it by the time they enter kindergarten. The purpose of grammar instruction, then, is to make this intuitive knowledge about the English language explicit and to provide labels for words within sentences, parts of sentences, and types of sentences. Children speak the dialect their parents and community members speak. Dialect, whether standard or nonstandard English, is informal and differs to some degree from the written standard English or "book language" that students will read and write in elementary school (Pooley, 1974; Edelsky, 1989). Figure 14–1 shows the cover and a page from a second grade ABC book that students developed while combining their study of adjectives and animals.

Applebee and his colleagues (1987) examined compositions written by nine-, 13-, and 17-year-olds as a part of the National Assessment of Educational Progress testing and were encouraged by the results. They concluded that most students make only a few grammatical errors in the compositions they write. Specially, they examined students' sentences and categorized them as simple, compound, complex, run-on, or fragment. They found that approximately a quarter of the sentences that nine-year-olds wrote were complex, and the proportion increased to 43 percent for 17-year-olds. The researchers also found that the proportion of sentence fragments and run-on sentences decreased with age, particularly between the ages of nine and 13. Moreover, even at age 9, many students had no run-on sentences (50 percent) or fragments (75 percent) in their writing. A major conclusion of this research was that "instructional procedures that encourage students to edit their work for grammar, punctuation, and spelling as a last stage in the writing experience would seem to reflect what the best writers do" (p. 7). They also noted that everyone makes some errors and, because patterns of error differed from student to student, small group instruction may be more effective than whole class instruction.

❖ THE CONTROVERSY ABOUT TEACHING GRAMMAR

Teachers, parents, and the community at large cite many reasons for teaching grammar. First, using standard English is the mark of an educated person, and students should be given a choice to use standard English. Many teachers feel that teaching grammar will

FIGURE 14–1

An Excerpt from a Second Grade Class Book on Adjectives

help students understand sentence structure and form sentences to express their thoughts. Another reason is that parents expect that grammar will be taught, and teachers must meet these expectations. Other teachers explain that they teach grammar to prepare students for the next grade or for instruction in a foreign language. Others pragmatically rationalize grammar instruction because it is a part of norm-referenced achievement tests mandated by state departments of education.

Language arts textbooks have traditionally emphasized grammar; often, more than three-quarters of the pages have been devoted to drills on parts of speech, parts of sentences, and sentence types. With the new emphasis on the writing process, language arts textbooks published within the past few years have reduced the number of pages focusing on grammar so that approximately half a book deals with grammar and the other half focuses on writing. Many teachers and parents assume that the content of a language arts textbook indicates what the curriculum should be, but it is important to separate the two so that the textbook is only one of many resources for implementing the curriculum.

Conventional wisdom is that knowledge about grammar and usage should improve students' writing, but research since the beginning of the century has not confirmed this assumption. Based on their review of research conducted before 1963, Braddock, Lloyd-Jones, and Schoer (1963) concluded that

Even though research does not support the formal teaching of grammar in the elementary grades, many teachers are required to teach it.

> The teaching of formal grammar has a negligible or, because it usually displaces some instruction and practice in actual composition, even a harmful effect on the improvement of writing. (pp. 37–38)

Since then, other studies have reached the same conclusion (cf. Elley et al., 1976; Hillocks, 1987).

Despite the controversy about teaching grammar and its value for elementary students, grammar is a part of the elementary language arts curriculum and will undoubtedly remain so for some time. Given this fact, it is only reasonable that grammar should be taught in the most beneficial manner possible. Researchers suggest that integrating grammar study with reading and writing produces the best results (Noyce & Christie, 1983). Elbow (1973) and Haley-James (1981) view grammar as a tool for writers and recommend integrating grammar instruction with the revising and editing stages of the writing process.

❖ TYPES OF GRAMMAR

Grammarians have described the structure of English in three different ways, and the three perspectives influence how grammar is taught in today's elementary schools.

GRAMMAR MINILESSONS

"Yes, I teach grammar. But I don't teach it from the front to the back of the textbook. I confer with students about their writing, and I determine what to teach from the grammatical errors they make in their writing."

Kaye Hicks, Sixth Grade Teacher,
Western Hills School

PROCEDURE

I spend ten minutes each day teaching a grammar minilesson on a topic that my students need. As I confer with students about their writing, I take notes on particular types of errors and add them to my list. I also note which students are having the problem, because those are the students that I want to attend the minilessons. Usually most students come, but those who are having trouble must attend. During the year, I cover most of the skills in the language textbook, but we rarely use the book. Instead I use my students' own writing, and of course, the language in books they are reading.

Traditional Grammar

Traditional grammar is *prescriptive*, providing rules for socially correct usage. This perspective dates back to medieval times and has its roots in the study of Latin. The major contribution of traditional grammar is its terminology—parts of speech, parts of sentences, and types of sentences—that teachers and students can use in talking about language. The shortcoming of traditional grammar is that the terms and rules are inadequate for English and cannot explain how language works.

Even though researchers have repeatedly concluded that the formal teaching of grammar is not effective, traditional concepts about grammar continue to be taught in

I begin a minilesson by presenting information—introducing a new concept or reviewing one we've worked on before. Then I present two or three sentences on the overhead projector as examples. I take the sentences from my students' writing—anonymously—and students take turns identifying the errors and making corrections. I have the students come up and use proofreader's marks to make the changes on the transparency.

Our current topic is comparisons. We've been working on it all week. First, we identified and corrected comparisons (for example, using *more* or *-er,* as in *more beautiful* and *faster*) in sample sentences from students' writing that I've collected. Then students look for examples in books they are reading and in their own writing. They share their examples and explain how the author applied the concept correctly. Today we finished the process by having a test—isn't that traditional? The difference is that my students create the sentences for the test. Tomorrow we'll move on to incomplete sentences; at least, that's what we'll do if my students do well on the test.

ASSESSMENT

I have a checklist with each student's name listed down one side and a list of grammar topics across the top. When I find errors in student writing, I make a checkmark under the topic by the student's name. When several students have demonstrated that they are having problems with one topic, I circle that topic and plan a minilesson. If students still seem to be making errors on that topic, I reteach; if they don't do well on a quiz, I reteach. I don't consider a topic mastered until I see consistent evidence that they are doing it correctly in their writing.

I also have students keep a special grammar section in their language arts notebooks. When I present information about grammatical concepts in the minilessons, students take notes. Then they can refer to the notes when they write and edit their writing.

REFLECTIONS

I really believe that grammar is a tool for writers. It makes more sense to tie grammar instruction to writing than to talk. I've learned not to ask students if a sentence with a grammatical error sounds right, because it often does to them. I focus instead on writing, because it is formal language, and clear communication of their ideas requires adherence to grammatical conventions. I want to help my students learn how to diagnose errors that interfere with clear communication. Sharing their writing in a writing group is one of the best ways I've found for students to realize the impact of their errors on communication.

elementary classes. The three most common types of information taught are the parts of speech, parts of sentences, and types of sentences.

Grammarians have sorted English words into eight groups, called *parts of speech:* nouns, pronouns, verbs, adjectives, adverbs, prepositions, conjunctions, and interjections. Words in each group are used in essentially the same way in a sentence. Nouns and verbs are the basic building blocks of sentences, and pronouns substitute for nouns. Adjectives, adverbs, and prepositions build upon and modify the nouns and verbs. Conjunctions connect individual words or groups of words, and interjections express strong emotion or surprise.

According to the traditional viewpoint, a sentence is made up of one or more words to express a complete thought and, to express the thought, must have a subject and predicate. Sentences are classified in two ways. First, they are classified according to structure, or how they are put together. The structure of a sentence may be simple, compound, complex, or compound-complex. A *simple* sentence contains only one independent clause, and a *compound* sentence is made up of two or more simple sentences. A *complex* sentence contains one independent clause and one or more dependent clauses. A *compound-complex* sentence contains two or more independent clauses and one or more dependent clauses.

Second, sentences are classified according to the type of message they contain. Sentences that make statements are *declarative,* those that ask questions are *interrogative,* those that make commands are *imperative,* and those that communicate strong emotion or surprise are *exclamatory*.

Structural Grammar

The second approach is structural grammar, an attempt to describe how language is really used. Proponents of the structural approach have distinguished between spoken and written language and analyzed the patterns of sentences unique to English, taking into account differences among language users. The study of structural linguistics has provided detailed information about both standard and nonstandard forms of English, but this approach focuses on form and does not explain how meaning relates to use.

The seven basic sentence patterns described in structural grammar can help students learn the structure and function of sentence elements. The basic sentence parts consist of nouns, verbs, and complements. The noun by itself serves as the subject of the sentence; the verb by itself or with complements serves as the predicate of the sentence. Modifiers are added to the nouns, verbs, and complements. Connectives are used to join words, phrases, and clauses. The seven basic patterns are as follows.

Pattern 1: Noun-Verb. This pattern consists of a subject and predicate with no complements. The verb is intransitive, so it does not take any complements. Both the noun and the verb may take modifiers that will expand the possible sentences and make them more interesting. This N-V sentence pattern (and all the succeeding sentence patterns) may be expanded by adding adjectives, adverbs, prepositional phrases, participial phrases, and absolute phrases. We will illustrate each basic sentence pattern and show one expanded sentence in the pattern.

Lions roared.

Hungry *lions,* searching for food, their mouths open wide, *roared* angrily in frustration.

Pattern 2: Noun-Verb-Noun. The N-V-N pattern consists of subject, transitive verb, and direct object complement. The direct object receives the action initiated by the subject and specified by the verb. The verb carries the action from the subject to the object, as the following sentences illustrate:

The lion stalked the jungle.

The hungry *lion,* swaying from side to side, his skin stretched taut, *stalked the jungle* menacingly.

Pattern 3: Noun-Linking Verb-Noun. In this pattern, the complement is a subjective complement because it completes the meaning of the subject. The linking verb links a description to the subject. The subjective complement further identifies the subject:

Lions are animals.

Lions, penned in cages, their freedom taken from them, *are* very unhappy *animals.*

Pattern 4: Noun-Linking Verb-Adjective. The N-LV-Adj pattern consists of a subject, a linking verb, and a predicate adjective. The predicate adjective is a subjective complement that points out a quality of the subject. The linking verb links the description of the adjective to the subject:

Lions are cautious.

The young *lions,* stalking their prey in the African grasslands, their tails twitching nervously, *are* extremely *cautious.*

Pattern 5: Noun-Verb-Noun-Noun. The fifth pattern, N-V-N-N, consists of subject, transitive verb, and two complements—an indirect object and a direct object. The verb specifies an action that is passed from the subject to the object, but another person or thing is also involved in the action. The subject passes the object on to someone or something else, the indirect object:

Lions give cubs meat.

Moving away from the kill, the *lions,* their paws red with blood, *give* their hungry *cubs meat.*

Pattern 6: Noun-Verb-Noun-Noun. This pattern consists of subject, transitive verb, and two complements—a direct object and an objective complement. The objective complement completes the meaning of the object by identifying what the verb has passed on to the object. The objective complement refers to the same person or thing as the object:

Lions make cubs hunters.

Lions, living at the edge of the jungle, painstakingly *make* their young *cubs hunters* of small game.

Pattern 7: Noun-Verb-Noun-Adjective. This pattern consists of subject, transitive verb, and two complements—a direct object and an objective complement. The objective complement in this pattern is an adjective; it still, however, completes the meaning of the action passed on from the subject to the object. The adjective points out a quality of the object. If the objective complement is a noun, as in pattern six, it renames the object rather than pointing out a quality of the object:

Lions make cubs happy.

The old *lions,* pacing back and forth, their heads swinging from side to side, *make* the *cubs* very *happy.*

These seven basic sentence patterns are summarized in Figure 14–2.

The sentence patterns can be expanded even further by using phrases and clauses as the subjects of the sentences. The sentences can also be joined by coordinating and subordinating conjunctions. A potential problem with an approach based on building sentences from basic patterns is that the sentences often sound stilted; the sample sentences about lions are in some respects awkward. The value of the exercises, however, lies in the practice they give students in manipulating language structures for different effects.

Variations and combinations of the seven basic sentence patterns are used to produce almost all sentences that we speak and write. Sentences can be changed from positive to negative, for example, by adding a form of *not* and an auxiliary verb, and

Pattern	Description	Sample Sentence
1. N-V	Subject and intransitive verb with no complements	Lions roared.
2. N-V-N	Subject, transitive verb, and direct object	The lion stalked the jungle.
3. N-LV-N	Subject, linking verb, and complement	Lions are animals.
4. N-LV-Adj	Subject, linking verb, and predicate adjective	Lions are cautious.
5. N-V-N-N	Subject, transitive verb, indirect object, and direct object	Lions give cubs meat.
6. N-V-N-N	Subject, transitive verb, direct object, and objective complement	Lions make cubs hunters.
7. N-V-N-Adj	Subject, transitive verb, direct object, and objective complement	Lions make cubs happy.

FIGURE 14–2

Seven Basic Sentence Patterns

questions are formed by transposing the subject and an auxiliary verb or by adding *who, what,* or other *wh-* words. Sentences are made more complex by joining two sentences or embedding one sentence within another. Linguists have identified a number of transformations that change sentences from one form to another; a list of the most common transformations appears in Figure 14–3. Although the transformations are presented separately, several transformations can be applied to a sentence simultaneously. Elementary students already know and use most of the simple transformations, but the more complex joining and embedding transformations are often taught through sentence combining activities.

Transformation	Description	Sample Sentence
Simple Transformations		
1. Negative	*Not* or *n't* and auxiliary verb inserted	Lions roar. Lions don't roar.
2. Yes-No Question	Subject and auxiliary verb switched	The lion stalked the jungle? Did the lion stalk the jungle?
3. *Wh-* Question	*Wh-* word *(who, what, which, when, where, why)* or *how,* and auxiliary verb inserted	Lions roar. Why do lions roar?
4. Imperative	*You* becomes the subject	Lions give cubs meat. Give cubs meat.
5. There	*There* and auxiliary verb inserted	Lions are cautious. There are cautious lions.
6. Passive	Subject and direct object switched and the main verb changed to past participle form	Lions make cubs hunters. Cubs are made hunters by lions.
Complex Transformations		
1. Joining	Two sentences joined using conjunctions such as *and, but, or*	Lions roar. Tigers roar. Lions and tigers roar.
2. Embedding	Two (or more) sentences combined by embedding one into the other	Lions are animals. Lions are cautious. Lions are cautious animals.

FIGURE 14–3

The Most Common Transformations
Malmstrom, 1977

Transformational Grammar

Transformational grammar is the third and most recent approach. Transformational linguists attempt to describe both how language works and the cognitive processes we use to produce language. They refer to two levels or structures, called *surface* and *deep levels,* to explain how meaning in the brain (deep level) is transformed into the sentences we speak and write (surface level). This approach also explains how standard and nonstandard surface-level sentences (e.g., *I don't have any money* and *I ain't got no money*) can be generated from the same deep-level thought.

The rise of transformational grammar has led many educators to seek ways to operationalize it for classroom use. The method that seems most promising is sentence combining, wherein students focus on sentence construction as they analyze, combine, select, rearrange, elaborate, organize, refocus, and edit their writing (Strong, 1986). The term *sentence combining* obviously suggests that one combines sentences to make them longer or conceptually more dense, but Strong argues that it should be thought of more broadly to include both "tightening" and "decombining" (p. 6). Making sentences longer does not always promote better writing, but it is a good way to help students manipulate sentences.

Mellon (1969) suggested that sentence combining activities might be a profitable way to increase the rate of students' syntactic development. Work by Hunt and O'Donnell (1970) and O'Hare (1973) showed that students could improve their writing when sentence combining exercises were taught. Since these studies, many teachers have introduced sentence combining activities to their students.

Students use complex transformations in sentence combining activities. Sentences can be joined or embedded in a variety of ways. Two sentences (S) are transformed to create a matrix (or combined) sentence (M) in these examples:

(S)   Tom found a wallet.

(S)   The wallet was brown.

(M1)   Tom found a wallet that was brown.

(M2)   Tom found a brown wallet.

The two possible matrix sentences (M1 and M2) show embedding of the adjective *brown*. Matrix sentence M1 uses a relative clause transformation; M2 uses an adjective transformation. Neither matrix sentence is right or wrong; rather, they provide two options. The goal of sentence combining is for students to experiment with different combinations. Examples of other sentence combining exercises are shown in Figure 14–4.

Teachers can incorporate sentence combining activities with the study of the syntactic patterns authors use. Analyze the authors' writing for sentences that readily demonstrate sentence combining. For example, this sentence about Wilbur from *Charlotte's Web* (White, 1952) can be broken down into three short sentences:

"He crawled into the tunnel and disappeared from sight, completely covered with straw." (p. 9)

Sentence Joining

1. (S)*   Joe is tall.
   (S)   Bill is tall.
   (M)**   Joe and Bill are tall.

2. (S)   John fell off his bike.
   (S)   Mary screamed.
   (M)   When John fell off his bike, Mary screamed.

3. (S)   Tom hit the ball over the wall.
   (S)   Tom ran around the bases.
   (M)   Tom hit the ball over the wall and ran around the bases.

Sentence Embedding

1. (S)   The boy is fat.
   (S)   The boy is eating cake.
   (M)   The boy who is eating cake is fat.
   (M)   The fat boy is eating cake.

2. (S)   John fights fires.
   (S)   John is a fireman.
   (M)   John who is a fireman fights fires.
   (M)   John, a fireman, fights fires.

3. (S)   The bird is beautiful.
   (S)   The bird is flying over the tree.
   (M)   The bird which is flying over the tree is beautiful.
   (M)   The bird flying over the tree is beautiful.

FIGURE 14—4

Examples of Sentence Combining
 *S = sentence to be combined
**M = matrix or combined sentence

1. He crawled into the tunnel.

2. He disappeared from sight.

3. He was completely covered with straw.

When you use sentences from children's literature for analysis, always stress what effect the author was trying to have on the reader. Sentence combining activities become "busywork" if the effect on potential readers is not emphasized. Students can ask themselves these questions:

- Would the effect be different if I combined these sentences?
- Which way of combining these sentences would be most effective?

Sentence combining activities give students opportunities to manipulate sentence structures; however, they are rather artificial. They are most effective when combined with other writing assignments. Weaver (1979) cautions that "sentence combining activities are only an adjunct to the writing program and the writing process and should never be used as substitutes for actual writing" (pp. 83–84). The drawback of the transformational approach is that it is difficult to apply the phrase structure rules, which explain how sentences are created, in grammar instruction for elementary students.

❖ TEACHING GRAMMAR

The traditional way to teach grammar is to use language arts textbooks. Students read rules and definitions, copy words and sentences, and mark them to apply the concepts presented in the text. This type of activity often seems meaningless to students. Instead, the teacher should use literature and the students' own writing; the study of words and their arrangement into sentences allows students to manipulate language (Cullinan, Jaggar, & Strickland, 1974; Tompkins & McGee, 1983).

Teachers have two ways to determine which grammatical concepts they will teach: they can identify the concepts they are supposed to teach from a list in a language arts textbook, or they can identify concepts they need to teach by assessing students' writing and noting what types of grammar and usage errors they are making. The concepts can be taught to the whole class or to small groups of students, but they should only be taught to students who don't already know them—it is a waste of time

Students use proofreader's marks to correct grammar and other mechanical errors in sentences the teacher writes on the chalkboard.

to teach something to a student who already knows it. Atwell (1987) suggests using "minilessons" that are brief, to the point, and meaningful because of their immediate connections to reading and writing.

Teaching Strategy

This six-step strategy for minilessons is based on the instructional model described in Chapter 1, and it can be used for teaching traditional, structural, or transformational grammar concepts to small groups of students or to the whole class. You will notice that no worksheets are recommended; instead, plan to use excerpts from books students are reading or from students' own writing.

1. Introduce the concept, using words and sentences from children's literature or students' writing.

2. Provide additional information about the grammatical concept and more examples from children's literature or students' writing.

3. Provide activities to help students establish relationships between the information presented in the first and second steps. Five activities to use in this strategy are word hunts, concept books, sentence slotting, sentence expansion, and moving language around.

Word Hunts.   Students can identify words representing one part of speech or each of the eight parts of speech from books they are reading or from their own writing. A group of fifth graders identified words representing each part of speech from Van Allsburg's *The Polar Express* (1985):

nouns: train, children, Santa Claus, elves, pajamas, roller coaster, conductor, sleigh, hug, clock, Sarah

pronouns: we, they, he, it, us, you, his, I, me

verbs: filled, ate, flickered, raced, were, cheered, marched, asked, pranced, stood, shouted

adjectives: melted, white-tailed, quiet, no, first, magical, cold, dark, polar, Santa's

adverbs: soon, faster, wildly, apart, closer, alone

prepositions: in, through, over, with, of, in front of, behind, at, for, across, into

conjunctions: and, but

interjections: oh, well, now

Similarly, students can hunt for parts of sentences or sentence types in books of children's literature.

Concept Books.   Students can examine concept books that focus on one part of speech or another grammatical concept. For example, Barrett describes the essential characteristics of a variety of animals in *A Snake Is Totally Tail* (1983), and most of the descriptions include an adverb. After students read the book and identify the adverbs, they can write their own sentences, following the same pattern, and illustrate the sentences on posters, mobiles, a mural, or in a class book. Useful books for teaching traditional grammar concepts are listed in Figure 14–5.

   Sentence Slotting.   Students can experiment with words and phrases to see how they function in sentences by filling in sentences that have slots, or blanks. Sentence slotting teaches students about several different grammatical concepts. They can first experiment with parts of speech using a sentence like this:

>   The snake slithered _____ the rock.
>   over
>   around
>   under
>   to

Students can brainstorm a number of words to fill in the slot, all of which will be prepositions; adjectives, nouns, verbs, and adverbs will not make sense. This activity can be repeated to introduce or review any part of speech.

   Sentence slotting also demonstrates to students that parts of speech can substitute for each other. In the following sentence, common and proper nouns as well as pronouns can be used in the slot:

>   _____ asked his secretary to get him a cup of coffee.
>   The man
>   Mr. Jones
>   He

A similar sentence-slotting example demonstrates how phrases can function as an adverb:

>   The dog growled _____ .
>   ferociously
>   with his teeth bared
>   daring us to reach for his bone

In this example, the adverb *ferociously* can be used in the slot, as well as prepositional and participial phrases. Sentences with an adjective slot can be used to demonstrate that phrases function as adjectives. The goal of this activity is to demonstrate the function of words in sentences. Many sentence-slotting activities, such as the last example, also illustrate that sentences become more specific with the addition of a word or phrase. Through these activities, students experiment with the grammatical options they have been learning. Remember, however, that the purpose of these activities is to experiment with language; they should be done with small groups of students or the whole class, not as individual worksheets.

   Sentence Expansion.   Students can expand simple, or kernel, sentences, such as *A frog leaps* or *The car raced,* by adding modifiers. The words and phrases with which

Nouns	Heller, R. (1987). *A cache of jewels and other collective nouns.* New York: Grosset & Dunlap. Hoban, T. (1981). *More than one.* New York: Greenwillow. Terban, M. (1986). *Your foot's on my feet! and other tricky nouns.* New York: Clarion. Wildsmith, B. (1968). *Fishes.* New York: Franklin Watts.
Verbs	Beller, J. (1984). *A-B-Cing: An action alphabet.* New York: Crown. Burningham, J. (1986). *Cluck baa, jangle twang, slam bang, skip trip, sniff shout, wobble pop.* New York: Viking. Heller, R. (1988). *Kites sail high: A book about verbs.* New York: Grosset & Dunlap. Hoban, T. (1975). *Dig, drill, dump, fill.* New York: Greenwillow. McMillan, B. (1984). *Kitten can . . . A concept book.* New York: Lothrop. Maestro, B., & Maestro, G. (1985). *Camping out.* New York: Crown. Neumeier, M., & Glasser, B. (1985). *Action alphabet.* New York: Greenwillow. Shiefman, V. (1981). *M is for move.* New York: Dutton. Terban, M. (1984). *I think I thought and other tricky verbs.* New York: Clarion.
Adjectives	Boynton, S. (1983). *A is for angry: An animal and adjective alphabet.* New York: Workman. Duke, K. (1983). *Guinea pig ABC.* New York: Dutton. Hoban, T. (1981). *A children's zoo.* New York: Greenwillow. Maestro, B. & Maestro, G. (1979). *On the go: A book of adjectives.* New York: Crown. McMillan, B. (1989). *Super, super, superwords.* New York: Lothrop.
Adverbs	Barrett, J. (1983). *A snake is totally tail.* New York: Atheneum.
Prepositions	Bancheck, L. (1978). *Snake in, snake out.* New York: Crowell. Berenstain, S., & Berenstain, J. (1968). *Inside, outside, upside, down.* New York: Random House. Berenstain, S., & Berenstain, J. (1971). *Bears in the night.* New York: Random House. Hoban, T. (1973). *Over, under, and through and other spatial concepts.* New York: Macmillan.

FIGURE 14–5

Books that Illustrate Traditional Grammar Concepts

they expand the basic sentence can add qualities and attributes, details, and comparisons. The "5 Ws plus one" help students focus on expanding particular aspects of the sentence; for example:

Basic sentence	A frog leaps.
What kind?	green, speckled
How?	high into the air
Where?	from a half-submerged log and lands in the water with a splash
Why?	to avoid the noisy boys playing nearby
Expanded sentence	To avoid the noisy boys playing nearby, *a* green, speckled *frog leaps* high into the air from a half-submerged log and lands in the water with a splash.

Depending on what questions one asks and the answers students give, many other expanded sentences are possible from the same basic sentence. Students enjoy working in small groups to expand a basic sentence so they can compare their expanded versions with the other groups. Instead of the "5 Ws plus one" questions to expand sentences, the teacher can ask older students to supply a specific part of speech or modifier at each step of expansion.

The students or the teacher can create basic sentences for expansion or take them from children's literature. Very few basic sentences appear in stories, but one can identify and use the basic sentence within an expanded sentence. Students enjoy comparing their expanded versions of the basic sentence with the author's. When students are familiar with the story the sentence was taken from, they can try to approximate the author's meaning. Even so, it is likely that they will go in a variety of directions, and because students' expanded sentences may vary greatly from the author's, they come to realize the power of modifiers to transform a sentence.

Moving Language Around.   Hudson (1980) suggests "moving language around" to help students learn about the structure of English and how to manipulate language. Students begin with a sentence and then apply four operations to it: they add, delete, substitute, and rearrange. With the sentence "Children play games," these manipulations are possible:

Add	Children play games at home.
	Children like to play games.
Delete	Children play.
Substitute	Adults play games.
	Children like games.
	Children play Nintendo.

Rearrangement   Games are played by children.

Games play children.

The last sentence is nonsensical, but thought-provoking, nonetheless.

These activities help students learn more about the relationship between changes in form and changes in meaning. After practicing the concepts with these activities, the teacher completes the final steps of the strategy:

4. Review the major points related to the grammatical concept. Students can freewrite about the concept to summarize and clarify their thinking or make notes in their learning logs.

5. Ask students to locate examples of the concept in books they are reading or in their writing as a comprehension check. They should also share the examples they locate with classmates.

6. Students apply the newly learned grammatical concept in their writing. In writing groups, students can focus on how the writer used the grammatical concept. They can compliment the writer for using the concept or make suggestions as to how the writer can revise the writing to incorporate the concept. As teachers grade students' writing, they can award points to students who have used the grammatical concept in their writing.

This teaching strategy can be used to teach any grammatical concept. A language arts textbook can supplement the steps, but it is not necessary. To illustrate the teaching strategy, Figure 14–6 lists the six steps of the teaching strategy and how they would be adapted for a series of minilessons to teach students to identify subjects and predicates in sentences. Other minilessons might focus specifically on subjects or on predicates.

Assessing Students' Knowledge about Grammar

The traditional way to assess knowledge about grammar is by giving students a written test that asks them to identify parts of speech or to write sentences that are simple, compound, or complex. As we discussed regarding spelling and handwriting, however, a better gauge of students' understanding of writers' tools is to observe how they use them in their writing.

Teachers can develop checklists of grammar and usage skills to teach at a particular grade level or list errors they observe in students' writing. Then teachers observe students as they write and examine their compositions to note errors, plan and teach minilessons based on students' needs, note further errors and plan and teach other minilessons, and so on. As teachers identify grammar and usage problems, they should plan minilessons to call students' attention to the problems that make a bigger difference in writing (Pooley, 1974). For example, in the sentences *Mom leave me go outside* and *I fell off of my bike,* the use of *leave* for *let* is a more important problem than the redundant use of *of.*

Teaching Middle Grade Students to Identify Subjects and Predicates

1. Introduce the concept.

   Explain, using ten sentences written on sentence strips, that a sentence is made up of a subject and a predicate. Choose sentences from *Sarah, Plain and Tall* (MacLachan, 1985), which the class is reading as part of a unit on pioneers. Have students take turns highlighting the subject of each sentence with a yellow highlighter pen and the predicate with a blue highlighter pen.

2. Provide additional information about the grammatical concept.

   Review information presented earlier (that sentences are made up of a subject and a predicate) and reread the sentences on sentence strips. Then ask students to work in small groups to write a sentence about *Sarah, Plain and Tall* on a sentence strip. Have the groups present their sentences to the class and highlight the subject and predicate. Next, ask students to examine the subjects of the sentences to determine what goes into the subject and what goes into the predicate.

3. Provide activities.

   Have students work in small groups to write two sentences on sentence strips about pioneers. Next, students cut their sentences into two pieces, separating the subjects and the predicates. Then students can experiment with the sentence parts and combine the pieces to form both sensible and nonsense sentences.

4. Review major points.

   As a class, develop a bulletin board display to review that sentences are composed of subjects and predicates. Use some of the sentence pieces from the previous activity.

5. Locate examples in literature.

   Have students copy two sentences from informational books on pioneers available in the classroom and highlight the subject and the predicate. Then have students share their work in small groups.

6. Apply in writing.

   Students work on mobiles, charts, dioramas, displays, and other projects related to the pioneer unit. Students write at least five sentences to describe their projects and meet in writing groups to review the sentences and, specifically, to check that each sentence includes a subject and a predicate. Part of the assessment for the project will focus on whether their project descriptions are complete sentences with subjects and predicates.

FIGURE 14–6

Teacher's Notebook Page: Using the Teaching Strategy

The most useful way to teach grammar is when students are editing their writing and want to communicate as effective as possible.

❖ LEARNING GRAMMAR THROUGH WRITING

Because children's knowledge of grammar and usage is dependent on the language spoken in their homes and neighborhoods, some primary- and middle-grade students do not recognize a difference between *me and him* and *he and I*. When the error is brought to their attention, they do not understand, because semantically—at a meaning level—the two versions are identical. Moreover, *me and him* sounds "right" to these students because they hear this construction at home. When other corrections are pointed out to middle- and upper-grade students, they repeat the correct form, shake their heads, and say that it doesn't sound right. *Real* sounds better to some than *really* because it is more familiar. An explanation that adverbs rather than adjectives modify adjectives is not useful either, even if students have had traditional grammar instruction. Correction of nonstandard English errors is perceived as a repudiation of the language spoken in children's homes rather than an explanation that written language requires a more formal language register or dialect. Jaggar (1980) recommends that teachers allow for language differences, acknowledging that everyone speaks a dialect and one is not better or more correct than another.

A better way to deal with grammar and usage errors is to use a problem-solving approach during the editing stage of the writing process. Locating and correcting errors in students' writing is not as threatening as correcting their talk, because it is not as personal. Also, students can more easily accept that "book language" is a different kind of English. During editing, students are error-hunting, trying to make their papers "optimally readable" (Smith, 1982). They recognize that it is a courtesy to readers to make their papers as correct as possible. Through revising and editing, classmates note errors and correct each other and teachers point out other errors. Sometimes teachers explain the correction (e.g., the past tense of bring is *brought,* not *brung*), and at other times they simply mark the correction, saying that "we usually write it this way." Some errors should be ignored, especially young children's errors; correcting too many errors only teaches students that their language is inferior or inadequate. Guidelines for correcting students' grammar and usage errors are summarized in Figure 14–7.

The goal in dealing with nonstandard English speakers is not to replace their dialects, but to add standard English to students' language options. (We will discuss teaching students who do not speak English or who speak nonstandard English in Chapter 16.)

HOW TO DEAL WITH STUDENTS' GRAMMAR AND USAGE ERRORS

- Use a problem-solving approach to correct grammar and usage errors.
- Correct errors during the editing stage of the writing process.
- Consider the function, audience, and form of the composition when determining whether to correct errors or which errors to correct.
- Let students know that correcting grammatical and usage errors is a courtesy to readers.
- Keep explanations for corrections brief.
- Sometimes, simply make the change and say that in writing it is done this way.
- Don't ask students if the correction makes the writing "sound better."
- Use sentence slotting and sentence combining activities to rid the composition of lackluster and repetitious words and short, choppy sentences.
- Ignore some errors, especially young children's.
- Respect the language of children's home and community, and introduce standard written English as "book language."

FIGURE 14–7

Teacher's Notebook Page: Guidelines for Correcting Students' Grammar and Usage Errors in Compositions

❖ REVIEW

Grammar is the structure of language. Usage, in contrast, is the socially accepted way of using words in sentences. Great controversy exists today about teaching grammar. Our position is that grammar is a writer's tool and is best taught by means of children's literature or as part of the editing stage of the writing process. There are three types of grammar: traditional, structural, and transformational. Each type has a contribution to make to grammar instruction. With the instructional model developed in Chapter 1, teachers use children's literature and students' own writing to teach grammar concepts. This approach requires no worksheets.

❖ EXTENSIONS

1. Examine your feelings about whether grammar should be taught in elementary schools. If you decide it should be, how should it be taught? Compare your opinions with the arguments you find for and against teaching grammar in Davis's "In Defense of Grammar" (1984) and Small's "Why I'll Never Teach Grammar Again" (1985) or in "Grammar Should Be Taught and Learned in Our Schools" (Goba & Brown, 1982).

2. Examine language arts textbooks to see how they present grammar. What percentage of the textbook pages is devoted to grammar instruction? What types of activities are included? Is grammar instruction tied to literature and writing activities?

3. Interview students about their knowledge of grammar and how they apply it in their writing. Use questions such as these:

   Do you study grammar in school?
   What kinds of grammar activities does your teacher assign?
   What have you learned about grammar?
   Do you think it's important to learn about grammar? Why or why not?
   Do authors need to know about grammar? Why or why not?
   Do you use what you know about grammar when you write? Why or why not?

4. Plan and teach a grammar lesson using one of the activities suggested in the chapter.

❖ REFERENCES

Applebee, A. N., Langer, J. A., & Mullis, I. V. S. (1987). *Grammar, punctuation, and spelling: Controlling the conventions of written English at ages 9, 13, and 17.* Princeton, NJ: Educational Testing Service.

Atwell, N. (1987). *In the middle: Writing, reading, and learning with adolescents.* Upper Montclair, NJ: Boynton/Cook.

Barrett, J. (1983). *A snake is totally tail.* New York: Atheneum.

Braddock, R., Lloyd-Jones, R., & Schoer, L. (1963). *Research in written composition.*

Champaign, IL: National Council of Teachers of English.

Cullinan, B., Jaggar, A., & Strickland, D. (1974). Oral language expansion in the primary grades. In B. Cullinan (Ed.), *Black dialects and reading.* Urbana, IL: National Council of Teachers of English.

Davis, F. (1984). In defense of grammar. *English Education, 16,* 151–164.

Edelsky, C. (1989). Putting language variation to work for you. In P. Rigg & V. G. Allen (Eds.), *When they don't all speak English: Integrating*

the ESL student into the regular classroom,
pp. 96–107. Urbana, IL: National Council of
Teachers of English.

Elbow, P. (1973). *Writing without teachers.* New
York: Oxford University Press.

Elley, W. B., Barham, I. H., Lamb, H., & Wyllie,
M. (1976). The role of grammar in a secondary
school English curriculum. *Research in the
Teaching of English, 10,* 5–21.

Fraser, I. S., & Hodson, L. M. (1978). Twenty-one
kicks at the grammar horse. *English Journal, 67,*
49–53.

Goba, R. I., & Brown, P. A. (1982). Grammar
should be taught and learned in our schools.
English Journal, 73, 20–23.

Haley-James, S. (Ed.). (1981). *Perspectives on
writing in grades 1–8.* Urbana, IL: National
Council of Teachers of English.

Hillocks, G., Jr. (1987). *Research on written
composition: New directions for teaching.*
Urbana, IL: National Conference on Research in English and the ERIC Clearinghouse on Reading and Communication
Skills.

Hudson, B. A. (1980). Moving language around:
Helping students become aware of language
structure. *Language Arts, 57,* 614–620.

Hunt, K. W., & O'Donnell, R. C. (1970). *An
elementary school curriculum to develop better
writing skills.* Washington, DC: U.S.
Government Printing Office.

Jaggar, A. (1980). Allowing for language
differences. In G. S. Pinnell (Ed.), *Discovering
language with children,* pp. 25–28. Urbana, IL:
National Council of Teachers of English.

Malmstrom, J. (1977). *Understanding language: A
primer for the language arts teacher.* New York:
St. Martin's Press.

Mellon, J. C. (1969). *Transformational sentence
combining: A method for enhancing the
development of syntactic fluency in English
composition* (NCTE Research Report No. 10).
Urbana, IL: National Council of Teachers of
English.

Noyce, R. M., & Christie, J. F. (1983). Effects of an
integrated approach to grammar instruction on
third graders' reading and writing. *Elementary
School Journal, 84,* 63–69.

O'Hare, F. (1973). *Sentence combining: Improving
student writing without formal grammar
instruction* (NCTE Research Report No. 15).
Urbana, IL: National Council of Teachers of
English.

Pooley, R. C. (1974). *The teaching of English
usage.* Urbana, IL: National Council of Teachers
of English.

Small, R. (1985). Why I'll never teach grammar
again. *English Education, 17,* 174–178.

Smith, F. (1982). *Writing and the writer.* New
York: Holt, Rinehart & Winston.

Strong, W. (1986). *Creative approaches to sentence
combining.* Urbana, IL: ERIC Clearinghouse on
Reading and Communication Skills and the
National Council of Teachers of English.

Suhor, C. (1987). Orthodoxies in language arts
education. *Language Arts, 64,* 416–419.

Tompkins, G. E., & McGee, L. M. (1983).
Launching nonstandard speakers into standard
English. *Language Arts, 60,* 463–469.

Van Allsburg, C. (1985). *The polar express.* Boston:
Houghton Mifflin.

Weaver, C. (1979). *Grammar for teachers:
Perspectives and definitions.* Urbana, IL:
National Council of Teachers of English.

White, E. B. (1952). *Charlotte's web.* New York:
Harper and Row.

15 EXTENDING LANGUAGE ARTS ACROSS THE CURRICULUM

◆ THIS CHAPTER EXTENDS THE TEACHING OF LANGUAGE ARTS
from language arts class across the curriculum into literature, social studies, and
other content areas.

◆ AS YOU ARE READING, THINK ABOUT THESE QUESTIONS:

Which language arts activities can be integrated across the curriculum?

What is a language arts across-the-curriculum thematic unit?

How do teachers plan thematic units?

S tudents listen, talk, read, and write across the curriculum every day in elementary classrooms, but greater learning and excitement about learning are not always the outcomes. The language arts across-the-curriculum movement, a new way of developing curriculum, focuses on using language to learn. This approach works best when the curriculum is organized into thematic units. Social studies, science, language arts, and other content areas are integrated into units that focus on broad themes, such as communication, explorers, mystery stories, the oceans, or Dr. Seuss's stories. Instead of reading content area textbooks and answering the questions at the end of each chapter, teachers and students are actively involved in researching to find answers and responding to what they learn.

Gamberg and her colleagues (1988) describe theme study as "the core of what children do in school" (p. 10). At their elementary school in Halifax, Nova Scotia, students participate in large-scale themes; one focuses on houses. Students at different grade levels studied different aspects, but all students focused on houses. One class of primary students, for example, studied homes around the world; a class of middle-grade students investigated how homes have changed through history; and a class of upper-grade students learned about building a house. Based on experiences teaching thematic units, teachers list these characteristics:

- The unit involves in-depth study.
- The topic is of interest to students.
- The topic is broad enough that it can be divided into subtopics.
- The topic lends itself to comparing and contrasting ideas.
- The unit includes opportunities for investigation and use of concrete materials and other resources.
- The unit allows for cross-disciplinary activities.
- The unit encourages students to use community resources.

Teachers work together to plan the units and to integrate content area study, language arts, and skills so that students are involved in meaningful, functional, and genuine learning activities. Theme studies are successful with all children because they help them become responsible, independent learners who cooperate with classmates at the same time that they become self-disciplined. One of the most important outcomes is that students gain self-confidence and self-esteem as they become successful and motivated to learn and apply what they are learning.

Language is a powerful learning tool, and reading, writing, listening, and talk activities are valuable ways to learn in all content areas. When students use language in meaningful ways in content area study, they learn the content information better and develop language competencies, and critical thinking skills are activated. Through listening, talking, reading, and writing activities, students develop their own knowledge of the subject. Thaiss (1986) identifies three benefits students gain from studying across the curriculum:

1. Students understand and remember better when they use listening, talking, reading, and writing to explore what they are learning.

521

❖ "PRO" FILE

PROCESS: SCIENCE AND WRITING

"Doing a science project is one of the best ways I know to practice the writing process."

Brian Bennett, Fifth-Sixth Grade Teacher, Heaton Elementary School

PROCEDURE

Beginning in September, my students conduct science experiments and record the results in lab reports. One of the things I stress is to keep accurate records of what is happening. We began with a unit on air and then went to units on water, the human body, plants, and machines. In each unit, my students use the scientific method; after conducting ten or more experiments in each unit, they can apply this approach to their own experiments.

In January, we begin to talk about science fair projects to present at our science fair in April. Students brainstorm a list of things that interest them, and their science fair projects develop from these ideas. This year some students chose to explore which brand of paper towels absorbs the most water, how to recycle paper, and behavioristic training of animals. Most students work in

small groups, and the whole class is involved in each project because of our sharing sessions, which function much like the Author's Chair. I try to keep most of the project work at school, but it is necessary to involve parents in some projects.

Using the scientific method, students identify the problem and write a hypothesis and research question. Next, they assemble the materials and conduct the experiment. They collect data using a chart and then interpret the data. This is probably the toughest part for them. We spend a lot of time talking about what the data show. Then they write the reports for their displays and put them together. It takes two months or more to complete the projects.

ASSESSMENT

I keep a notebook on each student with entries about his or her work on the project. When I review my entries, it is easy to see who is having difficulty. Then I talk with students, one at a time or in small groups if several students are having the same problem, to get them back on track. There are always a few students that I must work with closely. I also use a checklist that includes each of the components of the experiment and the pieces of information that must be included in the display. I give students this checklist when they begin, and they check off each step as they complete it. Then I assign points and give a grade for the project.

REFLECTIONS

My students use the writing process in creating their science fair projects. At each step of the process, students share their work with their classmates. We all sit in a circle, and students take turns talking about their projects and reading the drafts of problems, research questions, and other parts of their reports. Other students ask questions and give compliments and suggestions. This sharing also helps me keep tabs on each student's work. Science fair projects take a lot of time and hard work for the students and for me, but I think it's worth it because my students really apply the scientific method and learn how science affects their daily lives.

SCIENCE PROJECT CHECKLIST

STEPS	POINTS	
1. Identify a problem.	10	____
2. Write a hypothesis.	15	____
3. Collect the materials and make a list of them.	5	____
4. Write a research question.	15	____
5. Conduct the experiment.	10	____
6. Collect the data on a chart.	5	____
7. Interpret the data.	15	____
8. Report the conclusion.	10	____
9. Prepare the display.	15	____
TOTAL		____

Comments

2. Students' language learning is reinforced when they listen, talk, read, and write about what they are learning.

3. Students learn best through active involvement, collaborative projects, and interaction with classmates, the teacher, and the world.

❖ LEARNING THROUGH LANGUAGE

Halliday (1980) described three components of the language arts curriculum: learning language, learning through language, and learning about language. The first component, learning language, might seem to be language arts teachers' primary responsibility. Certainly, students do need to develop communicative competence in listening, talking, reading, and writing, and instruction in each of the four language modes is essential. The third component, learning about language, involves "coming to understand the nature and function of language itself" (Halliday, 1980, p. 16). Students develop intuitive knowledge about language and its forms and purposes while they use the four language modes, and through vocabulary, spelling, and grammar instruction, their knowledge is made more explicit. But language learning does not occur in isolation, and the second component is just as important.

Learning through language is described as "how we use language to build up a picture of the world in which we live" (Halliday, 1980, p. 13). It involves using language to learn in content areas across the curriculum. Students learn content area material through language at the same time they are learning, applying, and refining language through content area study. The language arts activities that we have discussed throughout this text are applied through literature and content area study. Rather than learn about listening for the sake of listening, students learn about it so they can listen more effectively to learn math or science. Similarly, they learn to read and write for content area study.

Two students work cooperatively to make a poster about the parts of a plant.

Learning Science Through Language

In learning about science, students participate in a wide variety of language activities (Hansen et al., 1985). They listen to information presented in filmstrips and videotapes, information presented by the teacher, and information read aloud. They use informal writing strategies to take notes and organize information. Clusters, note-taking/note-making sheets, learning logs, and lab reports are four forms that recording may take. Students read concept books, informational books, reference books, and magazine articles as a part of research projects and share what they are learning through oral reports, debates, written reports, "All about . . ." books, posters, charts, and diagrams. Interviewing can also be used in science; students can interview a scientist or other knowledgeable person and then share what they have learned by writing a newspaper article or other report.

In a unit about plants, for example, students might be involved in the following types of activities. Listening activities might involve these:

- Listen to the teacher share poems about plants with the class.
- Listen to the teacher read informational books about plants.
- Listen to films, videotapes, and filmstrips about plants.
- Listen to a botanist or gardener talk about plants.

Talk activities include these possibilities:

- Participate in discussions about plants.
- Talk about the plant experiments they are conducting.
- Ask a botanist or gardener questions about plants.
- Give oral reports about plants.
- Retell or dramatize a plant story, such as *The Giving Tree* (Silverstein, 1964).

Reading activities would include these:

- Read concept books and informational books about plants.
- Read seed packets and planting guides.
- Read maps showing where different kinds of plants live.
- Read aloud poems about a plant.
- Read a classmate's hardbound book about plants.
- Share learning log entries and freewrites about plants.

These are writing activities that might be part of a science unit on plants:

- Brainstorm a list of plant-related words.
- Make a cluster about plants, flowers, trees, or some other topic.

- Freewrite or write in a learning log about plants.
- Cube *plant, tree,* or another word related to the unit.
- Make a poster comparing deciduous and evergreen trees.
- Write a letter inviting a botanist to be interviewed.
- Record a seed's growth in a learning log.
- Make plant or ecology posters.
- Write invitations to a tree-planting ceremony.
- Write an "All about . . ." book.
- Write an ABC book about plants.
- Conduct a science experiment about plants and write a lab report.
- Research and write a report about plants.
- Write poems about plants.

Figure 15–1 shows two writing samples fourth graders wrote as part of a unit on plants. One sample is a lab report about a science experiment; the other is a cluster about nonflowering plants based on *Plants That Never Ever Bloom* (Heller, 1984). It would not be possible to list all the listening, talking, reading, and writing activities that can be related to a unit on plants, but these examples suggest the range of activities teachers should consider when planning instruction. Most importantly, our listing illustrates that the language modes are the vehicles through which students learn about plants.

Learning Social Studies Through Language

Like science, social studies lends itself to language activities. To study history, geography, political science, or another of the social studies, children read picture books, concept books, informational books, reference books, magazines, and newspapers. They talk and write informally about their learning, and they talk and write to organize their learning and to share it through reports, poems, stories, and other activities. Upper-grade students who are studying the American Revolution, for instance, might be involved in these language–social studies activities. For listening:

- Listen to the teacher read aloud books about the American Revolution
- Listen to songs of the period
- View and listen to films, filmstrips, and videotapes
- Listen to classmates share their writing

Students might participate in these talk activities:

- Discuss issues of the American Revolution.
- Dramatize events from the period.
- Give oral reports.

- Debate in the role of a Tory or a Patriot.
- Pretend to be someone from the period and be interviewed by their class-mates.

They might read from among these possibilities:

- Fritz's biographies of Revolutionary personalities, such as *Why Don't You Get a Horse, Sam Adams?* (1974)
- Informational books about the American Revolution
- Chapter books set in Revolutionary War days
- Poems such as "Paul Revere's Ride"
- Maps, charts, and diagrams about the Revolutionary War
- Classmates' stories, reports, and other writings

Writing activities might include these:

- Keeping a simulated journal as Paul Revere, Betsy Ross, or another personality from the period
- Keeping a learning log with lists of words, clusters, and note-taking/note-making pages
- Making a KWL chart listing what they know about the American Revolution, what they want to learn, and finally, what they have learned
- Writing poems about the American Revolution
- Researching and writing a report about life in the 1700s
- Writing a simulated newspaper that might have been published during the American Revolution
- Writing a biography of an American Revolutionary War personality

An excerpt from a fifth grader's biography of Benjamin Franklin is presented in Figure 15–2. In this biography, entitled "The Life of the Great Inventor," Matthew writes four chapters focusing on Ben's childhood, his experiments with electricity, *Poor Richard's Almanack,* and Franklin's role in the Revolutionary War period. Matthew read Aliki's *The Many Lives of Benjamin Franklin* (1988), d'Aulaires' *Benjamin Franklin* (1950), and Jean Fritz's *What's the Big Idea, Ben Franklin* (1976) to gather information about Franklin. He then developed a lifeline showing key events and accomplishments. With this background of information, Matthew chose topics for each chapter and used the writing process to cluster his ideas, write rough drafts of each chapter, revise the chapters in writing groups, edit to identify and correct mechanical errors, and, finally, to publish his biography in a hardbound book. His finished book included a title page, table of contents, four chapters, a bibliography, and an "All about the Author" page. A unit on the American Revolution with activities such as these can be extended to include the times allocated for both language arts and social studies.

My Experiment on Plants

My Question

Will plants grow without light?

My Prediction

No, plants cannot grow without light because if plants didn't have light the water wouldn't soak in and they wouldn't live because too much water would be on top. of the plant.

My Log

April 9
I planted my seeds in a row and watered them after it. My seeds' color is brown. They are about half an inch long. Their texture is very smooth.
They are an oval shape. They are bean seeds.

April 11
Mine has been in the dark for 2 days and nothing has changed.

April 14
My plants have grown half an inch tall in the dark. It really surprises me.

April 15
My plants are 4 inches tall (20 cm) according to what I can see.

April 16
My plants have grown 1 inch more.

April 17
Mine have grown 2 more inches longer in length

April 21
Mine have grown 5 more inches and are now 12 inches tall.

April 22
Mine have grown half an inch. I planted another one and can't water it.

April 23
Mine have grown one inch taller. The other is growing too, even without water.

April 24
Mine are now 15 inches tall. My unwatered plant is 4 inches tall.

April 25
Mine have grown 2 more inches and the other 1 inch.

April 29
My plants are dying out after they've grown a lot.

May 1
My plants are dying and they smell terrible.

FIGURE 15–1

Two Writing Activities from a Fourth Grade Plants Unit

May 2
My plants have died and they look terrible.

May 6
My plants have been dying since a while ago. I have taken good care of them.

May 7
My plants have died and we will talk about them on Monday.

May 8
My plants have died and there's not even a root left.

My Conclusion

Now I know that the plants grew so tall because they were reaching for sunlight.
They died because they were in the dark.

–Aaron

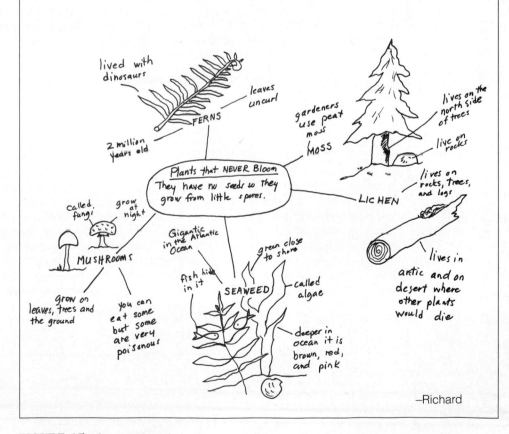

–Richard

FIGURE 15–1   (*continued*)

Chapter 1: In Which a Genius Is Born

In 1706 a young genius was born. His name was Benjamin Franklin. At the time the streets of Boston, Massachusetts were still being named. Luckily, the street Ben lived on had already been named Milk Street. Ben had 17 brothers and sisters. When Ben was 9 or 10, he bought a whistle with all his money. That was the last time he spent his money unwisely. That whistle drove his family crazy.

When Ben was 12, he made a swimming machine. He got two boards and cut a hole in the middle of them. When he tested out his invention, he raced his friend Tom. Ben beat him by 10 yards.

At the age of 12, Ben's father wanted him to become a candle maker, but Ben wanted to be a sailor. Ben's father talked him into being an apprentice for his brother James. James was a printer. Back then you had to work until you were 21 if you were an apprentice.

Ben got tired of reading the same old thing from the newspaper every single day. So he wrote letters to James about things so James would put them in the newspaper. He didn't want James to know it was him so he signed it Widow Dogood. Everytime a letter came, everybody got excited. His letters made newspapers sell faster. When James found out what Ben did, he got angry and didn't let Ben give him things to put in the newspaper.

Chapter 2: Ben Discovers Electricity

On a day in 1748 it was on the front cover of the newspaper that a man had died trying to prove electricity was in lightning. The man died instantly when lightning hit the tower the man was in. The newspaper said there was machinery in the tower. So Ben figured that there was electricity in lightning. He wanted to know for sure so he got a handkerchief, 6 sticks, wire, string, and a key. He made a kite. He took the 6 sticks and used 4 of them to made a diamond. He took 2 sticks and used them for a cross for the center of the diamond. Then he used the handkerchief to wrap around the diamond. After that he tied a wire to the end of it. The he tied some string to the end of the wire. After that he slid a key to about the center of the wire. He waited until a storm came with lightning. Then he flew the kite and lightning hit the top of the kite. A streak of electricity zoomed down the wire, but then it hit the string. When it hit Ben it was not so great but it still gave him a great shock. After he found out that electricity was in lightning he made up the lightning rod. Then he got a lot of people to become witnesses. Then he did it again and that's how we have electricity now.

–Matthew

FIGURE 15–2

An Excerpt from a Fifth Grader's Biography of Ben Franklin

Learning Literature Through Language

Literature units that focus on a single book, an author, a collection of books by the same author, a theme, or a genre can be developed the same way. Rather than just read and discuss the books, students can participate in a variety of reading, writing, talking, and listening activities (Hancock & Hill, 1987; Moss, 1984; Somers & Worthington, 1979). For a unit on Van Allsburg's fantasy picture books, middle-grade students might be involved in these listening activities:

- Listening to the teacher read aloud some of Van Allsburg's books
- Listening to other books at the listening center
- Listening to classmates share ideas about the books
- Listening to classmates share their writings in response to the books

Talk activities might include these:

- Discussing the books
- Telling stories based on the illustrations in *The Mysteries of Harris Burdick* (1984)
- Retelling a familiar story from an unusual viewpoint, as Van Allsburg did in *Two Bad Ants* (1988)
- Dramatizing one of Van Allsburg's stories

Students might do these reading activities:

- Read Van Allsburg's books independently.
- Read *Jumanji* (1981) as guided or shared reading.
- Read other fantasies, such as *The Lion, the Witch, and the Wardrobe* (Lewis, 1950) to compare to Van Allsburg's books.
- Examine a collection of ABC books to compare to *The Z Was Zapped* (1987).
- Read books about magic, after reading *The Garden of Abdul Gasazi* (1979).
- Share students' writing about Van Allsburg's books.

Students may participate in these writing activities:

- Keeping a reading log
- Clustering the beginning-middle-end of one of Van Allsburg's books
- Writing a letter to Van Allsburg
- Cubing Van Allsburg
- Writing a sequel to *Jumanji* (1981)
- Writing an ABC book similar to *The Z Was Zapped* (1987)
- Writing plans for a trip around the world, after reading *Ben's Dream* (1982)
- Writing directions for playing a game or researching a favorite game, after reading *Jumanji* (1981)

- Making posters about the four seasons, after reading *The Stranger* (1986)
- Writing stories to accompany the illustrations in *The Mysteries of Harris Burdick* (1984)
- Writing in response to the question "Is there a Santa Claus?", after reading *The Polar Express* (1985)
- Making posters, charts, or murals about the books

These listening, talking, reading, and writing activities illustrate some of the possible ways literature can be extended. In a fourth grade class, students wrote letters to Van Allsburg; one student's letter appears in Figure 15–3. As students read Van Allsburg's books, they might choose to learn more about magic, games, the seasons, ABC books, holidays, fantasies, or point of view. Students can make choices and pursue activities that interest them and involve using language to learn. Some students wrote sequels to *Jumanji;* one story is also shown in Figure 15–3.

Pioneer Intermediate School
P.O. Box 127
Noble, OK 73068
February 22

Mr. Chris Van Allsburg
114 Lorimer Avenue
Providence, RI 02906

Dear Chris,

I really like all of your books. But I wanted to know why there is a dog like Spuds MacKenzie in every book. Also, I'd like to know why almost every woman in your books looks the same.

Are you Harris Burdick or is the story true about him? I kind of believe you. But if it was true, it would probably be on Unsolved Mysteries. By the way, I think you ought to be the host. All right, I guess that's enough of Unsolved Mysteries.

Now let's get back to your books. I've been studying your writing. I have a folder full about you and your books. So does my class. My friend and I are doing a sequel to your book *Jumanji*. We're also tracing Ben's trip in *Ben's Dream* around the world on a big map in our classroom. My favorite book is *Two Bad Ants*.

My name is Annie. I'm ten years old. I've got two bratty sisters and one dog. It's the pits. I wanted to write to you to tell you all of this. Please write back.

Your friend,

Annie Picek

FIGURE 15–3

Two Student Samples from a Fourth Grade Unit on Chris Van Allsburg

Return to Jumanji

The next day on the way home from school Walter asked Peter if he would like to play a game that he had found in the park. Peter started to act weird and said, "Ah, well, ah . . . I got homework. Ah . . . I'm really tired . . . maybe, another time . . ." and he ran home as fast as he could.

At Walter and Daniel's house, Daniel opened the big long box and saw the directions and said, "Oh, how stupid—directions. Don't they have a game without directions?" "I don't know," said Walter.

Daniel rolled the dice and started to play. Move 10 spaces. Volcano eruption. Suddenly there was the loudest noise and then all of a sudden lava started filling the room. Daniel said, "Ah . . . Walter, I don't think, ah . . . I want to play this game, ah . . . any more."

"Oh, come on ya big baby. This is exciting!" said Walter. "Let's keep on playing and see what happens next."

Daniel agreed and Walter rolled the dice and moved two spaces. Laughing season. Move one space back. Suddenly Walter started laughing. He was laughing so hard his face turned red and fell out of his chair and landed in the lava. Daniel's chair fell over too and he was in it. They just could not stop laughing.

Daniel could hardly roll the dice. He rolled an 8. Dog and cat thunderstorm. Move 2 spaces back. All of a sudden dogs and cats started falling from the sky. A dog fell on Walter's head and a cat fell on Daniel's head. They stopped laughing. There were the strangest noises of meows and bow-wows. A dog got caught on the ceiling and his ears were dangling in Walter's face. The room sounded like a circus with all the meows and bow-wows of course.

Walter rolled the dice. He rolled a 9. Earthquake attack. Move 8 spaces back. The walls started shaking. Pictures fell from the mantle. Pans and pots fell from the kitchen cupboard. The table started shaking. The game fell but then Walter got it in his hands and put it back on the table.

Daniel rolled the dice. He rolled a 7. Music season. Move 5 spaces back. All of a sudden music started playing really loud. It was so loud they couldn't hear themselves think.

Walter rolled the dice. He rolled a 3. Flowers attack. Move 1 space back. Suddenly flowers started growing everywhere. A flower grew under Walter's chair. He went up to the sky. A flower grew under Daniel's chair and he went up to the sky too. Walter jumped out of his chair and landed in the lava. He said, "Im leaving." Daniel followed him. They walked out the door and closed it. Walter said, "I don't want to play this game anymore."

At 5:00 when Walter and Daniel's mom and dad got home they nearly fainted. The family moved far away from that house. But when Walter got old he got married and had two sons named Bradley and Ben. One day when Bradley and Ben were walking home from school, Bradley saw a house and tried the door. It was open. They walked in and music was blaring in their ears and dogs fell from the sky. They tried to run out but they slipped in the lava and fell down. The door closed and they never came out.

—Lori, grade 4

FIGURE 15–3 (continued)

Learning Other Content Areas Through Language

Listening, talking, reading, and writing can be connected to math and other content areas as well. Two language activities for use in math class, for example, are keeping learning logs and writing story problems. Students can keep learning logs in which they write about what they are learning during the last five minutes of class (Salem, 1982; Schubert, 1987). They can write about what they have learned during that class, the steps in solving a problem, definitions of mathematical terms, and things that confuse them. Writing in learning logs has several advantages over class discussion. All students participate simultaneously in writing, and teachers can review written responses more carefully than oral ones. Also, students use mathematical vocabulary and become more precise and complete in their answers.

Students can write story problems in which they apply the mathematical concepts they have been learning. In the process of writing the problems, students consider what information to include and how to phrase the question. Audience is especially important in writing story problems, because if students do not write clearly and completely, classmates may not be able to solve the problem. In a sixth grade class, students clipped advertisements from the local newspaper to use in writing story problems. One student used an ad for aspirin: the 72-count package was on sale for $2.99 and the 125-count package for $4.66; from this information, she composed the following problem:

> Sarah went to the drugstore to buy some aspirin. She found a bottle of 125 aspirin for $4.66 and a bottle of 72 aspirin for $2.99. Which one should she buy to get the most for her money? (Answer: the bottle of 125)

To learn more about incorporating language in math class, see Richards's (1990) article in *Language Arts,* in which she describes how she uses language activities to introduce math themes, investigate math concepts, and conclude the unit. Some of the writing activities her students use are summaries, definitions, reports, freewrites, notes, lists, evaluations, predictions, arguments, and explanations. One of Richards's students sums up the value of language in math class this way: "Language helps our maths [sic] by being able to write, use words, use symbols, being able to read and listen . . . It helps explain things" (p. 14).

Students use many of the same listening, talking, reading, and writing activities in other content areas. They use informal writing strategies to take notes and organize what they are learning, and they share their learning through oral and written reports, role playing, and other activities.

❖ THEMATIC UNITS

Teachers must plan to consciously involve students in a variety of activities to facilitate learning and higher-level, critical and application thinking. It is too easy to assign textbook readings and consider that content area study. Students read the textbook, discuss it (talking and listening), and write the answers to the questions at the end of the chapters. They are using the four language arts, but not as effectively as they might.

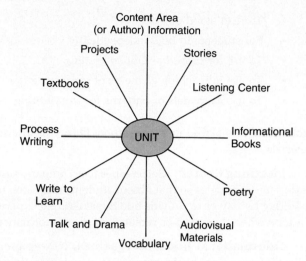

FIGURE 15—4

Possible Resources for Developing a Thematic Unit

A better method is to treat the textbook as one of a variety of resources for teaching a thematic unit.

Planning Thematic Units

To plan thematic units, teachers think about the types of materials and activities they want to incorporate. The cluster in Figure 15—4 illustrates twelve possible resources for developing a thematic unit, whether it focuses on social studies (e.g., California gold rush, explorers, American Revolution), science (hibernation, machines, weather), health (parts of the body, drugs, nutrition), geography (continents, the Mississippi River), literature (mystery stories, fables, myths, Halloween stories) or an author (Beverly Cleary, Tomie de Paola, Katharine Paterson).

Content Area (or Author) Information.   Here you consider what students will learn in the unit and develop objectives. You also decide how to present the information, using reading, writing, listening, talking, and audiovisual materials. For literature units, you would include information about authors and illustrators here as well.

Stories.   Teachers locate picture book and chapter books to use in connection with the unit. Some stories will be read aloud to students (or tape-recorded for the listening center), some will be read independently, and others students will read together as shared or guided reading. Investigating the topic in a library card catalog will suggest picture books and chapter books as well as other books by the same author. Textbooks sometimes list supplemental reading, and the reference books listed in Figure 4—9 are another source for stories. The stories you find will be used for a variety of purposes, including these:

- To read aloud to students
- For students to read independently
- To use for shared or guided reading
- To use in teaching elements of story structure
- To use as models or patterns for storywriting

Books should be placed in the classroom library or in a special area for theme-related materials.

Listening Center.   Select tapes to accompany stories or informational books or create your own tapes so that absent students can catch up on a book you are reading aloud day by day or to provide additional reading experiences for students who listen to a tape when they read or reread a story or informational book.

Informational Books, Magazines, Newspapers, and Reference Books. Collect informational books, magazines, newspaper articles, and reference books. Add these to the classroom library or put them in a special area for materials related to the theme. You can also use these materials to teach students about expository text structure patterns, how to use an index and table of contents, as models or patterns for student writing, and to provide information for reports or other process writing projects.

Poetry.   Locate books of poetry or individual poems that are appropriate to the unit theme to share with students. Also plan poetry writing activities using a variety of poetic forms described in Chapter 11.

Audiovisual Materials.   Plan the films, videotapes, filmstrips, charts, time-lines, maps, models, posters, and other displays you will use in connection with the thematic unit. You can display some of these, and students can make others as they learn the content area material during the unit. Four excellent resources for locating audiovisual materials (cassette tapes, filmstrips, films, and videotapes) of children's books and authors who write for children are:

Listening Library, Inc., One Park Avenue, Old Greenwich, CT 06870

Random House Media, Department 520, 400 Hahn Road, Westminster, MD 21157

Spoken Arts, Dept. B, 310 North Avenue, New Rochelle, NY 10801

Weston Woods, Weston, CT 06883

Vocabulary.   Select words related to the theme and from stories and informational books. Hang a vocabulary chart in the classroom and invite students to add new words as they encounter them. Have students write the words in their learning log. After students learn the words, they can serve as spelling words.

Talk and Drama.   Students can use talk and drama to learn and to demonstrate their learning (Erickson, 1988; Nelson, 1988; San Jose, 1988). These are possible activities:

- Giving oral reports
- Interviewing someone with special expertise on the theme
- Participating in a debate related to the theme
- Role-playing an event or a personality
- Participating in a reader's theater presentation of a story or poem
- Telling or retelling a story, biography, or event
- Using a puppet show to tell a story, biography, or event
- Writing and performing a skit or play

Write to Learn.   Students use brainstorming, clustering, freewriting, and cubing as they take notes, list vocabulary words, write questions, make observations, clarify their thinking, and write reactions to what they are learning (Tompkins, 1990). Plan activities in which students will keep learning logs, simulated journals or reading logs.

Process Writing.   At least one activity during the thematic unit should involve students in the writing process to draft, revise, edit, and share their writing. These are some possible process writing activities:

Biographies	Essays
Newspaper articles	Stories
Collaborative reports	Advertisements
Poems	Myths and legends
ABC books	"All about . . . " books
Letters	Concept books
Individual reports	Cartoons
Scripts	Posters

Textbooks.   You can teach themes without textbooks; however, when information is available in a literature or content area textbook, you should consider it. Upper-grade students, in particular, can read and discuss the textbook or use it as a reference for concepts, vocabulary, and directions for further study.

Projects.   Teachers plan whole class, small group, and individual projects related to the unit. Students usually complete one project independently and present their project to the class at the end of the unit. Projects should involve listening, talking, reading, and writing, as well as art, music, drama, cooking, or other activities. Figure 15–5 lists possible activities for unit projects that can be adapted for various thematic units.

Teachers brainstorm ideas for thematic units and then develop clusters of possible activities. The goal in developing unit plans is to consider a wide variety of resources that integrate listening, talking, reading, and writing with the content of the unit (Pappas, Kiefer & Levstik, 1990). We will discuss three sample thematic units for primary-

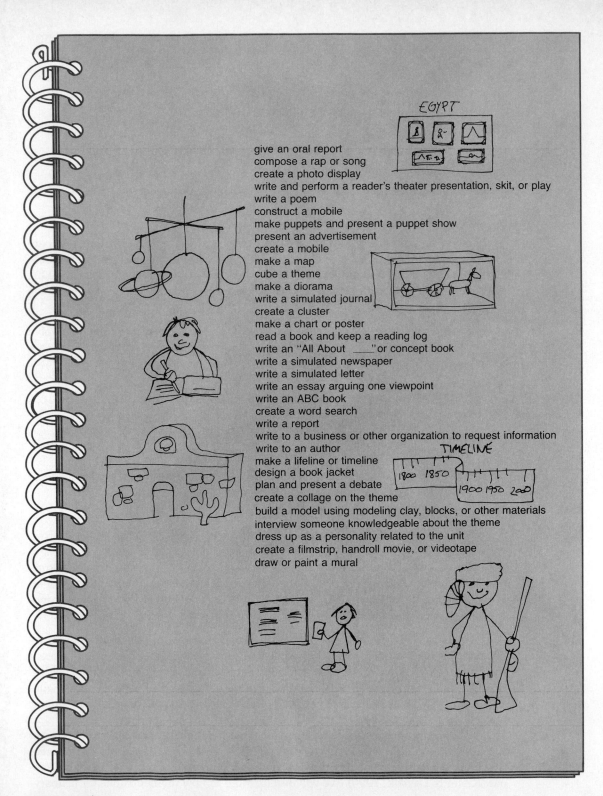

give an oral report
compose a rap or song
create a photo display
write and perform a reader's theater presentation, skit, or play
write a poem
construct a mobile
make puppets and present a puppet show
present an advertisement
create a mobile
make a map
cube a theme
make a diorama
write a simulated journal
create a cluster
make a chart or poster
read a book and keep a reading log
write an "All About _____" or concept book
write a simulated newspaper
write a simulated letter
write an essay arguing one viewpoint
write an ABC book
create a word search
write a report
write to a business or other organization to request information
write to an author
make a lifeline or timeline
design a book jacket
plan and present a debate
create a collage on the theme
build a model using modeling clay, blocks, or other materials
interview someone knowledgeable about the theme
dress up as a personality related to the unit
create a filmstrip, handroll movie, or videotape
draw or paint a mural

FIGURE 15–5

Teacher's Notebook Page: Activities for Unit Projects

grade students, three for middle-grade students, and three for upper-grade students. These units integrate the four language modes with literature, social studies, and science, and utilize many of the resources outlined in Figure 15–4.

Primary-grade Units

Three primary-grade units, designed for students in kindergarten, first, or second grade, are presented in Figure 15–6. One unit focuses on "The Gingerbread Boy" (a literature unit), the second on Sending and Receiving Mail (a social studies unit), and the third on Arnold Lobel's Frog and Toad Stories (an author and literature unit). The

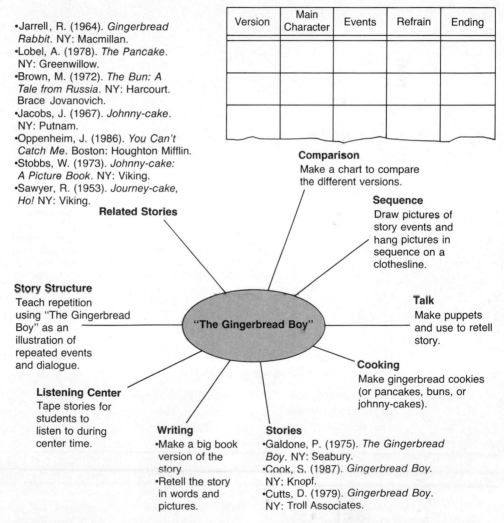

FIGURE 15–6

Clusters for Three Primary-Grade Units

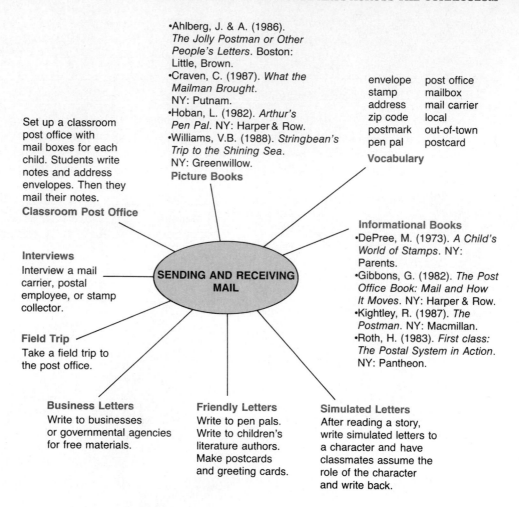

Set up a classroom post office with mail boxes for each child. Students write notes and address envelopes. Then they mail their notes.
Classroom Post Office

Interviews
Interview a mail carrier, postal employee, or stamp collector.

Field Trip
Take a field trip to the post office.

•Ahlberg, J. & A. (1986). *The Jolly Postman or Other People's Letters*. Boston: Little, Brown.
•Craven, C. (1987). *What the Mailman Brought*. NY: Putnam.
•Hoban, L. (1982). *Arthur's Pen Pal*. NY: Harper & Row.
•Williams, V.B. (1988). *Stringbean's Trip to the Shining Sea*. NY: Greenwillow.
Picture Books

envelope	post office
stamp	mailbox
address	mail carrier
zip code	local
postmark	out-of-town
pen pal	postcard

Vocabulary

SENDING AND RECEIVING MAIL

Informational Books
•DePree, M. (1973). *A Child's World of Stamps*. NY: Parents.
•Gibbons, G. (1982). *The Post Office Book: Mail and How It Moves*. NY: Harper & Row.
•Kightley, R. (1987). *The Postman*. NY: Macmillan.
•Roth, H. (1983). *First class: The Postal System in Action*. NY: Pantheon.

Business Letters
Write to businesses or governmental agencies for free materials.

Friendly Letters
Write to pen pals. Write to children's literature authors. Make postcards and greeting cards.

Simulated Letters
After reading a story, write simulated letters to a character and have classmates assume the role of the character and write back.

FIGURE 15–6   (*continued*)

unit clusters suggest eight or more types of activities and resources from which teachers can choose in developing lesson plans.

Literature Unit: "The Gingerbread Boy."   This folktale can be the basis for a unit for kindergarten and first grade students. The story, available in many versions (several are listed in the cluster), can be used to teach students about repetition—an element of story structure. The different stories follow the same general plot, but vary as to the characters the Gingerbread Boy runs past. Even young children can identify the variations from story to story. For additional experiences with the stories, students can listen to them at the listening center. Students enjoy listening to other journey stories, such as *You Can't Catch Me!* (Oppenheim, 1986), *Johnny-cake* (Jacobs, 1967), and *Gingerbread Rabbit* (Jarrell, 1964) because of their similarity to "The Gingerbread Boy." The repetitious form of the stories makes them easier to remember, and children enjoy pointing out differences among the stories.

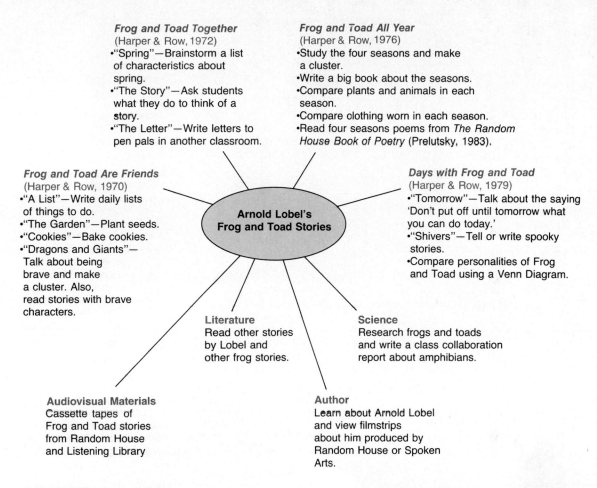

Frog and Toad Together
(Harper & Row, 1972)
•"Spring"—Brainstorm a list
of characteristics about
spring.
•"The Story"—Ask students
what they do to think of a
story.
•"The Letter"—Write letters to
pen pals in another classroom.

Frog and Toad All Year
(Harper & Row, 1976)
•Study the four seasons and make
a cluster.
•Write a big book about the seasons.
•Compare plants and animals in each
season.
•Compare clothing worn in each season.
•Read four seasons poems from *The Random
House Book of Poetry* (Prelutsky, 1983).

Frog and Toad Are Friends
(Harper & Row, 1970)
•"A List"—Write daily lists
of things to do.
•"The Garden"—Plant seeds.
•"Cookies"—Bake cookies.
•"Dragons and Giants"—
Talk about being
brave and make
a cluster. Also,
read stories with brave
characters.

Arnold Lobel's Frog and Toad Stories

Days with Frog and Toad
(Harper & Row, 1979)
•"Tomorrow"—Talk about the saying
'Don't put off until tomorrow what
you can do today.'
•"Shivers"—Tell or write spooky
stories.
•Compare personalities of Frog
and Toad using a Venn Diagram.

Literature
Read other stories
by Lobel and
other frog stories.

Science
Research frogs and toads
and write a class collaboration
report about amphibians.

Audiovisual Materials
Cassette tapes of
Frog and Toad stories
from Random House
and Listening Library

Author
Learn about Arnold Lobel
and view filmstrips
about him produced by
Random House or Spoken
Arts.

FIGURE 15—6 (*continued*)

After reading several versions of "The Gingerbread Boy" or related stories, students and the teacher can make a chart to compare the different versions, as shown on the cluster. Students compare the main character, the events, the refrain, and the ending. In some stories, the gingerbread boy (or similar character) doesn't get eaten.

Other after-reading activities are possible. Students can draw pictures of the story events and hang the pictures in sequence on a clothesline as they retell the story (Tompkins & McGee, 1989). Similarly, students can make puppets to use in retelling the story or creating a new version of the story. They can bake gingerbread cookies or cook pancakes, buns, johnny-cakes, or other foods and act out the story before eating the main characters.

Students can also write in response to the story. They can work together to make a big book version, drawing the illustrations and dictating the text for the teacher to print in the book. Students can also make individual story booklets, by drawing pictures and dictating their stories to the teacher or writing by themselves.

Young children use pictures and words to retell the story of "The Gingerbread Boy."

Social Studies Unit: Sending and Receiving Mail.   This unit connects letter writing with social studies, as shown in Figure 15–6. Students write friendly and business letters and learn how mail is collected, sorted, and delivered. Students write friendly letters to pen pals and children's authors and notes to classmates that are "mailed" through a classroom post office. Students can also write to businesses and governmental agencies for free materials. Simulated letters are another possibility. After reading a story, students assume the role of a character and write letters to another character in the story, then exchange letters, change roles, and answer the letters as the other story character.

Picture books and informational books about letters, mail, and the post office are available for primary-grade students; some books are listed in the unit cluster. *The Jolly Postman* (Ahlberg & Ahlberg, 1986) is a delightful book in which the Jolly Postman delivers letters to characters from well-known folk tales and fairly tales. Each letter or card is tucked into an envelope bound into the book. Informational books such as *The Post Office Book* (Gibbons, 1982) tell what happens to letters after they are mailed. Other activities include taking a field trip to the post office and interviewing a mail carrier, a postal employee, or a stamp collector.

Author and Literature Unit: Arnold Lobel's Frog and Toad Stories.   Some of primary students' first chapter books are Lobel's easy-to-read Frog and Toad books: *Frog and Toad Are Friends* (1970), *Frog and Toad Together* (1972), *Frog and Toad All Year* (1976), and *Days with Frog and Toad* (1979). This unit, also shown in Figure 15–6, includes activities to accompany the four books plus additional literature, author, and science activities. The activities relate to stories in each book; for example, *Frog and Toad All Year* is about the two amphibians' activities throughout the year, so a good extension is to build on the idea of seasons—by studying the seasons, making a cluster, writing a big book, comparing animals and people in each season, comparing clothing worn in each season, and reading poems about the seasons. One of the activities could be used before beginning the book, another between chapters, and others after reading.

Additional literature activities involve reading other of Lobel's stories, other stories about frogs and toads, and viewing the Frog and Toad stories on filmstrips and videotapes and listening to the stories on cassette tapes.

Author activities include learning about Arnold Lobel by viewing filmstrips about him, examining promotional materials from the publisher, and reading other books he has written (or illustrated).

Science activities focus on frogs and toads. Students can read informational books, take a walking field trip to a nearby pond to see live frogs and toads, and write an informational book about amphibians.

Middle-grade Units

The three middle-grade units appear in Figure 15–7. One unit focuses on Fables (a literature unit), one on Insects (a science unit), and one on Beverly Cleary (an author unit). These unit plans suggest eight or more types of resources for teachers to choose among in developing lesson plans.

Literature Unit: Fables.   Fables are short stories that teach a lesson, and a number of collections of Aesop's fables as well as contemporary fables have been written for children. As shown in Figure 15–7, this unit provides reading, writing, and talk activities while students learn about this traditional form of literature. Teachers may choose from among the list of picture book versions of fables for shared or guided reading or independent reading activities. (Several of the books are available in paperback, so class sets can be purchased.) After students read fables, they write their reactions in reading logs or make clusters of the beginning, middle, and ends of the fables. Another option is for students to make posters of the morals that have become popular sayings. Students can also retell fables orally, using puppets, or in writing.

Students can compare versions of the same fable. For instance, a number of versions of "The Tortoise and the Hare" are currently available as picture books. Students can divide into small groups to read the stories and compare how authors elaborated the beginning, middle, or end in the different versions. Students can also compare the traditional fables to modern ones, such as those of Lobel, and report their findings on a Venn diagram.

After reading and retelling fables, students can write their own fables; their first fables might be written as a class or in small groups. After this experience, students can choose a moral and write their own fables using the writing process. Some students may write traditional fables using animals as characters, and others may use well-known people, classmates, or family members as characters.

Students who become interested in these traditional stories might research Aesop or de La Fontaine, two great authors of fables. Other projects are also possible: students might make mobiles of a favorite fable, paint a mural, update and rewrite a fable with modern characters, or any of the other project possibilities listed in Figure 15–5.

Science Unit: Insects.   In this unit, listening, talking, reading, and writing activities extend students' learning about insects, as shown in Figure 15–7. Students read informational books about insects, use choral reading to enjoy *Joyful Noise: Poems*

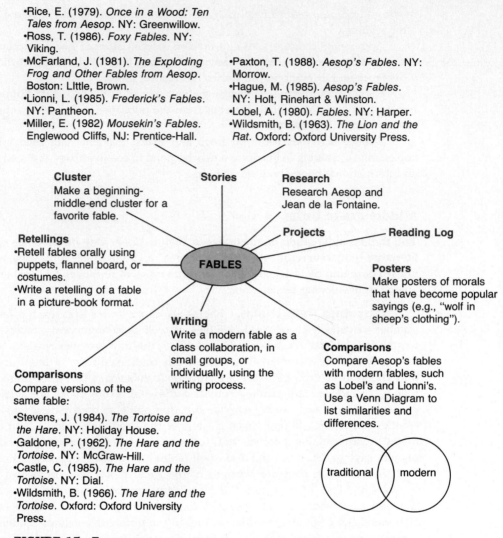

•Rice, E. (1979). *Once in a Wood: Ten Tales from Aesop*. NY: Greenwillow.
•Ross, T. (1986). *Foxy Fables*. NY: Viking.
•McFarland, J. (1981). *The Exploding Frog and Other Fables from Aesop*. Boston: LIttle, Brown.
•Lionni, L. (1985). *Frederick's Fables*. NY: Pantheon.
•Miller, E. (1982) *Mousekin's Fables*. Englewood Cliffs, NJ: Prentice-Hall.

•Paxton, T. (1988). *Aesop's Fables*. NY: Morrow.
•Hague, M. (1985). *Aesop's Fables*. NY: Holt, Rinehart & Winston.
•Lobel, A. (1980). *Fables*. NY: Harper.
•Wildsmith, B. (1963). *The Lion and the Rat*. Oxford: Oxford University Press.

Cluster
Make a beginning-middle-end cluster for a favorite fable.

Stories

Research
Research Aesop and Jean de la Fontaine.

Projects

Reading Log

Retellings
•Retell fables orally using puppets, flannel board, or costumes.
•Write a retelling of a fable in a picture-book format.

FABLES

Posters
Make posters of morals that have become popular sayings (e.g., "wolf in sheep's clothing").

Writing
Write a modern fable as a class collaboration, in small groups, or individually, using the writing process.

Comparisons
Compare versions of the same fable:

•Stevens, J. (1984). *The Tortoise and the Hare*. NY: Holiday House.
•Galdone, P. (1962). *The Hare and the Tortoise*. NY: McGraw-Hill.
•Castle, C. (1985). *The Hare and the Tortoise*. NY: Dial.
•Wildsmith, B. (1966). *The Hare and the Tortoise*. Oxford: Oxford University Press.

Comparisons
Compare Aesop's fables with modern fables, such as Lobel's and Lionni's. Use a Venn Diagram to list similarities and differences.

traditional   modern

FIGURE 15—7

Clusters for Three Middle-Grade Units

for Two Voices (Fleischman, 1988), and listen to a chapter book, *The Cricket in Times Square* (Selden, 1960), read aloud. Reading is a valuable way for middle-grade students to learn about science. They connect reading and writing by keeping a learning log in which they reflect on the book being read aloud and record scientific information from informational books and teacher presentations.

Each student chooses an insect to study in depth, and then students write a class report, with each one reporting on the insect he or she studied. They can also make charts to illustrate the life cycles or body parts of insects. As individual projects, students might make insect collections or choose one of the activities listed in Figure 15—5. Other possible activities include making a chart to classify insects as helpful or harmful, or creating imaginary insects and writing about them.

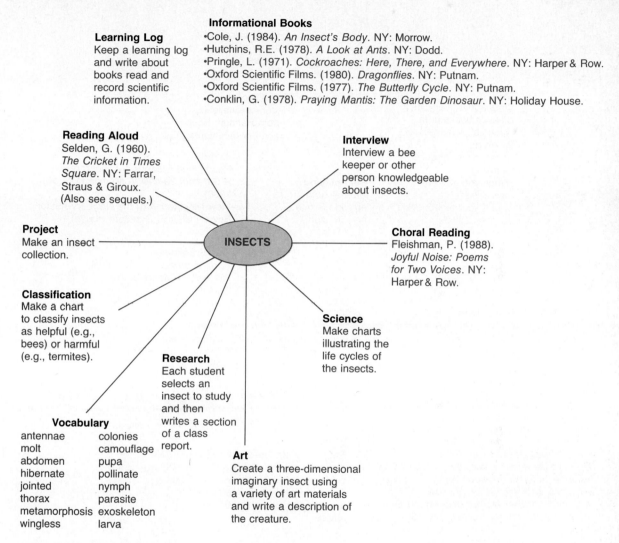

Informational Books
•Cole, J. (1984). *An Insect's Body*. NY: Morrow.
•Hutchins, R.E. (1978). *A Look at Ants*. NY: Dodd.
•Pringle, L. (1971). *Cockroaches: Here, There, and Everywhere*. NY: Harper & Row.
•Oxford Scientific Films. (1980). *Dragonflies*. NY: Putnam.
•Oxford Scientific Films. (1977). *The Butterfly Cycle*. NY: Putnam.
•Conklin, G. (1978). *Praying Mantis: The Garden Dinosaur*. NY: Holiday House.

Learning Log
Keep a learning log
and write about
books read and
record scientific
information.

Reading Aloud
Selden, G. (1960).
*The Cricket in Times
Square*. NY: Farrar,
Straus & Giroux.
(Also see sequels.)

Interview
Interview a bee
keeper or other
person knowledgeable
about insects.

Project
Make an insect
collection.

INSECTS

Choral Reading
Fleishman, P. (1988).
*Joyful Noise: Poems
for Two Voices*. NY:
Harper & Row.

Classification
Make a chart
to classify insects
as helpful (e.g.,
bees) or harmful
(e.g., termites).

Science
Make charts
illustrating the
life cycles of
the insects.

Research
Each student
selects an
insect to study
and then
writes a section
of a class
report.

Vocabulary

antennae	colonies
molt	camouflage
abdomen	pupa
hibernate	pollinate
jointed	nymph
thorax	parasite
metamorphosis	exoskeleton
wingless	larva

Art
Create a three-dimensional
imaginary insect using
a variety of art materials
and write a description of
the creature.

FIGURE 15–7 (*continued*)

Author Unit: Beverly Cleary. Beverly Cleary is a popular children's author and a good choice for a unit because she has written many books, most of which are available in paperback. This unit cluster also appears in Figure 15–7. Teachers may want to begin the unit by reading one of Cleary's Ramona books aloud. *Ramona the Pest* (1968) is a favorite of middle-grade students; this book introduces students to the Quimby family. Then students choose one or more of Cleary's books to read independently or as guided reading with the teacher. Students may also listen to Cleary's stories at a listening center or view filmstrips or videotapes of some books. They keep a reading log and respond to each Cleary book that they read. After reading, students can prepare a project related to the book they read, role-play a favorite episode from a story, or create an advertisement or commercial to "sell" their book.

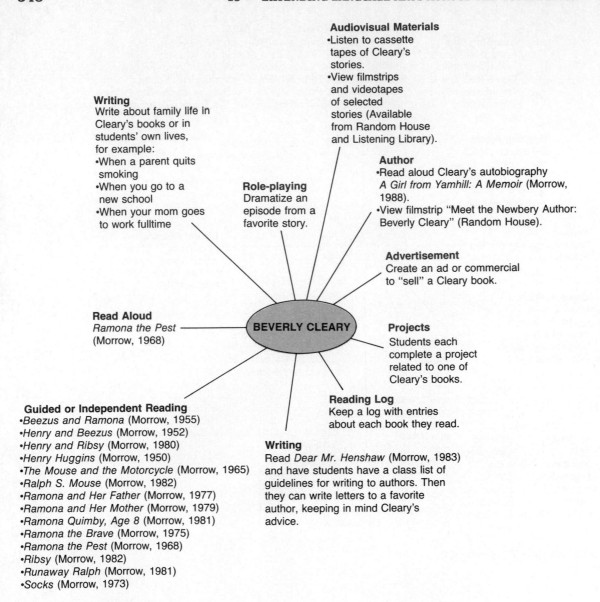

Audiovisual Materials
•Listen to cassette tapes of Cleary's stories.
•View filmstrips and videotapes of selected stories (Available from Random House and Listening Library).

Writing
Write about family life In Cleary's books or in students' own lives, for example:
•When a parent quits smoking
•When you go to a new school
•When your mom goes to work fulltime

Role-playing
Dramatize an episode from a favorite story.

Author
•Read aloud Cleary's autobiography *A Girl from Yamhill: A Memoir* (Morrow, 1988).
•View filmstrip "Meet the Newbery Author: Beverly Cleary" (Random House).

Advertisement
Create an ad or commercial to "sell" a Cleary book.

Read Aloud
Ramona the Pest (Morrow, 1968)

BEVERLY CLEARY

Projects
Students each complete a project related to one of Cleary's books.

Reading Log
Keep a log with entries about each book they read.

Guided or Independent Reading
•*Beezus and Ramona* (Morrow, 1955)
•*Henry and Beezus* (Morrow, 1952)
•*Henry and Ribsy* (Morrow, 1980)
•*Henry Huggins* (Morrow, 1950)
•*The Mouse and the Motorcycle* (Morrow, 1965)
•*Ralph S. Mouse* (Morrow, 1982)
•*Ramona and Her Father* (Morrow, 1977)
•*Ramona and Her Mother* (Morrow, 1979)
•*Ramona Quimby, Age 8* (Morrow, 1981)
•*Ramona the Brave* (Morrow, 1975)
•*Ramona the Pest* (Morrow, 1968)
•*Ribsy* (Morrow, 1982)
•*Runaway Ralph* (Morrow, 1981)
•*Socks* (Morrow, 1973)

Writing
Read *Dear Mr. Henshaw* (Morrow, 1983) and have students have a class list of guidelines for writing to authors. Then they can write letters to a favorite author, keeping in mind Cleary's advice.

FIGURE 15–7 *(continued)*

Other activities include reading *Dear Mr. Henshaw* (1983) and inviting students to write to a favorite author (after making a class list of things to remember when writing to authors). Or, students can write about family life in Cleary's books or about their own lives. They might compare events in their own lives to events in Ramona's life; possible parallels are her father's quitting smoking, her mother's going to work full time, and her moving to a new school. If students want to learn more about this author, teachers may read aloud Cleary's autobiography, *A Girl from Yamhill: A Memoir* (1988) or show a filmstrip about her.

For his project, this third grader rewrote the front page of his hometown newspaper to spread the word that Beverly Cleary's *Ramona* is now a movie.

Upper-grade Units

Three units designed for students in grades six, seven, and eight are presented in Figure 15—8. The first is a literature unit focusing on *Anne Frank: The Diary of a Young Girl*. Connected to this modern classic is a study of the Holocaust. The second cluster is a social studies unit on the Middle Ages, and the third is a biography unit featuring Martin Luther King, Jr. and other famous Black Americans.

Literature Unit: *Anne Frank: The Diary of a Young Girl*.   Anne Frank's autobiographical diary is a modern classic that many eighth graders read (Figure 15—8). For young adults to understand the book's complex historical and psychological implications, they need a background of experiences related to World War II. At the center of the unit is *Anne Frank: The Diary of a Young Girl* (Frank, 1952) which students read together as a class (shared and guided reading). Students keep a reading log to reflect on and respond to their reading. Students can also read informational books to gain more understanding of World War II and the Holocaust and read other stories with Jewish characters set during the war. Two highly recommended books are *Upon the Head of a Goat* (Siegal, 1981), the story of the Davidowitz family of Hungary, who are sent to the Auschwitz concentration camp; and *The Borrowed House* (Van Stockum, 1975), the story of twelve-year-old Janna, who lives with her family in a rented Dutch house and finds a Jewish Dutch boy hiding in the attic. Students might want to keep a simulated journal as they read these stories independently so they can more fully walk in these people's footsteps.

Students learn a variety of words through their reading, including *ghetto, concentration camp, intolerance, genocide,* and *anti-Semitism.* These words are added to a list hanging in the classroom and students write them in their unit folders. Some of the words can also be used as spelling words, and students are encouraged to use the words when they write informally in their reading logs and simulated journals.

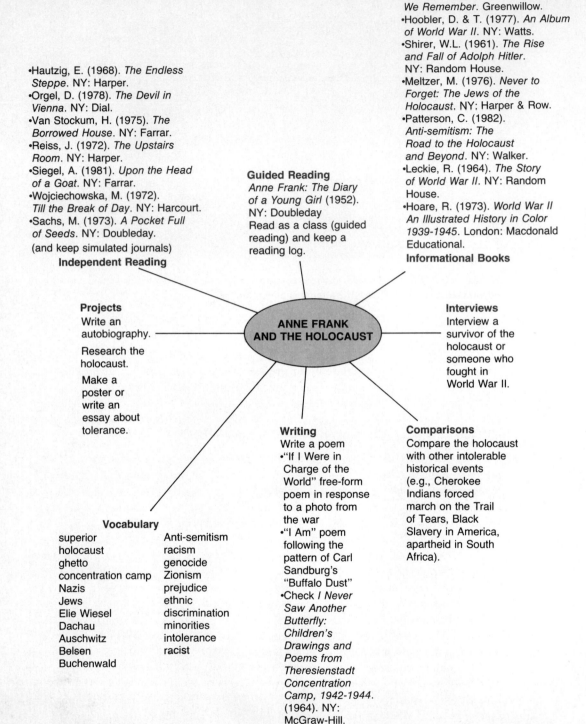

•Abells, C.B. (1986). *The Children We Remember*. Greenwillow.
•Hoobler, D. & T. (1977). *An Album of World War II*. NY: Watts.
•Shirer, W.L. (1961). *The Rise and Fall of Adolph Hitler*. NY: Random House.
•Meltzer, M. (1976). *Never to Forget: The Jews of the Holocaust*. NY: Harper & Row.
•Patterson, C. (1982). *Anti-semitism: The Road to the Holocaust and Beyond*. NY: Walker.
•Leckie, R. (1964). *The Story of World War II*. NY: Random House.
•Hoare, R. (1973). *World War II An Illustrated History in Color 1939-1945*. London: Macdonald Educational.
Informational Books

•Hautzig, E. (1968). *The Endless Steppe*. NY: Harper.
•Orgel, D. (1978). *The Devil in Vienna*. NY: Dial.
•Van Stockum, H. (1975). *The Borrowed House*. NY: Farrar.
•Reiss, J. (1972). *The Upstairs Room*. NY: Harper.
•Siegel, A. (1981). *Upon the Head of a Goat*. NY: Farrar.
•Wojciechowska, M. (1972). *Till the Break of Day*. NY: Harcourt.
•Sachs, M. (1973). *A Pocket Full of Seeds*. NY: Doubleday.
(and keep simulated journals)
Independent Reading

Guided Reading
Anne Frank: The Diary of a Young Girl (1952). NY: Doubleday
Read as a class (guided reading) and keep a reading log.

ANNE FRANK AND THE HOLOCAUST

Projects
Write an autobiography.

Research the holocaust.

Make a poster or write an essay about tolerance.

Interviews
Interview a survivor of the holocaust or someone who fought in World War II.

Comparisons
Compare the holocaust with other intolerable historical events (e.g., Cherokee Indians forced march on the Trail of Tears, Black Slavery in America, apartheid in South Africa).

Writing
Write a poem
•"If I Were in Charge of the World" free-form poem in response to a photo from the war
•"I Am" poem following the pattern of Carl Sandburg's "Buffalo Dust"
•Check *I Never Saw Another Butterfly: Children's Drawings and Poems from Theresienstadt Concentration Camp, 1942-1944.* (1964). NY: McGraw-Hill.

Vocabulary

superior	Anti-semitism
holocaust	racism
ghetto	genocide
concentration camp	Zionism
Nazis	prejudice
Jews	ethnic
Elie Wiesel	discrimination
Dachau	minorities
Auschwitz	intolerance
Belsen	racist
Buchenwald	

FIGURE 15–8

Clusters for Three Upper-Grade Units

•McGovern, A. (1988). *Robin Hood of Sherwood Forest*. NY: Scholastic.
•De Angeli, M. (1989). *The Door in the Wall*. NY: Doubleday.
•Grey, E.J. (1942). *Adam of the Road*. NY: Viking.
•Eager, E. (1954). *Half Magic*. NY: Harcourt. Brace Jovanovich.
•Babbitt, N. (1969). *The Search for Delicious*. NY: Farrar, Straus & Giroux.
•Bulla, C.R. (1956). *The Sword in the Tree*. NY: Harper & Row.
•Fleischman, S. (1987). *The Whipping Boy*. Mahwah, NJ: Troll.

Guided or Independent Reading

Reading Aloud
McCaughrean, G. (1984). *The Canterbury Tales* Chicago: Rand McNally.
Sutcliff, R. (1981). *The Chronicles of Robin Hood*. NY: Oxford Univ. Press.
Pyle, H. (1952). *The Merry Adventures of Robin Hood*. NY: Grosset & Dunlap.

Research
Research and make a class book on the Middle Ages.

Timeline

•Goodall, J.S. (1986). *The Story of a Castle*. NY: Macmillan.
•Miquel, P. (1980). *The Days of Knights and Castles*. Morristown, NJ: Silver Burdett.
•Glubok, S. (1969). *Knights in Armor*. NY: Harper & Row.
•Black, I. (1963). *Castle, Abbey and Town: How People Lived in the Middle Ages*. NY: Holiday House.
•Sancha, S. (1983). *The Luttrell Village: Country Life in the Middle Ages*. NY: Crowell.
•Unstead, R. (1973). *Living in a Castle*. Reading, MA: Addison-Wesley.
•Macauley, D. (1977). *Castle*. Boston: Houghton Mifflin.

Informational Books

Projects
ABC book
dress doll in costume
create castle or village
make a tapestry
coat of arms
mural

MIDDLE AGES

Comparisons
•Compare life in villages and in manors or castles.
•Make a chart or a book similar to J.S. Goedall's (1983) *Above and Below Stairs*. NY: Atheneum

Charts, maps and drawings

Medieval Feast
Plan and hold a medieval feast in the classroom. Each student role-plays a medieval person. Check Brandenburg, A. (1983). *A Medieval Feast*. NY: Crowell and Cosman, M.P. (1981). *Medieval Holidays and Festivals*. NY: Scribner.

Examine Middle English and French loan words

Vocabulary

apothecary	melee
bailiff	mercenary
feudalism	Moors
fief	tithe
fresco	troubadour
guild	vassal
heretic	villain
journeyman	yeoman
manor	Black Death
	Crusades

Simulated Journals
Keep a simulated journal as Charlemagne, William the Conqueror, a lord, lady, fief, vassal, king, pope or other historical person

Fairy Tales
Hodges, M. (1984). *Saint George and the Dragon*. Boston: Little, Brown.
Mayer, M. (1978). *Beauty and the Beast*. NY: Macmillan.
Hyman, T.S. (1977). *The Sleeping Beauty*. Boston: Little, Brown.

FIGURE 15–8 (*continued*)

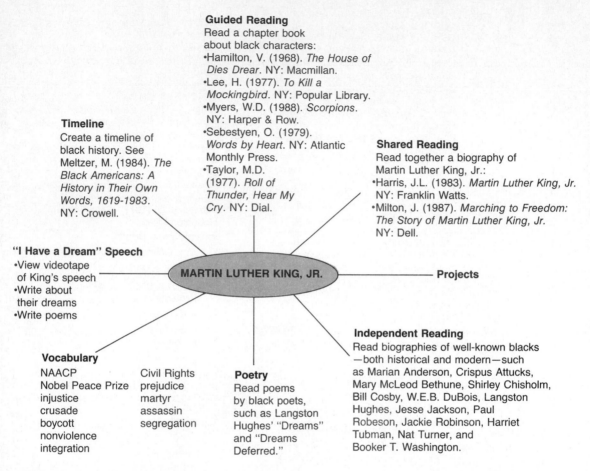

Guided Reading
Read a chapter book
about black characters:
•Hamilton, V. (1968). *The House of Dies Drear*. NY: Macmillan.
•Lee, H. (1977). *To Kill a Mockingbird*. NY: Popular Library.
•Myers, W.D. (1988). *Scorpions*. NY: Harper & Row.
•Sebestyen, O. (1979). *Words by Heart*. NY: Atlantic Monthly Press.
•Taylor, M.D. (1977). *Roll of Thunder, Hear My Cry*. NY: Dial.

Timeline
Create a timeline of
black history. See
Meltzer, M. (1984). *The Black Americans: A History in Their Own Words, 1619-1983*. NY: Crowell.

Shared Reading
Read together a biography of
Martin Luther King, Jr.:
•Harris, J.L. (1983). *Martin Luther King, Jr.* NY: Franklin Watts.
•Milton, J. (1987). *Marching to Freedom: The Story of Martin Luther King, Jr.* NY: Dell.

"I Have a Dream" Speech
•View videotape of King's speech
•Write about their dreams
•Write poems

MARTIN LUTHER KING, JR.

Projects

Vocabulary
NAACP
Nobel Peace Prize
injustice
crusade
boycott
nonviolence
integration

Civil Rights
prejudice
martyr
assassin
segregation

Poetry
Read poems
by black poets,
such as Langston
Hughes' "Dreams"
and "Dreams
Deferred."

Independent Reading
Read biographies of well-known blacks
—both historical and modern—such
as Marian Anderson, Crispus Attucks,
Mary McLeod Bethune, Shirley Chisholm,
Bill Cosby, W.E.B. DuBois, Langston
Hughes, Jesse Jackson, Paul
Robeson, Jackie Robinson, Harriet
Tubman, Nat Turner, and
Booker T. Washington.

FIGURE 15–8 (*continued*)

Poetry provides a good outlet for students' emotions during this unit; they can write "If I Were in Charge of the World" poems and "I Am" poems as if they were Anne Frank, Adolf Hitler, or other personalities from the war. They can also model the form of Sandburg's poem "Buffalo Dust" and write about the concentration camps or after the Nazis have gone and what is remembered. They can write a free form poem in response to a stark black-and-white photo of the war. Students will also be interested in examining *I Never Saw Another Butterfly* (1964), a collection of poems and drawings made by children in the Theresienstadt Concentration Camp.

Other possible activities related to this unit include inviting a concentration camp survivor to visit the classroom to be interviewed or to interview other persons who remember the war. Students can also investigate other intolerant events in history (e.g., the Cherokee Indians' forced march on the Trail of Tears, slavery in America, apartheid in South Africa) and compare them to the Holocaust.

Students also develop a project related to the unit; they may choose from the list of projects in Figure 15–5, or they may write an autobiography (perhaps in diary format), research the Holocaust and prepare an oral or written report, or make a poster or write an essay about tolerance.

Reading *Anne Frank: The Diary of a Young Girl* in isolation is difficult because the students are unfamiliar with the events of World War II and the Holocaust. Connecting history with literature in this unit makes the literature more meaningful and students have a variety of opportunities to respond to what they are learning through listening, talking, reading, and writing.

Social Studies Unit: The Middle Ages.   In a unit on the Middle Ages, teachers integrate reading, writing, listening, and speaking with history, as shown in Figure 15–8. Students use informational books to learn about the historical era, then use what they are learning for a variety of purposes. They can keep a simulated journal as a well-known person of the period, such as Charlemagne or William the Conqueror, or they may become an unrecorded personality—a lord, a lady, knight, vassal, pope, or troubadour.

Students add information to a class timeline that circles around the classroom or they can make their own using several sheets of computer paper. At the beginning of the unit, the teacher sets the limits of the time period (i.e., 1066–1485) and other key dates, then students add other dates as they read and learn more about the period.

Individual students or small groups can draw maps of the countries during the Middle Ages with an overlay of the modern countries, and they can make maps of the Crusades. They can make other types of charts, such as diagrams of castles, cathedrals, and villages, and they can also make drawings of costumes, modes of transportation, weapons, and other items related to the era. Students can also compare life in villages and in manors and castles and report the differences they find on a chart or by making a book similar to Goodall's *Above and Below Stairs* (1983).

As students research the Middle Ages, they each choose a topic for in-depth study, then write a report to share what they have learned. These reports are collected to form a larger class book on the Middle Ages.

Some novels written for older students are set in the Middle Ages, and students can read these stories independently or class sets can be purchased (e.g, *Robin Hood of Sherwood Forest* [McGovern, 1968] for directed reading). There are also some fairy tales set in the period, such as *Saint George and the Dragon* (Hodges, 1984) and *The Pied Piper of Hamelin* (Mayer, 1987), that students can read to retell or rewrite. Some stories set in the Middle Ages can be shared when read aloud by the teacher.

Word study activities can also be related to the unit. Words should be chosen from the informational books and stories students are reading; possible words are listed in the cluster in Figure 15–8. Another related activity is to study the history of English, particularly the Middle English period, and learn what French words were added to English during that time. Many of the vocabulary words show the impact the Norman kings had on English.

Students independently read the chapters and take notes using a cluster. Students each prepare a project to apply what they are learning in the unit. They choose projects, which may come from the list in Figure 15–5, in consultation with the teacher. Other possible projects are creating a castle or village, making a small tapestry, creating a coat of arms, dressing a doll in a medieval costume, or painting a mural.

As the culminating activity for the unit, students can plan and hold a medieval feast. Each student assumes the role of a medieval person, dresses in clothing of the era, and shares something (e.g., a poem, a simulated journal entry, a song, a reading, a piece of art, a skit) as that person. Students should plan food that might have been served and use music and typical activities of the time. Students can share their projects during the feast. For more information about medieval feast and festivals, check *A Medieval Feast* (Aliki, 1983) and *Medieval Holidays and Festivals* (Cosman, 1981).

Biography Unit: Martin Luther King, Jr.   In this unit, students learn about a great Black American, Martin Luther King, Jr., at the same time that they learn about Black history in general and about biographies. The cluster for the unit appears in Figure 15–8. The unit begins with shared reading (or reading aloud) of a book about Martin Luther King, Jr., and learning about his life. Students view a videotape of King's "I Have a Dream" speech and write about their own dreams; they can share Hughes's poems "Dreams" and "Dreams Deferred" along with poems by other Black poets. Students apply vocabulary words that are introduced in their own reading.

Students might choose another prominent Black—historical or modern—such as Harriet Tubman, Mary McLeod Bethune, or Jesse Jackson—for independent reading and report on that person's contribution to America. Together students might develop a timeline of Black history and share it with an elementary school as part of Martin Luther King's birthday celebration or during Black History Month (in February).

Students might read chapter books by Black authors or with Black main characters under the teacher's direction, or the teacher can read one aloud. Two books listed in the cluster are *Roll of Thunder, Hear My Cry* (Taylor, 1977) and *Words by Heart* (Sebestyen, 1979). Students keep a reading log to reflect on their reading.

Developing Lesson Plans

From these unit clusters, teachers choose the activities they plan to use and develop lesson plans. They can plan special activities to initiate or conclude the unit. The plans may be part of content area classes or language arts class, or they may extend throughout the school day. There are always difficult choices to make in selecting and sequencing activities for the unit. Rarely can teachers include all the activities outlined in a unit cluster; instead, they must choose activities that are most appropriate for their students within the time and material constraints imposed on them. Teachers often identify so many possible activities and projects that students could spend six, nine, or even twelve weeks on a unit, which is simply not possible, given the great number of units that must be taught during the school year. Limited supplies of trade books, models, films, and other materials also have an impact on teachers' planning.

Planning for Assessment

After developing the lesson plans, teachers need to consider how to assess students' work during the unit. They can identify particular activities and projects that students will complete during the unit. Some activities will be assessed simply as completed or not completed; others might be assessed according to the level of quality displayed. Some activities require individual work, and others involve small group and class work.

Activities should represent all four language modes: listening, talking, reading, and writing. Both informal writing activities, such as learning logs or freewrites, and process writing activities should be included.

One way to organize the assessment plan is to develop a checklist identifying the activities that will be assessed or graded. Checklists can be distributed to students at the beginning of the unit so they will understand what is expected of them. Teachers who use checklists have found that their students become more responsible in completing assignments. An assessment checklist for a middle-grade unit on insects is shown in Figure 15–9. Students receive this checklist at the beginning of the unit and keep it in their unit notebooks or file folders. Students check off each of the nine activities after completing it. At the end of the unit, the teacher collects and assesses students' work on each activity.

INSECT UNIT CHECKLIST

Name _____

____ 1. Keep a learning log.

____ 2. Read five informational books about insects and write about them in your learning log.

____ 3. Help your group to make an insect life-cycle chart.

____ 4. Construct an imaginary insect and write a description of it. (Make sure your insect has the characteristics of an insect.)

____ 5. Listen to *The Cricket in Times Square* and write or draw in a reading log about each chapter.

____ 6. Do a choral reading with a friend from *Joyful Noise*.

____ 7. Make a page for our class ABC book on Insects. Your page? ____

____ 8. Study spelling words from our insect unit word wall.

____ 9. Learn more about insects and do a project to share your learning. What is your project? _____

FIGURE 15–9

Teacher's Notebook Page: Assessment Checklist for a Middle-Grade Science Unit

❖ REVIEW

Language arts can be integrated into thematic units for across-the-curriculum study. Integration of listening, talking, reading, and writing into science, social studies, literature, and other areas of the curriculum enhances students' learning of the content area as well as their language abilities.

Teachers plan thematic units by considering their available resources and the types of activities that would enhance content area learning. Then teachers develop clusters, outlining possible resources and activities, and write lesson plans from the clusters.

❖ EXTENSIONS

1. Plan a thematic unit using a cluster. Choose a grade level and develop a literature, social studies, science, biography, or author unit.

2. Plan a thematic unit for literature or author study using the procedure in this chapter.

3. Examine a content area textbook and find ways to expand one of the chapters or units beyond the textbook.

4. Choose a grade level that you teach or hope to teach and identify the thematic units you will teach throughout the school year.

5. Make a collection of poems you could use for teaching three different thematic units.

❖ REFERENCES

Ahlberg, J., & Ahlberg, A. (1986). *The jolly postman or other people's letters*. Boston: Little, Brown.

Aliki. (1983). *A medieval feast*. New York: Crowell.

Cleary, B. (1968). *Ramona the pest*. New York: Morrow.

Cleary, B. (1983). *Dear Mr. Henshaw*. New York: Morrow.

Cleary, B. (1988). *A girl from Yamhill: A memoir*. New York: Morrow.

Cosman, M. P. (1981). *Medieval holidays and festivals*. New York: Scribner.

Erickson, K. L. (1988). Building castles in the classroom. *Language Arts, 65*, 14–19.

Fleischman, P. (1988). *Joyful noise: Poems for two voices*. New York: Harper and Row.

Frank, A. (1952). *Anne Frank: The diary of a young girl*. New York: Doubleday.

Fritz, J. (1974). *Why don't you get a horse, Sam Adams?* New York: Coward.

Gamberg, R., Kwak, W., Hutchings, M., Altheim, J., & Edwards, G. (1988). *Learning and loving it: Theme studies in the classroom*. Portsmouth, NH: Heinemann.

Gibbons, G. (1982). *The post office book*. New York: Harper and Row.

Goodall, J. S. (1983). *Above and below stairs*. New York: Atheneum.

Halliday, M. A. K. (1980). Three aspects of children's language development: Learning language, learning through language, learning about language. In Y. M. Goodman, M. M. Haussler, & D. S. Strickland (Eds.), *Oral and written language development research: Impact on the schools*, pp. 7–19. (Proceedings from the 1979 and 1980 IMPACT Conferences sponsored by the International Reading Association and the National Council of Teachers of English.) Urbana, IL: National Council of Teachers of English.

Hancock, J., & Hill, S. (1987). *Literature-based reading programs at work*. Portsmouth, NH: Heinemann.

Hansen, J., Newkirk, T., & Graves, D. (Eds.). (1985). *Breaking ground: Teachers relate reading and writing in the elementary school.* Portsmouth, NH: Heinemann.

Heller, R. (1984). *Plants that never bloom.* New York: Grosset & Dunlap.

Hodges, M. (1984). *Saint George and the dragon.* Boston: Little, Brown.

I never saw another butterfly: Children's drawings and poems from Theresienstadt Concentration Camp, 1942–1944. (1964). New York: McGraw-Hill.

Jacobs, J. (1967). *Johnny-cake.* New York: Putnam.

Jarrell, R. (1964). *Gingerbread rabbit.* New York: Macmillan.

Lewis, C. S. (1950). *The lion, the witch, and the wardrobe.* New York: Macmillan.

Lobel, A. (1970). *Frog and toad are friends.* New York: Harper and Row.

Lobel, A. (1972). *Frog and toad together.* New York: Harper and Row.

Lobel, A. (1976). *Frog and toad all year.* New York: Harper and Row.

Lobel, A. (1979). *Days with frog and toad.* New York: Harper and Row.

Mayer, M. (1987). *The pied piper of Hamelin.* New York: Macmillan.

McGovern, A. (1968). *Robin Hood of Sherwood Forest.* New York: Scholastic Books.

Moss, J. F. (1984). *Focus units in literature: A handbook for elementary school teachers.* Urbana, IL: NCTE.

Nelson, P. A. (1988). Drama, doorway to the past. *Language Arts, 65,* 20–25.

Oppenheim, J. (1986). *You can't catch me!* Boston: Houghton Mifflin.

Pappas, C. C., Kiefer, B. Z., & Levstik, L. S. (1990). *An integrated language perspective in the elementary school: Theory into action.* New York: Longman.

Richards, L. (1990). "Measuring things in words": Language for learning mathematics. *Language Arts, 67,* 14–25.

Salem, J. (1982). Using writing in teaching mathematics. In M. Barr, P. D'Arcy, & M. K. Healy (Eds.), *What's going on? Language/learning episodes in British and American classrooms, grades 4–13,* pp. 123–134. Montclair, NJ: Boynton/Cook.

San Jose, C. (1988). Story drama in the content areas. *Language Arts, 65,* 26–33.

Schubert, B. (1987). Mathematics journals: Fourth grade. In T. Fulwiler (Ed.), *The journal book,* pp. 348–358. Portsmouth, NH: Boynton/Cook.

Sebestyen, O. (1979). *Words by heart.* New York: Atlantic Monthly Press.

Selden, G. (1960). *The cricket in Times Square.* New York: Farrar, Straus & Giroux.

Siegal, A. (1981). *Upon the head of a goat: A childhood in Hungary, 1939–1944.* New York: Farrar, Straus & Giroux.

Silverstein, S. (1964). *The giving tree.* New York: Harper and Row.

Somers, A. B., & Worthington, J. E. (1979). *Response guides for teaching children's books.* Urbana, IL: National Council of Teachers of English.

Taylor, M. D. (1977). *Roll of thunder, hear my cry.* New York: Dial.

Thaiss, C. (1986). *Language across the curriculum in the elementary grades.* Urbana, IL: ERIC Clearinghouse on Reading and Communication Skills and the National Council of Teachers of English.

Tompkins, G. E. (1990). *Teaching writing: Balancing process and product.* Columbus, OH: Merrill.

Tompkins, G. E., & McGee, L. M. (1989). Teaching repetition as a story structure. In K. D. Muth (Ed.), *Children's comprehension of text: Research into practice,* pp. 59–78. Newark, DE: International Reading Association.

Van Allsburg, C. (1979). *The garden of Abdul Gasazi.* Boston: Houghton Mifflin.

Van Allsburg, C. (1981). *Jumanji.* Boston: Houghton Mifflin.

Van Allsburg, C. (1982). *Ben's dream.* Boston: Houghton Mifflin.

Van Allsburg, C. (1984). *The mysteries of Harris Burdick.* Boston: Houghton Mifflin.

Van Allsburg, C. (1985). *The polar express.* Boston: Houghton Mifflin.

Van Allsburg, C. (1986). *The stranger.* Boston: Houghton Mifflin.

Van Allsburg, C. (1987). *The Z was zapped.* Boston: Houghton Mifflin.

Van Allsburg, C. (1988). *Two bad ants.* Boston: Houghton Mifflin.

Van Stockum, H. (1975). *The borrowed house.* New York: Farrar.

16 TEACHING STUDENTS WITH SPECIAL NEEDS

MILDLY HANDICAPPED STUDENTS
    Learning Disabled Students
    Mentally Retarded Students
    Emotionally Disturbed Students

LANGUAGE DIFFERENT STUDENTS
    Language-delayed Students
    Bilingual and Non-English-Speaking Students
    Nonstandard-English-Speaking Students

GIFTED STUDENTS

◆ IN CHAPTER 16, WE EXAMINE THE LEARNING CHARACTERISTICS of exceptional students who are mainstreamed in regular classrooms and suggest ways to modify the language arts program to meet these students' needs.

◆ AS YOU ARE READING, THINK ABOUT THESE QUESTIONS:

What types of exceptional students might be mainstreamed in regular classrooms?

What are the learning characteristics of mildly handicapped students?

What teaching strategies can be used with these special learners?

What are the learning characteristics of language different students?

What teaching strategies can be used with these students?

What are the learning characteristics of gifted students?

What are the teaching strategies that can be used with these students?

In 1975 Congress passed the Education for All Handicapped Children Act (PL 94-142). This act requires that handicapped children be educated "to the maximum extent appropriate with children who are not handicapped" and that "removal of handicapped children from the regular educational environment occurs only when the nature or severity of the handicap is such that education in regular classes with the use of supplementary aids and services cannot be achieved satisfactorily" (*Federal Register,* August 23, 1977, p. 821). This legislation does not stipulate that every exceptional child will be placed in regular classrooms; it does mean, however, that mildly handicapped children who can benefit from being in regular classrooms will spend part or all of each school day in the mainstream of education, in the regular classroom.

Mainstreaming is the placement of handicapped students in the least restrictive environment. For many mildly handicapped students, such as learning disabled and emotionally disturbed students, the least restrictive environment may be the regular classroom with or without supplemental "pull-out" programs. This placement involves more than just the physical integration of handicapped students into a regular classroom. Exceptional students have educational and social needs that must also be met. Classroom teachers can modify their language arts programs to meet the students' individual needs and to integrate them socially into the classroom by allowing them to participate fully in classroom activities.

We will consider the learning characteristics and instructional needs of the exceptional students who are most likely to be placed in regular classrooms. Because it is not possible to examine all categories of exceptional learners, we will focus on only three categories of students with special learning needs: mildly handicapped, language different, and gifted. Although school districts may use slightly different labels, we use the terms specified in federal guidelines. For exceptionalities not defined by federal legislation, we use the currently accepted terminology. Of course, students do not always fit neatly into the identified categories; for example, some students may be both bilingual and gifted, and others may have multiple handicapping conditions, such as cerebral palsy.

Our position is that students with special needs benefit from the same language arts content and teaching strategies that other students do. Instructional strategies that allow students to use their natural language ability and concrete, real-life activities facilitate all students' oral and written language development. The material in this book capitalizes on the natural ways children learn, and it can be used effectively with exceptional students. Glass, Christiansen, and Christiansen (1982) point out that no one way exists to teach students with special needs that is significantly different from how nonhandicapped students are taught. Moreover, educators recommend a holistic, integrated approach as especially valuable for learning disabled and remedial learners (Rhodes & Dudley-Marling, 1988) and for non-English-speaking students (Heald-Taylor, 1986).

❖ MILDLY HANDICAPPED STUDENTS

Mildly handicapped students are those identified as learning disabled, mentally retarded, or emotionally disturbed. PL 94-142 mandates that these youngsters be mainstreamed as much as possible; thus, it is likely that teachers will have one or more of these students in their classrooms. These students' handicapping conditions have an impact on their communicative competence both linguistically and socially. Their messages are linguistically less complex and differ in content from their nondisabled classmates'. At the same time, these students are less able to interact socially with classmates—to ask questions, to direct a conversation, or to respond to others' questions. When they read, they are less able to interpret a character's behavior, and when they edit their compositions, they are less able to identify and correct mechanical errors. Special educators are concluding that mildly handicapped students do not employ the same sociolinguistic strategies as do their nonhandicapped peers.

Learning Disabled Students

Learning disabled (LD) students exhibit severe and specific learning difficulties in areas related to language or mathematics. Learning disability is defined as follows:

> A disorder in one or more of the basic psychological processes involved in understanding or in using language, spoken or written, which may manifest itself in an imperfect ability to listen, think, speak, read, write, spell, or to do mathematical calculations. The term includes such conditions as perceptual handicaps, brain injury, minimal brain disfunction, dyslexia, and developmental aphasia. The term does not include children who have learning problems which are primarily the result of visual, hearing, or motor handicaps, of mental retardation, of emotional disturbance, or of environmental, cultural, or economic disadvantage. (*Federal Register,* August 23, 1977, p. 786)

Characteristics of LD students that affect language arts instruction include, in the area of behavior:

- the student moves constantly
- the student has difficulty beginning or completing tasks
- the student is generally quiet or withdrawn
- the student has difficulty with peer relationships
- the student is disorganized
- the student is easily distracted
- the student displays inconsistencies in behavior
- the student seems to misunderstand oral directions
- In the area of oral language:
- the student hesitates often when speaking
- the student has poor verbal expression for age

In the area of reading:

- the student loses place, repeats words
- the student does not read fluently
- the student confuses similar words and letters

- the student uses fingers to follow along
- the student does not read willingly

In the area of spelling:

- the student uses incorrect order of letters in words
- the student has difficulty associating correct sound with appropriate letter
- the student reverses letters and words

In the area of handwriting:

- the student cannot stay on line
- the student has difficulty copying from board or other source
- the student uses cursive and manuscript handwriting in same assignment
- the student is slow in completing written work

In the area of writing:

- the student uses poor written expression for age (Summers, 1977, p. 42)

These characteristics suggest an academic handicap, and language arts disabilities, particularly in reading, are common academic problems. In addition, these students frequently exhibit socially inappropriate behaviors and may have difficulty relating to their classmates. Certainly, not all learning disabled students exhibit all these characteristics, and some of the characteristics are also associated with other learning problems and handicapping conditions.

Many different diagnostic labels have been applied to LD students; the term *learning disabilities* is relatively new. It was coined by a special educator, Samuel Kirk, in 1963 (Lerner, 1985). Depending on the labels and criteria used, the prevalence of learning disabilities has been estimated to range from three to five percent of the school-aged population.

Instructional Implications. Learning disabled students are typically mainstreamed in regular classrooms for much of the school day and "pulled out" to a resource room for special instruction. Perhaps the most important consideration in planning instruction for learning disabled students is that the approach be structured. The strategy described in Chapter 1 is a structured approach that, when applied to listening, the writing process, the elements of story structure, and expository text structures, is especially beneficial for LD students. Englert, Raphael, Fear, and Anderson (1988) point out that "LD students may not readily recognize strategies that they have merely practiced . . . unless they are explicitly labeled and taught as a strategy" (p. 44). Making strategies explicit is a good teaching practice for all students, and it is crucial for LD students.

Because LD students are frequently inactive learners (Torgesen, 1982), teachers must design activities that allow them to actively experiment with language and to use language in genuine, meaningful, and functional ways.

Another important consideration is that learning disabled children must be allowed to experience success, even in nontraditional ways. For example, students can compose stories orally, using a tape recorder, or prepare oral reports rather than written reports. It is essential that teachers develop innovative strategies to work around LD students' handicapping conditions.

Other strategies and activities we have discussed that are appropriate for LD students include the following:

Try predictable books with LD students because the repetitive patterns allow them to feel immediate success as well as to learn prediction strategies (McClure, 1985). Vocabulary study and writing activities can grow out of the reading experiences.

Allow LD students with severe handwriting problems to use a typewriter or a microcomputer with word-processing software to write compositions and practice spelling words. Few studies have examined the usefulness of word-processing programs with disabled students, but several have found that writing improves along with students' attitudes about writing. The value of word processing seems to depend on how effectively the instructional program takes advantage of the computer capabilities in supporting students as they draft, revise, and edit (MacArthur, 1988). Also, because poor handwriting skills contribute to many children's spelling errors, using a typewriter or microcomputer eliminates that part of the problem.

Teach the writing process and involve students in a wide range of activities that promote their interest in writing and the acquisition of writing skills. In their instructional recommendations, Graham and Harris (1988) identify components similar to those in this book. A notable addition is the recommendation that teachers find ways to help students automatize skills for getting language onto paper. For many middle- and upper-grade LD students, the mechanical considerations of getting words onto paper may interfere with the cognitive processes involved in writing. Ways to alleviate this problem include providing daily writing opportunities to develop fluency; taking students' dictation; deemphasizing mechanical correctness during drafting; and teaching spelling, handwriting, and other mechanical skills during separate minilessons and quickly applying the skills in genuine writing activities.

Students can use wordless picture books to tell stories based on the pictures, learn vocabulary words related to the stories, and dictate or write their own stories based on the books (D'Angelo, 1980; McGee & Tompkins, 1983). Refer to the list of wordless picture books in Figure 8–7.

Provide extensive prewriting activities (e.g., brainstorming and clustering) to give LD students the necessary warm-up before writing (Tompkins & Friend, 1986). Even though the prewriting stage of the writing process is valuable for all students, learning disabled students especially benefit from prewriting activities in which they generate ideas and organize them for writing. A third grader's cluster and autobiographical writing appear in Figure 16–1. Notice how the student gathered and organized ideas in the cluster and expanded the ideas in the autobiography.

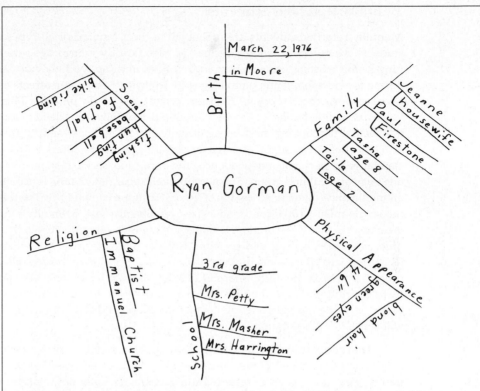

My name is Ryan Gorman. I was born March 22, 1976. I was born in Moore, Oklahoma. I have blond hair. My eyes are green. I am 4'6".

My favorite sports are football and baseball. I like bike riding. I like fishing. I like hunting.

My mom's name is Jeanne. She is a housewife. My dad's name is Paul. He works at Firestone. I have two sisters. One's name is Tasha. She is 8. My other sister's name is Talia. She is 2.

I am Baptist. I go to Immanuel Church.

The school I go to is Southgate. I am in third grade. My homeroom teacher is Mrs. Petty. My lab teacher is Mrs. Harrington. I have a science teacher. Her name is Mrs. Masher. My favorite subject is math. My worst subject is reading.

FIGURE 16–1

A Student's Cluster and Autobiography

Use listening rather than reading whenever possible, because LD students are usually better at listening. For instance, students can proofread their writing aloud or have another student read aloud the writing. Espin and Sindelar (1988) have shown that students identify more mechanical errors when they listen to the piece read aloud than when they read the draft silently. Also, LD students tend to locate fewer errors in their writing than do nonhandicapped students.

Mentally Retarded Students

Mentally retarded students are probably the most familiar of all types of exceptional students. *Mental retardation* is defined as "significantly subaverage general intellectual functioning existing concurrently with deficits in adaptive behavior, and manifested during the developmental period [ages 0–18], which adversely affects a child's educational performance" (*Federal Register,* August 23, 1977, p. 785). This definition involves two dimensions: (1) to be considered mentally retarded, a student's general intellectual functioning must be significantly below average; and (2) the student must also have deficits in adaptive behavior. *Adaptive behavior* refers to the ability to meet standards of personal independence, self-care, and social responsibility expected of one's age and cultural group. *Subaverage intellectual functioning* is usually indicated by an intelligence quotient score (IQ) of 70 or less (approximately two standard deviations below the mean, 100) on a standardized intelligence test. Mentally retarded students are classified into three or more levels according to severity. Psychologists use the terms *mild, moderate, severe,* and *profound* to label the categories, but educators typically use terms with educational implications: *educable mentally retarded* (EMR) (55–70 IQ range); *trainable mentally retarded* (TMR) (40–55 IQ range); and *severe/profound mentally retarded* (less than 40 IQ). School districts, however, may use different IQ scores to define the categories of mental retardation and to identify which students they will serve in each program.

Instructional Implications. Programs for the mentally retarded focus on helping students develop the functional skills considered essential to living independently. The more severely retarded students are typically not mainstreamed into elementary classrooms. Educable mentally retarded students, in contrast, are often placed in a regular class for most of the school day and go to a resource room for special instruction.

Educable mentally retarded students can be included in many regular instructional activities with slight modifications. The most valuable activities for EMR students, as well as for other students, are those that are concrete, meaningful, and based on personal experience. When the pace of classroom activities is too fast, individualized instruction with peer-tutors can be provided. This individualized instruction should involve more repetition and practice than is necessary for other students. EMR students need to "overlearn" a concept or skill by continuing to practice even after they have demonstrated proficiency.

The most valuable language arts activities for EMR students are functional and involve skills that they really need to know. These students are capable of learning to communicate through oral and written language, and they need to learn many of the same basic skills that other students learn in the elementary grades. Activities that are appropriate for educable mentally retarded students include the following.

Have peer-tutors read with EMR students using the assisted reading strategy presented in Chapter 8. The strategy allows students to move naturally into reading and provides the necessary repetition and practice. Encourage peer-tutors to reread favorite books; studies show that repeated readings provide needed practice for EMR students and allow them to delve more deeply into literature (O'Shea & O'Shea, 1988).

Have EMR students tell and dictate stories using wordless picture books. These books without words are useful for introducing book handling skills and the concept of "story." Lisa, a 14-year-old mildly handicapped student, retold Alexander's wordless picture book *Out! Out! Out!* (1968) this way:

The little boy is pulling the train. The mother is feeding porridge to the baby while the baby feeds the porridge to a bird. The mother screams and the bird flies into the cabinet. The bird is getting into everything. A man is bringing groceries to mom. The bird flies out of the bag. The trashman shoos the bird out with a broom. The bird is trying to run away from the men. The little boy is spilling food. The bird is eating the food the little boy spilled. The little boy puts food on the window and the bird follows it. The mother is happy because the bird went away. The mother hugs the little boy.

Focus on functional learning through reading, spelling, and writing activities. For example, on a walking field trip through the community, take pictures of functional words (e.g., *STOP, exit, women*) that students spot. Paste the photos in a booklet and add students' dictated sentences below the pictures to show the word in context. Figure 16–2 lists essential survival words and phrases. Share concept books, such as *Signs* (Goor & Goor, 1983), which include photos of signs with the accompanying survival words and phrases.

Use pattern books to teach oral language patterns such as *wh-* questions and past-tense markers. In addition, students can dictate or write their own books following the patterns. (Pattern books are predictable books in which a phrase or sentence is repeated again and again.)

Try writing without a pencil (Tompkins, 1981). EMR students can practice handwriting skills using clay, fingerpaint, sand, shaving cream, and shaping their bodies like letters. They can also practice spelling words with these techniques, or use magnetic letters, foam letters, and letter stamps.

Invite EMR students to write "I wish" poems, color poems, "If I were . . ." poems, and other formula poems discussed in Chapter 11. Although EMR students may not be successful with haiku, limericks, and other more difficult syllable-counting and rhyming poetic formulas, they can write poems with repetitive patterns.

Emotionally Disturbed Students

Emotionally disturbed students (ED) are children with behavior disorders that interfere with learning. Typically, they are either aggressive, demonstrating acting-out behaviors, or withdrawn, showing nonresponsive behaviors. The term *emotionally disturbed* is defined as

A condition exhibiting one or more of the following characteristics over a long period of time and to a marked degree, which adversely affects educational performance:

- An inability to learn which cannot be explained by intellectual, sensory, or health factors;

- An inability to build or maintain satisfactory interpersonal relationships with peers and teachers;

50 Most Essential Survival Words		50 Most Essential Survival Phrases	
1. Poison	26. Ambulance	1. Don't walk	26. Wrong way
2. Danger	27. Girls	2. Fire escape	27. No fires
3. Police	28. Open	3. Fire extinguisher	28. No swimming
4. Emergency	29. Out	4. Do not enter	29. Watch your step
5. Stop	30. Combustible	5. First aid	30. Watch for children
6. Hot	31. Closed	6. Deep water	31. No diving
7. Walk	32. Condemned	7. External use only	32. Stop for pedestrians
8. Caution	33. Up	8. High voltage	33. Post office
9. Exit	34. Blasting	9. No trespassing	34. Slippery when wet
10. Men	35. Gentlemen	10. Railroad crossing	35. Help wanted
11. Women	36. Pull	11. Rest rooms	36. Slow down
12. Warning	37. Down	12. Do not touch	37. Smoking prohibited
13. Entrance	38. Detour	13. Do not use near	38. No admittance
14. Help	39. Gasoline	open flame	39. Proceed at your
15. Off	40. Inflammable	14. Do not inhale fumes	own risk
16. On	41. In	15. One way	40. Step down
17. Explosives	42. Push	16. Do not cross	41. No parking
18. Flammable	43. Nurse	17. Do not use near	42. Keep closed
19. Doctor	44. Information	heat	43. No turns
20. Go	45. Lifeguard	18. Keep out	44. Beware of dog
21. Telephone	46. Listen	19. Keep off	45. School zone
22. Boys	47. Private	20. Exit only	46. Dangerous curve
23. Contaminated	48. Quiet	21. No right turn	47. Hospital zone
24. Ladies	49. Look	22. Keep away	48. Out of order
25. Dynamite	50. Wanted	23. Thin ice	49. No smoking
		24. Bus stop	50. Go slow
		25. No passing	

FIGURE 16–2

A List of Survival Words and Phrases
Polloway & Polloway, 1981, pp. 446–447.

• Inappropriate types of behavior or feelings under normal circumstances;

• A general pervasive mood of unhappiness or depression; or

• A tendency to develop physical symptoms or fears associated with personal or school problems. (*Federal Register*, August 23, 1977, pp. 785–786)

Although any student can exhibit one of these behavior patterns for a brief period, children who are identified as emotionally disturbed exhibit one or more age- or context-inappropriate patterns to a marked degree or consistently over time.

Approximately two percent of students have an emotional handicap, but usually only the most severely maladjusted students are identified and served. Emotionally disturbed students are frequently underachievers, because their emotional problems interfere with learning.

Drawing is an especially valuable prewriting activity for students with special learning needs.

Instructional Implications. Scant attention has been given to developing teaching strategies and instructional materials to meet the special needs of ED students. The behavior of these exceptional learners suggests, however, that they need a structured and positive school environment. Instruction in oral language skills may help ED students to express their emotions more appropriately. Teachers must closely monitor ED students' frustration levels and help them find ways to communicate their frustration. Behavior modification is an effective technique for helping students learn to control disruptive and socially inappropriate behavior. Also, teachers must consider the ED students' social and emotional needs as well as their academic needs.

Many of the oral and written language strategies and activities discussed in this book can be used effectively with ED students. The following are some recommended activities:

To develop ED students' oral language and socialization skills, involve them in a variety of functional oral language activities. Younger children can participate in dramatic play, and children at all ages can engage in informal conversations with classmates and with the teacher.

SUCCESS WITH "AT-RISK" STUDENTS

"Children at risk are children who are not learning. They can't understand assignments and they don't complete them. My students are not at risk because they are learning."

Sue Wuestner, Special Education Teacher, Western Hills Elementary School

PROCEDURE

I work with six boys aged 9 to 12. They have behavior and emotional problems and range academically from first to eighth grade levels. Right now we're doing a unit on fables. I use trade books—real books they like and can read. After reading, my students share with each other. For many of them, it's the first time they've ever been up in front of the class. Lots of sharing and talking go on in our classroom because it is a social environment. They write informally in learning logs and use the writing process as they retell favorite fables and write original fables.

We began the unit by reading and discussing fables. The boys are continuing to read and re-read fables and listen to others at the listening center. Now my students are writing a retelling of their favorite fable. Two boys have finished edit-

ing and are making corrections before printing out their final copies on the computer. Justin has already printed out his final copy and is now making a shoebox diorama to accompany it. This is his retelling of "The Lion and the Mouse."

Once there was a lion sleeping in his den. A mouse not looking where he was going ran over the lion's nose and woke the lion up. When the lion saw him and was about to eat him, the mouse said in a frightened voice, "Please, don't hurt me. I will repay you someday." "Ha! repay me? What an idea." But soon he fell into a trap set for him and let out a roar. The mouse rushed to the spot and set to work nibbling on the ropes. Soon the lion was free. Now the lion is wiser.

The moral of this story is kindness is never wasted.

My three other boys are meeting together in a writing group to revise their retellings. This schedule is working well because as soon as the two boys are done at the computer, these three will be ready to edit.

After retelling their favorite fables, my boys are going to write and illustrate their own fables. We've talked about the elements of fables, and, after the experiences they've had reading and retelling fables, I think they are ready to create their own. They'll use the writing process to revise and edit their writing, and they'll bind their finished fables into books.

ASSESSMENT

I use unit checklists that list the activities the boys will be involved in for the unit. I pass out file folders and the checklists at the beginning of the unit, and the boys staple the checklists inside the folders. As we do each activity, they check it off. It's important that my students understand what is expected of them, and checklists work well.

REFLECTIONS

I use units just like the other teachers at Western Hills School do. The main difference is that I have to set very explicit guidelines and provide more structure so my students can be successful. I can do anything the other teachers do with these students as long as I keep the pressure low, set clear expectations, and provide a structured classroom environment.

FABLES

Name_____

Required Activities

1. Read five fables and write in your reading log.

2. Listen to five fables at the listening center and write in your reading log.

3. Write a retelling of your favorite fable on the computer and make a diorama to go along with it.

4. Write and illustrate your own fable and make a hard-bound book of it.

Your Choice Activities
(Choose one, but you can do more than one!)

1. Write a poem about a fable you've read.

2. Read a fable that's new to you and make a poster about it.

3. Direct a play about a fable.

4. Choose an animal from a fable, research the animal, and then give an *oral* report.

5. Choose an animal from a fable, research the animal, and then do a *written* report.

6. Make an ABC book about fables.

7. Choose a different activity (but check with the teacher first).

Emotionally disturbed students can express themselves with less anxiety if they use puppets, so encourage them to use puppets in developing oral reports and retelling stories.

Have students record their feelings or behaviors in journals. This activity provides ED students with a pressure-release valve, as well as with necessary writing practice.

Use drawing and other art activities as a prewriting strategy for ED students. Art is an alternative form of communication for children who have trouble expressing themselves. Students might also try creating their own wordless picture books.

Some ED students benefit from reading books with characters who exhibit behavior and learning problems similar to their own. These kinds of stories help them recognize that other children cope with similar problems. Figure 16–3 is a list of books with characters who exhibit aggressive or withdrawn behavior. Students can write in reading logs as they read the books or listen to them read aloud. These books, as opposed to those suggested in Chapter 9, may also be more appropriate for ED students to use in examining elements of story structure.

Special care is necessary when introducing ED students to the revising and editing stages of the writing process. Some ED students will find it difficult to allow classmates to critique their writing. Teachers must nurture the writing process and demonstrate the importance of revising and editing to improve writing quality. Begin with one-on-one revising and editing, then move slowly into group work.

❖ LANGUAGE-DIFFERENT STUDENTS

Language-different students are children who cannot communicate effectively in standard English for reasons other than physical or emotional. They may be delayed in developing language, live in non-English-speaking communities and have limited proficiency in English, have recently arrived in the U.S. and not speak English, or speak a nonstandard English dialect.

Language-delayed Students

Students are classified as *language-delayed* when their language development is significantly slower than the rate for others their age. Despite a chronological delay, the students' language development usually follows the same stages as other children's development, but at a slower rate. Scofield (1978, p. 720) lists these characteristics of language-delayed students: "They may speak in markedly childlike phrases, lack the sentence-producing ability of their classmates, lack the ability to use language purposefully, talk very little in school situations, and lack many concepts that are part of day-to-day living." Many of these same language problems are also exhibited by learning disabled, mentally retarded, and emotionally disturbed learners.

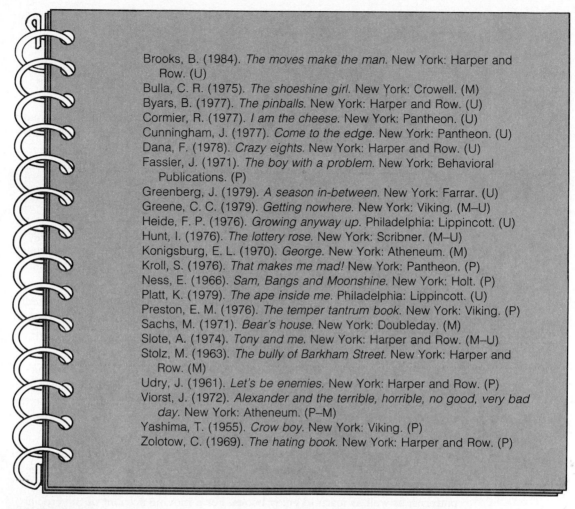

Brooks, B. (1984). *The moves make the man*. New York: Harper and Row. (U)

Bulla, C. R. (1975). *The shoeshine girl*. New York: Crowell. (M)

Byars, B. (1977). *The pinballs*. New York: Harper and Row. (U)

Cormier, R. (1977). *I am the cheese*. New York: Pantheon. (U)

Cunningham, J. (1977). *Come to the edge*. New York: Pantheon. (U)

Dana, F. (1978). *Crazy eights*. New York: Harper and Row. (U)

Fassler, J. (1971). *The boy with a problem*. New York: Behavioral Publications. (P)

Greenberg, J. (1979). *A season in-between*. New York: Farrar. (U)

Greene, C. C. (1979). *Getting nowhere*. New York: Viking. (M–U)

Heide, F. P. (1976). *Growing anyway up*. Philadelphia: Lippincott. (U)

Hunt, I. (1976). *The lottery rose*. New York: Scribner. (M–U)

Konigsburg, E. L. (1970). *George*. New York: Atheneum. (M)

Kroll, S. (1976). *That makes me mad!* New York: Pantheon. (P)

Ness, E. (1966). *Sam, Bangs and Moonshine*. New York: Holt. (P)

Platt, K. (1979). *The ape inside me*. Philadelphia: Lippincott. (U)

Preston, E. M. (1976). *The temper tantrum book*. New York: Viking. (P)

Sachs, M. (1971). *Bear's house*. New York: Doubleday. (M)

Slote, A. (1974). *Tony and me*. New York: Harper and Row. (M–U)

Stolz, M. (1963). *The bully of Barkham Street*. New York: Harper and Row. (M)

Udry, J. (1961). *Let's be enemies*. New York: Harper and Row. (P)

Viorst, J. (1972). *Alexander and the terrible, horrible, no good, very bad day*. New York: Atheneum. (P–M)

Yashima, T. (1955). *Crow boy*. New York: Viking. (P)

Zolotow, C. (1969). *The hating book*. New York: Harper and Row. (P)

FIGURE 16–3

Teacher's Notebook Page: Stories with Characters Who Exhibit Aggressive or Withdrawn Behaviors

P = primary grades (K–2)
M = middle grades (3–5)
U = upper grades (6–8)

Instructional Implications. Language-delayed students need intensive experience with language, and the regular classroom can offer them many meaningful opportunities for learning language, both directly and indirectly. Scofield (1978) suggests three strategies for working with language-delayed children: they need systematic instruction, experience with a range of language functions, and opportunities for spontaneous speech in the context of genuine interpersonal relationships.

Many of the activities suggested for talk and drama can be used effectively with language-delayed students. The list of seven language functions mentioned in Chapter

1 can be used to plan language experiences for special learners. The following is a list of activities for language-delayed students:

> Encourage language-delayed students to participate in conversations, daily sharing time, and small group interactions. Primary-grade students can use talk spontaneously as they participate in dramatic play.

> Use predictable books to provide structured practice of targeted language patterns. Bromley and Jalongo (1984) recommend using song picture books with particular language patterns. Keats's *Over in the Meadow* (1971), for instance, can be used to practice person-number agreements. Other song picture books are *Six Little Ducks* (Conover, 1976), *Roll Over! A Counting Song* (Peek, 1981), and *She'll Be Comin' Round the Mountain* (Quackenbush, 1973).

> Involve language-delayed students in dramatic play, role-playing, and puppetry (Hurvitz, Pickert, & Rilla, 1987). Retelling familiar stories with puppets is one possible activity, and movement activities can be used to teach language concepts such as opposites, prepositions, and directional terms.

> Teach language and content area concepts by applying Piaget's theory of cognitive development. Introduce concepts to language-delayed students, provide concrete experiences, and help students identify both the features of the concept and the relationships between the concept and the child's other experiences. Drawing cluster diagrams may also be helpful.

> Have language-delayed students write caption books in which they draw pictures or cut pictures from magazines and add word or phrase captions. Students can read the captions in the books and talk about the pictures, or use the captions in complete sentences. Students thus learn concepts about written language while preparing materials for oral language practice.

> Involve language-delayed children with books. Read and reread books to them and use the assisted reading strategy. Through experiences with books, these students will hear and perhaps repeat a rich variety of words and language patterns, as well as learn to enjoy books. For a moving account of the crucial role books played in the early development of a severely handicapped and nonverbal child, read Butler's *Cushla and Her Books* (1979).

Bilingual and Non-English-Speaking Students

Because many children living in the U.S. come from Hispanic, French, Asian, and Native American backgrounds, they acquire a native language at home that is different from the language their teachers use at school. These children are *bilingual speakers* because they speak one language in the home and English in the outside world. They speak some English, but often mix it with their native language, shifting back and forth even within sentences. This often-misunderstood phenomenon is called *code-switching;* rather than a confusion between the two languages or a corruption of the native language, code-switching is a special linguistic and social skill (Troika, 1981).

One conflict for bilingual students is that learning and speaking standard English are often perceived by family and community members as a rejection of family and culture. Cultural pluralism has replaced the "melting pot" point of view. People in minority ethnic groups are no longer as willing to give up their primary culture and language to join the mainstream Anglo culture. They want to live and function in both cultures, with free access to their cultural patterns, and switch from one culture to the other as the situation demands.

Millions of immigrants enter the U.S. each year speaking Spanish, Farsi, Vietnamese, and other languages from around the world. These immigrant children who do not speak English are *non-English speakers*. They become immersed in an English-language environment as soon as they enter this country and learn to speak English with varying degrees of success, depending on a variety of factors.

In 1986, voters in California approved Proposition 63, which declared English as the official language in the state; since then, more than a dozen other states have enacted similar laws. Some interpret this English-only movement to mean that bilingual programs and the use of languages other than English in elementary classrooms are not permissible. Many educators are concerned about the initiative, because they believe bilingual education offers non-English-speaking children their greatest opportunity for success. At its convention in 1986, the National Council of Teachers of English responded to the English-only movement by passing a resolution to condemn "any attempts to render invisible the native languages of any Americans or to deprive English of the rich influences of the languages and cultures of any of the peoples of America" and to actively oppose "any actions intended to mandate or declare English as an official language or to 'preserve,' 'purify,' or 'enhance' the language [because] any such action will not only stunt the vitality of the language, but also ensure its erosion and in effect create hostility toward English, making it more difficult to teach and learn" (NCTE, 1988). This is a controversial issue; as this revision is being written, legislation is pending in the U.S. Congress that would make English the official language in America.

Research suggests that second-language acquisition is similar to first-language acquisition. Urzua (1980) lists three principles culled from the research:

1. When people learn languages, they use many similar acquisition strategies; this is true whether they are small children learning their first (or native) language or older children or adults learning a second language.

2. Second-language learners go through several stages as they acquire their new language.

3. First- or second-language learning can take place only when and if the learner is placed in a situation that has meaning for that individual. (p. 33)

These stages of second-language acquisition are listed in Figure 16–4. At the same time that students are acquiring the syntactic structures, they are also progressively using longer and more complex sentences. You will note many similarities to the stages of first-language acquisition discussed in Chapter 1.

Instructional Implications. Educational programs for bilingual and non-English-speaking students usually take one of two forms: (1) transitional programs, in which instruction in students' native language is used as a bridge to learning English

FIGURE 16–4

Stages of Second-Language
Acquisition
Gonzales, 1981a, pp. 156–157.

Stage 1

Yes:no answers
Positive statements
Subject pronouns (e.g., *he, she*)
Present tense/present habitual verb tense
Possessive pronouns (e.g., *my, your*)

Stage 2

Simple plurals of nouns
Affirmative sentences
Subject and object pronouns (all)
Possessive (*'s*)
Negation
Possessive pronouns (e.g., *mine*)

Stage 3

Present progressive tense (-ing)
Conjunctions (e.g., *and, but, or, because, so, as*)

Stage 4

Questions (*who? what? which? where?*)
Irregular plurals of nouns
Simple future tense (*going to*)
Prepositions

Stage 5

Future tense (*will*)
Questions (*when? how?*)
Conjunctions (e.g., *either, nor, neither, that, since*)

Stage 6

Regular past tense verbs
Questions (*why?*)
Contractions (e.g., *isn't*)
Modal verbs (e.g., *can, must, do*)

Stage 7

Irregular past tense verbs
Past tense questions
Auxilliary verbs (*has, is*)
Passive voice

Stage 8

Conditional verbs
Imperfect verb tense
Conjunctions (e.g., *though, if, therefore*)
Subjunctive verb mood

Classroom teachers can modify their language arts programs and provide special assistance to meet exceptional students' needs.

and the native language is phased out as their English proficiency increases; and (2) maintenance programs, in which instruction in both English and the native language continues through school. No single approach has been found to be most successful for all students; however, Troika (1981) urges that instruction in the students' native language continue until they are ten or eleven years old. More recently, experts have concluded that it is valuable for both English language development and for academic achievement for instruction to continue in the native language during the elementary grades (Hudelston, 1987). When students reach age 11 or 12 and have consolidated their linguistic skill development, the transfer to instruction primarily in English is easier.

To help bilingual and non-English-speaking students learn English as a second language, teachers need to develop an understanding and appreciation of the culture and language the students bring with them. Teachers' attitudes toward students' language and culture will be the key to success or failure in teaching language-different students.

The first priority in instructing a non-English-speaking student is to teach survival vocabulary and to orient the child to the school and classroom environment. English-speaking students can serve as peer-tutors and "buddies" for the new students. Wagner (1982) reports that her students took turns teaching the non-English-speaking students in her class. The program was terminated after one semester because the non-English-speaking students had learned to speak English! Suggestions for orienting non-English-speaking students into an English speaking class include these:

Teach the non-English-speaking student survival vocabulary, including courtesy words and phrases such as "hello," "thank you," "my name is," and "I need to go to the bathroom."

Try to locate an adult or older student who speaks both the child's native language and English to teach English-speaking students a few survival words and phrases in the child's native language and to serve as a volunteer aide to ease the non-English-speaker's transition to the classroom.

Orient the non-English-speaking student to the school setting and the classroom. Take the child on a "survival tour" of the school, pointing out the cafeteria, library, bathroom, principal's office, and other essential locations. Continue with a classroom "survival tour," and add labels for classroom objects. If possible, write the labels in both the child's native language and English. Draw maps of the classroom and school with the student.

Ask students to volunteer to serve as peer-tutors for the non-English-speaking student. Peer-tutors serve as "buddies" and involve the non-English-speaking student in hands-on and natural-language activities, such as playing basketball, erasing the chalkboard, delivering messages to other classrooms, or working on a jigsaw puzzle (Gonzales, 1981b).

Speaking in English is a necessity when children in one classroom speak a variety of languages or when teachers or aides who speak the child's language are not available.

In the regular classroom, bilingual and non-English-speaking students at the second grade level or above should be immersed in both oral and written language, but bilingual educators suggest that younger students concentrate first on oral language (Rodrigues & White, 1981). Language-different students can be immersed in oral language by means of conversations, discussions, and informal drama activities. Students can be immersed in written language by reading to them and by using assisted reading. Edelsky (1986) recommends allowing students to develop reading and writing competencies in their native language before receiving formal instruction in English. This recommendation is easier to implement for children who speak Spanish than for those who speak Thai or other languages that few teachers or aides speak and write fluently. Other strategies for immersing these language different students in oral and written language include the following:

Have students write in journals. Journal writing is an effective way to help students develop writing fluency (Rodrigues & White, 1981). Shea and Fitzgerald (1981) report that non-English-speaking kindergartners can draw pictures in their journals and gradually grow into dictating and later writing labels and captions to accompany their drawings.

Teach the survival words and phrases. Non-English-speaking students and those with limited English proficiency need to learn these words and phrases quickly to function successfully in the mainstream culture.

Use concept books such as Gibbons's *Trucks* (1981) and Hoban's *A, B, See* (1982) to teach basic vocabulary words. A list of concept books appropriate for elementary students appears in Figure 16—5. In addition, students can draw pictures or cut pictures from magazines and add labels to create their own concept books.

Show filmstrip versions of stories to limited-English-speaking students before asking them to read the story. (Filmstrip versions of many stories are available from Weston Woods, Weston, CT 06880). Have students pantomime stories or retell them using puppets. Another possibility is to tape-record reading materials or have limited-English-speaking students read with a peer-tutor who can answer questions as they arise.

Anno, M (1975). *Anno's counting book*. New York: Crowell.

Banchek, L. (1978). *Snake in, snake out*. New York: Crowell.

Beller, J. (1984). *A-B-C-ing, An action alphabet*. New York: Crown.

Burningham, J. (1969). *Seasons*. Indianapolis: Bobbs-Merrill. (See also *Sniff shout* and other books about sounds by the same author.)

Carle, E. (1974). *My very first book of colors*. New York: Crowell. (See other concept books by the same author.)

Crews, D. (1982). *Harbor*. New York: Greenwillow. (See other beautifully illustrated concept books by the same author.)

Gibbons, G. (1981). *Trucks*. New York: Crowell. (See other concept books including *The boat book, Fire! Fire!* and *New road* by the same author.)

Goor, R., & Goor, N. (1983). *Signs*. New York: Crowell.

Hoban, T. (1982). *A, B, see.* New York: Greenwillow. (See *More than one, Over, under & through (and other spatial concepts), Push-pull, empty-full: A book of opposites,* and other concept books by the same author.)

Maestro, G. (1974). *One more and one less*. New York: Crown.

Oxenbury, H. (1981). *Dressing*. New York: Simon & Schuster. (See other basic concept books by the same author.)

Robbins, K. (1981). *Trucks of every sort*. New York: Crown.

Rockwell, A. (1984). *Trucks*. New York: Dutton. (See *Cars* and other concept books by the same author.)

Rockwell, A., & Rockwell, H. (1972). *Machines*. New York: Macmillan. (See other concept books by these authors.)

Rockwell, H. (1975). *My dentist*. New York: Greenwillow. (See *My doctor* and other concept books by the same author.)

Supraner, R. (1978). *Giggly-wiggly, snickety-snick*. New York: Parents.

Wildsmith, B. (1962). *Brian Wildsmith's ABC*. New York: Watts. (See *Brian Wildsmith's circus* and other concept books by the same author.)

FIGURE 16—5

Teacher's Notebook Page: Concept Books to Use with Non-English-Speaking Students

Involve students in sentence pattern and sentence-combining activities to refine oral language skills after they have developed some fluency in English.

Non-English-speaking and bilingual students often have difficulty understanding our idioms (e.g., "rocks in his head," "out in left field"). Use pantomime to act out literal and figurative meanings. Later, have children develop a class collaboration book in which they draw pictures and write sentences using both meanings. Books such as *Put Your Foot in Your Mouth and Other Silly Sayings* (Cox, 1980), *In a Pickle and Other Funny Idioms* (Terban, 1983), and *Easy as Pie: A Guessing Game of Sayings* (Folsom & Folsom, 1985) can be used as examples. A student's drawing of the literal meaning of "butterflies in my stomach" is shown in Figure 16–6.

Invite students to retell stories, especially stories with repetitions and predictable language, through talk, art, and writing. Franklin (1988) found that kindergarten and first grade Hispanic, bilingual children responded well to two repetitive stories, *The Gingerbread Boy* (Galdone, 1974) and *The Day Jimmy's Boa Ate the Wash* (Noble, 1980). Through retelling activities, the students developed increased fluency in English syntactic patterns and learned more about reading and writing.

FIGURE 16–6

A Student's Literal Drawing of an Idiom
Robert, age 10.

Nonstandard-English-Speaking Students

A single "pure" form of English does not exist; all English speakers speak one dialect or another. Dialects vary across geographic regions, ethnic backgrounds, and socioeconomic levels. Speakers of particular dialects are distinguished by their pronunciations, word choices, and grammatical forms. Consider the different pronunciations of Bostonians, New Yorkers, and Texans; the different words—*pop, soda, soft drink, soda pop,* and *tonic*—to describe the same carbonated beverage; and the double negatives of some dialects. This diversity reflects society's cultural pluralism. Some dialects, however, command more respect than others. The dialect of television reporters and commentators, authors of books and newspaper and magazine articles, and of school is known as standard English (SE). The other dialects are collectively termed nonstandard English (NSE). Students who use nonstandard speech patterns in 20 to 30 percent of their conversation are generally referred to as nonstandard-English-speakers.

In the past, Black students, Appalachian students, and others who spoke a dialect different from standard English were considered to have little language ability. Myths about Black English and other nonstandard dialects that were perpetuated for generations have been disproved. Nonstandard English dialects are not inferior language systems; rather, they are different, rule-governed systems that have patterns of their own (Labov, 1969). Children and adults who speak these dialects are neither cognitively nor linguistically deficient.

Children who speak NSE dialects develop language competency in the same way and at a rate parallel to standard English development. Distinctive phonological and syntactic features of Black English and other nonstandard dialects are listed in Figure 16–7. Researchers have found that NSE speakers gradually incorporate some features of standard English into their speech and writing during the elementary grades. The increasing use of SE features may be due to peer interaction, exposure to standard English on television, or instruction in standard English at school.

Instructional Implications.   Labov (1966) has identified eight areas of language arts instruction necessary for NSE students; they are, in order of priority:

- Understanding spoken SE
- Reading books written in SE
- Communicating effectively through talk
- Communicating effectively through writing
- Using SE forms in writing, spelling words correctly
- Using SE forms in talk
- Using SE pronunciation

Notice that the sequence moves from competency in basic oral and written communication to the acquisition of standard English syntactic and phonological features. Using standard English in writing precedes oral language proficiency.

The teacher's role is threefold: to become sensitive to the needs of NSE speakers; to learn about the distinctive features of NSE so as to understand the difficulties and

Contrast	Standard English	Nonstandard English
Phonological Contrasts		
1. *r*-lessness	guard, fort	god, fought
2. *l*-lessness	help, you'll	hep, you
3. Final consonant cluster simplified	past, desk, meant	pass, des, men
4. Substitutions for /th/	then, mouth	den, mouf
5. Substitution of /n/ for /ing/	coming	comin'
Syntactic Contrasts		
1. Plural marker	two girls	two girl
2. Possessive marker	a dog's bone	a dog bone
3. Double negatives	don't have any	don't got none
	doesn't have	ain't got no
4. Preposition	at his friend's house	to his friend's house
	lives on 3rd Street	live 3rd Street
5. Indefinite article	an apple	a apple
6. Pronoun form	we have	us got
	his ball	he ball
7. Double subjects	John runs	John he run
8. Person-number agreement	she walks	she walk
	Bill has	Bill have
9. Present participle	he is coming	he comin'
10. Past marker	Mother asked	Mother ask
11. Verb form	I said	I say
12. Verb "to be" (present tense)	she is busy	she busy
		she be busy
13. Verb "to be" (past tense)	we were happy	we was happy
14. Future form	I will go	I'ma go, I gonna go
15. "If" construction	I asked if	I ask did

FIGURE 16–7

Contrasts Between Standard and Nonstandard English

frustrations that NSE students face in learning to read, write, and spell in standard English; and to accept and show respect for students' language. Rejection of nonstandard dialects as well as teachers' confusion about nonstandard English interferes with students' learning (Goodman & Buck, 1983). Teachers should establish a climate in their classrooms where students will feel that their language is accepted. Students' language reflects their culture, and it is essential to respect them. Teachers should also demonstrate that they truly believe their students capable of handling two or more dialects. Teachers usually assume that non-English-speakers who have recently arrived in the U.S. will learn to speak standard English, but this same confidence is rarely shown to NSE speakers.

Students naturally use their NSE dialect in reading aloud. Even though students comprehend the standard English they are reading, they often "translate" the language of the textbook into their dialect. This phenomenon can be explained using transformational grammar terminology: whereas the surface structures of NSE and SE are different, the deep, meaning levels are the same, and the dialectal errors do not interfere with meaning (Goodman & Buck, 1983).

Accepting students' linguistic differences, however, is not synonymous with not teaching standard English. Students who speak a NSE dialect need to participate in oral language activities to be able to use the forms of standard English. Many of the oral language activities can be used to help these students expand their use of sentence patterns and grammatical structures. Interrupting students while they are speaking or reading aloud to correct their NSE "errors," however, is not an effective practice. In fact, students may choose not to talk or read aloud if they do not feel their language will be accepted. Activities to teach standard English are as follows.

Use children's literature that involves SE patterns in teaching standard English. Programs using children's literature as a model have been found to be successful in expanding students' language repertoire (Strickland, 1973; Cullinan, Jaggar & Strickland, 1974). A three-step approach has been developed to introduce NSE speakers to SE syntactic patterns:

1. Introduce an SE pattern by reading a predictable book that repeats the syntactic pattern.
2. Provide extensive practice with the pattern through reading, role-playing, puppetry, and dictating or writing the story.
3. Have students manipulate the pattern by inventing new content for the pattern they are practicing. (Tompkins & McGee, 1983)

Emphasis in this approach is on imitating and repeating the pattern. At first, students will use their own dialect in repeating the pattern, but as they feel comfortable with it, they should be encouraged to substitute the SE form. Emphasize the specific contrast between the dialect and the standard form. The list of predictable books with patterns and sample activities to teach some NSE/SE contrasts is presented in Figure 16–8. Teachers can locate additional predictable books to use in introducing other NSE/SE syntactic and phonological contrasts.

Teachers can use stories and short pieces of children's writing or dictate to teach standard English (Gillet & Gentry, 1983). The four steps of this approach are to (1) compose a story with a child; (2) present an SE version of the story; (3) revise the original story using SE forms; and (4) expand selected sentences from the story using a transformation strategy. The teacher begins by writing a story with a child or selecting a story the child has already written. Next, an SE version of the story is developed in which the teacher replaces the NSE sentence patterns and grammatical structures with standard English but retains as many of the child's words as possible. This version is

SE/NSE Contrast	Sample Book	Book's Pattern	Steps 2 and 3 Sample Activities	Other Books
Plural	*The Very Hungry Caterpillar*	The very hungry caterpillar eats through: 1 apple 2 pears 3 plums, etc.	Have children draw pictures of more foods for the caterpillar to eat. Use a hole punch to make holes in the foods. Record children's dictation to accompany the pictures.	*Goodnight Moon* *Millions of Cats*
Possessive	*Ask Mr. Bear*	Danny asks Mr. Bear and other animals, "Can you give me something for my mother's birthday?"	Have children make labels using possessives for their desks, pencils, and other belongings. Then have them read the labels aloud.	*Whose Nose Is This?*
Person-Number Agreement	*The Judge*	Each prisoner describes the horrible thing in more detail: It growls, it groans It chews up stones It spreads its wings And does bad things	Have children use collage materials to construct their own horrible things. Then record children's descriptions of their horrible things.	*Over in the Meadow* *The Green Grass Grows All Around* *Seven Little Monsters* *The Maestro Plays* *When It Rains . . . It Rains*
Past Tense	*I Know an Old Lady Who Swallowed a Fly*	This is a cumulative tale about an old lady who swallows a fly and a series of other animals to catch the fly.	Have the children make a set of finger puppets to use in retelling the story.	*Elephant in a Well* *Too Much Noise* *Goodnight, Owl* *Where the Wild Things Are* *The Haunted House* *Roll Over!* *The Enormous Turnip*

FIGURE 16–8

Pattern Books and Sample Activities to Teach some SE/NSE Contrasts
Tompkins & McGee, 1983, pp. 466–467.

Present Participle	*Chicken Licken*	Chicken Licken warns everyone that "The sky is falling!"	Have the children act out the story	*Someone Is Eating the Sun* *The Chick and the Duckling* *Crocodile and Hen* *Henny Penny* *The Fat Cat* *Brown Bear, Brown Bear, What Do You See?*
Negative	*A Flower Pot Is Not a Hat*	This pattern is repeated on each page: A___ is not a ___.	Have children compose new sentences and record them on a chart or in individual booklets. Have children draw pictures to illustrate the sentences.	*It Looked Like Spilt Milk* *Never Hit a Porcupine* *Have You Seen My Cat?* *One Monday Morning* *The Grouchy Ladybug* *Crocodile and Hen*
Verb "to be" (Present tense)	*Where in the World Is Henry?*	Two children use questions and answers to look for Henry: Where is the bed? The bed is in the bedroom.	Have children compose new questions and answers following the same pattern. Record them on sentence strips for children to match.	*A Ghost Story* *King of the Mountain* *The Judge* *The House That Jack Built*
Verb "to be" (Past tense)	*10 Bears in My Bed*	A little boy tries to get 10 bears out of his bed. Each page begins: There were (number) in his bed and the little one said, "Roll over!"	Tape-record the story leaving space on the tape for children to repeat the sentence pattern.	*There Was an Old Woman* *The Very Hungry Caterpillar* *What Good Luck! What Bad Luck!*

FIGURE 16—8 (*continued*)

introduced as "another story" and the child reads it aloud. The second story is compared to the original story, then the student revises the original story by expanding the sentences. Even in the revisions, several nonstandard elements are likely to remain. In the final step, sentences selected from the revised story are used to generate new sentences by substituting words and phrases:

Original sentence: It sits on a log.

Transformation: A rabbit sits on a log.

Transformation: A rabbit *with long ears* sits on a log.

Transformation: A rabbit with long ears *hops* on the log.

The sentence transformations allow students to expand their vocabularies and invent new, more elaborate sentences while modeling SE sentence patterns and grammatical structures.

Use the editing stage of the writing process to correct NSE "errors" in students' writing and to teach selected NSE/SE contrasts. Emphasize that the purpose of these changes is to communicate more effectively, not to criticize the student's language. It may be helpful for students to keep a checklist of NSE/SE contrasts they have learned to locate their own errors. Sometimes students will write dialogue in a nonstandard dialect to more fully develop the characters and setting of a story. Many adult authors use this strategy to depict characters and settings more authentically, and teachers should be supportive of this writing strategy.

While NSE students' writing is less influenced by their dialects than is their oral language, dialect does have an impact on students' writing. Research indicates that the two NSE features that have the greatest influence on spelling errors are verb marker omissions and consonant omissions (Cronnell, 1984). One strategy for helping NSE speakers keep track of standard English errors involves the use of spelling and grammar logs (VanDeWeghe, 1982). Students divide pages in their learning logs (a section in their journals or a special notebook) into columns, as shown in Figure 16–9, and record spelling errors in one section and grammar errors in the other. In their learning logs, students record errors and corrections, then analyze possible reasons for the errors. This is a strategy that many students use intuitively, but by formalizing the strategy in their learning logs, NSE students are more likely to learn SE patterns.

Because of pronunciation differences between dialects, students may have difficulty with pairs of words that are not homonyms in standard English, but are homonyms in their dialects. These pairs of words, for example, are homonyms for some students: *poke/pork, told/toll, pin/pen, all/oil* (Barnitz, 1980). Teachers who are sensitive to students' spelling and word choice errors can catch homonym confusions and develop activities to help students distinguish between the pairs. One possible activity is the class collaboration homonym book.

Introduce students to the variety of dialects spoken in the U.S. Play records such as "Our Changing Language" (Burack & McDavid, 1965) so that students can hear the phonological, syntactic, and semantic differences among dialects. (For a list of language recordings, check *The Sound of English: A Bibliography of Language Recordings* compiled by Linn and Zuber [1984]). Books of children's literature with dialogue written in different dialects can also be used. These experiences help students learn about the richness and variety of language as well as the prestige associated with some dialects. Research suggests that, before adolescence, children are not even aware that standard English is the prestige dialect (Labov, 1970).

SPELLING LOG ENTRY			
Correct Spelling	My Misspelling	Why the Word Confuses Me	Helps for Remembering the Correct Spelling
meant	ment	I spell it like I think it sounds.	It's the past of *mean*.
demonstrate	demenstrate	I use *e* instead of *o*.	A dem*o* is used to dem*o*nstrate.
coarse	course	I get it mixed up with *course* as a class.	a = co*a*rse is h*a*rd.

GRAMMAR LOG ENTRY		
Personal Grammar	Written Grammar	Reasons for Differences
my brothers house	my brother's house	I need to put in an apostrophe (') to show ownership.
We took the following items, a camera, a backpack, and a canteen.	We took the following items: a camera a backpack, and a canteen.	I should use a colon (:) when I introduce a series of things.

FIGURE 16—9

Sample Spelling and Grammar Logs
Van DeWeghe, 1982, pp. 102–103.

❖ GIFTED STUDENTS

In contrast to mildly handicapped students who have intellectual or emotional problems that interfere with their learning and language-different students who have language barriers, *gifted students* are academically advanced. Because they learn quickly and have advanced language skills, these students also require special programs to meet their needs.

National interest in gifted students was sparked in 1957 with Russia's launch of the Sputnik satellite, and federal programs were soon developed to encourage students to excel academically. Gifted children usually score two standard deviations or higher (approximately 130+) above the mean IQ score of 100 on intelligence tests, and their level of academic functioning is often two or more grade levels above that of their classmates. Many school districts, however, set their own guidelines for identifying students to include in gifted programs.

Educators acknowledge that giftedness is more than an IQ score and are working to broaden the concept and definition of giftedness by including other dimensions of intelligence. Certainly, intelligence is far more than a single ability. Guilford (1967) identified 120 specific abilities related to intelligence! In general, gifted students tend to:

- Have a unique learning style
- Learn faster than most children do
- Develop earlier (e.g., walking, talking, reading)
- Ask complex questions and display a high degree of curiosity
- Give complicated, detailed explanations
- Grasp relationships quickly
- Organize information in new ways
- See many solutions to a problem
- Have unusually good memories
- Use abstract thought processes
- See ambiguity in factual materials (e.g., true-false questions)
- Have a large vocabulary
- Express themselves well
- Have varied interests
- Delight in discovery and problem solving
- Enjoy working independently
- Have a longer attention span than peers
- Persevere in areas of interest
- Have a highly developed sense of humor (e.g., punning)
- Be perfectionistic
- Be highly energetic
- Prefer the company of older children and adults
- Exhibit strong personal values
- Be highly sensitive about self and others
- Show a high level of self-awareness (Silverman, 1982, p. 494)

Not all gifted students are high achievers. Some are underachievers who do not work up to their potential because of lack of motivation, peer pressure, or fear of success. Teachers sometimes tend to identify students who are well behaved or who complete their assignments accurately and punctually as possibly gifted; in contrast, students who appear to be bored or who exhibit a lack of interest in class activities may be gifted but have not demonstrated their potential.

Instructional Implications.   Gifted students have special needs just as other exceptional learners do, and the greater the student's ability, the more the student needs an individually tailored program. Four options are available to meet the needs of gifted students: (1) segregating gifted students in a special "gifted class" or in magnet schools; (2) accelerating gifted students by "telescoping" or "skipping" them to a higher grade; (3) mainstreaming gifted students in regular classrooms; and (4) enriching mainstreamed gifted students through special pull-out programs (Schwartz, 1984).

Cohen (1987) suggests a variety of tips to help classroom teachers meet the needs of their gifted students:

Establish a classroom setting that is noncompetitive and individualized.

Provide an environment that encourages risk-taking and learning by trial and error.

Change the teacher's role from "information-giver" to "organizer of resources" to give students greater responsibility and control of their learning.

Promote interactions with classmates to help gifted students develop a more realistic view of themselves.

Expect students to do their best.

Harness gifted children's desire to do something to improve their world through community projects.

Provide students with the tools for learning, including research skills, higher-level thinking skills, and problem-solving skills.

Gifted students can create learning centers and other curricular materials for their classmates to use.

Investigate real problems, so that students become producers rather than consumers of information.

Look for the uniqueness of each student.

Vary the formats (e.g., reports, scripts, stories) students use in completing projects.

Independent study assignments are recommended as the best way for classroom teachers to work with mainstreamed gifted students (Silverman, 1982). For example, Krogness's sixth graders (1987) participated in a family folklore unit in which they researched their cultural and linguistic heritage and shared what they learned through reports, plays, stories, cartoons, and other writing forms. Before assigning independent study activities, though, teachers should be certain that students know how to study independently. They need to know how to collect resources, use study skills, manage time, and complete products. Teachers should teach or review these skills before allowing students to work individually. Gifted students, like other students, need teacher supervision as they work, and they need to know their teacher is interested in their work and available for guidance.

In designing independent study activities, the teacher must consider the following variables:

> *Pacing.* Instruction for gifted students should be rapidly paced to suit their learning style.
>
> *Level of abstraction.* Gifted students can engage in hypothetical reasoning, discuss complex issues, make higher order inferences, and utilize systematic procedures in their quest for knowledge.
>
> *Type of subject matter.* Interdisciplinary units are well suited to the complex minds and synthesizing abilities of the gifted.
>
> *Depth of study.* For gifted students, depth is preferable to breadth.
>
> *Range of resources.* Gifted students can be given access to a greater variety and more advanced level of resources than the norm. . . . Human resources should also be used to a greater extent.
>
> *Dissemination.* High quality student products should be shared with the community in some way—through science fairs, editorials, speeches to parents, learning centers for other classes, submitting work for publication, and so on. (Silverman, 1982, pp. 505–506)

One approach to self-directed, independent study is Renzulli's *enrichment triad* (1977), three steps for leading gifted students through a series of experiences that culminate in products that have value for society. Through the enrichment triad, prospective scientists, artists, or young historians, writers, or computer programmers can have an impact on the adult world.

Step 1. The first step consists of exploratory activities, in which students investigate one or more avenues of interest and then decide on a topic or problem they would like to study further. Through an interview, the teacher and the gifted student discuss a topic and together develop a written plan of study listing the activities the student will engage in, the types of resources he or she will consult, and a timeline for completing the activities.

Step 2. Experiences in this step provide students with the technical skills and tools they will need to complete their scientific investigations and other products. The technical skills each student learns depend on the topic or problem identified earlier. After completing the training activities, students brainstorm products, which they complete in the third step.

Step 3. In the third step, students investigate real-life problems, working individually or in small groups. Using appropriate methods of inquiry, they develop a product that is meaningful to them and to society. Products could include reports of scientific investigations that are submitted for publication, computer programs, artistic creations and productions, or serving as docents at a local museum.

Throughout this book, we have encouraged the notion of independent study assignments without calling them by name. We have discussed oral history projects, research reports, class newspapers, writing biographies, and composing and performing scripts. All these activities are appropriate for gifted students; these are other possibilities:

Invite community members with particular areas of expertise to serve as mentors for gifted students (Boston, 1976; Jackson, 1981). Mentors offer enthusiasm as well as expertise and can guide and counsel students as they work on independent study assignments. Mentors can provide assistance in almost any area in which students indicate interest—from aerospace engineering to computer programming to writing for publication.

Encourage students to publish their writing in a variety of ways. They can compile class anthologies, publish class newspapers, and produce plays or puppet shows from scripts they write. They can create books with pop-ups or movables on each page and share these or other stories they write with younger children (Abrahamson & Stewart, 1982).

Gifted students can write and produce story and informational films (Cox, 1983). Students begin by brainstorming a film and developing it into a cohesive composition. Next, they write the script using a storyboard. Finally, they collect or create the film properties (e.g., illustrations, title card, credits list, and other props) and shoot the film with a movie or video camera.

Besides using microcomputers for writing, gifted students can learn computer languages such as BASIC and PASCAL and create computer programs. Gifted students are often encouraged to study a foreign language, an alternative form of communication. Similarly, computer languages are alternative forms of communication, and learning to program computers gives students an additional communication mode.

Encourage gifted students to use higher-level thinking skills. Bloom's *Taxonomy of Educational Objectives* (1956) identifies six levels of thinking skills ranging from knowledge to evaluation. Instruction often focuses on the lower-level thinking skills (knowledge and comprehension), but gifted students especially should be led to the higher levels (analysis, synthesis, and evaluation). In planning independent study assignments, teachers should design activities that involve the higher-level thinking skills. An example of an interdisciplinary unit on ancient Egypt, with activities planned at each of the six levels of Bloom's taxonomy, is shown in Figure 16–10.

Provide opportunities for gifted students to create curricular materials for classroom use. Developing these materials provides students with the opportunity to apply their knowledge in particular content areas and to create a functional product. For instance, two upper-grade gifted students developed a unit on survival. They began by collecting survival stories (e.g., Defoe's *Robinson Crusoe* and Taylor's *The Cay* [1969]), autobiographies and biographies (e.g., Read's *Alive* [1984]), and informational trade books such as *Outdoor Survival Skills* (Olsen, 1973). Next, the students developed the unit and organized it according to six hazardous geographic environments: arctic, sea, swamp, forest, tropical forest, and desert. They developed activities for each environment

---

Level 1: Knowledge

Make a flow chart showing the power structure of government during the New Kingdom.
Learn about at least five Egyptian gods. Write a paragraph on each.

Level 2: Comprehension

Write biographical sketches of five famous Egyptians.
Draw a crosscut diagram of a pyramid.

Level 3: Application

Make a scrapbook of gods and goddesses.
Make an annotated bibliography of 10 sources about ancient Egypt.

Level 4: Analysis

Write a poem that describes the ancient Egyptian army.
Make a chart of sacred animals showing their purposes.

Level 5: Synthesis

Write a fairy tale about the flooding of the Nile River.
Create your own writing system using hieroglyphics.

Level 6: Evaluation

Solve the problem of how to play "senet." Write your own rules and teach others to play.
Write a report about the motifs of ancient Egyptian art.

FIGURE 16–10

Activities from an Interdisciplinary Unit on Ancient Egypt at the Six Levels of Bloom's *Taxonomy* (1956)

Mrs. Diane Lewis, Irving Middle School, Norman, OK.

Knowledge	Make a list of all the materials you would need to construct a shelter in a tropical forest. Explain why the materials are needed.
Comprehension	Explain why you need more preparation concerning first aid and insects in a tropical forest than in a regular forest.
Application	Draw a picture to illustrate at least 10 dangers of a tropical forest and tell how you can avoid them.
Analysis	Survey 10 adults and ask them what they think are the 10 most essential items for survival in a tropical forest.
Synthesis	Collect facts and make a scrapbook on surviving in a jungle and other tropical rain forests.
Evaluation	Compare the necessities for surviving in a forest to the necessities for surviving in a tropical forest.

FIGURE 16–11

Tropical Forest Survival Activities from a Unit Developed by Gifted Students
Brian and Brady, age 14.

based on Bloom's taxonomy and produced the unit as a center with survival books and related activity cards. Activities on tropical forest survival that the students developed for the unit are listed in Figure 16–11. After the unit was constructed, it was set out in the classroom for other students to use.

❖ REVIEW

We have discussed three categories of students with special learning needs: mildly handicapped students, language different students, and gifted students. Our approach is that the content and teaching strategies presented throughout this book are appropriate (with some modifications) for all students who are mainstreamed.

Learning disabled, mentally retarded, and emotionally disturbed students are three types of mildly handicapped students who are frequently mainstreamed in regular classrooms. These students benefit from structured environments in which they can learn more easily and feel successful. Language-different students are students who are language-delayed, students who do not speak English or have limited English proficiency when they come to school because they speak another language at home, and nonstandard-English-speaking students. These students need involvement in language activities to expand their use of language patterns and develop their knowledge of the world in general. The third category of special needs is gifted students. In contrast to other groups of exceptional learners, gifted students have advanced language development and accelerated academic achievement. In the regular classroom, these students benefit from independent study assignments and interdisciplinary units of study.

❖ EXTENSIONS

1. Observe mildly handicapped students, language-different students, or gifted students working in regular classrooms as well as in supplemental "pull-out" programs. Which of the activities recommended in this chapter are teachers using with these special students?

2. Develop and teach a lesson to one or more mildly handicapped students. Choose one of the activities listed in this chapter for learning disabled, educable mentally retarded, or emotionally disturbed students. Keep a log describing the students you are working with and how you adapt the activity to meet their needs. After teaching, evaluate the lesson and describe in your log how students benefited from it.

3. Repeat extension 2 with language-different students and with gifted students.

❖ REFERENCES

Abrahamson, R. F., & Stewart, R. (1982). Movable books—A new golden age. *Language Arts, 59,* 342–347.

Alexander, M. (1968). *Out! out! out!* New York: Dial.

Barnitz, J. G. (1980). Black English and other dialects: Sociolinguistic implications for reading instruction. *The Reading Teacher, 33,* 779–786.

Bloom, B. S. (1956). *Taxonomy of educational objectives, handbook I: Cognitive domain.* New York: McKay.

Boston, B. O. (1976). *The sorcerer's apprentice: A case study in the role of the mentor.* Reston, VA: The Council for Exceptional Children and the ERIC Clearinghouse on Handicapped and Gifted Children.

Bromley, K. D., & Jalongo, M. R. (1984). Song picture books and the language disabled child. *Teaching Exceptional Children, 16,* 114–119.

Burack, E. G., & McDavid, R. I., Jr. (1965). *Our changing language* (record). Urbana, IL: National Council of Teachers of English.

Butler, D. (1979). *Cushla and her books.* Boston: Horn Book.

Cohen, L. M. (1987). Thirteen tips for teaching gifted students. *Teaching Exceptional Children, 20,* 34–38.

Conover, C. (1976) *Six little ducks.* New York: Crowell.

Cox, C. (1983). Young filmmakers speak the language of film. *Language Arts, 60,* 296–304, 372.

Cox, J. A. (1980). *Put your foot in your mouth and other silly sayings.* New York: Random House.

Cronnell, B. (1984). Black-English influences in the writing of third- and sixth-grade black students. *Journal of Educational Research, 77,* 223–236.

Cullinan, B. E., Jaggar, A. M., & Strickland, D. (1974). Language expansion for black children in the primary grades: A research report. *Young Children, 39,* 98–112.

D'Angelo, K. (1980). Wordless picture books and the learning disabled. In G. Stafford (Ed.), *Dealing with differences: Classroom practices in teaching English 1980–1981,* pp. 46–49. Urbana, IL: National Council of Teachers of English.

Defoe, D. (1966). *Robinson Crusoe.* New York: Penguin.

Edelsky, C. (1986). *Writing in a bilingual program: Habia una vez.* Norwood, NJ: Ablex.

Englert, C. S., Raphael, T. E., Fear, K. L., & Anderson, L. M. (1988). Students' metacognitive knowledge about how to write informational texts. *Learning Disabilities Quarterly, 11,* 18–46.

Espin, C. A., & Sindelar, P. T. (1988). Auditory feedback and writing: Learning disabled and nondisabled students. *Exceptional Children, 55,* 45–51.

Federal Register (vol. 42). (1977, August 23). Washington, DC: Department of Health, Education, and Welfare.

Folsom, M., & Folsom, M. (1985). *Easy as pie: A guessing game of sayings*. Boston: Houghton Mifflin.

Franklin, E. A. (1988). Reading and writing stories: Children creating meaning. *The Reading Teacher, 42,* 184–190.

Galdone, P. (1974). *The gingerbread boy*. New York: McGraw-Hill.

Gibbons, G. (1981). *Trucks*. New York: Crowell.

Gillet, J. W., & Gentry, J. R. (1983). Bridges between nonstandard and standard English with extensions of dictated stories. *The Reading Teacher, 36,* 360–364.

Glass, R. M., Christiansen, J., & Christiansen, J. L. (1982). *Teaching exceptional students in the regular classroom*. Boston: Little, Brown.

Gonzales, P. C. (1981a). Beginning English reading for ESL students. *The Reading Teacher, 35,* 154–162.

Gonzales, P. C. (1981b). How to begin language instruction for non-English-speaking students. *Language Arts, 58,* 175–180.

Goodman, K. S., & Buck, C. (1983). Dialect barriers to reading comprehension revisited. *The Reading Teacher, 27,* 6–12.

Goor, R., & Goor, N. (1983). *Signs*. New York: Crowell.

Graham, S., & Harris, K. R. (1988). Instructional recommendations for teaching writing to exceptional students. *Exceptional Children, 54,* 506–512.

Guilford, J. P. (1967). *The nature of human intelligence*. New York: McGraw-Hill.

Heald-Taylor, G. (1986). *Whole language strategies for ESL students*. Toronto, Ontario (Canada): Ontario Institute for Studies in Education Press.

Hoban, T. (1982). *A, B, see*. New York: Greenwillow.

Hudelston, S. (1987). The role of native language literacy in the education of language minority children. *Language Arts, 64,* 827–841.

Hurvitz, J. A., Pickert, S. M., & Rilla, D. C. (1987). Promoting children's language interaction. *Teaching Exceptional Children, 19,* 12–15.

Jackson, L. A. (1981). Enrich your writing program with mentors. *Language Arts, 58,* 837–839.

Keats, E. J. (1971). *Over in the meadow*. New York: Scholastic.

Krogness, M. M. (1987). Folklore: A matter of the heart and the heart of the matter. *Language Arts, 64,* 808–818.

Labov, W. (1966). *The social stratification of English in New York City*. Washington, DC: Center for Applied Linguistics.

Labov, W. (1969). The logic of non-standard English. *The Florida FL Reporter, 7,* 60–74.

Labov, W. (1970). *The study of nonstandard English*. Urbana, IL: National Council of Teachers of English.

Lerner, J. (1985). *Learning disabilities: Theories, diagnosis, and teaching strategies* (4th ed.). Boston: Houghton Mifflin.

Linn, M. D., & Zuber, M. (1984). *The sound of English: A bibliography of language recordings*. Urbana, IL: National Council of Teachers of English.

MacArthur, C. A. (1988). Computers and writing instruction. *Teaching Exceptional Children, 20,* 37–39.

McClure, A. A. (1985). Predictable books: Another way to teach reading to learning disabled children. *Teaching Exceptional Children, 17,* 267–273.

McGee, L. M., & Tompkins, G. E. (1983). Wordless picture books are for older readers, too. *Journal of Reading, 27,* 120–123.

National Council of Teachers of English. (1988). *SLATE starter sheet: English as the official language*. Urbana, IL: National Council of Teachers of English.

Noble, T. (1980). *The day Jimmy's boa ate the wash*. New York: Dial.

Olsen, L. D. (1973). *Outdoor survival skills*. New York: Pocket Books.

O'Shea, L. J., & O'Shea, D. J. (1988). Using repeated readings. *Teaching Exceptional Children, 20,* 26–29.

Peek, M. (1981). *Roll over! A counting song*. Boston: Houghton Mifflin.

Polloway, C. H., & Polloway, E. A. (1981). Survival words for disabled readers. *Academic Therapy, 16,* 443–448.

Quackenbush, R. (1973). *She'll be comin' round the mountain*. Philadelphia: Lippincott.

Read, P. P. (1984). *Alive: The story of the Andes survivors*. New York: Harper and Row.

Renzulli, J. S. (1977). *The enrichment triad model: A guide for developing defensible programs for the gifted and talented.* Mansfield Center, CT: Creative Learning Press.

Rhodes, L. K., & Dudley-Marling, C. (1988). *Readers and writers with a difference: A holistic approach to teaching learning disabled and remedial students.* Portsmouth, NH: Heinemann.

Rodrigues, R. J., & White, R. H. (1981). *Mainstreaming the non-English speaking student* (TRIP Booklet). Urbana, IL: ERIC Clearinghouse on Reading and Communication Skills and the National Council of Teachers of English.

Schwartz, L. L. (1984). *Exceptional students in the mainstream.* Belmont, CA: Wadsworth.

Scofield, S. J. (1978). The language-delayed child in the mainstreamed primary classroom. *Language Arts, 55,* 719–723, 732.

Shea, P., & Fitzgerald, S. (1981). Raddara's beautiful book. *Language Arts, 58,* 156–161.

Silverman, L. (1982). Giftedness. In E. L. Meyen (Ed.), *Exceptional children in today's schools: An alternative resource book,* pp. 485–528. Denver: Love.

Strickland, D. S. (1973). A program for linguistically different, black children. *Research in the Teaching of English, 7,* 79–86.

Summers, M. (1977). Learning disabilities . . . A puzzlement. *Today's Education, 66,* 40–42.

Taylor, T. (1969). *The cay.* New York: Doubleday.

Terban, M. (1983). *In a pickle and other funny idioms.* Boston: Houghton Mifflin.

Tompkins, G. E. (1981). Writing without a pencil. *Language Arts, 58,* 823–833.

Tompkins, G. E., & Friend, M. (1986). On your mark, get set, write! *Teaching Exceptional Children, 18,* 82–89.

Tompkins, G. E., & McGee, L. M. (1983). Launching nonstandard speakers into standard English. *Language Arts, 60,* 463–469.

Torgesen, J. K. (1982). The learning disabled child as an inactive learner: Educational implications. *Topics in Learning and Learning Disabilities, 2,* 45–52.

Troika, R. C. (1981). Synthesis of research on bilingual education. *Educational Leadership, 38,* 498–504.

Urzua, C. (1980). Doing what comes naturally: Recent research in second language acquisition. In G. S. Pinnell (Ed.), *Discovering language with children,* pp. 33–38. Urbana, IL: National Council of Teachers of English.

VanDeWeghe, R. (1982). Spelling and grammar logs. In C. Carter (Ed.), *Non-native and nonstandard dialect students: Classroom practices in teaching English, 1982–1983,* pp. 101–105. Urbana, IL: National Council of Teachers of English.

Wagner, H. S. (1982). Kids can be ESL teachers. In C. Carter (Ed.), *Non-native and nonstandard dialect students: Classroom practices in teaching English, 1982–1983,* pp. 62–65. Urbana, IL: National Council of Teachers of English.

APPENDIX A

Joint Statement on Literacy Development and Pre-First Grade

A Joint Statement of Concerns about Present Practices in Pre-First Grade Reading Instruction and Recommendations for Improvement ▪ Association for Supervision and Curriculum Development ▪ International Reading Association ▪ National Association for the Education of Young Children ▪ National Association of Elementary School Principals ▪ National Council of Teachers of English

Prepared by the Early Childhood and Literacy Development Committee of the International Reading Association*

❖ OBJECTIVES FOR A PRE-FIRST GRADE READING PROGRAM

Literacy learning begins in infancy. Reading and writing experiences at school should permit children to build upon their already existing knowledge of oral and written language. Learning should take place in a supportive environment where children can build a positive attitude toward themselves and toward language and literacy. For optimal learning, teachers should involve children actively in many meaningful, functional language experiences, including *speaking, listening, writing,* and *reading.* Teachers of young children should be prepared in ways that acknowledge differences in language and cultural backgrounds and emphasize reading as an integral part of the language arts as well as of the total curriculum.

*From *The Reading Teacher,* April 1986, v. 39, no. 8, pp. 819-820.

❖ WHAT YOUNG CHILDREN KNOW ABOUT ORAL AND WRITTEN LANGUAGE BEFORE THEY COME TO SCHOOL

1. Children have had many experiences from which they are building their ideas about the functions and uses of oral language and written language.
2. Children have a command of language, have internalized many of its rules, and have conceptualized processes for learning and using language.
3. Many children can differentiate between drawing and writing.
4. Many children are reading environmental print , such as road signs, grocery labels, and fast food signs.
5. Many children associate books with reading.
6. Children's knowledge about language and communication systems is influenced by their social and cultural backgrounds.
7. Many children expect that reading and writing will be sense-making activities.

❖ CONCERNS

1. Many pre-first grade children are subjected to rigid, formal pre-reading programs with inappropriate expectations and experiences for their levels of development.
2. Little attention is given to individual development or individual learning styles.
3. The pressure of accelerated programs do not allow children to be risk-takers as they experiment with language and internalize concepts about how language operates.
4. Too much attention is focused upon isolated skill development or abstract parts of the reading process, rather than upon the integration of oral language, writing and listening with reading.
5. Too little attention is placed upon reading for pleasure; therefore, children often do not associate reading with enjoyment.
6. Decisions related to reading programs are often based on political and economic considerations rather than on knowledge of how young children learn.
7. The pressure to achieve high scores on standardized tests that frequently are not appropriate for the kindergarten child has resulted in changes in the content of programs. Program content often does not attend to the child's social, emotional and intellectual development. Consequently, inappropriate activities that deny curiosity, critical thinking and creative ex-

pression occur all too frequently. Such activities foster negative attitudes toward communication skill activities.

8. As a result of declining enrollment and reduction in staff, individuals who have little or no knowledge of early childhood education are sometimes assigned to teach young children. Such teachers often select inappropriate methodologies.

9. Teachers of pre-first graders are conducting individualized programs without depending upon commercial readers and workbooks need to articulate for parents and other members of the public what they are doing and why.

❖ RECOMMENDATIONS

1. Build instruction on what the child already knows about oral language, reading and writing. Focus on meaningful experiences and meaningful language rather than merely on isolated skill development.

2. Respect the language the child brings to school, and use it as a base for language and literacy activities.

3. Ensure feelings of success for all children, helping them see themselves as people who can enjoy exploring oral and written language.

4. Provide reading experiences as an integrated part of the broader communication process, which includes speaking, listening and writing, as well as other communication systems such as art, math and music.

5. Encourage children's first attempts at writing without concern for the proper formation of letters or correct conventional spelling.

6. Encourage risk-taking in first attempts at reading and writing and accept what appear to be errors as part of children's natural patterns of growth and development.

7. Use materials for instruction that are familiar, such as well-known stories, because they provide the child with a sense of control and confidence.

8. Present a model for students to emulate. In the classroom, teachers should use language appropriately, listen and respond to children's talk, and engage in their own reading and writing.

9. Take time regularly to read to children from a wide variety of poetry, fiction and non-fiction.

10. Provide time regularly for children's independent reading and writing.

11. Foster children's affective and cognitive development by providing opportunities to communicate what they know, think and feel.

12. Use evaluative procedures that are developmentally and culturally appropriate for the children being assessed. The selection of evaluative measures should be based on the objectives of the instructional program

and should consider each child's total development and its effect on reading performance.

13. Make parents aware of the reasons for a total language program at school and provide them with ideas for activities to carry out at home.

14. Alert parents to the limitations of formal assessments and standardized tests of pre-first graders' reading and writing skills.

15. Encourage children to be active participants in the learning process rather than passive recipients of knowledge, by using activities that allow for experimentation with talking, listening, writing and reading.

APPENDIX B

Award Winning Books of Children's Literature

❖ CALDECOTT MEDAL BOOKS, 1964-1990

Each year since 1938, the American Library Association has awarded the Caldecott Medal to the most distinguished picture book for children published the preceeding year. The Caldecott Medal was named for Randolph J. Caldecott, an English illustrator. One or more books are also named as "honor" books.

1990 *Lon Po Po, A Red Riding Hood story from China,* Ed Young (Philomel). Honor books: *Bill Peet: An autobiography,* William Peet (Houghton Mifflin); *Color zoo,* Lois Ehlert (Lippincott); *Herschel and the Hanukkah goblins,* Eric A. Kimmel, illustrated by Trina Schart Hyman (Holiday House); *The talking eggs,* Robert D. San Souci, illustrated by Jerry Pickney (Dial).

1989 *Song and dance man,* Jane Ackerman, illustrated by Stephen Gammell (Knopf). Honor books: *Goldilocks,* James Marshall (Dial); *The boy of the three-year nap,* Diane Snyder, illustrated by Allen Say (Houghton Mifflin); *Mirandy and Brother Wind,* Patricia McKissack, illustrated by Jerry Pickney (Knopf); *Free Fall,* David Wiesner (Lothrop).

1988 *Owl Moon,* Jane Yolen, illustrated by John Schoenherr (Philomel). Honor book: *Mufaro's beautiful daughters: An African tale,* John Steptoe (Morrow).

1987 *Hey, Al,* Arthur Yorinks, illustrated by Richard Egielski (Farrar, Straus & Giroux). Honor books: *Alphabatics,* Suse MacDonald (Bradbury); *Rumplestiltskin,* Paul O. Zelinsky (E. P. Dutton); *The village of round and square houses,* Ann Grifalconi (Little, Brown).

1986 *The polar express,* Chris Van Allsburg (Houghton Mifflin). Honor books: *King Bidgood's in the bathtub,* Andrew Wood (Harcourt Brace Jovanovich); *The relatives came,* Cynthia Rylant (Bradbury).

1985 *Saint George and the dragon,* Margaret Hodges, illustrated by Trina Schart Hyman (Little, Brown). Honor books: *Hansel and Gretel,* Rika Lesser, illustrated by Paul O. Zelinsky (Dodd, Mead); *Have you seen my duckling?* Nancy Tafuri (Greenwillow); *The story of jumping mouse,* John Steptoe (Lothrop, Lee & Shepard).

1984 *The glorious flight: Across the channel with Louis Bleriot,* Alice and Martin Provensen (Viking). Honor books: *Little red riding hood,* Trina Schart Hyman (Holiday); *Ten, nine, eight,* Molly Bang (Greenwillow).

1983 *Shadow,* Blaise Cendrars, translated and illustrated by Marcia Brown (Scribner). Honor books: *A chair for my mother,* Vera B. Williams (Greenwillow); *When I was young in the mountains,* Cynthia Rylant, illustrated by Diane Goode (E. P. Dutton).

1982 *Jumanji*, Chris Van Allsburg (Houghton Mifflin). Honor books: *On Market Street*, Arnold Lobel, illustrated by Anita Lobel (Greenwillow); *Outside over there*, Maurice Sendak (Harper & Row); *A visit to William Blake's inn: Poems for innocent and experienced travelers*, Nancy Willard, illustrated by Alice and Martin Provensen (Harcourt); *Where the buffaloes begin*, Olaf Baker, illustrated by Stephen Gammell (Warne).

1981 *Fables*, Arnold Lobel (Harper & Row). Honor books: *The Bremen-Town musicians*, Ilse Plume (Doubleday); *The grey lady and the strawberry snatcher*, Molly Bang (Four Winds); *Mice twice*, Joseph Low (Atheneum); *Truck*, Donald Crews (Greenwillow).

1980 *Ox-cart man*, Donald Hall, illustrated by Barbara Cooney (Viking); Honor books: *Ben's trumpet*, Rachel Isadora (Greenwillow); *The garden of Abdul Gasazi*, Chris Van Allsburg (Houghton); *The treasure*, Uri Shulevtiz (Farrar, Straus & Giroux).

1979 *The girl who loved wild horses*, Paul Goble (Bradbury). Honor books: *Freight train*, Donald Crews (Greenwillow); *The way to start a day*, Byrd Baylor, illustrated by Peter Parnall (Scribner).

1978 *Noah's ark: The story of the flood*, Peter Spier (Doubleday). Honor books: *Castle*, David Macaulay (Houghton); *It could always be worse*, Margot Zemach (Farrar, Straus & Giroux).

1977 *Ashanti to Zulu*, Margaret Musgrove, illustrated by Leo and Diane Dillon (Dial). Honor books: *The amazing bone*, William Steig (Farrar, Straus & Giroux); *The contest*, Nonny Hogrogian (Greenwillow); *Fish for supper*, M. B. Goffstein (Dial); *The Golem: A Jewish legend*, Beverly Brodsky McDermott (J. B. Lippincott); *Hawk, I'm your brother*, Byrd Baylor, illustrated by Peter Parnall (Scribner).

1976 *Why mosquitoes buzz in people's ears*, Verna Aardema, illustrated by Leo and Diane Dillon (Dial). Honor books: *The desert is theirs*, Byrd Baylor (Scribner), illustrated by Peter Parnall; *Strega Nona*, Tomie dePaola (Prentice-Hall).

1975 *Arrow to the sun*, Gerald McDermott (Viking). Honor book: *Jambo means hello: A Swahili alphabet book*, Muriel Feelings, illustrated by Tom Feelings (Dial).

1974 *Duffy and the devil*, Harve and Margot Zemach (Farrar, Straus & Giroux). Honor books: *Cathedral: The story of its construction*, David Macaulay (Houghton); *The three jovial huntsmen*, Susan Jeffers (Bradbury).

1973 *The funny little woman*, Arlen Mosel, illustrated by Blair Lent (E. P. Dutton). Honor books: *Hosie's Alphabet*, Hosea, Tobias, and Lisa Baskin, illustrated by Leonard Baskin (Viking); *Snow-White and the seven dwarfs*, translated by Randall Jarrell from the Brothers Grimm, illustrated by Nancy Ekholm Burkert (Farrar, Straus & Giroux); *When Clay sings*, Byrd Baylor, illustrated by Tom Bahti (Scribner).

1972 *One fine day*, Nonny A. Hogrogian (Macmillan). Honor books: *Hildilid's Night*, Cheli Duran Ryan, illustrated by Arnold Lobel (Macmillan); *I fall the seas were one sea*, Janina Domanska, (Macmillan); *Moja means one: Swahili counting book*, Muriel Feelings, illustrated by Tom Feelings (Dial).

1971 *A story, a story*, Gail E. Haley (Atheneum). Honor books: *The angry moon*, William Sleator, illustrated by Blair Lent (Atlantic-Little), *Frog and Toad are friends*, Arnold Lobel (Harper & Row); *In the night kitchen*, Maurice Sendak (Harper & Row).

1970 *Sylvester and the magic pebble*, William Steig (Windmill/Simon & Schuster). Honor books: *Alexander and the wind-up mouse*, Leo Lionni (Pantheon); *Goggles!* Ezra Jack Keats (Macmillan); *The judge: An untrue tale*, Harve Zemach, illustrated by Margot Zemach (Farrar, Straus & Giroux). *Pop Corn and Ma Goodness*, Edna Mitchell Preston, illustrated by Robert Andrew Parker (Viking); *Thy friend, Obadiah*, Brinton Turkle (Viking).

1969 *The fool of the world and the flying ship*, Arthur Ransome, illustrated by Uri Shulevitz (Farrar, Straus & Giroux). Honor book: *Why the sun and the moon live in the sky: An African folktale*, Elphinstone Dayrell, illustrated by Blair Lent (Houghton Mifflin).

1968 *Drummer Hoff*, Barbara Emberley, illustrated by Ed Emberley (Prentice-Hall). Honor books: *Frederick*, Leo Lionni (Pantheon); *Seashore story*, Taro Yashima (Viking); *The emperor and the kite*, Jane Yolen, illustrated by Ed Young (Harcourt Brace Jovanovich).

1967 *Sam, Bangs & Moonshine*, Evaline Ness (Holt, Rinehart & Winston). Honor book: *One wide river to cross*, Barbara Emberley, illustrated by Ed Emberley (Prentice-Hall).

1966 *Always room for one more*, Sorche Nic Leodhas, illustrated by Nonny Hogrogian (Holt, Rinehart & Winston). Honor books: *Hide and seek fog*, Alvin Tresselt, illustrated by Roger Duvoisin (Lothrop, Lee & Shepard); *Just me*, Marie Hall Ets (Viking); *Tom Tit Tot*, edited by Joseph Jacobs, illustrated by Evaline Ness (Scribner).

1965 *May I bring a friend?* Beatrice Schenk de Regniers (Atheneum). Honor books: *A pocketful of cricket*, Rebecca Caudill, illustrated by Evaline Ness (Holt, Rinehart & Winston); *Rain makes applesauce*, Julian Scheer, illustrated by Marvin Bileck (Holiday); *The wave*, Margaret Hodges, illustrated by Blair Lent (Houghton Mifflin).

1964 *Where the wild things are*, Maurice Sendak (Harper & Row). Honor books: *All in the morning early*, Sorche Nic Leodhas, illustrated by Evaline Ness (Holt, Rinehart & Winston); *Mother Goose and nursery rhymes*, Philip Reed (Atheneum); *Swimmy*, Leo Lionni (Pantheon).

❖ NEWBERY MEDAL BOOKS, 1964-1990

Since 1922, the American Library Association has awarded the Newbery Medal to the most distinguished contribution to children's literature published the preceeding year. The Newbery Medal was named for John Newbery, the first English publisher of books for children. One or more books are also named as "honor" books.

1990 *Number the stars*, Lois Lowry (Houghton Mifflin). Honor books: *Afternoon of the elves*, Janet Lisle Taylor (Orchard); *Shabanu: Daughter of wind*, Suzanne Fisher Staples (Knopf); *The winter room*, Gary Paulsen (Orchard).

1989 *Joyful noise: Poems for two voices*, Paul Fleishman (Harper & Row). Honor books: *In the beginning*, Virginia Hamilton (Harcourt Brace Jovanovich); *Scorpions*, Walter Dean Myers (Harper & Row).

1988 *Lincoln: A photobiography*, Russell Freedman (Clarion). Honor books: *After the rain*, Norma Fox Mazer, (Morrow); *Hatchet*, Gary Paulsen (Bradbury).

1987 *The whipping boy*, Sid Fleischman (Greenwillow). Honor books: *A fine white dust*, Cynthia Rylant (Bradbury); *On my honor*, Marion Dane Bauer (Clarion); *Volcano: The eruption and healing of Mount St. Helen's*, Patricia Lauber (Bradbury).

1986 *Sarah, plain and tall*, Patricia MacLachlan (Harper & Row). Honor books: *Commodore Perry in the land of the Shogun*, Rhoda Blumberg (Lothrop, Lee & Shepard); *Dog song*, Gary Paulsen (Bradbury).

1985 *The hero and the crown*, Robin McKinley (Greenwillow). Honor books: *Like Jake and me*, Mavis Jukes (Alfred A. Knopf); *The moves make the man*, Bruce Brooks (Harper & Row); *One-eyed cat*, Paula Fox (Bradbury).

1984 *Dear Mr. Henshaw*, Beverly Clearly (Morrow). Honor books: *The sign of the beaver*, Elizabeth George Speare (Houghton Mifflin); *A solitary blue*, Cynthia Voigt (Atheneum); *Sugaring time*, Kathryn Lasky (Macmillan); *The wish giver*, Bill Brittain (Harper & Row).

1983 *Dicey's song*, Cynthia Voigt, (Atheneum). Honor books: *The blue sword*, Robin McKinley (Greenwillow); *Doctor DeSoto*, William Steig (Farrar, Straus & Giroux); *Graven images*, Paul Fleischman (Harper & Row); *Homesick: My own story*, Jean Fritz (Putnam); *Sweet Whispers, Brother Rush*, Virginia Hamilton (Philomel).

1982 *A visit to William Blake's inn: poems for innocent and experienced travelers*, Nancy Willard (Harcourt Brace Jovanovich). Honor books: *Ramona Quimby, age 8*, Beverly Clearly (Morrow); *Upon the head of the goat: A childhood in Hungary, 1939-1944*, Aranka Siegal (Farrar, Straus & Giroux).

1981 *Jacob have I loved*, Katherine Paterson (Crowell). Honor books: *The fledgling*, Jane Langton (Harper & Row); *A ring of endless light*, Madeleine L'Engle (Farrar, Straus & Giroux).

1980 *A gathering of days: A New England girl's journal, 1830-1832*, Joan W. Blos (Scribner).

Honor book: *The road from home: The story of an Armenian girl*, David Kerdian (Greenwillow).

1979 *The westing game*, Ellen Raskin (Dutton). Honor book: *The great Gilly Hopkins*, Katherine Paterson (Crowell).

1978 *Bridge to Terabithia*, Katherine Paterson (Crowell). Honor books: *Anpao: An American Indian odyssey*, Jamake Highwater (Lippincott); *Ramona and her father*, Beverly Clearly (Morrow).

1977 *Roll of thunder, hear my cry*, Mildred Taylor (Dial). Honor books: *Abel's Island*, William Steig (Farrar, Straus & Giroux); *A string in the harp*, Nancy Bond (Atheneum).

1976 *The grey king*, Susan Cooper (Atheneum). Honor books: *Dragonwings*, Laurence Yep (Harper & Row); *The hundred penny box*, Sharon Bell Mathis (Viking).

1975 *M. C. Higgins, the great*, Virginia Hamilton (Macmillan). Honor books: *Figgs and phantoms*, Ellen Raskin (E. P. Dutton); *My brother Sam is dead*, James Lincoln Collier and Christopher Collier (Four Winds); *The perilous gard*, Elizabeth Marie Pope (Houghton Mifflin); *Philip Hall likes me, I reckon maybe*, Bette Greene (Dial).

1974 *The Slave Dancer*, Paula Fox (Bradbury). Honor book: *The dark is rising*, Susan Cooper (Atheneum).

1973 *Julie of the wolves*, Jean C. George (Harper & Row). Honor books: *Frog and Toad together*, Arnold Lobel (Harper & Row); *The upstairs room*, Johanna Reiss (Crowell); *The witches of worm*, Zilpha Keatley Snyder (Atheneum).

1972 *Mrs. Frisby and the rats of Nimh*, Robert C. O'Brien (Atheneum). Honor books: *Annie and the old one*, Miska Miles (Atlantic–Little); *The headless cupid*, Zilpha Keatley Snyder (Atheneum); *Incident at Hawk's Hill*, Allan W. Eckert (Little, Brown); *The planet of Junior Brown*, Virginia Hamilton (Macmillan); *The tombs of Atuan*, Ursula K. LeGuin (Atheneum).

1971 *The summer of the swans*, Betsy Byars (Viking). Honor books: *Enchantress from the stars*, Sylvia Louise Engdahl (Atheneum); *Kneeknock rise*, Natalie Babbitt (Farrar, Straus & Giroux); *Sing down the moon*, Scott O'Dell (Houghton Mifflin).

1970 *Sounder*, William Armstrong (Harper & Row). Honor books: *Journey outside*, Mary Q. Steele (Viking); *Our Eddie*, Sulamith Ish-Kishor (Pantheon); *The many ways of seeing: An introduction to the pleasures of art*, Janet Gaylord Moore (Harcourt Brace Jovanovich).

1969 *The high king*, Lloyd Alexander (Holt, Rinehart & Winston). Honor books: *To be a slave*, Julius Lester (Dial); *When Shlemiel went to Warsaw and other stories*, Isaac Bashevis Singer (Farrar, Straus & Giroux).

1968 *From the mixed-up files of Mrs. Basil E. Frankweiler*, E. L. Konigsburg (Atheneum). Honor books: *The black pearl*, Scott O'Dell (Houghton Mifflin); *The Egypt game*, Zilpha Keatley Snyder (Atheneum); *The fearsome inn*, Isaac Bashevis Singer (Scribner); *Jennifer, Hecate, Macbeth, William McKinley, and Me, Elizabeth*, E. L. Konigsburg (Atheneum).

1967 *Up a road slowly*, Irene Hunt (Follett). Honor books: *The jazz man*, Mary Hays Weik (Atheneum); *The King's Fifth*, Scott O'Dell (Houghton Mifflin); *Zlateh the goat and other stories*, Isaac Bashevis Singer (Harper & Row).

1966 *I, Juan de Pareja*, Elizabeth Borton de Trevino (Farrar, Straus & Giroux). Honor books: *The animal family*, Randall Jarrell (Pantheon); *The black cauldron*, Lloyd Alexander (Holt, Rinehart & Winston); *The noonday friends*, Mary Stolz (Harper & Row).

1965 *Shadow of a bull*, Maia Wojciechowska (Atheneum). Honor book: *Across five Aprils*, Irene Hunt (Follett).

1964 *It's like this, cat*, Emily Neville (Harper & Row). Honor books: *The loner*, Ester Wier (McKay); *Rascal*, Sterling North (E. P. Dutton).

APPENDIX C

Questions about the Elements of Story Structure

❖ BEGINNING-MIDDLE-END

Beginnings of Stories

What kinds of information does an author put in the beginning of a story?

Which characters do you meet?

What do you learn about the setting or where the story takes place?

What happens in the first part of the story?

Is there a problem that will need to be solved?

Does the author give you any ideas about what will happen next?

Middles of Stories

What kinds of information does an author put in the middle of a story?

What happens to the characters?

Does the author add new characters?

What happens to the problem?

Does it get worse?

Is it solved?

What happens during the second part of the story?

How do you feel during this part of the story?

Ends of Stories

What kinds of information does an author put in the end of a story?

What happens to the characters?

What happens to the problem?

How do you feel during this part of the story?

❖ REPETITION

Are some words repeated over and over in the story?

Which words are repeated?

Why are they repeated?

Is an event repeated over and over with different characters?

What event is repeated?

Who are the different characters?

Why is the event repeated with different characters?

What effect does the repetition have on the story?

Is an event repeated over and over with different objects?

Is a feeling repeated over and over as different characters strive to accomplish a task?

❖ SETTING

Is the setting elaborated in great detail or barely sketched?

Is the setting of much importance to the story, or could the story take place anywhere?

Does the author take a great deal of effort to establish the authenticity and description of the environment?

Does the weather or time play an important role in the story?

Is the scenic description interspersed with character description? How?

Is the mood engendered by the setting important to the story?

Would the story have as strong an effect if the setting were less involved?

Is the setting necessary for plot development?

Could the story characters be found in other kinds of settings?

Do the conflict situations depend as much on the setting as on the characters for the complications and resolutions of the problems?

Does the author use the setting to provide the kinds of complications that are believable?

Is the setting sometimes more important than the action or character description?

❖ CHARACTERS

What is the character's main goal?

What problems do the characters face?

What conflict situations does the author use?

How does the author introduce the plot and get the story started?

What roadblocks (or complications) do the characters face in trying to reach the goal?

If one attempt is not successful, do the characters have the chance to try again to reach their goal?

Does the main character or one of the supporting characters resolve the conflict?

Do the characters gain in skill, strength, wisdom as each roadblock is overcome? How?

Are the opposing characters endowed with powers that would make the outcome or resolution of the conflict doubtful? What kinds of powers?

Are the characters left to their own devices or does some outside force or character come to rescue or help them find new sources of strength within themselves?

How much complication does the author use before the high point (or climax) of the story?

Is there a shift from one form of conflict to another form?

Does the author use the device of foreshadowing? How?

Which character is developed the most?

Does the main character seem to be a real person?

How many supporting characters does the author include in the story?

Which characters support (or oppose) the main character?

How does each character get involved with the main character?

What does each character look like?

How do those physical characteristics affect the character's role in the story?

If the character had been bigger (smaller, older, stronger, etc.) would the character have behaved the same in the story?

Does the character use any specific mannerisms or gestures?

Is there a special relationship between how the character is described and how the character acts and talks?

Does the author use dialogue in the story? How?

Does the dialogue help you predict what might happen because of what is said?

What do a character's actions tell us about that character?

Can we expect a character to behave in a certain way when we get to know that character?

❖ THEME

What does the story mean to you?

What is the most important idea the author tried to get across in the story?

Is this idea or theme explicitly stated or implied in the story?

Does the primary theme unfold primarily through the speech, thoughts, or actions of the characters?

Does the conflict the characters encountered help you to determine what the theme is? How?

Is the theme similar to the motif or rather different? How?

Are there other themes besides the primary one?

Are these other themes related to the primary theme or are they different? How?

❖ POINT OF VIEW

First-Person Viewpoint

Who is telling the story?

Is the story told in first person?

Is the main character telling the story, or is another character telling it?

Is the narrator speaking as an eyewitness as well as a participant in the events?

Do we learn about the other characters only through what the narrator sees and what the other characters tell the narrator?

Omniscient Viewpoint

Who is telling the story?

Do we know what the characters are thinking?

Does the narrator tell us how the characters feel?

Does the narrator tell what the character's ideas are before he or she tells anyone else?

Is the story told in third person?

Limited Omniscient Viewpoint

Who is telling the story?

Are we limited to overhearing the thoughts of just one or two characters?

Does the narrator tell us how these characters feel?

Is the story told in third person?

Does the author stick to dialogue, action, and physical description when discussing the other characters in the story?

Objective Viewpoint

Who is telling the story?

Is what we learn about the story only by what we see and hear as eyewitnesses?

Are we restricted to only hearing dialogue and seeing actions and settings?

Can we listen in on a character's thoughts?

APPENDIX D

Spelling Options for Phonemes

Phoneme	Grapheme	Example	Phoneme	Grapheme	Example
ă	a	apple	b	b	bug
	ai	plaid		bb	rabbit
	al	calf			
	au	laugh	ch	ch	church
				che	niche
ā	a	age		t	picture
	ai	aid		tch	watch
	au	gauge		te	righteous
	ay	say		ti	question
	a-e	game			
	ea	break	d	d	dog
	eigh	eight		dd	add
	et	bouquet		ed	filled
	ei	vein			
	ey	they	ĕ	a	any
				ai	said
ar	a	care		ay	says
	ai	hair		e	end
	ay	prayer		ea	head
	e	where		ei	heifer
	ea	bear		eo	leopard
	ei	their		ie	friend
	hei	heir		u	bury
ä	a	father			
	ah	ah			
	al	calm			
	e	sergeant			
	ea	heart			

Phoneme	Grapheme	Example	Phoneme	Grapheme	Example
ē	ay	quay	ĭ	ea	near
	e	equal		ee	been
	ea	peach		ei	weird
	ee	meet		i	igloo
	ei	receive		ie	sieve
	eo	people		o	women
	ey	key		u	busy
	e-e	these		ui	build
	ea-e	breathe		y	myth
	i	machine	ī	ais	aisle
	ie	believe		ay	bayou
	is	debris		ei	eider
	oe	phoebe		eigh	height
	y	city		eye	eye
er	ea	earth		i	ice
	er	her		ie	lie
	err	err		igh	high
	ir	first		is	island
	irr	whirr		uy	buy
	olo	colonel		y	sky
	our	courage		ye	rye
	or	word	j	d	gradual
	ur	church		dg	judgment
	urr	purr		dge	bridge
	yr	myrtle		di	soldier
f	f	fat		g	general
	ff	cuff		gg	exaggerate
	gh	laugh		ge	large
	ph	telephone		gi	allegiance
g	g	go		j	job
	gg	egg	k	c	cat
	gh	ghost		cc	account
	gu	guest		ch	chemistry
	gue	catalogue		che	ache
h	h	he		ck	clack
	wh	who		cq	acquire
				cu	biscuit
				k	keep
				q	quill
				qu	liquor
				que	pique
				x	luxury

Phoneme	Grapheme	Example	Phoneme	Grapheme	Example
l	l	last	ō	au	chauffeur
	ll	hill		eau	beau
	le	automobile		eo	yeoman
syllabic l	le	able		ew	sew
	al	animal		o	go
	el	cancel		oa	oak
	il	civil		oe	toe
m	gm	diaphragm		oh	oh
	m	me		ol	folk
	mb	climb		oo	brooch
	mm	comment		ou	soul
	mn	solemn		ough	though
	me	come		ow	own
n	gn	gnat		o-e	note
	kn	knight	ô	a	tall
	n	no		al	walk
	nn	manner		au	author
	ne	done		augh	taught
	pn	pneumonia		o	office
syllabic n	an	important		oa	broad
	ain	certain		ou	cough
	en	written		ough	bought
	in	cousin		wa	saw
	on	lesson	oi	oi	oil
	contrac-tions	didn't		oy	boy
ŏ	a	watch	o͝o	o	women
	ach	yacht		oo	look
	ho	honest		ou	could
	o	odd		u	put
			o͞o	o	to
				oo	tool
				ou	group
				o-e	lose
				u	cruel
				ue	blue
				u-e	rule

Phoneme	Grapheme	Example	Phoneme	Grapheme	Example
ou	hou	hour	sh	ce	ocean
	ou	out		ch	machine
	ough	bough		che	chace
	ow	cow		ci	ancient
p	p	pig		psh	pshaw
	pp	puppet		s	sure
r	r	rock		sch	schwa
	rh	rhyme		sci	conscience
	rr	marry		se	nausea
	wr	write		sh	she
stressed				si	tension
syllabic r	er	her		ss	issue
	ur	church		ssi	admission
	ir	first		ti	national
	or	world	t	bt	doubt
	ear	heard		ed	stopped
	our	courage		pt	ptomaine
unstressed				t	tell
syllabic r	ar	dollar		th	Thomas
	er	better		tt	button
	or	favor		te	definite
	ure	picture	ŭ	o	son
s	s	city		oe	does
	ce	nice		oo	flood
	ps	psalm		ou	country
	s	sick		u	up
	sc	scent	ū	eau	beauty
	se	else		eu	feud
	ss	class		eue	queue
	s(ks)	box		ew	few
				iew	view
				u	union
				ue	value
				u-e	use
				yew	yew
				you	you
				yu	yule
			v	f	of
				ph	Stephen
				v	very
				ve	have

Phoneme	Grapheme	Example	Phoneme	Grapheme	Example
z	cz	czar	schwa e	a	alone
	s	present		ah	rajah
	sc	discern		ai	bargain
	se	applause		e	moment
	ss	scissors		eo	dungeon
	x	xylophone		i	April
	z	zero		o	complete
	ze	gauze		oi	tortoise
	zz	buzz		ou	cautious
				u	circus
zh	ge	garage			
	s	measure			
	si	division			

❖ REFERENCES

Horn, E. (1957). Phonetics and spelling. *The Elementary School Journal, 57,* 424–432.

Personke, C. R. (1987). Spelling as a language art. In C. R. Personke & D. D. Johnson, *Language arts instruction and the beginning teacher: A practical guide,* pp. 75–85. Englewood Cliffs, NJ: Prentice Hall.

APPENDIX E

"Let's Go on a Bear Hunt"

"Let's Go on a Bear Hunt" is a favorite language game of young children, and it can also be adapted for a handwriting activity. The teacher takes the children on a bear hunt using the basic handwriting strokes to represent the actions of the hunt. Straight sticks become grass and forests to hike through, slanted sticks become hills and mountains to conquer, and circles become bears' paw-prints to track. As the teacher tells the story and demonstrates the handwriting strokes on the chalkboard, the children practice making the strokes on their papers.

❖ TEACHING STRATEGY

The steps in the teaching strategy are:

1. Provide students with lined or blank paper and crayons or pencils.
2. Explain that you are going to tell the students a story, and they will draw lines and pictures for the story.
3. Tell the first section of the story and demonstrate the first handwriting stroke on the chalkboard.
4. Have students copy the stroke on their papers and practice making the stroke several times.
5. Circulate to check that students are making the stroke correctly.
6. Repeats steps 3, 4, and 5 with each section of the story.
7. At the end of the story ask students to draw a picture about the story. Also, record their dictation about the pictures or have them write a sentence about the story on their papers.

Let's Go on a Bear Hunt*

The teacher says:

The teacher demonstrates, and the children copy on their papers:

1. Let's go on a bear hunt! Here we are hiking through the grass looking for a bear. Let's make a row of grass on our papers.

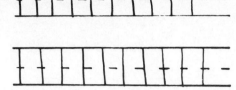

2. Shh! Do you hear anything? No? Let's keep hunting. Now we're walking through a forest. The forest is filled with many trees.

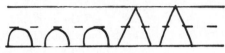

3. Do you see any bears? No? Let's keep walking. Oh, the walking is getting harder and harder. We're climbing over hills and mountains. Let's make some hills and mountains.

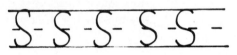

4. Watch out for bears! These mountains are so curvey and dangerous. Be careful! Stay on the trail!

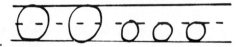

5. Look! I see some marks that look like circles on the ground. Let's make big and little circles.

6. These circles look like paw-prints to me. Could they be bear paw-prints? Make circles into paw-prints by adding little claw marks.

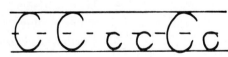

7. These paw-prints lead up to a cave. Do bears live in caves? Let's make some big and little caves.

8. Listen! Do you hear a bear? Do you see a bear? Draw a picture of what you think the bear might look like.

*Adapted from Tompkins, G.E. (1980). Let's go on a bear hunt! A fresh approach to penmanship drill. *Language Arts, 57,* 782–786.

The bear hunt activity can be adapted to other topics; children can hunt for dinosaurs, Santa Claus, ghosts, the Easter Bunny, other animals, or even Big Foot. Below are examples of how children have made their own variations on the bear hunt activity.

❖ ADAPTATIONS OF CIRCLE AND STICK STORIES

Teachers can make up new and different stories by adapting the basic circle and stick stories to represent other pictures. Here are two variations, a Halloween and a snow story:

Jack-o-Lanterns

The teacher says: The teacher demonstrates:

1. Let's make a jack-o-lantern. We need a nice round pumpkin. Let's make a pumpkin patch full of big and little pumpkins.

2. When we turn a pumpkin into a jack-o-lantern, we give it a face. Let's make triangle eyes and noses. This way.

3. And this way.

4. Let's add happy and sad mouths.

5. And lots of teeth to fill the mouths.

6. Now draw a picture to show how the jack-o-lantern might look.

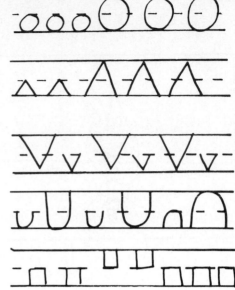

A Snowy Day

The teacher says: The teacher demonstrates:

1. One day it began to snow. At first it was just a snow flurry. Then it began to snow very hard. (Remind children to have the snowflakes come from the sky down to the ground.)

2. At first the snow wasn't very deep. Then, as it snowed harder and harder, the snow got deeper and deeper.

3. Then we decided to go outside and make a snowman. We started rolling snowballs. At first the snowballs were very small. Then they got larger and larger.

4.   After we made the snowballs, we needed some things to make our snowballs become a snowman. Can you guess what we needed? We needed sticks for arms, a hat, a pipe, and a carrot.

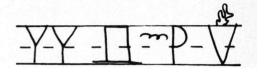

5.   Now draw a picture to show how you think our snowman looked when he was all put together.

This is a 5-year-old's version of the snow story:

Children can compose their own handwriting stories using the basic strokes. This is a fossil hunt written by Robbie, a 7-year-old who cleverly manages to involve dinosaurs in almost every activity.

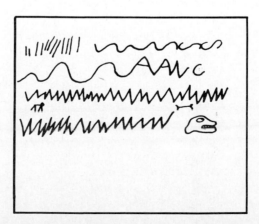

Robbie describes his fossil hunt this way:

A paleontologist was going on a fossil hunt. He went over short grass and long grass and over little hills. (See, I made the hills with a sideway S's). Then he came to mountains and high mountains and high mountains with snow on them. Then he went in a cave. It had lots of icicles. He crawled down low. He crawled some more. Then he found it—a Tyrannosaurus skull.

The teacher's excitement makes these stories believable. By setting the mood and responding to the children's comments, the teacher stimulates children's interest in the handwriting activity. The rapid tempo of the activity allows for intensive drill without losing the children's interest. As the children practice each letter form, the teacher can instruct individual children about proper letter formation and spacing between letters.

SUBJECT INDEX

TITLE & AUTHOR INDEX

Gail E. Tompkins is an Associate Professor at California State University, Fresno, in the Department of Literacy and Early Education. She teaches courses in reading, writing, and language arts for preservice and inservice teachers. Previously Dr. Tompkins taught at the University of Oklahoma and in 1986 she received the University of Oklahoma's prestigious Regent Award for Superior Teaching. She was also an elementary teacher in Virginia for eight years.

Dr. Tompkins is also the author of *Teaching Writing: Balancing Process and Product* (Merrill, 1990) and co-author of *Answering Students' Questions about Words* (National Council of Teachers of English, 1986). She has written numerous articles related to language arts that have appeared in *Language Arts, The Reading Teacher, Journal of Reading, Childhood Education,* and other professional journals. In addition, Dr. Tompkins serves on the Review Board of *The Reading Teacher.*

Dr. Tompkins is married and lives in Fresno, California, with her husband, two step-children, two dogs, and a cat. Her hobbies include swimming, needlework, and traveling in Europe.

Dr. Kenneth Hoskisson teaches courses in reading and language arts at Virginia Tech in Blacksburg, Virginia. He has published in the *Elementary School Journal, Language Arts,* and *The Reading Teacher.* Dr. Hoskisson is well known for his conceptualization and development of assisted reading. He earned a Ph.D. in curriculum and instruction with emphasis in reading and language arts at the University of California, Berkeley. His major interests are writing and helping teachers examine the relationships between theory and practice. Dr. Hoskisson was both a teacher and administrator with the Department of Defense schools in Europe for 10 years.